MONEY TALK

PREVIOUS TITLES

Money Clips: 365 Tips—
from the Simple to the Sophisticated—
for Making, Saving, and Investing Your Money

From Alphabet Stock
to the Naked Sale—
The Words and Phrases
that Control Your Money

MONEY TALK

LORRAINE SPURGE

HYPERION

NEW YORK

Legal Counsel

Homer, Kirsch & Mitchell

Important Caution to Our Readers

Please keep the following important cautions in mind when reading and using this book. Because of differences in the laws of various states and countries, the constant changes in tax law, and the unique circumstances that might apply to the individual reader, as well as other factors, the publisher and the author cannot guarantee that the information and advice discussed in this book are appropriate and accurate for every reader. For that reason, readers are strongly cautioned to consult an accountant, attorney, or other professional adviser before making financial decisions. This book is not intended to replace such professional advice.

Accordingly, this book and its contents are sold without warranties or guarantees of any kind, express or implied, and the publisher and the author disclaim any liability, loss, or damage caused by the contents of this book or its use by readers.

Library of Congress Cataloging-in-Publication Data

Spurge, Lorraine.
    Money talk : from alphabet stock to the naked sale—the words and phrases that control your money / by Lorraine Spurge.—1st ed.
        p.   cm.
    ISBN 0-7868-8498-3
    1. Money market—Terminology.   2. Finance—Terminology.   I. Title.

HG226 .S68 2001
332'.03—dc21

                                                            00-040967

FIRST EDITION

10   9   8   7   6   5   4   3   2   1

To my children,
Nicole and Renee,
who have made my life worthwhile . . .

CREDITS

Managing Editor and Creative Director
Debra Valencia

Research Consultant
Pamela Nelson, CFA

Copy Editors
Mari Florence, Back Bone Books
Janis Hunt Johnson
Stephanie Keenan
Christine Stewart

Research Assistant
Tamera Rogers

Proofreading
Ask Janis Editorial & Rewrite Services

Photo Captions
Susan Sabel Advertising

Graphic Production Support
Vannika Bell
Brad Frost
John Gibson
Mark Heliger
Sean P. Riley

Contents

MONEY TALK

INTRODUCTION

"**B**asis points," "currency futures," "net present value"—as anyone who's tried to decipher an investment account statement knows, the lingo of finance can sound like a completely foreign language. There you are, with all of your 401k, mutual fund, and bank account statements spread out, determined to put your financial house in order, when the terrible truth dawns on you: you don't know what any of these words mean. Resolutely, you read the definitions in the tiny print on your statement. Now you're even more confused. Can't people just tell you what a call option is in plain English?

Of course they could, but they don't. Because they're more concerned with sounding official than with showing you the ropes. That's where *Money Talk* comes in. This is the book that will tell you what a call option is (in the plainest English) and even give you an example to boot. How many times have I wished someone would give me the real lowdown instead of a formal definition—and that's exactly why I compiled this book.

Money Talk is packed with the kind of plain-spoken definitions, examples, and illustrations that I would have liked to have during those late nights with my calculator. Even though I spent all of my days on the front lines of high finance, I could still be stumped by the lingo in my pension fund statement. I couldn't tell the difference between a "defined benefit" and a "defined contribution" plan, and the literature was doing nothing to make things easier.

Even today, when I think I've tackled every investment issue there is, I often run across a new term that baffles me. That's because Wall Street continues to invent weird and complex instruments with even weirder names (and nicknames) to match. And acronyms—who can keep up with the acronyms? Between LIBOR, LYONs, and LEAPS, there are days when the alphabet soup of the finance pages makes me run for my definition guide, which never seems to include what I'm looking for. That's why I've put together *Money Talk*.

I almost always find that, once you've got the right translation, these terms aren't so complicated at all. Heck, none of this stuff is really that confusing once you get past the two-dollar terminology. A call option? Really just another way to bet that a stock will go up. Net asset value? Essentially, the price of your mutual fund shares. Now, that's not so baffling, is it?

As always, I am a firm believer in the sensible mind of the "small" investor. With a little common sense and the right translation, all of us can master our financial lives. So get out those mutual fund statements one more time—with your copy of *Money Talk* firmly in hand. Now you can be your own expert.

A: Abatement to Average Life

abatement

Reduction of a property tax.

See also **property tax assessment.**

accelerated cost recovery system (ACRS)

Method of depreciating fixed assets for tax purposes. The most recent version is called the modified accelerated cost recovery system (MACRS).

ACRS and MACRS are forms of accelerated depreciation. Congress created ACRS in 1981 and MACRS in 1986. Assets placed in service after 1980 and before 1987 fall under ACRS; those placed in service after 1986 fall under MACRS. The purpose is to encourage investment by letting companies recover the cost of acquiring productive assets more quickly with relatively greater depreciation deductions early in an asset's life.

Under the ACRS system, instead of basing depreciation deductions on the individual useful life of a particular asset, you can group assets into eight basic property classes. The salvage value is ignored when calculating depreciation deductions.

The 3-, 5-, 7-, and 10-year property classes take a variation on the double-declining-balance depreciation method. The 15- and 20-year classes use another modification called the 150 percent declining-balance method. The remaining two property classes (depreciable over 27.5 and 39 years) use straight-line depreciation.

Did You Know?

You manage a small supermarket. A&P hires you away and gives you a $50,000 hiring bonus, payable over 3 years. Because your contract has an acceleration clause, you get the entire bonus if A&P goes out of business before the 3 years are up or if you're discharged without just cause.

A company with property in any of the classes may stretch out, rather than accelerate, depreciation by opting for straight-line depreciation with a feature called the half-year convention. That is, the company may deduct half the normal straight-line annual depreciation in the first year and deduct the other half in a year added at the end of the asset's economic life.

You would use the depreciation table like this: Say you have property that falls under a 3-year classification. In the first year you would depreciate it by 33.3 percent of its cost, in the second year by 44.5 percent, and so on. A property in the 20-year category would be depreciated similarly, and so on.

accelerated depreciation

Accounting methods that, in comparison with the straight-line method, recognize greater amounts of depreciation in the initial years of an asset's life and lesser amounts as the asset ages.

These methods recognize that some assets are more efficient and productive in their early years and become more costly to maintain, or even obsolete, as they age. Because accelerated depreciation gives businesses tax benefits early in an asset's life, it is sometimes used for tax reporting. For financial reporting, companies can then choose another method that suits them better.

The most common forms of accelerated depreciation are the 200 percent, or double-declining-balance method; the 150 percent declining-balance method; and the sum-of-the-years'-digits method. All methods recover the same amount of depreciation over the entire life of the asset.

See also **accelerated cost recovery system (ACRS)** and **depreciation.**

acceleration clause

Provision for immediate payment of money that's otherwise due over time. An acceleration clause might be found in a loan agreement or other contract. It says the money is due if certain things happen.

account executive (AE)

1 In marketing, a mid-level employee of an advertising agency or public relations firm who looks after the interests of one or more clients.

Among the AE's duties are analyzing problems and working with the client to create an advertising or public relations strategy. The AE makes sure all the client's advertising or public relations activities harmonize at the agency and serves as liaison to the agency's services, such as its media, research, and creative operations.

Use of the term has grown in other fields as well. A financial services firm, for instance, might have account executives looking after the interests of designated clients.

2 AE can also refer to a retail broker at an investment firm.

accountant

Person trained in accounting.

Accountants often specialize in a particular area, such as financial accounting, cost accounting, managerial accounting, taxes, or auditing. Their skills are needed for both internal analysis and external reporting. An accountant's work might range from calculating company earnings and preparing monthly financial statements to auditing financial records and developing capital expansion plans.

See also **audit.**

accountant's responsibility

Moral and professional obligation of a public practitioner to adhere to a code of ethics and conduct established by the various state boards of accountancy. In general, these codes recognize that an accountant occupies a position of trust and that investors, creditors, and others rely on the accountant to provide information that truly reflects a company's economic condition.

Just the Facts

What's a CPA?

A certified public accountant (CPA) has advanced training and must pass a rigorous certification process. A CPA usually offers a considerably higher level of service than a bookkeeper. Bookkeepers usually record daily numbers such as sales, receivables, and expenses, while a CPA analyzes the records of these activities to determine their financial consequences for a company.

accounting change

Switch in accounting principles, estimates, or the reporting entity.

One of the main reasons for an accounting change is when, as often happens, the Financial Accounting Standards Board (FASB) changes generally accepted accounting principles (GAAP). A new FASB standard might call for a company to make adjustments in the current year. Those adjustments have absolutely no impact on operations or cash flow, but they can make an enormous difference in the year's reported results.

See also **cumulative effect of accounting change.**

accounting equation

Formula that expresses the central relationship in accounting:

$$\text{assets} = \text{equities}$$

It is more commonly shown in a form that distinguishes between the equity of creditors and that of owners.

This equation gives rise to a system known as "double-entry bookkeeping." Each accounting transaction affects at least two accounts

---

There are three broad types of accounting changes:

1 A change from one generally accepted accounting principle to another, such as changing from one method of depreciation to another.

2 A change in estimates as the result of new information or additional experience, such as when collections on accounts receivable do not materialize as expected and the allowance for doubtful accounts must be increased.

3 A change from reporting as one type of entity to reporting as another type, such as after two companies merge.

in an equal but opposite manner. Anything that changes one side of the equation has to show up on the other side as well.

accounting method

How you keep your books—on a cash, a modified cash, or an accrual basis.

Here are the different accounting methods:

Cash Accounting

The simpler of the two cash methods. Revenues are reported when they are actually received; expenses are reported when they are paid.

Modified Cash Accounting

Contains certain items such as accounts receivable, accounts payable, depreciation, and so on, which are added to the cash balances, but accounts for these items are not maintained on a continuous basis.

Accrual Accounting

Revenues are recorded as they are earned, regardless of when you collect the money. Similarly, expenses are recorded as they are incurred, without regard to when you really pay out the money.

Many companies have to use the accrual basis, at least for external reporting. Generally accepted accounting principles (GAAP) require the use of the accrual method, and the Securities and Exchange Commission (SEC) mandates it for publicly traded corporations. For income tax purposes, most individual taxpayers can use the cash basis, but not for their inventories. The Internal Revenue Service (IRS) has been trying to force all substantial businesses to use the accrual method.

accounting period

Interval covered by a financial statement.

Companies typically close their books and prepare financial

statements at the end of a 12-month period, although interim reports may be published more frequently—say, quarterly. The 12-month period may conform to the January 1 to December 31 calendar year, or it may be a fiscal year, meaning it can be any continuous 12-month period, such as July 1 through June 30.

For tax purposes, owners of sole proprietorships and S-corporations do not have the option of electing a fiscal year that differs from the calendar year. Some partnerships and most corporations do have that option.

accounting rate of return (ARR)

Quick way to measure the potential profitability of an investment.

ARR is calculated by dividing annual net income by the amount of the investment:

$$\text{net income} \div \text{investment} = \text{ARR}$$

Financial managers and project analysts often use accounting rate of return to compare the potential profitability of different investment opportunities.

Example
You are considering an investment in a two-family home that you will rent out:

initial investment	$300,000
estimated life	30 years
cash flow per year	$36,000
annual depreciation (straight-line method)	$10,000

The ARR for this investment is:

$$(\$36,000 - \$10,000) \div \$300,000 = .0867\ (8.67\%)$$

See also **internal rate of return (IRR), net present value (NPV),** and **present value.**

accounts payable

Amount owed to vendors for goods and services received but not yet paid for.

An account payable is a liability to a creditor. It is listed as a current liability or a long-term liability on your balance sheet, depending on when the payment is due.

accounts receivable

Amount owed to you by customers who purchase goods or services on account.

This is a current asset, or short-term asset, on your balance sheet. There may be other types of receivables, such as notes receivable.

accretion

1   Increase in value of assets.
2   Difference between the price of a bond purchased at a discount and the par value of the bond.

Example
Real estate 20 miles from a growing city becomes more valuable as development gets closer. Autographs of famous people are worth more after the signers' deaths. Still, most assets—such as computers and cars—decrease in value over time.

If an investor pays $900 for a newly issued bond that has a par value of $1,000, that bond has an accretion of $100.

accrual basis

Method of accounting in which revenues are recorded as they are earned, regardless of when the money is actually received.

See also **accounting method.**

accrued expense

Any expense you have incurred but have not paid for by the end of your accounting period. Accrued expenses may also be called accrued liabilities.

See also **balance sheet.**

accrued interest

Earned interest that hasn't been paid to you yet.

Interest accrues on promissory notes, commercial paper, and bonds. When you sell a security with accrued interest, the buyer pays the amount that has accrued as well as the market price of the security.

accrued liabilities

Expenses a company has incurred but not yet paid for by the end of its accounting period.

See also **accrued expense** and **balance sheet.**

accrued revenue

Money earned that is neither received nor past due. It creates a receivable listed in the current asset section of the balance sheet.

accumulated depreciation

Total amount of depreciation taken on an asset or asset group, based on the use of a particular method and on estimates of the useful lives of the asset(s).

The conventional method in accounting is to record the acquisition of plant assets in one account and to record and accumulate the

annual depreciation charges in an offsetting account, known as a con-
tra account.

See also **depreciation**.

accumulated dividend

Overdue dividend on cumulative preferred stock.

A corporation carries the unpaid dividends on its books as a liability until they're paid. A dividend in arrears is likely to depress the
market price of both the issuer's common stock and its preferred
stock. You can't collect a dividend on your common shares until the
company has settled up with the holders of the cumulative preferred
stock.

See also **arrearage**.

ACHs

Automated clearinghouses.

See also **electronic funds transfer (EFT)**.

The Advantages of Being Preferred

Accrued dividends apply only to preferred stock, not common
stock. That's because the company isn't obligated to pay dividends to common shareholders.

---

acid test ratio

A measure of liquidity, or the company's ability to pay what it owes,
roughly over a 30-day period. Also called a quick ratio.

Different companies might give the categories slightly different
names, but the numerator is cash and those things that can easily be
converted to cash. The information can be found on a company's balance sheet.

The rule of thumb for the acid test ratio is 1:1; that is, you should have one dollar in quick assets for each dollar of current liabilities. The acid test ratio is a more restrictive version of the current ratio, which includes prepaid expenses as well as inventories.

acquisition

When one company buys another. Usually, the acquired company gives up its independent existence; the surviving company assumes all assets and liabilities.

See also **merger/acquisition (M&A)**.

ACRS

See **accelerated cost recovery system (ACRS)**.

active portfolio management

Using investment strategy—the opposite of buy-and-hold, or passive portfolio management. An active strategy can include changing the asset mix during cycles in the investment markets, shifting between stocks in different industries, and buying and selling individual shares based on under- and overvalued target prices.

Conservative investors tend to favor a buy-and-hold strategy, characterized by a stable, long-term asset mix of stocks, long-term and short-term bonds, and cash; broad diversification across industries; and a low portfolio turnover rate (very little switching in and out of investments).

In contrast, passive portfolio management involves less decision making on the part of the manager—it is often a "buy-and-hold," or indexing, strategy in which the portfolio is simply constructed to match a popular index.

The more actively one trades, the greater the transaction costs, such as brokerage commissions. The active investor is also likely to spend considerable time and money on research.

In your accounting system, some cash gets reported along with the marketable securities, and some marketable securities show up as cash. The amounts involved are small, and there is no reason for you to explain it.

See also **conservatism concept, consistency concept,** and **matching concept.**

additional paid-in capital

Part of shareholders' equity on the balance sheet that shows what investors paid above (or below) par value for shares in a company.

Things to Think About

Believers in the efficient market theory have no use for active portfolio management: if securities prices already reflect everything that's known, and if future changes will be random, what's to be gained by making a lot of trades?

---

adequate disclosure concept

Financial reporting convention requiring that, along with your financial statements, you provide whatever materials are needed to understand them.

The additional information may be in notes to the financial statements or in supplementary schedules. Adequate disclosure goes hand in hand with the materiality concept: if it does not make much difference, you don't need to provide the details, as they might overwhelm readers. Companies court potential problems if they do not disclose information a reasonable person would consider material.

Although a company may issue shares to investors at $20 per share, the par value of the shares might be only $1. The $19 difference would be the additional paid-in capital.

adjustable rate

Interest rate that changes periodically.

The adjustments are based on a standard market rate, such as the prime rate, or the rate on Treasury bills. Also called a floating rate, increasing rate, or exchangeable rate, the rate can change quarterly, monthly, or semiannually. A floor puts a limit on how low the interest rate can fall; a ceiling limits the rise.

An adjustable rate note (also known as a resettable or exchangeable note) may be used by a company to lengthen a bond's maturity. In the event that the maturity date shifts out, bondholders will often have the option of selling their bonds back to the company or they may receive a new "adjusted" coupon rate, which makes the bond trade at a certain price (usually above par value). This structure may also apply to preferred stock.

In your accounting system, some cash gets reported along with the marketable securities, and some marketable securities show up as cash. The amounts involved are small, and there is no reason for you to explain it.

See also **conservatism concept, consistency concept,** and **matching concept**.

adjustable rate mortgage (ARM)

A loan (also called a variable rate mortgage or a floating rate mortgage) whose interest rate fluctuates with prevailing market rates.

An ARM's initial interest rate might be 1 to 3 percentage points cheaper than conventional fixed rate mortgage rates. A 2 percentage point differential on a $100,000 mortgage can shave more than $140 off monthly payments. But after the first year or two, the rate is usually pegged 2 to 4 percentage points higher than the market rate it is based on. ARMs are most often linked to one-year Treasury bills, the national average mortgage rate (calculated by the Federal Home Loan Bank), the prime rate, or the Eleventh District cost of funds rate (the average cost S&Ls pay on deposits). The shorter the term of the index an ARM is linked to, the more your payments will tend to fluctuate. Some ARMs change rates annually, although some loans adjust as seldom as 3 to 5 years or as often as every month. In the mid-1990s, 5-to-1 adjustables, which lock in the initial rate for 5 years and then adjust annually, became popular.

Some ARMs come with a payment cap guaranteeing that monthly payments won't increase more than, say, 7.5 percent in any year. That may sound reassuring, but it can be dangerous. If rates rise and your payments stagnate, you will run into a dangerous pitfall: negative amortization. That's when monthly payments aren't enough to cover interest and principal payments, causing the size of the loan to increase at a compounded rate.

Don't confuse payment caps with rate caps, which are good. They limit interest rate increases—and decreases—in a given period. Some ARMs also have aggregate, or lifetime, caps. Standard rate caps used to be 2 and 6 (for period and lifetime adjustments, respectively). Now an increasing number of ARMs offer 1 and 5 percentage point caps.

See also **hybrid mortgage**.

adjustable rate note

See **adjustable rate**.

adjustable rate preferred stock

Variety of preferred stock whose dividends fluctuate with prevailing interest rates. Also called floating rate preferred stock.

The dividend on this type of preferred stock is tied to an interest rate benchmark, such as the Treasury bill rate. Most of these preferred stocks have a built-in ceiling and floor: the issuer will never have to pay more than the ceiling interest rate, and the buyer will never have to accept less than the floor.

See also **collar**.

adjustable rate security

See **adjustable rate note** and **adjustable rate preferred stock**.

adjusted gross income (AGI)

An individual's total taxable annual gross income minus any allowable losses.

What you must include in your AGI: wages, profits from a small business, annuity income, pension income, profits from the sale of investments, interest or dividend income, rental income, royalty payments.

What you can subtract: losses from a small business from an investment in a limited liability, deductible contributions to an IRA or Keogh, contributions to a pension plan or an S-corporation, alimony (but not child support) payments, premature withdrawal penalties from CDs, and deductions from real estate investments.

The more you can reduce your AGI, the more AGI-based Schedule A deductions you can claim. For instance, you can deduct medical expenses up to 7.5 percent of AGI, and miscellaneous expenses (such as job-related expenses) only in excess of 2 percent of AGI.

adjustment bond

A bond issued by a company during financial reorganization.

See also **income bond**.

ADRs

See **American Depository Receipts (ADRs)**.

adverse opinion

An auditor's negative recommendation.

See also **audit**.

adverse selection

1 An exchange of goods, services, or currency that's off balance because either the buyer or the seller has hidden information.

The prior knowledge puts the other side at a disadvantage, which makes it more difficult for that side to get a fair deal. Adverse selection disrupts the workings of a marketplace that may be considered fair and equitable on the whole.

2 In marketing, adverse selection refers to a pricing policy that results in less-desirable customers.

An example in the auto insurance market is the higher rates in high theft areas.

affinity card

Credit card that offers some reward for its use. As financial institutions fight each other for customers, they might offer everything from contributions to a charity to frequent flyer mileage, and even cash rebates, based on the use of their cards. One of the best known is the General Motors MasterCard, initiated in 1993, which gives its users credit toward the purchase of a new GM car.

AFR

See **applicable federal rate (AFR)**.

against the box

Another term for a covered sale. For example, if shares are sold short but are held in the account so that they could be delivered later (to eventually complete the trade), they are considered sold "against the box."

See also **call**.

agent

Intermediary that routes goods or services from a producer to consumers.

See also **distribution channel**.

AGI

See **adjusted gross income (AGI)**.

AICPA

See **American Institute of Certified Public Accountants (AICPA)**.

all or none

1 In securities brokerage, an investor's requirement that it's all or nothing: the broker must cancel the transaction if he or she can't buy or sell the whole enchilada.

2 In investment banking, a provision that sales of a securities offering will become final only if the entire issue is sold by a certain date.

If the offering is undersubscribed, it will be withdrawn. That protects investment bankers from getting stuck with securities they can't sell. They'll seek an "all or none" provision when the market climate for a particular deal looks uncertain. But most U.S. offerings are underwritten issues, meaning the investment banker agrees to buy the whole issue and assume the risk.

allowance

1 In taxes: the number of dependents, including yourself, that you claim on a W-4 form when you are first hired (and whenever your tax circumstances change).

The employer uses this number to calculate how much money to withhold from every paycheck for personal income taxes. The amount withheld from your paycheck decreases for each allowance you claim. How much each allowance saves you in withholding depends on your tax bracket. (Self-employed people, who have no withholding, must list their allowances on a worksheet to determine the amount of quarterly estimated taxes they have to pay.)

2 Regular payments from an income earner to a dependent. For instance, parents often give their children weekly allowances, which may be based on completion of household chores.

Exemptions versus Allowances

An allowance is different from an exemption, which is a tax deduction for each dependent (including the taxpayer).

---

alpha (α)

1 Measure of a stock's price movements in response to factors specific to a company.

To help explain alpha, we will start with beta (β). Beta is a measure of how a particular security performs in response to changes affecting the whole stock market—like shifts in the economy, interest rates, and inflation. Alpha eliminates the effect of general market fluctuations and examines how the stock would do if the market were flat—as though securities rose and fell entirely on their own merits. These merits include such things as anticipated growth in earnings per share, management effectiveness, and labor relations. In other words, while beta measures response to the stock market's behavior, alpha responds to a company's behavior.

2 Long-established stocks on the London Stock Exchange having a solid record of paying dividends. In the United Kingdom,

the term "alpha stocks" applies to what are called blue chips in the United States.

3 When used in reference to mutual funds, alpha represents the relationship between a fund's performance and its beta, usually over a three-year period.

To calculate a historical alpha (α), you need the following values:

$\rho\varphi$	the security's rate of return
β	the security's historical beta
$\rho\mu$	the historical return of the market
$\rho\phi$	the risk-free rate of return

The formula:

$$\rho\varphi - [\beta\ (\rho\mu - \rho\phi)] = \alpha$$

Let's say a company's stock had a 20 percent return last year. The stock's historical beta is 1.5, the rate of return for the market was 10 percent, and the risk-free rate was 5 percent.

$$20\% - [1.5 \times (10\% - 5\%)] = 12.5\%$$

The stock's historical alpha is 12.5 percent.

alphabet stock

Categories of stock within the same stock-issuing corporation. For example, someone might own "E" shares of a particular company, while someone else owns "B" shares. These different categories often have different prices and voting rights.

alternative minimum tax (AMT)

Uncle Sam's way of limiting how much income you can shield from the tax collector.

The AMT can apply to individuals, corporations, limited partnerships, estates, and trusts. Because regular partnerships and S-corporations don't pay federal income taxes on their own, the AMT doesn't apply to them.

The AMT is figured slightly differently for individual and corporate taxpayers. Here's how it works for individuals: you calculate a new AMT base-income figure, on Form 6251, by adding back some of the deductions you took figuring your taxes the conventional way, and make other related adjustments. Then you subtract a $45,000 statutory exemption, if you're married, filing jointly ($33,750 if you're single). You pay 26 percent on the first $175,000 of AMT income (after subtracting exemptions) and 28 percent on anything over that amount. If the final number exceeds your regular federal income tax liability, that's what you'll have to pay.

Congress continues to wrestle with the AMT, and it's unlikely to survive unchanged for very long. But while it's on the books, if you're in its range, think about deferring some expenses and possibly accelerating income. You might also elect alternative depreciation methods that don't have AMT consequences.

American Depository Receipts (ADRs)

Certificates representing stake in a foreign company held in the United States.

ADRs, also called American Depository Shares, are traded on U.S. stock exchanges and through U.S. brokers, eliminating the need for U.S. residents to deal in foreign currencies on foreign markets. Transactions are the same as for U.S. shares, although one ADR does not necessarily represent one share; it can correspond to multiple shares or fractional shares.

American Institute of Certified Public Accountants (AICPA)

National professional society for those who have met the requirements to be certified public accountants (CPAs).

The AICPA prepares and grades the Uniform CPA Examination, which is given by state licensing bodies to accountants who want to be CPAs. The organization also wields considerable influence in setting accounting and auditing standards and in formulating and policing rules of ethical conduct throughout the accounting profession. Founded in 1887, the AICPA has more than 300,000 members.

American option

The option traders use to buy or sell commodities, securities, or other assets at future dates and at specified prices.

A European option must be exercised on a specific date. The American option allows the owner to exercise the option any time before its expiration date.

See also **derivatives** and **hedge**.

American Stock Exchange (AMEX)

Smaller of New York's two stock exchanges.

Because of more lenient listing requirements than those of the New York Stock Exchange (NYSE), the companies whose common shares are traded on the AMEX are usually smaller. The AMEX now specializes in the trading of foreign issues, American Depository Receipts (ADRs), and options on many NYSE and some over-the-counter (OTC) stocks.

amortization

1 Periodic write-down of intangible assets, such as patents or goodwill. The cost basis of the assets is gradually reduced through regular charges to income. Amortization also refers to the gradual extinction of any debt over time, such as the amortization of a mortgage.

See also **depletion** and **depreciation**.

2 In bond investments, amortization is apportioning, over the life

of the investment, any premium you might have paid above par value.

3 In corporate financing, it means repaying a loan in installments that will cover the entire principal and interest by maturity.

AMT
See **alternative minimum tax (AMT)**.

angels
In finance, a term for investors in start-up companies.

announcement effect
A theory that the price of a company's common stock tends to fall when the company announces that it will issue new shares and rise when it announces a new debt issue.

The presumption is that management, which has better information than investors have, will sell its equity only when it's pessimistic about the future. If management is optimistic, according to this theory, it will raise money by borrowing rather than give up any ownership in the company.

annual meeting
Gathering of a corporation's shareholders in which directors are elected, other key matters are voted on, and business issues are discussed.

This is a once-a-year, legally required rite for publicly held corporations. Since most U.S.-based corporations operate on a calendar-year basis, the season for annual meetings centers on early May, allowing enough time after year's end for the annual report and proxy statement to be prepared and mailed to shareholders.

In practice, only a small percentage of the outstanding stock is represented by shareholders who attend the meeting in person. Most individuals and institutions that hold the company's stock vote by proxy in advance.

Although the annual meeting is necessary in its current form for various legal reasons, there is an increasing desire among corporate executives to find an alternative. Since it is common for some 90 percent of the votes to be cast by mail, the physical meeting is usually symbolic. And it is expensive, not only in costs like transportation, accommodations, and catering, but in the time that management must set aside from business operations to prepare for unpredictable questions.

annual percentage rate (APR)

Measurement of the true cost of credit.

The APR is more exact and higher than the stated interest rate for installment loans, because it considers the compounding of interest during the loan period. Since 1969, federal law has required disclosure of the APR and total finance charges on all financial contracts in the United States. Essentially, the APR restates the full cost of the loan as a simple, effective annual interest rate.

There are four ways to calculate the APR for installment loans:

1 actuarial method
2 direct-ratio method
3 constant-ratio method
4 N-ratio method

The actuarial method, generally used by lenders, gives the most accurate results but involves complicated computerized calculations. Lenders calculate interest using a fixed rate on the unpaid balance of the principal of a loan. The borrower pays an installment, the lion's share of which is applied to the interest. As the loan matures, interest payments decline as those on the principal increase.

annual report

Publication prepared by a company—primarily for its shareholders and bondholders—at the end of its reporting year.

Most U.S. corporations operate on a calendar-year basis, so most annual reports are prepared during January and February and are distributed to security holders by late March or early April. As a rule, the annual report is mailed along with the company's proxy statement and proxy card, which enables the shareholder to vote by mail in advance of the annual meeting.

The Securities and Exchange Commission (SEC) requires distribution of the annual report, which must include the company's income statement, balance sheet, cash flow statement, statement of shareholders' equity, and the audit report. The Financial Accounting Standards Board (FASB) also requires companies to submit information about contracts and sales to foreign sources and government agencies.

All of this required information must be sent to shareholders before the company's annual meeting. Most publicly held corporations also include, as the front part of the annual report, a letter from the top one or two executives, an operating review focusing on the company's achievements and prospects, and photographs. In addition to the security holders, who are the primary audience for the annual report, potential shareholders, stock analysts, creditors, employees, job applicants, business associates, government officials, and others seeking information on the company might have an interest in its contents.

See also **10-K**.

annuity

An investment contract sold by an insurance company, which guarantees future payments to the buyer on a monthly, quarterly, or annual basis. Annuities are often used to provide retirement income.

When payments are made at the beginning of a specified period, the contract is called an annuity due or an annuity in advance;

if payments are made at the end of the period, it is an ordinary annuity or an annuity in arrears.

In accounting terms, a mortgage with monthly payments qualifies as an annuity, as does a trust account into which are made quarterly deposits for a child's future education.

See also **future value of an annuity**.

antitrust law

Body of laws and court precedents designed to protect citizens and companies against unfair business practices, including the formation of monopolies.

Key congressional legislation has resulted in the following:

Sherman Antitrust Act of 1890

The first major piece of legislation designed to prevent monopolies.

Clayton Act of 1914

Closed some of the loopholes in the Sherman Act by pinpointing specific things businesses could not do, including purchasing large quantities of a competitor's stock and using discriminatory pricing.

Federal Trade Commission Act of 1914

Established a policing agency—the Federal Trade Commission (FTC)—for the increasingly complex world of big-time business. It was expected not only to track down offenders but also to counsel companies on how to avoid antitrust violations.

Robinson-Patman Act of 1936

Eliminated loopholes and reduced the amount of proof required to make a case of illegal pricing. Also outlawed price discrimination.

Wheeler-Lea Act of 1938

Broadened the FTC's powers to police bad business practices, such as deceptive advertising, that are harmful not only to the public but to competitors as well.

Celler-Kefauver Act of 1950

Forbade mergers through the acquisition of a competitor's assets. Since the Celler-Kefauver Act, most of the major changes in antitrust law have evolved from court decisions. The most recent trend has been to impose fewer restraints on vertical integration.

APB

Directive handed down regarding accounting practices.

See also **generally accepted accounting principles (GAAP)**.

applicable federal rate (AFR)

Set by the IRS, this is the minimum interest rate that family members and friends are required to charge each other on personal loans.

appraisal

1 An expert opinion about the value of personal or real property.
   For collectibles, the Appraisers Association of America (212-889-5404) and the International Society of Appraisers (206-241-0359) certify member appraisers and hold them to a code of ethics. Call these groups to find names of local members if you need an appraisal on a collectible you want to buy or sell, or to prove your cost basis to Uncle Sam when you report a profit or loss from the sale of a collectible. Appraisers should submit a written, signed report explaining the factors upon which they set the value.

2 In human resources, an assessment of an employee's job performance.

For real estate, both buyer and seller should obtain their own independent appraisals. Buyers must submit an appraisal when they apply for a mortgage, which banks use to determine how much they are willing to loan (a certain percentage of the property's appraised value). The National Association of Master Appraisers (1-800-229-NAMA) or the Appraisal Institute (312-335-4100) can help you find an appraiser in your area. Buyers can also use their appraisal, if it is lower than the seller's, as a bargaining chip for negotiating the price of property.

appreciation

1 Increase in the value of property over time.

2 The excess of the fair value of assets over the book value.

APR

See **annual percentage rate (APR)**.

APT

See **arbitrage pricing theory (APT)**.

arbitrage

Buying a security, currency, or commodity on one market and simultaneously selling it (or an equivalent) at a higher price on another market.

A simple arbitrage deal might involve buying a silver contract in Chicago for $4.70 an ounce and selling an equal contract in Hong Kong for $4.72. A more complicated arbitrage strategy might involve several variables such as currency rates, interest rates, and derivatives such as options. For example, an arbitrageur (known also as an arb)

Did You Know?

A company might own land that has become more valuable over time. Generally, it is required to carry its assets on its books at the historical cost—what it actually paid to acquire the property. But when a business changes hands or goes through a restructuring, appreciation may be recognized by marking up book value to fair value.

---

might buy a stock with French francs in Paris while selling an option on it in U.S. dollars in New York and hedging the foreign exchange exposure.

Because markets tend toward equal prices, arbitrageurs must act quickly to take advantage of temporary differentials. Also, because the price differences are small, arbitrageurs need to trade in big blocks to reap sizable profits. Some investors argue that arbitrageurs destabilize the markets because they trade so quickly in such large blocks. Others contend that the arbitrageur's trading helps equalize the markets by pushing the price up in the weaker market and down in the stronger one.

arbitrage pricing theory (APT)

A way to understand and control risk in securities portfolios.

This highly quantitative system, developed by Stephen Ross, a Yale professor of economics and finance, is based on theorems from linear algebra. It focuses on macroeconomic factors that can explain the risk of each security in an investment portfolio. According to Professor William Goetzmann, a colleague of Ross at Yale, no one knows how many factors affect stock market returns. Some of the likely suspects include:

- Investor confidence, as measured by the spread between government and corporate bond rates. A smaller spread means greater investor confidence. The idea is that the more confident investors become in corporations' ability to pay their bills, the lower the premium they will demand for buying corporate bonds.
- Interest rates, with higher rates usually attracting money away from the stock market and depressing stock prices.
- Gross National Product (GNP) and stage of the business cycle.
- Unexpected inflation, measured by deviations from economic forecasts of inflation.
- Evolving expectations about inflation.

Each factor is assigned a risk premium based on past changes in the security's return as the factor fluctuated. Different analysts may use different sets of factors.

The theory expands the idea of beta (β), which compares a security to the average performance of the stock market as measured by an index, usually Standard & Poor's (S&P) 500. Although few analysts today rely on a single factor like beta, the trick is picking the right factors to use.

Investment managers use APT to adjust the risk of their portfolios. Arbitrageurs use it to attempt to earn rates of return in excess of the market risk factor. APT also helps investment bankers determine a security's value at a given time.

arbitration

Submitting a dispute for settlement by an impartial individual or panel. When the individual arbitrator or a board of arbitration makes a decision, it is binding. That is what distinguishes arbitration from mediation, where the third party has no authority to impose a settlement.

Although commonly referred to as the preferred alternative to litigation, arbitration predates the organization of court systems and was recognized 25 centuries ago by the Greeks as a means to quickly and efficiently settle disputes. Today, many business contracts, especially in the securities industry, contain provisions for arbitration. The benefits include reduced legal expenses and faster settlement than in court cases. Plus, unlike most court proceedings, arbitration is carried out in private. That means dirty linen does not get washed in public, and trade secrets are less likely to become public knowledge. Usually, an arbitrator's award can be appealed to the courts only if there is a question over whether proper procedure was followed, not over the facts of the case.

The securities industry keeps arbitrators busy with client grievances against brokerage companies, complaints by registered representatives about employers, and disputes between securities companies.

arm's-length transaction

A transaction in which each party is able and free to act in its own best economic interest.

If both parties are fully informed, neither is under any special compulsion to complete the transaction, and both are equally capable of negotiating the transaction, the resulting price should be at fair market value. A loan, lease, or other agreement between two parties is considered an arm's-length transaction if the terms are the same as for unrelated parties. Goods sold to a parent company by a subsidiary at cost would not be considered at arm's length. Many tax laws related to deductions and adjustments are affected by whether a transaction is deemed to be at arm's length.

ARR

See **accounting rate of return (ARR)**.

arrearage

Overdue payments, especially those involving interest on bonds or dividends on preferred stock.

A company cannot pay dividends on its common stock as long as bond interest or dividends on cumulative preferred stock are in arrears.

See also **accumulated dividend**.

articles of incorporation

Document individuals must file with their secretary of state to form a corporation.

The document typically gives:

- the corporation's name
- its officers, purposes, and fiscal year
- the amount of paid-in capital; that is, how much people paid for the stock
- other information on the stock, such as the number of shares authorized and outstanding

See also **bylaws** and **charter**.

asked price

The price at which a commodity or security is offered for sale.

In mutual funds, this is also called the offering price, which is calculated by taking the current net asset value (NAV) per share of the fund and adding on any commission or front-end load.

See also **bid price**.

asset

In accounting, a company's resource that has future value. There are two broad types of assets:

1 *Tangible:* These assets include such things as buildings, cash, inventories, land, supplies, and vehicles.
2 *Intangible:* Copyrights, goodwill, and patents are examples.

Assets are reported on a company's balance sheet in two categories: current (likely to be converted to cash within one year or within the company's normal operating cycle, whichever is longer) and fixed (likely to have utility beyond one year).

asset allocation

A method of diversifying investments by keeping a set percent of the value of a portfolio in stocks, bonds, cash, and other investment vehicles.

asset coverage

Relationship between the value of a company's assets and a particular obligation.

A potential lender might consider the asset coverage before deciding on a loan. To calculate asset coverage, he or she takes the value of the company's assets as expressed on the balance sheet, then subtracts intangible assets, current liabilities, and any obligations that are ahead in line. The lender weighs the resulting number against the potential loan obligation.

Since a bond is another form of loan, you would examine the asset coverage for a particular bond issue just as you would for a loan. And although preferred stock is not technically a loan, it is an obligation that can be looked at the same way. When it comes to common stock, which is last in line for a claim on the company's assets, asset coverage is usually expressed as book value per share.

asset stripping

A term used for a type of financial surgery on a takeover target. Various parts of the company are removed and sold in an effort to recover the cost of acquiring the company.

asset-backed security

A form of borrowing secured by assets and the income attached to them.

Mortgage-backed bonds may be considered a form of asset-backed security, but these have come to be regarded as a class of their own. Usually, the term "asset-backed security" refers to automobile loans, credit card receivables, home equity loans, and leases that have been bundled together and then sold as securities. The underlying assets will provide the cash stream to pay these instruments.

See also **securitization**.

asset-based lending

Using balance sheet assets, such as accounts receivable or inventories, to secure a senior note.

The lender will closely monitor the company's collateral and financial data.

assignment loan

A loan that a bank partially transfers to other lenders.

Large money center banks, whose demand for loans tends to exceed their supply of funds, might sell some of their loans to smaller banks. This secondary market for bank loans replenishes lenders' liquid funds, enabling them to make loans to other borrowers. With an assignment, the borrower must agree; the institution buying part of the loan has a direct claim on the borrower. This is by far the most common way for a bank to sell part of a loan.

A less common, and more risky, arrangement is called a participation loan. The borrower isn't part of the deal and has no direct legal relationship with the one or more institutions buying part of the loan. If the lead bank goes belly-up, the other lenders might have trouble recovering their money.

asymmetric information

A theory that different groups of market participants might have different information about a particular company, causing their expectations about that company—and their investment behavior—to differ.

See also **announcement effect**.

at the market

A phrase indicating the market price. If a broker is told to execute a trade "at the market," it means that the order will go through at whatever price the market happens to be trading.

at the open

A phrase indicating the first opening price of the market. If a broker is told to execute an order "at the open," it means that you want the earliest available trade when the market opens on the next trading day.

ATM

See **automated teller machine**.

auction rate preferred

Variation of floating rate preferred stock where the dividends are reset through a Dutch auction.

The auction is held every 49 days to allow investing corporations to keep their 70 percent exclusion from income taxes on dividends. To qualify for an exclusion, the corporations must hold the stock for at least 46 days.

Shareholders can participate in the auction by submitting a bid for the minimum dividend they will accept. If their bid is higher than the lowest rate needed to sell the issue, these shareholders can sell their shares to new investors at par value. American Express issued the first auction rate preferred stock in 1984.

audit

Examination of a company's books or operations.

We will deal here primarily with the financial audit. In performing a financial audit, an accountant must conduct the work in accordance with generally accepted auditing standards (GAAS). These standards are set by the Auditing Standards Board, an arm of the American Institute of Certified Public Accountants (AICPA). The auditor's report or opinion will appear in the company's annual report and in its annual 10-K filing with the Securities and Exchange Commission (SEC).

Aside from financial audits, other types are:

1 *Internal audit:* Where an auditor within the company investigates its procedures to ensure that they meet corporate policies.
2 *Management audit:* Examines management's efficiency.
3 *Compliance audit:* Determines whether a company is following specific rules.

authorized shares

The maximum number of common and preferred shares a company can issue.

Companies aren't required to issue the entire amount. They can periodically issue shares as needed—say, for distributed dividends—up to the amount of their authorized shares. This figure, which appears in the company's articles of incorporation, can be increased only by a vote of shareholders. The company must then file an amendment to its charter and obtain approval from the appropriate state officer or agency, often the secretary of state.

automated clearinghouses (ACHs)

Electronic interchange systems among banks.

See also **electronic funds transfer (EFT)**.

automated teller machine (ATM)

A machine provided by a financial institution that allows bank customers to complete a variety of transactions, such as withdrawals and deposits, without interacting with a bank teller.

average life

The length of time from a bond's release until its maturity.

See also **yield to average life (YTAL)**.

B: Baby Bond to Bylaws

baby bond

A bond with a par value of less than $1,000.

Baby bonds open the bond market to small investors, but they can be more expensive relative to the dollar value because of the higher administrative costs. Brokerage costs might be high, too.

In fact, new issues of baby bonds are rare. Nevertheless, in the early 1990s the Midwest Securities Trust Company, a subsidiary of the Chicago Stock Exchange, began the first program for registered municipal and corporate baby bonds. The Baby Bond Safekeeping Program holds the certificates, keeps records, and arranges automated payment of interest and redemption money.

back-end load

The fee a mutual fund investor must pay when selling his or her shares. A front-end load is paid when the shares in the fund are originally purchased.

backwardation

1 In commodity futures and foreign exchange trading, when contracts with the nearest deliveries cost more than those with later deliveries.

This occurs when demand is greater for commodities that can be delivered soon. The opposite situation, when contracts with the longer maturities command higher prices (i.e., corn to be delivered in six months costs more than corn to be delivered this month), is called contango. Contango is considered the more "natural" state of the market, because it's assumed that storage and administrative fees should make a more distant delivery date more expensive.

2 London Stock Exchange term for the fees and interest a seller of a security pays to a buyer for deferring delivery.

bad debt expense

Amount included as an expense on a company's income statement based on an estimate of accounts receivable that will not be collected. These estimates are reviewed annually in light of actual experience.

At the end of every quarter, you take a look at all of the debts you're owed by your clients. You reasonably assume that 5 percent of them will never be paid and move that amount from accounts receivable on your balance sheet to bad debt expense on your income statement.

bad debt recovery

Receivable you previously wrote off as uncollectible, but you have now collected.

balance forward

Bookkeeping or billing method in which individual charges are itemized on the statement where they first appear, but show up only as a balance on later statements.

Under the alternative to the balance forward method—known as open invoice billing—all unpaid charges are itemized on each succeeding bill until they're finally paid.

Although there's no hard-and-fast rule, monthly bills that are presented directly to the consumer—such as credit card and telephone bills—generally follow the balance forward format. Bills from one business to another—for goods that will later be resold, for example—tend to use the open invoice method.

balance sheet

Snapshot of a company's finances at a given time, usually at the close of a fiscal quarter or year.

The balance sheet portrays the basic accounting equation:

assets = liabilities + owner's equity

The left side of the equation shows the company's resources (assets), and the right side shows the amount it owes (liabilities) and the amount belonging to the owners (including their capital contributions and earnings retained in the business). It is called a balance sheet because the left and right sides of the equation balance out, which is another way of saying that your company's assets equal the sources of those assets.

Because this is a corporation, owner's equity here is shareholders' equity. The only other difference between the format of this balance sheet and the accounting equation is that it is laid out vertically rather than horizontally.

assets = liabilities + shareholders' equity
$24,900,000,000 = $15,800,000,000 + $9,100,000,000

Assets are listed in the balance sheet in order of decreasing liquidity—that is, the speed with which a particular asset can be turned into cash should the need arise.

An example of a balance sheet for a large corporation on December 31, 1995, would contain the following:

Assets are divided into two types:

1 *Current assets:* These will be converted into cash or used
   within a year or within the company's normal operating cycle,
   whichever is longer. Listed in order of proximity to cash,
   current assets typically consist of cash and cash equivalents,
   followed by marketable securities such as government notes,
   bankers' acceptances, and commercial paper. Next are accounts
   receivable, inventories, deferred income taxes, and prepaid
   expenses.

2 *Fixed assets:* These are less liquid than current assets and not
   likely to be converted to cash within a year. Typically, these
   assets are not acquired for resale but are viewed as productive assets. They include properties, plants, and equipment;
   investments; and other resources, including intangibles such
   as patents, franchises, goodwill, and exploration permits.

The second part of the balance sheet contains the right-hand
side of the equation—liabilities and shareholders' equity. Like assets,
liabilities are divided into current and long-term, the difference being
whether they will be paid off within a year.

Here is how liabilities and shareholders' equity break down:

Current Liabilities

These include accounts payable, accrued liabilities (expenses
incurred but not yet paid at the end of the accounting period),
taxes payable, short-term debt, and the current portion of long-
term debt.

Noncurrent Liabilities

These consist of long-term debt (mostly loans, mortgages, and
bonds), other liabilities, and deferred income taxes.

Shareholders' Equity

This is shown in the following accounting equation:

assets − liabilities = shareholders' equity

Listed first under shareholders' equity is the par value of outstanding preferred stock and common stock. Next comes additional paid-in capital, which is what people paid for the stock over its par value. Retained earnings—what it takes to balance the equation—represent all the accumulated earnings of the company minus the dividends it has paid to shareholders. Taken together, the owner's equity section of a balance sheet represents the company's net assets.

See also **income statement** and **statement of financial position**.

balanced mutual fund

A mutual fund that mixes bonds, cash, preferred stocks, and common stocks.

Although balanced mutual funds share the most attractive features of other types of mutual funds—diversification, a relatively small minimum investment, and ready conversion to cash—they also have several advantages all their own. Because of their bond component (depending on the fund, 30 to 50 percent of the portfolio usually consists of bonds and cash, with stocks making up the remainder), balanced funds are less subject to short-term price swings that might bedevil funds composed solely of stocks.

There's considerable overlap in the conditions that cause stocks and bonds to perform well—if interest rates are low and stocks are booming, bonds will usually do nicely, too. But they don't move in lockstep. Even if one half of the portfolio is stagnating—or actually heading south—the other might be doing reasonably well.

balancing

A way to determine that financial information from one source corresponds to a related source.

A familiar example is balancing a checkbook. At the end of each statement period, account holders would be wise to compare their record of how much is left in the account with the bank's monthly statement. First you subtract from the previous balance the value of any checks you wrote during the month, add that month's deposits, and compare the result—less the value of any outstanding checks and plus any outstanding deposits—to the adjusted bank balance. Unless the two sums are equal, some sort of error has been made (perhaps on the part of the bank, but more often, alas, by the account holder) that must be found and corrected.

You can apply the same general procedure to other types of accounts, such as money market funds or savings accounts, to ensure that you and those managing your money at the other end are working with the same information.

balloon payment

A payment on a loan that is particularly large relative to any other payments. A balloon payment is usually the last payment on a loan and usually retires the balance of the loan.

BAN

See **bond anticipation note (BAN)**.

bank

A financial institution that receives money from individuals or businesses—depositors—and pays them a modest rate of interest. The bank earns a profit by lending money from this pool to other individuals or businesses at a higher rate of interest.

When most of us think "bank," we think of a commercial

bank, which offers other familiar services as well, such as checking and savings accounts and automated banking. Other types of banks include:

- *Investment banks:* essentially securities wholesalers (i.e., Merrill Lynch, Salomon Brothers, Morgan Stanley Dean Witter). When a company issues new stocks or bonds, they are initially sold to investment banks, which resell them to the investment public at a higher price, turning a profit on the transaction.

- *Credit unions:* depositor-owned cooperatives—usually associated with a large employer, a professional association, or some other group—that accept deposits from members and offer them low-interest loans.

- *Savings and loan associations (S&Ls):* accept deposits from the general public and loan money to borrowers planning to build or buy a home. In return for investing a large proportion of their assets in home mortgages, S&Ls receive federal tax benefits. However, many S&Ls also make business loans and general consumer loans as well.

- *Mortgage banks:* like S&Ls, mortgage banks are in the business of providing home mortgages. Unlike S&Ls, however, they don't accept money from individual depositors. The mortgage bank borrows the money it needs to provide a mortgage from another financial institution, such as a commercial bank, and loans it to the consumer. It then resells the resulting mortgage to a company that wishes to hold it as a secure long-term investment.

These types of banks provide a variety of specialized services not always available from commercial banks. However, the line between these institutions has become blurred as the government has continued to deregulate the financial services industry over the last 15 or so years.

See also **banking regulation**.

bank draft

Paper withdrawal authorization from a bank account.

See also **bill of exchange**.

bankers' acceptance

A draft drawn on and accepted by a bank that orders payment to a third party at a later date.

Bankers' acceptances are a common method of financing import and export transactions. Backing by the bank assures the seller that the funds for payment will be available.

banking regulation

A number of federal actions have kept banks, the securities industry, and insurance companies regulated and out of one another's businesses for most of the twentieth century.

Three key regulations were:

1 *The Bank Holding Company Act, also known as the McFadden Act, of 1927:* This law prohibited federally chartered banks from operating across state lines in most cases. The Douglas Amendment of 1956 restricted the ability of banks to use holding companies to get around the McFadden Act.

2 *The Glass-Steagall Act of 1933:* It established the Federal Deposit Insurance Corporation (FDIC) to insure bank deposits and separated commercial and investment banking, reasoning that federally insured deposits shouldn't be exposed to the whims of Wall Street.

3 *Regulation Q:* A cap set by the Federal Reserve System ("the Fed") on the interest rates banks could pay on time and savings deposits.

With the fixed cost of funds and little product and geographic competition, the banking industry was quiet and safe after the

Depression—until 1978. That's when President Carter signed legislation to create money market certificates and small saver's certificates, allowing variable interest rates tied to Treasury bills. This increased banks' cost of funds—and their risks. Coupled with the high inflation that followed, it left many banks and other depository institutions unable to compete.

Deregulation became the watchword of the 1980s. A series of new laws, beginning with the Depository Institutions Deregulation and Monetary Control Act of 1980 (DIDMCA), started to unravel a half century of strict regulations. Among other things, DIDMCA:

- Phased out interest rate ceilings on deposits at commercial banks, savings and loan associations, mutual savings banks, and credit unions.
- Permitted banks to offer interest-bearing checking accounts, technically called negotiable orders of withdrawal (NOW).
- Let S&Ls and mutual savings banks write consumer installment loans and create trust departments.
- Established uniform reserve requirements for all depository financial institutions.

One effect of deregulation has been the proliferation of new financial products for consumers and investors. On the other side of the coin, greater competition has caused an increasing number of banks to go under. Those able to react quickly and aggressively, though, have flourished with their newfound freedom.

In 1982, the number of commercial bank failures reached forty-two, compared with thirty-two in 1981 and sixteen in 1980. The Garn–St. Germain Depository Institutions Act of that year responded with yet more deregulation. Among other things, it allowed a limited amount of interstate banking to save troubled banks. But the banks didn't wait for the bill's provisions to broaden their activities. They took advantage of a loophole at the state level that allowed interstate reciprocity agreements between banks.

With commercial bank failures increasing at an alarming rate—184 in 1987—the Competitive Equality in Banking Act (CEBA) that year essentially redefined banks by placing all depository institutions under the purview of the Federal Reserve. It also allowed further product and geographic deregulation by allowing all depository institutions to offer money market deposit accounts and by eliminating rate ceilings on all deposit accounts.

With yet more red ink spilling over the banking landscape, the Financial Institutions Reform, Recovery, and Enforcement Act (FIRREA) in 1989 established the Resolution Trust Corporation (RTC) to liquidate or sell off about 1,000 S&Ls that were insolvent at the time. FIRREA also curtailed the lending powers of S&Ls and required higher capitalization. The deregulation fury continues.

bankruptcy

When an individual or a company is insolvent—that is, unable to pay debts as they come due.

A court-appointed trustee liquidates the debtor's assets under Chapter 7. In Chapter 11, a company attempts to reorganize while the courts provide some protection from creditors.

Barron's Confidence Index

An index of corporate bond yields published by *Barron's* weekly newspaper.

The idea behind the index is that when investors are worried about the economy they buy high-quality bonds; when they're more optimistic they risk buying lower-quality bonds in order to get higher yields. Barron's calculates the index by dividing the average yield on a selected group of ten top-grade corporate bonds by the Dow Jones forty-bond average yield.

Because of their top grade and low risk, Barron's bonds will have a lower yield than the Dow Jones bonds, so the ratio will always be below 100 percent (or 100 points). When bond investors are bullish about the economy, the yield difference between the Barron's and Dow Jones bonds will be small and the index high, perhaps near 95. When investors are bearish, the index will fall, dropping to around 85.

Barron's Confidence Index

When the Barron's bonds are yielding 8 percent and the Dow Jones bonds 9 percent, the Barron's Confidence Index is 89 percent, or 89 points ($8 \div 9 = .89$), a somewhat bearish sign.

Many analysts think that stock market performance follows the confidence index by several months.

---

bartering

1 Trading products or services directly for another's products or services without using money.

A company with excess inventory, for example, can obtain a needed product or service without eating up cash. In some foreign transactions, a barter arrangement in a needed commodity is preferable to cash payment in a soft currency. In other instances, agreeing to a trade is the only way a company can finalize a transaction because of a country's restrictions on exporting currency. A company agrees to take goods or commodities produced in that country and then sells them in other markets.

A more complicated form of barter is sometimes arranged

by smaller companies within the United States that cannot get
needed credit. These agreements with suppliers and others
might involve directly reciprocal trade or complex three- or
four-party transactions.

2   In advertising, trading products or services for advertising time
or space.

See also **parallel trade**.

basis

A tax term that describes the adjusted cost of a piece of property, as
used in calculating the capital gain or capital loss that the owner experiences when the property is sold.

basis point

Measure of yield of interest rate equal to .01 percent.

If a bond's yield moves from 8.25 percent to 8.50 percent, it has
moved 25 basis points.

basket

See **consumer price index (CPI)**.

bear hug

When one company comes to the rescue of another in helping to fend
off a hostile takeover. This "embrace" eventually tightens into a death
grip that kills the company, when the rescuer proceeds to take over
the company.

bear market

A financial market—such as the stock, bond, or commodities market—in which prices are falling.

While declining prices are bad news, or "bearish," for most
investors, some professional traders—identified, naturally enough, as
bears—might profit at such times by taking a speculative position in

Bulls and Bears

The terms "bull" and "bear" were first used to describe different types of stock traders in England during the 1700s. They're derived from a pair of brutal pastimes of the day—known, respectively, as bull baiting and bear baiting—in which spectators amused themselves by watching specially bred dogs attack a tethered bull or bear confined in a pit. (This was before the invention of professional football.) The styles of the unwilling combatants differed markedly: while a bear defended itself by batting the attacking dogs to the ground with its paws, a bull sought to toss them upward with its horns. Because the frenzied atmosphere of the trading floor was thought to resemble that of the bear or bull pit, stock traders came to be described as bears or bulls, depending on their approach to the business. Both terms survive today—as does the breed of dog we know as the English bulldog.

the market, such as selling short. The opposite of a bear market—one in which prices are rising—is called a bull market.

bearer bond

A bond not registered to a specific holder.

These securities have coupons attached, and each interest payment is made to whomever presents the coupon for that payment. Today, most bonds are registered bonds, which means that interest payments go automatically to your bank or broker, which then forwards them to you.

bearish

An investment position based on expectation that prices will fall.

See also **bear market**.

bells and whistles

Noise on the sidelines intended to distract a purchaser to take attention away from the price.

bellwether

Security whose price is widely viewed as an indicator of a market's direction.

There are almost as many bellwether stocks as there are analysts and commentators on the stock market, but IBM is one that has carried the label many times over the years. Microsoft and Intel have been considered bellwethers in the 1990s. In the bond market, the 20-year U.S. Treasury bond is widely viewed as the bellwether.

belly-up

A capsized enterprise whose mutilated underside is visible only to its creditors.

beneficial owner

One who gets the benefits and rights of a security that isn't listed in his or her name.

This term is used when securities are held in a street name at a brokerage company or by a bank or other financial institution. It doesn't apply, of course, to securities in a mutual fund.

beneficiary

A recipient of benefits.

The beneficiary of a life insurance policy, for example, is the person—or organization—that will receive benefits upon the death of the insured. The principal beneficiary is the policyholder's first choice to receive benefits. Most policies also name one or more contingent beneficiaries, who benefit if the primary beneficiary is no longer living.

When you name your children (or anyone else) in your will as beneficiaries to a trust, insurance policy, IRA, or other pension plan, make sure that they are also listed as beneficiary with the issuer of those financial vehicles. If, before your children were born, you designated your sister as beneficiary on your life insurance policy, and you never filed a change of beneficiary form with the insurance company, even if your will specifies that you want your children to receive the proceeds, your sister gets the dough.

best effort

When an investment banker takes on the sale of a new security without committing its capital or resources to complete the total amount of the issue.

This arrangement is in contrast to an underwriting, when investment bankers buy the entire issue and then sell it to the public. When an investment banking company takes an issue on a best effort basis, it tries to sell the securities but does not promise to buy the entire issue from the client. The banker can also sell a partial offering or increase the offering if demand permits and the client agrees.

After the investment banker determines how much it can sell, it either buys the securities from the client or cancels the deal, forgoing its fee. Although common in the past and in some other countries, in the United States today best effort arrangements generally apply only to the more speculative securities of new companies.

beta (β)

Measure of a security's volatility, or how much its price moves in relation to the overall stock market.

You can calculate beta by comparing a security's historical price movements with the movements of a general index, usually the Standard & Poor 500. (Or better yet, you can usually get the beta coefficients for actively traded stocks from published sources such as the Value Line Investment Survey or through brokerage firms.)

A security with a beta of 1.0 carries exactly the same risk as the market in general. When the market rises 4 percent, a stock with a beta of 1.0 is expected to rise 4 percent as well. When the market falls 4 percent, such a stock ought to fall to the same degree. With a beta of 2.0, a security should rise 10 percent whenever the market increases 5 percent and fall 10 percent whenever the market dips 5 percent. A stock with a beta of less than 1.0 rises or falls less sharply than the overall market.

You can also use beta to measure the price movements of your portfolio or of the holdings of a mutual fund versus the market.

Beta looks at what is called systematic risk, or market risk. A related measurement, alpha (α) considers internal risk factors that relate to the individual company and its unique business risk.

betterment assessment

See **property tax assessment**.

bid price

In options and the over-the-counter market for stocks and bonds, the price a dealer will pay to purchase a given security at a particular moment in time.

Should the seller immediately decide to turn around and buy it back, he or she would have to pay the dealer a higher asked price. The difference between the bid and asked price—akin to the retail markup on consumer goods—is known as the spread. Taken together, the current bid and asked prices for a given security are known as a quotation, or quote.

Big Board

Nickname for the New York Stock Exchange (NYSE).

Stock traders were once kept informed of fluctuating prices by means of a large chalkboard above the trading floor. This big board came to symbolize the exchange itself, much as the White House symbolizes the presidency.

Big Five

The major accounting firms in the United States as measured by revenues.

These are the names you see under the audit reports of just about every publicly traded Fortune 500 corporation. Each has offices throughout the world. In addition to auditing, these firms perform tax services for their clients, Securities and Exchange Commission (SEC) reviews, and consulting services.

The Big Five firms are:

> Arthur Andersen
> Deloitte & Touche
> Ernst & Young
> KPMG Peat Marwick
> PricewaterhouseCoopers

Once known as the Big Eight, mergers among the eight consolidated the list to five. In 1989, Deloitte, Haskins & Sells merged with Touche Ross to form Deloitte & Touche, and Ernst & Whinney joined with Arthur Young to create Ernst & Young.

bill

1 In accounting, an itemized list of accounts payable or receivable (in the former case, the bill is incoming; in the latter, outgoing) for goods (or services) sold or received.

2 In finance, often a slang term for a T-bill.

See also **audit**.

bill of exchange

If it's made out to you, you've got money coming. Also called a draft.

A bill of exchange is an order written by one party instructing another to make a payment. The payment might be to a third party (payee) or to the drawer. Bills of exchange are negotiable; they can be bought, sold, and given in payment for goods or services. A bill of exchange payable on a specific future date is called a time draft. These are often traded in the open market.

binder

A symbolic good-faith payment that obligates two or more parties to an agreement that they have not yet finalized.

Example
You write a check, which is also called a sight draft or a bank draft. It's a bill of exchange telling a bank to pay the party you've named as payee.

One common type of binder is the deposit a prospective purchaser makes to an escrow account when deciding to buy a home. If the seller accepts the offer, the binder—ordinarily several percent of the price being offered—remains in the account while the details of the sale are worked out. The buyer typically needs time to arrange for financing, and may impose other conditions or contingencies as well, such as requiring that the property pass a detailed structural inspection.

If the contingencies in the contract are met and the sale goes through, the binder is returned to the buyer. If the contract becomes void because one of the contingencies is not met—for instance, if the buyer is unable to get a loan or the house fails the inspection—the binder reverts to the buyer. But if the buyer backs out for other reasons, the binder is forfeited to the seller.

BIR (Business Information Report)

See **Dun & Bradstreet reports**.

Black Monday

The nickname for October 19, 1987, when the Dow Jones Industrial Average fell by 508 points (more than 20 percent).

blank check

1   Security, usually offered by a start-up company, that doesn't specify in its prospectus what the funds will be used for.

Often these companies don't yet have operations, so investors must rely on the issuer's word that the proceeds will be used wisely. Many scams, resulting in serious losses for investors, historically have involved blank check offerings, so a lot of states have prohibited them. Others have such stringent rules that blank check offerings have almost disappeared.

2   A check that's signed but has no dollar amount specified. Used in transactions where the final dollar amount hasn't been settled, blank checks should be used only when the account holder thoroughly trusts the payee. Like a signed credit card slip with the card imprinted but no amount entered, this is a negotiable instrument—and a potentially dangerous one. If the amount filled in doesn't match your expectations, you could be in for a nasty shock. There are better alternatives that still don't delay the seller. Credit cards, checks by fax, even COD orders may be preferable.

blind pool

An offering by a company or limited partnership that does not list the specific properties to be acquired. (An industry is usually indicated, such as oil and gas, real estate, or technology.)

Blind pool ventures are often set up to buy equity stakes in small, private companies, and might have high risks because the investor doesn't know what the manager of the money pool is going to do with the money raised. Because of this additional risk, investors usually charge a premium to the issuing company. However, blind pool ventures provide a way to invest in small, potentially profitable companies that need financing to develop their product or distribution. Investors can evaluate these ventures on the track record of the general partner or chief executive and the potential for the targeted industry.

Bloch, Henry Wollman

Chairman of H&R Block, the Kansas City–based, $1.2 billion tax preparation and computer services firm.

Bloch's 9,500 (company-owned and franchised) income tax preparation offices around the world fill out tax forms every year for more than 12.9 million people—some 12 percent of all filings. The company owns CompuServe, the 3-million-plus-member on-line information service.

Bloch was born in 1922 and earned a bachelor of science degree in mathematics at the University of Michigan. In 1946, he and his brother, Richard, started United Business Co. (UBC), offering bookkeeping, management assistance, and collection services to local businesses. They provided income tax preparation as a freebie to bookkeeping clients, but it became so popular that they folded UBC in 1955 and launched H&R Block (with a *k* for simpler spelling).

Bloomberg Financial Markets

Named for its founder, Michael Bloomberg, this system is used widely by investment professionals to track and price securities, as well as to obtain general information on the markets. The most common system is to place a Bloomberg machine—with computer screen and separate keyboard—in the offices of the user.

blowout

An initial public offering (IPO) that goes through the roof on its first day of trading.

Sometimes the demand is apparent even before the stock starts trading, as people call brokers to place their orders. When trading opens, the offering is snatched up so quickly that the buyers can't get as many shares as they'd like. Then the people who did get shares at the offering price can sell them immediately to the hungry investors who are bidding up the price.

See also **going public**, **underwriting**, and **underwriting syndicate**.

blue chips

Considered to be the most tried and true performers among stocks. In the United Kingdom, blue chips are called alpha stocks.

Blue chips are not necessarily the most expensive stocks on the market or the fastest short-term earners. That distinction goes to whatever industry group is hottest at the moment. But blue chips are not cheap, either. And even blue chips can steer you wrong. In the early 1970s, the "nifty fifty," as they were called, were a group of rapidly growing companies whose stocks were selling at high price earnings ratios. They were commonly believed to be the key to superior investment performance but faltered by the end of the 1970s.

Blue List

Daily municipal bond quotation service. Also called blue sheet.

Each weekday, the Blue List gives prices for municipal bond issues on the secondary market. The number of bonds offered depends on what's available. Their total value has reached around $3 billion. The companies that deal in, or make a market for, a particular issue cite the bid and asked prices in transactions among brokerage houses. The bid price to the public will be a little higher and the asked price a little lower, to reflect the spread the broker keeps. (Some brokerage houses publish their own lists with retail prices.)

This Standard & Poor's (S&P) publication is still printed in dark blue ink on light blue paper, but you no longer have to read it that way. Like the pink sheets, where you find prices for smaller over-the-counter (OTC) stocks, the Blue List is available via computer services. Its full title is the Blue List of Current Municipal Offerings. It also lists a few corporate bonds.

See also *Bond Buyer, The*.

blue sky laws

State securities laws dealing with registering new issues, licensing salespeople, and prosecuting those who make a fraudulent sale.

Today, every U.S. state has legislation regulating the securities industry within its jurisdiction, and the federal government's laws apply to securities offerings and deals that cross state borders. These laws mesh pretty well with one another, in part because most states have adopted parts of the Uniform Securities Act, first proposed in 1956.

board of arbitration

The people who decide the merits of an arbitrated dispute.

See also **arbitration**.

Board of Governors of the Federal Reserve System

Seven people who, as a body, wield great influence over U.S. banking, interest rates, and money supply. Informally called the Federal Reserve Board.

The U.S. president appoints the governors to 14-year terms on the board, which administers the Federal Reserve System (the Fed). The president also appoints one of the governors to a 4-year term as chairman of the Federal Reserve. Although the governors are appointed by the president, their mandate is to operate independently of political influence.

The seven governors—along with the president of the New York Federal Reserve Bank and four of the other eleven regional Federal Reserve Bank presidents—comprise the Federal Open Market Committee (FOMC). That body sets goals regarding interest rates and the money supply, and directs the Fed in meeting those goals.

boilerplate

Standard wording in a document, particularly in legal contracts.

Most boilerplates consist of important words, phrases, and clauses that have survived many years of close inspection by lawyers. They save everyone's time since the lengthy texts do not need rewriting.

Example
Investment bankers often use boilerplates to describe the legal aspects of a bond offering in the prospectus.

Office supply companies, such as Office Depot and Office Max, sell standard (boilerplate) rental agreements, bills of sale, and other everyday legal documents, where you simply fill in the blanks. Software that provides a wide range of fill-in-the-blank legal documents, including leases, corporate minutes and resolutions, and copyright and trademark agreements now is also available.

bond

Debt security issued by a corporation or government entity, usually in multiples of $1,000, obligating the issuer to pay bondholders a fixed amount of interest at specific intervals, usually semiannually, and to repay the principal of the loan at maturity.

Since bondholders are creditors, not stockholders, they have no ownership privileges, such as voting, but they do have a senior claim to assets in the event of a firm's liquidation or bankruptcy.

See also **bond ratings**, **bond valuation**, **bond yield**, **convertible security**, **debenture**, **high-grade bonds**, and **high-yield bonds**.

bond anticipation note (BAN)

Short-term debt instrument used by states and municipalities to fund daily operations. The principal and interest on these BANs are repaid from the proceeds of long-term bond issues.

BANs usually have higher yields than other tax-free debt instruments of the same maturity.

Bond Buyer's Index

A bond index published by *The Bond Buyer*.

Bond Buyer, The

A century-old daily newspaper that prints key information used primarily in the municipal bond market.

The Bond Buyer's Index of 40 actively traded general obligation and revenue bond issues provides a benchmark against which yields in the tax-exempt market are measured.

The 30-day visible supply is published weekly and shows the total dollar volume of new municipal issues expected in the following

30 days. It includes bonds with maturities of 13 months or more. The newspaper also compares the after-tax return on long-term Treasuries with that from tax-free municipals. Investors use the information to gauge relative interest rate trends.

See also **Blue List**.

bond ratings

Classifying bonds by sizing up their risk of default. Also called quality ratings.

Several organizations publish bond ratings, most prominently Moody's Investors Service and Standard & Poor's (S&P). Other rating agencies include Fitch Investors Service; Duff & Phelps; and McCarthy, Crisanti & Maffei. Bonds considered high-grade, or investment-grade, have ratings of Aaa through Baa3 in the Moody's system; in the S&P rankings they have AAA through BBB–. Bonds with ratings below those are considered non–investment grade, or high-yield bonds.

bond ratio

1 Proportion of company assets financed with long-term debt as opposed to equity.

Bonds usually represent most of a corporation's long-term debt. The ratio is calculated with this formula:

$$\textbf{long-term debt} = \textbf{bond ratio}$$
$$\textbf{long-term debt + shareholders' equity}$$

2 Ratio of downgraded municipal bonds to all of an issuer's municipal bonds.

Example
The real estate slump in Colorado in 1991 and 1992 led to the downgrading of many of the state's municipal bonds. The ratio

in 1991 hit 4:1 (four issues downgraded for every one issue not downgraded). It improved to 2:1 (two issues downgraded for every one issue not downgraded) in 1993.

See also **bond ratings** and **interest coverage ratio**.

bond valuation

A calculation to figure out the current price of a bond.

Bond valuation looks at the present value of all the bond's anticipated cash flow to tell you how much it is worth today. If you know the current yield of similar bonds, this calculation establishes the price a buyer will pay or a seller will get.

Bond valuation requires five key pieces of information:

1 The number of interest payments in one year—most bonds pay semiannually, but some pay quarterly or annually.

2 The dollar amount of each periodic interest payment.

3 The face value of the bond—how much you will get when it matures.

4 The date the bond matures.

5 The interest rate currently being paid for bonds of similar risk and similar maturity.

Adding the present value of the bond's future interest payments and the present value of the money you will receive at maturity gives you the bond's value today. The money you will get at maturity, the bond's face value, is usually $1,000.

See also **bond yield**.

bond yield

Return an investor gets on a bond investment, expressed as an annual percentage.

Usually, when a bond is issued, its interest rate is based on market conditions and it sells at or very close to its par value, or face value. If the bond sells at par value, its yield is the same as its stated interest rate, or coupon rate. But during the bond's life market interest rates will rise and fall. If you want to resell a bond, you will have to price it so that it yields the prevailing interest rate.

The bond market tables in the *Wall Street Journal* and other newspapers usually list the current yield as well as the coupon rate.

Since calculating a bond's yield to maturity is complex and involves trial and error, it's easier to use a bond calculator or a computer.

bond/warrant unit

Security in which a bond and a set number of equity warrants are sold as a unit. Sometimes called a synthetic convertible.

In accounting for these units, the issuer records the bond as debt and the warrants as equity. In contrast, traditional convertible bonds are recorded entirely as debt until exchanged. The bond portion can be used as currency—generally at par value—to exercise the warrants.

Unlike conventional convertible securities, the bonds and the warrants can be traded separately.

book value

1 In accounting, the original cost of an asset (plant or equipment) less its accumulated depreciation. More generally, it is the dollar figure of an asset that appears on the balance sheet. It is sometimes called the carrying amount.

2 In securities analysis, the per-share valuation of the equity that holders of common stock have in a company. Also called book value per share. It is calculated by deducting from shareholders' equity the liquidation value of any preferred stock and any preferred dividends that are owed, then dividing the result by the number of common shares outstanding.

bookkeeping

Recording daily transactions in an accounting system.

To keep track of transactions, bookkeepers use a general journal, which is a chronological listing of transactions showing debits and credits to particular accounts. Most businesses use special journals as well, determined largely by the specific transactions of the business involved.

Three common types of bookkeeping systems are:

1 *Cash payments journal:* lists entries for all cash paid out.
2 *Cash receipts journal:* in which all cash received by the business is recorded.
3 *Sales journal:* contains entries for all sales of merchandise on account (sales of merchandise for cash are listed in the cash receipts journal).

See also **book value**.

bootstrap effect

Rise in earnings per share for an acquiring company in a merger because of the consolidation of financial statements.

See also **merger/acquisition (M&A)**.

bottom line

A figure that represents the difference between what was attempted and what actually happened.

See also **net income**.

bottom-up investing

Investment approach that looks at the growth and earnings potential of stocks before considering the impact of economic trends. The assumption is that some companies can thrive in hard times even when competitors are faring poorly.

See also **top-down investing**.

Brady Bonds

Bonds named after Nicholas Brady, the secretary of the Treasury during the Latin American debt crisis in the 1980s. The bonds were sponsored by the U.S. government and used to assist Latin American countries in restructuring their debt.

bridge loan

Short-term loan that's meant to be replaced by more permanent financing.

Many companies used bridge loans in the 1980s as they acquired other companies. They retired the bridge loans by issuing bonds, which often commanded high interest rates, so they were left with enormous debt. A survey by *Institutional Investor* magazine put the volume of bridge loans in the mid-1990s at about a quarter of what it was in the 1980s.

See also **leveraged buyout (LBO)**.

broker

1 Intermediary that routes goods or services from a producer to consumers. See also **distribution channel**.

2 In finance, the salesperson who deals with a brokerage firm's customers. Also referred to as an account executive (AE).

buffalo chip

A blue chip company that has gone through a leveraged buyout. Here proliferation of share certificates in former blue chips in the recent past is likened to "buffalo chips," which pioneers of the American West gathered to use as fuel (they were a good source of heat, but not light).

Buffett, Warren Edward

Most actors have to earn their keep waiting tables; this occasional soap opera actor has a day job investing his billions and running his holding company, Berkshire Hathaway. The stock of Berkshire Hathaway, his 41 percent–owned holding company, boasted a whopping 33 percent annual rate of return to investors for the years 1982 through 1994. Its subsidiaries range from See's Candies to National Indemnity Company, from several shoe companies to the publishers of the World Book Encyclopedia and the *Buffalo News* newspaper. The company also has minority stakes in Capital Cities/ABC, Coca-Cola, Geico, Salomon Brothers, USAir, and many other companies.

Berkshire Hathaway's annual meetings at the Omaha, Nebraska, headquarters have attracted as many as 4,000 devotees from around the world who scramble to catch Buffett's fleeting, 10-minute address that is filled with understated, folksy humor and modesty. His long and rambling chairman's letters in the company's annual reports are a model of honest business writing.

Buffett started as an investment salesman in 1951, then became a securities analyst in 1954. He co-launched an investment partnership at age twenty-five with $100,000. He dissolved that company in 1969 at a market peak after its 30-fold increase in value.

In a biography, *The Warren Buffett Way*, author Robert Hagstrom Jr. says Buffett preaches: "Unless you can watch your stock holdings decline by 50 percent without becoming panic-stricken, you should not be in the stock market."

See also **diversification** and **dividend**.

bull market

Sustained, general rise in the value of financial assets; usually used in reference to the stock market.

There's no official definition of how much the stock market has to rise—or for how long—before it can be termed a bull market. Technical market analysts beg the question by saying that a bull market is one in which the "primary trend" is upward and there has been no "reversal of the primary trend."

bulldog bond

A bond issued in Britain by a non-British company.

See also **Yankee bond**.

bulletin board system (BBS)

Messages posted and read by people using computers linked by a telecommunications network.

See also **electronic bulletin board**.

bullion

Refined gold or silver in bulk, usually in the form of bars or ingots, rather than in minted coins.

Nations store their gold reserves in bullion form, usually in bars or bricks. And although gold no longer is the standard by which the world's currencies are evaluated, a nation's financial strength is based, in part, on its gold reserves. The United States keeps most of its gold bullion at Fort Knox in Kentucky. It, as well as many other nations, also stores gold at the Federal Reserve Bank in New York. Gold stored there is used primarily to settle international debts. In fact, the use of gold reserves is limited almost exclusively to international transaction settlements.

bullish

An investment position based on the expectation that markets will rise in value.

bundling

Selling a package of products for one total price.

For example, travel services offer a variety of packages for Walt

Disney World that might include, in addition to airfare, admission to the park, lodging, some meals, and shuttle service. If your price is competitive and is used as an enticement, bundling becomes important in marketing the product because it provides extras that the customer might not get from a competitor at the same price.

Increasingly, bundling has been used in the computer hardware and software industries to make products more attractive. A Packard Bell computer, for instance, might come bundled with a monitor, a fax modem, an operating system, Windows, and several software applications. Operating systems themselves come bundled with applications.

See also **cherry picking** and **pricing**.

business cycle

Short-term fluctuations of the aggregate economy around its long-run growth path. Various indicators such as Gross Domestic Product (GDP), employment, and housing starts are used to gauge business cycles.

Recurring patterns of expansion and contraction also occur in particular industries and in regional economies. The business cycle of a particular industry and the larger economy do not always move in the same direction. When crude oil prices dip modestly, oil companies slump, but the overall economy gets a boost from cheaper energy prices. A more severe drop in crude prices, though, cuts oil company profits so sharply that the companies reduce spending, pinching the overall economy.

To plan for a company's future—its financing, pricing, and employment policies—it is necessary to understand both an industry's and the overall economy's cycles and how they will likely affect sales, inflation, labor availability, interest rates, and so on.

Business Week 1,000

Annual roster of America's most valuable companies, published by *Business Week* magazine. The largest public companies are ranked according to their market value.

buy and hold

Strategy of withstanding market swings by keeping investments for a long time.

See also **active portfolio management**.

buyback

Company's purchase of its own securities.

A company might decide to buy back some of its common stock if it thinks that the price is too low and that a buyback is the most efficient use of its money. The repurchased shares become treasury stock or are retired and are no longer used in calculating per-share figures, such as earnings. So the buyback improves per-share measures of the company's performance.

Companies sometimes buy back their bonds on the open market. They might be motivated to do this when they have spare cash and rising interest rates have reduced the market price of the bonds significantly below their face value. A buyback sends a signal to existing and prospective shareholders that management thinks the securities are undervalued, and tends to boost the price by reducing the supply of shares on the market while also increasing the demand for them.

See also **call feature** and **capital stock**.

buydown

Prepayment of interest at closing to lower the interest rate on a mortgage loan.

Buydowns are a form of creative financing that enables home buyers to lower their mortgage interest rate—and hence their monthly house payment—particularly when interest rates are high. The lower payment allows them to qualify for a loan they might not otherwise be able to afford based on their income.

Buyers may prepay the interest at closing, but sellers—especially home builders—often foot the bill as a way of sweetening the deal for the buyer. Some buydowns lower the interest rate for the life of the loan; others lower it temporarily.

A popular approach is the 3-2-1 buydown; enough money is prepaid at closing to lower the interest rate 3 percent during the first year of the loan, 2 percent during the second year, and 1 percent during the third year.

If the seller offers you a buydown, consider how long you plan to own the house and how much you'll save over time. It might be that

For Example

You have your eye on a $100,000 house. You're putting down $20,000, but you can't quite afford the monthly payments on an $80,000 mortgage at the current 9 percent—not while you're also paying for all the new furniture, carpeting, and drapes you'll need. Luckily, the builder is offering a 3-2-1 buydown as an incentive.

At closing, the builder turns $3,600 over to the mortgage company for the buydown. Your interest rate and payments will look like this:

Year	Interest Rate	Payment
1	6%	$479.64
2	7%	$532.24
3	8%	$587.01
4–30	9%	$643.70

you'd be better off with a cash rebate at closing. If you think so, ask the seller, who might be willing to give you—instead of the mortgage company—the cash cost of the buydown.

bylaws

Rules for governing a corporation or other organization.

A corporation's bylaws spell out such things as how directors are elected; how board committees are formed; the duties of the board's officers; and how, when, and on what issues shareholders get to vote. The bylaws conform to the laws of the state where the company is incorporated.

See also **articles of incorporation** and **charter**.

C: Cafeteria Plan to Current Yield

cafeteria plan

Employee benefits package that lets workers pick and choose among a "menu" of benefits, so that those with different goals can better accomplish their objectives.

Employees have a certain number of dollars to spend on themselves, and can decide where they want those dollars to go.

See also **withholding**.

call

An option contract that gives the owner the right to buy a stock at a specified price on or before a certain date.

The premium, or the price of the call, is determined by a large number of factors, including the strike price, the option period (i.e., the amount of time before the option expires), and the volatility of the asset—the more volatile the stock is the higher the premium. Even if two stocks have identical strike prices and option periods, they could command very different premiums.

Call options are handled through a brokerage firm, which executes the transaction through one of the nation's five exchanges that deals in options. In 1973, the Chicago Board Options Exchange (CBOE) was the first to list options.

call feature

Provision of a bond agreement that allows the issuing company to repurchase the bond before it matures.

The price an issuer pays to redeem a bond is the call price, which is usually higher than the bond's face value. The call premium is the difference between a bond's call price and its face value. Companies or other bond issuers may exercise their call features when interest rates have fallen. They repurchase their high-interest bonds and issue new ones at lower interest rates. The call feature also gives management flexibility in controlling its capital structure.

call option

Gives the holder of a stock the right to buy an asset at a particular price before a certain date. A European option would allow the option to be exercised only on the expiration date.

See also **call** and **derivatives**.

call premium

The difference between the call price of a bond and its face value.

Example
In the example of a call feature mentioned above, the company "recalls" your bonds (i.e., pays you your money back) at a higher price than the $1,000 face value of the bonds. They might pay you a call price of $1,050 rather than $1,000, in which case the call premium would be $50. It's kind of a consolation prize for having your bonds taken back earlier than you'd planned.

See also **call feature**.

call price

The price the issuer pays to buy back a bond.
   See also **call feature** and **call premium**.

call provision

A provision of a bond agreement that allows the issuer to repurchase the bond before it matures. Also referred to as a call feature.

cap

Highest allowable interest rate or regular (e.g., monthly) payment amount—or a limit on out-of-pocket medical costs.

   Example
   An adjustable rate mortgage may be linked to a standard interest rate like the 10-year Treasury bond, but it will have a cap
   of, say, 12 percent, to protect you from skyrocketing interest
   rates.

   See also **adjustable rate mortgage (ARM)** and **collar**.

capital appreciation

A rise in stock price.

capital asset pricing model (CAPM)

An academic method of determining a security's fair return.
   "CAP-M" (as it is pronounced) is based on this principle: the return you get on a security should equal the "risk-free return" (like that on U.S. Treasury bills) plus a risk premium. The tricky part, of course, is figuring out what the risk premium should be. Most fund managers use the security's beta (β), which is a measure of how it moves with the general market index (like the S&P 500). The higher the risk, the higher the required premium.

Managers sometimes use CAPM internally to calculate the rate of return they will try to get for shareholders.

capital gain

The money you make when you sell an investment for more than you paid. That difference is taxable as a capital gain.

Short-term capital gains are profits made on assets held for less than a year. They are taxed at the regular income rate. Long-term capital gains are those profits made on assets held for longer than a year, and are taxed at a more favorable rate.

capital loss

What happens when you sell something for less than you paid for it.

Sadly, some investments don't quite work out the way investors hope. The silver lining in the cloud is that the government will absorb part of the loss. A capital loss on any investment (other than on your primary residence) can be used to offset any capital gain. Investors can also use capital losses to offset other income—but only up to $3,000 in any tax year. Additional losses can be carried forward and used to offset other income in future years.

capital markets

All the markets where securities are traded, including both debt and equity, for corporations, government entities, and municipalities.

The primary market involves the sale of new debt and equity issues, such as initial public offerings (IPOs). The secondary market is for trading previously issued securities. (That's where you buy most of your stocks.) The organized secondary markets in the United States include the New York Stock Exchange (NYSE), the NASDAQ Stock Market, the American Stock Exchange (AMEX), the Chicago Board Options Exchange (CBOE), and regional exchanges.

When businesses want funds for start-up or expansion, they can try to attract savers' money by issuing new debt, such as corporate bonds, or new equity, such as common stock. Governments also participate in the capital markets when issuing new debt securities to fund their expenditures.

See also **money markets**.

capital stock

Common or preferred stock that represents ownership, authorized by a company. A company's articles of incorporation specify a set number of authorized shares. When stock is sold, it is called issued stock. As long as it remains in the hands of stockholders, it is outstanding. If it's bought back by the company, it becomes treasury stock.

As a rule, an owner of capital stock may claim the following:

1   A percentage of the company profits in the form of dividends— although these are paid out at management's discretion.
2   A claim (subordinated) on the assets if the company goes out of business.
3   The right to vote on membership of the board of directors and on fundamental company changes.
4   The right to maintain the same proportion of ownership should additional stock be issued.

Unlike partners or sole proprietors of a business, holders of capital stock have no liability beyond the price they paid to buy their shares.

capitalization ratio

A way of measuring how debt-laden a company is. It's calculated by adding up the proportions of common stock, preferred stock, and debt that make up a company's capital structure.

CAPM

See **capital asset pricing model (CAPM)**.

carrying amount

See **book value**.

cash basis

Accounting method that recognizes revenue when it is actually received.

See also **accrual basis**.

cash cow

A company's division or subsidiary that has achieved such rewarding profits that the parent company no longer sees a need to reinvest the profits in order to keep the operation current.

cash flow

A way of measuring the actual cash that flows through a business during a specific period.

On a company's income statement, noncash charges such as depreciation are deducted from revenues along with other expenses to arrive at net income. So, to determine cash flow from operations, you would add them back.

Cash flow is the lifeblood of any business and may be considered its most important financial statistic. In the mergers and acquisitions of the 1980s and early 1990s, companies with substantial cash flow were prime targets for takeovers. The people looking for takeover candidates are aware that the cash coming in can be used to help pay the cost of the acquisition.

cash flow coverage

The ratio of a company's cash flow to its outstanding debt used as a measure of bond safety.

Companies with a AAA rating from Standard & Poor's tend to have more than three times as much cash flow as they do long-term debt. The cash flow of companies rated A tends to be approximately 75 percent of their long-term debt.

cash management systems

In corporate finance, methods for determining the optimal amount of cash that a company should have on hand.

These systems look at the company's cash flow, returns on short-term investments, the cost involved in making those investments, and the opportunity cost of maintaining any cash balances that do not pay interest.

cash value insurance

The part of life insurance that's also an investment tool: part of the premium is used to provide death benefits, and the remainder is placed in an investment vehicle to earn interest.

It's more expensive than protection-only (i.e., term) insurance, because it allegedly provides a greater value. Until recently, *allegedly* was the key word. Most financial advisers once considered the investment value of this insurance a bad joke, just a step up from an under-the-mattress plan. Today, however, things are different. Most insurance companies offer high-yield investments, such as mutual funds. And if held until death, no tax is ever paid. Another advantage is that you can get access to your money by borrowing against the cash value.

There are three types of cash value policies:

1 *Whole life:* The cash value is closely tied to the yield of bonds and mortgages. Annual premiums don't rise with age.
2 *Universal life:* It's hooked to short-term cash yields. In this type, premiums are flexible, protection is adjustable, and insurance company expenses and charges are disclosed to the purchaser. The death benefit can be a locked-in amount.

3 *Variable life:* It offers a choice of investment funds. The death benefit fluctuates in relation to the performance of the chosen securities, but it never goes below a guaranteed minimum.

If you're seriously thinking about replacing your policy, you should consider a second opinion. The Consumer Federation (202-387-6121) offers a $40 policy analysis service. Also, don't forget to give your current policy carrier a chance to explain why you should stick with the insurance you've already got. And never cancel one policy until your new policy is in force.

CBOE
See **Chicago Board Options Exchange (CBOE).**

CD
See **certificate of deposit (CD).**

certainty equivalents
Method of determining when an investor with a low-paying, safe investment will be willing to opt for a higher-paying, more risky investment.

certificate of deposit (CD)
A debt instrument issued by a bank to individuals and institutions that lend it money for a set period of time.

CDs are time deposits, meaning they cannot be withdrawn until their term is up. There's a secondary market, though, for large CDs with short-term maturities that are bought by money market funds and other institutional investors. Those reach maturity in anywhere from 14 days to a year. They're sold in denominations of more than $100,000, but most often trade in units of $1 million. Banks often auction off these negotiable CDs in lots as large as $50 million. Individual CDs start as low as $100.

certified financial planner (CFP)

A person who has passed a two-year tax planning and personal finance program from the College of Financial Planning in Denver, Colorado.

CFPs can provide many services, including portfolio management and planning for insurance, taxes, and estates. Although certified financial planners do provide valuable services, not everyone needs them. If you're in the process of socking away your first few thousand, frankly, you don't have much to work with. But if you have investment assets in excess of $100,000 and are confused about how to handle your money, a CFP can help put your financial house in order.

Most CFPs don't charge for an initial meeting. Once you hire them, they will bill you in one of two ways: commissions or fee only. With commissions, CFPs make their money when you purchase a financial product. This isn't inherently bad—most CFPs are reputable—but you should be aware of their financial interest in the product they're selling you. Other CFPs charge clients an hourly rate (anywhere between $50 and $200), a flat rate for a particular service, or a rate based on assets under management.

When choosing a CFP, don't confuse them with garden-variety financial planners. Virtually anyone with a shingle and a calculator can use the title "financial planner." Not all of these people are scurrilous, but they don't have to be to lose your money. A 1989 Consumer Federation of America report stated that more money is lost through incompetence and self-interested advice than through outright fraud. The report estimated that in 1986 (the last year studied), financial planners lost more than $540 million of their clients' money. Stockbrokers, CPAs, and insurance agents sometimes call themselves financial planners too. Most do provide legitimate financial services but can't provide the same kind of broad-based planning that a CFP can.

Don't be taken in by financial planners who tout that they're registered with the Securities and Exchange Commission. They don't need any special education to register—$150 and a completed application are the only requirements for registration.

See also **investment adviser**.

certified public accountant (CPA)

An accountant who has met licensing requirements in a particular state.

The requirements for becoming a CPA usually include:

- Passing the Uniform CPA Examination, which is prepared and graded by the American Institute of Certified Public Accountants (AICPA).
- Practicing as an accountant within the state for a given period, often two years.

The Securities and Exchange Commission (SEC) requires that an independent CPA audit the financial statements of every publicly held corporation.

CFP

See **certified financial planner (CFP)**.

Chapter 7

The most common form of bankruptcy for individuals and privately owned companies. Also referred to as straight bankruptcy.

In Chapter 7, either there is no attempt at a reorganization or one has been attempted and failed. A court-appointed trustee gathers and liquidates all assets that are not exempt from a bankruptcy order, then distributes any proceeds (after fees and expenses) to the creditors. With few exceptions, all remaining debts are discharged: the debtor is not required to pay them.

For a company or individual to file under Chapter 7, debts usually exceed assets. So it is almost certain that the liquidation proceeds will not cover all debts. A business will file Chapter 7 when it sees no possibility of salvaging its assets and operations. If it believes a reorganization is possible, the company will use Chapter 11.

See also **common stock** and **preferred stock**.

Chapter 11

Bankruptcy filing involving an attempt to reorganize. This is the most common form of bankruptcy filing for larger companies.

When a business has substantial assets, it is likely to try a Chapter 11 reorganization rather than a Chapter 7 bankruptcy. In a Chapter 11 proceeding, the business may continue to operate—in most cases, without a trustee—while senior managers negotiate a financial reorganization and payment plan. Usually, the terms of debt repayment will be extended over a longer period. Creditors accept this reorganization because the eventual return is better than what would be available under the fire sale provisions of Chapter 7. During the Chapter 11 process, the company suspends payments on its past debts. If the bankruptcy court decides that the company has no chance of viability as a going concern, it will order a Chapter 7 proceeding, appoint a trustee, and liquidate the business's assets.

After a decade of litigation, a U.S. Supreme Court decision in 1991 granted Chapter 11 coverage to individuals as well as to businesses. Individuals may opt for Chapter 11 when they have one or more assets they want to protect from seizure and sale. The reorganization may allow them to keep those assets, sell others, and adopt a modified repayment schedule for their remaining debts.

Chapter 13

Also called the wage earner plan, this form of personal bankruptcy allows you to keep most of your assets and discharge a large portion of your unsecured debt. It generally gives you 3 to 5 years to repay the rest.

Secured debt (such as your home mortgage or loans on your car or furniture) must still be paid or you will forfeit the property. You can file a Chapter 13 as long as your secured debt does not exceed $750,000 and your unsecured debt (such as unpaid credit card balances) is less than $250,000.

A Chapter 13 petition includes a suggested repayment plan and a list of all your income, assets, and debts, along with the names and addresses of your creditors. A court-appointed bankruptcy trustee will make sure your plan and your budget are realistic. The plan will not fly unless your creditors agree to accept the terms. Once they do, you send a check every month to the trustee to cover the payment to your creditors, plus a trustee fee.

As long as you keep to the plan, a Chapter 13 filing might smudge your credit rating for only 7 years.

charitable deduction

A way of simultaneously doing good and reducing your federal income tax bite.

If you contribute money or other property to a qualified charity, you can deduct the amount of the gift from your adjusted gross income on your federal tax return. Taking a charitable deduction, however, might not always be as simple as it seems, particularly for the wealthy and for big givers. Section 501(c)(3) of the tax code, for example, divides charitable organizations into two groups. Those that rely mainly on public support, such as the United Way, are called 50 percent–type organizations, meaning that the giver can deduct only up to 50 percent of his or her adjusted gross income for contributions. For other types of organizations, such as private and community foundations, the corresponding figure is 30 percent.

Recent changes have also tightened the reigns on documentation. As of 1994, you need a written receipt from the charity for gifts of $250 or more; no longer will a canceled check serve as proof that you made a donation. For any noncash gift worth more than $5,000—artwork donated to a museum is a good example—the giver must have an appraisal done by the due date of the income tax return. An appraisal summary—Form 8283—must be attached to the return and signed by both the appraiser and the charitable donee. Only if the gift is in excess of $20,000 must the actual appraisal be attached to the return.

If a charity provides a gift in return for a donation, the value of the gift must be subtracted from the donation. So, if you attend a $250-a-plate dinner to benefit an environmental group, you have to exclude the value of the dinner from the charitable deduction.

Charitable giving can be a good way to eliminate capital gains taxes on stock and mutual fund shares. Assume that you have $10,000 worth of stock for which you paid $1,000. If you sell the stock, you'll have to pay capital gains taxes of $2,520 on the appreciated value of the stock ($9,000 times 28 percent). But if you donate the $10,000 to a charity instead, you can avoid the capital gains tax and still give the money to your favorite charity. Many mutual fund companies are geared to transfer shares from your account to that of a charity.

chart of accounts

A numbered list of a company's accounts that gives order and consistency to its bookkeeping system.

This numbering system will reflect the order of the balance sheet and income statement. The numbering should start with the accounts that go into current assets, the first section of the balance sheet, and end with the last category of expenses in the income statement.

Chart of Accounts (partial sample)

Category	Account	Description
Cash	1100	Cash-Operating Account
		Cash-Payroll
Accounts Receivable	1200	Accounts Receivable
		Allowance for Doubtful Accounts
		Credit Card Receivables
Inventory	1300	Inventory-Retail / Parts
		Inventory Warehouse-Retail / Parts
Prepaid Expenses	1400	Prepaid Expenses

charter

A certificate of incorporation issued by a state and the articles of incorporation filed by individuals. Legally establishes a corporation.

charting

See **technical analysis.**

chartist

See **technical analysis.**

checking account

Demand deposit account held at a bank, in which all or a portion of the account is payable on demand to a person who presents a check drawn on the account.

This feature distinguishes checking accounts from time deposits, otherwise known as savings accounts, from which funds can be with-drawn only by the owner of the account and only upon presentation of a passbook or withdrawal slip. Banks are not obligated to pay funds from a time deposit immediately; they legally have 30 to 60 days to honor the withdrawal.

Checking accounts come in three basic packages:

1　Regular checking accounts pay no interest on their bal-ances, and they usually charge a monthly fee.
2　NOW (meaning "negotiated orders of withdrawal") accounts waive service charges for depositors who are willing to maintain a minimum balance, and in return pro-vide a modest interest rate.
3　Super-NOW accounts, as the name suggests, provide higher interest and require higher minimum balances than regular NOW accounts. But even on Super-NOW accounts, the interest rate is lower than that of a money market account.

---

cherry picking

1　A buyer's selection of only some items in a vendor's line. This practice is common in the computer market.

Retailers often cherry-pick items from different manufac-turers to create packages that offer the features and prices con-sumers want. In contrast, a manufacturer might also bundle its products, offering a complete system at a discounted price.

See also **bundling**.

2　Another form of cherry picking occurs when HMOs enroll only the healthiest individuals, allowing the HMOs to remain prof-itable in a competitive market.

Chicago Board Options Exchange (CBOE)

The most active options exchange in the United States. The CBOE was founded in 1973 as the nation's first organized marketplace for trading options contracts. Before that time, options were traded through a limited number of specialized securities firms.

See also **derivatives**.

Chicago Board of Trade

Major securities exchange based in Chicago on which a number of futures and futures options trade.

Chicago Mercantile Exchange (CME)

National marketplace, established in 1919, for the organized trading of futures contracts in numerous agricultural commodities, such as hogs, cattle, and lumber. In addition, the CME's International Monetary Market (IMM) division, which was organized in 1972, trades financial instruments, such as futures in foreign currencies, U.S. Treasury bills, and Eurodollars.

See also **derivatives**.

Chicago school

See **monetarism**.

Chinese wall

In a financial institution, an imaginary barrier between different departments to maintain confidentiality for clients (and to avoid conflicts of interest).

CHIPS

See **Clearinghouse Interbank Payments System (CHIPS)**.

churning

1 A term used to describe unusually high activity in an investment account. For example, unscrupulous brokers might be
   accused of "churning" a client's account in order to generate
   more commissions.

2 In insurance, the shady practice of some agents who sell new
   policies to boost their commissions, even though an existing
   policy is as good as or better than the new one.

See also **whole life insurance**.

circuit breakers

Limits imposed by the stock exchanges that shut down the market
once they've moved by a certain amount.

Example
The New York Stock Exchange circuit breakers are as follows
(as of 1998): if the first circuit breaker (Dow Jones Industrial
Average down 350 points) is reached prior to 3:00 P.M., trading
would be halted for a half hour. If the first circuit breaker is
reached at or after 3:00 P.M., trading would continue uninter-
rupted until the second circuit breaker (DJIA down 550 points)
is reached.

classification of directors

See **staggered terms**.

clear title

See **title insurance**.

clearing

Approving—or being approved for—a transfer of assets.
   See also **clearinghouse**.

clearinghouse

1 In securities trading, a facility that delivers certificates and payments for transactions executed by brokers, dealers, banks, and mutual funds.

2 In banking, an organization that settles checks between member banks. The three major securities exchanges—the New York Stock Exchange (NYSE), the American Stock Exchange (AMEX), and the NASDAQ Stock Market—clear their trades through the National Securities Clearing Corporation (NSCC), a clearinghouse they jointly own. As the industry continues to automate, the brokerage houses and exchanges have been increasingly matching buyers and sellers themselves; the clearinghouse gets the money and the certificates to where they have to go.

Clearinghouse Interbank Payments System (CHIPS)

See **electronic funds transfer (EFT)**.

closed-end lease

A lease for a car in which both the lease period and the monthly payments are fixed. You also have a fixed price for the car if you wish to purchase it at the end of the lease period.

With an open-end lease, both the lease period and the price you'd have to pay to purchase vary with the market value and the car's condition at the end of the lease period.

closing tick

A term referring to the number of stocks that last traded on an uptick minus those that traded on a downtick. (*Uptick* means that the last trade price was higher than the previous trade price; *downtick* means that the last trade price was lower than the previous trade price.) A negative closing tick (i.e., more downticks) is considered to be bearish, and a positive closing tick (i.e., more upticks) is considered to be bullish.

clouds

See **title insurance**.

CMA

See **comparative market analysis (CMA)**.

CME

See **Chicago Mercantile Exchange (CME)**.

CMO

See **collateralized mortgage obligation (CMO)**.

COGS

See **cost of goods sold (COGS)**.

coincident economic indicators

Index, comprising four components, that serves as a mirror on the current state of the U.S. economy.

The four index components are:

1 Employees on nonagricultural payrolls.
2 Personal income minus payments such as Social Security, veterans' benefits, and welfare payments.
3 An index of industrial production.
4 Manufacturing and trade sales in constant dollars.

The index of coincident economic indicators is published monthly by the U.S. Commerce Department's Bureau of Economic Analysis.

See also **lagging economic indicators** and **leading economic indicators**.

COLA

See **cost of living adjustment (COLA)**.

cold call

An attempt to sell something, either in person, or over the phone, to a person or company totally unfamiliar with you, your company, or your product.

cold comfort letter

See **comfort letter**.

collar

A maximum and minimum interest rate, or dividend, to be paid on an adjustable rate security.

The interest rate can't fluctuate beyond the high and low (known as the cap and floor) of the collar.

See also **adjustable rate preferred stock**.

collateral

An asset used to ensure the security of a loan. The lender often has the right to claim the asset should the borrower fail to pay the debt.

collateralized mortgage obligation (CMO)

Mortgage-backed security offering a choice of maturity dates.

See also **mortgage-backed security**.

comfort letter

An attachment to a securities registration or legal agreement saying that certain conditions have been or will be met.

In a securities underwriting, the letter comes from an independent auditor and states that the information in the registration statement and prospectus was correctly prepared and that there have been no material changes since its preparation. The letter does not say that the information is correct, only that there is no evidence that it is incorrect. For this reason, it is sometimes called a cold comfort letter.

In a legal agreement, a comfort letter usually specifies actions—not listed in the formal agreement—that will or will not be taken. It is also called a declaration of intent, because it states what one of the parties intends to do. It is not part of the legally binding contract.

commercial paper

Short-term securities sold by large corporations and other institutions.

These unsecured notes, with maturities of from 2 to 270 days, usually provide short-term working capital for the issuer. Commercial paper is bought mostly by other large institutions. These investors like commercial paper because it lets them put their cash to work in a relatively secure way (it is almost always backed by a bank letter of credit) without tying it up for very long.

Commercial paper is rated by both Moody's Investors Service and Standard & Poor's (S&P).

commodity

The products underlying the contracts traded on the commodity exchanges. Examples include metals (such as aluminum, copper, or gold), grains (such as wheat), or foods (such as corn).

See also **commodity futures** and **futures**.

commodity futures

Standardized contracts that lock in a commodities transaction at a certain price on a specific future date. These are traded on the

Chicago Mercantile Exchange; the Chicago Board of Trade; and the New York Coffee, Sugar, and Cocoa Exchange, among others.

See also **derivatives**.

common stock

Share in a company's ownership.

Common stockholders supply equity capital, usually have voting rights, and elect the board of directors. This allows majority shareholders to indirectly control the company. Shareholders may benefit from a company's success through the receipt of income (in the form of dividends) and through capital appreciation (a rise in the stock price). If a company declares bankruptcy, holders of common stock have only a residual claim to assets—behind creditors, debtholders, the IRS, and preferred shareholders—making them the last in line to collect.

See also **capital stock** and **equity**.

comparative market analysis (CMA)

See **property tax assessment**.

completion bond

Money put up to guarantee that a job will be finished to the client's satisfaction.

See also **performance bond**.

compound interest

Earning or paying more interest on your reinvested interest.

Let's say that you're making 5 percent annually on an account in which you have $10,000. If it's compounding annually, then your interest would be calculated like this:

Beginning balance	$10,000
Interest (5% × $10,000)	$ 500
Ending balance	$10,500

But if your interest were compounding quarterly, the calculation would look like this:

Beginning balance	$10,000
1st quarter interest	$10,000 × 1.25% = $125
Balance end of 1st quarter	$10,125
2nd quarter interest	$10,125 × 1.25% = $126.56
Balance end of 2nd quarter	$10,251.56
3rd quarter interest	$10,251.56 × 1.25% = $128.14
Balance end of 3rd quarter	$10,379.70
4th quarter interest	$10,379.70 × 1.25% = $129.75
Balance end of 4th quarter	$10,509.45

Interest can be compounded monthly, quarterly, semiannually, or continuously. The more frequently your interest compounds, the faster it grows over time.

Compound Interest

Say you plunked $1,000 into a one-year CD earning 5 percent interest. You'd make $51.16 by year's end if the CD compounded monthly and $51.27 if it compounded continuously—okay, it's only an 11-cent difference. But over time, the effect does become more pronounced:

$1,000 CD at 5% Interest Value After	Simple Interest	Compounded Monthly	Compounded Weekly
1 year	$1,050.00	$1,051.16	$1,051.27
5 years	1,276.30	1,283.36	1,283.87
10 years	1,628.90	1,647.01	1,648.33
15 years	2,078.90	2,113.70	2,116.24

The different yield on simple versus compound interest is more significant. With simple interest you just get a straight percentage on your money; so $1,000 at 9 percent would earn you $90 a year. If you compounded your interest continuously, you'd make $95.12 the first year and more in the years to come.

comprehensive coverage

Insurance policies that cover most standard medical procedures or accidents.

Insurance companies rarely, if ever, offer coverage that is "comprehensive" in the literal sense of the word.

Most auto insurance policies have two parts: collision and comprehensive. The comprehensive portion encompasses just about anything that can happen to your car besides getting hit by another vehicle or running into a stationary object, including fire, flood, theft, hail, mischief, riot, or simply smashing into a deer. An "act of God," such as a hurricane or another similar unforeseen disturbance, rarely falls under a comprehensive plan, so be sure to look into additional coverage if you live in a place where grand-scale problems happen often. The deductible—the amount you have to pay before the insurance kicks in—can range from $50 to $500. The higher the deductible you're willing to live with, the lower your premium will be.

For health insurance policies, comprehensive coverage includes basic hospital and surgical costs, infant care, most doctor bills, as well as a portion (depending on your co-payment) of your costs for prescription drugs and home health care your doctor orders. But such deals may limit expenses relating to a preexisting condition, substance abuse, mental illness, cosmetic surgery, dental problems, pregnancy, or even routine checkups.

So "comprehensive" actually means the best blanket policy you can get without paying extra for special coverage (such as maternity).

In the United States, a more comprehensive option might be a Health Maintenance Organization (HMO). Many of these cover routine physicals, pregnancy, and maternity, and—depending on the plan—perhaps prescription drugs with a low co-payment. But you can only use the HMO's doctors and facilities, and there might still be gaping holes in coverage.

conservatism concept

A term for the idea that accountants should be pessimists by anticipating all losses but no gains.

Whenever there is doubt about which estimate to use in accounting, an accountant will pick the one that yields less net income or a lower asset value. Another way of looking at it is that bad news is accounted for as soon as it can be given a number, but good news is recognized only when the money has been collected.

Example
Kaiser Permanente, an HMO with health centers in many parts of the country, covers prenatal care, birth, and postnatal care—even including complications. But it doesn't cover chiropractic, and its coverage of prescription drugs and dental care varies depending on the plan.

See also **adequate disclosure concept**, **consistency concept**, **matching concept**, and **materiality concept**.

consistency concept

A term for the idea that the same accounting methods are used year after year unless there is good reason to change, perhaps to more accurately reflect a company's performance.

The reader of a company's financial statements should be able to assume that the numbers provided this year are based on the same accounting procedures as last year's numbers, and so on. If a company chooses to alter its accounting method—say, its way of valuing inventories—the company needs to disclose its method and show the effects in its financial reports. Sometimes an earlier year's results will be restated to maintain consistency.

See also **adequate disclosure concept**, **conservatism concept**, **inventory valuation**, **matching concept**, and **materiality concept**.

consolidation

Reporting the financial statements of the parent company and its subsidiaries as if they were one entity in terms of assets, liabilities, and operating results.

In general, accounting principles call for consolidation when one company owns more than 50 percent of another's common stock. The precept applies even if the businesses are so dissimilar that it might seem to make more sense to report them separately. Therefore, even conglomerates such as Berkshire Hathaway report their businesses on a consolidated basis. General Electric makes a separate category for General Electric Capital Services and some other units, but then totals them to a consolidated number.

Consolidation does not mean that important information on a company's various businesses is obscured, however. If, among other things, a publicly held company gets 10 percent or more of its revenue from a second industry, it must make separate disclosures concerning revenues, operating profits, and assets somewhere in the annual report, in a process called segment reporting.

consumer price index (CPI)

The most common measure of inflation in the United States, usually expressed on an annualized basis.

The Bureau of Labor Statistics computes the change in the level of consumer prices monthly, based on changes in the prices of a representative "basket" of goods and services that a typical urban consumer is believed to buy. Surveys are used to determine what items and how much of them make up the basket, but the basket changes more slowly than consumers do. When prices for fresh fish rise, for example, many consumers switch immediately to beef or chicken, but basket adjustments lag far behind. Similarly, when gasoline prices rise, people drive less, carpool, and use more public transportation, while the basket still includes a set quantity of gasoline.

In addition, the CPI does not account for changes in retailing, such as the huge popularity of discount stores in recent years, nor does it assess product quality changes or the introduction of new goods and services. For these reasons, the CPI tends to overstate inflation, or changes in the "cost of living."

consumption tax

A tax paid on money spent rather than on money earned—like the sales tax you pay on items you purchase.

The sales tax (in force in all but a handful of U.S. states) is the simplest form of consumption tax. The value-added tax (VAT) is another form, common outside the United States.

A tax on money earned that we are all familiar with is the income tax. In recent years, economists have debated the merits of replacing all or part of the U.S. income tax with a comprehensive consumption tax—a national sales tax, a VAT, or a third alternative: a tax on the difference between what you earn and what you add to savings each year.

contango

See **backwardation**.

contingent liabilities

Liabilities that might or might not become due.

A lawsuit that might result in your company's paying a large settlement would result in a contingent liability on the balance sheet.

See also **liability**.

Continuous Net Settlement

A system to keep constant track of which brokers owe each other how much over the course of the trading day.

See also **clearinghouse**.

contrarian

In general, an investor who likes to bet opposite the market, with the idea that less-popular investments offer more value.

contribution

1 Earnings that you or your employer invest in your retirement plan.

See also **vested/vesting**.

2 Donation to charity, often tax-deductible.

See also **charitable deduction**.

conversion price

The price at which conversion of a security can be exercised, usually expressed as a dollar value.

For a convertible bond, for example, you might have a $1,000 bond that is convertible into common shares at $20 per share. Thus, your conversion price would be $20, and you would be able to exchange your bond for fifty shares.

If the price is not stated, you can calculate it by dividing the face value of the security by the conversion ratio—the number of shares you will receive.

conversion ratio

Number of common stock shares that an investor can get in return for a convertible security—usually a convertible bond or a share of convertible preferred stock.

If the ratio is not stated, you can calculate it by dividing the face value of the security by the conversion price—the per-share value of the stock you will receive:

conversion ratio = bond face value ÷ conversion price
See also **conversion price** and **convertible bond**.

convertible bond

A bond that can be exchanged for a specified number of shares of common stock, usually at a predetermined price in the future.

A convertible bond is typically an unsecured debt obligation of a company and would rank above preferred and common stock in the event of a bankruptcy. In addition to scheduled interest payments, equity participation is offered to the investor by convertibles if the stock price rises above the conversion price.

Because of the equity kicker (you're getting some play on the company's share price), the coupon rate of a convertible bond is typically lower than that of a comparable straight bond. Although convertible bonds can be short term, they are typically long-term obligations (15 years or longer).

See also **conversion price**, **conversion ratio**, **convertible preferred stock**, and **convertible security**.

convertible preferred stock

A security that is similar to a convertible bond, except that it's a preferred stock (rather than a bond) that's convertible to common stock.

The preferred shareholder receives dividend income while retaining the opportunity to gain from stock appreciation.

See also **conversion price, conversion ratio, convertible bond,** and **convertible security.**

convertible security

A bond or preferred stock that can be exchanged at the holder's option for a specified number of shares of common stock.

Usually, a company issues convertible rather than straight securities because it wants to obtain a lower interest rate. For investors, the conversion feature offers the opportunity to benefit from a future increase in the common stock price in return for giving up a little of the interest rate.

See also **conversion price, conversion ratio, convertible preferred stock,** and **convertible bond.**

corporate bonds

See **bond.**

corpus

1 All the assets (such as property or cash) originally put in a trust.

A person may open a trust for any number of reasons: to scoot around the IRS, to provide for a relative, or to avoid creditors, probate, or any number of other things that might drain money from an estate. Sometimes the corpus (also called Principal of Trust) is doled out to one person or organization and the interest on the assets to someone else.

2 The principal portion of a bond, so named to distinguish it from its interest coupons.

If you are at risk for racking up huge medical costs because of some illness or simple old age, be sure any trust you form clearly states that the medical community must first apply for government benefits such as Medicaid and Medicare before it tries to tap into the principal of your trust. In many states, health care providers can go after the assets you've locked in a trust if your bills go unpaid.

correlation coefficient

Measure of how one factor relates to another in either a positive or a negative way.

Statisticians express the correlation coefficient in values ranging from +1 (the highest level of positive correlation) to −1 (the highest level of negative correlation), with 0 representing no correlation at all between the two factors.

See also **elasticity**.

cost of capital

1 In accounting, the payments that a company makes for its various sources of capital—such as interest payments on its debt and dividends on its stock.

   It is also the minimum rate of return an investor would require to buy into a business or venture. Analysts use cost of capital in evaluating an investment or project such as building a plant or introducing a product.

2 In corporate finance, the minimum rate of return a company would be willing to earn if it invested in another venture with equal risk.

cost of goods sold (COGS)

See **income statement**.

cost of living adjustment (COLA)

Adjustment made when analysts or the government calculate economic indicators such as the consumer price index.

See also **indexing**.

co-trustee

See **trustee**.

coupon rate

The stated interest rate on a security, referred to as an annual percentage of face value. Also called the nominal rate.

It is called the coupon rate because bonds once carried actual coupons that holders would redeem for interest payments. (Those bonds are called bearer bonds.) Today, most bonds are registered in holders' names, and interest payments are sent to the registered holder, but the term coupon rate is still widely used.

covenant

A restriction placed on a security issuance, usually on bonds being issued by a company.

Debt covenants are found in the indenture (which is filed with the Securities and Exchange Commission) at the time of a debt offering. Typical covenants include restrictions on borrowing over a certain amount or from letting liquidity or operating ratios cross certain thresholds. For example, a covenant will require that a company maintain a minimum net worth, below which the company must redeem its bonds at par value.

Three important covenant categories are:

1 *Net worth requirement:* Protects investors by requiring a minimum net worth to be maintained on a periodic (usually quarterly) basis. If a company's net worth falls significantly, the covenant usually requires the issuer to tender for a portion of its bonds at par value.

2 *Limitation on dividend and stock repurchase:* Specifies the maximum amount that can be used for dividends or stock buybacks. This covenant protects bondholders' priority over that of equity holders.

3 *Merger/sale of assets:* Describes under what conditions a merger or substantial asset sale can occur. This covenant gives some protection against adverse impact on the bonds from fundamental changes in the company.

covered sale

The practice of selling a security short while owning the underlying stock. (If you do not own the security, then it's called a naked sale.) Also referred to as selling against the box.

See also **call**.

CPA

See **certified public accountant (CPA)**.

CPI

See **consumer price index (CPI)**.

credit

In accounting, an entry on the right side of an account, offsetting the corresponding debit. Asset and expense accounts are decreased on the credit side; and liability, revenue, and capital accounts are increased on the credit side.

See also **bookkeeping** and **debit**.

credit bureau

Organization that provides information about how promptly you pay your bills.

Credit bureaus act as clearinghouses for businesses that want to know your payment history before they give you credit. There are three national bureaus—Equifax, Experion (formerly TRW), and Trans-Union—as well as 750 or so local and regional bureaus, to which you can write or call for your credit history. The reams of numbers you will receive will not contain any rating or summary; they will just matter-of-factly list your payment record for basic lines of credit, such as your Visa card or student loan.

In theory, the clearinghouse also taps into any public records when it does a check on you, which would uncover bankruptcies, foreclosures, tax liens, or court judgments, but the searches are not always that thorough. Federal law imposes limits on how long you can be penalized for having gone through something like a bankruptcy, with 10 years marking the outer range and 7 years the norm.

Your credit record will not include your payment record for short-term expenses such as utilities, doctor's appointments, telephone bills, and such. So if you are tight on cash and want to be sure you are not damaging your credit history, give that credit card bill priority over the dentist's bill.

credit card

Banks and other vendors hook up with credit associations, such as Visa or MasterCard, to issue plastic cards that consumers can use to buy now and pay later. Although American Express is often called a credit card, it works a bit differently, as you'll see in a moment. Cardholders get to repay the debts at their own pace as long as they pay a minimum balance each month—but they pay dearly for the privilege.

The associations market their product and act as a clearinghouse for receipts, while the banks actually shell out the cash for the incoming bills and then send an invoice to the cardholder. If you can't pay your bill in full, finance charges accrue. Some lenders also charge annual fees, though that's become less common as competition for cardholders has intensified. Indeed, many of the banks and credit associations offer all sorts of perks to entice people with good credit. Travel insurance, shopping discounts, extended warranties on products you buy, deferred payments, cash advances, and car rental insurance are just some of the carrots dangled in front of potential cardholders.

Don't confuse your credit card with other types of plastic on the market, including debit cards (which essentially function like checks), charge cards (which can only be used at the store that issued the card), and travel and entertainment cards (such as American Express and Diners Club, which require you to pay in full each month but don't charge interest). A credit card has a float period between the date you purchase something and when you have to pay for it—sometimes as long as 45 days—that serves as a free loan if you pay off your bill in full each month.

credit history

Record of how faithfully you pay your bills.

See also **credit bureau**.

credit-sensitive note

A bond whose interest rate is tied to credit ratings assigned by agencies like Standard & Poor's (S&P) and Moody's Investors Service.

It's simple: if the rating declines, then the price of the bond probably will too (and vice versa). For the investor, credit-sensitive notes act as a hedge against falling ratings. The issuer gets a way to make its bonds more marketable by extending a degree of protection to the buyer.

See also **bond ratings**.

cumulative effect of accounting change

Item on your income statement that shows the catch-up cost, or benefit, of making an accounting change.

When a company changes its accounting methods, it affects not only the current period but all prior periods that are used in making comparisons. Most annual reports contain several years of comparable income statement and balance sheet data.

cumulative preferred stock

Stock that continues to accumulate dividends even if the company can't pay them. Unlike the case of common stock, a company is obligated to pay dividends on preferred stock. If they're forced to stop for any reason, the unpaid dividends will accrue, to be paid later.

See also **accumulated dividend** and **preferred stock**.

cumulative voting

A system of voting for elective bodies, such as boards of directors, that ensures sizable minority views or representation.

Under cumulative voting, each voter gets a number of votes equal to the number of positions to be filled and can cast all of the votes for one candidate. As a result, a voter can concentrate his or her voting power and might be able to elect one or more candidates. Basically, any group that holds a percentage of votes equal to the percentage of total board seats represented by one seat can elect at least one board member. Although it's not common for publicly held companies, cumulative voting is often used in electing boards for private companies and organizations such as condominium associations.

In recent years, shareholders have introduced proposals at the annual meetings of many large publicly held corporations calling for cumulative voting in the election of directors. These proposals have almost invariably been opposed by the company's management and defeated. The idea behind the proposals is that cumulative voting would make it easier to elect directors to represent a particular point of view. A labor union, for example, or an environmental organization could encourage its members and sympathizers to cast all of their cumulative votes for one candidate.

See also **staggered terms.**

Curb Exchange, or "The Curb"

The nickname for the American Stock Exchange (AMEX).

currency futures

Financial instruments whose value is based on currency indexes; traded on exchanges such as the International Monetary Market (IMM).

See also **derivatives.**

current assets

Assets that can quickly be converted into cash or that will be used by the end of a year or within the company's normal operating cycle, whichever is longer. Current assets would include a company's marketable securities, cash accounts, and accounts receivable.

See also **balance sheet.**

current liabilities

Short-term obligations, due before the end of the next accounting period. Current liabilities typically include accounts payable and any debt that's payable within a year.

See also **balance sheet.**

current ratio

Measure of liquidity, or the company's ability to meet currently maturing or short-term obligations.

The ratio is:

current assets ÷ current liabilities

The information can easily be found on a company's balance sheet.

current yield

Percentage return on a bond, arrived at by dividing the dollar amount of annual interest by the market price.

See also **bond yield**.

D: Daisy Chain to
Dun & Bradstreet Reports

daisy chain

A scheme in which a group of unscrupulous "investors" bids up a stock in order to create the illusion of higher value, then sells to unwitting buyers.

D&B

See **Dun & Bradstreet reports**.

day order

An order to be executed that day only, otherwise to be canceled. For example, you might want to buy a stock at, say, $20. If the stock doesn't dip that low that day, then your day order would be automatically canceled.

See also **good-till-canceled (GTC)** and **limit order**.

DCF

See **discounted cash flow**.

debenture

A bond backed by the issuer's "full faith and credit," but not by any hard assets.

Debentures are backed by a document called an indenture, which details the covenants, terms, and obligations of the issuing company. Debentures are by far the most common form of corporate bond, usually issued by large companies that have strong credit records.

Debentures often include provisions or warrants that permit their holders to convert the bonds or warrants to common stock under certain terms. These rights allow the debenture holders to increase returns by participating in the growth of the business.

debit

Entry on the left side of an account, opposite the credit entry on the right. All asset and expense accounts are increased on the debit side, while all liability, revenue, and capital accounts are decreased on the debit side.

See also **bookkeeping** and **credit**.

debit card

Similar to a credit card, except that purchases are deducted directly from the cardholder's account, rather than being added to a debt balance.

debt security

A security representing money borrowed that must be repaid, having a fixed amount, a specific maturity, and usually a specific rate of interest or an original purchase discount—such as a bill, bond, commercial paper, or note.

debt-to-capital ratio

Measure of a company's debt load, intended to reflect creditworthiness.

There are variations on exactly what goes into this ratio, but the most common procedure is to divide total debt by total capitalization. (Capitalization is usually defined as total debt plus shareholders' equity.)

For the debt-to-capital ratio, a low number indicates better financial stability than a high one does—but like all ratios, it needs to be evaluated against those of other companies in your industry, and against your own company's numbers over time. When calculating the ratio, some prefer to use the market value of the debt and equity rather than the book value.

debt-to-equity ratio
See **debt-to-capital ratio**.

deductible
In an insurance plan, the amount that a policyholder must pay "out of pocket" before the insurance company begins covering expenses. For example, a health insurance plan might cover expenses only above $1,000 for a given year, giving the policyholder a $1,000 deductible.

deduction
An amount subtracted from your income for tax purposes, therefore lowering your tax bill.

Although the 1986 Tax Reform Act pared back the number and largesse of deductions, quite a few juicy ones remain:

Homeownership Deductions
Interest paid on mortgage loans together with property and school taxes paid on a house; they make home ownership the fattest deduction for most taxpayers.

IRAs AND 401ks

Despite restrictions in recent years, these basic instruments are still the best ways to shield your hard-earned dollars from Uncle Sam. Essentially, with either a 401k or an IRA (the most popular tax-free savings plans), you can shield a portion of your income from taxes until you withdraw the funds (preferably during retirement, when you're in a lower tax bracket).

Charitable Donations

Charitable contributions not only give you a warm, fuzzy feeling, they give you a tax deduction. Just be sure that you document exactly what you give to a charity and when, and have a fair estimate of its value. Generally speaking, for gifts of more than $250, the charity must send you a receipt for your donation and an estimate of the value of whatever you received in return for the donation.

deep discount bond

A bond with a purchase price well below face value. Most zero-coupon bonds, for example, are deep discount bonds—so the face value might be $1,000, but your purchase price could be much less.

default

Failure to meet a required payment on a loan or other debt. Whether you're the lender (i.e., a bond in your portfolio has gone into default) or lendee, this is an unhappy outcome.

From the lendee's perspective, the consequences of defaulting on a major loan, such as a mortgage or a car loan, can be dire. At best, your credit rating will be hurt, and at worse you could be forced into bankruptcy. Consider what the U.S. government can do if you default on a student loan: seize tax refunds, garnish wages, and report you to credit agencies. "You can't get a mortgage, a car loan, or a credit card," says Leo Kornfeld, U.S. deputy assistant secretary of education for student financial assistance. "We literally push you out of society if you default."

deferred compensation

Receiving pay or other compensation for a job after you've left.

Executives and their companies increasingly opt for deferred compensation for a couple of reasons. First, it can save taxes for both the corporation and for the executive. Second, in an era when employees and shareholders take a dimmer view of mammoth executive paychecks, deferring compensation adds an air of frugality to executive compensation.

defined benefit pension plan

A kind of pension plan in which the money you receive is set (or defined) ahead of time. That's in contrast to the defined contribution pension plan, in which your payout depends on your own contributions, as well as on the plan's investment performance. With a defined benefit plan, your payments will probably be based on your pay level and length of employment.

See also **pension plans**.

defined contribution pension plan

A kind of pension plan in which the money you receive depends on your own contributions, as well as on the plan's investment performance. That's in contrast to the defined benefit pension plan, in which your payout is set from the beginning.

See also **pension plans**.

delta

See **hedge ratio**.

demand deposits

Just what they say: you put your money in and you can get it back whenever you want, without prior notice, in cash or check form, and without any penalties or loss of interest.

See also **withdrawal**.

deflation

See **inflation**.

demand loan

A loan for which the lender can demand payment at any time.

A demand loan has no fixed maturity date. Banks and other financial institutions often require this form of lending for smaller companies, or for large ones that are considered higher risks. Some demand loans carry onerous obligations for the borrower—that all profits be applied to repay the loan, for example, or that the lender must approve any actions that exceed day-to-day decision making. (For example, corporate acquisitions and plant closings would be subject to review.) When a demand loan is drawn up as a negotiable instrument, one that can be bought and sold, it is called a demand note.

demand note

See **demand loan**.

depletion

Accounting procedure by which the cost of a natural resource—such as coal, oil, or timber—is expensed as the resource is sold.

Depository Institutions Deregulation and Monetary Control Act of 1980 (DIDMCA)

See **banking regulation**.

depreciation

An accounting method that extends the cost of an asset—such as a building or equipment—over its estimated useful life.

Although accountants, engineers, and economists might each define depreciation differently, everyone can agree that most assets will inevitably lose value. So some means is needed to show, for accounting and tax purposes, that the asset's usefulness has declined. To accountants, depreciation is not so much a matter of valuation as a means of cost allocation.

When buying a fixed asset, a company has three decisions to make about depreciation:

1 Which depreciation method to use; for financial reporting, the most common are straight-line, double-declining-balance, and the sum-of-the-years' digits.
2 What the life of the asset is.
3 What the estimated salvage value of the asset is (or what it can be sold for at the end of its useful life).

Below are the primary methods of determining depreciation:

Straight-line depreciation is the most commonly used method, and the simplest. It assumes that the asset provides constant benefits, so the cost is spread in equal amounts over the asset's useful life. The annual amount of depreciation is calculated by subtracting the salvage value from the cost and then dividing by the useful life.

Double-declining-balance depreciation is a form of accelerated depreciation in which you write off most of an asset's value early on. Essentially, you use twice the straight-line rate in the first year and then continue to use that rate going forward. Here's an example: Under this method, you don't consider salvage value in your beginning depreciation calculation, although you can't let the asset value drop below salvage value. Alternatively, you can switch to the straight-line method at the optimal point. There is a variation on this method called 150 percent-declining-balance depreciation.

The sum-of-the-years' digits is another method of accelerated depreciation. It's a little more complicated, but it goes something like this: First, you assign a number to each year of the asset's useful life—1, 2, 3, etc. Then you total those numbers to come up with your SYD (sum-of-the-years' digits). For example, an asset with an 8-year life would have thirty-six digits:

$$1+2+3+4+5+6+7+8 = 36$$

So 36 is the denominator you'll be using. Or, there's a shortcut to arrive at the SYD. Just take the last number (in this case, 8) and plug it into this formula, where n = number of years:

$$n(n + 1) \div 2$$

So, using this formula, the calculation for our example would be:

$$8(8 + 1) \div 2 = 36$$

Your numerator will be the number of years your asset has left. So, for our asset with an 8-year life, our first year's numerator would be 8, for the second year it would be 7, and so on. You simply apply that fraction to the depreciable cost of the asset every year.

See also **amortization**.

Here's what the schedule would look like:

Year	Cost	Fraction	Depreciation	Cumulative Depreciation	Balance
1	$36,000	8/36	$8,000	$ 8,000	$32,000
2	$36,000	7/36	$7,000	$15,000	$25,000
3	$36,000	6/36	$6,000	$21,000	$19,000
4	$36,000	5/36	$5,000	$26,000	$14,000
5	$36,000	4/36	$4,000	$30,000	$10,000
6	$36,000	3/36	$3,000	$33,000	$ 7,000

Year	Cost	Fraction	Depreciation	Cumulative Depreciation	Balance
7	$36,000	2/36	$2,000	$35,000	$ 5,000
8	$36,000	1/36	$1,000	$36,000	$ 4,000

derivatives

A financial instrument that's based on an underlying asset, like a stock or index.

Derivatives are often used to offset risk, but they can also be traded in more speculative ways to profit from everything from swings in interest rates to prices of commodities or currencies. Examples range from stock options (which are based on the underlying stock) to index options (which are based on a particular index, like the S&P 500) to futures (which can be based on currencies, indices, or commodities).

Derivatives fall into five basic categories:

1 *Futures* are standardized contracts that lock in a transaction at a certain price on a specific future date. Futures contracts can be for (a) financial instruments, such as currencies, Eurodollars, or interest rates; (b) indices, such as the S&P 500; or (c) physical commodities, such as corn and gold. The contracts change hands many times on the market where they are listed, and, at maturity, contracts to buy can offset contracts to sell. So in most cases, the underlying transaction actually never takes place.

2 *Forwards* are contracts that call for delivery of a specific amount of an underlying asset on a future date at the spot price (the current cash price) or at another negotiated price. Forwards differ from futures in that they are less standardized (each aspect of the contract—such as time and place of delivery—is negotiable). They're also only available to large hedgers with enough collateral to satisfy an underwriting bank.

3 *Options* come in two basic flavors—a call option and a put
option. A call option gives the holder the right, but not the
obligation, to buy an asset at a particular price before a certain
date. If the asset does not climb to that value, or strike price,
the option does not need to be exercised. A put option gives
the holder the right, but not the obligation, to sell an asset at a
particular price before a certain date. If the asset does not fall
to the strike price, the holder will not exercise the option.
Options represent two thirds of all the derivatives trading based
on equities, but trading is larger still in interest rate options.

   See also **call option** and **put option**.

4 *Swaps* are private agreements between two companies to
exchange cash flows in the future. For instance, firms that
have branches in each other's home countries might exchange
some of their accounts receivable to reduce costs and foreign
exchange risk. In interest rate swaps, traders may take responsibility for each other's loans. That makes sense when one
company can get good terms on, say, a fixed rate loan, and
another can do well on a floating rate. Swap contracts last
longer than most other derivatives, covering from 1 to 10
years.

5 *Hybrids* and *synthetics* are derivative securities that combine
the other four forms into one complex instrument. For example, you might buy a call option on a forward contract, crazy
as it sounds. (Leave that transaction to the pros.) Synthetics
allow firms to construct derivatives not covered by existing
markets.

See also **arbitrage**.

diluted earnings per share

A method of calculating earnings per share that assumes the conversion to common stock of everything that can be converted—such as
convertible bonds and warrants.

dilution

Issuing more shares of stock so that the ownership of the company is divided among more shareholders.

Dilution can result from stock offerings, the exercising of warrants or options, or the conversion of preferred stock or bonds.

disclaimer of opinion

Indicates that an auditor cannot give an opinion, usually because the audit could not be completed. If your company's annual report has a disclaimer of opinion from your accountant, chances are it's in hot water.

disclosure

A term used to indicate fully divulged information. Public companies, for example, are obligated to provide enough disclosure to their auditors and investors for them to adequately understand their businesses.

See also **adequate disclosure concept**.

discount rate

1 Interest rate the Federal Reserve System (the Fed) charges its member banks.

If you've watched the way the market reacts to decisions by the Fed, you know that they wield plenty of influence with their control over the discount rate. This is why, when they lower the discount rate, banks are encouraged to borrow more reserves, which they can then use to make more interest-earning loans and investments, thus expanding the money supply. Conversely, when the Fed raises the discount rate, it can trigger a contraction in the supply of money and credit.

2   Another use of the term "discount rate" is in the calculation of present value. It's the rate used to discount a series of future cash payments.

See also **internal rate of return (IRR)**.

discounted cash flow

The current value of an investment's future cash flow.

See also **net present value (NPV)**.

disinflation

See **inflation**.

disposable income

What is left of your personal income after taxes are paid.

See also **personal income** and **savings**.

dissavings

If you spend more than you earn, the negative balance is sometimes called dissavings.

See also **savings**.

distribution channel

An integrated system of channel members that influences the movement of goods and services and has direct impact on the end consumer.

A product's distribution channel usually involves a network of interdependent organizations, such as transportation companies, storage facilities, wholesalers, and retailers needed to move the product along. What one organization adds to the process might be tangible (as when a factory converts raw material into a product) or intangible (as when a wholesale distributor handles the logistics of getting a product to retail stores).

Four forms of distribution channels are:

1 *Direct sales or direct marketing:* When the product goes from the producer directly to the ultimate consumer.

2 *One intermediary:* Often a retailer that might buy its goods directly from the manufacturers and sell them to the consumer via retail stores.

3 *Multiple intermediaries:* Typically, a wholesaler and a retailer are involved, plus in all likelihood some transportation and possibly storage companies.

4 *Industrial channels:* In the industrial market, the producer might sell directly to the customer. Or the producer might use intermediaries such as manufacturer's representatives or distributors.

The distribution channel, taken together, performs a variety of functions: transporting and storing goods, financing operations, gathering information through market research and contact with the various customers, fitting the product or service to the customers' needs, promoting the product or service, identifying potential buyers, reaching those buyers, negotiating the transaction, and in general taking on elements of financial risk.

Distribution channels were once mainly loose collections of independent producers, wholesalers, and retailers—each member having its own way of doing business and each out to make maximum profit for itself. Recently, though, vertical marketing systems have been on the rise, with the elements of the channel working cooperatively.

diversifiable risk

Price swings in one company's stock for reasons specific to that company (versus, say, general market conditions). This risk can be somewhat reduced in an overall portfolio through diversification.

See also **alpha (α)**, **beta (β)**, **market risk premium**, and **nonmarket risk**.

diversification

Strategy for spreading risk by investing in a variety of markets, industries, or types of securities.

For most investors, the primary categories of diversification will be cash, bonds, and stocks. Although every investor is different, a typical allocation table might look like this:

10%	CASH	
40%	BONDS	
		• Government bonds
		• High-grade bonds
		• High-yield bonds
50%	STOCKS	
		• Blue chips
		• Small stocks
		• International stocks

Don't put all your eggs in one basket. True diversification doesn't mean three or four different investments. As painful as it might be, you have to think of the worst-case scenario. Force yourself to consider how much you could lose without ruining your life. Five percent? Then make sure you're in twenty different investments. Ten percent? Then find ten investments you like.

dividend

Payment made to shareholders at the discretion of a company's management.

Dividends are most often granted in cash (like the $1 dividend you might get every quarter from one of your stocks). But they can also come in different forms, including additional securities. (So you might receive more shares in your company instead of cash—that's called a stock dividend.) Companies that pay regular dividends traditionally issue them quarterly, but they can be granted or terminated at any interval.

An increasingly popular way for companies to reward their shareholders without increasing the dividend is via a stock buyback. A company that buys up its shares on the open market is adding value to the shares still outstanding. That is because the buyback increases demand for the stock and, by reducing the number of shares outstanding, improves all per-share calculations.

Many investors forget that a company can choose to cut or eliminate its dividends to common shareholders at any time. They usually don't like to (because it typically hurts their share price). Still, there are no guarantees with dividends.

See also **stock split**.

dividend policy

How a company chooses to pay out dividends.

Dividend policy varies greatly from company to company. Most fall into one of the following three categories:

1 *No dividends:* Some companies believe that the thing to do with extra cash is to invest it right back into the company. The idea is that if your company cannot make better returns for its investors than they can make for themselves, you've got no business tying up their money in the first place. Besides, the company's earnings have already been taxed once. Paying them out to investors gets them taxed again.

   If a company maintains a no-dividend policy and continues to grow, any time an investor needs cash, he or she ought to be able to sell some stock profitably.

2 *Moderate Dividends:* This approach tries to accommodate those investors who want some current income. The dividends represent a much smaller cash return than investors could earn in other ways, and increases in the payout are rare.

Even so, companies are reluctant to reduce or eliminate a dividend because that action often sends investors fleeing.

3 *Steadily growing dividends:* Many successful companies like to please their income-oriented investors with growing payouts. The most successful can pull that off and still plow plenty back into growth as well. Of course, investors are hoping to see growth in the share price, too, but that dividend is a bird in the hand as they anticipate those in the bush.

DJIA

See **Dow Jones Industrial Average (DJIA)**.

dog and pony show

A CEO with entourage in tow makes a tour of the country, meeting with bankers and investment dealers to give them a sample of their skills in dealing with the funds they all hope to raise by selling large amounts of their stock.

DOJ

The U.S. Department of Justice.

dollar-weighted rate of return

Another term for internal rate of return (IRR).

double-declining-balance depreciation

A method that writes off more of an asset's value in the early years.
See also **depreciation**.

Dow Jones Industrial Average (DJIA)

The oldest and most commonly followed U.S. stock market index.

When people say, "The market rose ten points today," they are usually referring to the Dow Jones Industrial Average. The DJIA is a price-weighted average of thirty widely traded stocks on the New

York Stock Exchange (NYSE). The companies change from time to time, but they usually represent between 15 percent and 20 percent of the market value of all actively traded stocks on the NYSE. The DJIA is adjusted for the substitutions, mergers, stock dividends, and splits that have occurred since it was first published in 1896. Because of its 100-plus years of adjustments, it has more value as a measure of price movements than as a measure of absolute price levels.

See also **Russell 2000 Index**, **Standard & Poor's (S&P) 500**, and **Wilshire 5000 Equity Index**.

downtick

A term referring to the direction of a trade versus the trade just before it. For example, if a stock trades at $30, and the trade price before that was at $32, then the stock has traded on a downtick. (Conversely, an uptick means that the last trade price was higher than the previous trade price.)

See also **closing tick**.

draft

Order to transfer money.

See also **bill of exchange**.

dual-currency bonds

Bonds issued in one country using another country's currency.

See also **Eurobonds**.

due diligence

Gathering and verifying data before making a final commitment to a course of action.

In a public offering, due diligence is essentially the process in which the underwriters check the background and viability of the issuing company. In a merger or acquisition, due diligence calls for assembling materials that verify financial statements. The process might go so far as investigating potential legal or ethical problems of the other company. In banking, it involves investigating the viability of the borrower and the adequacy of the collateral.

See also **underwriting**.

Dun & Bradstreet reports

Information sold to subscribers of Dun & Bradstreet, a private credit rating agency.

When people talk about "pulling a D&B," they are referring to Dun & Bradstreet's Business Information Report (BIR). The BIR gives credit information to help assess the risks and opportunities involved in doing business with another company. The reports include information such as credit rating, sales, net worth, number of employees, payments to suppliers, financials, suits, judgments, current debts, history, and operations. D&B also sells business-to-business marketing information.

E: Ear Candy to Extraordinary Item

ear candy

Catchy but empty platitudes that sound good but mean little, and are fitted to the occasion for which they are spoken.

earnings before interest and taxes (EBIT)

Just what it says—how much a company made before it paid its income taxes and the interest on its loans.

It is usually easy to arrive at this figure from a company's income statement, and it is often listed as a separate line item. If not, just add the tax and interest figures to the one for net earnings like this:

```
Example
Interest expenses     ($20,000)
Taxes paid            ($45,000)
Net income            $120,000
```

The EBIT would be $185,000 ($120,000 + $20,000 + $45,000).

Analysts use EBIT to determine a company's ability to meet interest and principal payments. Many analysts also use EBITDA, which simply adds depreciation and amortization to the list of items "added back" to a company's income.

earnings per share (EPS)

A company's net earnings divided by the number of shares outstanding. It's calculated simply enough:

Net income	$120,000,000
Outstanding shares	200,000,000
Earnings per share	$0.60 = $120 million ÷ $200 million

You'll often see different versions of EPS on a company's income statement. That's because they might want to point out the effects of "extraordinary items" that they don't think should reflect on the ongoing business. For example, if a company made $1 per share from normal operations but had to pay out after a huge lawsuit that resulted in an accounting loss of $0.50 per share, they'd probably show you both numbers.

See also **income statement**.

earnings report

Summary of a company's income and expenses for an accounting period.

See also **income statement**.

EBIT

See **earnings before interest and taxes (EBIT)**.

EBITDA

See **earnings before interest and taxes (EBIT)**.

economic indexes

See **coincident economic indicators**, **lagging economic indicators**, and **leading economic indicators**.

economic value added (EVA)

Measuring corporate performance against what shareholders could earn elsewhere.

This technique was developed by management consultant G. Bennett Stewart III. Using Stewart's approach, you depreciate investments such as training, and research and development, as well as traditional ideas of capital—such as plants and equipment. It all goes into your capital base. Then you look at how much you are earning from that base.

In the mid-1990s, if your business entailed average risk, you should probably have been earning more than 13.5 percent. That's the 7.5 percent investors could get on long-term Treasury bonds plus the 6 percentage points they earn, on average, for the extra risk of a typical stock.

Unless you were making at least that much on your shareholders' money, Stewart would have said you were doing poorly. The point is not whether you paid it out in dividends or reinvested it—if you were not making it, your shareholders were losing out. Says Stewart: "When you are making more money than your cost of doing business plus your cost of capital [e.g., at least that 13.5 percent], you are creating wealth for your shareholders."

See also **depreciation**.

economies of scale

The concept that larger volumes reduce per-unit costs.

Economies of scale are generally achieved by distributing fixed costs, such as general and administrative expenses, advertising, distribution, insurance, and so on, over a larger number of products. Even in industries where economies of scale are a major factor, there might be room for a small niche player to operate profitably.

EDGAR
See **Electronic Data Gathering, Analysis, and Retrieval (EDGAR)**.

effective interest rate
Actual percentage rate paid on borrowed money after taking into account the terms of the loan; it can differ from the stated interest rate.

efficient market theory
Hypothesis that capital markets operate so efficiently that you can assume everyone knows the same information and that such knowledge is already reflected in the prices.

See also **random walk theory**.

efficient portfolio
Assortment of securities that gives you the most return for a certain level of risk, or at least a set return for a minimum amount of risk.

See also **diversification, market risk**, and **nonmarket risk**.

elasticity
In economics, how various elements respond to changes in others. The form of elasticity most commonly referred to is price elasticity, which measures the change in demand in reaction to a change in price.

Defined as the percentage change in the quantity demanded divided by the percentage change in price:

elasticity = % change in quantity demanded ÷ % change in price
Other forms of elasticity include:

Income Elasticity of Demand
Measures how responsive demand is to a change in income. If demand rises when income rises, the goods are considered normal. Goods with high income elasticity are considered luxuries.

On the other hand, if demand falls when income rises, the goods in question are termed inferior and have negative income elasticity.

Cross-Price Elasticity

Measures how the change in one item's price affects demand for another. If cross-elasticity is positive, an increase in the price of one item sparks more demand for the other.

Take butter and margarine, for example. Because they are substitutes, they have a positive elasticity. Cross-elasticity is negative if a price hike for one item causes less demand for another. Bread and butter, for example, would have a negative elasticity. Products with this kind of relationship are called complements.

Supply Elasticity

Measures the responsiveness of producers to price changes. It indicates how much prices must change to get suppliers to increase their output by a given amount. A key factor here is the time producers have to adjust output.

For example, an increase in the price of coffee beans is not likely to get more onto the market, at least in the short run (coffee plants take many years to mature). However, if prices stay at inflated levels, the quantity supplied will eventually increase; that is, supply elasticity increases with time.

electronic bulletin board

Messages posted and read by people using computers linked via a network or over phone lines.

See also **bulletin board system (BBS)**.

Electronic Data Gathering, Analysis, and Retrieval (EDGAR)

Electronic database of documents filed with the Securities and Exchange Commission (SEC), which makes EDGAR available for research and inquiries. Anyone with a computer, a modem, and access to commercial on-line services can electronically obtain the EDGAR documents.

electronic funds transfer (EFT)

Nimble, paperless way to move money around.

Virtually every bank in the United States can send and receive money by wire or computer, and these transactions add up to trillions of dollars a day. There are three major wholesale systems banks use to move money:

1 *Fed wire:* Run by the Federal Reserve System, it's the biggest of the networks. It links some 10,000 U.S. banks to the Fed, its twelve regional Federal Reserve Banks and their branches, some Treasury Department offices, and the Commodity Credit Corporation. The Fed wire specializes in large transactions, and it is the way banks settle their accounts with each other each day as they process checks.

2 *Clearinghouse Interbank Payments System (CHIPS):* Operated by the New York Clearing House, it has around 140 large U.S. and foreign banks at its core. Those banks act as correspondents for many others around the world. CHIPS specializes in international transactions.

3 *Automated Clearinghouses (ACHs):* These are to banks what the automated teller machines (ATMs) are to their customers. They're private processing systems that serve as an alternative to paper checks. They handle direct deposit of payroll and Social Security payments. The U.S. Treasury makes almost 40 percent of its payments via ACHs.

eleventh district cost of funds rate

The average cost S&Ls pay on deposits.

emerging market stock

A stock issued by a country with a less developed or "emerging" economy, expected to show dramatic future growth (with greater risk).

Employee Retirement Income Security Act (ERISA)

Legislation passed in 1974 that regulates pension plans.

employee stock ownership plan (ESOP)

A way of giving employees an equity stake in their company. Occasionally the stocks are regular voting shares, but often they're a special class of nonvoting stock.

ESOPs financed by bank loans have facilitated employee leveraged buyouts of companies. In those cases, stock dividends are used to pay back the loans; as the debt decreases, the employee equity increases.

employment

Stated simply, employment is the use of human resources to produce goods and services for exchange in the market.

Employment differs from work or labor because some work yields goods and services that are not for sale. (The substantial quantity of goods and services produced within households illustrates work or labor, but not employment.) The number of people employed depends both on the total population aged 16 years and older and on the proportion of people who choose to work. This proportion is called the employment-population ratio.

See also **unemployment rate**.

enrolled agent

A person who has passed an IRS examination and is officially recognized as a tax preparer.

EPS

See **earnings per share (EPS)**.

equipment obligation bond

Another name for an equipment trust certificate.

equipment trust certificate

A very secure form of bond backed by a company's equipment as collateral. Also called an equipment obligation bond.

These are common in industries where the equipment is fairly standard, such as the railroad industry. What makes these bonds so secure is that the title to specific pieces of marketable equipment is held in trust until the bonds are paid. If the company fails, the bondholders can claim the equipment and sell it fairly readily.

Equipment trust certificates, like mortgage bonds, are forms of senior secured debt. But many consider the equipment trust certificates more secure, since the equipment can so easily be sold.

equity

Ownership interest in a company. Owner's equity or shareholders' equity on a balance sheet is the company's net worth, or assets minus liabilities.

equity kicker

Attaching an offer of stock ownership to a loan or debt instrument.

You might offer lenders an opportunity for an equity stake in your business to reduce the interest rate or to improve other terms of your loan.

Equity kickers attached to bonds might include warrants, rights, and options. The convertibility provisions for convertible securities are also equity kickers. In other loan agreements, a borrower might offer a lender a small ownership position in the project or acquisition that is being financed. In that case, when the property is sold, the lender is likely to get additional income.

equity REITs

Publicly traded companies that buy real estate.

See also **real estate investment trust (REIT)**.

equity-release

A financing method where part of your monthly payment is credited toward your eventual purchase price.

ERISA

See **Employee Retirement Income Security Act (ERISA)**.

escrow

Something of value held by a neutral third party until conditions in a contract are met.

An escrow agent holds the loot—usually cash, deeds, or securities. An escrow agreement spells out who gets the escrow and when. Once the parties to the contract do what they agreed to do, the escrow is closed.

Most mortgage insurers require an escrow for prepaid private mortgage insurance (PMI) premiums whenever the borrower puts down less than 20 percent.

ESOP

See **employee stock ownership plan (ESOP)**.

Escrow

The escrow agreement in a contract to buy real estate makes the listing broker an escrow agent who holds the buyer's deposit. Since the buyer's ability to get a mortgage is a condition of the sale, the escrow is returned to the buyer if the loan is denied. If it's approved, the escrow goes to the seller as part of the purchase price. But if either party defaults, the broker may hold the escrow until a judge decides who gets it.

Lenders open escrow accounts to hold mortgage customers' prepaid property taxes, private mortgage insurance (PMI), and sometimes homeowner's insurance and/or flood insurance. The Real Estate Settlement Procedures Act (RESPA) makes lenders pay a minimal amount of interest on escrow balances and refund overcharges once a year.

estate tax

A tax on the value of your estate at death. This should be a key concern of anyone setting up an estate, will, or trust. The first $600,000 worth of property and valuables is tax-free, but the rest will be taxed at an estate tax rate. That means that if you leave your beautiful house to your favorite daughter, and the IRS values it at $1,000,000, your daughter will need to come up with as much as $220,000 within 9 months after your death. If she can't find the money, she could lose the house you wanted her to have.

See also **transfer tax.**

Euro

Name for the inter-European currency.

See also **European currency unit (ECU).**

Eurobank

A bank that holds currency deposited from outside its nation's borders; the name comes from the common practice in Europe, but applies to any bank worldwide.

See also **Eurocurrency**.

Eurobonds

Corporate bonds denominated in one country's currency but issued in another country. Also called international bonds.

For example, a German company might issue Eurobonds through a U.S. investment bank, and the bonds will then be purchased by investors in many different countries.

Eurocurrency

Currency deposited in a financial institution outside its home country.

The name relates to the fact that a European country is often involved, but that is not always the case. Similarly, the institution holding the money is called a Eurobank even if it is not in Europe.

The most common form of Eurocurrency is Eurodollars. These U.S. dollars deposited in banks outside the United States are often used in international business transactions. Some securities are denominated in Eurodollars, meaning that all interest, dividends, and other payments are made in dollars deposited overseas. U.S. companies sometimes find better terms for borrowing in the Eurodollar market than for borrowing at home.

Eurodollars

U.S. dollars deposited in banks outside the United States.

See also **Eurocurrency**.

European currency unit (ECU)

Common currency used by the fifteen member countries of the European Economic Community (EEC) to help them simplify monetary transactions among themselves. The value of the ECU is calculated by a weighted index of the members' currencies. The ECU is used as part of each country's foreign exchange reserves.

See also **exchange rate**.

European option

An option that can be exercised only on a specific date.

See also **American option**.

EVA

See **economic value added (EVA)**.

exchange rate

Price at which one country's currency can be traded for another's.

The U.S. dollar, for example, has an exchange rate with the Mexican peso, the French franc, the Japanese yen, and every other currency. These rates are influenced by a complex set of factors and can vary daily; on any given day, the dollar might strengthen against one currency while weakening against another.

Today, most exchange rates "float" in the world market, moving up or down with changes in their demand and supply. Of course, governments might try to influence their currencies' values through actions of their central banks, perhaps by raising domestic interest rates or directly buying a currency on the open market to prop up its price by increasing its demand.

See also **foreign exchange**.

How Do Exchange Rates Really Work?

Prices of currencies are determined by supply and demand, just like prices for other goods. Factors that change the demand for or supply of a given currency will also change its world "price," or exchange rate.

For example, if a government causes inflation by printing too much money, foreigners will demand less of its currency. At the same time, the increase in the money supply will make more currency available to foreigners. The combination of increased supply and reduced demand will cause the currency's price, or exchange rate, to fall.

Other factors, such as interest rates, can produce similar effects. If interest rates rise compared with those throughout the world, foreigners are likely to demand more of the currency to buy the nation's interest-paying assets. The increased demand can then push up the currency's price.

exchangeable rate

See **adjustable rate**.

ex-dividend

Term for a stock dividend that will no longer be paid to the buyer. When a stock has passed its ex-dividend date, the current owner of the stock is entitled to the dividend. A stock's price will often fall by the amount of the dividend on that date.

executive compensation

The total pay package given to the top officers of a corporation.

Compensation can be divided into four categories:

1 *Base salary:* In many cases a relatively small portion of the total package.

2 *Bonuses:* Usually tied in some way to the performance of the company.

They are granted by the board of directors, which often establishes a formula based on such things as profits and total return to shareholders.

3 *Stock options:* The right to buy shares in the future at a set price, usually the price prevailing when the option is granted. The Securities and Exchange Commission (SEC) counts the value of options as executive compensation during the year that they are exercised.

4 *Severance payments:* Special compensation made available if the executive's employment has ended under certain conditions, such as a takeover. The most lucrative of these have come to be known as golden parachutes.

Packages, of course, vary widely by industry, company size, and other factors. Sometimes the value of executive compensation rises markedly during a year when the company's profits dip. In many cases, this is because the stock price remained high and the executive exercised a large number of stock options.

executor
An institution or a person designated to facilitate the directions of a will or last testament.

expected rate of return
Way of evaluating competing investments or portfolios based on the probability of future events. Because it involves predictions, the expected rate of return is commonly used along with a calculation of standard deviation, which measures the average deviation from

an expected result. The larger the deviation, the riskier the investment.

See also **alpha (α), beta (β), market risk**, and **nonmarket risk**.

expenses

Cost of goods and services that are used in a business's attempt to gain revenue.

See also **income statement**.

external reporting

Disclosures of public information to potential investors, creditors, government agencies, and so on.

See also **management accounting**.

extraordinary item

See **earnings per share (EPS)** and **special item**.

F: FAF to Futures

FAF

See **Financial Accounting Foundation (FAF)**.

fair market

In common usage, another term for the market, or going, rate. Technically, it's the price at which a buyer will buy something from a seller, given that they're both rational and aware of all relevant details.

fallen angels

In finance, a derogatory term for securities that were once considered of high quality (even blue chips) but are now thought of as riskier investments.

Fannie Mae

The nickname for the Federal National Mortgage Association (FNMA). Fannie Mae is a quasi-government corporation that buys mortgages (like yours), combines them, and packages them into securities to sell to investors. We say "quasi-government" because it's sponsored by the government but is actually a public corporation.

You can even buy shares in Fannie Mae—it's publicly traded on the New York Stock Exchange.

Fannie Mae buys mortgage lenders' residential mortgages, packages them into securities, and resells them to investors in the United States and, increasingly, overseas. Without Fannie Mae and her cousins Ginnie Mae and Freddie Mac, mortgages would be harder—and more expensive—to come by.

The Story of Fannie Mae

Congress created Fannie Mae in 1938 to ensure a source of credit for low- and moderate-income home buyers. In the early 1950s its role expanded to include the purchase of guaranteed loans for veterans. Then, in 1954, Fannie Mae became partly owned by private shareholders and partly a federal agency. The organization split into two separate entities in 1968: Fannie Mae and Ginnie Mae, which is a direct government agency.

Since Fannie Mae fortunes are so dependent on interest rates, you'll generally find that the stock does well when interest rates fall.

FASB
See **Financial Accounting Standards Board (FASB)**.

FDIC
See **Federal Deposit Insurance Corporation (FDIC)**.

Fed, The
See **Federal Reserve System (Fed)**.

Fed wire

The largest wire service for domestic money exchanges.
See **electronic funds transfer (EFT)**.

Federal Deposit Insurance Corporation (FDIC)

The organization protecting depositors against bank failure.
See **banking regulation**.

Federal Home Loan Mortgage Corporation

See **Freddie Mac**.

Federal Insurance Contribution Act (FICA)

Federal legislation mandating that employers make contributions to Social Security through payroll deductions.

When people refer to "FICA," they usually mean the amount taken out of their paycheck for Social Security.

Federal National Mortgage Association

See **Fannie Mae**.

Federal Open Market Committee (FOMC)

The key decision-making group in the Federal Reserve System. It's the top-secret meetings of the FOMC that decide interest rate policy, which analysts and journalists are always trying to anticipate. The FOMC is actually made up of the seven Federal Reserve governors and the presidents of six Federal Reserve Banks.

Federal Reserve Board

See **Board of Governors of the Federal Reserve System**.

Federal Reserve System (Fed)

The central bank of the United States.

The Fed is a nonprofit, government-created institution made up of the Board of Governors in Washington, D.C., twelve regional Federal Reserve Banks, their twenty-five branches, and the Federal Open Market Committee (FOMC), a major policymaking group. It is owned by its many member banks. All nationally chartered banks are required by law to belong to the Fed, and many state-chartered banks are also members.

The primary function of the Fed is to regulate the nation's money in a way that fosters price stability, economic growth, and moderate long-term interest rates. These objectives are, however, often at cross-purposes, so the Fed must typically choose more of one and less of the others. Moreover, economists debate the ability of the Fed to promote goals other than price stability, and not surprisingly, they also disagree about which goals should be pursued.

The Fed also handles transfers of funds among banks, regulates the banking system, helps banks in trouble, and participates in negotiations with other governments on banking and economic issues.

See also **monetary policy** and **regional bank**.

Federal Savings and Loan Insurance Corporation (FSLIC)

Established in 1934, the FSLIC insured deposits at savings institutions. When the Financial Institutions Reform, Recovery, and Enforcement Act (FIRREA) was established in 1989, the FSLIC was abolished. The FSLIC Resolution Fund was established by FIRREA to assume all the assets and liabilities of the FSLIC.

Federal Securities Act of 1964

See **securities laws**.

Federal Trade Commission Act of 1914

Law setting up the Federal Trade Commission (FTC).

Congress gave the FTC the power to promote and enforce "free and fair competition in interstate commerce in the interest of the public through the prevention of price-fixing agreements, boycotts, combinations in restraint of trade, unfair acts of competition, and unfair and deceptive acts and practices."

FICA

See **Federal Insurance Contribution Act (FICA)**.

FIFO

See **inventory valuation**.

Financial Accounting Foundation (FAF)

The parent of the FASB, the FAF appoints the FASB's members.

Financial Accounting Standards Board (FASB)

Agency that, since 1973, has been primarily responsible for overseeing GAAP. Its primary means of enforcement is through the issuance of numbered standards.

financial audit

When an independent certified public accountant (CPA) examines a company's accounting records and gives a formal opinion on whether it complies with accounting standards and principles.

See also **audit**.

financial engineering

Development of creative financial instruments to attract capital and enhance investor wealth.

Deregulation and increased competition have inspired investment bankers, brokerage houses, and other financial institutions to engineer new and attractive ways to raise capital and package investments. There's an almost confusing array of financial instruments—from asset-backed securities to zero-coupon bonds—that can make sweet music in the hands of an artistic financial engineer.

See also **asset-backed security, convertible security, mortgage-backed security, pass-through security, securitization**, and **stripped bond**.

financial futures

A futures contract with a financial instrument behind it, not a commodity. Rather than wheat or gold, a financial futures contract would be backed by a Treasury bond, for example, or a foreign currency.

See also **derivatives** and **futures**.

Financial Institutions Reform, Recovery, and Enforcement Act of 1989 (FIRREA)

Legislation that imposed wide-ranging changes in the investment operations and choices of thrifts and of savings and loans. FIRREA also created the Resolution Trust Corporation to dispose of failed thrifts, as well as the Office of Thrift Supervision.

financial leverage

Relationship of debt to equity in your company's capital structure—the greater the proportion of long-term debt, the greater the degree of leverage.

See also **debt-to-capital ratio** and **debt-to-equity ratio**.

financial public relations

A division of public relations dealing with individual investors and financial professionals, such as securities analysts and portfolio managers; also called investor relations.

Financial public relations specialists work to maintain communication between their companies and the investment community.

financial statements

Standard set of reports that document a company's financial status.

Produced at least once a year, the key statements are the income statement, the balance sheet, the cash flow statement, and explanatory notes. Financial statements are included in the annual reports that companies provide to shareholders. The Securities and Exchange Commission (SEC) also requires publicly held companies to file annual 10-K financial statements; interim quarterly reports are filed on form 10-Q.

finite-life REIT

A REIT that expects to dissolve itself at a specified future time.

See **real estate investment trust (REIT)**.

FIRREA

See **Financial Institutions Reform, Recovery, and Enforcement Act of 1989 (FIRREA)**.

first mortgage bond

A bond backed by a lien on real estate.

See also **mortgage bond**.

first-in, first-out (FIFO)

See **inventory valuation**.

fiscal policy

The exercise of government tax-and-spend policies to achieve economic goals, such as economic growth, increased employment, or stable prices.

See also **Federal Reserve System (Fed)**, **monetarism**, and **supply-side economics**.

fiscal year

The 12-month accounting period a company uses for financial reporting purposes.

Two thirds of publicly traded U.S. companies use the calendar year (ending December 31), but it makes sense for some companies to use a different 12-month period. Retail stores, for example, use a fiscal year that runs through January, when the holiday season is behind them. Many other industries also have fiscal years that fit their businesses.

fixed annuity

An annuity whose payments are always equal.

See **annuity**.

fixed asset

An asset that is not likely to be converted into cash or used within a year.

See also **balance sheet**.

fixed costs

Those costs or expenses that remain constant over a range of activity. For example, if you own a bookstore, your rent will remain the same regardless of how many hours you stay open or how many books you sell.

That's in contrast to your variable costs, such as your light bill, which will change with your hours.

See also **sunk costs** and **variable costs**.

fixed rate mortgage

A type of mortgage in which the interest rate does not fluctuate with general market conditions.

See also **adjustable rate mortgage (ARM)** and **hybrid mortgage**.

fixed stock fund

A stable fund without much buying and selling of underlying stocks.

flat

Trading "flat" means without accrued interest or dividends.

flexible premium variable life insurance

See **variable universal life insurance.**

flight to cash

When investors' panic causes them to sell—exchanging tomorrow's stock possibilities for the solidity of bank deposits that day.

flip/flipping

The practice of buying shares through an initial public offering (IPO) and then selling them very quickly—often all in the same day. This technique is thought to be the reason many IPOs have such volatile price swings when they first hit the market.

float

1   The portion of company shares that can be bought by the public.

A small float means the stock will be more volatile, since a large buy or sell order can have a dramatic impact on the share price. A large float means the stock will be less volatile, since the price cannot be as easily influenced by large transactions.

2   The term also refers to bringing a new issue to market, or to the portion of a new issue that remains unsold at a given time.

3   In banking, the time that funds are in transition from one bank or one account to another.

Because of the float, after you write a check to your supplier, you may continue to earn interest until the payee deposits the check and your bank removes the money from your account. Your supplier's bank may get the funds the next day but withhold the money from his or her account for a specified number of days. So the bank is then earning interest on the float. Your supplier's bank justifies this practice because it is still possible you did not have enough money in your account to cover the check. If that is the case, your bank will reclaim the money from your supplier's bank. Some states have regulations limiting the float that banks can impose on their depositors.

floating rate
See **adjustable rate**.

floating rate mortgage
See **adjustable rate mortgage (ARM)**.

floating rate preferred stock
See **adjustable rate preferred stock**.

floor
Lowest allowable interest rate on an adjustable rate security.
    See also **collar**.

FNMA
See **Fannie Mae**.

FOMC
See **Federal Open Market Committee (FOMC)**.

Forbes 500
A ranking of the 500 largest publicly owned companies in the United States, published annually by *Forbes* magazine. The companies are ranked according to their assets, profits, sales, and market value of shares.
    See also **Business Week 1000, Fortune 500,** and **Inc. 500**.

forced conversion

When an issuing company calls in a convertible security.

Despite the name, holders of the security are not really forced to convert it to the underlying common stock. They can accept the issuer's call price or sell the security on the open market during the call's notice period. If the common stock price is higher than the call price, most people will choose to convert their security into stock.

foreign exchange

Trading of various currencies in the international marketplace.

These currency exchanges arise when people trade goods and services, real assets, or financial assets such as stocks and bonds. To implement such trades, people use the currencies themselves or short-term credit instruments such as bills of exchange. A typical day sees more than a trillion dollars' worth of foreign exchange transferred throughout the world, much of it occurring electronically via computer.

Fortune 500

List published yearly by *Fortune* magazine of the 500 largest public companies (as measured by revenues).

From 1955 through 1994, the list included only industrial companies. In 1995, recognizing that a changing economy had boosted the importance of nonindustrial businesses such as Wal-Mart and AT&T, *Fortune* began classifying all corporations on its Fortune 500 list.

See also **Business Week 1000**, **Forbes 500**, and **Inc. 500**.

forward contract

A contract to buy or sell a foreign currency, security, or commodity at its current price at a specified date.

forward cover

A contract that eliminates one party's risks by locking in a price for the future.

See also **derivatives**.

forwards

See **forward contract**.

401k plan

A type of pension plan that allows you to set aside money for your retirement. The key advantage to a 401k plan is that it is a tax-free vehicle. That means you don't pay taxes on the money that goes into your 401k account until you withdraw it (usually after you've retired and you're in a lower tax bracket).

See also **defined benefit pension plan** and **pension plans**.

Freddie Mac

A federal lending agency (Federal Home Loan Mortgage Corporation) that issues securities.

See also **mortgage-backed security**.

Friedman, Milton

American economist and Nobel laureate most widely known for his views on monetarism.

front-end load

The fee a mutual fund investor must pay when purchasing shares in the fund. A back-end load is paid when the investor sells the shares.

FSLIC

See **Federal Savings and Loan Insurance Corporation (FSLIC)**.

FSLIC Resolution Fund
See **Federal Savings and Loan Insurance Corporation (FSLIC)**.

FTC
See **Federal Trade Commission Act of 1914**.

future value
The amount to which an investment will grow if it earns a set rate of interest, compounded regularly, until a specific date.

The basic formula for future value is:

$$FV = PV \, [1 + I]^n$$

Where FV = future value, PV = present value, I = interest rate, and n = the number of time periods.

Example

You deposit $100,000 in a savings account that earns 5 percent annual interest. In 10 years, your investment will be worth:

$$\$100{,}000 \, (1.05)^{10} = \$162{,}889$$

future value of an annuity
Value to which an investment will grow if you make regular payments into it. For example, you might wish to set aside $100 per month for your child's education—that plan would called be an annuity stream.

The basic formula when annual payments are made at year-end can be written as:

$$FV = A(1 + r)^{n-1} + A(1 + r)^{n-2} \ldots A(1 = r)^0$$

See also **annuity**.

futures

A type of derivative based on the prices of various underlying assets. Futures may be based on:

1 Physical commodities, such as corn and gold.
2 Financial instruments, such as currencies and Eurodollars.
3 Indices, such as the S&P 500.

They are traded as standardized contracts and might change hands many times before they expire. At maturity, contracts to buy can offset contracts to sell. So in most cases, the underlying transaction never takes place (a contract for 100 bushels of corn usually doesn't result in the actual delivery of any corn).

See also **derivatives**.

G, H: GAAP to Hypertext

G

GAAP

See **generally accepted accounting principles (GAAP)**.

GAAS

See **generally accepted auditing standards (GAAS)**.

GDP

See **Gross Domestic Product (GDP)**.

general ledger

Basis for an accounting system—the location in which all of your active accounts are collected.

This is a book or a computer database that contains a full set of your accounts, such as cash, sales, and so on, each with its debit side and its credit side. The ledger's function is to classify transactions so that all those affecting, say, cash are recorded in the cash account.

Since a general ledger system is based on offsetting entries, it should be in balance at all times, with aggregate debits equaling aggregate credits.

See also **chart of accounts**, **journal entry**, and **trial balance**.

general lien

Claim on all property owned by a borrower, used to back up a loan in case of default.

See also **lien**.

general mortgage bond

A bond backed by all of a company's fixed assets that aren't pledged as collateral for other debts.

See also **mortgage bond**.

general obligation bonds

Also known as GO-bonds, these bonds are backed by the full faith and credit of a municipality or government entity. Other types of municipal bonds are often backed by funds from a specific project (such as a new bridge or tunnel).

general partner

Person who manages a limited partnership business and who assumes liability for its debts. General partners are different from limited partners, who are investors only and have no liability or role in the business's day-to-day operations.

See also **limited partnership**.

generally accepted accounting principles (GAAP)

Official criteria for financial reporting by U.S. companies.

At the broadest level, GAAP is based on published rules, such as Accounting Research Bulletins and Accounting Principles Board Opinions. In the absence of any published rules, substantial industry support may be derived from industry practices, books, and treatises.

Since 1973, the Financial Accounting Standards Board (FASB) has been primarily responsible for overseeing GAAP, and its primary means of enforcement is through the issuance of numbered standards.

The audit opinion included in every publicly held company's annual report tells whether a company's financial statements are presented fairly (in all material respects) in conformity with GAAP.

generally accepted auditing standards (GAAS)

These standards are set by the Auditing Standards Board, an arm of the American Institute of Certified Public Accountants (AICPA).

gift tax

A tax paid when a person transfers assets to someone for free during his or her lifetime.

You are allowed to give tax-free gifts of $10,000 a year (in cash, securities, property, or other assets) to as many people as you wish. Gifts that exceed that limit will need a gift tax return filed by the donor.

Ginnie Mae, GNMA
(Government National Mortgage Association)

Mortgage-backed securities that were introduced in 1970 by the *Government National Mortgage Association (Ginnie Mae)*. Ginnie Mae, a federal agency, bundles residential mortgages **insured by the Veteran's Administration (VA) and Federal Housing Agency (FHA)** and pools them into securities (guaranteed by Uncle Sam, even if homeowners default on mortgages in the pool). By 1994, more than 16.3 million homes had been financed through Ginnie Mae securities. And more than 95 percent of all FHA and VA mortgages originated by local lenders in the primary mortgage market are repackaged as securities by Ginnie Mae.

Ginnie Mae sells these securities to investors in minimum lots of $25,000.

Glass-Steagall Act of 1933

See **banking regulation**.

GNP

See **Gross National Product (GNP)**.

go naked (going naked)

See **naked sale**.

GO-bonds

See **general obligation bonds**.

going private

A company's purchase of all of its publicly held stock.

This converts the company from a publicly owned entity to a privately owned one. Often, a family owning a large share of a company's stock buys the rest of the shares and takes the company private. Also, management sometimes identifies an investment group that might take a company private.

Companies often go private when they believe that their shares are undervalued in the marketplace. In that case, a management group might buy all outstanding shares because its members see them as a good deal. Another reason for going private is to remove the shares from the market so they cannot be bought in an unfriendly takeover.

See also **initial public offering (IPO)** and **leveraged buyout (LBO)**.

going public

Selling to the public—via a common stock offering—an ownership stake in a company that's been privately owned.

After the initial public offering (IPO), the publicly held shares may be traded on a stock exchange or on the over-the-counter (OTC) market. A company might go public when it needs more capital to support or expand operations. Or the company's private owners might want to sell part of their stake.

Companies selling shares to the public must register them and meet the disclosure requirements of the Securities and Exchange Commission (SEC).

See also **going private** and **investment banker**.

golden handcuffs

A generous package of pay and benefits created to prevent an employee from being lured away to another company.

golden parachute

A generous severance payment that can amount to anywhere from 3 to 5 years' salary that is given to a company's top executive when that person retires or is discharged from the company.

good-till-canceled (GTC)

An order to trade a security that has no expiration. For example, you might place a good-till-canceled order with your broker to sell a stock at $20 per share, should the market price go that high. Your order would remain valid until you told your broker otherwise, making it good until canceled. Also called an open order. (This is opposed to a day order, which is valid only until the end of the trading day.)

goodwill

1 In general, goodwill is the value that comes from intangibles such as your business's location, product quality, name recognition, and employees' skills. A company such as Wal-Mart Stores, Inc., for example, is worth much more than the value of its hard assets. The brand name has enormous marketplace recognition and would warrant a considerable price for goodwill in the event of a buyout. This is an asset that a potential buyer of your business will consider, but it will not show up in your financial statements unless it meets the accounting definition that follows.

2 In accounting, the amount you pay for a company you are acquiring in excess of the fair market value of the company's assets less liabilities assumed. This applies only when a company is acquired under the purchase method of consolidation. Goodwill is an intangible asset on the balance sheet and will be amortized over its estimated useful life, but not over more than 40 years.

See also **amortization**.

government bond

A bond issued by a municipal or state government, or by the federal government, as a means of acquiring capital.

Government National Mortgage Association (Ginnie Mae)

See **mortgage-backed security**.

GPM

See **graduated payment mortgage (GPM)**.

grace period

1 The period of time when a lendee is given some kind of break from a lender. For example, you might be exempt from making payments on a student loan during a grace period after your graduation.

2 In finance, a grace period may also be the amount of time you can miss payments (on a loan or on an insurance policy) without being considered in default.

graduated payment mortgage (GPM)

Also nicknamed jeeps, these are mortgages that start with low payments that increase over time. Young people, who expect their income to increase over time, often prefer GPMs.

Below-market interest rates or payment caps keep costs down initially. Payments eventually rise to market levels, where they remain for the rest of the loan life.

See also **adjustable rate mortgage**.

grandfather clause

A provision that gives exemption to people or companies prior to the passing of a rule or law. For example, a new requirement for a professional title might include a grandfather clause for those who've already been practicing for a number of years. In accounting, new accounting rules sometimes include grandfather clauses. For example, a new rule about write-offs could exempt assets acquired before a set date.

grantor

In the investment world, the person who sells a call or put option.

grazing

A miscellaneous amassing of acquisitions.

green fund

A nickname for a mutual fund with an environmental focus. Many green funds only invest in companies with environmentally sound practices.

See also **socially conscious investing**.

green shoe

The extra shares sold during a public offering after the initial allotment has run out. A standard green shoe allotment is 15 percent of the original amount. Underwriters will exercise this option if it looks like the offering is likely to be oversubscribed and can support a higher price.

greenmail

Practice through which a target company buys back its own shares from a potential acquirer. Since the suitor usually makes a profit on the deal, some industry experts consider it to be a cousin to black-mail—or greenmail.

Gross Domestic Product (GDP)

The chief measure of a nation's overall economic activity during a given period. The GDP measures goods and services produced by all resources located within a nation (even if those resources are owned by people in other nations).

GDP is measured in two ways: as the total market value of all so-called final goods and services produced, or as the total income received from those goods and services. Both measures are identical, since the market value must equal the money received for produc-ing them. GDP also includes a nation's exports minus its imports.

See also **Gross National Product (GNP)**.

Gross National Product (GNP)

The measure of a nation's overall economic activity over a given period. In contrast to the Gross Domestic Product (GDP), the GNP measures goods and services produced by all resources owned by a nation's citi-zens, whether located at home or abroad. Thus, production from foreign plants owned by U.S. citizens would be included in the U.S. GNP but not in the GDP. Production from a foreign-owned plant in the United States would be excluded from the U.S. GNP but included in the GDP. The actual GNP figure is adjusted for inflation and expressed annually.

gross proceeds

Total funds raised through the issuance of securities or the sale of assets.

To arrive at net proceeds, you would deduct the costs of the transaction—such as an underwriter's fees and registration expenses.

gross profit

Net sales minus cost of goods sold.

See also **profit margin**.

gross profit margin

Ratio of gross profit to net sales.

See also **profit margin**.

gross spread

See **investment banker**.

growth stock

A stock that has shown better-than-average earnings growth in recent years. The catch is that you'll probably have to pay dearly for that kind of momentum—growth stocks usually have higher price/earnings ratios than other stocks.

If you're interested in dividend income, don't look to growth stocks. Since these are companies in their early stages of development, they typically plow earnings back into the company rather than pay them out to shareholders.

GTC

See **good-till-canceled (GTC)**.

hard currency

A currency that is considered stable; usually the currency of a politically and economically established country.

The German mark, the Japanese yen, and the U.S. dollar are examples. Although they move in value, they tend to fluctuate less than many other currencies. Hard currency can usually be exchanged with currencies of other countries. Typically, when loans are taken out in hard currency, they must be repaid in hard currency.

Multinational companies doing business in less-developed countries (which have soft currency) might have profits that don't mean much because they can't be converted to hard currency. During extreme periods of monetary instability, citizens might prefer to receive other types of currency than their own. (In the former Soviet Union, for example, many businesspeople would prefer to deal in U.S. dollars than in rubles.) The difficulty might arise from the lack of a market for the country's currency or simply from laws preventing the transfer of profits outside that nation's borders.

hedge

A position that reduces the risk of a business transaction or investment, often through the use of a derivative product. Hedging can be used as an insurance policy for traders and investors.

Watch out for the tax consequences inherent in some hedges. The holding period of the investment, for example, could be altered by the hedge. Check with your tax adviser.

Suppose you decide to hedge a stock position by buying a put on the stock, which will move in the opposite direction. Let's say your stock price does indeed fall, from $25 to $23—and your put price increases, from $3 to $4. That means your hedge ratio would be:

$$(\$3 - \$4) \div (\$25 - \$23) = -1 \div 2 = -0.5$$

Essentially, that means your hedge is offsetting 50 percent of your losses.

---

hedge ratio

Measure of the proportionate relationship between a security or commodity and its hedge. The ratio expresses the position needed in, say, options or futures contracts to cover $1 of the investment you hold.

A hedge ratio might also be referred to as a delta, and usually refers to the relationship between an option being used as a hedge and the underlying stock. The formula would be:

HR = change in option price ÷ change in underlying stock price

The ideal hedge (one that allows for no profit or loss) is −1. That means that any move in the stock price is perfectly offset by the move in the option price.

hedging

Taking offsetting positions to reduce the risks associated with investing or other business transactions.

See also **derivatives**.

herd instinct

In investing, the tendency of investors to follow the crowd, or continue to invest in those stocks that have done well in the recent past.

See also **momentum investing/investors**.

high-grade bonds

Debt rated as Aaa through Baa3 by Moody's Investors Service and AAA through BBB− by Standard & Poor's.

See also **bond ratings** and **investment-grade bonds**.

high-yield bonds

Debt rated below investment grade by the major rating agencies. Also nicknamed junk bonds.

Although high-yield bonds have a risky reputation, they are simply the bonds issued by companies that are still growing. They typically pay higher interest rates to compensate investors for their lower rating.

holding period return

A return on an investment during the time that it is held. This includes both income from the investment and any profit or loss upon its disposal—any capital gain or loss. Here is how you calculate it:

Suppose you held two investments, Stock X and Stock Y, for 1 year.

	Stock X	Stock Y
Purchase price	$100	$100
Cash dividend	$ 16	$ 10
Selling price	$ 94	$110
Capital gain (loss)	($ 6)	$ 10

The holding period return for each stock is:

Stock X: ($16 − $6) ÷ $100 = 0.10, or 10%
Stock Y: ($10 + $10) ÷ $100 = 0.20, or 20%

home equity loan

A loan based on the equity built up by a home owner, which makes it a type of secured loan.

housing completions

Number of new houses that have been built in a given time period as reported by the U.S. government. Considered to be an important indicator of economic health.

See also **housing starts**.

housing permits

Number of new houses local governments have authorized during a period of time. Watched closely as an indicator of economic health.

See also **housings starts**.

housing starts

Number of new housing units workers have started building in a given period, usually 1 month.

Since residential construction accounts for roughly 3 percent of the total U.S. Gross Domestic Product (GDP), this is an important economic indicator. In addition to housing starts (determined to have occurred when the foundation of the house or multifamily building is dug), other housing activities monitored by the Commerce Department include:

- housing permits—when new housing units are authorized by local governments
- housing completions—the end of construction
- new home sales—completion of the transaction

Residential construction is highly cyclical, because a new house is a major expenditure for a typical family, and because the role played by mortgage interest rates is significant.

Hulbert Financial Digest

A publication that monitors the performance of investment advisory newsletters.

Hulbert tracks approximately 160 investment newsletters, as well as 450 model portfolios based on securities their authors recommend. The monthly newsletter reports 5-year, 10-year, and (where possible) 15-year compound rates of return, adjusted for risk and unadjusted, and compares their performance to the Standard & Poor's 500 Index.

hybrid

A type of transaction that combines various types of securities. A hybrid derivative might involve a call option on a forward contract.

hybrid mortgage

Also referred to as a multiyear mortgage. Offers an initial fixed rate for about 5 to 10 years (just like a traditional fixed rate mortgage) and then adjusts like a traditional adjustable rate mortgage.

hyperinflation

See **inflation**.

hyperlink

See **hypertext**.

hypertext

In a document on your computer screen, highlighted text (underlined, a different color, boldfaced, etc.) that brings up a new set of data, or hyperlink, when clicked on with the mouse. The standard on Internet web sites.

I: Illiquid to Issued Stock

illiquid

Deficient in liquid assets, not readily convertible into cash.

IMF

See **International Monetary Fund (IMF)**.

IMM

See **International Monetary Market (IMM)**.

in play

When a group of bidders attempting to acquire a company toss the company among them in an effort to determine which one of them is superior.

in the money

A term describing an option with an underlying price that has passed the strike price cutoff point. For example, if you held a call option with a $20 strike price, and the underlying stock price rose to $21, your option would be in the money. Conversely, if you held a put option with a $20 strike price, and the stock fell to $19, your option would be in the money.

Inc. 500

A listing of the 500 fastest-growing privately held companies in the United States, as measured by *Inc.* magazine. The annual ranking is based on the companies' sales growth over a 5-year period.

See also **Business Week 1000**, **Forbes 500**, and **Fortune 500**.

incentive pay

Broadly speaking, any type of compensation based on performance.

In the financial world, the most common type of incentive pay is an executive package that includes options on the company's stock.

income bond

A type of bond whose interest payments depend on the company's earnings.

When a company can't make interest payments on income bonds, it's not considered to be in default. Investors usually buy bonds specifically because they want regular payments, but income bonds are used in unusual situations.

When a company is reorganizing in the face of a possible bankruptcy, bondholders might agree to exchange their securities for income bonds in order to keep the company going. The income bonds issued in that sort of reorganization are also called adjustment bonds. Or, when a company wants to sell a subsidiary, it sometimes will accept income bonds as partial payment.

With income bonds, the interest must be paid if the company makes enough profit. As with preferred stock, the interest will often be cumulative—unpaid amounts add up until the company can pay. Some income bonds have a limited cumulative feature, where only some of the unpaid interest carries over. With noncumulative interest, the company doesn't have to make up skipped interest payments.

income statement

Summary of a company's revenues and expenses for an accounting period. Also called earnings report, profit and loss statement, or statement of operations.

While the balance sheet shows the company at a fixed point in time, the income statement covers the period from one balance sheet date to the next. It explains, in broad terms, how the company arrived at its bottom line, or net income.

Consider the categories an income statement for a large fictional corporation (in millions). While formats for the income statement vary from company to company, the major categories are:

1 *Revenues:* Also called net sales. This category is a summary of the sales your company made during the period net of returns, allowances, and discounts.

2 *Cost of goods sold:* What it cost to buy or make the merchandise you sold.

3 *Operating expenses:* This goes by a variety of names, including selling, general, and administrative expenses. It is a summary of all expenses attributed to operating your business other than the cost of merchandise. It includes salaries and rent, selling and marketing expenses, depreciation and amortization, and general expenses—such as those for telecommunications, equipment repair, and so on.

4 *Operating income:* The earnings from your company's regular business activities.

5 *Interest expense:* Interest you have paid out on money borrowed, most likely on bank loans or issued bonds.

6 *Other items:* After you calculate your operating income, you deduct interest expenses and add interest income. You also add or subtract any other items not part of your regular business.

7 *Pre-tax earnings:* Also called earnings before income taxes.

8 *Income taxes*

9 *Net income:* Also called net earnings or net profit. This is the bottom line. In some years, when you have had an extraordinary item like the sale of a major asset or an accounting change, net income might not represent the company's true earning power.

10 *Earnings per share (EPS):* Net income after taxes divided by the weighted average number of common shares outstanding during the year. If your company has convertible securities outstanding, you might need to compute fully diluted earnings per share as well. That assumes conversion to common stock of everything that can be converted.

See also **cumulative effect of accounting change** and **special item**.

income stock

The partner of capital stock in an arrangement where a stock is split between two types of holders. (Usually for a dual-purpose fund or split investment group.) The income stockholders will receive income-oriented payments from a stock (such as dividends), while the capital stockholders will receive the benefit of long-term capital gains.

increasing rate

See **adjustable rate**.

increasing rate indenture

A written agreement detailing terms of a bond and the rights and responsibilities of the issuer and of the bondholder.

See also **debenture**.

index

See **stock index**.

index funds

Mutual funds that invest in the same securities that make up market indices such as the Dow Jones Industrial Average.

See **indexing**.

index option

See **derivatives**.

indexing

1 Tying wages, taxes, other payments, or any dollar amount over time to an economic indicator such as the consumer price index (CPI).

   If a labor contract, for example, has a provision to boost wages along with any sizable increase in the CPI over 2 years, the contract could be referred to as indexed for inflation. A provision like this is known as a cost of living adjustment (COLA).

2 A form of passive portfolio management in which the portfolio is designed to match the movement of a market index.

   Common indices are the Dow Jones Industrial Average or the Standard & Poor's 500. A number of mutual funds have been set up and maintained this way. They are called index funds. One reason they are so popular is that they have lower fees because they are easier to manage.

Individual Retirement Account (IRA)

A retirement account through which savings may be accrued on a tax-free basis. As of 1998, an individual is allowed to set aside up to

$2,000 into a tax-free IRA. Any gains from underlying investments are also tax-free until they're withdrawn after age 59½. (Early withdrawals will accrue a 10 percent penalty.)

industrial development bond

Municipal bond (issued by a state or local government) used to finance revenue-generating projects. Also called an industrial revenue bond.

Interest payments on these bonds come from the project's revenue and are backed by the credit of a private company. These bonds' ratings are based on the creditworthiness of the backing organization. At one time, they were a popular way for a state or local government to give a boost to a project that businesses wouldn't otherwise pursue.

industrial revenue bond

A bond issued by a state or local government to finance a facility that will generate revenue to make bond payments. The payments are guaranteed by the lease to the private company that will use the facilities.

See also **industrial development bond**.

inflation

Sustained, overall increase in the prices of goods and services. Inflation is usually expressed as an annual percentage.

Inflation generally results when supply and demand are out of sync—when the money available to spend grows faster than products available to buy. An inflation rate of up to approximately 2.5 percent is not considered a serious economic or social threat, but higher rates worry people.

Because inflation most often moves in small annual increments, its effects over time are often underestimated. For example, the same item that cost $1 in 1913 cost more than $15 in 1995.

Hyperinflation

In those very rare cases when inflation becomes so extreme that it is apparent on a day-to-day basis, it is called hyperinflation, and it is a big problem. During periods of hyperinflation, people are reluctant to save their money because its value is so rapidly diminishing. Instead, they tend to buy tangible assets such as real estate or gold.

The opposite of inflation is deflation, which is a decrease in the prices of goods and services. Deflation should not be confused with disinflation, which is when the rate of price increases slows down.

---

initial public offering (IPO)

The first public sale of common stock, usually by a privately owned company that wants to go public.

After the IPO, the publicly held shares may be traded on a stock exchange or on the over-the-counter (OTC) market. A company might go public when it needs more capital to support or expand operations. This is particularly true when market conditions make it more advantageous for a company to sell stock rather than borrow funds. Or a company might decide to go public when its private owners want to sell part of their stake.

See also **going private** and **investment banker**.

insider trading

Making stock market transactions based on private information that is unavailable to the public.

Insider trading might be unlawful, depending on the relationship between the individual who has the inside information and the companies involved in the insider trading. Many cases are not clearcut. It is generally agreed that directors, officers, key employees, and major shareholders are insiders who need to take special care not to trade in anticipation of news the public does not yet know. But during the workday, insiders might talk with financial printers, consultants, lawyers, and Wall Street professionals. And after hours, there is no limit to the kinds of people to whom they may spread information. A cabdriver, a cop, a dentist, and the psychiatrist of an executive's spouse have all been charged in insider trading cases. Sometimes the insider might not have any direct connection to the company at all.

Directors, officers, and major shareholders of publicly traded companies are required to report their trades in their company's stock to the Securities and Exchange Commission (SEC), which publishes the information monthly so the public can at least keep tabs on what insiders are doing.

Insider Trading Sanctions Act of 1984
See **securities laws**.

Insider Trading Sanctions Act of 1988
See **securities laws**.

insolvent
Unable to pay debts when due.
   See also **bankruptcy**.

installment loan
A transaction in which the purchase price and interest charges are paid over time.

institutional investor
Large investing entities, such as banks, mutual funds, or pension plans. Other examples are insurance companies, unions, and university endowment funds.

As individual investors have turned more and more to institutions such as mutual funds, the individual's influence on the market has shrunk (although individuals now affect the market indirectly).

intangible assets

Assets without physical substance, such as patents, copyrights, leases, and goodwill.

See also **tangible assets**.

inter vivos trust

Another name for a living trust.

interest coverage ratio

Measure of how well a company's pretax operating profit covers its debt payments.

Example

Your company reported interest expense of $800,000 in fiscal 1994. Its pretax profit that year was $20,000,000, so interest payments were covered by a multiple of 25:

$20,000,000 ÷ $800,000 = 25 (interest coverage ratio)

If a company's operating profits remain strong and interest rates are low, borrowed money can help finance a company's growth. But if operating profits are weak and interest rates are high, too much debt can lead a company to default on its payments.

What's the best interest coverage ratio? That depends on the steadiness of a firm's earnings. There's no magic number. For a company whose profits are extrasensitive to cyclical ups and downs, less borrowed capital is best, analysts maintain.

interest expense

Money paid out by a company for interest payments.

See also **income statement** and **interest coverage ratio**.

interest income

Money collected on securities owned that pay interest.

See also **income statement**.

interest rate

The rate, expressed as an annual percentage, charged on borrowed money. Interest rates are quoted on consumer and business loans, of course, but also on bonds, notes, bills, and credit cards.

Two lending rates play a big role in your cost to borrow money. The discount rate, which is what the Federal Reserve System charges on loans to its member banks, sets a floor under lending rates. The prime rate, which is what banks charge their best, most creditworthy corporate customers, is a key determinant for other commercial and consumer loans. When you get your loan, what the bank charges you is called the nominal, or stated, interest rate. But that can differ from the actual rate paid, also known as the effective interest rate.

Here is how a nominal rate can be the same as, or different from, the actual rate:

If you borrow $1,000 at 10 percent for a year, and the interest is paid when the loan matures, you receive $1,000 at the start of the period and return it plus $100 interest at the end. You have paid an actual rate of 10 percent ($100 ÷ $1,000 = 0.1, or 10%)—the same as the nominal rate. But if you must pay the 10 percent, or $100, interest in advance, you get $900 at the start of the year and return $1,000 at the end, so the effective interest rate is 11.11 percent ($100 ÷ $900 = .1111, or 11.11%).

The real interest rate is the nominal rate minus inflation. The real rate is of particular interest to investors in fixed rate instruments such as bonds, notes, and bills, because it gives them a way to see if the interest they are earning will keep them ahead of inflation-caused erosion in the value of their money.

See also **annual percentage rate (APR)**.

interest rate futures

See **derivatives**.

interest rate swaps

When two parties agree to exchange periodic interest payments. For example, traders might take responsibility for each other's loans because one company can get good terms on, say, a fixed rate loan and another can do well on a floating rate. Or one company might trade long-term debt for another's short-term debt.

See also **derivatives**.

internal audit

When an auditor within a company investigates its procedures to make sure they meet corporate policies.

See also **audit**.

internal rate of return (IRR)

Measure of the return of an investment over time, expressed as an annual percentage rate; sometimes referred to as a discount rate.

IRR is the interest rate at which the net present value of an investment equals the cost of the investment. For example, suppose that you were considering investing in a new pizza van for $8,677 that you figured would net your delivery business $5,000 in each of the next 2 years.

Solving for r, here's how the numbers would look:

$$\$8,677 = [(\$5,000 \div (1 + r)^1] + [(\$5,000 \div (1 + r)^2]$$

Thus, you'd calculate (with the help of a bond calculator) that the IRR for the pizza van above was only 10 percent. Is that good enough? It depends—you might have decided that any new investments should yield at least a 15 percent return. (You can get 7 percent or so by putting the same money in a T-bill, after all.) In that case, you might opt against the new pizza van, or at least try to get a lower price.

In this way, managers and financial planners often use IRR to evaluate a possible venture, such as expanding a plant or buying a company. But how do you decide your minimum IRR? If you were deciding on a project, you might determine the cost of capital (what the money you're using is costing you) and then establish it as the minimum IRR that is acceptable for your company. If the expected IRR for your proposed project exceeds the minimum you set, the project is a go.

international bonds

Corporate bonds denominated in one country's currency but issued in another. Also called dual-currency bonds.

See also **Eurobonds**.

International Monetary Fund (IMF)

Multinational organization working to stabilize currencies, to lower trade barriers, and to help countries that are having financial problems.

Conceived at the Bretton Woods Conference in 1944 and established in 1947 as part of the United Nations, the IMF is financed by its more than 100 member nations. When the IMF was formed, developed nations had their currencies pegged to the U.S. dollar. That policy was largely abandoned in 1971, and since then most of the world's currencies have operated with floating exchange rates.

Although the IMF has little control over these currency rates, it still exerts great influence. Member nations are encouraged to follow IMF rules of conduct that promote order in their currency dealings—that is, if they wish to continue receiving IMF funds. And when the IMF helps a developing nation pay off its debt or build its infrastructure, the IMF usually imposes strict guidelines designed to reduce inflation, cut imports, and raise exports. These are called structural adjustment policies.

International Monetary Market (IMM)

Division of the Chicago Mercantile Exchange that trades currency and interest rate futures.

See also **derivatives**.

Internet

Huge on-line network of computers linked for the exchange of information, products, and ideas. Also called "the Net."

In 1997, the estimate was that 30 million to 50 million people worldwide had access to the Internet, with the number expected to double every year. The Internet's most popular feature is the World Wide Web, where users can "surf" through screens of data offered by businesses, colleges, libraries, museums, political entities, and so on. As you are reading, you can click on a highlighted word or phrase to bring up more screens of information, which might have been obtained from yet another computer. Each organization offering data starts out with a home page, often with sophisticated graphics. Companies have been flooding onto the World Wide Web for publicity as well as to sell products.

The term "Internet advertising" is being used to mean a specific marketing strategy involving promotion of products and services on the Net. Consumers can window-shop, research various products, or even place orders using computer interfaces. Companies should not depend, however, on consumers' simply coming across an advertisement while casually surfing the Net. This medium lends itself to use by those investigating specific services and companies.

See also **hypertext**.

intestate

Dying without having made a legal will.

When that happens, the intestate succession statutes guide the deceased person's state in divvying up his or her property based on spousal and blood relationships. The state will also impose the maximum amount of taxes and transfer costs if there is no will or estate plan to help take advantage of legal estate tax reduction strategies. If there are no relatives, the state takes it all.

See also **probate** and **will**.

inventory valuation

How one measures the cost of the goods one has in stock.

Like many other things in accounting, inventory valuation is a lot more complicated than it might seem. A method of costing is used to determine how much was paid for the goods. How much of the cost went into the goods sold and how much is still in inventory are determined. If the cost never changed, there is no problem. The cost of each unit is known, whether it was sold or still in inventory. But because values differ the world over, a method for valuing the inventory must be selected, such as specific identification; weighted-average cost; first-in, first-out (FIFO); or last-in, first-out (LIFO).

See also **conservatism concept** and **consistency concept**.

inverted yield curve

Rare situation in which long-term interest rates fall below short-term rates.

An inverted curve usually foreshadows a recession, as it did in late 1980, when short-term Treasury bill rates were 16.55 percent, compared with 11.89 percent for long-term bonds—the country's steepest yield curve inversion.

See also **yield** and **yield curve**.

investment adviser

Person or organization that offers investment advice for a fee.

The Investment Advisers Act of 1940 requires investment advisers to register with the Securities and Exchange Commission (SEC), which has primary oversight responsibility for the investment industry. The form that an investment adviser must file with the SEC is known as an ADV Part II. Registered investment advisers are required by law to release this form to prospective clients. Be sure to ask for it, because it can tell you a lot, including whether any disciplinary actions have been taken against the adviser by the SEC.

See also **registered representative**.

Investment Advisers Act of 1940

See **securities laws**.

investment banker

Middleman or agent between an organization issuing securities and the public.

In most cases, the investment banker buys the securities from the issuer at a discount and sells them to investors and other dealers. The price difference is called the gross spread. This arrangement is called underwriting, and often it is carried out by a syndicate of investment bankers. If the securities are overpriced, or if the market falls before they are sold, the underwriters take the loss.

For certain securities, such as U.S. Treasury issues and municipal bonds, underwriters must be chosen by competitive bidding. For most other securities, the issuer negotiates an arrangement with an investment banker, who may then form a syndicate to spread the risk.

Investment bankers also advise clients on all aspects of issuing a new security or on other large capital transactions such as mergers and acquisitions. They might be called on to handle the sale of secondary offerings or to act as finders, arranging the private placement of large blocks of a security.

See also **best effort**.

Investment Company Act of 1940
See **securities laws**.

investment leverage
Using other people's money to multiply the potential for investment gains. Margin loans, options, and warrants increase investment leverage, but also the chance for losses if you guess wrong. In commercial real estate, your mortgage is a form of investment leverage.

The first rule of leveraged investing is to remember that prices can fall as fast as they can rise. The leverage increases the impact on you in both directions.

See also **leverage** and **operating leverage**.

investment-grade bonds
Debt rated as Aaa through Baa3 by Moody's Investors Service and AAA through BBB- by Standard & Poor's.

See also **bond ratings**, **high-grade bonds**, and **high-yield bonds**.

investor relations
The division of a company that serves the investment community—especially shareholders of the company's stock.

Although big institutional investors get most attention from investor relations departments, small investors can call with questions too. And many companies have web sites where questions can be answered by E-mail.

See also **financial public relations**.

involuntary exchange

Sudden loss of an asset that doesn't occur in the ordinary course of your business.

A building destroyed by fire qualifies as an involuntary exchange. So does land seized by a state highway department for use in the construction of a road. If you're compensated for your loss, the exchange is treated like any other transaction.

IPO

See **initial public offering (IPO)**.

IRA

See **Individual Retirement Account (IRA)**.

IRR

See **internal rate of return (IRR)**.

irrevocable trust

Essentially, a trust that the benefactor can't take back. An irrevocable trust can be changed or terminated only with the permission of the beneficiary. A revocable trust, on the other hand, can generally be changed while the donors are still living.

issued stock

The number of authorized shares that have been sold and are out-standing.

See also **capital stock**.

J, K, L: Joint Venture to LYON

J

joint venture

A business enterprise developed by two or more unrelated companies. Often one company acts as manager of the venture; or, each might supply a number of employees to fill management positions.

Joint ventures help spread financial risk, help companies enter a new market, and help companies take advantage of each other's complementary areas of expertise.

journal entry

The recording of a business transaction in an accounting book or ledger. The entry usually consists of the accounts and the amounts to be debited and credited, along with the date and an explanation.

See also **bookkeeping**.

junk bonds

Bonds with a rating lower than investment grade.

See also **high-yield bonds**.

K

Keogh plan

A Keogh is a retirement plan similar to a 401k, intended for the self-employed.

The self-employed have, since 1962, had the Keogh plan, named for Eugene Keogh, the congressman who sponsored the legislation. Anyone with self-employment income can set up one of these plans to put aside tax-deferred money for retirement.

See also **pension plans**.

kicker

See **equity kicker**.

kiddie tax

A tax paid by children under the age of fourteen. The standard tax rate is 15 percent, but you should consider this before you transfer all of your income-earning assets to your kids—the limit they may earn is $1,300. Any amount over that limit will be taxed at the parents' tax rate.

L

lagging economic indicators

The seven components of an index that tell analysts where the economy has been in recent months.

The index components are:

1 The average duration of unemployment (in weeks).
2 The ratio of inventories (manufacturing and trade) to sales.
3 The ratio of consumer installment credit to personal income.

4   The average prime rate.
5   The change in the consumer price index (CPI) for services.
6   The total amount of commercial and industrial loans outstanding.
7   The change in the index of labor cost per unit of output
    (manufacturing).

The index of lagging economic indicators is published monthly
by the U.S. Commerce Department's Bureau of Economic Analysis.

See also **coincident economic indicators** and **leading economic indicators**.

last-in, first-out (LIFO)

See **inventory valuation**.

LBO

See **leveraged buyout (LBO)**.

leading economic indicators

The eleven parts of an index that usually change months before corresponding changes in overall economic activity.

The index components are:

1   The average length of the work week for production workers.
2   The number of new state unemployment insurance claims.
3   New orders for consumer goods, adjusted for inflation.
4   An indicator of vendor performance based on the percentage
    of companies receiving slower deliveries from suppliers.
5   Contracts and orders for plants and equipment.
6   An index of permits for new private housing units.
7   The change in manufacturers' unfilled orders for durable
    goods.
8   The change in certain materials prices that are considered economically sensitive.
9   An index of stock prices.

10 The money supply.

11 An index of consumer expectations based on surveying.

Many of these indicators—housing permits, for example—represent commitments to future economic activity. The index of leading economic indicators is published monthly by the U.S. Commerce Department's Bureau of Economic Analysis.

See also **coincident economic indicators** and **lagging economic indicators**.

LEAPS
See **long-term equity anticipation securities (LEAPS)**.

lease rate
Also called the money factor. The interest rate that applies to your leasing term.

letter stock
Shares of common stock that are restricted because they aren't registered with the Securities and Exchange Commission (SEC). Also called restricted stock.

These shares, which might have been sold via a private placement, can't be traded on the open market unless they are first registered. They're called letter stock because the buyer has to sign a letter stating that the stock is not for public sale. Some companies have granted letter stock to key employees as part of their executive compensation.

leverage
1 In finance, using borrowed funds to generate a greater return on invested capital. Companies employ leverage by taking on debt to increase earnings. Banks employ leverage when they use depositors' funds to finance lending, on which the banks then expect to earn a profit-producing amount of interest.

2 In terms of a company's operations, the relationship of fixed costs (such as those for rent and insurance) to variable costs (such as those for materials and wages). If a company's costs are virtually all fixed, every dollar of sales beyond the break-even point will increase earnings. Such a company is said to have high operating leverage.

leveraged buyout (LBO)

Typically, when an investment group buys a company with money raised from debt.

In this kind of buyout, the assets of the acquired company are used as collateral for the loans. The amount of borrowing, or leverage—sometimes more than 70 percent of total capitalization—allows the buyer to get control of the company with less equity capital. If all goes well, the loans are repaid from the cash flow generated by the acquired company or from the sale of assets. Many widely publicized takeovers in the 1980s by investor groups, individuals, and investment/LBO firms made the term popular.

Sometimes, managers of a company use a leveraged buyout to take over a company and go private, or to acquire a business they think is undervalued by the stock market. That's an example of a management buyout (MBO). In other cases, a company's employees have taken over a company, or a large share of it, in an LBO involving their employee stock ownership plan (ESOP). Another form of LBO, a tender offer buyout, is completed through a tender offer rather than a merger.

See also **going private**.

liability

Amount owed to another person or entity.

You might know the actual sum, such as what you owe to vendors for goods and services you have purchased. Or you might know only an estimate, such as income taxes payable or the estimated costs of warranties.

Liabilities are reported on a company's balance sheet within two major categories: current liabilities (expected to be paid during the year) and long-term liabilities (not expected to be paid during the year). Contingent liabilities are those that might or might not materialize, such as possible costs regarding a lawsuit against the company that is not yet resolved.

LIBOR

See **London Interbank Offered Rate (LIBOR)**.

lien

Creditor's claim against property.

A mortgage is a lien against a house: if the mortgage is not paid on time, the house can be seized to satisfy the lien. A secured bond is a lien against a company's assets: if interest and principal are not paid when due, the assets may be seized to pay the bondholders.

LIFO

See **inventory valuation**.

limit order

An order to trade a stock at a targeted price. On the other hand, an order placed at the market would trade at the first available market price.

See also **day order**.

limited liability company (LLC)

A company form that gives limited legal protection to the owner(s). An LLC is similar to an S-corporation in that income flows through to the personal returns of shareholders, but an LLC allows for more shareholders, including some who aren't U.S. citizens.

limited partners

See **limited partnership**.

limited partnership

Ownership structure with one or more general partners and a number of limited partners.

The general partners manage the business and are liable for its debts. The limited partners are simply investors who have no role in the business's day-to-day operations and no liability. In most cases, limited partners get a percentage of the business's income, some tax benefits, and capital gains. General partners may also receive fees.

Limited partnerships are common in equipment leasing, oil and gas, real estate, movie financing, and research and development, often in start-up situations. A company making an acquisition might also use a limited partnership to help finance the deal, with itself as the general partner.

See also **partnership**.

liquid yield option note (LYON)

A zero-coupon bond convertible into common stock.

Like other zero-coupons bonds, LYONs don't make annual or semiannual interest payments and are sold at a deep discount. LYONs, however, can be converted into common stock at a future date—usually at a premium to the stock's price at issuance. Because of this convertible feature, yields on LYONs are lower than on straight zero-coupon notes (investors are willing to accept a lower coupon rate in exchange for the potential gain on the underlying stock).

See also **convertible security**.

liquidating dividend

Distribution of a company's assets as dividends when the company is going out of business.

To the extent that the dividend is from paid-in capital rather than retained earnings, it's not taxable to the recipient. Liquidating dividends are used most often by utility or real estate companies.

liquidity

1 In accounting, solvency, or the ability to pay your obligations as they come due and still fund your business operations.

2 In finance, whether the market for a security is big enough that it can trade easily. If the market is liquid, you can probably sell your holdings without depressing the price or incurring large transaction costs.

3 In general business use, whether you have enough cash, or assets that can be easily converted to cash.

See also **balance sheet**.

liquidity premium

Extra cost that investors often pay for a short-term asset that can be converted into cash with little trouble or delay.

Liquidity Premium

A commercial bank receives $500,000 in short-term deposits that it would like to invest for just a few months before the accounts close. By paying a liquidity premium on a short-term investment option, it can earn interest but still retain easy access to the cash. On the other hand, an insurance company that makes a tidy profit from the sale of some long-term annuity contracts has no reason to pay a liquidity premium, because it stands to gain the most from investments with long maturities. The interest is more important to investors than access to the money.

---

living trust

A trust created while the donors are living. Also called an inter vivos trust.

See also **trust**.

LLC

See **limited liability company (LLC)**.

load fund

A mutual fund bought through a brokerage firm in which the cost includes a commission.

See also **no-load fund**.

London Interbank Offered Rate (LIBOR)

Interest rate that international banks usually charge each other for large Eurodollar and Eurocurrency loans.

Like the prime rate for dollar loans in the United States, LIBOR is also a base rate for Eurodollar and Eurocurrency loans to the international banks' customers. A developing Third World country, for example, might have to pay a risk premium of 2 points over LIBOR when it takes out a loan in Eurodollars.

See also **adjustable rate** and **exchange rate**.

long bond

A bond with a maturity of 10 years or more.

Long bonds typically pay a higher yield than shorter-term bonds of the same quality if the yield curve is normal, or upward curving. (When the yield curve is inverted, short-term bonds will pay a higher yield than long-term bonds.) Long bonds, such as the 30-year U.S. Treasury bonds, often serve as a benchmark from which other bonds are priced. That differential between the yield on a U.S.

Treasury bond and the yield on a municipality or corporation bond is called the yield spread.

long-term capital gain

Profit made on assets held for longer than a year, which is taxed at 28 percent (as of 1998), compared to short-term capital gains, which are taxed at personal income tax rates, which range from 15 to 39.6 percent.

See also **capital gains**.

long-term equity anticipation securities (LEAPS)

Long-term option contract that gives the owner the right to buy an asset (stock) at a specified price at a distant time in the future.

Unlike conventional options that last a few months, LEAPS can last up to 2 years. If you're right about where a stock is going, but can't pinpoint exactly when, LEAPS cut you the slack that conventional options don't.

Since their introduction in 1990, LEAPS have become a red-hot options product. The five U.S. options exchanges offer them on more than 150 stocks, with more to come. Plans are also under way to introduce LEAPS on every major index, including Standard & Poor's.

LEAPS premiums typically cost more than conventional options: 1-year LEAPS cost about twice as much as a 3-month option on the same stock.

loophole

A technicality that allows the spirit or intent of a law or contract to be violated.

Just what constitutes a loophole is a matter of endless debate (and tax law). In the case of taxes, if you can qualify for it, it's a deduction. If somebody else qualifies for it, it's a loophole.

lump sum distribution

Withdrawal of the entire cash value of a company pension or 401k plan, usually as you leave a job.

Since this withdrawal is subject to tax, most people opt to roll over the lump sum into an individual retirement account (IRA) for tax-deferred status, and start withdrawing without penalty after age 59½. Lump sum distribution is in contrast to the pension management option of an annuity, or receiving your retirement income in monthly payments rather than as one lump sum.

LYON

See **liquid yield option note (LYON).**

M: Macroeconomics to Mutual Fund

macroeconomics

The study of an economic system from an overall perspective.

A macroeconomist would, for example, examine nationwide data on industrial production, inflation, price levels, and unemployment. Microeconomics, on the other hand, studies the behavior and interactions of the individuals, households, businesses, and other decision-making units that make up the economy.

MACRS

See **accelerated cost recovery system (ACRS)**.

make a market

See **market maker**.

Maloney Act of 1938

See **securities laws**.

management accounting

A branch of accounting directed at internal management operations, usually under the direction of a controller. Also called managerial accounting.

Broadly defined, it includes activities such as cost accounting, budgeting, financial forecasting, cash management, and asset utilization. Management accounting contrasts with external reporting, which is concerned primarily with disclosures to outside audiences such as potential investors, creditors, and government agencies. Managerial accounting, as long as the information stays entirely within the company, need not adhere to the rules and regulations governing external reporting.

management buyout (MBO)

See **leveraged buyout (LBO)**.

M&A

See **merger/acquisition (M&A)**.

margin

Amount of money a customer may borrow in his or her brokerage account to buy more securities.

The amount that may be borrowed is based on the market value of the account. The required margin percentage is set by the Federal Reserve Board. If the balance in a margin account falls below the required minimum—which usually results from a price drop in the security—the brokerage firm issues a margin call, meaning the customer must deposit more funds or face liquidation of the securities.

margin account

A line of credit or loan account established for you by a brokerage firm. This account enables investors to use securities equity as collateral to buy more, up to the 50 percent allowable margin (you can buy $20,000 in stock by pledging $10,000 in stock as collateral). The brokerage will charge interest on the loan, usually a point or two above the prime rate. You will also sign a margin agreement outlining the lending and interest terms. This agreement also gives the brokerage firm the power to sell your securities to other brokerage clients for the purpose of selling short or to sell your securities from your account in the case of a margin call.

margin call

See **margin**.

mark to the market

The value of any portfolio based on the most recent closing prices. At the end of each trading day, most portfolio managers receive a valuation of their holdings that is marked to the market.

Frame of Reference: Margin Accounts and the Crash

Margin accounts get people into trouble during big market drops. In fact, before the 1929 market crash, banks would lend up to 90 percent of the value of a client's holdings. That meant that a 5 percent decline could wipe out an investor—a phenomenon that many believe was responsible for amplifying the crash. Even as recently as the 1987 crash (when the market lost more than 20 percent of its value), many investors were hit with big margin calls. Many large brokerage firms sent out representatives door-to-door to collect margin account monies due.

market capitalization

The current value of a company's common stock, determined by multiplying the share price by the total number of shares outstanding.

Example
If the current price of a company's stock is $20 per share, and there are 2 million shares outstanding, then its market capitalization would be $40 million ($20 × 2 million).

See also **market value**.

market maker

The entity or person who facilitates trading in a security by agreeing to buy or sell a stock as needed to "make a market." Such a person generally makes a profit by keeping the spread (the difference between the bid and asked prices).
See also **broker**.

market risk

The sensitivity of a stock's price to the things that affect all stocks—such as shifts in the economy, interest rates, inflation, and general investor confidence. This is also known as systematic risk.
A stock's market risk is measured by its beta (β).
See also **alpha (α)**, **market risk premium**, and **nonmarket risk**.

market risk premium

The return a stock pays, or should pay, to compensate investors for market risk.
For the overall market, the premium is the difference between average annual returns for stocks and the interest rate for risk-free investments such as Treasury bills. For example, if the average annual return for stocks is 13 percent, and for T-bonds it's 7 percent, then

the market risk premium you would want for investing in stocks would be 6 percent. For an individual stock, the market risk premium can be calculated using the capital asset pricing model (CAPM).

market value

1   In general, the worth allocated to a security or asset in a publicly traded market arena. The market value of your stock would be the price at which it trades in the major stock exchanges.

2   In accounting, the value of a company's assets based on their worth in the marketplace (versus historical or book value). Some analysts use a market value balance sheet, which revalues all assets based on their current value.

matching concept

A fundamental concept in accounting that links expenses with their associated revenues or with the time periods in which benefit from the expenditures occurs.

The matching concept is also part of the reason for depreciation. Say you bought a pizza-delivery truck at the end of December 1995 and plan to use it in 1996 through 2000. You will depreciate it, recognizing part of the cost each year.

See also **adequate disclosure concept**, **conservatism concept**, **consistency concept**, and **materiality concept**.

materiality concept

Legal or accounting standard that determines information that must be disclosed to investors.

Basically, information is considered material if the average investor would need to know it to make an informed decision. In a publicly held company, you do not have to report everything you are doing, just items that will have a material impact on your results. The problem, of course, is defining what is considered material. Materiality is also relative. What might not be material to a company with

$100 billion in revenues might well be material to one with revenues of less than $100 million.

See also **adequate disclosure concept**, **conservatism concept**, **consistency concept**, and **matching concept**.

MBO

See **management buyout (MBO)**.

MDA

See **multiple discriminant analysis (MDA)**.

mechanic's lien

Claim against a building that enables the holder to stand in line before other creditors in the event that a construction project fails and is liquidated.

See also **lien**.

mediation

Nonbinding dispute resolution by an impartial third party.

See also **arbitration**.

medium-term note (MTN)

Bond with a maturity between 2 and 10 years. As the terms are generally understood, an MTN falls between a short-term note (with a maturity of 2 years or shorter) and a long bond (with a maturity of 10 years or longer).

megabank

Term used to describe a very large institution that conducts banking activities in a specific region of the United States. An example is NationsBank Corporation, which had 1996 revenues of $17.4 billion and has more than 3,000 banking offices across the southern and midwestern United States.

See also **regional bank**.

merger

Combination of two or more companies in which the acquired company gives up its independent identity.

Types of M&A

There are three basic types of mergers and acquisitions:

1 *Horizontal:* The fusing of two or more companies involved in the same type of business. The Price Club/Costco merger is an example.
2 *Vertical:* A merging of two or more companies engaged in different stages of the same business. A company that manufactures nylon, for example, might buy a company that makes the chemical feedstocks needed.
3 *Conglomerate:* The combination of two or more companies whose products are not related. In these situations, even if one company buys the other, the management structures might remain separate because of the different natures of the businesses. The 1995 acquisition of CBS by Westinghouse is an example.

---

merger/acquisition (M&A)

Two or more companies fusing into one.

Usually, one company buys another, and the acquired company gives up its independent existence; the surviving company assumes all assets and liabilities. Not all acquisitions come about in a friendly fashion. Sometimes a spurned suitor will launch a hostile bid for its desired partner.

See also **tender offer**.

microeconomics

See **macroeconomics**.

mill rate

See **property tax assessment**.

minimum pension liability

Balance sheet shortfall when the value of a company's pension plan assets is lower than its future payout estimate.

When the assets in a company's pension plan do not cover the present value of the pensions to which the workers are eventually entitled, this is a liability that must be included in the company's balance sheet.

momentum investing/investors

An investing strategy that bets on securities that have performed well in the past, and often in the recent past. Momentum investors believe that high-performing stocks have built up the momentum to continue to be high performers. This strategy is usually at odds with value investing, which often bets on recent underdogs.

M_1

See **money supply**.

monetarism

A school of economic thought that holds that inflation is largely the result of increases in the money supply. Monetarists believe that manipulating the money supply to promote economic stability is a bad idea.

More specifically, monetarism—which is widely associated with the American economist and Nobel laureate Milton Friedman—is founded on at least three basic propositions:

1 Periods of persistent inflation usually happen because of sustained increases in the money supply that exceed the growth of real output.

2 Increases in an economy's anticipated inflation cause interest rates to rise and the exchange rate to fall.

3 Increases in the growth of the money supply produce only temporary changes in real production but lasting changes in the rate of inflation.

Monetarists are usually skeptical of the government's ability to use fiscal and monetary policies to improve an economy's performance. Instead, they tend to believe that government has the best chance of promoting economic stability by acting predictably and by avoiding efforts to steer the economy in one direction or the other.

See also **monetary policy**, **price controls**, and **supply-side economics**.

monetary aggregates

Measures of the supply of money in an economy.

The Federal Reserve, for instance, calculates three measures of the amount of money in circulation in the United States: M_1, M_2, and M_3.

See also **money supply**.

monetary policy

In the United States, use of the Federal Reserve System to regulate the money supply and thus influence the nation's economy. The Fed implements monetary policy through open market operations, changes in bank reserve requirements, and changes in the discount rate.

See also **fiscal policy**, **monetarism**, **price controls**, and **supply-side economics**.

money center bank

A bank in a key financial center—such as London, New York, or Tokyo—that conducts major national and international dealings.

Money center banks, also called money market banks, are major economic players because they handle large deposits from and loans to both governments and corporations, and they buy large quantities of securities. Through their policies and their interest rates, these banks are highly influential worldwide. The eleven acknowledged United States money center banks control almost a quarter of the assets of all U.S.-based banks.

See also **regional bank**.

money factor

See **lease rate**.

money manager

A person who is paid a fee to supervise the investment decisions of others. This term most often refers to managers of large financial institutions, such as bank trust departments, pension funds, insurance companies, and mutual fund companies. Also known as a portfolio manager.

An investor adviser does not need permission from investors to trade and is usually compensated by a fee of .5 to 2 percent of total assets under management. The money manager might also receive some commissions on purchases and sales and/or be compensated based on performance measures of the portfolio. One of the most high-profile money managers of recent years is Peter Lynch, who managed the high-growth Magellan Fund in the boom 1980s.

money market banks

Banks in major financial centers such as New York, Tokyo, and London.

See **money center bank**.

money market mutual fund

An open-end mutual fund that invests in commercial paper, bankers' acceptances, repurchase agreements, government securities, certificates of deposit, and other highly liquid and safe securities paying money market rates of interest. The fund's net asset value remains a constant $1 a share—only the interest rate goes up or down.

money market securities

See **money markets**.

money markets

Where you can buy and sell short-term bonds, or those with terms of less than 1 year. These arenas for short-term lending and borrowing are really electronic markets similar to over-the-counter (OTC) stock markets. Short-term U.S. Treasury bills, certificates of deposit, and commercial paper, among other things, are traded on money markets.

money supply

Total stock of money available, consisting in the United States of currency in circulation and various types of deposits at commercial banks, savings and loans, and other institutions.

Money Supply

According to the Federal Reserve, there are at least three measures of the money supply:

1 M_1 includes all the dollar bills and coins in circulation (outside of bank vaults), plus travelers' checks, demand deposits, and NOW accounts.

2 M_2 includes M_1 and then adds other savings accounts and time deposits. It also includes general-purpose money market mutual funds and other instruments.

3 M_3 includes M_2 plus most additional forms of savings.

Both M_2 and M_3 tend to be more stable than M_1. When banks are offering high interest rates on checking accounts, people shift funds from their money market and savings accounts to checking. That has no effect on M_2 or M_3, but M_1 increases sharply.

Moody's Investors Service

The company best known for its bond rating service, along with Standard & Poor's and Dun & Bradstreet. Moody's issues ratings on corporate bonds, commercial paper, municipal bonds, and preferred and common stocks.

See also **bond ratings**.

mortgage

A loan made to purchase a home, usually with the home used as collateral.

Aside from this simple arrangement, there are a number of other financial instruments that can be constructed around a mortgage. An original mortgage can become leverage for an equity line, or second mortgage. And the equity of a paid-up home can be turned into a reverse mortgage, with regular payment checks sent from the mortgageholder back to the homeowner.

The entire arena of mortgage lending has, in fact, become quite a financial marketplace all its own. The multibillion-dollar mortgage-backed securities market includes such investment options as the Government National Mortgage Association (Ginnie Mae) and Real Estate Investment Trusts (REITs).

mortgage bond

A debt security backed by a company's real estate and other fixed assets.

A first mortgage bond is secured by a lien on specific real property. A general mortgage bond is backed by a claim on all of a company's fixed assets that aren't pledged as collateral for other debts. If the mortgage is closed, no more bonds may be issued against it. An open mortgage may have additional bonds issued against it.

See also **bond** and **equipment trust certificate**.

mortgage REITs

Type of real estate investment trust (REIT) that sells stocks and bonds to the public and invests the proceeds in mortgages or construction loans.

Mortgage REITs behave more like bonds than stocks, and have a less appealing track record.

mortgage-backed security

A security made up of a pool of mortgages whose monthly payments of interest and principal pass through to investors.

These were introduced in 1970 by the Government National Mortgage Association (Ginnie Mae). Ginnie Mae, a federal agency, bundles residential mortgages insured by the Veteran's Administration (VA) and the Federal Housing Agency (FHA), and pools them into securities (guaranteed by Uncle Sam, even if home owners default on mortgages in the pool). By 1994, more than 16.3 million homes had been financed through Ginnie Mae securities.

More than 95 percent of all FHA and VA mortgages originated by local lenders in the primary mortgage market are repackaged as securities by Ginnie Mae. Ginnie Mae sells these securities, also called mortgage backs, to investors in minimum lots of $25,000. Banks and other financial institutions often continue to service the loans they sell to Ginnie Mae and her cousins, collecting payments and channeling them (net of service charges) to the government agency. A collateralized mortgage obligation (CMO) is a slightly more complex form of mortgage-backed security. The pool of mortgages is divided into different maturities—each one called a tranche—so that investors can choose among them.

Mortgage backs are generally cheaper to buy on the secondary market. That's because these certificates, which have experienced some degree of prepayments, cost significantly less. You can even buy shares in some mutual funds or unit trusts that invest in Ginnie Mae's for as little as $1,000. The buyers get the interest payments (typically 1 to 2 percentage points higher than Treasuries with similar maturities) and—when the mortgages are paid off—the principal. Monthly payments to investors, though, are unpredictable, because when home owners prepay their mortgages or refinance their homes, that money is passed through to investors in the pool.

Mortgage-backed securities work best when interest rates are stable. When they fluctuate, investors lose—whether rates head up or down. When interest rates fall, blocks of mortgages are refinanced and investors receive large chunks of principal, which they will not be able to reinvest at the higher rate they had expected. When market rates rise, prepayments and refinancings slow down—just when investors would love extra principal to reinvest at those juicier rates.

See also **asset-backed security**, **Fannie Mae**, and **securitization**.

M₃

See **money supply**.

MTN

See **medium-term note (MTN)**.

M₂

See **money supply**.

multiple discriminant analysis (MDA)

A system used to evaluate the creditworthiness of borrowers, usually for consumer loans.

Factors evaluated include:

- income
- length of time with present employer
- bank account balances
- time in present residence

The system uses statistical techniques considering these factors to obtain a score for each loan applicant.

municipal bonds

Bonds issued by a state or local government entity. Examples of municipal bonds are industrial development bonds, revenue bonds, and general obligation bonds.

The most attractive feature of munis is that many have tax-exempt interest—usually from state and local taxes, and some from federal taxes, too.

munis

See **municipal bonds**.

mutual fund

A fund operated by an investment company that raises money from shareholders and invests it in stocks, bonds, options, commodities, or money market securities. A mutual fund offers the advantages of diversification and professional management.

N, O: Naked Call to Owner's Policy

N

naked call

See **naked sale**.

naked sale

The practice of selling a security short without owning the underlying stock—also referred to as an uncovered sale, or going naked. (If you do own the security, then it is a covered sale.) This technique is considered to be especially risky, since there is essentially no limit to potential losses.

See also **call**.

NASD

See **National Association of Securities Dealers, Inc. (NASD)**.

NASDAQ Stock Market

The world's first computerized stock market and the second-largest market in the United States; based in Washington, D.C.

In 1998, the NASDAQ listed more than 5,000 companies, many of which are eligible to be listed on the New York Stock Exchange (NYSE) or the American Stock Exchange (AMEX). These include such giants as Microsoft, Intel, MCI, and Amgen.

See also **National Association of Securities Dealers, Inc. (NASD)**.

National Association of Securities Dealers, Inc. (NASD)

Largest self-regulatory organization in the U.S. securities industry. The NASD is the corporate parent of the NASDAQ Stock Market.

National Exchange Market System Act

See **securities laws**.

National Securities Clearing Corporation (NSCC)

See **clearinghouse**.

NAV

See **net asset value (NAV)**.

negative amortization

The insidious offspring of certain mortgages that allows the principal balance to grow, instead of shrink, as prescribed monthly payments are made.

Neg-am, as it is called among lenders, happens when an adjustable rate mortgage (ARM) has a payment cap but not an interest rate cap. When the adjustable rate rises, a capped monthly payment won't cover the entire principal, causing the size of the loan to increase at a compounded rate.

To avoid negative amortization, look for loans without payment caps. If you already have a loan with a payment cap, you are free to make higher monthly payments than the terms of your loan require. When rates move up, it's wise to make the biggest payment you can afford.

negotiable orders of withdrawal (NOW)

See **checking account**.

Net

See **Internet**.

net asset value (NAV)

An accounting term similar in meaning to net worth; most often used in reference to the value of a mutual fund and similar investment shares.

net current assets

See **working capital**.

net earnings

See **net income**.

net income

Often referred to as net earnings or net profits. For a company, it is the difference between revenues and expenses. It is typically an after-tax number, although net income before taxes is also a popular measure. Dividends are paid out of net income.

See also **earnings before interest and taxes (EBIT)** and **income statement**.

net present value (NPV)

Current worth of future amounts of money. Also called discounted cash flow (DCF).

You might want to calculate NPV for a number of reasons, including:

- to calculate the benefits of a potential project or investment, including buying a business
- to determine the price of a partnership or a minority interest when an investor's interest is being bought

- to compare the true cost of leasing equipment to an outright purchase

To arrive at the NPV, you need to find the cost of capital, or the discount rate, you feel your investment should get. The basic formula for NPV is:

$$NPV = P_0 + P_1 \div (1 + r) + P_2 \div (1 + r)^2 + \ldots + P_n \div (1 + r)^n$$

$P_0, P_1, \ldots P_n$ **are the payments in periods 0 through** n, **and** r **is the required rate of return.**

See also **opportunity cost**.

net proceeds

Total funds raised (usually through the issuance of securities or the sale of assets) less the costs of the transaction—such as underwriters' fees and registration expenses.

See also **gross proceeds**.

net profit margin

Ratio of net income to net sales.

See also **profit margin**.

net profits

See **net income**.

net sales

See **revenues**.

net working capital

Current assets minus current liabilities.

This is important to lenders and analysts as a measure of a company's ability to pay its bills. Loan agreements often mandate that the company keep a certain level of working capital. But the number is significant only in relation to other variables, such as the company's sales and industry standards.

net worth

In general, assets minus liabilities.

For an individual, net worth is the value of everything you own (such as your house, car, and portfolio) less all of your debts (such as your mortgage and credit card debt). For a company, the net worth is also called shareholders' equity, which is the assets less liabilities on the balance sheet.

See also **owner's equity**.

New York Clearing House

Established in 1853, the first and largest bank clearinghouse in the United States. The primary function of this institution is to process payments electronically among domestic financial institutions.

New York Coffee, Sugar, and Cocoa Exchange

Large futures exchange based in New York. The primary futures contracts traded are coffee, sugar, and cocoa.

New York Stock Exchange (NYSE)

Largest dollar-volume stock exchange in the world. It is also known as the Big Board.

More than 2,700 companies are listed on the Big Board. With a few exceptions (such as Microsoft Corporation and Apple Computer, which are listed on the NASDAQ), the companies listed on the NYSE are the biggest publicly held corporations in the country. The NYSE listing requirements are generally more strict than those of other exchanges, which is why the companies are bigger. But in 1995 the NYSE eased some of its listing requirements and now will consider listing companies without reported profits as long as they have market capitalizations of at least $500 million and revenues of at least $200 million.

936 companies

See **Section 936**.

no-load fund

A mutual fund offered by an investment company that imposes no sales charge (load) on its shareholders. Investors buy shares in no-load funds directly from the fund companies, rather than through a broker.

nominal rate

See **coupon rate**.

noncash charges

See **cash flow**.

noncompetitive bids

See **Treasuries**.

noncumulative interest

See **income bond**.

noncumulative preferred stock

See **preferred stock**.

noncurrent assets

See **balance sheet**.

nonmarket risk

Potential price swings in one company's securities for reasons specific to that company. Also called diversifiable risk.

Nonmarket risk factors include anticipated growth in earnings per share, management effectiveness, labor relations, and so on. They contrast with market risk factors, which affect all securities. Market risk factors include shifts in the economy, interest rates, inflation, and general investor confidence.

A security's nonmarket risk is reflected by its alpha (α). An investor can diversify a portfolio to minimize nonmarket risk, which is why it is also called diversifiable risk.

Example
The sudden resignation of a company's CEO would be a nonmarket risk, but a negative economic report that caused the stock to dip (along with many others) would be a market risk.

See also **beta (β)** , **capital asset pricing model (CAPM)** , and **diversification**.

no-recourse loan

See **recourse**.

normal distribution

In statistics, a division of data points that produces the bell-shaped curve. Also called Gaussian distribution, after Karl Friedrich Gauss (1777–1855), who identified the pattern of a bell curve.

In a normal distribution, most of the points on a graph are gathered around the high center. They trail off rapidly—and more or less symmetrically—to each side. In general, the larger the sample, the more likely it is that the data will follow this pattern and the closer it will come to total symmetry. For instance, the Dow Jones Industrial Average (DJIA) charts only thirty securities. As a result, it is less likely to follow the bell curve than the Standard & Poor's (S&P) 500 or broader indexes.

A company's dividend actions might be expected to follow a normal distribution over time, with a few very sharp increases or decreases in the rate and the majority clustered between those extremes.

note

See **promissory note**.

NOW (negotiable orders of withdrawal)

See **checking account**.

NPV

See **net present value (NPV)**.

NSCC

See **National Securities Clearing Corporation (NSCC)**.

NYSE

See **New York Stock Exchange (NYSE)**

O

OCC

See **Options Clearing Corporation (OCC)**.

odd lot

A trade of 100 shares or less. A round lot is a trade of a multiple of 100 shares.

offering price

See **asked price**.

OID

See **original issue discount bond (OID)**.

open interest

The number of open futures contracts on the market.

open invoice billing

See **balance forward**.

open mortgage

See **mortgage bond**.

open order

See **good-till-canceled (GTC)**.

open-end lease

See **closed-end lease**.

operating expenses

All costs that can be attributed to regular business activities.
See also **income statement**.

operating income

Earnings from a company's regular business activities.
See also **income statement**.

operating leverage

The relationship of a company's nonfinancial fixed costs to its variable costs.
See also **leverage**.

operating ratio

A ratio that measures a company's operating health. Examples include net income to revenues, or net income to shareholders' equity.

operating review

See **annual report**.

opportunity cost

Value of the best alternative given up by choosing one course of action over another.

Assessing opportunity cost offers decision makers a quantitative way to make informed choices between competing options.

The same concept can be applied to money tied up in accounts receivable. If it takes 3 months for a company to collect $100,000 from a client, the opportunity cost of the tied-up money is the amount of interest that would have been earned if the money had been invested.

See also **cash management systems** and **cost of capital**.

option

A contract that gives you the right to buy an asset (such as a stock) at a given price before an expiration date.

See also **call option**, **derivatives**, and **put option**.

option period

Amount of time before an option expires.

See also **call**.

Options Clearing Corporation (OCC)

Organization in Chicago that guarantees the transactions that take place on the nation's organized options exchanges.

Established in 1972, the OCC substitutes its own credit for that of the parties undertaking the options transactions.

See also **clearinghouse**.

ordinary life insurance

See **whole life insurance**.

original issue discount bond (OID)

Bond initially sold below its par value, or its redemption value at maturity. The difference between par value and the purchase price is the original issue discount. Investors must pay regular income tax, not capital gains tax, on this amount.

Companies like to issue bonds with an OID—especially zero-coupon bonds—because they can deduct the value of the interest as they go along even though they don't shell it out until maturity. Investors, though, must pay income tax on the amount they realize on paper even though they don't get the payments until later.

OTC

See **over-the-counter (OTC) stocks**.

outstanding stock

See **capital stock**.

over-the-counter (OTC) stocks

Shares in companies traded outside of organized stock markets such as the New York Stock Exchange (NYSE) and the American Stock Exchange (AMEX).

owner's equity

Item on a balance sheet expressing the value of the company's assets after liabilities are deducted. For a corporation, it is called shareholders' equity.

See also **accounting equation**.

owner's policy

See **title insurance**.

P: Pac Man Defense to Pyramid Scheme

Pac Man defense

A term for an anti-takeover tactic. The company targeted for the take-over defends itself by making an offer to take over the firm attempting to buy it.

paid-in capital

See **shareholders' equity**.

par value

Face value of a security.

For bonds, the par value is the amount you will be repaid at the maturity date. (For most bonds, the par value is $1,000.)

With common stock, par value does not mean a whole lot. It is an arbitrary amount (often 1 cent per share) that is specified for legal reasons and is represented on the company's balance sheet along with additional paid-in capital. Together, the two items add up to what investors paid when they bought the stock from the company as a new issue.

Example

If the par value of common stock is set at $0.01, and the company sells shares for $10.00 each, then the additional paid-in capital is listed as $9.99.

parallel trade

In international trade, linked transactions for exchanging goods between two companies.

This is a form of countertrade that involves two agreements. Each agreement is distinct and individually enforceable.

See also **bartering**.

participating preferred stock

Type of preferred stock that gives holders the right to receive, under certain conditions, additional earnings payouts over and above the specified dividend rate. In that sense, holders may participate in special dividend distributions to common shareholders. For example, a participating preferred shareholder might receive a stated dividend of $1.50 a year and also receive a share in any extra dividends given to common shareholders over the current rate.

participation loan

A loan a local bank or financial institution makes to a small business that is guaranteed by the Small Business Administration (SBA).

See also **assignment loan**.

partnership

When two or more people come together as co-owners of a business, pooling funds and sharing in profits or losses.

In accounting for a partnership, the parties involved must agree on how to value any noncash assets contributed by each partner. A partnership can be general or limited. In a general partnership, each party is personally liable for all of the entity's debts.

See also **limited partnership**.

passive investment

Stake in a business in which you are not active on a regular, continuous, or significant basis. The two most common examples of passive investment are limited partnerships and the rental of real estate.

This term also refers to a policy of portfolio management in which you or your broker select diversified securities that will remain relatively unchanged over a period of years. This is considered a passive rather than an active investment, since you are assuming you can't beat the market and want to passively participate in a modest rate of return on your investments.

Any net income from a passive investment is taxable, but net losses from a passive investment can be deducted from net income. Also, net losses can be accumulated over time and deducted as soon as a passive investment finally makes a profit (when you finally sell and make a profit on a rental property on which you had previously been taking losses, for example).

passive portfolio management

See active portfolio management.

pass-through security

Debt security, usually a bond, representing a portion of an overall loan pool, where payments are passed through to the debtholders.

The loan pool might be a portfolio of mortgages, for instance, or a package of credit card receivables. The payments to the security holders are made up of the funds received from many individual borrowers and might include both interest and principal. Each investor receives his or her share of the total pool with each distribution.

The checks to each investor may vary from pay period to pay period, both in amount and in the proportion derived from interest versus principal. That's because some borrowers repay their loans early, some skip payments, and so on.

See also **asset-backed security**, **mortgage-backed security**, and **securitization**.

payback period

How long it takes to recover one's investment in a project.

Although this is a meaningful number, it is not a very good measure of profitability. A project can have a short payback period but low profitability.

See also **rule of 72**.

Payback Period

You are considering buying an office building that needs some work. The building and improvements will cost around $500,000. The work will take a year. You believe you could then sell the building, recover your investment, and make a profit of $30,000. So your payback period is a year. If you hold on to the building, though, you believe you could make $80,000 a year in rent. Then your payback period for $500,000 is 6 years and 3 months. But, in the meantime, you would be making a good return on your money ($80,000 ÷ $500,000 = 16 percent annual return) and you would still have a building to sell.

---

pay-in-kind (PIK) securities

Bonds or preferred stock that pay interest or dividends—either cash or more shares—in the early years.

It's the issuer that makes the choice about the form of payment. The security usually allows PIK interest for from 1 to 6 years after the date of issue. This allows issuers to manage their cash flow flexibly during periods when capital needs are high and revenue is not yet established. By paying interest in the form of more securities, a company increases its debt pending the revenue growth it expects once capital investments are in place.

> Example
> Cellular telephone and cable television companies issued PIKs in the 1980s, when they needed lots of cash and flexibility to build infrastructure.

> PIK securities are considered to be relatively risky.

payout ratio
The relationship between the dividend and earnings per share.

The idea is to measure the amount of earnings a company pays out in dividends. To get the payout ratio, you divide the dividend by the earnings per share.

PBGC
See **Pension Benefit Guaranty Corporation (PBGC)**.

P/E ratio
See **price/earnings ratio**.

penny stocks
High-risk stocks that generally sell for less than a dollar per share.

Penny stocks are traded between brokers in over-the-counter (OTC) markets. Because these companies typically have erratic results and a small number of shares outstanding, their stock prices can be highly volatile. Denver, Colorado; Salt Lake City, Utah; and Vancouver, British Columbia, have traditionally been hot markets for penny stocks, often involving mining ventures.

See also **float** and **pink sheets**.

Pension Benefit Guaranty Corporation (PBGC)

Retirement fund insurer established by the Employee Retirement Income Security Act (ERISA).

See also **pension plans**.

pension plans

Investment plans that set aside money for future retirement income.

There are two broad classifications of pension plans:

1 *Defined benefit:* In this type of plan, the money you receive is defined ahead of time. Your payments will probably be based on your pay level and length of employment. There is no separate account for each employee, so the company meets its obligations by setting money aside in a pension fund.

2 *Defined contribution:* In this case, the money you receive depends on your own contributions, as well as on the plan's investment performance. Here, each employee has an account. Typically, both the employer and the employee make contributions, usually a percentage of the employee's pay. What is contributed and the money earned by the contributions accumulate in the account until the employee retires. The retirement benefit is simply what is in the account at that time. Defined contribution plans require less regulatory attention to ensure adequate funding.

There are maximum amounts that you can contribute to either kind of pension plan. The government also establishes rules for equity among workers, so the plans aren't skewed for the brass.

perfect hedge

See **hedge**.

performance bond

Guarantee from a third party that one person or organization will meet its obligations to another.

Performance bonds are often required in construction projects, where a contractor will have to buy a surety bond from an insurance company to guarantee its work. Other forms of performance bonds are issued by government agencies, banks, and individuals.

permanent life insurance

See **whole life insurance**.

perpetuity

An annuity that goes on indefinitely.

personal income

The total income received by an individual.

Personal income in the United States is measured by the Commerce Department, which deducts Social Security taxes, but not other taxes, from its calculations. Personal income includes wages and salaries and other labor income, rental income, interest, dividends, proprietors' income from noncorporate business ownership, and government transfer payments.

Pickens, Thomas Boone, Jr.

First of the new breed of activist investors, he is seen as both a shareholder rights savior and a swashbuckling corporate raider.

Pickens, born in 1929, grew up in Oklahoma and started out as a geologist, working from his car. His first job after graduating Oklahoma State University in 1951 was with Phillips Petroleum, a company for which he later made a hostile bid. In 1956, with a $2,500 loan, he and two partners founded a company that eventually became natural gas and oil producer Mesa Inc., where he remains general partner.

Pickens earned millions from greenmail—the practice of buying up huge blocks of stock of a company, announcing a takeover bid, and then selling the shares to the company at a high price while withdrawing as a suitor. His most profitable targets included Cities Service, Gulf, General American, Phillips, and Unocal. A statue of Pickens, ready to take a swing with a racquetball racket, greets visitors to Mesa's Irving, Texas, headquarters.

In early 1995 the tables turned for Pickens. He was forced to defend Mesa itself from a hostile takeover attempt by three raiders, including his own former top takeover strategist.

PIK

See **pay-in-kind (PIK) securities**.

pink sheets

Daily publication (pink, of course) that lists the bid prices and asked prices of thousands of over-the-counter (OTC) stocks. Many of the shares are so-called penny stocks that are not listed in daily newspapers. The pink sheets are published by the National Quotation Bureau.

The prices in the pink sheets do not necessarily reflect transactions; instead, the listings are paid advertisements from brokerage firms wanting to buy and sell the stocks. Trading is conducted directly between brokers, also called market makers.

play, in

See **in play**.

PMI

See **private mortgage insurance (PMI)**.

points

Prepaid finance charge that a lender might require a borrower to pay for the use of money loaned. Each point equals 1 percent of the loan amount, so on a $100,000 mortgage, 1.5 points equals $1,500.

Points are paid only once, usually at the closing of the loan. But points may be rolled into some loans and paid, with interest, over the term. This is a popular option among consumers who refinance an existing mortgage or buy a home with no money down, but it costs them big bucks over the long term of a mortgage.

There's always a trade-off between the interest rate and the points you'll pay your lender. (The more points you pay, the lower interest rate you'll get.) If you plan to stay in your house fewer than 4 years, opt for the higher rate with fewer points. If you plan to stick around for the long haul, choose a loan with some extra points—the lower rate, over the years, will save you more than the points will. Points are sometimes disguised as origination fees or discount points. If these costs are computed as a percentage of the loan amount, regardless of what they're called, they're still points.

Borrowers who pay points to buy, build, or improve a primary residence can usually claim them as tax-deductible expenses, just like mortgage interest, on their federal income tax returns. Buyers can even deduct points paid by the seller on the buyer's behalf.

poison pill

An anti-takeover device. In its simple form, it is a hastily made acquisition by a company facing a hostile takeover in order to make itself undesirable to possible attackers. In a more complex version, a company fearing for its life issues warrants to stockholders, giving them the right to purchase stock at a bargain price in case a hostile party buys a set percentage of the company's shares, aimed at making a takeover prohibitively expensive.

Ponzi scheme

An investment scam in which investors, promised fabulous returns, are paid off not from investments but from money contributed by subsequent investors.

A Ponzi scheme is beautiful in its simplicity and comes with a built-in advertising campaign that practically guarantees early success: word-of-mouth promotion from your friends, family, or neighbors who are reaping big rewards and getting you involved.

Fortunately, any one Ponzi scheme can do only so much damage because, past a certain point, the number of suckers must increase at a fabulous rate to pay off the previous suckers. For example, if Sucker A invests $100 and is promised a 50 percent return in one month, he must be paid back his own $100 plus $50 from the next sucker. But Sucker B must receive his own $50 back plus $50 each from suckers C and D. The number of rubes must increase geometrically to keep the scam alive, meaning that by the time you reach suckers X, Y, and Z thousands of additional rubes must be drawn into the deal. Also called a pyramid scheme.

The Ponzi Namesake

Charles (a.k.a. Carlo) A. Ponzi might have become an immortal fixture in finance for lending his name to a particular scam, but that's about all he got. Ponzi began his checkered career selling nonexistent Postal Union Coupons that promised a 50 percent return in 45 days. The scam collapsed in less than a year. He then left Boston for Florida, where he sold bogus real estate and landed in jail. The Italian-born Ponzi was deported and died broke in Rio de Janeiro at age seventy-one.

Check any suspicious or too-good-to-be-true investment with state or federal authorities before parting with your money. And remember to diversify your investments, so even if you're caught in a scam you won't lose your shirt.

portfolio

Your holdings of stocks, bonds, and other investments. The balance of investments in a portfolio should take into account your investment goals and your tolerance for risk and capital loss.

portfolio manager

See **money manager**.

preferred stock

Security that, like common stock, shows ownership in a corporation.

For most investors, the most important aspect is that preferred dividends are usually paid in fixed amounts. That means that your dividend of, say, $1 per quarter will always be paid. That's much different from a common stock dividend, which comes entirely at the discretion of the company (but which often increases over time).

Preferred stockholders have priority over those who own common stock in terms of dividend payments and in the case of any liquidation of the company. Most preferred stock is cumulative, meaning that unpaid dividends that the company can't pay must be paid in full before common stockholders can receive any dividends.

See also **convertible security**.

premium

Term used when a bond is selling above its par value.

See also **bond yield**.

prepayment

Payment of all or part of an installment debt before it's due.

Principal prepayment, also known as principal acceleration, means making advance payments—in any amount at any time—on the outstanding balance of your simple interest loan. This increases equity and dramatically reduces interest expense. With a fixed rate loan, it also shortens the loan term.

A prepayment penalty might be charged by some lenders if a borrower pays off an entire loan balance within the first few years of the loan. The amount of the penalty is generally a maximum of 3 months' worth of interest. Another type of prepayment penalty is charged when payments in a given year exceed 20 percent of the loan balance. Prepayment penalties are illegal in some states and are not allowed on mortgages sold to Fannie Mae or other secondary market investors. The absence of a prepayment penalty is called a prepayment privilege.

Prepayment penalties, when they legally exist, are exercised at the lender's discretion and may be waived or negotiated. Read the fine print before you apply for a loan. Or use the penalty as a bargaining chip—offer to accept a prepayment penalty clause in exchange for a lower interest rate.

prepayment penalty

See **prepayment**.

prepayment privilege

See **prepayment**.

present value

Current worth of money to be received in the future.

The present value of a future payment is calculated like this:

$$PV = FV \div (1 + r)^n$$

PV = present value
FV = future value
r = interest rate
n = number of time periods

See also **annuity**, **discount rate**, and **net present value (NPV)**.

present value of an annuity

See **present value**.

price controls

Government actions to set price levels for an industry or for the entire economy.

Control may be exerted to either reduce or increase prices from the going, market-determined level. An example of an effort to raise a price above the market equilibrium level, or the price that would prevail if the government did not intervene, is the federal minimum wage law; the government has, in effect, set a price floor for labor services.

Price controls are controversial, because interference with the free-market allocation of resources creates imbalances between demand and supply. Artificially high prices generate surpluses because the amount actually demanded is below that being supplied. Similarly, when prices are set artificially low, the amount people want to buy exceeds the amount available and shortages emerge.

See also **monetarism**, **monetary policy**, and **supply-side economics**.

price/earnings ratio (P/E)

A company's common stock price divided by its earnings per share for the year.

The P/E ratio is simply:

share price ÷ earnings per share

So if a company's share price is $40 and its earnings per share (the earnings-per-share figure most commonly used is from the most recent four quarters) is $2, the P/E would be 20.

This ratio is often used by investors and investment analysts to decide whether a stock is a good buy. Often it is given along with the price in newspaper and other stock listings.

See also **cash flow coverage**.

pricing

The process of determining how much to charge consumers in relation to what they will spend for the quality and value involved.

The pricing of a good or service depends on several internal factors—costs and marketing strategy, for example—and on external factors such as competition, demand, government regulations, and consumers' value judgments about the product.

See also **distribution channel**.

primary market

See **capital markets**.

prime rate

The interest rate banks typically charge their most creditworthy commercial customers.

The prime rate is a benchmark for other loans. With a prime rate of 8 percent, for example, a company might negotiate a loan at prime plus 2, or 10 percent. Some adjustable rate securities also are

priced against the prime rate, with periodic adjustments determined
by the prevailing level of that key interest rate.

Changes in the prime are linked to Federal Reserve System
adjustments in the discount rate. When that happens, major money
center banks will raise or lower their prime rates, which then tends to
ripple across the banking industry.

See also **London Interbank Offered Rate (LIBOR)**.

principal

The face amount of a loan or bond, apart from the interest. If you
receive a mortgage loan, for example, the principal would be the purchase price of the house. Over the course of the loan, you might pay a
total of $250,000—$100,000 might be for the principal, and the
other $150,000 would be for interest.

principal acceleration

See **prepayment**.

Principal of Trust

See **corpus**.

principal prepayment

See **prepayment**.

private mortgage insurance (PMI)

A policy that insures the lender against financial loss if you default on
your mortgage.

Borrowers prepay PMI premiums up front at the closing of the
loan, and then monthly with principal and interest payments. Prepaid
PMI premiums are placed in an escrow account by the lender.

Both the requirement to pay PMI and the amount of the
expense depend on:

- type of mortgage
- amount of equity
- mortgage insurer
- type of payment plan
- amount of lender coverage

In general, the greater the equity and the more stable the interest rate, the lower the PMI premium.

Eventual elimination of the monthly PMI cost is up to the lender. But a lender will usually agree to drop PMI when the property's equity has grown to at least 20 percent due to major home improvements or to principal prepayment.

Find out what the lender will require in order to give up the PMI escrow requirement before you apply for a mortgage. Some lenders won't drop PMI ever. Others might require a professional appraisal, at the borrower's expense, to document the amount of equity.

private offering

Selling securities not available to the general public.

There are a number of reasons for a private offering, not the least being the ability to simplify or eliminate registration requirements. Smaller companies can make a private offering to no more than twenty-five people without having to file a registration statement with the Securities and Exchange Commission (SEC).

private placement

Sale of unregistered securities, including stocks and bonds, directly to an institutional investor.

To qualify as a private placement, an offering must be made to accredited investors, big institutions such as mutual funds and banks. Under SEC Rule 144, a private placement investor must hold the securities for at least 2 years, after which they may be sold into the secondary market. All proceeds of a secondary offering go to the selling investor, not to the company whose stock is involved.

Securities sold in a private placement do not trade and are usually illiquid. Private placements do not have to be registered with the Securities and Exchange Commission (SEC), but the investor can later register and sell the securities in a secondary offering.

privately held company

A company that does not have publicly traded stock. It can be a corporation, partnership, limited partnership, joint venture, sole proprietorship, or limited liability company. In the United States, privately held companies are normally not obligated to disclose their financial statements publicly.

See also **publicly held company**.

pro forma

In accounting, an unaudited financial statement involving assumptions, usually taking the form of projections that include upcoming important events.

probate

A court order process through which the provisions of a will (generally transferring assets) are carried out.

profit and loss statement

See **income statement**.

profit margin

Net earnings divided by revenues. Also called net profit margin or return on sales. Some analysts calculate a gross profit margin. That is gross profit divided by net sales. (Gross profit is net sales minus cost of goods sold.)

program trading

A trade automatically completed by computer programs, usually by a large institutional investor.

promissory note

A legal document signed by a borrower that contains the loan principal, the interest rate, and the time and place for payments.

By borrowing money from a bank via promissory notes and repaying it, a company can establish a track record and eventually obtain a line of credit. Promissory notes, which may be short or long term, also give a company a way of dealing with an overdue account. Getting the customer to sign a promissory note means a formal acknowledgment of the debt and a firm commitment to a schedule of payment.

property tax assessment

The value assigned to real estate by an assessor, also known as the tax valuation.

State tax authorities require tax assessments to reflect the fair market value of the real estate, evidenced by local property sales. Property tax assessments might include the value of personal property, too; but cities usually limit such assessments to commercial or income-producing property with salable inventories.

When a city or town makes costly improvements that benefit property owners, such as new street lighting or town water/sewer lines, it might sell bonds to finance the cost. Then the city or town will assess property owners for the betterment by adding a betterment assessment to property tax bills. These betterment taxes become a lien on the real estate, just like uncollected property taxes do, preventing the sale of the property, except by foreclosure, until the debt is repaid.

To calculate an annual property tax bill, property tax assessments are multiplied by the tax rate, or mill rate (expressed in dollars per thousand).

Example
A property tax assessment of $180,000 with a tax rate of
$15/M (per thousand) equals annual property taxes of $2,700
(180×15).

Before spending time and money on a professional appraisal to
support your tax abatement request, check the assessor's field card to
be sure the written description of the property matches reality. Common errors include extra rooms, amenities, outbuildings, and acreage.
If your property description is accurate, get a comparative market
analysis (CMA) from a local real estate broker—it costs much less than
a professional appraisal. The CMA lists recent comparable property
sales and can be used to support your case for a tax abatement.

prospectus

1 Formal written document giving the facts about a new offering
   of securities. In the prospectus, a company issuing stocks or
   bonds describes in detail what it plans to do with the money it's
   raising.
        A prospectus should include, among other things, the
   financial details of the offering at hand, as well as the financial
   standing and history of the company. Also included should be a
   discussion of the company's business, the use of proceeds of
   the offering, information about management, and any pending
   litigation or liabilities.
        Ordinarily, after the filing with the SEC, the company
   must wait at least 20 days before offering the securities for sale
   (although this waiting period may vary depending on whether
   the SEC opts for a full review). During that time, a tentative preliminary prospectus can be distributed without pricing information or the issue date. That prospectus, which can be changed, is
   called a red herring, since portions are printed in red ink.

2 A prospectus may also be issued by a mutual fund, with information about its products and the overall company, to attract potential investors.

See also **underwriting** and **underwriting syndicate**.

proxy card

Shareholders use it to cast their votes on directors and other resolutions without having to attend the annual meeting.

See also **proxy statement**.

proxy statement

A document sent to shareholders before a company's annual meeting.

The proxy statement accompanies a proxy card, on which shareholders can mark their votes on issues to be decided at the meeting. The Securities and Exchange Commission (SEC) sets the rules for: (1) what information must be in the proxy statement to help shareholders decide how to vote, and (2) when the statements must be sent out.

Companies send the proxy material to shareholders of record (those people and institutions that hold stock in their own names). Brokerage houses that hold stock for others normally send out the proxy materials to investors.

A typical proxy statement includes:

- a letter of invitation from the board chairman and a notice from the secretary with details of the annual meeting
- information on the election of directors, their compensation, their committee assignments, brief biographical material, and a small photo of each
- disclosure of each director's stock ownership
- other issues proposed by management for a vote—such as approval of special compensation arrangements (bonus plans for the top brass, for example)

- resolutions proposed by shareholders and opposed by the board—usually involving social responsibility (such as adopting a code for environmental performance) or corporate governance (such as calls for cumulative voting or staggered terms)
- data on compensation of the highest paid executives and how compensation is determined
- a graph depicting the common stock's performance
- a supplement with the full text of any compensation plans up for a vote

See also **annual report** and **executive compensation**.

publicly held company

Corporation whose common shares are traded on a public exchange.

Publicly held companies are subject to reporting requirements from regulatory agencies such as the Securities and Exchange Commission (SEC). They must reveal detailed information about their business, finances, and operations.

See also **privately held company**.

purchase method

See **consolidation**.

put option

A contract that gives the holder the right to sell an asset at a particular price before a certain date. Buyers of a put option are betting that the value of the underlying asset will fall.

See also **derivatives**.

pyramid scheme

See **Ponzi scheme**.

Q, R: Qualified Opinion to Russell 2000 Index

Q

qualified opinion

A report by an accountant that indicates some reservation about the examination of a company's financial statements. For example, an auditor's opinion might include a statement about a lawsuit that, if lost, would substantially change the financial condition of the company.

See also **audit**.

quality ratings

Security rankings—both debt and equity—that attempt to rank a company's potential risk.

See also **bond ratings**.

quick ratio

Measures a company's ability to pay what it owes over a 30-day period. The formula used to calculate this ratio appears in the entry for acid test ratio.

quotation

Taken together, a current bid and asked price for a given security. Also called a quote.

R

random walk theory

Essentially a less-stringent form of the efficient market theory. The random walk way of thinking says that the markets are entirely unpredictable and certainly can't be forecast.

The theory came from the idea that security price movements are a random walk. It discounts the value of technical analysis, which relies heavily on past prices through charting. Many people use the theory to point out that long-term investment is not really an art; rather, your best bet is to pick almost any good stock and stick with it.

real estate investment trust (REIT)

A publicly traded company that sells stocks and bonds, and invests the proceeds in real estate (such as shopping centers, office buildings, apartment complexes, or hotels) or mortgages.

Because REITs distribute pretax earnings, their current yield tends to be high. However, sometimes a yield is unusually high because the share price has dropped—a possible signal that it might own troubled properties.

real interest rate

Stated interest rate on a loan minus inflation. It's basically a way of adjusting for inflation. So if you received a 12 percent return on an investment, but inflation was 4 percent, your real interest rate would be 8 percent.

See also **interest rate**.

recession

An economic slump. While people argue about what exactly makes up a recession, the National Bureau of Economic Research defines it

Types of REITs

- *Equity REITs* buy properties. These tend to be the most profitable to investors, especially those that specialize in particular types of real estate and do their own developing.
- *Mortgage REITs* invest mostly in mortgages or construction loans. These behave more like bonds than stocks, and have a less-appealing track record.
- *Hybrids* combine investments in real properties and mortgages.
- *Finite life REITs* plan to dissolve after a specified number of years, but like the limited partnerships that bombed in the 1980s, many are unable to do so at good prices, if at all.

as a period of at least two consecutive quarters of decline in inflation-adjusted Gross Domestic Product (GDP). It is also characterized by rising unemployment rates.

recessionary trough

See **business cycle**.

recourse

Lender's ability to collect assets in the event of a borrower's default. In a secured loan, of course, the lender can seize the assets the borrower put up as collateral.

In a no-recourse loan, the lender has a claim only on the assets that are directly involved. Two major companies forming a joint venture to build a plant will typically seek no-recourse financing, which the banks will give if the prospects for the plant look good.

When a company issues an equipment trust certificate, equipment (such as railroad cars) is the collateral. The lender collects the cars if the borrower defaults. But the term "recourse" is more properly used for secondary assets, which the lender can go after in cases like the following:

- When an individual proprietorship or partnership borrows money, the lender might be able to go after bank accounts and other assets of the firm's principals.
- When someone guarantees a loan, his or her assets will be vulnerable if the borrower defaults.

red herring

Tentative, preliminary version of a prospectus. It's called this because of a statement attached, printed in red ink, advising that it's been filed with the Securities and Exchange Commission (SEC) but has not yet become effective.

regional bank

1 Each of the twelve Federal Reserve Banks of the Federal Reserve System.

2 A bank that makes loans and collects deposits throughout a region of the United States. Many U.S. regional banks and bank holding companies have become so large they are known as superregionals or megabanks. An example is Union Bank of California, a commercial bank holding company and among the oldest banks on the West Coast, having roots as far back as 1864.

Regional banks are influential but not on the national and international level of a money center bank.

See also **Federal Reserve System (Fed)**.

registered representative

Probably the most correct name for the securities industry employee who's also called an account executive (AE), broker, investment adviser, stockbroker, or vice president of investments, among other things.

Registered representatives are the salespeople who deal with the customers of a brokerage company. They're called registered because these reps are registered . . . and registered . . . and registered. Among the organizations they must register with are the National Association of Securities Dealers (NASD), the Securities and Exchange Commission (SEC), the agencies that regulate securities transactions in the states where they do business, and the stock exchanges where their companies trade.

regression analysis

Statistical technique for predicting how a dependent variable, the unknown, relates to one or more independent variables, the known.

Suppose you were trying to decide whether the scores job applicants received on an aptitude test were an accurate predictor of their job performance. You would set up a regression analysis in which the test scores were your independent (or known) variable and job performance was the dependent (or unknown) variable. Then you would take past results and compare to decide if the two factors were correlated in a significant way.

Simple regression analysis involves the comparison of only one variable against another, but in multiple regression analysis there might be several variables involved. (In the above example, you might use the test score, interview rating, and education level to predict job performance.)

Regulation A

A Securities and Exchange Commission (SEC) provision based on the Securities Act of 1933, which lets small companies issue up to $1.5 million in securities to the public under somewhat relaxed registration and disclosure requirements. Also called the small-issues exemption.

Regulation D

Rules established by the Securities Act of 1933, which governs private placement offerings.

Regulation Q

Federal Reserve Board rule that formerly put a ceiling on how much interest savings institutions could pay on time and savings deposits. The Depository Institutions Deregulation and Monetary Control Act of 1980 gradually phased out Regulation Q.

reinvested dividends

The dividends that are added back to one's total investment amount.

If you have $1,000 in a mutual fund that automatically reinvests your dividends, and you receive a $10 dividend—it will be used to buy more units in the mutual fund instead of being distributed to you.

reinvested interest

Similar to reinvested dividends, except it's interest payments that are being used to buy more of the base investment product. So if you receive $10 in interest from a bank account, it will be added to your savings rather than distributed to you. That way your $10 will also generate interest.

See also **compound interest**.

REIT

See **real estate investment trust (REIT)**.

repurchase agreement (repo)

A transaction, usually with Treasury issues, in which the seller agrees to a buyback of the security at a set price. The deal might set a date for the repurchase, or it might be an open repo. In effect, a repo is a low-risk, short-term loan to a bank or securities dealer. The duration is typically from overnight to 1 or 2 weeks.

In a reverse repo, the bank or securities dealer buys the securities and agrees to sell them back later. This provides short-term cash for the securities' owner.

The Federal Reserve System often uses repurchase agreements to temporarily adjust the money supply.

reserve requirement

The minimum fraction of a bank's deposits that the Federal Reserve System must hold in reserve.

Resolution Trust Corporation (RTC)

See **banking regulation**.

restricted stock

See **letter stock**.

retained earnings

Earnings accumulated on a company's balance sheet after dividends have been paid out. Retained earnings are a part of the shareholders' equity on the balance sheet, and might also be referred to as an earned surplus.

For example, if a company's net income were $5 million, and it paid out dividends of $1 million, that would leave $4 million to add to its retained earnings on the balance sheet, thus adding to the total value of shareholders' equity and the company's net worth.

return on sales

Another term for profit margin.

return on shareholders' equity (ROE)

Ratio of net income to average shareholders' equity for the accounting period. This is one measure of a corporation's performance.

To get the average shareholders' equity, you add the number from the balance sheet at the start of the period to the one for the end of the period, and divide by 2.

Toys for Tots has a net income of $12,000,000. Shareholders' equity was $60,000,000 on December 31, 1997, and $64,000,000 on December 31, 1998. So, the average shareholders' equity is $62 million:

$$\$60,000,000 + 64,000,000 = \$124,000,000$$
$$\$124,000,000 \div 2 = \$62,000,000$$

Return on shareholders' equity is 19.4 percent:

$$\$12,000,000 \div \$62,000,000 = 0.194 \ (19.4\%)$$

A variation on this measure singles out common shareholders' equity.

---

revenue bond

See **tax-exempt bonds.**

revenues

A company's sales in dollars. Revenues, sometimes referred to as net sales, should be expressed net of all returns, allowances, and discounts.

See also **income statement**.

reverse repo

See **repurchase agreement (repo)**.

reverse split

The opposite of a stock split, a reverse split is a way of reducing the number of a company's shares outstanding. A company exchanges one share of stock for a larger number of shares outstanding. Although the total value of the stock remains the same, the per-share price increases because fewer shares are now outstanding.

See also **stock split**.

revocable trust

See **irrevocable trust**.

right

Short-term entitlement to buy shares of stock. Also called subscription right.

Rights normally have a life of a few weeks and usually give the holder the opportunity to buy the shares at a price lower than the current market price. If registered with the Securities and Exchange Commission (SEC), the rights can be traded on the open market.

Issuing rights to current shareholders allows them to retain their proportional ownership in the company. Shareholders exercising their rights will not have their equity diluted.

See also **warrant**.

risk capital

See **venture capital**.

risk premium

See **capital asset pricing model (CAPM)** and **market risk premium**.

risk-free rate

The rate of return considered to be generally without risk. Within calculations for measures such as alpha (α), beta (β), and the capital asset pricing model (CAPM), the 3-month Treasury bill rate is often used as the risk-free rate.

risk-free return

See **risk-free rate**.

Robinson-Patman Act of 1936

See **antitrust law**.

ROE

See **return on shareholders' equity (ROE)**.

round lot

A trade of 100 shares or a multiple thereof. An odd lot is a trade of less than 100 shares.

Rule 144

See **private placement**.

rule of 72

A formula for determining how long it will take for a sum of money to double at a given compound interest rate. The formula is simple: 72

divided by the interest rate. So, $1,000 earning 6 percent will double in 12 years ($72 \div 6 = 12$).

See also **future value**.

	Years to Double Investment	
Annual Return	**Rule of 72 Estimate**	**Actual**
1%	72.0	69.7
5%	14.4	14.2
10%	7.2	7.3
15%	4.8	5.0
20%	3.6	3.8
25%	2.9	3.1

Russell 2000 Index

An index of price performance of smaller and midsize publicly held corporations, published by Frank Russell & Company. The index eliminates the 1,000 largest companies in terms of market capitalization (the value of all the stocks outstanding) and then tracks the stock prices of the 2,000 next-biggest companies.

See also **Dow Jones Industrial Average (DJIA)** and **Standard & Poor's (S&P)**.

S: S&Ls to Systematic Risk

S&Ls

Savings and loan institutions.

S&P 500

See **Standard & Poor's (S&P)**.

salvage value

Estimate of what an asset can be sold for at the end of its useful life.
See also **depreciation**.

samurai bond

See **Yankee bond**.

savings

Earnings that are not spent.

After taxes and other payments are subtracted from personal income, what's left is called disposable income, and in essence only two things can happen to it. The money will either be spent, thus becoming part of personal consumption expenditures, or it will be saved. Whether you stuffed the money into your mattress, ignored it as it sat in your checking account, earned interest on it by putting it in a savings account, bought stocks and bonds with it, or did almost anything else with it short of giving it away, an economist would call it savings.

If you spend more than you earn, the savings will be a negative number, and that's called dissavings.

savings rate

Proportion of personal disposable income that goes into savings.

See also **savings**.

SBA

See **Small Business Administration (SBA)**.

scorched-earth policy

A form of anti-takeover defense. The firm targeted for the takeover sells off the assets that have attracted the attention of those trying to acquire it in an effort to make the company worthless and unattractive.

S-corporation

Corporation taxed like a partnership or sole proprietorship.

Under subchapter S of the Internal Revenue Code, a domestic company with thirty-five or fewer shareholders can elect to have its corporate income treated as the income of its shareholders. Thus, as with a partnership, the corporation pays no income tax; instead, shareholders include their proportionate share of the corporation's income or losses on their individual tax returns. The shareholders still enjoy the protection from liability they get from incorporation, but they avoid the double taxation that happens when a company pays taxes on its income and then the investor pays taxes on dividends.

SEC

See **Securities and Exchange Commission (SEC)**.

secondary market

See **capital markets**.

secondary offering

The most common way securities are traded, it's simply the sale of a company's previously issued securities. (When you buy shares of Microsoft, they're traded on the secondary market.) A secondary offering is distinguished from an initial public offering (IPO), in which the company issues new shares to the public.

Sometimes a company wanting to raise capital will sell a block of securities to a large investor through a private placement. In this case, the investor must hold the securities for at least 2 years, after which they may be sold into the secondary market. All proceeds of a secondary offering go to the selling investor, not to the company whose stock is involved.

Section 936

A section of the U.S. tax code giving incentives to companies with operations in Puerto Rico. These organizations, known as 936 companies, are exempt from U.S. income tax on money earned and remaining in Puerto Rico.

secured debt

Debt backed up by some type of collateral. Examples of secured debt would be a mortgage or a car loan.

Unsecured debt, as the name implies, has no such collateral beneath it. Examples include a promissory note to your parents, or your credit card balance.

See also **Chapter 13**.

secured loan

See **recourse**.

Securities Act of 1933

See **securities laws**.

Securities Acts Amendments of 1975

See **securities laws**.

Securities and Exchange Commission (SEC)

Federal agency created by the U.S. Congress to administer U.S. securities laws.

The Securities Exchange Act of 1934 created the SEC to regulate securities markets, including the flow of information to investors and potential investors. The SEC historically has deferred to the Financial Accounting Standards Board (FASB) on the rules accountants must follow when preparing financial statements. But the SEC has a lot to say about exactly what information must be disclosed, when and how, and the contents of its required documents, such as annual reports, 10-Ks, and prospectuses.

Securities Exchange Act of 1934

See **Securities and Exchange Commission (SEC)** and **securities laws**.

Securities Investor Protection Act of 1970

See **Securities Investor Protection Corporation (SIPC)** and **securities laws**.

Securities Investor Protection Corporation (SIPC)

Nonprofit company that insures investors' accounts against brokerage company failures.

The SIPC is funded by brokerage companies, which are required to be members. It also can borrow from the Securities and Exchange Commission (SEC) if it cannot meet its obligations. Many brokerage companies buy additional insurance for their customers.

securities laws

Federal and state statutes that regulate the industry and try to eliminate fraud.

All states have laws dealing with registering new issues, licensing salespeople, and prosecuting those who make a fraudulent sale. These blue sky laws apply to offerings and transactions within a state's borders. Federal laws apply to deals and offerings that cross state lines.

The major federal securities laws are:

- *Securities Act of 1933:* Also called the Truth in Securities Act. Mandated a registration statement for new issues of securities. The statement gives financial data and information on the company's management and its business. The act also requires that a summary of the registration statement be published as a prospectus.
- *Securities Exchange Act of 1934:* Created the Securities and Exchange Commission (SEC) to regulate the securities markets and impose standards on people who sell securities. This law also covers the updating of registration statements.
- *Maloney Act of 1938:* Set up self-regulation of the over-the-counter (OTC) securities market under the National Association of Securities Dealers (NASD).
- *Investment Company Act of 1940:* Gave the SEC authority over companies that sell mutual funds.
- *Investment Advisers Act of 1940:* Brought investment advisers under the regulation of the SEC. This law requires advisers to disclose to their clients any conflict of interest, such as when advisers hold shares in a company they're recommending.

- *Federal Securities Act of 1964:* Extended the SEC's reach to most companies with assets of at least $1 million whose stocks are traded over the counter.
- *Securities Investor Protection Act of 1970:* Created the Securities Investor Protection Corporation (SIPC), which insures investors' accounts against brokerage company failures.
- *Securities Acts Amendments of 1975:* Also called the National Exchange Market System Act. Wide-ranging amendments to the 1934 law that directed the SEC to work with the industry on a unified, nationwide system for price quotations, trade executions, clearance, and settlement. Other provisions increased competition by eliminating fixed brokerage commissions, and established regulations for trading in municipal securities.
- *Insider Trading Sanctions Act of 1984:* Toughened the 1934 law's rules on insider trading and increased the penalties.
- *Insider Trading Act of 1988:* Made management of brokerage companies responsible for reporting to the SEC any insider trading it discovers.

securitization

A way to spread risk by pooling debt instruments, then issuing new securities backed by the pool.

This term became popular in the 1970s to describe the mortgage-backed security business, which bundled mortgages and passed the income from home owners' principal and interest payments through an intermediary, such as a government agency or an investment bank, to investors in the pool. Other types of accounts receivable, such as credit card debt, have now been securitized into bonds and notes as well. Junk bonds have been pooled and repackaged, creating a form of securitized commercial loan.

See also **asset-backed security**.

security

In investing, an instrument such as a stock, bond, or option that represents either ownership (stock), a creditor obligation (bond), or a right to ownership (option).

selling short

See **short/shorting**.

senior debt

Owed money that is first in line in claims on the borrower's assets.

Senior debt ranks below secured debt in the event of default or liquidation, but above subordinated debt, preferred stock, and common stock. Senior debt may also be secured, in which case it's called senior secured debt.

Senior debt usually includes loans from banks or insurance companies, and any bonds or notes not clearly designated as junior or subordinated.

senior preferred stock

See **preferred stock**.

senior secured debt

See **senior debt**.

serial bonds

Debt securities issued at the same time but with staggered maturities.

Most municipal bonds are issued this way, and so are some corporate bonds. The issuer redeems the bonds, or pays back the principal, on a regular schedule over time.

See **common stock**.

shareholders' equity

Item on a balance sheet showing the value of a corporation's assets after liabilities are deducted. Also called stockholders' equity. For an unincorporated business, it is called owner's equity.

There are two major categories within shareholders' equity on a balance sheet:

1 *Paid-in capital:* What investors paid for shares, both common stock and preferred stock. These are broken into par value and additional paid-in capital, or what investors paid above (or below) par value.

2 *Retained earnings:* This is the company's accumulated earnings over the years after dividends have been paid.

shareholders of record

See **proxy statement**.

shelf registration

Registering securities for public sale at a future date.

Under SEC Rule 415, a company may file a registration statement as much as 2 years before it actually offers the securities. The registration must be updated quarterly, but it can be used quickly when the company decides that market conditions are right for making the public offering.

shogun bond

See **Yankee bond**.

short squeeze

A market phenomenon in which the price of a security rises, putting those investors in a "squeeze" who have sold the stock short (bet that the stock would go down). This dynamic can often drive the market even higher, as those investors will be forced to buy back the stock to close their trades.

short/shorting

A trade in which an investor sells a security he or she doesn't own with the intention of making a profit if the security price drops. The investor later buys the stock for delivery on the sale, thus realizing the difference between the two prices. This type of trade might be either a covered or an uncovered (naked) sale.

short-term capital gains

See **capital gain**.

short-term note

A bond with a maturity of 2 years or less.

See also **commercial paper** and **medium-term note (MTN)**.

sight draft

See **bill of exchange** and **travelers' checks**.

simple interest

Calculation of interest paid on a loan or a deposit without compounding.

simple interest = principal amount × interest rate per time period × number of time periods

See also **interest rate**.

sinking fund

Money a company puts aside to redeem bonds or other obligations prior to maturity.

The company issuing the debt puts a sum of cash into a separate custodial account that is then used to buy back the securities. The idea is that by gradually redeeming the bonds the company is enhancing the safety of the bonds. This added degree of safety often allows the issuer to pay a lower interest rate.

In private placement bonds, a sinking fund is usually mandatory. Sometimes preferred stock is also issued with sinking fund provisions.

SIPC

See **Securities Investor Protection Corporation (SIPC)**.

sleeping beauty

A company marked for takeover, as its assets are not performing up to par, its shares are bargain-priced, and management has not created sufficient, or any, takeover defenses.

Small Business Administration (SBA)

Government agency that provides support to small companies and businesses. In addition to gathering information, the SBA also provides financial assistance to small businesses through direct loans and bank guarantees.

small-capitalization stock

Also called small cap, a stock with a lower market capitalization and price, as opposed to blue chip stock. There are no general guidelines, but small caps are often defined as those stocks with share prices below $20.

small-issues exemption

See **Regulation A**.

smart card

A card issued by travel and credit card companies that stores specialized facts about the cardholder such as travel preferences and other personal information.

socially conscious investing

A field of finance that allows you to factor in personal feelings about various social issues and causes. For example, there are a number of green funds that invest only in companies deemed to be environmentally responsible.

soft currency

Money that cannot be converted easily to the currency of another country. It might be difficult to convert because a rapid fall in value has made outsiders mistrustful of holding it, or because it is offered only at an unrealistic exchange rate.

See also **hard currency**.

soft landing

Swing of the nation's business cycle, after a period of high growth, that does not lead to a recession or high inflation.

This is an elusive concept, much talked about but seldom—if ever—achieved. Many economists define it as a sustained period with 2 to 2.5 percent annual growth in the Gross Domestic Product (GDP), and many will also tell you that it has never happened. The term tends to be used when the Federal Reserve System raises interest rates to slow down a growth period.

sole proprietorship

Unincorporated business owned by one person, or by a husband and wife. Sole proprietors are liable for their company's debts and pay taxes as though they and their business are one entity.

See also **S-corporation**.

S-1 filing

The most comprehensive of the detailed disclosure statements that have to be filed with the Securities and Exchange Commission (SEC) before a stock offering.

See also **prospectus**.

special item

Something that affects a company's income statement but is not part of its regular business and does not ordinarily happen. Also called an extraordinary item.

Special items get a line of their own on the income statement. To be considered special items, they must be both unusual and infrequent.

Example
In 1994, General Electric liquidated its Kidder, Peabody securities operation and sold off some of the assets. It reported a loss of almost $1.2 billion as a special item on its income statement.

specific invoice prices

See **inventory valuation**.

specific lien

See **lien**.

spin-off

1 When a corporation divests itself of a division or subsidiary by setting it up as a stand-alone entity. It's then owned directly by the shareholders of the parent. The parent company distributes shares in the new company to its shareholders on a proportional basis.

2 Sale of part of a company to employees.

A company may spin off a subsidiary by selling it to the subsidiary's Employee Stock Ownership Plan (ESOP) in a leveraged buyout (LBO).

spot interest rate

See **spot price**.

spot market

Place where you pay cash for commodities and take immediate delivery. See also **spot price**.

spot price

Current cash price on the free market. The term is often used for commodities also traded under contract.

spread

The difference between the bid price and the asked price on a security, akin to the retail markup on consumer goods. In exchange for providing a market for the security, the market maker (broker) will receive that difference in price.

staggered terms

Electing a portion of the board every year. Also called classification of directors.

With staggered terms, directors usually are elected to 3-year terms, with a third of the directors up for election at each annual meeting.

See also **cumulative voting**.

Standard & Poor's (S&P)

1   Division of the McGraw-Hill Companies that publishes financial and statistical data and background information about companies.

S&P is best identified with:

- *Standard & Poor's 500 Stock Index (S&P 500):* A comprehensive index of 500 stocks designed to show price movements.
- *Standard & Poor's Bond Guide:* A monthly publication of S&P's bond ratings.
- *Standard & Poor's Confidence Indicator.*

2   A measurement of investor confidence in the securities markets. When investors buy more low-priced stocks, the indicator rises. The likely explanation is that they are more willing to take risks. If investors are buying more high-priced stocks, the indicator falls, indicating less confidence.

See also **Dow Jones Industrial Average (DJIA)** and **Russell 2000 Index**.

Standard & Poor's (S&P) 500

See **Standard & Poor's (S&P)** and **stock index**.

standard deviation

Calculates the average variation from an expected result.

See also **expected rate of return**.

statement of financial position

A summary of assets and liabilities at a particular time.

See also **balance sheet**.

statement of operations

A summary of a company's revenues and expenses for an accounting period. It explains, in broad terms, how the company arrived at its bottom line, or net income.

See also **income statement**.

statutory exemption

See **alternative minimum tax (AMT)**.

stock dividend

A dividend payout in the form of stock rather than cash.

Stock dividends are used in pay-in-kind preferred stocks, or PIKs. A PIK preferred stock will pay dividends in additional preferred stock instead of cash. There might also be PIK bonds, which pay interest in the form of additional bonds. This structure can be onerous to the issuer and advantageous to the security holder.

PIK securities trade flat (that is, without accrued interest or dividends). Their price is expected to reflect accrued interest since the last payment. PIKs generally trade at higher yields than their cash-paying counterparts because of the lower perceived valuation of non-cash payouts.

See also **stock split**.

stock index

Any of a number of indicators used to measure stock market price movements.

Stock market indicators include the following:

- *The Dow Jones Industrial Average (DJIA):* Tracks the shares of thirty major corporations traded on the New York Stock Exchange (NYSE). Dow Jones also maintains averages for transportation and utility stocks.
- *The Standard & Poor's 500:* Tracks 500 widely held stocks.
- *The New York Stock Exchange Composite Index:* Measures the market value of all shares traded on the NYSE.
- *The NASDAQ Composite Index:* Measures the market value of all equity shares traded on the NASDAQ Stock Market.
- *The AMEX Market Value Index:* Measures the performance of more than 800 issues traded on the American Stock Exchange (AMEX).

Some investors and mutual funds build their portfolios on the basis of a market index, and many traded derivatives are based on an index.

stock option

Right to buy or sell a stock at a particular price before a given date. Stock options are often included in the compensation packages offered to senior executives of public companies.

See also **derivatives, warrant**, and **executive compensation**.

stock picking

The process of evaluating and selecting individual stocks for investments. An example of stock picking is active portfolio management.

stock split

Increasing the number of a company's outstanding shares without changing shareholders' equity.

The immediate result is that the number of shares held by each shareholder increases, but the total values involved do not. If the company pays a dividend, it will be reduced in proportion to the split. In executing a stock split, the company reduces the par value of each share and probably needs to increase the number of authorized shares, so shareholder approval is required. A stock split can be in any proportion: two-for-one, three-for-one, three-for-two, and so on.

Another way of increasing outstanding shares is through a stock dividend. This does not involve a change in the par value and is usually done on a smaller scale, so shareholder approval might not be needed. A company declaring a 10 percent stock dividend would issue another share to each holder of ten shares. Although a stock dividend involves some changes within shareholders' equity on the balance sheet, total shareholders' equity remains the same.

See also **reverse split**.

So What's the Point of a Stock Split?

Why declare a stock split if the overall values do not change? Many companies believe that a lower stock price is at least a psychological encouragement to investors. It also makes stock ownership more affordable to a larger number of people and increases liquidity. In addition, a split enables smaller shareholders to buy in lots of 100 shares and therefore might reduce their brokerage commissions.

---

stockbroker

See **registered representative**.

stockholders' equity

See **shareholders' equity**.

stored value card

A prepaid calling card or spending card that takes the place of a cash card or credit card. As the card is used, the dollar value stored on it is decreased until spent.

straight bankruptcy

See **Chapter 7**.

straight bond

A bond with no optional features.

A straight bond can't be called, it's not convertible, and it has no warrants or other sweeteners attached. You can calculate the value of a straight bond simply by determining the present value of its future cash flows—the interest you'll receive periodically and the principal you'll get when the bond matures.

See also **bond valuation** and **convertible security**.

straight life insurance

See **whole life insurance**.

straight-line method

The simplest method of depreciation, it spreads the cost of an asset in equal amounts over the asset's useful life.

See also **accelerated depreciation** and **depreciation**.

street name

Refers to securities registered to, or held by, a brokerage company or other outfit for an individual investor. The individual is known as the beneficial owner, and the security is that person's asset, not the brokerage's.

The street name account is basically for convenience. When transactions are made or dividends are paid, for example, the account is adjusted without the beneficial owner's needing to take any action. The securities in the account can also be used as collateral if the investor trades on margin, meaning with money borrowed from the broker. When it's time for the company's annual meeting, the brokerage firm will mail the company's annual report, proxy statement, and proxy card to the owner.

Investors with securities in street names probably have to tell the IRS what they own, but in most cases they don't need to tell anyone else.

strike price

Point at which the asset underlying an option can be bought or sold.

See also **derivatives**.

stripped bond

A bond whose pay-to-bearer interest coupons have been physically removed, so what's left is only the principal—the capital value of the bond.

Typically, these bonds are sold at a deep discount and are redeemed at face value at maturity, while the interest coupons are sold separately. The reason? Some investors prefer to gain appreciation for long-term needs such as retirement or the children's education. They don't want the current income, so they'll buy what amounts to a zero-coupon bond. Other investors need the immediate, ongoing return and aren't concerned about recovering the principal at maturity. So they buy the income stream in the form of the coupons.

A brokerage house or other financial institution will strip bonds and sell them as two units when they think investors prefer them that way.

Subchapter S

See **S-corporation**.

subordinated debt

Unsecured debt obligations that are junior in liquidation preference to senior secured debt and secured debt.

Because subordinated debt is farther down in the capitalization ladder, it carries more risk than senior debt. This means that the interest rate, or yield, that a company must pay on subordinated debt is usually more expensive.

subordinated preferred stock

See **preferred stock**.

subscription right

Authorization to buy newly issued common stock at a discount price.

See also **right**.

subscription warrant

Security that lets its holder buy a certain number of a company's shares at a set price.

See also **warrant**.

sunk costs

Those costs that are permanent, like the money your company has paid for a new manufacturing plant. Sometimes it's helpful to separate sunk costs from variable costs in making a decision to continue operations. For example, even if you're not making enough money to cover all of your costs, it might be worth it to stay open if you're simply covering your variable costs (since you can't get your sunk costs back anyway).

See also **fixed costs** and **variable costs**.

superregional bank

Very large institution that conducts banking activities in a specific region of the United States.

See also **regional bank**.

supply-side economics

School of economic thought that emphasizes a connection between government policies and aggregate supply.

Supply-siders gained attention during the 1980s, when the Reagan administration promoted the notion that lower taxes would actually increase government revenues. The idea was that lower marginal tax rates would give people the incentive to work more and less incentive to find loopholes. Conversely, supply-siders argued that higher marginal tax rates would reduce incentives to work, save, and invest, thereby constraining the growth of productivity and aggregate supply.

See also **fiscal policy**, **monetarism**, **monetary policy**, and **price controls**.

surety bond

See **performance bond**.

sushi bond

See **Yankee bond**.

swaps

See **derivatives**.

syndicate

A group of investment bankers who join together to buy and resell a new issue of securities.

See also **underwriting syndicate**.

synthetic convertible

See **bond/warrant unit**.

synthetics

See **bond/warrant unit**.

systematic risk

Sensitivity of a stock's price to things like shifts in the economy, interest rates, inflation, and general investor confidence.

See also **market risk**.

T: Takeover to Tuition Reimbursement

takeover

When one company takes over controlling interest of another. A takeover can be friendly or hostile. A hostile takeover, one that is originally unsolicited by the target company, is often initiated through a public tender offer for the company's shares. A hostile takeover might eventually become a friendly one.

See also **acquisition** and **merger/acquisition (M&A)**.

tangerine

A company with the potential to be separated into juicy segments.

On Wall Street, the whole is often worth less than the sum of its parts. In recent years, a number of companies have increased their value to shareholders by breaking themselves up. Shareholders have found that two (or sometimes more) stocks representing different businesses have been worth more than the single stock was before.

See also **spin-off**.

tangible assets

Assets involving physical property, such as land, buildings, equipment, or inventory.

See also **intangible assets**.

tape

See **ticker tape**.

tax haven

A country offering low or no taxes for foreign companies and individuals.

The Cayman Islands, for example, have no income tax. One measure of the international business flowing through the Caymans is the more than 500 banks registered there—more than one for every fifty citizens. Other well-known tax havens include the Bahamas, Bermuda, the Channel Islands, Liechtenstein, Luxembourg, Panama, and the Turks and Caicos Islands.

tax lien

See **lien**.

tax lien bonds

See **lien**.

tax valuation

See **property tax assessment**.

tax-exempt bonds

Bonds whose interest is not taxed, also known as tax-exempts, tax-free bonds, or tax-frees.

In the past few years, tax-exempt institutions have been issuing tax-free bonds with increasing frequency. (The Norton Simon

Museum and the New York Public Library are two examples.) But the overwhelming majority of tax-exempt bonds are municipal bonds. This has led to a general impression that a municipal bond equals a tax-exempt bond. That's often the case, although there are exceptions for certain types of municipal bonds that are deemed not really for the public purpose.

There are two main types of tax-free bonds: general obligation bonds and revenue bonds. The former type is backed by the full faith and credit of the issuer. That means that if a state government has trouble meeting its interest payments as planned, it's supposed to dip into tax coffers to make good on the debt. Revenue bonds are tied to something more specific—such as building an airport or a water system. Once the project is completed, it's supposed to generate enough revenue to pay off the bonds.

tax-free bonds

See **tax-exempt bonds**.

T-bill

See **Treasuries**.

technical analysis

A type of investment approach that relies on computer programs and charts rather than on the fundamentals of individual companies. Investors who take this approach don't really care about factors such as earnings—instead they study the chart patterns of a security's past performance. By doing that, they hope to predict future trends, the theory being that patterns usually repeat themselves.

A type of technical analysis is trend analysis, which often looks at overall indices (such as the S&P 500) and the market's general movements. Technical investors are often called chartists, and their type of investing is called charting.

tender offer

Public offer to buy a company's shares.

Tender offers are sometimes made by a company for some of its own shares, but more often they are part of a takeover attempt. An offer for another company's shares is called friendly when it is approved by the management of the target company, and hostile when it is not. The bidder is usually referred to as the acquirer and the other company is the target. The acquiring company might offer to buy shares in the target company for a fixed price, which is virtually always above the market price.

The offer is made to all shareholders, although sometimes the bidder seeks less than 100 percent of the target company. If so, the bidder might accept a proportionate number of shares from each stockholder accepting the offer by the set date. Sometimes bidding wars develop between two or more suitors, or shareholders will hold out for a higher price. In those cases, if the bidder raises the price during the offer, the new price will be paid for all accepted shares, including those tendered earlier.

See also **acquisition, leveraged buyout (LBO), merger/acquisition (M&A),** and **takeover.**

10-K

Annual filing that publicly traded corporations make with the Securities and Exchange Commission (SEC).

Unlike the annual report, the 10-K need not be mailed to every shareholder, but it is made available on request. The SEC requires more information in the 10-K than in the annual report. In practice, companies usually put the supplementary data in the 10-K and include an index showing where other required information can be found in the annual report.

1099-MISC

There are a number of 1099 forms, ranging from 1099-C to 1099-R, but they are relatively obscure. Usually, when people refer to a 1099 they mean a 1099-MISC, called the freelancer's W2. And as the job market in America has shifted away from a full-time focus, more of us are receiving 1099-MISCs (84 million were filed in 1995, according to the IRS).

1099s and W2s

If you're new to the world of 1099s, you should be aware that it's not just a substitute for a W2—it means you have a whole different tax status. For instance, instead of paying regular Social Security tax, you have to pay self-employment tax. What's the difference? Self-employment tax costs you more, because it includes the share that would have been paid by your employer. Other tax authorities will share that opinion. So you might be subjected to local taxes you never heard of—such as New York City's Unincorporated Business Tax. Also, you will have to withhold from yourself by filing quarterly estimated taxes—form 1040-ES.

But the tax news isn't all negative. You can now deduct business expenses on your Schedule C and reduce your total tax burden. These expenses can range from gas for the car to home office costs. But make sure that you keep good records and that your expenses conform to the sometimes bewildering IRS guidelines.

If you've worked as any sort of independent contractor, the 1099-MISC forms arrive from your client(s) once a year, in January or February, showing the dollar amount you earned for commissions, stipends, royalties, and/or freelance work. Whether you get a 1099 in the mail or not, you are required to report the income, no matter how small. If you don't, and it comes to the attention of the IRS, things will get messy. Misreported 1099 income is considered one of the quickest ways to trigger an audit. So, if you're doing a few different jobs, keep track of what you're earning and don't depend on your 1099s.

Individuals who purchase your services are not required to file 1099s. For example, if you do a thousand dollars' worth of plumbing for your next-door neighbor, she doesn't have to file anything. And businesses that pay you under $600 a year have no obligation to file, either.

10-Q

Similar to the 10-K, except it's a quarterly filing rather than an annual one.

The SEC is charged with protecting investors, and these quarterly reports are an important tool for doing just that. Information contained in a 10-Q ranges from financial data to legal proceedings. And though 10-Qs are less detailed, they follow the format of the annual 10-K. But there is one important difference. Unlike 10-Ks, 10-Qs are not required to be audited (although many are reviewed by independent accountants, as the SEC recommends).

All stocks sold on nationally traded exchanges must be accompanied by at least three 10-Qs per year (the last quarter can be included in the annual 10-K). Copies are kept at the SEC and at stock exchanges. In addition, they are available on microfiche at business libraries. Recently, a large number of 10-Qs went on-line on the SEC's EDGAR database.

If you own shares in a business, you don't want to ignore its 10-Q. Companies have been known to drop bombshells in their 10-Qs. PNC Bank is a case in point. In mid-1994, it was pegged by top analysts as a growth stock. Then its third quarter 10-Q came out. In it, PNC forthrightly predicted that net interest income (its main source of profit) would drop 7 percent in the next and final quarter. With that, the financial wizards quickly deep-sixed their buy ratings. And shares fell from the $30 level to approximately $20.

term insurance

See **cash value insurance**.

testamentary trust

A trust created by a will.

The main purpose of a testamentary trust is to avoid estate and inheritance taxes. Instead of leaving money to your relatives in your will, you leave instructions to put your estate in a trust. Then the trust disposes of your assets in the manner you've intended. Since no one receives money directly from you, no one has to pay estate and inheritance taxes.

Testamentary trusts don't eliminate all costs. Your will must go through probate before the trust is created, which can be costly. Depending on the size of your estate and where the will is probated, between approximately 6 and 9 percent of an estate will be lost.

If you want to avoid both taxes and probate, you might consider a living trust. It is similar to a testamentary trust, except that no will is involved. Living trusts cost money to administer, however. So you should evaluate whether paying a lawyer to take care of your trust while you're living will cost less than paying for probate after you're gone. The basic rule of thumb is: the larger the estate, the more you save from a living trust.

thirty-day visible supply

See ***Bond Buyer, The***.

3-2-1 buydown

See **buydown**.

thrift

A virtuous form of cheapness.

Thriftiness has long been admired in America. Benjamin Franklin's best-selling pamphlet, "The Way to Wealth," has thrift as its centerpiece. But thrift has seldom been practiced. Old Ben himself had some lapses—that is, if John Adams's accounts of Franklin's escapades as ambassador to France are accurate. And small wonder, since sacrificing small pleasures to slowly accumulate wealth is easier to talk about than to do. Especially when you know that all those pinched pennies can't be spent on something frivolous. They have to go for something important, mind you, or it's not really thrift.

So Oseola McCarty, the eighty-seven-year-old washerwoman who, in 1995, donated her life savings of $150,000 to an African American scholarship fund at the University of Southern Mississippi, is thrifty. But Donald Duck's Uncle Scrooge, who uses his carefully hoarded cash to swim in, is just plain stingy.

thrifts

Savings banks and savings and loans.

The thrifts might seem like an inevitable aspect of American banking. But the thrifts industry is a relatively recent invention that might have outlived its usefulness. Before the Glass-Steagall Act of 1933 there were no such things as thrifts. That legislation created overarching regulations for what had previously been two separate types of institutions—savings and loans and savings banks.

Under Glass-Steagall, both of them were restricted to fixed rate mortgage loans as their sole form of lending. And both were allowed to offer higher interest rates on deposits than commercial banks. From there on in, savings banks and savings and loans were in the

same boat, and collectively they became known as thrifts. But Glass-
Steagall didn't create uniformity among different thrifts. Assorted
state and federal charters and insurance funds created a crazy quilt of
certification and regulation. For the most part a consumer went to a
thrift to get a little extra interest on the passbook or to make a down
payment on a mortgage. That was all there was to thrifts, and that was
all there needed to be. The thrifts industry financed the American
dream of homeownership—and made a bundle doing it.

But by the late 1970s that was no longer true. High-interest
money funds were pulling customers away from low-interest passbook accounts. And inflation made fixed rate, 30-year mortgages a
losing proposition. The thrifts industry was solvent, but profits were
drying up. A crisis seemed to be approaching.

So the thrifts sought help. It came in the form of deregulation.
In a series of changes between 1980 and 1982, down went the
deposit interest ceilings and loan restrictions. Now thrifts could make
auto and personal loans, and get into commercial real estate. What's
more, there was an incentive to take risks. The thrifts were paying top
interest rates to get deposits in a highly competitive market. They had
to take in more than they were paying out. So they needed high-
paying (risky) loans to turn a profit. Inexplicably, along with deregulation came a decrease in oversight. Accounting requirements were
loosened, and examinations were cut back; between 1980 and 1984
the rate of examinations by the FSLIC Resolution Fund per billion
dollars of assets was slashed in half.

By 1982, the year that deregulation was completed, the percentage of thrifts that were unprofitable hit 85 percent. (It had been 3
percent in 1978.) And the hemorrhaging didn't stop. Thrifts went
belly-up all throughout the 1980s. The federal government had to
step in. Its efforts to pay off depositors and resurrect, or close down,
thrifts has cost an estimated half a trillion dollars. Thrifts must now
pay more to secure deposits than commercial banks, and they have
been reregulated. According to 1989's FIRREA act, federally char-

tered thrifts were supposed to put 70 percent of their assets into housing loans and related investments.

The net effect of the bailout is that the thrifts industry is back on its feet. The number of thrifts dropped from about 3,000 in 1990 to about 2,000 in 1994, but of those left, 94 percent were profitable.

ticker tape

1 Stock transaction data, also known as tape or ticker.

2 Paper tape that runs through stock tickers.

Nowadays on Wall Street, unless there's a parade, ticker tape refers to stock market quotations—the continuous record of stock market transactions that is carried on various forms of electronic media. Why has this reference to an outdated piece of equipment endured so long? Perhaps because stock tickers and ticker tape are more than quaint artifacts. They are cornerstones of the modern securities industry.

Ticker tape allowed for timely, accurate information to be disseminated across unlimited distances. Anyone who could read a tape could participate in a market. This meant access to amounts of capital that previously would have been unimaginable. So it's not going too far to say that, without ticker tape, there would not be a Wall Street as we know it today.

ticks

The smallest increments of price change allowed by an exchange.

The sizes of ticks vary: ⅛ of a point for stocks, ¹⁄₁₆ for options, ¹⁄₃₂ for bond futures. But however small ticks might be, they are significant. Traders who operate strictly on the basis of market trends (as opposed to evaluating a company's growth potential or some other measure of its worth) keep careful track of each tick. Under the right market conditions, just a few upward or downward ticks will set these traders off on a buying (or selling) spree.

time deposits

Money invested in an Individual Retirement Account, 401k, Keogh plan, or certificate of deposit (CD), which can't be withdrawn before a specified date without paying penalties.

See also **certificate of deposit (CD)** and **withdrawal**.

time draft

See **bill of exchange**.

time to maturity

In investing, the time before a bond matures and the face value is due.

time value of money

The principle that a sum of money received today is worth more than the same sum received in the future, because of its potential earning benefit.

See also **inflation** and **present value**.

time-weighted rate of return

A measurement of investment performance. It's a way of evaluating the investment performance of, say, a pension fund that takes into account factors such as when money was contributed and when it was withdrawn.

title

A written record proving real estate ownership.

See also **title insurance**.

title insurance

Insures the policyholder against loss due to unrecorded defects in a title.

Most title defects are discovered during a title search, when the buyer's attorney examines all land records involving transfer of ownership in the past 50 years. Any errors or discrepancies, called clouds, should be eliminated before the next owner takes title to the property.

Not all title glitches are obvious from searching public records. Easily overlooked defects include forged documents, undisclosed heirs, unknown creditors, and mistakes in recording (errors such as "Boyle" indexed as "Doyle"). The attorney who searches the title is not responsible for finding and fixing such problems. That is where title insurance comes in. To cure a claim, you usually have to hire a lawyer and defend the title in court. Luckily, title insurers pay legal costs as well as other financial losses incurred by the policyholder.

title search

See **title insurance**.

top-down investing

Investment approach emphasizing trends in the general economy and stocks that will benefit from those trends.

Bottom-up investing focuses on the companies first and then looks to more general factors (such as the economy) later.

total return to shareholders

Combination of everything you gain from holding a stock—including dividends and price appreciation. So if you own a stock that rises from $50 to $60 in one year, and you receive $2.50 in dividends, your total return would be $12.50 ($10 + $2.50), or 25 percent ($12.50 ÷ $50).

Total return is often shown on a 5-year basis, assuming that all dividends were reinvested in additional shares of the stock and making no allowance for income taxes. It might also be expressed as an annualized percentage.

The Securities and Exchange Commission (SEC) requires

publicly traded corporations to include in their proxy statements a graph showing the company's total return to shareholders over 5 years and the total return for a stock index, along with a peer industry group.

total shareholder return
See **total return to shareholders**.

tranche
See **mortgage-backed security**.

transfer tax
A tax paid when certain types of property are transferred from one person to another, often as a gift, an inheritance, or through a sale.

Transfer taxes usually come into play in three situations:

1 *The selling of real estate:* In this case, transfer taxes go to a state agency to pay for the cost of recording the new deed. The tax is usually paid by the seller when the property is sold and is recorded by special tax stamps placed on the deed. Sometimes, transfer taxes are levied in cases where a business license is sold or given by one person to another.

2 *Settling of estates:* In estate settlements, estate taxes are due usually within a year of the person's death. The amount of the tax depends on the value of the estate. In 1998, the tax-free amount was $600,000.

   See also **estate tax**.

3 *Transfer of securities from one investor to another:* A federal tax is levied on the sale of all stocks and nongovernment bonds. The tax is paid by the seller and usually amounts to a few cents for each $100 of value. Some states also impose a transfer tax on stock sales.

travelers' checks

Prepaid vouchers that can be used like cash.

The key selling point of travelers' checks is safety—they're insured against loss or theft. If they disappear, the holder files a report with one of the issuer's many sales agents around the world and usually gets a replacement within 24 hours.

Consumers pay a small fee (usually about 1 percent of the total) to get the checks, which in financial parlance are known as sight drafts. The checks are usually sold in denominations of $10 to $100 and can be denominated in either U.S. dollars or the major foreign currencies. Once cashed, they are payable by the issuing company.

Remember that you'll have to sign them twice: once in the presence of the teller, when you buy the checks; and again in front of the retailer, restaurant host, or store cashier, when you cash the checks or use them to settle a bill.

Treasuries

Marketable debt securities issued by the federal government to help finance the nation's debt.

Treasuries are backed by the full faith and credit of the government—so they're considered just about the safest securities you can buy. Plus, their interest is exempt from state and local income taxes. Treasuries come in three basic forms:

	Maturities	Denominations
1. Treasury bills	Up to 1 year	At least $10,000
2. Treasury notes	1 to 10 years	$1,000 and up
3. Treasury bonds	10 years or more	$1,000 and up

Treasury bills (T-bills) are sold at a weekly auction conducted by the Federal Reserve System. Their interest rate is discounted from the price of the bill, so you get no payments until the bill expires. Then you get your principal and interest. You might pay, say, $9,750 for a 6-month, $10,000 T-bill, collecting the $10,000 value when you redeem it. Treasury notes and bonds, also sold at auction, work like conventional bonds, with interest paid semiannually.

Individuals can buy Treasuries directly from a Federal Reserve Bank without a fee. If you have a lot to buy, it might be worth it to avoid the commissions at your bank or brokerage house.

Treasury bills

See **Treasuries**.

Treasury bonds

See **Treasuries**.

Treasury notes

See **Treasuries**.

treasury stock

Issued shares that have been reacquired by a company, either through repurchase or donation. It is called treasury stock because it is held in the corporate treasury until it is resold or retired.

See also **capital stock**.

trend analysis

A type of technical analysis.

trial balance

List of all open accounts in a ledger and their balances. A trial balance can be prepared at any time, but it is one of the first things done when closing the books at year's end. It proves that debits and credits are equal.

triple witching day

The third Friday in March, June, September, and December. These are the 4 days a year on which three types of options expire simultaneously—stock options, index options, and index futures. So they can often be particularly volatile trading days.

trust

A legal arrangement in which a person or organization (the trustee) holds title to property for the benefit of others, called beneficiaries.

A typical trust might be created by parents who, upon their demise, want their assets managed by a trustee until their children become adults. This type of trust could be specified in a will, making it a testamentary trust.

If the trust is created while the parents (the donors) are living, it would be a living trust or inter vivos trust. Such a trust can generally be changed while the donors are still living, making it a revocable trust. An irrevocable trust, however, locks away assets under the trustee's control for good—except in special circumstances.

Trusts can be created for a single person, for an organization, or even for a pet. They can last for a limited time or for a lifetime.

See also **corpus** and **probate**.

trust department

Group of people within a financial institution—usually a bank—that manages trust funds. A trust department often is made up of experts who specialize in different types of investments. So it might have corporate bond experts, stock experts, and tax-free municipal bond experts, among others.

Traditionally, laws required trust departments to concentrate on preservation of capital. This limited investments to the bluest of blue chip stocks; U.S. Treasury bills, notes, and bonds; and top-grade corporate bonds. However, the effects of inflation and taxes tend to eat away at very conservatively managed portfolios. Because of this, and a need for greater flexibility in how trust money is managed and spent, many states have moved toward more liberal policies governing trust departments. Even the riskiest of investments, such as derivatives, might find their way into some trust portfolios.

trust protector

See **trustee**.

trustee

The person or organization that holds title to property for the benefit of another person.

A trustee can be anyone from your Uncle Ned to a CPA to a bank (which manages trusts through its trust department). You can also choose more than one trustee. For example, Uncle Ned might be a stand-up guy, but he might not know much about investments. In such a case, you might want to make Uncle Ned and First National Bank co-trustees. Ned will make decisions about when to pay money to the beneficiary of the trust, while First National will invest the trust's assets.

Truth in Securities Act

Federal law that requires lenders to clearly spell out the true cost of a loan or credit card.

A key requirement of the act is that lenders' contracts or advertisements disclose the interest rates being charged in terms of the annual percentage rate (APR). That's a more accurate measure of the interest charges than the straight interest rate. The APR makes it easier to compare loan rates when shopping around for a mortgage or credit card. The act also gives you the option of breaking a contract (within 3 business days) that involves pledging your home as security.

When buying a house, be sure to take out the garbage, those last-minute fees tacked onto a mortgage transaction that many experts argue should be disclosed by the lender up front but sometimes aren't. They go by many names:

- underwriting fees
- loan disbursement charges
- tax service fees
- amortization schedule charges
- truth-in-lending disclosure preparation fees
- processing fees
- loan assignment fees
- flood plain determination fees
- document transportation
- courier fees

If you're ambushed by these fees at the last minute, have your attorney challenge them.

See also **securities laws**.

tuition reimbursement

Employees' college costs paid for by an employer—typically for courses directly related to the job.

In today's job-switching market, it's important that skills be kept on a cutting edge. For this reason, it's hard to find a reason not to take advantage of tuition reimbursement. Education makes you more valuable to your employer and will make you more marketable should you lose your job, or just want a new position.

U, V, W: Uncovered Sale to World Wide Web

U

uncovered sale
See **naked sale**.

underfunded
See **unfunded**.

underwriter
See **underwriting**.

underwriting
1 In finance, an agreement by investment bankers to buy a new issue of securities at a fixed price and then to sell to the public in an offering.

See also **best effort, secondary offering**, and **underwriting syndicate**.
2 In insurance, underwriting refers to the assumption of risk in exchange for the premium.

underwriting syndicate

A group of investment bankers who join to purchase an issue of securities from a corporation or government entity for resale to the public.

These syndicates are formed to spread the risk in larger offerings. One investment banker will act as lead underwriter or syndicate manager, finding other firms to take parts of the offering. The lead underwriter is also called the book runner, because he keeps the book on the securities sold. In the biggest offerings, the lead underwriter might seek a second lead underwriter to help form the syndicate.

See also **underwriting**.

unemployment rate

The percentage of the labor force that is out of work.

In the United States, the size of the labor force and the unemployment rate are measured by the Labor Department's Bureau of Labor Statistics based on data from a household survey. A sample of households is asked:

- whether household members age sixteen or older were employed for the previous 4 weeks
- whether they left employment voluntarily or involuntarily during the previous 4 weeks
- whether they actively sought employment during that period

The survey results are projected nationally. The labor force is the total of all three groups—those employed, those recently unemployed, and those looking for work. In the 1990s, the labor force has comprised about 66 percent of the total population of those age sixteen and older. The unemployment rate is the percentage of the labor force that falls into the latter two categories in the list above—those who have recently lost jobs and those who are seeking jobs.

Rising unemployment is one of the most important signs of an underperforming economy. It's considered to be a lagging economic indicator—that is, after a recession starts, it might take a couple of months before the unemployment rate rises. More important, as the economy begins recovering from the recession the unemployment rate might actually rise for a few months as reentrants and new entrants join the labor force, believing that jobs are opening up.

See also **employment**.

unfunded

Lack of money set aside to pay a future obligation.

If no money has been set aside, the obligation is unfunded. If there is a reserve, but its balance is not enough to cover the future costs, it is underfunded. These terms are often applied to pension plans.

Uniform Securities Act

See **blue sky laws**.

universal life insurance

A type of whole life insurance that unbundles the insurance, the investment, and the expense factors of your policy and allows you to alter them to meet your changing needs.

In the early 1980s, when low returns on the investment portion of policies began to tarnish the luster whole life had enjoyed for decades, insurance companies came up with universal life, which promised greater returns on the surplus portion of the premium. Ted Bernstein, president of Assured Enterprises, an insurance consulting firm in Chicago, puts it like this: "Whole life insurance can only be whole life insurance. Term insurance can only be term insurance. Variable life insurance can only be variable life insurance. Universal life insurance can be all of those." This, he qualifies, assumes no conversion.

Universal, he says, can be turned into any one of those three forms of insurance (if the company offering universal life also offers variable life). With whole life, you have fixed premiums and fixed death benefits; you can't adjust your premium up or down. The insurance company has all the control and the consumer has none. If you like this philosophy, take a universal life chassis and design it as a whole life policy. In other words, Bernstein says, you can't predict your life needs 4 years or 20 years down the road. So with universal, you've retained the flexibility to change your policy design.

See also **term insurance**, **variable life insurance**, **variable universal life insurance**, and **whole life insurance**.

universal life II
See **variable universal life insurance**.

unqualified opinion
A report by an accountant that says a company's financial statements fairly present its position and operations in conformity with generally accepted accounting principles (GAAP).

See also **audit** and **qualified opinion**.

unsecured debt
See **Chapter 13** and **secured debt**.

uptick
A term referring to the direction of a trade versus the trade just before it. For example, if a trade occurs at $35, and the trade just before that was at $33, then the security has traded on an uptick. (Conversely, a downtick means that the last trade price was lower than the previous trade price.)

See also **closing tick**.

V

value investing

A form of investing involving careful study of the fundamentals of individual stocks. It's similar to bottom-up investing and the opposite of top-down investing (or technical analysis).

As a value investor, you spend a lot of time poring over the financial documents of the companies you're interested in, such as the balance sheet, the income statement, and the cash flow statement.

Value Line Investment Survey

Investment advisory service that tracks the financial and stock market performance of 1,700 large companies.

Value Line ranks stocks for their safety as an investment and their timeliness as a purchase. Using complicated computer models, Value Line projects the expected price performance of the issues over the projected 12 months and ranks them.

value stock

A stock considered to be a good value because of its fundamentals— its financial stability, core business, and management team.

Value stocks are often contrasted with growth stocks, which are primarily judged on their future growth potential rather than on their current business qualities.

value-added tax (VAT)

A form of national sales tax common outside the United States.

The VAT is added to the price each time a product changes hands during its manufacture and delivery to the customer, who picks up the final tab. The VAT is common in European countries and most other developed nations of the world. It differs from the sales tax collected in most U.S. states, whose taxes are levied at the retail level on the entire price. Although a VAT might seem much more complicated to administer, one advantage is that there are more checks and balances against cheating, because the tax is collected in stages throughout the process.

See also **consumption tax**.

Value-Added Tax

Here's how VAT usually works: Daisy Clothing Company makes dresses. The value Daisy adds to the product is the difference between its cost for materials and the price it charges its customer, Trend Wholesale. The VAT is a percentage of that added value, and Daisy folds the tax into its prices. Daisy also gets a rebate from the government for the VAT it paid as part of the price for its materials. Trend Wholesale will collect the tax on the value Trend adds and will get a rebate for the VAT included in the price it paid. So Trend, Daisy, and the mill that supplied the materials all act as tax collectors. In turn, so does the retail store selling the dress. At the end of the process, the retail price includes all the VATs collected along the way. A provider of a service—an accountant, for example—might collect a VAT on his or her entire fee.

---

variable annuity

See **annuity**.

variable costs

Those costs that tend to fluctuate in direct proportion to the level of business activity.

Supplies, parts, and the wages of hourly employees are all

variable costs. Although these change from month to month depending on the business volume, per-unit variable costs stay about the
same.

See also **economies of scale**, **fixed costs**, and **sunk costs**.

variable life insurance

Type of whole life insurance with several investment options you can
choose from, and whose death benefit and cash value depend on how
your investment performs.

If it's control over your investments you're after, look to a variable policy. As with regular whole life, annual premiums are level.
There is a cash value, and policyholders can receive low-rate loans.
But instead of the fixed rate of return from a plain vanilla whole life
policy, variable policies let you choose from a menu of investment
options such as a portfolio of stocks, bonds, money markets, and
other blends.

The insurance company does not guarantee the return on your
investment or the amount of the death benefit, as it does with regular
whole life. Variable policies, which account for perhaps fewer than 10
percent of total policies, nevertheless are becoming more popular
with younger buyers, who feel more comfortable making their own
investment decisions.

See also **universal life insurance**, **variable universal life
insurance**, and **whole life insurance**.

variable rate mortgage

See **adjustable rate mortgage (ARM)**.

variable universal life insurance

A type of whole life insurance that combines the control of choosing
your investments (variable life insurance) with the flexibility of struc-
turing the type of policy you need to meet your changing needs (universal life insurance). Also known as flexible premium variable life

insurance or universal life II. This policy must be registered with the Securities and Exchange Commission (SEC) and can be sold only by agents who've passed their National Association of Securities Dealers (NASD) exam.

See also **term insurance**.

VAT

See **value-added tax (VAT)**.

venture capital

Funding for start-up companies and private research and development (R&D) projects. Also known as risk capital.

A number of private investors, investment companies, and limited partnerships provide venture capital. Because of the risks involved with start-up companies—whose failure rate estimates are as high as 80 percent—venture capitalists look for high rates of return, usually between 25 and 40 percent. But start-ups seldom generate enough cash flow to pay those returns, so the investors get shares in the new company as part of their return. They hope to get their profits by selling the shares when the company goes public.

vertical integration

The extent to which a company controls all the steps of a business. This means everything from product design to procuring parts and supplies, to manufacturing, to finalizing a deal with the end user.

Vertical integration is described as downstream when it moves from manufacturing along the distribution channel toward the consumer. It is upstream when it moves toward control over the sources of supply, which can also be called backward vertical integration.

vested/vesting

Term for an employee who has passed the cutoff point in order to be eligible for pension plan benefits. For example, you might be vested— eligible for your company's matching contributions to your pension plan—once you've worked there for 10 years. There are often different degrees of being vested—you might be 50 percent vested after 5 years, and 100 percent vested after 10 years.

vice president of investments

See **registered representative**.

vulture fund

A term for an investment fund that invests in securities that have seriously declined in value.

wage earner plan

See **Chapter 13**.

warrant

A security that gives a person the right to buy shares in a company at a set price in the future. Also called a subscription warrant.

Warrants are usually attached to another security, such as a bond or preferred stock. Used in that way, warrants are a type of equity kicker that makes the security more attractive. For the investor, a warrant works like a call option, except that warrants usually have longer terms (and occasionally have a perpetual life).

See also **equity kicker**, **right**, and **stock option**.

wash sale

A term for a simultaneous transaction that cancels itself out. Many investors use wash sales for tax reasons—perhaps selling a stock for a loss (to claim on taxes) and then buying it again soon after. (The IRS has very specific rules to prevent direct wash sales.)

Wheeler-Lea Act of 1938

See **antitrust law**.

white knight

A savior in a hostile tender offer.

Two things might cause you to search for a white knight if you're targeted for takeover. One is a lowball price for your company, and the other is a company you simply don't like.

If the price is right, and your company's management thinks the new boss will be okay to work for, it isn't a hostile tender offer. Your company will agree to recommend the deal to the shareholders. But when the suitor and its offer aren't to your company's liking, the real question becomes: What are the odds of success? If your company stands a good chance of being bought, it might as well be by a company you're comfortable with and at a price you like. That's where the white knight comes in.

whole life insurance

Life insurance with a savings component that lasts for the lifetime of the insured.

Also called cash value, ordinary life, permanent life, or straight life, whole life is insurance for the long run. You pay a level premium each year, build up savings, and receive a guaranteed death benefit. Unless you plan on keeping a whole life policy for at least 15 to 20 years, it's generally wiser to buy term insurance. Whole life is more expensive than term because you pay extra money to build up a surplus (cash value), which you can borrow from in later years or use to pay the insurance component of your policy.

Traditional whole life products include continuous premium, graded premium, joint, limited payment, modified premium, and single premium. Nontraditional whole life products include adjustable life, current assumption whole life, indeterminate premium life, universal life, variable life, and variable universal life. All these whole life products are considered cash value insurance, as opposed to term insurance, which almost never has a cash value, is issued for a set number of years, and runs up to a specific age. The premium you pay for term insurance rises each year, so it eventually becomes prohibitive.

Whole life earnings are tax-deferred (the policyholder doesn't pay taxes on the cash value until he or she is older, presumably retired, and in a lower tax bracket). When the policy is held until the death of the insured, no taxes are paid on the earnings. If you're young, or you're on a tight budget, term insurance will provide more coverage for less money.

Agents frequently will try to steer you toward whole life, using rosy illustrations of how much you'll earn and how soon you'll be able to stop paying your premiums and let the savings pay for your insurance. One reason they do this is the higher commission they receive on whole life: as much as 50 to 90 percent of your first year's premium beyond the cost of insurance. Several major insurers were investigated in 1994 and 1995 following complaints that their agents misrepresented projected earnings. Investigators also looked into the practice of churning, or selling new policies to boost commissions when an existing policy was as good as or better than the new one. If you already have a cash value policy, think twice before cashing it in for a new one.

widows and orphans

In investing, a term for those investors who are thought to be extremely conservative.

Investments with secure dividends and solid track records are sometimes referred to as widows and orphans investments.

will

A legal document that lays out in detail how you want your estate distributed after you die. A will must be properly witnessed and notarized to be valid.

When you make out a will you're acknowledging, in writing, the fact that you're going to die one day. It's not something people do with great relish. But the more stuff you accumulate in life, the older you get, and the more people rely on you, the more important it is to have a will. An estimated seven out of ten people die without a proper will. If you are one of them, your survivors will watch the state carve up your estate in ways that have nothing to do with your wishes.

A well-planned will can minimize estate taxes (up to 55 percent), as well as other expenses, thus maximizing what your heirs receive. It's important to run your will by a lawyer, whose job is to imagine the worst things that can go wrong and fix them in advance. You want your will to be bedrock solid. Failure to meet legal requirements may be the same as having no will at all.

When choosing an executor, look for someone younger than you and your spouse. Such a person is more likely to be around after you die, to implement your wishes. Consider choosing co-executors. One can be a trusted friend and the other an expert in legal and financial matters. Consider hiring an organization, such as a bank or law firm, as an executor. These entities not only have expert knowledge, they are likely to be around in corporate form long after you're gone.

Review your will every couple of years—and especially if there is a major change in your circumstances. Important events such as births, deaths, marriages, divorces, and illnesses could be reason enough for a review. A move should always prompt your attention: if you move to a different state, the laws will be different. You'll need to have a local attorney review your will.

Wilshire 5000 Equity Index

Widely followed measure of price movements of approximately 6,500 stocks listed on the New York Stock Exchange (NYSE), the American Stock Exchange (AMEX), and the over-the-counter (OTC) market.

Created in 1974, the Wilshire 5000 uses capitalization-weighted returns to gauge the performance of U.S.-based equity securities. Changes are measured against its base value as of December 31, 1980. Its capitalization is about 81 percent NYSE, 2 percent AMEX, and 17 percent OTC.

withdrawal

Removal of money from a bank account, investment, or retirement fund.

"Substantial penalties for early withdrawal"—you've heard that one before. When you put your money into an IRA, 401k or Keogh plan, or certificate of deposit (CD) or other form of time deposit, you can't withdraw it before a specified date without paying penalties and sacrificing interest. Demand deposits, on the other hand, are just what they say: you put your money in and you can get it back whenever you want, without prior notice, in cash or check form, and without any penalties or loss of interest. Checking account deposits are demand deposits. Funds in NOW (negotiable order of withdrawal) accounts are also available on demand. Passbook savings accounts require 30 to 60 days' advance notice. CDs are time deposits that pay a higher rate of interest than passbook accounts because you're required to leave the money in the account for a longer time. Some banks will let you withdraw the interest without incurring a penalty, but you cannot dip into the principal without paying a price.

withholding

Money earned that an employer deducts from an employee's paycheck.

Some withholding is mandatory: federal, state, and city taxes; Social Security; and FICA/Medicare. Your employer forwards this money directly to the taxing or collecting agency. Other withholding is voluntary: pension plans; 401k plans; health, life, or disability insurance premiums; and other employee benefits offered through your company. Your employer directs this money according to your instructions.

Your goal as a wage earner is to set up your withholding allowances to match your predicted tax bill as closely as possible. Savvy taxpayers shake their heads each spring when their friends celebrate a $2,000 refund as if they'd just won the lottery. In fact, they're just receiving back an interest-free loan they've made to the government during the previous year, money that could have been working for them. (And not a word of thanks from Uncle Sam!) Some taxpayers, who know they have trouble saving money, willingly allow extra withholding each paycheck as a type of forced savings plan.

If you claim too many allowances, you might be liable not only for a large tax payment on April 15 but also for penalties and interest if you fall below 90 percent of your tax liability or 100 percent of the previous year's tax bill (110 percent for an adjusted gross income [AGI] above $150,000). A quick check on your status in June and September will allow you to increase or decrease your withholding.

An estimated 70 percent of the 100 million U.S. tax filers overpaid their taxes in 1994, averaging about $1,000 each.

See also **allowance**.

working capital

Current assets minus current liabilities. Also called net current assets or net working capital.

Working capital is used by lenders and analysts as a measure of a company's ability to operate its business and pay its bills. Loan agreements often mandate that the company keep a certain level of working capital. But the number is significant only in relation to other variables, such as the company's sales and industry standards.

Sources of working capital in a typical business arise from:

- an increase in long-term borrowing
- a sale of stock
- a sale of fixed assets
- net income from operations

Uses of working capital include:

- repayment of debt
- buyback of treasury stock
- purchase of fixed assets

World Wide Web (WWW)

Screens of data offered by businesses, colleges, financial institutions, libraries, museums, political entities, and so on, available on the Internet.

X, Y, Z: X-Dividend to Zero-Coupon Bonds

X

X-dividend

See **ex-dividend**.

Y

Yankee bond

A bond issued in U.S. dollars in the United States by a foreign company. Yankee bonds are typically issued when market conditions are better in the United States than in the Eurobond market or in the issuer's home market.

Similar bonds:

- A bulldog bond is issued in London by a non-U.K. company.
- A samurai bond is issued in yen by a non-Japanese borrower (for sale mainly in Japan).
- A shogun bond is issued in Japan by a foreign company (but denominated in a currency other than yen).
- A sushi bond is a Japanese company's Eurobond.

yield

Actual, as opposed to nominal, rate of return on an investment.
See also **internal rate of return (IRR)** and **bond yield**.

yield curve

For bonds, a graph showing the relationship between yield and time to maturity.

Bond investors use yield curves to help them determine trends and plan their buying and selling strategies. A normal yield curve is considered to be upwardly sloping, since short-term rates are typically lower than long-term rates (a 30-year bond will have a higher interest rate than a 10-year bond).

In rare circumstances, when long-term rates fall below short-term rates, the yield curve is inverted, sloping downward as it moves out in time. An inverted curve is thought to suggest an unstable economy.

A flat yield curve occurs when short- and long-term rates are approximately the same. That's generally considered to be a neutral economic sign.

yield spread

The difference between the yield on a U.S. Treasury bond and the yield on a municipality or corporate bond, often expressed in basis points. For example, if the yield on a treasury bond is 7.2 percent and the yield on a corporate bond is 8 percent, the yield spread between the two would be 0.8 percent, or 80 basis points.

See also **long bond**.

yield to average life (YTAL)

See **yield to maturity (YTM)**.

yield to call

See **yield to maturity (YTM)**.

yield to maturity (YTM)

The annual return on a bond that takes into account its current price, par value, coupon interest rate, and time to maturity. YTM can be approximated with a bond yield table, but since calculating a bond's yield to maturity is complex and involves trial and error, it is usually done using a calculator equipped for bond calculations.

Essentially, the yield to maturity is the discount rate in a present value calculation, where the present value is the bond's current price. The future cash flows are both the bond's interest payments and its value at maturity.

See also **bond yield**.

yield-curve swap

See **derivatives**.

YTAL

See **yield to average life (YTAL)**.

YTM

See **yield to maturity (YTM)**.

Z

zero-based budgeting (ZBB)

A method of setting budgets for corporations and government agencies that requires justification of all expenditures, not only those that exceed the prior year's allocations.

Thus all budget lines are said to begin at a zero base and are funded according to merit. Many investors use zeroes for very specific investment goals—such as a specific amount of money needed for college tuition in 10 years.

The IRS thinks of your interest payments as more real than implied. They expect you to pay interest on your phantom interest, even though you won't receive it until the bond matures. That's why zeroes are often placed into IRAs or other tax-sheltered instruments.

zero-coupon bonds

Bonds that pay no interest until maturity—also known as zeroes.

Zero-coupon bonds are sold at deep discounts to face value—even though investors receive the full face value when the bond matures. For example, you might buy a zero-coupon bond for $450 that matures in 10 years, when you'll receive the full $1,000 face value. In this manner, the interest is implied.

Zeroes might be sold by a company, or a brokerage house might create them by separating out the interest stream and selling it as another security. Zero-coupon bonds can be particularly attractive to investors who believe that interest rates will decline, since the absence of interest payments takes away the reinvestment risk inherent in other bonds.

The Trillion Dollar Budget

THE
TRILLION
DOLLAR
BUDGET

How to Stop the
Bankrupting of America

GLENN PASCALL

With a chapter on "The Fiscal Collision"
by **DAYNA HUTCHINGS**

UNIVERSITY OF WASHINGTON PRESS
Seattle and London

In memory of Noble D. Stutzman, 1890–1983

Library of Congress Cataloging in Publication Data

Pascall, Glenn R.
  The trillion dollar budget.

  Bibliography: p.
  Includes index.
  1. Budget—United States.   2. Budget deficits—United
States.   I. Title.
HJ2051.P36   1985   336.73   84-40665
ISBN 0-295-96217-8
ISBN 0-295-96237-2 (pbk.)

Contents

Foreword

1985 MAY BE the most important year in the fiscal history of the federal government. Congress for the first time will debate a trillion dollar budget. We will do so against a background of growth in the national debt from $900 billion in 1980 to twice that amount in 1985.

There are many causes for the surge in annual deficits which have produced this doubling. Revenues were reduced by tax rate relief in 1981 and by the recession of 1981–82. Spending was increased by the defense buildup and by continued growth in domestic programs such as Social Security and Medicare.

In combination, the major budgetary events of this decade have created a serious imbalance which is expressed by the deficit. Much has been made of the debate between supply side and traditional economists. But both sides in this debate agree that the deficit must be brought down dramatically by the end of the decade or interest costs will consume an unacceptable share of our fiscal resources.

Congress will be the focus of the search for budget solutions in 1985. Congress has often been criticized for "pork barrel" bills which fund projects and provide the benefits of federal spending to communities across the country. This problem persists because each project, when viewed in isolation, seems to offer more benefit to its recipients than the share of taxes they must pay to fund it.

Equally serious has been the problem of a polarizing between those who want to reduce spending by trimming defense and those who concentrate on cuts in "entitlement" programs. Too often, members of Congress calling for stricter cost-benefit standards and tighter management of our military buildup have had to face the accusation that they are "soft on defense." By the same token, those who have sought prudent controls over future pension and health care costs have been branded as lacking in compassion.

Each political party has scored certain gains from this exchange of charge and counter-charge. But in 1985 we must lay aside these weapons of partisan warfare and join in a common effort to reduce the deficit.

Only a broad-based and even-handed approach can succeed. Every area of the budget must be looked at with the same fair and level vision. Sacrifices must not fall on those unable to bear them. But for most of us, there is room to moderate our demands on the federal budget. And there is reason to do so. We must unmortgage the economic future both for ourselves and for our children.

A broad-based approach to deficit control is essential because it is a fair-share approach which singles out no one to bear a disproportionate burden from the actions we must take. And by including all areas of the budget as a source of savings, we will maximize the opportunity for savings which are based on moderate changes. By contrast, if the focus of cuts is narrow, the risk increases that actions of doubtful merit might be taken.

There is also a place for changes to make the tax system more fair—and to increase revenues. But this step should be taken only after Congress has proven its good faith on spending control. If we can beat the deficit down to a lower level, then taxes can play an appropriate role in finishing off the deficit threat.

Like the approach we must take, this book plays no favorites. It is neither apologist nor hostile in examining programs. Again and again, it asks two questions: Is the program working? Can money be saved in ways which are fair and practical?

This book tackles the issue squarely. It does not pretend we can balance the budget by eliminating unnamed examples of "waste." Instead it turns to the biggest areas of spending and searches for ways to get the job done with less money.

Neither of us could personally verify every finding or endorse every recommendation in these pages. But the key to effective action on the deficit is to hammer together a package which reflects *everyone's* priority concerns. This means including many ideas which would not be on the priority list of *each* member of Congress. It is the combination, the balance, the overall benefit versus the overall cost, that is crucial. This book offers a "road map" to those who feel we must act.

The Trillion Dollar Budget is not dry or technical. It is a colorful story of the politics of our time. Large problems and bold new directions have created dramatic debates and disagreements over policies. Each of us has been part of those debates—and not always on the same side. But we agree that this book helps tell a story which needs to be told and helps prepare Americans as citizens, taxpayers, and users of public services to understand the challenge with which Congress must grapple in 1985.

SENATOR SLADE GORTON   CONGRESSMAN MIKE LOWRY
Senate Budget Committee   House Budget Committee

Preface

IN 1980 a three-person team from the Washington State Research Council spent nine months interviewing budget experts in Washington, D.C. and writing up their ideas for reducing federal spending. On January 9, 1981 Congressman Barber Conable hosted a Capitol press conference which released the report. It contained ninety-eight "expenditure control opportunities" worth over $100 billion in annual savings.

The report was given to Budget Director Stockman, and was later said to have provided a basis for as much as $35 billion of the $50 billion in spending cuts proposed by the President and enacted by Congress in 1981.

This was certainly a source of satisfaction to the research team, on which I served as project director. But amidst the rare experience of being involved with a study that had major impact, there was also a disappointment. The report called for an equal balance of savings in the three major areas of spending: defense, transfer payments, and the domestic budget. None of the $50 billion in cuts for 1981 came from defense, even though the proposed savings were consistent with a military buildup. None of the cuts came from nonmeans-tested entitlements, such as Social Security, Medicare, and military and civil service retirement, even though these are the most expensive transfer payments. Instead, all reductions were in the federal domestic budget and in means-tested entitlements—transfer payments to the poor.

Politics is the art of the possible, and the cuts made in 1981 were far larger than prior experience would suggest was possible. Perhaps the biggest factor in the success of that package was its very size. So many interests were affected that no single interest could collar members of Congress and claim it was being singled out for sacrifice.

Thus the 1981 package is a paradox. It excluded many areas of spending that, to serve the causes of fairness and fiscal control, should have been included. Yet it was broad enough to reach "critical mass"—that political dimension that gives a proposal the appearance of serving a broad public need rather than being either an attack on or a favor to a select few.

Four years have passed. The areas of spending that were untouched in 1981 continue to grow rapidly. The areas that were pruned back in 1981 continue to be restrained. But the increase in the former has far outstripped the decrease in the latter. Federal spending as a share of the national economy continues to climb.

In June 1983 I was asked by Senator Slade Gorton to update the 1980 study. As in the previous effort, there is no shortage of savings opportunities. In many areas the quality of spending, the return per tax dollar, is disappointing. And concern over the quantity of spending, the economic threat posed by the combination of taxes and deficits needed to fund the budget, is far greater today than it was four years ago.

Concerns about both the quality and quantity of spending create a political basis for action to restrain budget growth. But in one regard things have gotten worse since 1980–81. Then, many spending control options were new. Now, most of them have been badly chewed upon. It is like comparing the Western Front in 1914 with what it became by 1916. Open ground, with room for maneuver, has taken direct hits. In this no man's land, troops are hunkered down in their foxholes.

That does not mean the issues cannot be addressed. But a different approach is required. In 1981, a laundry list could do the job: here are the programs; here's what's wrong with them; here are the cuts. The case could be presented compactly. Our 1980 report averaged only about a page of typeset copy for each $1 billion in savings.

Today, to make a credible case for reductions, one must get into the heart of each major program and deal with the forces driving costs. Horror stories can no longer serve as the basis of reform plans; at best, they can illustrate symptoms. Only in a few areas, notably subsidy programs, can important savings opportunities be put forth in the old, straightforward way.

In defense, vast savings are possible and urgently need to be made. In Medicare and Social Security, huge future costs can and must be avoided. To make the correct course of action persuasive, one must offer a precise statement on the source of spending pressures and on paths to reform that protect basic values such as national security and retirement security. Piecemeal "hit lists" that fail to provide this context will fail to have impact.

The experience of research and writing for this study has been a fresh challenge. After the 1980 report, I worked for three years on state and local fiscal issues in Washington State. To return after this lapse of time to the federal budget was in one sense ideal. The earlier study had given me a basic knowledge of major programs but I had forgotten the details and had not kept current on the issues. To immerse myself in the facts and debates of 1984 was to feel the impact that time and change had worked on once-familiar topics. I hope the reader will find in these pages a perspective which reflects that experience.

When one first looks into today's fiscal problems, it is easy to react in irritation. How could these huge deficits develop? Why is the budget so big and so far out of whack? Why hasn't all the talent in Washington straightened out the mess?

But as one gets into the issues, there is an overwhelming mass of detail, an enormous range of choices, a wide range of legitimate interests. So *that's* why they haven't solved the problem, says the maturing analyst.

If that were the end of the matter, there might be little to hope for. But a third realization dawns. It is that those who know the most about each issue tend to agree the most on what needs to be done. There is a small army of dedicated, capable, and knowledgeable people in Washington who have struggled to understand the big issues. Among them they have developed something like a coherent program for action.

Why, then, don't we see more movement toward solutions? One of the best answers I've heard comes from James Lynn who was budget director for President Ford. Lynn says there are two crucial shortcomings in government. First, elected officials do not make the use they could of their own policy experts. There is a lot of talent that never gets properly tapped. Second, the public doesn't get explanations of problems which are in terms that relate to the things that would have to be done to solve them. There is a complete imbalance between sensational and technical aspects; the first gets too much coverage, the second too little. As a result, the public lacks the facts about how to make real reforms.

Why don't politicians make better use of their idea people to help them "tell it like it is" to the electorate?

Thomas Jefferson once remarked, "Private life holds no terrors for me." One suspects his sentiment is not shared by many elected officials. Their aversion toward losing elections leads them to a dim view of the public's ability to maturely accept unpleasant truths and to reward an official's responsible action in casting tough votes. In short, zero tolerance for the prospect of defeat leads to zero risk in riling up the folks out there.

Against this general climate of caution, those numerous acts of political courage which occur are even more notable. The risk involved is double: first to oneself, for the act; second to the good idea which may not get the support it deserves from the cautious.

Part of the fault lies with "we the people." Too seldom do we speak to our representatives as individual citizens and taxpayers. Too often do we implore them through pressure groups. It is not surprising politicians can come to believe the nation is a collection of lobbies.

The agendas of each interest group are frequently focused to a white heat on specific items of spending. The budget is sometimes said to be a sum total of what "the people" want. But it is more nearly a sum total of what the pressure groups demand. Each group cares everything for its own agenda and nothing for the combined cost of all agendas. The result is a budget whose total cost startles us, and whose imbalance between what is being spent and what we are willing to pay is dismaying.

The public and those we elect are two of the forces at work on the budget. But there is a third force, whose importance rises to the point of dominance in programs so technical that only the experts are said to understand them. This is the force of those hired to deliver the program, whether as part of the bureaucracy or through government contracts. In huge areas such as defense and health care, service professionals call the shots to a much greater degree than we often realize.

This book tells the story of an emerging collision between our spending commitments and our economic future. It raises questions about the quality of spending—what we are getting for our money. It looks at the impact of the quantity of spending—what big deficits and a trillion dollar budget can do to our vitality.

The quality of spending is often disappointing and at its worst is scandalous. The quantity of spending is damaging and at its worst could be disastrous.

That is the problem. The solution is a new American social contract. It calls for moderating our demands so we will not mortgage the future. It calls for sharing sacrifice so the budget is balanced on everybody's back, and thus nobody is unfairly singled out. It calls for a recognition that we can't beat the system because we are the system. If we try to break the bank, we will be bankrupting ourselves.

There are those who say that all democracies must sink under the weight of over-promise and under-performance, of choosing to do everything until they are finally unable to do anything. We can prove them wrong, we can give the lie to this notion through our own capacity for moderation and self-restraint.

The new social contract may be our last chance to avoid the stresses and distortions imposed by a mechanical rule such as the balanced budget amendment, which would be an admission in the Constitution that the form of government designed by the Constitution no longer worked on budgetary matters.

More important, the new social contract may be vital if we are to avoid a train of economic events resulting from the explosion in the national debt and in annual interest payments on the debt. These events could carry us beyond the turning point—not in the sense that one can predict certain pieces of bad news on specific days, but that we are ever more burdened with liabilities that will narrow economic choices and diminish economic prospects for future generations.

If as Americans we believe an essential part of our dream is a capacity to shape events and an essential part of our responsibility is to leave the future in better shape than we found it, the challenge of budget and deficit control can be met and cannot be avoided.

Acknowledgments

PUBLIC POLICY IN A DEMOCRACY is developed through the exchange of many viewpoints, interests, and concerns. Major policy issues cannot be understood or analyzed in a vacuum. The author is grateful to those named below who shared their knowledge and perspectives. Many are both political practitioners and technical specialists. Their contribution to the text comes not only from comments quoted directly but from leads on topics that deserved research in secondary sources. My thanks to all these individuals for the insights they offered.

First, to the Washington State congressional delegation, with whom it was my pleasure to work in one degree or another. Particular recognition is due to Senator Slade Gorton and to Congressmen Mike Lowry, Joel Pritchard, and Norm Dicks. Among the staff my special appreciation to John Wills and Dan Goldfarb of Senator Gorton's office; to Don Wolgamott of Congressman Lowry's office; and to Paul Roberts and Terry Freese of Congressman Dicks's office.

Among that marvelous pool of talent that serves the nation through private research institutes and through the policy arms of government, my thanks to the following persons:

Tom Bell, William Bell, Irving Leveson, and Merit Janow of the Hudson Institute; Charles Bingman of the National Academy for Public Administration; J. P. Bolduc of the Grace Commission; Michael Burns of Business Executives for National Security; Robert Carlson, Special Assistant to the President; Bruce Chapman of the White House Office of Planning and Evaluation; Pat Choate of TRW Systems, Inc.; Carol Cox and Susan Irving of the Committee for a Responsible Federal Budget; Bowman Cutter of Coopers and Lybrand; Bruce Davy of the House Ways and Means Committee staff; Paul Feldman and F. J. "Bing" West of the Center for Naval Analysis; Steve Hoffman and Ted Van Der Meid of the House Wednesday Group; James Lynn of the Aetna Corporation; James McIntyre of Hansell and Post; Don Moran, Dale MacComber, and Peter Modlin of the Office of Management and Budget; William Niskanen of the Council of Economic Advisors; Van Ooms of the House Budget Committee; Rudolph Penner, Robert Hale, and Nancy Gordon of the Congressional Budget Office; Roger Porter of the White House Office of Policy Development; Dina Rasor, Paul Hoven, and Joseph Burniece of the Project on Military Procurement; Alice Rivlin of the Brookings Institution; John Shannon and Mark Menchik of the Advisory Commission on Intergovernmental Relations; Franklin "Chuck" Spinney and Rebecca Paulk of the Department of Defense; defense consultant Pierre Sprey; Jacob Stockfish of the American

Petroleum Institute; Ronald Utt of the U.S. Chamber of Commerce; and Charls Walker of Charls Walker and Associates.

The author also received valuable guidance and encouragement from a distinguished advisory committee at the University of Virginia. Its members were: Dennis Barnes of the Office of Intergovernmental Relations; James Dunstan of the Darden School of Business; Frederick Mosher of the Miller Center for Public Affairs; James "Dolph" Norton of the Institute of Government; and Neil Snyder of the McIntire School of Commerce.

My gratitude to that group of Seattle and Tacoma firms and foundations without whose faith and financial support this book would not have come to be. Thanks to the Boeing Company, Burlington-Northern Foundation, Cheney Foundation, Medina Foundation, Pacific Northwest Bell, Rainier Bancorporation, Safeco Insurance, and the Weyerhaeuser Company Foundation, for paying the expenses of research and writing, and to Dorothy and Hunter Simpson and the Bullitt Foundation for the funding that made possible the publication of the book by the University of Washington Press.

At the University Press, my appreciation for the extraordinary efforts of director Donald Ellegood, editors Julidta Tarver and Leila Charbonneau, and production manager Veronica Seyd, to publish the text on a schedule far tighter than they wished. And my special thanks to Dean Hubert Locke of the Graduate School of Public Affairs and to Betty Jane Narver of the Institute of Public Policy, University of Washington, for their belief in the book. Finally, that respect verging on awe that one accords a great editor: Lucille Fuller of the Institute for Public Policy.

Introduction

The Summer of Our Discontent

THE YEARS 1983 AND 1984 were an unusual and perhaps unique time in American history. The economy was in a robust recovery. But long-term worries were on the rise. The mood among many who follow economic events most closely was almost the reversal of a traditional American attitude. Optimism when times are tough has often marked our history. Pessimism when times are good seems almost foreign to our character. But that was the mood.

Its cause was the specter of deficits. From the end of World War II to the early 1970s the federal budget had shown either a small deficit or a small surplus each year. In 1975 a "deficit plateau" was reached in the $50 billion range. This lasted for seven years until 1982 when the deficit doubled. But the new level was not a plateau. It lasted only one year and the deficit doubled again in 1983. Many analysts concluded that the amount of red ink for that year defined the future; $200 billion deficits seemed to stretch as far as the eye could see.

The deficit creates big problems for the Treasury, the budget, and the economy. The Treasury must find buyers for $200 billion in new securities each year, and must "roll over" (resell) half the $1.8 trillion total debt every 15 months. The budget faces the threat of being eaten alive by debt interest costs, which by decade-end could eliminate all flexibility and choice in spending decisions. The economy faces an even more ominous threat: a national debt that is growing faster than the economy itself.

Why should anyone care if the Treasury faces a challenge in marketing securities? They are professionals and that is their job.

We should be concerned because it is the "full faith and credit" of the United States that is pledged in repayment of each Treasury bill. This fine phrase is not an abstraction. Consider what happened on May 11, 1984.

The Treasury was holding one of its frequent "auctions"—a session where bond dealers make bids on federal securities and government sells to whomever makes the best offers. On this day, dealers had just bought about half the $4.75 billion in 30-year bonds being auctioned when they discovered to their horror that, even with a return of 13 percent interest, they could find almost no investors to take the securities off their hands.

Panic-stricken, dealers slashed prices. In two dizzying hours the new bonds plunged $143 million in value. Then, as if to taunt those who had swiftly unloaded at a loss, the market inexplicably rocketed almost all the way back up.

Bond traders had not seen such volatility since the market recoiled in dread at Jimmy Carter's budget in 1980, forcing him to rip it up when the red ink was barely dry. (He had proposed a deficit of $30 billion, which was rejected as a sign of inadequate fiscal control.)

May 11, 1984 was "the kind of day in the government bond market that can generate aftershocks for years to come. . . . The gulf between the economy's current strong condition and the investor's somber assessment of the future—as tangibly expressed in bond prices—has never been wider," *Business Week* reported at the time, and added, "After a weekend of reflection, the market resumed a year-long slide, treating the world's safest securities with a frostiness usually reserved for the shakiest corporations."[1]

Since then the bond market has had its ups as well as downs. But the Treasury had a glimpse of its ultimate nightmare: What if we held an auction and nobody came?

The basis for a "somber assessment of the future" has grown. A climb in market interest rates which began in January 1984 had by June added $12 billion to the projected cost of debt service for 1985, $24 billion for 1986, and $35 billion for 1987, invalidating federal budget estimates made by the Office of Management and Budget as recently as February 1984.[2] Surveying the new situation, OMB estimated that each one percent rise in interest rates would add $10 billion to the deficit by 1986.[3]

During 1984 the debt-service bill rose by $1 to $2 billion a month. Part of this was caused by additions to the national debt from the current deficit, and part by rising interest costs on both new and old debt. The "rollover" of old securities can be painful because they often carry low interest rates from the good old days, but must be refinanced at today's rates.

By August 1984, the federal government with the best credit in the land was paying more than 10 percent to borrow money for just three months. Its most recent 30-year loan had just cost 13.3 percent.[4]

The Treasury is caught in a debt-deficit spiral. Its credit needs are expanding much faster than the U.S. savings pool. It must therefore either attract more of that pool or get more money from overseas—or both. This requires paying a premium rate of interest, which is added to the deficit, increasing the amount of securities that must be sold at still higher interest rates in the future.

Like other economic barometers, rates fluctuate. But thanks to the debt-deficit spiral, they face steady, even inexorable, upward pressure. The challenge is not only to the skill and professionalism of the Treasury but to the "full faith and credit" of the United States.

The deficit creates big problems for the budget because of some brutally simple arithmetic. Revenues are stuck at about 19 percent of Gross National Product (GNP) and spending is stuck at about 24 percent of GNP. Over time, both are projected to rise gradually. But the gap between the two will remain and in fact will increase.

Each year the government runs a deficit equal to 5 percent of GNP, this amount (currently about $200 billion) is added to the national debt. To borrow this much extra money requires paying at least $20 billion more each year in interest costs. With only a modest rise each year in the deficit as a percent of GNP, the Congressional Budget Office (CBO) projects the tab for net interest on the debt as follows:

Fiscal year	Net interest	Fiscal year	Net interest
1984	$109.6 billion	1987	$167.0 billion
1985	125.6	1988	193.3
1986	144.5	1989	217.0

There are two ways to put these figures in perspective. They can be compared to either taxes or spending. The CBO says that in 1989 the income tax—personal and corporate combined—is expected to raise $563 billion.[5] The interest figure shown above will consume well over one-third this amount, 38.5 percent, for no purpose other than to satisfy our creditors. Not a single dollar of this cost will strengthen national security or provide public services. Instead it goes into what has been called a "fiscal black hole."[6]

The impact of a growing interest tab stands out starkly when it is compared to other spending. If Congress had wanted to wash out the one-year rise in interest from 1984 to 1985, it would have had to cancel the B-1 and eliminate Aid to Families with Dependent Children, or as an alternative, wipe out food stamps, close the FBI, and abolish the Department of Interior. At $20 billion a year, the rise in interest costs is equivalent to adding a new Veterans Administration or Department of Agriculture annually.

The real damage this does is to demoralize Congress at the very time when fiscal discipline is vital. "Congressmen and White House people sweat bullets to get minor reductions in the deficit, and when you point out to them that the interest expense will offset it, they just throw up their hands," reports former OMB chief economist Lawrence Kudlow. Senator William Proxmire says this is making a "mockery" of modest deficit reduction packages proposed in Congress. "The federal government is being forced to run harder and harder just to say in place."[7]

The debt-deficit spiral is at work here. "When deficits are $150 billion instead of, say, $30 billion, there is a tendency for the President and members of Congress to ask, why should we take the heat to save $5 billion? Why should we get the pressure groups fired up just to do something that's scarcely a dent in the deficit?" observes former OMB Director James McIntyre.

He contrasts this debilitating mood with the days when deficits were much smaller. Then a fight over $5 billion was worth it. Red ink would be reduced by a respectable percentage. The budget would come noticeably closer to balance. Now, there is no such political reward for taking on the interests.

The high plateau on which current-year deficits are stuck weakens the will to make the kind of mid-sized cuts that were once an important way to hold the deficit down. This drives the spiral. A failure of fiscal control translates into $20 billion annual growth in interest costs. In polite terms this surge "is going to be a significant factor in preventing any new initiatives in the budget during the mid-1980s." In more direct terms, debt interest is eating the budget alive, foreclosing not only attractive choices but imperiling the prudent minimum of flexibility the President and Congress should have on spending decisions.

Ultimately, "the big worry, though, is that growth in debt service costs could overwhelm the government's political will to cut spending or raise taxes."[8] Congress must confront a paradox: the only way to prevent a loss of all spending options tomorrow is to make deliberate spending reductions today. Here is where some much-needed good news comes in.

"The miracle of compounding works in both directions," notes CBO Director Rudolph Penner.[9] Just as every dollar the government has to borrow is compounded by added interest payments, so every dollar of reduced red ink trims deficits further by the amount of prospective interest the government will not have to pay.

The effect is powerful. In a typical deficit reduction plan, about 30 percent of the impact over a five-year period comes from interest savings rather than from the pain of spending cuts or the cold cash of tax increases.

The enemy of this good news is delay. As the government borrows to cover a $200 billion deficit, the bill for debt services goes up $20 billion if interest rates are 10 percent. After two years, $400 billion has been added to the debt and $40 billion to interest. After three years, even without compounding, the numbers are $600 billion and $60 billion. So if you wait three years, you have thrown away the first $60 billion of the spending cuts or tax hikes in any plan to solve the deficit problem.

Even if budget outlays were stable at 24 percent of GNP and revenues were stable at 19 percent of GNP, there would probably be a fiscal collision rather than (to use an economists' term) a steady-state disequilibrium. For a number of reasons, the odds are high that even with these fixed shares, the sterile expense of debt interest would consume an ever-larger portion of the budget.

To House Budget Committee chief economist Van Ooms, "There is no realistic economic model that can easily generate savings and investment numbers which will accommodate future years' debt service costs. As the burden climbs, much higher tax burdens or massive service cuts become possibilities. . . . The crunch will come—when is uncertain, but the arithmetic makes it inescapable."[10]

Congress may well be faced with this challenge: make decisive choices now or lose the capacity for choice in the future.

What is the impact of the deficit on the economy? Is it somehow possible that red ink can be a beneficial form of stimulus even while it is causing headaches on the budget front?

In the short term, the answer is yes; such a paradox is possible. Despite his concerns about the longer term, Ooms sees the deficit as compatible with the 1983–84 recovery: "The recession was a lot deeper and longer than anyone predicted. This set the stage for a strong recovery by creating a lot of running room in credit markets. In the short term, the demand by government for credit didn't create problems. Interest payments on the debt go back into savings flows and are recycled into the pool of available credit. This, together with strong cash flow generated by corporate tax cuts, meant less pressure on interest rates than some gloomy forecasts had predicted."[11]

The long-range picture is far different. It "could lead to 75 percent of all public and private credit being used by the federal government." To attract that large a share of investment, "it could take 20 percent interest rates to buy our way out of the problem." At some point, renewed inflation looms as the only option: "Congress understands the common sense notion that you can get so deeply in debt you can't pay it off."[12]

These views of Ooms' are seconded by others. Former Budget Director James McIntyre sees "the cat chasing its own tail" if no progress is made on the deficit before the next recession. At that point most analysts expect a $300 billion deficit and debt interest heading rapidly to $200 billion a year. "This scenario," says McIntyre, "is an even more difficult situation than we face today."[13]

How about the flow of world capital into the U.S. to buy Treasury bills? Is this a painless way to float ever-larger debt? Ooms believes not. "It's unsustainable because the size of this country in the world economy makes it impossible to finance a growing debt without increasing interests costs."[14] Rudolph Penner of CBO says simply, "We are heading for deficits that are a dramatically large part of world capital markets."[15] This means not only greater interest rate pressures on the Treasury but on other nations. To cite a single example, when the U.S. prime rate rose one and one half percent in two months during the spring of 1984, this added $600 million to Argentina's debt service cost—an amount equal to the value of that nation's best known export, beef.[16]

The 1983–84 economic boom caused some to hope that the U.S. could "grow its way" out of deficits. "If you believe that, I have several Brooklyn Bridges I might sell you," says Peter Peterson, former Secretary of Commerce and head of a deficit-reduction coalition.[17]

The basis for Peterson's assertion is this stark fact: Even if prosperity continues through the 1980s, the national debt will grow faster than Gross National Product. In 1980 it was equal to 28 percent of GNP. In 1983 it was 37 percent. It is headed toward 49 percent in 1989.[18]

As an inevitable result, interests costs have risen from 1.5 percent of GNP in the 1970s to 3.3 percent in the 1980s and are headed to 5.5 percent in the 1990s.[19] The ultimate in fanciful projections (based nonetheless on simple arithmetic) would carry debt-service costs to one hundred percent of the national economy in the year 2472.

This obviously isn't going to happen and even if it were, such a calculation merely offers an extreme illustration of John Maynard Keynes' observation that, "In the long run, we're all dead." In the much shorter run, concerns persist. "At a minimum, we need to reduce the deficit to the point where annual additions to the debt do not exceed the growth in GNP," says Council of Economic Advisors member William Niskanen. "The deficit must be reduced to $100 billion in fiscal 1986 just to keep the debt sustainable."[20]

Why aren't alarm bells ringing loud and clear in every quarter of government? Why aren't policy-makers marching arm in arm in the deficit-cutting army?

There are two reasons. One is hope. The other is belief. Hope is fed by the lack of obvious calamity. "The consequences of the deficit are not precipitous; this makes them more difficult to deal with," observes Niskanen.[21] Former Council Chairman Charles Schultze adds, "The catastrophe is that there is no catastrophe." Instead, Schultze sees the economy as headed for a "plateau of stagnation."[22] To Felix Rohatyn, architect of the New York fiscal rescue plan, deficits are a "financial cancer" which does not announce itself but makes a stealthy approach.[23] In short, those disinclined to see are not forced to see the trouble which lies ahead.

Beyond this, there are those who have seen the future and have decided it does work—just as it is. They believe deficits will go away on their own and will not do any harm while they're here.

A classic formulation of this view is offered by former Treasury official and leading supply-side economist and tax specialist Norman Ture. He sets forth this thesis:

> "To put the deficit in a realistic perspective, the administration and Congress alike will have to recognize that the budget deficits
>
> —have not been the source of the recovery; they have not spurred a boom in consumer demand; capital formation in the business and household sectors has been the driving force behind this recovery;
>
> —do not crowd out private investment by forcing up interest rates; interest rates plunged in 1982 as budget deficits soared, and interest rates have been going up as budget deficits have been coming down;
>
> —do not crowd out capital formation by preempting private saving; government purchases of goods and services do the preempting;
>
> —are not responsible for the 'strength of the dollar,' the strong capital inflows, or the increasing and very large balance of trade deficits;
>
> —have, in fact, been the only major constraint on more rapid increases in government spending; and
>
> —are an accounting residual rather than an active fiscal force influencing economic activity; governments spend, governments tax, governments do not deficit."[24]

This remarkable enumeration reduces the deficit to a shadowy and vaguely benign existence, a friendly phantom which is only a "residual"— except when it steps forward to do battle with unwise spending.

Ture's list of what the deficit is not finds its basis in what mainstream economists say it is. To them, describing the deficit as a sum of negative attributes is the essence of "voodoo economics," which balances the budget with "smoke and mirrors"—and then tells you the deficit doesn't matter anyway.

Much of the appeal of supply-side economics is that it provides an intellectual superstructure to defend something we all want: lower taxes. The famous Laffer curve had the virtue of illustrating an obvious truth: taxes can be so high they depress individual initiative. Not so obvious is figuring out which side of the curve we are on at any time. Are we where tax cuts will increase revenues or where they will decrease revenues?

The supply-side emphasis on incentives, on entrepreneurship, on what John Maynard Keynes called the importance of "animal spirits," is all to the good. But the attempt to go farther, to a world where economic cause and effect dissolve in apparent vapor, only to emerge governed by a new set of relationships, has created among many a sense of philosophic unease and an active concern as these doctrines have been embraced by some high-level policy makers.

Even before the current debate, the role of deficits as a policy tool had changed a great deal. Keynes had proposed that budgets should be balanced over the economic cycle. Deficits would offer a stimulus during downturns, but surpluses would provide restraint during recoveries. These swings in fiscal policy would offset each other. Government revenues and spending over each period of five years or so would be equal.

The budget numbers of the last twenty years suggest another approach has come into vogue. To some extent it merely reflects what happened, but it may also be a cause of what happened.

This post-Keynesian doctrine seems to call for running a deficit at all times: in a recession to promote recovery; in a recovery to avoid "choking off" the upswing; in a boom to let the good times roll. At every point in the economic cycle, there has been an excuse for deficits.

Partly as a result of this comfortable notion, we now have a budget which seems to run itself, limiting real options and raising the question of whether fiscal policy—the deliberate use of deficits and surpluses of various sizes— still has any meaning. Instead, we may be stuck with a single-option budget—one that demands of us certain actions unless we wish to be confronted with a zero-option budget—one that denies us all meaningful choices on taxes and spending and threatens to steadily chew up the entire economy.

Even if there is an equal chance that supply-side or traditional doctrines will prove correct, we must assess the risk of following each course if it proves in error. To take a hard look at all areas of federal spending, to eliminate what we do not need and to raise the performance and control the cost of the rest, would not seem to be a course damaging to the national well-being even if the deficit turns out to be Puff the Magic Dragon. But the risk in betting that red ink is no more real than the flames from a dragon's mouth must be judged grave indeed.

Optimism for the future is a fine thing. Yet, such optimism to be sound must be grounded by a faith in America's best qualities of energy, responsibility, and excellence. Taking the prudent course on deficits does these qualities more honor than assuming that everything will turn out all right without the restoration of fiscal discipline.

The Trillion Dollar Budget

Chapter 1

Setting the Stage

AMERICANS HAVE BECOME ACCUSTOMED to presidents who bemoan the economic and fiscal policy errors of their predecessors. It was not always so. As recently as the Eisenhower and the Kennedy years, the economy and the budget were dealt with on a current basis. Seldom was an action or proposal put forth as a way to correct some blunder made by those previously in power.

One reason the blaming game was not much in evidence is that the years from 1945 to 1965 were a time of steady, noninflationary growth—an economic golden age in which all things seemed possible. In a graceful tribute to John Kennedy on the twentieth anniversary of his death, Robert Samuelson recalled a president who had made us feel we were on the last lap of a marathon. America was about to cross the finish line—a society whose values were the hope of mankind, unsullied by the crude use of power yet a presence on the world stage; a society able to afford the cost of assuring economic justice without creating a burden which reduced economic opportunity.[1]

In the two decades following that moment of hope, we seemed in our worst moments to be moving from the last lap to the last chance. Part of our sense of decline was that we may have swathed Kennedy's fine rhetoric in a golden haze that transformed words into a reality we could almost touch. But there has been real damage done to the dream, above all by Vietnam and Watergate.

Much has been written of the moral and political anguish these events produced. Less has been said about their effect on our economic strength and on our ability to use the federal budget as a flexible policy tool.

The price of Vietnam was paid in all these ways. From 1965 to 1968 military spending rose by two-thirds. The budget went from a $1.4 billion surplus to a $12.3 billion deficit—the most red ink in any year since World War II.[2] President Johnson hesitated in the face of an unpopular war to ask

3

for taxes to close this gap. As a result, the federal government entered the economically tumultuous 1970s in a weakened fiscal condition.

President Nixon tried to overcome the tendency toward deficits by using the full array of federal policy tools. He put the economic accelerator to the floor with stimulative fiscal and monetary policies. He slammed on the brakes with restrictive wage and price controls. In the Kennedy era economists talked of "fine tuning"—precise shifts in the money supply and in federal surpluses or deficits to keep growth on course. By the Nixon era subtlety had given way to a slam-bang style that began to raise fears of the British "stop-go" syndrome—constantly changing signals and a confused economy.

Richard Nixon was the first president since Franklin Roosevelt who had some cause to blame his predecessor for economic and budgetary problems. He responded vigorously and even with an excess of zeal, according to some. Then came Watergate and a vast erosion of presidential power.

For a full year and a half, from about March 1973 until he resigned in August 1974, Nixon's ordeal preoccupied the nation. A policy paralysis set in as Washington was engrossed by the drama of a man slipping down a greased slide and trying to clamber back up again.

The bureaucracy's routine functions ground on as usual. But the higher functions of government slowed to a crawl. Major issues were put on hold. Months passed in which the policy tools that had earlier been used so vigorously lay idle. Even more serious, as the nation began to be gripped by the idea that we had again been lied to by a president, doubt arose as to whether the chief executive had a right to use the tools of power vigorously. In this sense, the memory of Vietnam increased the price that had to be paid for Watergate.

Johnson and Nixon were succeeded by Ford and Carter. Two men capable of great political competence had been done in by defects of character. They were followed by two men of honor who suffered from public doubts about their competence. Ford had an amiability that seemed to interfere with his ability to convey an understanding of the issues and a quality of decision that was often quite high. Carter suffered from being, as an earlier commentator once said of George McGovern, "the kind of man who gives virtue a bad name." A remarkable combination of brains, energy, and moral character translated into a remarkable inability to wield power.

Then came Ronald Reagan, a president with the clearest agenda since Lyndon Johnson's, and if anything, cut even more out of whole cloth. LBJ's program emerged from his long experience in Congress. At one level, it was the ultimate in log-rolling with the nation itself as a vast log. At another level, LBJ had a vision, as Reagan has had. In philosophic terms, the Great Society may have been to the New Beginning what matter is to anti-matter.

It has often been observed that a president's budget proposals are the clearest expression of what he believes government should do and be. The last five presidents have, perhaps by coincidence, illustrated five combinations of budget style and budget content. This variety in approach and substance helps provide a background to today's issues and helps explain how we have moved from the "last lap" in solving America's economic problems to what some say is a "last chance" to restore fiscal balance.

Johnson: A liberal approach to a liberal budget. Two decades of almost unbroken economic growth provided the background. A presidential temperament that was hard-driving and expansive provided the impetus. The result was an administration with more spending initiatives than any since FDR's New Deal.

New initiatives create new agencies, which tend to get more money than they need. When the national imagination is fired by ideas such as ending poverty or making America strong again, programs are put in place fast and often without much thought. Those parts of the budget that are most popular are treated most tolerantly with regard to waste, especially during periods of rapid buildup.

The Great Society moved on many fronts at once: Medicare and Medicaid, food stamps, aid to schools and colleges, mass transit. The tab for these programs was modest at first. The list just cited cost $5 billion initially in 1964–66. But by 1980 outlays for the same items had swelled to $72 billion.[3]

As in FDR's day, the President's staff was a major source of ideas that generated new spending. The budget office role tended to be peripheral because the budget at the "crucial margin" was shaped by the White House.[4]

Johnson's long years in Congress had given him a very personal style. He liked to make decisions by word of mouth and he liked to do his deciding down at the LBJ ranch. He did not like to spend a lot of time working on the budget. Kermit Gordon and Charles Schultze, his budget directors, would take boxes of decision memos to the ranch, which Johnson wouldn't read. But he would talk with them about the politics of the budget.

Even though times were good in the early years of his presidency, Johnson was under strong pressure from Congress to hold down spending. It was in these years that the budget office began to put out lists of potential cuts. Both when he sought to reduce taxes and when he asked for a surtax, LBJ was confronted by a Congress seeking spending restraint in return.

For 1965 Johnson struggled to produce a budget that would hold outlays under $100 billion. Every effort was made to find both accounting shifts and program trims to achieve this goal. At one point an exasperated President told his budget director he wanted a spending plan that was "larger on the inside and smaller on the outside."

Gradually the cost of fighting a war in Vietnam came into collision with the cost of his domestic initiatives. Every president since Eisenhower has worried about the level of spending for defense, and has found it almost equally painful to accept or to disagree with budgets proposed by the Pentagon. This pain was part of the reason LBJ decided not to run again.

Despite these pressures, the Johnson era is remembered as ambitious and expansive. It was the last time, at least for a while, when there seemed to be no limit on what money could do, nor on the amount of money a generous nation could apply to any purpose. The spirit of the era was summed up in a saying: If you must choose between A and B, choose both.

Nixon: A conservative approach to a liberal budget. As the phrase suggests, this was a time of crosscurrents, not so easily analyzed as its predecessor. The Nixon Administration emphasized management, but made big spending commitments. Even more potent in driving up budget totals, Great Society spending soared in these years. Programs which were camels' noses under the fiscal tent in LBJ's term were up and running in Nixon's.

This President found the business of the budget painful and difficult. He used Eisenhower-like task forces to sift out budget questions. He set up an extensive process for agencies to appeal on behalf of their spending requests. At times, cabinet secretaries camped outside Nixon's office to make their case.

The President and his Budget Director Robert Mayo thought in terms of a logical (if elaborate) process. The budget office knew where it stood, knew what to expect, knew what would actually occur. A philosophy had been articulated and was adhered to.

This philosophy emphasized management and the orderly procedures by which management is implemented. Nixon was a student of bureaucracy, and according to some old hands, understood what went on inside government better than almost any president.

The logical model was not perfectly implemented. Explosive growth in Great Society spending was a disruptive factor, and the Nixon Administration was a very political one, responsive to many constituencies. Particularly effective in these years were state and local government lobbies. Many new grant programs were created, and intergovernmental relations was a subject in great vogue.

Thus, the budget environment was complex, even contradictory. An emphasis on management gave it a conservative flavor. But while management dominated the focus on long-standing programs, there was a much more flexible and dynamic focus on newer areas of spending. This was forced by the steep expansion in Great Society costs and by a political response to favored constituencies. Budget numbers alone give the Nixon era a liberal flavor.

Ford: A conservative approach to a conservative budget. This President was clearer than any other recent chief executive on budget philosophy and therefore on actions. Ford's nonideological but conservative approach always led to a search for ways to hold down costs even in old-line programs like public works and agriculture characterized by congressional log-rolling.

Ford was fascinated by budget issues and was knowledgeable about them. He enjoyed the give and take of executive budget sessions, listened with intense interest to arguments pro and con, and talked with pleasure about policy directions and options. He was a clear favorite of the budget staff: accessible, easy to talk with, and willing to make decisions. Ford encouraged budget staffers to tackle controversial issues with members of Congress, while cautioning them that politics might make some cuts impossible even when they were desirable.

Ford and Budget Director James Lynn looked at all areas of spending with an equal emphasis on restraint: defense, transfer payments, and the domestic budget. One result of this was that Ford vetoed an extraordinary number of bills during his term. In a sense it can be said that he was ahead of Congress on the shift in national mood toward spending restraint—a reversal of LBJ's day when Congress had tried to rein in the President.

Carter: A liberal approach to a conservative budget. Complexity and contradiction returned to the fiscal sphere with this presidency. The Carter Administration was most unclear about its philosophy. In part this mirrored a struggle then under way between the liberal and conservative wings of the Democratic Party.

Carter was torn between a philosophic conservatism and a tendency to accede to arguments that spending in poor-performing programs must continue for political reasons. The tension between these two forces was so acute that it prevented the President from developing a general approach to the budget. For those in the budget office, "Carter was always choosing and we couldn't tell what he would choose."

One peril in the situation was that there was no formal process for the President to look at the economy except in the context of the budget. Carter began to lose political credibility as the economy got in trouble. Bad news and surprises on the economic front came to be a millstone for Charles Schultze, an LBJ budget director and Carter's chief economic advisor.

This was a factor in executive budget discussions where Carter was pulled between the enthusiasm of White House staff for new spending plans and the resistance of budget officials James McIntyre and Bowman Cutter, joined by Treasury Secretary Michael Blumenthal. The "swing" man in these discussions was Schultze—a delicate role made more difficult by bad economic news.

Many of today's highly visible budget trends began modestly under Carter—the real rise in defense, the real decline in federal aid to states and localities, the concern with waste. But he is more likely to be remembered for sounding an uncertain trumpet than as a harbinger of things to come.

Reagan: An agenda approach to a conservative budget. "The conservative agenda is an expensive agenda," says columnist George Will. And so it proved to be under an administration perhaps the most ideological in our history. Reagan has been consistent in pursuing his agenda, but from a budgetary standpoint the agenda itself may seem inconsistent. Something approaching a double standard has been applied to different areas of spending. Favored programs seem required to meet few cost-benefit criteria while those less favored have been subjected to strict standards of worth.

There was one striking success in the Administration's first year, a success which literally made budget history. Over $40 billion was cut from the spending base of domestic programs. How this was done is as instructive as the amount is impressive.

The budget in Reagan's first year was shaped in a way nearly opposite to Nixon's "appeals process." There was no agency input. No cabinet secretaries petitioned the President with claims from their constituencies for replacement of funds cut by the budget office. This is why, from the standpoint of enforcing reductions, the process worked so well.

In the process, Reagan like Nixon used Eisenhower's task force approach—groups of key persons who surface issues. And Reagan heard the arguments within each task force, not just the conclusions. To be sure, he was interested in the essence, not in the detail, of these arguments. But old budget hands felt the pros and cons were fairly and clearly presented by David Stockman. Indeed, some called his review an outstanding distillation of issues and an able synthesis of ideas.

The result was dramatic budget changes in 1981. Comparatively little has happened since then. Defense spending hikes canceled the value of domestic budget savings. Tax cuts took hold and caused a revenue decline. Recession cost the Treasury even more. The deficit soared. Then came a recovery and a debate over whether renewed economic growth could restore fiscal balance without help from further changes in spending or taxes. This debate continues. The experience of 1981 remains a historical example of decisiveness in budget policy.

A *"Carter-Reagan era"?* A common thread of peace and prosperity ran through the presidencies of two very different men. We speak of the "Eisenhower-Kennedy years" despite sharp contrasts in leadership style and policy substance. The catch-all phrase is valid because there was a continuity in the way the nation felt about itself.

Improbable as it may seem, historians may some day look back on a "Carter-Reagan era." At least, economic and fiscal historians may do so. Despite the great change in national mood which separates the two presidencies, Carter's uncertain trumpet announced several themes which Reagan was to sound with a full marching band.

These themes include elimination of waste and better management of government, imposing greater discipline over social programs, increasing defense spending in real terms, cleaning up the maze of grants to state and local government, and the politics of large deficits.

There are of course great differences between Carter and Reagan. The contrast in style is vast. One man seemed gripped by indecision, hesitancy, agonizing, and moralizing. The other's self-assurance was so broad that at times he seemed to present himself as a giant rabbit's foot, a big good luck charm, for the nation.

To paraphrase Lincoln, Carter frustrated many by an incessant concern about whether he and we were on God's side. Reagan exasperated many by his bland assumption that God was on our side. Somewhere in between, many sensed, was the leadership style that wears best.

The analysts who speak of a single Carter-Reagan era delight in plunging through the stylistic gulf and finding what they see as common substantive ground. This is a useful approach but it can easily be overdone. A visible thread runs between the two administrations on many spending issues, but there is a sharp break on tax policy. Concern over deficit growth and inflation control persists, but one problem has become three times as big while the other has shrunk to one-third its former size. These are significant changes.

In two crucial ways Jimmy Carter prepared the political world for his successor. To a much larger degree than we easily recall, he launched a new era in which the federal government's policy focus was no longer to solve problems by creating new programs, but to solve the problem created by federal spending growth. In this sense, Carter deserves part of the credit Reagan has received for changing the national agenda.

Carter's other assist was negative. He created a hunger for strong leadership. Carter was kicked around by Congress, by other nations, by impersonal economic forces, and most of all by his own conscience. He was, as a president, the reversal of Justice Holmes' famous characterization of FDR: "A second-rate intellect, but a first-rate temperament." In the years after 1981, the American people seemed to draw from an almost bottomless well of gratitude for Ronald Reagan, who had delivered us from the sad spectacle of the president as victim.

Reagan in turn had his own snare, less obvious but still damaging. The same broad-gauged approach that conveyed confidence and commanded the agenda created resistance among those in the public and in the political system who doubted his grasp of important details. The shift in style was reflected in a shift of concern about the presidency.

Johnson and Nixon had given us the imperial presidency. Ford for largely historical reasons and Carter for largely personal reasons gave us the enfeebled presidency. Under Reagan there was vast relief at the restoration of the chief executive's proper role. But disagreement with some of his policies, and criticism of how well they were thought out, found expression in an increasing number of deadlocks with Congress after 1981. This caused some scholars to dream of a parliamentary system in which voters would give the president a legislative majority at the same time they elected him.

This change is not likely to happen. The imperial presidency and the enfeebled presidency both called forth proposals to redesign our institutions. But as personalities come and go, yesterday's proposals look irrelevant and even misguided. So it probably is with the parliamentary plan: an idea that sounds attractive to some supporters of a personally popular president whose policy depth and substance are debated.

Perhaps the people prefer Reagan's leadership most when it is not exercised in relation to any specific issue. He does, however, receive strong support on taxes (reduce them), inflation (hold it down), and the Soviets (stand up to them). The political and historic verdict on Reagan appears to hinge on the threat posed by the deficit, especially on its growth and impact during the next downswing in the economic cycle.

The pages which follow set the stage for today's budget debate by tracing the contrast of style and the continuity of substance from Carter to Reagan. Carter recognized the new era but could not impose his will upon it. This was expressed fatally in his inability to control inflation. Reagan masters the new era but must navigate between the rocks of the "fairness issue" on one side and the shoals of stagflation that will becalm the economy if supply-side theories prove unsound.

The history of 1977–84 is one of political and economic stress, of a drift punctuated by lurches for four years, and then of an attempt to impose a blueprint by staying the course, or at least seeming to, for four years. These adventures in combination bring us to the present moment.

The Carter Legacy

JIMMY CARTER'S THEMES WERE "anti-government, anti-Washington, anti-big program," a senior White House staffer recalled in 1978. As President, Carter attempted to follow through "by pushing down the budget deficit and shaking up the bureaucracy."[1]

California's Proposition 13 passed a year and a half into Carter's term. The tax revolt had an enormous ripple effect on federal politics. Balancing the budget was an obsessive concern as voters reacted to the quantum leap in deficits that began in 1975. (Budget references are to fiscal years. Any budget year—such as 1978—is that of the last day in the budget year: September 30, 1978. Before 1976 the last day of the budget year was June 30.) Inflation, viewed as the inevitable result of red ink, was an equal concern.

Carter, like Reagan, campaigned on a painless solution. Better management of government would save tax dollars without cutting services. The tool: zero-based budgeting (ZBB) which promised to review spending from the ground up.

Experts warned Carter there was less to ZBB than met the eye. They cautioned against expecting changes to result automatically from a process. "The content of the budget is not necessarily different after zero-based budgeting than before," said Allan Schick of the Congressional Research Service.[2] "The budget process . . . is primarily the fine-tuning of an approved program, not . . . a ranking process," admonished Harvard professor of management control Robert Anthony.[3] And Maynard Waterfield of Tax Foundation, Inc. noted that "bureaucracies basically involve people who cannot be eliminated just by shifting or combining agencies,"[4] a fact that Carter himself underscored when as President he urged agency heads to find jobs for workers displaced by reorganization.

Zero-based budgeting played the same role in Carter's scheme of things as "waste, fraud, and abuse" has in Reagan's. It proved to be a marginal tool, a presidential hobbyhorse. ZBB was no substitute for the hard slogging needed to improve management or reorder priorities.

In terms of political symbolism, though, Carter was on the right track. Pollster Everett Carll Ladd found the tax revolt was "based on a genuine belief that government can and should do all it is doing—but much more efficiently." Ladd said Proposition 13-style protests were "a deliberately exaggerated expression of low regard for government's competence." Voters saw officialdom as "a very unresponsive animal . . . that will not pay attention until it gets a jolting shock." Ladd quoted an elderly resident of Des Moines: "Anytime you call the government, they put you on hold."[5]

In a key formulation, Ladd summed up the dilemma that was to plague Carter's approach to the budget: "Americans are institutional conservatives and operational liberals."[6] Carter struggled without final success to reach a balance between fiscal conservatism and social liberalism that would satisfy his country, his party, and himself.

It was Carter's fate to be forced simultaneously to confront these challenges: a major turning point in public finance; resistance in the Democratic Party to budgets which reflected the turning point; a personal identity crisis as he went from being a big frog in a little pond to a big frog in an enormous pond.

In facing these pressures, Carter sounded a wide range of fiscal themes and was left in the end without a theme. The process fell into three overlapping phases: "liberal" modification of budget policies left by Ford; a "blueprint for enlightened conservatism"; drift and loss of direction in the face of recession and reelection politics.

The 1978 budget. Each incoming president inherits a budget proposal from his predecessor. He has scant time to make changes, as the plan is due for submission to Congress virtually on inauguration day. Gerald Ford left a

1978 plan which Jimmy Carter changed and sent to Congress in February 1977. He was still making changes as late as January 1978, four months into the budget period. These late alterations were perhaps not remarkable in a first year. But they foreshadowed a pattern of midyear revisions that led to political damage later on.

The net effect of Carter's proposals was to add $27.2 billion on the domestic side and to trim defense by $5.5 billion.[7]

These shifts were in part a predictable Democratic response to a budget left by the most conservative president in 50 years. But the domestic spending hikes were given a kick by inflation, which had bounced off its 1976 low of 5.8 percent and had begun a climb that would carry it to 13.5 percent in 1980.[8] The specter of inflation hung over budget-building through the Carter years, producing large dollar increases without proportional growth in services.

The 1979 budget. No budget is more likely to reflect a president's priorities than the one written during his first full year in office. Yet Carter's plan seemed simply to roll forward spending patterns based on midyear revisions in a Ford budget. Nearly every program was held near current service levels. Among major outlays, defense rose 1 percent in real terms, income security was up 0.8 percent, and health declined 0.3 percent.[9]

Critics were puzzled. "It's hard to see how this pattern can continue for three more years if Mr. Carter wants to be reelected," wrote Dennis Farney, in the *Wall Street Journal.* "The budget is neither fish nor fowl. It offers no bold new programs because the economy can't afford them. At the same time, it offers no painful economizing because the Congress and interest groups won't accept it—and because spending cutbacks might endanger the economic recovery."[10]

Farney contrasted Carter's lack of options with the room for maneuver granted to Kennedy and Johnson: "They had trade-offs open to them. They could trade an increase in inflation for more jobs because inflation was relatively mild in those days. But with 6 percent inflation and 6.4 percent unemployment, Jimmy Carter has no such leeway."[11]

Michael Levy, analyzing the budget for the Conference Board, emphasized the narrow range of impacts it offered. Its $24 billion tax cut was "rather modest, if not minimal . . . in the present economic setting" of fragile recovery. The tax cut equaled only 1.1 percent of GNP and more than two-thirds of the relief it granted would be taken back in Social Security hikes.

On the spending side, real changes were so minor that Levy made much of national defense, "which is budgeted for significant real gains"·of $1 billion, or 1 percent (!). Sifting through the data, Levy concluded "as a matter of prudence . . . I am adding $2–3 billion to the official deficit estimate and, as usual, continuous monitoring seems appropriate."[12] The weight Levy gives to a billion dollars is a poignant reminder of the explosion in fiscal magnitudes during the Reagan era.

Carter's cautious approach did not spare him the charge that spending was out of control. The *Wall Street Journal* warned his proposed $500 billion budget would mark "the third consecutive annual increase of 11 percent, the fastest three-year spurt in peacetime history"—measured of course in current and not constant dollars.[13]

Time editorialists inveighed against "the dangers of budget bloat," charging that "Washington's free-for-all spending just makes inflation worse." *Time* noted that "though the nation has been at peace for the last five years, military spending has grown by 58 percent" (ironically, this was the period during which the defense share of federal outlays fell from 30 to 23 percent). *Time* also stated what was then felt to be an indisputable law of economics: "The dizzy growth of the deficit must be reversed because it condemns this U.S. to unending inflation."[14]

These responses to Carter's 1979 budget proposal underscore the dilemma he faced. The deficit for each year between 1975 and 1978 was twice as large as for any other year since 1945 and the three-year total was almost $170 billion. This far outstripped the 1971–73 Vietnam War deficit of $61 billion and even exceeded the 1943–45 total of $123 billion—without the excuse of a war to pay for.

Clearly, things couldn't go on this way. To do nothing, the apparent drift of Carter's 1979 budget, was to do something: admit the situation was out of control. "The man in the street has come to believe that 'government has gone crazy,'" *Fortune* informed its readers in the summer of 1978.[15] The stage was set for the most dramatic period in the fiscal history of Carter's presidency.

The 1980 budget. No one could blame Jimmy Carter for thinking he had a broad-based go-ahead to draft a tight budget. The deficit was at a level never before seen during an economic recovery. Business feared rising interest rates and a credit crunch. The Treasury was charged with siphoning off all growth in private saving for its own purposes. Only foreign capital prevented a crowding-out of investment. The prospect of a new recession raised the specter of record unemployment not seen since the Depression, and carried the awesome prospect of a $100 billion deficit. Pressure to hike defense spending conflicted with demands from groups which Carter wryly called "benevolent lobbies."[16]

The economy and the budget were in collision. Even George McGovern said it was time to call a halt to real spending growth. He proposed a "moratorium" for fiscal 1980. Congress would avoid new programs and focus on improving the quality of current services. "A Congress concentrating on the oversight of existing programs should have few problems working harmoniously with a President who is interested primarily in reorganizing and reducing the bureaucracy," wrote David Broder after interviewing McGovern. "Such a government might well be exactly what most of the voters want. But whether it can satisfy the interest groups that have important influence in the Democratic party is another—and far tougher—question."[17] Echoing this theme, Everett Ladd commented, "In a liberal democracy, 'benevolence' is nearly omnipotent because it doesn't give rise to countervailing forces."[18]

In the summer of 1978, Office of Management and Budget (OMB) Director James McIntyre was lamenting that the 1979 budget was too big, but he had not been able to "whip agency heads into line and impose tighter controls on spending."[19] By November of 1979 a different sort of budget was taking form under McIntyre's direction. "Draconian," said Rudolph Penner of the conservative American Enterprise Institute. "Difficult to defend from either a social welfare or a political viewpoint," said Carter's own HUD Secretary Patricia Harris. "If he's going to win, he's going to have to prove that he can't be out-bluffed," warned a top Senate aide.[20]

Carter's central dilemma had resurfaced: "Next year is supposed to be the year the Democratic party pulls its disparate elements together in advance of the 1980 presidential election," wrote *Business Week*. "Instead, it is shaping up as a year of fighting over the scraps of a bare-bones budget."[21]

Even before the budget was completed, debate over Carter's dilemma intensified. Citibank economists predicted that optimism about fiscal restraint "will undergo a trial by fire in the coming year and beyond—especially when real growth slows and the economy slides into recession." At that point, "the policy environment would surely change and the deficit would jump sharply upward."[22]

The *Wall Street Journal* judged Carter's plan for a trim in the deficit from $40 billion in 1979 to $30 billion in 1980 as no better than "elusive restraint"[23] while the *London Times'* Frank Vogl branded Carter's budget "a shoddy compromise. . . . It will likely add to inflation and may weaken his reelection chances. . . . Few economists believe the current U.S. economy needs any stimulus at all."[24]

The budget for 1980 was released on January 22, 1979. "The most austere blueprint for social services spending to be proposed by any Democratic President since before the New Deal," said the *Los Angeles Times*.[25] The plan cut at least $12 billion[26] off the amount needed to maintain current domestic programs. Carter "assured Congress, however, that his budget would provide adequate funds for 'those Americans most truly in need,'" perhaps the first use of a phrase his successor would make famous.

Among programs with real cuts were Medicare and Medicaid, aid to education, job training, and farm price supports. "The political risks in the budget revolve around the President's call for a 10 percent increase in military spending when he is proposing to slash federal jobs programs and reduce Social Security benefits," noted William Eaton of the *Los Angeles*

Times.[27] The defense hike fulfilled a NATO pledge to raise real outlays by 3 percent annually. As to the domestic cuts, "Our most important goal . . . is to control inflation, and this budget meets that requirement," Carter said in signing the budget message.[28]

Some analysts noted that the approach and the arguments were almost identical to Ford's last proposal. "The intriguing question is: Can a Democrat elected with the help of organized labor, blacks, and liberals, follow the same economic policy as a conservative Republican and still be reelected?" asked Eaton.[29]

Senator William Proxmire gave a hopeful answer: "Contrary to popular opinion, Congress will cut even a tightfisted presidential budget in the new fiscal year."[30] One reason for Proxmire's optimism was 97 new members "who are expected largely to agree with Carter's budget stringency." Many had campaigned "against wasteful spending."[31] *U.S. News* predicted, "Carter will succeed in increasing military spending and in reducing the budget deficit, but the infighting will be fierce over where the cuts in domestic outlays will be made."[32]

To complete the Carter parallel with Ford and Reagan, there was even a proviso that the Administration would consider a major tax cut if the economy required such a move. But Treasury Secretary Blumenthal said this would be "risky" until inflation was under control.[33]

The 1980 budget proposal was Carter's fiscal crescendo. It was a "high wire act"[34] denounced by a financial community unused to large deficits and denounced equally by a "benevolent" lobby unused to spending rollbacks. Economic analyst Frank Vogl could assail the President's "unwillingness to act with sufficient determination" against inflation[35] at the same time Jesse Jackson of Chicago's action organization Operation PUSH was charging that "anti-inflation is a domestic neutron bomb" that destroys those "who are less organized and therefore less able to defend themselves."[36]

After a decade of "stop-go" federal policies, with one foot on the gas and one foot on the brake, as the saying went, the economy could no longer deliver attractive trade-offs. Even those who doubted fine tuning had to admit that, compared to the 1950s and 1960s, Carter was faced with a "zero option" budget environment. In the 1980 proposal, he split the howls of protest about evenly.

And the President who had to face this bruising environment was a man whose agenda and philosophy had focused on a now-marginal issue: "management." The conflicting pressures would have tested a far more ideological leader than Carter.

For a moment it seemed he might survive the pulling and hauling intact. He had paid the price of proposing restraint; perhaps now he would reap the reward. "With this budget President Carter has at least pointed us in a different direction, and the people seem disposed to follow," wrote Vermont Royster. "Dare we hope that some day we can look back on 1979 as a turning point in the affairs of the nation?" Royster noted "this is the first time in many a year that the word 'restraint' appears in a President's budget message not as a mere gesture but as its primary thrust."[37]

Irving Kristol judged that "President Carter is now doing so many things right in the area of economic policy that, if he continues along this path, he could easily be renominated and reelected in 1980." But Kristol saw an irony: "He is doing [the right things] against his will and, apparently, against his own best judgment. His greatest danger at the moment derives from his own lack of assurance in all the right things he is doing."[38] The ranking Republican on House Ways and Means put the matter succinctly: Carter's budget was "a fairly tight structure built on somewhat shifting sands."[39]

In the end, the numbers that were to have given the 1980 budget its distinctive flavor spun wildly out of control. Instead of $532 billion in outlays, there were $576 billion. Instead of taking barely 21 percent of GNP, federal spending claimed almost 23 percent. Instead of the deficit declining from $40 billion to $30 billion, it rose from $27 billion (1979's final figure, lowest in five years) to almost $60 billion.[40] The numbers were moving in the wrong direction.

Carter's "lean and austere" budget was transformed into something else, but not by Congress. Proxmire and the other "optimists" had been right about political support for restraint. The budget numbers were blown by a combination of raging inflation and a stagnant economy.

Inflation rose steadily during the Carter years, but the great leap was from calendar 1978 to 1979, when the rate jumped from 7.7 to 11.3 percent. It was to notch up once more to a record 13.5 percent in 1980.[41]

"The unexpected inflation had two opposite effects: spending on indexed programs and interest rose, but some non-indexed programs eroded more rapidly" than had been planned.[42] Transfer payments are adjusted automatically for inflation and are paid to an eligible population. They soared over the year, but the real value of outlays tied to fixed appropriations dwindled as inflation ate into the purchasing power of each dollar.

Recession set in during the summer and fall of 1979. The Federal Reserve's new policy of October 6 "signaled retreat" in accommodating deficits through money supply growth. Revenues fell relative to spending. "Recession has simply tossed the balanced budget into the ashcan," said Walter Heller.[43] "If the slowdown or recession comes, as White House economists now expect," reported *Fortune*, "the 1980 budget could well come unglued."[44]

The Administration and Congress had agreed on a budget that seemed a model of fiscal responsibility. But as it was forcibly modified by events, the budget became a bewildering document. Inflation punched through the approved ceilings and shifted real spending in ways no one had foreseen. Some programs were boosted, others slashed. Inflation cut revenues by triggering recession, and then recouped part of the loss by ramming taxpayers into higher brackets.

The impacts of inflation were so complex, so confusing, that they sapped the energy that might otherwise have formed a basis for sustained commitment to fiscal moderation and responsibility. By 1979 a turning point indeed seemed to be reached. The stage had been set for a reorientation to new patterns. "If anyone had told me five years ago a Democratic President would submit a budget of $12 billion below the amount needed to sustain 1979 program levels, or that an overwhelmingly Democratic Congress would cut that budget, I wouldn't have believed it," said Rudolph Penner of the American Enterprise Institute and formerly with Gerald Ford's OMB.[45] At the same time (July 1979) a high Carter official, perhaps overstating the case, claimed "the days of Hubert Humphrey are over. There is no constituency for big government anymore."[46]

But the lack of political activism was not enough to hold down the budget in the face of inflation. Lawmakers felt buffeted by events. They had bitten the bullet and approved austerity. Now they were subjected to an exhausting ordeal. The budget was being rewritten by inflation and recession. It is not surprising that many in Congress began at this time to dwell on a claim that the bulk of the budget was "uncontrollable"—tied to benefit formulas rather than to spending limits. Less often mentioned was the fact that these formulas were in statute and could be amended by majority vote. Congress seemed to lack the stomach for such actions. Simple survival in the face of dizzying economic change was all it could manage.

The 1981 budget. Jimmy Carter's 1979 proposal had been "business as usual"—a carrying forward of midyear revisions in the 1978 budget. His 1980 plan was a fiscal policy crescendo. But, with perfect symmetry, the 1981 proposal was again "business as usual," a carrying forward of midyear revisions in the 1980 budget revisions, which had been forced by economic events rather than deliberately adopted.[47]

"It's going to be very tough," said OMB Director McIntyre as he announced a $600 billion ceiling for 1981 outlays.[48] McIntyre might have used the word "impossible" had he known the actual spending base and inflation rate he was facing. In the end, 1981 outlays would top revenues by $58 billion and would total $657 billion. But when McIntyre made his announcement, only ten days into the 1980 fiscal year, his hopes were "to stay within striking distance of the first balanced budget since 1969,"[49] a quest that dominated a good part of the debate that was to follow.

By the time the plan was sent to Congress at the end of January, spending had climbed to $616 billion with receipts at an even $600 billion. Of the $52 billion in estimated 1981 growth, $49 billion would simply pay the inflated cost of current programs[50] and defense would get almost all the real increase.

A new focus for critics was the level of taxes—21.7 percent of GNP. Only in 1944 had government ever exceeded this. Income taxes, which had taken a long-term average 10 percent of personal income, would go from 11.6 percent in 1980 to 12.2 percent in 1981.[51] Except for the windfall profits tax ($14 billion), no new laws were needed to capture added revenues from inflation-caused "bracket creep" on income taxes ($13 billion) and hikes in Social Security payroll taxes resulting from a 1977 law ($15 billion).[52]

"Apparently an old slogan is now being modified to inflate and tax; spend and spend," observed the Conference Board's Levy.[53] "Because of these massive tax increases the budget is extremely restrictive, whether judged from an old-fashioned Keynesian point of view or the newer supply side," judged Rudolph Penner of the American Enterprise Institute. He suggested a coalition of the two might form in Congress for a 1981 tax cut "to reduce the economic shock implied by the abrupt increase in tax burdens. . . . But it is hard to imagine a 'cut' large enough to keep the true burden from rising."[54]

The President had labeled his budget "prudent and responsible." *Wall Street Journal* editorialists rejected this characterization in their commentary on Carter's plan. "His spending proposals, combined with the tax increases . . . are a prescription for running the economy into the ground."[55]

To Penner, since real spending was up by less than 1.5 percent, "this budget is not irresponsible in the sense that Lyndon Johnson's budgets of the mid-1960s were irresponsible." But "when a growing defense burden is superimposed on growing elderly programs, it takes more than the avoidance of irresponsibility to make one sanguine about the long run. It will, in fact, take extraordinary political courage to make the cuts from current policy that are necessary to avoid ever-growing tax burdens. 'Business as usual' is no longer an appealing policy."[56]

The fiscal policy act now meant juggling five balls: defense spending pressures, social (i.e., elderly) spending pressures, tax relief demands, inflation demands, and deficit dangers.

Carter's budget got some praise for being "at least honest in laying out the problems facing the economy. It is the first federal budget ever to predict a recession. And it offers an unrelievedly gloomy inflation forecast."[57] But "instead of attacking the twin problems of inflation and recession" the budget "accepts them as facts of life. It is a stagflation budget, reflecting the dilemma instead of moving to solve it."[58]

Indeed this might be the fiscal epitaph of the Carter years. It is at least a question that will be debated by economic historians for a long time. Was Jimmy Carter the victim of inflationary forces, a man at the wrong place at the wrong time? Or did he endorse policies and fan expectations that assured an acceleration of inflation?

In Carter's 1981 budget, Robert Samuelson saw reflected the cumulative impact of Johnson's Great Society and Nixon's New Federalism, of inflationary "kickers" in entitlement payouts and income tax collections. "This is not policy, but evasion. . . . The theme is that there is no theme."

Samuelson judged that "Carter has willingly allowed himself to become the prisoner of short-term political pressures. . . . The White House is mostly drifting, accommodating the constituencies. . . . The budget is progressively less a tool to promote needed economic growth and change, and increasingly one used to redivide and apportion a national wealth that is expanding at a slower and slower rate."[59]

On March 14 the President announced a "totally revamped" 1981 proposal, spurred by an 18 percent annual inflation rate in data for January and February.[60] At the end of March, Carter sent the budget to Congress. It projected a $16.5 billion surplus—an all-time record.[61]

It did not take long for critics to find the plan's changes in spending "murky" and those on the tax side all too clear. "The Administration . . . has opened itself to the charge that it intends to balance the budget with mirrors," said Tax Foundation, Inc.[62]

Inflation seemed to be not only the stimulus for a new plan, but an active agent in the changes. The proposed spending cuts were offset by inflation-caused hikes. Despite claimed reductions of $17.2 billion, outlays declined just $4.3 billion. But on the tax side, there was $28 billion in new revenue, more than half of which came from the impact of inflation on existing taxes rather than from new levies.[63] As it had in January, inflation was "writing the budget."

The question now was, what would Congress do? Would the Democratic majority balk at cutbacks in education, health, mass transit, economic development, parks, water projects, and a delay in welfare reform? Would it accept OMB Director McIntyre's claim that "this Administration has not balanced the budget on the backs of the poor"? How much weight would it give to Carter's statement that he was "absolutely determined" to wipe out the red ink?[64]

What happened was in one sense remarkable and even historic. The House and Senate Budget committees asserted their role more than they had dared before. "In effect, the once-powerful barons who chair . . . committees were told they must cooperate in the effort to control federal spending, rather than ignore the budget panel's guidelines, as they have often done," was one enthusiastic assessment. House Budget Committee Chairman Robert Giaimo said, "This budget marks a departure from past years. It is not loaded with fiscal sweeteners . . ."[65]

On May 21 House and Senate negotiators agreed to $613 billion in spending with a razor-thin surplus. The budget contained $3.2 billion more than Carter had asked for defense and $5.7 billion less than he wanted for domestic spending. The White House and the Speaker announced they would fight the plan. On June 11 conferees from both houses agreed on a compromise that shifted $800 million from defense to social programs, and spent $300 million of the projected $500 million surplus.[66]

From the outset the claim of budget balance was denounced as a "sham,"[67] a "charade,"[68] and an "illusion."[69] Yet, even critics found some hope. "When you look at all the political energy that went into producing a balanced budget that is not really there, it tells you that even symbolic victories don't come cheap," stated the *Wall Street Journal*[70] while *Business Week* commented, "the simple fact that Congress endorses budgetary balance—even if it gives no more than lip service to the idea—represents a major change."[71]

But the bottom line was not encouraging. The *Journal* concluded that "Congress has provided a facade of a balanced budget by fiddling with the figures and raising taxes. It is guilty of both deceiving the public and crippling the economy."[72] Citibank economists judged "the big issue at the moment is tax cuts."[73]

A balanced budget had its brief shining moment. By seeming within reach, it strengthened the budget committees' role in enforcing fiscal discipline. Yet the outcome was an erosion of the numbers as bad as the year before with almost $60 billion of red ink.

There was a final, farcical incident in the fiscal history of the Carter era. It came just after Ronald Reagan had been elected President.

On November 11 the House Budget Committee approved a binding ceiling that would obligate the President-elect to cut 1981 outlays by 2 percent, except for defense, which was slated for a 16 percent hike, of which 6 percent was real growth. The resolution was passed on a straight party-line vote by majority Democrats.

"Mr. Reagan has said that a 2 percent cut can be made in the remainder of fiscal 1981 solely through the elimination of—and I quote—'waste, extravagance, abuse and outright fraud,'" said committee chairman Giaimo. Democratic member Stephen Solarz called the spending ceiling "a test of voodoo economics." Solarz said it would be interesting to see whether Reagan was "as good an alchemist as politician" and could turn the "base metal of waste into the gold of government savings." One strategist said the resolution enabled Democrats to take credit for making the cut themselves while exposing Reagan to embarrassment if the state of the economy forced him to recommend a lesser cut later on.[74]

The next day Reagan aide Ed Meese said there was no problem; the transition team had already found 6 percent in cuts and would "sift and choose" to select the required 2 percent.[75] Rather than grumbling about the resolution, as they proceeded to do, committee Republicans "would have looked better had they congratulated the Democrats on finally discerning the national mood after the voters had hit them over the head with a two-by-four," wrote the *Wall Street Journal*'s Robert Merry. "Instead . . . they raised questions about how serious the out-of-power party has been through all the years it was taking easy shots at Democratic profligacy."[76]

The Carter years were ending; the Reagan years had begun. A cynic might say that under Carter the problem was having a president who did not know what he wanted and under Reagan the problem was having a president who did know what he wanted. This is not quite fair to either man. Carter very badly wanted to end inflation and he tried a wide range of themes to do the job. But he used each for too short a time to achieve any consistent effect. One result was a sense of indecision that fed a climate of uncertainty. This in turn became part of those negative "expectations" that fueled inflation.

Americans feel uneasy when a president is controversial and possibly wrong. But they will not tolerate a president who seems to be a victim, tossed about by events and buffeted by contending pressure groups. Goodwill avails him little if he seems unable to impose his will. A president can talk about hard choices if they seem to be heroic or at least hopeful. But the president is in trouble if frank talk about tough times seems touched more with malaise than "manliness." The term is meant politically; Prime Minister Thatcher has this quality (the Latin word for "manliness" is of feminine gender).

Those are some cautionary political lessons of the Carter years. There were economic and fiscal lessons as well.

No one can recall the years 1977 to 1981 without being reminded that inflation can be a ravaging force that upsets calculations and defeats policies. Inflation indeed was a more active and devastating factor in Carter's term than deficits have been since. Inflation is right up there with unemployment as a "real" economic phenomenon rather than a theoretical danger.

Yet one cannot review the Carter era without a disquieting sense that in those days a billion dollars still meant something. True, the final figures for 1980 and 1981 were farther off the mark than they had ever been before— tens of billions in error. But politicians and fiscal analysts still fought seriously over amounts as small as one billion dollars, or even less. Witness the $800 million compromise that settled the initial 1981 budget debate.

The deficit has taken three quantum jumps: one in 1975, another in 1982, and yet another in 1983. Each time the deficit roughly doubled from previous levels. In the Carter era only the first of these jumps had occurred and people were not yet used to it. How far distant the earnest debate on a 1981 balanced budget now seems. The psychological value that a billion dollars used to carry can probably not be attained with less than five billion dollars today. The Carter era seems a paradox. In policy terms it was a time of drift punctuated by lurches. But despite massive forecasting errors, the numbers debate was carried on in a way that now seems almost exquisitely precise.

The Reagan Blueprint

ON FEBRUARY 18, 1981, PRESIDENT REAGAN announced "A Program for Economic Recovery." The President pointed to a dismal background of economic problems—high inflation and interest rates, eight million unemployed, a federal budget "out of control," a national debt approaching $1 trillion, a record tax load relative to income, and burdensome government regulations.

Reagan's action plan called for $41 billion in 1982 budget cuts, a major reduction in individual and business taxes, and measures to relieve the "cost, burden, and intrusion of government regulations."[1]

The results the plan would produce were claimed to include lower inflation, an increase in workers' real incomes through higher capital investment and productivity, lower interest rates "by reducing government borrowing made necessary to cover massive deficits," a lower tax burden, less regulation, and a reduction in "the size and role of the federal government, and its intrusion in decisions that could better be made by individuals, businesses, and state and local governments."[2]

How well did the Reagan blueprint succeed? There are three camps—those who believe he did what he pledged to do, and had set a new course for the nation by the end of 1981; those who believe the real change in fiscal and economic trends has been much less than the rhetoric would suggest; and those who see the Reagan program as having failed almost totally to deliver what it promised. Part but not all of the difference in view depends on whether the analyst focuses on taxes, spending, deficits, or the economy in evaluating the success of Reaganomics.

The new President's budget proposed a shift in priorities. His 1981 plan applied eight criteria to evaluate programs and funding levels. Entitlement programs (transfer payments) were to be revised to "eliminate unwarranted beneficiaries and payments." Subsidies and benefits for middle and upper income levels were slated for reduction. User fees would be assessed on those who benefited from specific services. "Sound economic criteria" were to be applied to evaluate the worth of subsidy programs. Capital investment in "infrastructure" would be stretched out and retargeted. Fiscal restraint was to be imposed on programs "that are in the national interest but are lower in priority than the national defense and safety net programs." Grants to state and local government would be consolidated into a few block grants. Federal personnel and overhead costs, and "waste and inefficiency," were to be reduced.[3]

These criteria were all aimed at saving money. But there would also be "a stronger national defense within restrained overall spending levels." The increase in defense spending was to be far less than the savings in other outlays.

The impact of the 1981 program is shown below in a comparison of what was planned versus the actual outcome or latest estimate:[4]

Item (in billions)	1982	1983	1984	1985	1986
Defense					
Planned	$+7	$+21	$+27	$+50	$+63
Actual/est.	+1	+17	+25	+36	+42
Other programs					
Planned	−41	−58	−74	−87	−96
Actual/est.	−39	−46	−48	−59	−71
Total outlays					
Planned	696	733	772	844	912
Actual/est.	728	796	853	928	1012

In one respect, the plan was an unqualified success. It did shift national priorities, as promised. It also managed to keep roughly the promised ratio between defense hikes and nondefense cuts. (Unfortunately, this ratio is slated to deteriorate in fiscal 1987–89. Nondefense savings will stagnate at about $78 billion while defense increases will soar to $77 billion by 1989.)[5]

The net impact of defense hikes and domestic program cuts on outlays has been very close to what was proposed. Why then has total spending soared?

The 1981 plan called for savings to be proposed "subsequently." These were to have accounted for lower outlays of $21 billion in 1983, $31 billion in 1984 and 1985, and $28 billion in 1986. Such savings never materialized.

At the same time, interest costs to finance the growing national debt were much greater than predicted. By far the most dramatic change in federal budget shares under Reagan has been debt interest. The 1981 plan called for it to fall from 9.8 percent of outlays in that year to 8.6 percent in 1984. Instead, debt service rose to over 12 percent of spending.[6]

The biggest factor driving debt interest costs upward was the surge in annual deficits produced by revenue declines. The 1981 plan predicted that unless tax laws were changed, federal receipts would climb from 21.4 percent of Gross National Product in 1981 to 24.1 percent in 1984.[7] A potent force behind this surge was the impact of inflation on "progressive" tax rate brackets. Taxpayers would be driven into higher brackets due to illusory earnings gains caused by the declining value of the dollar.

The President's plan proposed to reverse the trend and bring about an actual decrease in the share of GNP taken by federal taxes. Personal income taxes were to be cut 10 percent a year for three years and business would be able to write off capital investments more rapidly through an accelerated depreciation schedule.[8]

Congress reduced the total personal cut to 25 percent but added a provision adjusting the rate brackets for inflation (tax "indexing") beginning in 1985. This would put an end to the burden imposed by bracket creep. Congress also accepted the President's proposal for business tax relief.

Here is the planned versus actual impact (or latest estimate) of policy changes affecting federal revenues:[9]

Item (in billions)	1982	1983	1984	1985	1986
1981 tax cut					
Planned	−52	$−97	$−145	$−182	$−218
Actual/est.	−40	−91	−135	−166	−210
1982 tax hikes*	+1	+18	+38	+41	+49
1983 tax					
changes*		+1	+3	+8	+10
Net change	−39	−72	−94	−117	−151
Revenues					
Planned**	650	728	813	898	1000
Actual/est.	618	601	680	753	815

* The figures for 1982 and 1983 law changes include only actual figures and latest estimates. Since these changes were not anticipated in the 1981 plan, no estimate was then made of their impact.

** Planned revenues adjust the 1981 estimates for the actual impact of 1982 and 1983 law changes.

Why is there such an enormous gap between the revenues that were predicted in the President's 1981 plan and those which the government actually received?

The reason was the severity of the 1981−82 recession. The plan built its estimates on an optimistic projection of the amount of tax receipts under current law. These were overstated by about $48 billion for 1982, $135 billion for 1983, and $161 billion for 1984. The Congressional Budget Office made an estimate in January 1981 that was in error by a similar amount.[10]

The Reagan plan of February 18, 1981 was reasonably on-target in its projection of a shift in resources between defense and other programs, and it was close to the mark in its estimate of revenue losses from the 1981 tax cut. Where it went painfully wrong was in predicting a drop in the deficit to $45 billion in 1982 and $23 billion in 1983, with an actual surplus in 1984.[11]

The total divergence of these numbers from reality is the result of three factors. Most important was the violent effect on revenue flows by the recession. Next came the surge in debt interest costs, caused by rapid buildup in the debt and by the high rates which the Treasury had to pay to borrow money. Finally, there was the lack of follow-through on budget cuts after the first big package.

To what extent did the Reagan Administration deserve credit for policy leadership in shaping new budget priorities? To what degree did it bear the blame for bringing on the recession, or at least for failing to foresee its effects?

Two interesting documents bear on these questions. One is the final budget message of President Jimmy Carter, transmitted to Congress in January 1981. The other is a memo to the President-elect written by his budget director-designate in December 1980, titled "Avoiding a GOP Economic Dunkirk." In its own way, each of these documents pointed to the future.

Carter warned the Congress that "we have reached a point where uncontrollable spending threatens the effectiveness of the budget as an instrument of national economic policy."[12] In other words, spending pressures had become so great that the budget could no longer be used as a tool to stimulate or restrain the economy by deliberately "tuning" the level of outlays or deficits.

As if anticipating Reagan, the outgoing President made it clear that social programs were the heart of the problem. He offered a budget analysis which traced outlays rising from $42 billion in 1967 to $322 billion in 1982 for transfer payments. Their share of the budget during the same years climbed from 27 percent to 48 percent, and their claim on GNP doubled from 5.5 percent to 11 percent. Together with rising interest payments on the national debt, Carter put the share of "uncontrollable" outlays (those tied to formulas in law or contractual obligations) at 75 percent of the total budget, up from 60 percent fifteen years earlier.

Carter then turned to a series of Reaganesque solutions: correct the "implicit indexing" in Medicare—its automatic accommodation of medical care cost inflation; restrain annual cost-of-living increases in Social Security, which offer a similar guarantee of immunity; reform the "chaotic system" of grants to state and local government by moving toward block grants; act to contain subsidized loan programs, some of which are hidden off-budget.[13]

Can all this be dismissed as an attempt to carve out a niche in history, in the hope that one's contribution would eventually be recognized? Perhaps. But what gives Carter's statement some weight is how very different it is from the campaign themes that would be sounded against Reagan at the 1984 Democratic convention. Carter might have chosen to frame a liberal counterattack on the new administration, whose social philosophy was said to be to the right of Attila the Hun. Instead, Carter made it clear that he was something other than a traditional Democratic liberal on a number of issues including budget control, management of government, and social programs that entirely spared beneficiaries from sharing in the economic burdens imposed by inflation.

But there were two big differences between Carter and Reagan. Carter was fated to serve as a reminder that success in politics depends on a harmony between style and substance, between personality and program.

Hamlet in the White House was not going to clean the Augean stables, if one may risk a badly mixed mythical metaphor. It was as if, from the standpoint of the new agenda, Carter's mind was in the right place but his heart pulled him toward agonizing rather than toward action.

The other big difference is that in fiscal 1982 Carter would have let bracket creep continue to generate new revenue from the income tax, and he wanted $25 billion more from hikes in other taxes. The miracles of supply side economics did not exist for Carter; eliminating the deficit was his focus. But the range of tools available seemed to offer him no escape from the combination of high inflation and high joblessness known as stagflation. It remained for Reagan to take the great leap away from traditional options—into the future, according to some; into the abyss, according to others.

Carter did presage Reagan's themes on the spending side, in both transfer payments and defense (regarding the latter, see section on "The Permanent War Economy"). But he did not exude the fortress-storming sense of conviction that would reorient priorities at a single blow, as Reagan did in 1981. It can be argued that under Carter inexorable trends were making themselves evident while under Reagan they got a strong shove. History usually identifies emerging eras with those who have embraced and accelerated change rather than those who have analytically recognized and sought to manage change. Thus, Carter may never get his "due" for sounding the new themes.

On the tax side, Carter did not anticipate the supply-side experiment. In this regard, Reagan put forth a revolutionary game plan whose consequences are not yet played out.

Did Reagan and his budgeteers fail to anticipate the 1981–82 recession and thereby miss the arithmetic that would have told them huge deficits were on the way?

It can be charged that supply-side theory failed to allow for the time dimension—the period of transition—involved in a basic policy change. Instead, it claimed that we could simply move from one point to another on the famous Laffer curve. The curve argues that high tax rates can reduce revenues by undermining the incentives which generate taxable economic activity. In such a case, lower rates would serve to stimulate economic initiative and add to government receipts. Many advocates of supply-side theory felt that in 1981 the federal tax burden had reached this point of counter-productivity. "Less is more," they argued; lower rates would mean greater revenue.

Reagan's budget office did not adopt this interpretation of the Laffer curve. Instead it projected, very accurately, large revenue losses from the 1981 tax cut. But it erred in hoping the fact of tax cuts would boost economic morale and avert a recession. Continued growth would keep revenues high, tax cut advocates promised. Before the decline in tax receipts reached a point that added greatly to the deficit, new economic activity would replace the revenue. Thus there would be no pressure on interest rates from added government borrowing. Consumer credit purchases and business loans for capital investment would not be dampened by higher money costs.

There was a risk inherent in this model. It was that before tax cuts had a chance to work their benefit, a period of time might pass as consumers and businesses got their bearings in the new order of things. If this time lag were very long, the deficit would explode. To the extent that massive government borrowing put pressure on interest rates, it would dampen the economic growth that depended on available and affordable credit.

In short, supply-side theory seemed to offer a "simultaneous equation" without explaining what might happen if the process turned out to be a "sequential equation."[14]

Whether these categories explain what actually happened in 1981 and 1982, and the worries which persisted in 1983 and 1984, is a subject of raging debate. Traditional economists tend to see the kind of causal links described above, while supply-side economists see completely different factors at work.

There was one member of the incoming team who quickly predicted grim economic conditions "during the first 24 months of the Reagan administration." His picture in some regards actually exceeded reality—no small feat considering the severity of the 1981–82 recession.

David Stockman's December 1980 paper, "Avoiding a GOP Economic Dunkirk," must at the time have seemed a daunting document. Here is everybody at the bar, some celebrating with the champagne of recent victory, others quaffing the real gusto of a coming policy revolution, and one guy is claiming he has found hemlock cocktails among the set-ups.

"Economic Dunkirk" is not easy reading. It is an amalgam of policy concerns Stockman developed while in Congress, an analysis of the dizzying rate of spending revisions in Carter's last budget, and a warning that economic events could undermine Reagan's base of support. Its recommendations are also a mix of Stockman's own views and large, diplomatic allowances made to include the President's priorities and the supply-siders' prescriptions.

Stockman's greatest fear was that the Volcker tight money policy would collide with massive Treasury borrowing and bring on a credit crunch. The result would be high interest rates and "pervasive expectations of a continuing 'Reagan inflation.'"[15]

The new budget director saw a 50 percent risk of stagnant or declining real GNP in the first half of 1981, creating "staggering political and policy challenges." The Carter-era budget equation would worsen, and "intense pressure" would arise to bail out "wounded" sectors of the economy.[16]

Stockman sounded Carter's concern about uncontrollable entitlement spending, but in more colorful terms. "The federal budget has now become an automatic 'coast-to-coast soup line' that dispenses remedial aid with almost reckless abandon, converting the traditional notion of automatic stabilizers into multitudinous outlay spasms throughout the budget."[17]

Within the budget office, Stockman predicted "the first hard look at the unvarnished . . . budget posture . . . is likely to elicit coronary contractions among some, and produce an intense polarization between supply-side tax cutters and the more fiscally orthodox. An internecine struggle over deferral or temporary abandonment of the tax program could ensue."[18]

To avoid these perils, Stockman urged that President Reagan "should declare a national economic emergency soon after inauguration" and request that Congress "clear the decks for exclusive action during the first 100 days" on an emergency program.

The program would be based on an "inside" effort to cut spending and an "outside" effort to stimulate growth. Budget action would focus on "severe recission [elimination] of entitlement and new obligational authority." Stockman emphasized two points. Quick cuts could come only from that part of the budget which was nonentitlement and nondefense. Target programs would be trimmed an average 16 percent. He said "achieving this . . . hold-down will be tough and necessary." At the same time, the authority to spend in future years must be pruned as well. Otherwise, it would be a fiscal time bomb.[19]

The "outside" economic program would include tax cuts, and any "dilution" of the plan should be resisted as "counter-productive" since "weak growth . . . will generate soup-line expenditures equal to or greater than any static revenue gains from trimming the tax [cut] program."[20]

But tax relief alone would not spur capital investment. A "major 'regulatory ventilation'" was needed "to boost business confidence."[21] With fiscal and regulatory reform in hand, the President should then seek an accord with Federal Reserve Board (Fed) Chairman Paul Volcker. "The markets have now almost completely lost confidence in Volcker and the new monetary policy," said Stockman. The President's accord with the Fed would be in the form of a new, informal "charter" issued by Reagan. Volcker would "eschew all consideration of extraneous economic variables" and "concentrate instead on one exclusive task: stabilizing the growth of the money supply and the value of the dollar." As for the Fed, "restoration of its tattered credibility is the critical lynch-pin of the whole program."[22]

The details of Stockman's plan which held up best were those on budget-cutting. These substantially found their way into the President's 1981 plan and were the basis of many cuts approved by Congress that year. The tax cut of course did pass, and the President did stand by the Fed Chairman during the downturn of 1981 and 1982. One of Stockman's two great fears was realized; the other was not. There was a Reagan recession; there was no Reagan inflation.

Rating the Reagan Achievement

As a leader, Reagan would get an "A" from almost everyone for demonstrating that the President is still able to dominate the debate by setting its terms. In the words of an Urban Institute report: "The long cycle of dramatic growth in the social activism of the national government that began with Roosevelt's New Deal has ended. President Reagan has shifted the national agenda from problem-solving to budget-cutting, and as long as the federal deficit remains a serious problem, there is little room for the agenda to shift back."[23]

Reagan gets credit for setting the agenda. But the Urban Institute report is not a rave review of that agenda—or its results. Indeed, in the quote above, one reason why the new direction will persist is that it is locked in by the deficit. And the deficit is a "serious problem" of an administration which has "shifted the national agenda [away] from problem-solving."

Thus it is possible to rate Reagan high in dominating the debate and in setting a new direction—while giving him lower marks in achieving the results he promised.

The arguments of defenders and critics of Reagan's success on taxes, spending, deficits, and the economy are these:

Taxation. Three dimensions of the 1981 cut stand out: its impact of changes on the economy, on revenues, and on "fairness." Grades on the economy are mixed. Business tax cuts seem to have created a pool of retained earnings which contributed to a surge in capital investment. The stream of tax-sheltered profits was running about $50 billion in 1984. At a 46 percent tax rate, this means business's borrowing needs were reduced $23 billion.[24] A good share of these cash assets were spent on new plants and equipment.

More controversial is the fact that many major firms paid no taxes at all, thanks to 1981 changes in depreciation rules. In some cases, companies profited by refunds from previous years and by being able to sell tax credits they could not use. One study of 250 large corporations found that 128 of them paid no federal tax in at least one year since 1981, and seventeen firms paid no tax at all from 1981 through 1983. The latter group contained a notably large share of major defense contractors.[25]

Individual tax cuts do not seem to have made a clear contribution to productive investment. The personal savings rate fell instead of rising as supply-side theory said it would. Some tax law changes (IRAs, for example) cost the Treasury more revenue than they added to the pool of investment capital. Nor was it clear that productivity gains were due to people working "smarter"—another supply-side prediction related to tax cuts.

It was hoped that the effect of tax cuts would repeat the history of 1964–65, when a rate reduction was followed by more receipts for the Treasury.

This did not happen and, as noted on page 24, the President's own plan did not predict revenue gains, at least not directly. Large losses in receipts were expected from the rate cuts. But if the tax base remained strong, this loss could be handled. The prospect of tax relief could give a boost to the economy and stave off a recession. This of course did not happen. In 1981–82 production fell and unemployment reached more than 10 percent.

By far the trickiest tax issue was fairness. Did the rich get a big break, out of all proportion to that given any other group? Or was the cut in fact a boon to those of modest means, giving the lie to critics of President Reagan on the "fairness issue"? The figures flew on this topic in 1984.

Debate began in March when the Congressional Budget Office estimated that, as a result of tax and spending changes under Reagan, families with 1981 incomes of less than $10,000 would "lose" $820 in 1984 while families with 1981 income of more than $80,000 would "gain" $8,270.[26] The American Institute for Economic Research challenged the arithmetic on tax impact. It compared actual 1982 tax returns with the CBO estimate:[27]

Adjusted gross income	1982 Average tax payment	Change from 1981		Actual % relief
		CBO estimate	Actual	
Under $10,000	$ 210	$ −10	$ −14	6.7%
$10–20,000	1,410	−130	−162	11.5
$20–40,000	3,890	−460	−320	11.8
$40–75,000	9,070	−1,170*	−1,093	12.0
Over $75,000	43,900	−5,100*	−1,210	2.8

*The CBO data divide at $80,000, not $75,000, on these figures.

The American Institute's point was that "proportionally, the decrease in the top group is far and away the smallest." But this argument was made somewhat cleaner than the facts may justify by omitting the last column shown above. Apart from the top income group, the proportion of tax relief rises steadily.

Some analysts believe even the data showing less relief for the rich is misleading. They note that those whose Adjusted Gross Income (AGI) exceeded $1 million scored by far the highest rate of pre-tax income growth from 1981 to 1982. The apparent reason was a surge in capital gains income of about 20 percent in one year. This additional income created a tax liability which offset the lower tax bills the rich would have otherwise paid thanks to rate changes passed in 1981.[28]

Another analysis tended to confirm that tax relief was most potent at the upper end. It traced the history of annual increase in income taxes paid by those whose AGI exceeds $50,000:[29]

Year	Growth	Year	Growth
1971	13.8%	1977	21.4%
1972	19.0	1978	25.0
1973	16.1	1979	28.2
1974	20.9	1980	27.4
1975	9.1	1981	19.9
1976	24.0	1982	3.3

The reason for the huge annual percentage increase in taxes paid is an explosion in the number of taxpayers in the $50,000-plus group from less than half a million in 1971 to more than four and a half million in 1981. This ninefold increase was produced by a combination of inflation and real income gains. The dramatically low change in tax burden for 1982 had three causes—lower inflation, fewer real income gains (due to the recession), and a hefty chunk of tax relief for well-to-do Americans.

The *Wall Street Journal* offered a defense of "tricklenomics" in an editorial with that title. The share of total taxes paid by every income group under $50,000 went down while that for every group above $50,000 went up in 1982 compared to 1981. These numbers, said the *Journal*, "vindicate the supply-siders."[30]

But critics charge that a fairness issue is inescapable if one turns to the impact on lower-income families of the 1981–82 recession. Total personal income rose 4.2 percent in 1982. But for those families with an AGI below $25,000, it actually fell by 3 percent. Thus, one-third to one-half the claimed tax relief may have actually been due to a decline in taxable income rather than to rate reductions.[31]

Tax economist Kenneth Simonson adds a dimension to the debate. Each year inflation increases the portion of families with more than $50,000 income. A century from now the dollar may have depreciated so much that $50,000 will be a poverty-level income. A little of this change will occur each year through inflation.

Simonson found a way to allow for the dollar's decline in measuring the tax shift between those better-off and those less well-off. He divided the tax-paying public into ten equal-sized groups based on income (the poorest 10 percent, the next poorest 10 percent, and so on). Then he measured the shift in the share of total taxes paid by each of these ten groups. Simonson found that between 1977 and 1982 the maximum shift was no more than 2 percent of total taxes. The Urban Institute came to the same conclusion: "Tax rate cuts had no effect on tax shares."[32]

There was one enormous relative change. The share of taxes paid by the poorest 20 percent of Americans went up from 0.1 percent of the total to

0.4 percent. Defenders of the status quo argue that the absolute share paid by the poor is so low it proves our progressive tax system is working. Critics note the fourfold increase in share translates into a tax burden which rose from 4 percent to 10 percent of income for a family of four living at the poverty line between 1978 and 1983.[33]

The reason for this rising burden is that the poor didn't take part in 1981 tax relief. The features of the tax code that are vital to them are the earned income credit and personal exemptions. Neither of these was increased to give the poor the kind of relief which rate-bracket cuts gave those better off.[34]

Particularly hard hit were the working poor. Under new laws they lost eligibility for welfare and other benefits at a rate so steep that it amounted to a tax of more than 100 percent on some earnings. This is hardly the kind of productivity incentive which supply-side theory recommends. Indeed, Arthur Laffer himself concluded in a recent study that changes since 1981 "have imposed punitive tax rates on poor families seeking to increase their earnings."[35]

In fairness to the supply-siders, it should be noted that fairness was never a major focus of their argument for tax cuts. They felt that reshaping rate brackets to affect the distribution of net income was a liberal game that had been among the causes of stagflation.

The supply-siders did anticipate, however, that income tax cuts would enhance social equity in two ways. First, the rich would have less incentive to seek tax shelters if rates were lower. They would shift some of their dollars into taxable investments and, in the process, their tax share would go up. Second, these investments were likely to help the economy more than tax shelters do. The result would be growth and jobs and a better deal for those less well-to-do.

But the 1981–82 recession swelled unemployment and reduced the income of poorer Americans, while those with high incomes enjoyed a surge in capital gains and earned high rates of interest on their savings. When supply-siders were attacked, they noted that the tax cut was being phased in at such a slow pace that their theory was left untested and the economy was left without stimulus. Defects in the dosage, not in the medicine itself, had opened a crucial gap that undermined their plan for a smooth sequence of beneficial effects.

Those of more traditional economic views agree that tax cuts stimulate the economy. But that idea has been around since Keynes. It's called pump-priming. It has a proper use but the price you pay is deficits.

As for fairness, traditionalists urge supply-siders to forthrightly admit they intend for the rich to get the most relief, because investment by the rich is the supply-siders' engine of growth. It is disingenuous to go farther and argue, by a new slant on data, that the poor are the special beneficiaries of supply-side tax cuts. That is an attempt to make a case look good after the fact.

Spending. There are two dimensions to spending: its size and its shape. The first dimension deals with control of total spending and restraint of budget growth. The focus is on spending in the abstract, as it affects the demand for revenues and pressures on the deficit. The second dimension deals with program priorities and the mix of spending. Its focus is on spending in the concrete, as it affects national goals—including the apparently inescapable matter of fairness.

Here is a comparison of Carter's 1981 budget with Reagan's 1985 budget, as a percentage of Gross National Product:[36]

Category of spending	GNP share	
	1981	1985
Total outlays	23.6%	24.0%
Social Security and Medicare	6.0	6.9
National defense	5.5	6.7
Interest on the debt	2.4	3.2
All other outlays	9.7	7.2
Revenues	20.6	18.7
Current year deficit	3.0	5.3

For the four budget years from 1982 through 1985, the Office of Management and Budget estimates that spending growth will exceed inflation by an average 3.9 percent annually—exactly the same rate of growth as for the four years of the Carter Administration.[37]

Two of the Reagan-era changes in GNP share have clearly been deliberate—the increase in defense and the decline in "all other." The abstract argument for defense hikes is that the military share of GNP was much greater under Eisenhower (9.7 percent) and Kennedy-Johnson (9.1 percent) than today. We are merely climbing up from the low point reached under Nixon-Ford (5.2 percent).[38]

The decline in that category labeled "all other" reflects David Stockman's claim that "aside from defense, interest, and Social Security, we have shrunk the government by about 15 percent. The domestic budget is not growing seriously in real terms."[39]

The Congressional Budget Office bears Stockman out in an analysis of how much lower program costs would be in 1984 as a result of Reagan-requested law changes passed from January 1981 to August 1983:[40]

Program	Reduction in spending
Child nutrition	28%
Student loans	27
Public health services	22
Compensatory education	17
Aid to families with dependent children (AFDC)	13
Food stamps	13
Vocational education	12
Low-income energy assistance	8
Unemployment compensation	7
Medicare	5
Medicaid	5
Social Security	3
Civil service retirement	3
Veterans' pensions	1

The basis for these cuts runs the gamut from changes which were widely recognized as proper to those which have become part of the fairness debate. In the former category are the elimination of overlapping programs which provided double benefits to some recipients, cost-containment laws in areas such as health care, and restrictions on middle-class eligibility to receive some tax-funded services.

Not shown on the list above are Great Society anti-poverty programs in training and employment, and in community and regional economic development, which were virtually abolished. They had either outlived their usefulness or failed to achieve results, and appear unlikely to be revived by any future administration.

More controversial were shifts of greater responsibility to state and local government for health and welfare programs. The federal government saved money by combining numerous grants into a few large blocks of reduced total value. States were compensated for this cut by having more freedom to target funds. This was a trade-off which some found worthwhile and others judged inadequate. It was also an elegant way for the Administration to phase out low-priority programs without an open fight. Such programs were simply starved for funds and fell by the wayside as states made their decisions on spending the block grants. Some of the victims deserved this fate. Others fueled the fairness debate. The counter-strategy in Congress was to pull favored programs out of block grants and restore their protected status.

One respected analyst gives "Reagan federalism" high marks. Richard Nathan of Princeton University finds that "the changes made so far . . . add up to a significant increase in state influence. . . . Overall we are impressed that the Reagan period has seen a resurgence in the role of state governments." Nathan points to the greater discretion provided by block-grant programs, reduction in federal regulations on states, and enhanced state responsibility to run many social programs.[41]

Most controversial among Reagan's budget savings were the cuts in AFDC and basic health and nutrition programs for poor children. Welfare grants are not automatically adjusted for inflation each year as are Social Security pensions. Since 1970, the real value of an average AFDC check has declined by an estimated 13 percent. Combined with cuts in direct service programs, this illustrated the diminished political clout of the poor since the mid-1960s.

In 1983 the official poverty rate edged up for the fifth straight year to 15.2 percent of total population. The rate for Blacks was 35.7 percent; for Hispanics, 28.4 percent; for female-headed households, 36 percent.[42]

When these figures were released in August 1984, Democrats called them "the smoking gun of Reagan unfairness."[43] More temperate was the comment of Robert Samuelson: "Reagan's welfare cuts are debated legitimately. But Reagan is correct that changes in the economy affect the poor more. Recession increased poverty, but the blame lies with the high inflation that caused severe recession."[44] In other words, the root evil was price shocks in the 1970s and the inability of Carter's drifting policy to reestablish stability and confidence. Reagan would surely approve of this interpretation from a mainstream economist with a reputation for independent thinking. Samuelson sums it up this way: "We cannot reduce poverty simply by being generous. Ultimately, only economic growth and individual effort will suffice."[45]

Budget Director Stockman has also urged that if poverty measures are to be used as part of a debate, they be realistic. In the words of American Enterprise Institute fellow Terry Hartle: "Poverty rates for the 1980s and the 1960s are not strictly comparable because the poor now enjoy a greater range of benefits than before. Food stamps and Medicaid are not counted as income, but they contribute significantly to the recipient's well-being."[46]

Critics of this approach respond that some in-kind benefits, especially health care, do not increase disposable income. But if the Stockman-Hartle approach were used, it would cut the poverty rate from about 15 percent to about 11 percent.[47]

In September 1984 Stockman was summoned by two House Ways and Means subcommittees to explain his prediction 10 months earlier that the poverty rate would "decline dramatically" in 1983. After admitting that guess was off the mark, Stockman offered a dramatic illustration of the redistribution of wealth which does occur. He presented figures showing that "federal tax and spending policies boosted the income of the poorest one-fifth of the nation's households by $89 billion in 1983, while the same policies cost the richest one-fifth $179 billion."

After these income transfers, occupants of the richest households—who earned more than fifty times as much as the occupants of the poorest households—had only four times as much left to spend as their poorer counterparts.[48] This is a significant impact. But within two weeks of Stockman's testimony the Federal Reserve Board issued a study showing the top two percent of American families control 70 percent of the tax-exempt bonds, 50 percent of the stock, and 20 percent of the real estate.[49] Perhaps all one can glean from comparing Stockman's analysis with that of the Fed is that the debate on income redistribution may never end.

To some analysts, the most troubling issues deal not with the discipline which Reagan and Stockman imposed on outlays for the poor, but with their inability to impose discipline on outlays for the middle class.

"The absolute increase in military spending [under Reagan] was larger than those in the other areas. But even if the share . . . devoted to the military had not increased at all . . . , spending under Reagan would still claim a larger share of the GNP than ever before in peacetime," notes policy analyst and journalist James Fallows.[50] The reason is the growth of middle-class entitlements—transfers of income and medical services to those whose eligibility was unrelated to their economic means.

These programs have surged in cost despite modest Reagan-era trims. They include Social Security, Medicare, and civil service and military retirement. They also include hallowed tax breaks such as the home mortgage interest deduction. Half of its $28 billion in benefits went to the wealthiest 10 percent of households in 1984. A quarter of the relief—$7 billion—was enjoyed by the wealthiest 2 percent. Yet to speak of modifying middle- and upper-class welfare is to court defeat.

The result is an inability to prevent a huge flow of benefits to those who do not need them. This creates an entirely new focus for the fairness issue. "The only real redistribution Social Security effects is from one generation to another: those now under the age of forty or forty-five are transferring resources to their elders," says Fallows.[51] Herbert Stein, a former chairman of the Council of Economic Advisors, sounds the same theme: "The present debate about fairness does not focus on today's serious issue—fairness between present and future. To put it more sharply, the issue is one of fairness between today's middle-income people and the whole American population for generations ahead."[52]

In October 1984 the National Council of Senior Citizens charged that the state of the elderly during the Reagan Administration had been one of "broken promises." The Council cited benefit reductions of $24 billion, equal to $900 for each American over 65 years of age, and protested that "they should not have to pay for the misguided tax and military policies of this administration."[53]

The reduction of $24 billion is in fact based on an estimate of what federal spending would have been without any change since 1981. In other words, it is a slowing of the growth rate in increased outlays for seniors' programs.

Terry Hartle believes senior citizens have done rather well in receiving government aid, especially compared to poor children. "The Census Bureau reports that 22 percent of children under 18 lived in poverty in 1983, the highest percentage since the early 1960s. In contrast, the percentage of adults in poverty has fallen from 24 percent in 1970 to 14 percent last year (1983)."[54]

The Census Bureau study found that 66 million people, almost one-third the population, receive direct government benefits.[55]

Households receiving a Social Security check had an average monthly income of $1,054 while those receiving veterans' benefits averaged $1,432. By contrast, poor families headed by a woman and receiving child aid averaged $795 in monthly income, those receiving a housing subsidy averaged $485, and those with food stamps averaged $418.[56]

The number of beneficiaries in major programs, and their average income, appears to support the concern of those who believe it is middle-class welfare which represents the real challenge in controlling the cost of income transfers. This spending pattern may simply reflect a national mood described by David Broder: "It is not anti-government. That mislabels it. It is a mood that is perfectly willing to use government for goals that appeal to the personal self interest of the majority, while denying its assistance to the minority who may be victims."[57]

Perhaps Broder's assessment is unduly harsh. But there is no denying that government programs of cash assistance and medical care are heavily targeted on the basis of age alone with no income test. Programs for the poor are not negligible but they are distinctly smaller and slower-growing. Welfare has been capped and even cut back, while Social Security and Medicare continue to expand in real terms.

Deficits. The greatest burden imposed by the rise in spending for defense and middle-class benefits is not the high current taxes they require but the huge future taxes they will require. Borrowing one dollar of every five spent in the current budget means imposing on coming generations part of the payment for our programs. When interest is added, their "share" of the burden created by today's spending becomes shockingly large.

To most analysts, deficits have been the signal failure of Reaganomics. Stein believes "a large deficit . . . threatens growth and economic stability."[58] To Fallows, "by evading [the issue of soaring outlays], our elected leaders make the entire financial structure dangerously brittle. . . . What if the government decides that it can escape its mounting debts only by starting up the printing presses? Are the potential wounds less grievous because they would be self-inflicted?"[59]

Fortune's Anne Fisher asked, "What's left of Reaganomics?" and concluded that "little remains of the ambitious program." She cited Stockman's observation that tax cuts should never have been made without an all-out assault on middle-class entitlements—the "boulders" in the budget, the "untouchables." As a result, judged Fisher, as of 1984 only the tax cuts remained from the original grand scheme. And they were imperiled by the growth of deficits. "Unless Reagan finally makes the hard choices in a second term that the first-term Reagan has avoided, he could leave office in 1988 with an economy that looks dismayingly like that of 1980: high taxes, high spending, stop-go monetary policy, and overregulation."[60]

Robert Samuelson concluded that "by historical standards, Reagan has reduced taxes and nondefense spending as a proportion of GNP only slightly. But interest payments are exploding." To Samuelson, there was political skill involved. "Reagan's genius, so far, is to prevent deficits from being politically alarming simply by pretending they're not. . . . Reagan avoids [dealing with] deficits because the costs are immediate and obvious and the benefits are distant and obscure. If a president should promote necessary but unpopular changes, Reagan is derelict. He has not created a new consensus, but only exposed the deficiencies of the old. . . . The next president faces an awesome political adventure: to recreate consensus."[61]

But it would be wrong to leave the impression that Reagan ducked the issue simply out of cowardice. He was also being told by supply-siders that everything would turn out all right without action; indeed, that action on the tax-increase front could snatch defeat from the jaws of victory.

In June 1984, former Assistant Treasury Secretary Paul Craig Roberts, a leading supply-sider, announced, "The deficit scare has all but faded away." He offered this table to readers of *Business Week*:[62]

Fiscal year	Federal deficit	Down-payment	State-local surplus	Total govt. deficit	Percent of GNP
1985	$207 bil	$ 25 bil	$46 bil	$136 bil	3.5%
1986	219	53	50	116	2.7
1987	224	71	58	95	2.1
1988	207	93	61	53	1.1
1989	198	119	64	15	0.3

The table has its ironies. Most notable is the role played by state-local surpluses. These were achieved by tax rate hikes in 1981–82 to make up revenue losses caused by economic decline. Rate hikes are of course something supply-siders vehemently oppose. It is poetic to see them resurface as part of Roberts' arithmetic. One reason the surpluses look so healthy is that the figures allow for no more recessions in the 1980s.

Roberts' first column is from the Office of Management and Budget. In August 1984, OMB shaved those numbers by $40 to $60 billion per year. But this was done largely to reflect Roberts' second column, the budget cuts and tax hikes passed by Congress in 1984—another violation of supply-side doctrine. OMB's estimate isn't nearly as optimistic as Roberts'. His 1989 deficit, with downpayment included, is $79 billion; OMB's August 1984 figure is $60 billion higher.[63] And the Congressional Budget Office estimate is $124 billion above OMB's.[64] The variance between OMB and CBO is caused mostly by different projections of the interest rates which will have to be paid on the debt.

Even if there were no recession and state-local revenues held to Roberts' level, the total deficit in 1989 would be four times what he predicts if OMB is right and over thirteen times as large if CBO is on the mark.

Roberts had titled his table "The Incredible Shrinking Deficit." The *Wall Street Journal* editorialized during the same week in June 1984, "Deficit Monster, RIP." This analysis also put the red ink at $15 billion in 1989, and concluded, "It is certainly an oddity to watch America get bogged down in a debate over how and when to increase taxes to reduce the deficit just when, thanks to tax cuts, it is enjoying shrinking deficits and spreading prosperity."[65]

The risk for Roberts and the *Journal*, of course, was that their dramatic headlines and arguments might turn out to be the oddity. In the meantime, they must certainly be judged a factor in making President Reagan feel that a full-scale assault on the deficit was of less than compelling urgency.

Those who have taken the sanguine view sometimes say the deficit is "an effect, not a cause."[66] Why this should make the deficit less of a threat is not clear. Perhaps the phrase is meant to return our attention to spending control issues.

It would be more accurate to say that the deficit is an effect which has become a cause. Debt interest costs are one-eighth of total outlays and are rising rapidly. The deficit once may have been merely an expression of the gap between current year revenues and expenditures. But in the last 10 years it has taken on a life of its own. The interest on prior years' deficits has been in an amount that ranged from 40 to 127 percent of the current deficit. This suggests the risk of a debt-deficit spiral.

There is an obvious fairness issue regarding the debt and a more subtle fairness issue related to deficits. The debt is a bill we are passing on to future generations. Some have argued this is all right since current budgets include public works and other capital investments our children can use. But it turns out the total value of such items is only about $30 billion a year,[67] roughly one-sixth of the added debt. The other five-sixths is tax-supported consumption we have decided not to finance ourselves but to pass on, thus bestowing upon the unborn a form of "taxation without representation."

The fairness issue regarding current deficits is more subtle. It concerns the impact of high rates of real interest: the spread between the inflation rate and what borrowers are charged. This spread has been at a record level—about 6 percent—since 1981.

Supply-side economists argue no connection can be proven between deficits and interest rates. More traditional economists believe there is a link because heavy government borrowing demands make lendable funds scarce and drive up rates. When Treasury Secretary Donald Regan and then Chairman of the Council of Economic Advisors Martin Feldstein scrapped over this issue, fellow Council member William Niskanen said it was a shame to see them argue: "Don is right—there is no clear proof of a connection. But Marty is right too—there should be proof because such a connection probably exists."[68]

Recently supply-siders have offered another defense. The argument is that high interest rates are good because individuals, not government or corporations, are the big gainers. Individual income excluding interest rose only 45 percent in total dollars between 1979 and 1983, but interest income went up 89 percent.[69] The problem with this argument is that it is a "reverse Robin Hood" approach. The gains are at the top end of the income scale, where interest-bearing investments are heavily concentrated.

For the average American, the estimated 4 percent which the deficit may have added to real interest rates[70] is a problem, not a boon. It makes purchases more expensive and in the case of home mortgages can mean an inability to qualify. If deficits do affect interest rates, they create an advantage for those who have money to invest and a disadvantage for those who don't, as far as the eye can see.

The economy. Economic news was a political plus for Ronald Reagan in 1984. Herbert Stein recalls a similar situation from 1972, when he was chairman of the President's Council of Economic Advisors: "In the spring of that year I declared at a press conference that the economic statistics were the best combination in recorded history, or at least in the Christian Era. As far as economics was concerned, the Democrats could not lay a glove on Richard Nixon."[71]

Stein was among those enjoying the result. But he believes the focus was and is wrong. "A far more important issue, unlikely to get much attention from the candidates, relates to the future. What is the policy by which we can keep on the path of low inflation and reasonably steady growth of output—not just in 1984 and 1985 but into the long future?"[72]

Stein judges that there has been something seriously wrong with fiscal and monetary policy in the last 20 years. Until 1980 it was manifest in no-win trade-offs between unemployment and inflation; since then its symptoms have been high interest rates and the deficit threat. To judge administrations on the basis of quarterly statistics has been an exercise in misplaced, indeed meaningless, assignment of credit and blame. Ultimately all that matters is the impact of their policies on long-term trends and on broadening the range of choices which allow for price stability and steady growth.

The Urban Institute's 1984 evaluation of the Reagan record confirmed Stein's point in statistics. A typical middle-class family "experienced a negligible increase in real after-tax income between 1980 and 1984 and has at best only a modest increase to look forward to over the rest of the decade. . . . Even under optimistic assumptions, standards of living for most people will rise less in the 1980s than they did in the 1970s, and far less than they did in the 1960s."[73]

The Federal Reserve study offered an even less hopeful picture. It concluded that the income of an average American, adjusted for inflation, is lower now than in 1969 and even farther below the peaks reached in the mid-1970s. Inflation has swelled paychecks, hiding the real trend by "giving a deceptive illusion of progress."[74]

Data from the Tax Foundation present a picture of total stagnation. Median family income in current dollars doubled between 1974 and 1984. But when direct federal taxes are subtracted and after-tax income is expressed in constant 1974 dollars, here is the result:[75]

Year	Income	Year	Income
1974	$10,976	1980	$10,282
1975	11,145	1981	9,636
1976	11,049	1982	9,786
1977	11,025	1983	10,013
1978	11,000	1984	10,175
1979	10,869		

The classic question in presidential campaigns, "Are you better off than you were four years ago?", would seem to have had a positive answer in 1976 and a negative answer in 1980 and 1984.

The Urban Institute sees even the feeble upturn of 1982–84 as imperiled. "In a sense, we have bought whatever gains we now have with the deficits. Whatever economic growth we may get, the combination of future tax increases and benefit cuts will take it away," says John Palmer, coeditor of *The Reagan Record*.[76]

A dramatic illustration of the difference between long-term changes and election economics is offered by Princeton Professor Alan Blinder. In August 1984 Blinder noted that the average annual increase in GNP had been 2.95 percent under Carter and 3.04 percent under Reagan. The unemployment rate averaged 6.4 percent under Carter and 8.6 percent under Reagan.

But when one looks at the year preceding the election, the numbers change. In 1980 GNP slid 0.8 percent; in 1984 it grew 6.4 percent. Job creation was zero in 1980, but 5.4 percent in 1984. Blinder's tongue-in-cheek advice to presidents: have your recession early in the term.[77]

Commerce Department Chief Economist Robert Ortner took on Blinder by pointing out that Carter inherited "an economy that was growing strongly with moderate inflation" and by 1979 "had squandered his inheritance" while Reagan had to dig out of the hole created by Carter.

Ortner used the "misery index" developed by the late Arthur Okun, "a Democratic economist." The index combines the rates for inflation and unemployment. In 1980 it stood at 18; by 1984 it had dropped to about 11.[78]

Okun had said 9 percent was the "discomfort level" above which the country becomes "quite unhappy." Here is the misery index for years 1977–84:[79]

Year	Index	Year	Index
1977	13	1981	16
1978	15	1982	14
1979	14	1983	13
1980	18	1984	11

The reliability of the misery index "is implicit in its two components. . . . A low inflation rate suggests a high living standard, because the consumer's dollar is not losing value so rapidly. And a low unemployment rate is a sign of high living standards because it indicates that more people are working. . . ."[80]

The misery index itself may be open to question. Low inflation rates have often reflected a weak economy rather than a high living standard. Indeed, some skeptics ask why inflation in itself is a bad thing for consumers, especially if people are keeping up with it. The answer may be that inflation is bad, or at least unpopular, because constant change in the value of a dollar disorients people and makes it hard for them to know if they are keeping up or not. This breeds unrest even when the standard of living continues to rise.

Ronald Reagan caught a favorable swing of the misery index in 1984. But Stein reminds us the focus must be long-term: "Who is willing to stand up to say that in all fairness the current generation of middle-income Americans should make some sacrifice, in the form of higher taxes and lower entitlements, for the sake of future national security, economic growth and economic stability?" Stein concluded such questions were rare because no candidate, let alone a campaign consultant, would be inclined to bet on the willingness of the American voter to sacrifice "for any gain that is more than six months in the future."[81] Fallows agrees: "Most politicians obviously feel that it is impossible even to raise such questions."[82]

SUMMING UP THE REAGAN SCORECARD

There is effective politics and there are effective policies. Here is how Reagan might be graded:

Taxes. An "A" for defining the debate and for setting a new direction. Even the tax hikes of 1982 and 1983 do not undo the dramatic change in tax levels and tax growth brought about by the 25 percent personal income tax rate reduction, by indexing, and by the reduced tax load on business investment.

A "B+" for the impact of corporations' greater retained earnings on business investment. A "C−" for the impact of high-income individuals' reduced tax load on productive investment. A "D" for the supply-side theory that lower personal tax rates would surface money from the underground economy and would improve productivity by making people work harder.

Spending. An "A" for defining the debate, and for meeting his chosen goals in defense. The current military buildup is the largest in history, yet there isn't a war on. This is extraordinary. Congressional trims of amounts requested by the Administration don't diminish the grade for political impact.

An "A" for effectiveness in trimming nondefense, nonentitlement spending. This part of the budget has dropped by one-fifth to one-sixth in real terms, a historic reversal.

A "C" for affecting entitlement spending. Transfer payments and middle-class welfare remain as "boulders" in the budget. Much larger savings in these programs should have gone with the 1981 tax cut package. Tax-supported payments unrelated to means remain not only as a major source of fiscal pressure but as the ultimate test of political will to act responsibly on behalf of future generations.

Deficits. An "F" for 1981–84. The total federal debt at the end of 1985 will have doubled from its 1980 level—$1.8 trillion versus $900 billion. This is contrary both to Reagan's 1981 plan and to his then-stated philosophy.

The debate between supply-siders and traditional economists is not over whether large deficits are a bad thing but whether the stage is now set for their elimination through economic growth. Critics of this hopeful thesis note that the most credible sources project large deficits for 1989 even if no recession occurs. The CBO's $263 billion in red ink and the OMB's $139 billion, both call for a recovery lasting seven years—two years more than the longest boom on record. By contrast, the average recovery is 34 months and then there is a downturn. Recession in 1986 or 1987 could easily balloon a single year's deficit to $300 billion.[83]

At that point, "the U.S. wouldn't be able to spend its way back to recovery."[84] The cost of paying interest on the debt would climb by $30 billion or more a year, swallowing up all the options on spending and turning "fiscal policy" into a hollow phrase.

This is the mainstream view. Supply-siders respond with their own fear: haste to bring down the deficit will lead to the very tax increase that could choke off a boom of unprecedented duration. This is an attractive vision; it also involves a large penalty if the theory proves wrong.

Both schools of thought agree that spending cuts are a proper way to reduce the deficit, though supply-siders tend to hope the economic miracle will make it possible to avoid trims which are painful or divisive.

The years 1981–84 saw what some called a "battle for Reagan's soul." Paul Craig Roberts strenuously sought to demonstrate that Reagan was a supply-sider and Martin Feldstein insisted with equal energy that Reagan was not. This battle of the pens was perhaps less crucial than the President's own posture. It was an amalgam of traditional emphasis on spending cuts and supply-side enthusiasm for economic growth caused by tax cuts. Reagan also embraced, almost as a talisman, an idea neither Roberts nor Feldstein gave particular weight: the balanced budget amendment.

The proposed amendment carried the appeal of making the world over in one bold stroke. It carried the liability of providing endless possibilities for mischief and evasion in the budget process. Many seasoned observers concluded that the only way for an administration to express convincing support for a balanced budget is to submit a balanced budget, or something close to it. To submit spending plans with huge deficits, while calling for the amendment, is like the heavy drinker who announces he will go on the wagon when prohibition is enforced.

To offset earlier test scores and win a passing grade for the course, a second Reagan administration would have to take major steps toward budget balance. This means bringing out the heavy equipment to remove budget "boulders" and tackle some tough tax issues.

The economy. An "A" for standing by Fed Chairman Paul Volcker while he wrung out inflation, and an equal grade for the rate at which inflation has dropped. But while marks for fortitude are tops, the jury is still out on the matter of whether too much medicine was applied in 1981–82. National income would have been $600 billion higher in those years without the recession.[85] True, hyperinflation was a major cause of the downturn. But did the Fed need to slam on the brakes so hard? Could it have done better with less of a drop and more moderate growth thereafter? These questions will be debated for a long time.

Among the footnotes in this debate is the fact that a third of the drop in inflation was due to the worldwide slackening of food and energy prices and to the high exchange value of the dollar. Another 20 percent of the drop occurred because a defect was corrected in the way inflation had been measured. The rest of the drop—about half—was attributed to the creation of economic slack, with high unemployment and severe hardships for many Americans.[86]

A "B+" for the strength of the recovery. An "A" is denied because those large percentage gains were scored off the worst recession in 40 years. Also, the ravaging of American exports by an overvalued dollar denies the recovery a clean sweep. And by late summer of 1984, interest rates were knocking around in a range that had housing, forest products, and savings and loan industries in a cold sweat.

In a sense the jury is always out on the economy because the economy is like life itself. It goes on. There is no final parenthesis. And as Stein suggests, it is not easy to offer a verdict on the economic policies of an administration. At what point after it takes office does it affect the economy more than its predecessor? At what point after it leaves do its policies stop reverberating?

The budget imbalance which began in 1966 set off "stop-go" use of federal policy tools for fiscal stimulus and restraint. In the process, these tools have tended to become blunt instruments. Spending pressures in defense and transfer payments, together with the 1981 tax cut, have created what some believe is a "zero-option" budget, one that is no longer a policy tool at all but is instead a mere function of forces driving the numbers.

This relates to the politically convenient bad habit of each administration citing the mess it inherited as the explanation for all its actions. In the process, current responsibility is almost obliterated. The country will be better off when the sins of the past are no longer the rationale for today's economic policies.

In this regard, the Reagan Administration's grade is mixed. The supply-side experiment is often debated in terms of a new direction which will be judged on its own merits. If nothing else, this had made the debate more interesting. But the old political tendency persisted in 1981–84 to blame any shortfalls in current performance on the hole dug by past administrations.

A crucial test for Reaganomics is the next downturn. Supply-siders have been careful never to claim that economic cycles would end. But the next recession will put their theory on trial. Will the deficit explode? Will this lead to the Treasury soaking up so much of the savings pool that too little is left for private investment?

In this event, will the Fed have a choice between prolonging the recession and reigniting inflation? If it chooses the former course, what would be the economic, social, and political impact of another recession comparable to 1981–82? How would the world economy and third world debt be affected by a sharp slowdown in the U.S.? If the Fed chooses the second course, will it yield to the temptation to use inflation not only as a cure for recession but as a way to pay off the federal debt the easy way—with depreciated dollars resulting from long-term inflation?

In short, has supply-side economics uncovered a new calculus? Or has it created a zero-margin situation which will lead us back to stagflation if everything does not come up roses?

The jury is out. For most of the public, the issue is probably this stark and simple: If the last recession was an adjustment shock to a new and better era, it was a price worth paying. If it was just a violent swing on the same old roller-coaster, it was not worth the cost.

Chapter 2

What Everybody Knows about Defense

THIS CHAPTER AND THE NEXT are titled "what everybody knows." The phrase is used even though it carries a risk of overstatement. Obviously, everybody does not know a lot of detail about defense or transfer payments. Equally obvious is that those who do know don't always agree.

The phrase is used anyway, to emphasize the level of agreement that does exist and to underscore the fact that the issues which form the debate are widely known. This is especially important to realize in defense, where it is claimed one cannot judge what is going on without access to military secrets.

About one trillion dollars has been spent on defense since 1980. Not surprisingly, America's forces have grown stronger. Both surprising and worrisome, however, is that the gain in strength and particularly in security has been far less than one might suspect.

A major reason is that the Pentagon has been plagued by a number of crucial mismatches between intentions and reality. The five sections which follow focus on these mismatches:

—Our vast global commitments versus our actual willingness and ability to apply force;

—Our theoretical emphasis on conventional war capability versus our practical emphasis on nuclear war capability;

—The skills, talents, and abilities we need in our officer corps versus the basis for promotion in the service;

—The reliability and affordability we need in our weapons versus the temptation to maximize high technology;

—The businesslike spirit we need in our weapons industry versus the practices which actually prevail;

—The impact military spending is claimed to have on our economic and political life versus the impact it does have.

47

The Department of Defense is the world's largest enterprise. This has caused some to point out, correctly, that a certain amount of waste is inevitable and that a few horror stories should not obscure the good work done by many devoted people. The horror stories are just a flashy tip of the iceberg. Serious questions arise from the mismatches—questions involving tens of billions of dollars.

Some, but not all, of the critique which follows is based on ideas taken from the military reform movement. This loose coalition of members of Congress and defense analysts has been at work for several years. Many of their ideas make sense—for example, that new weapons designs should be realistically tested before being put in production. Other ideas are less obviously correct—for example, that simpler weapons are almost always to be preferred to more complex ones.

The Office of the Secretary of Defense has proposed and implemented a number of cost reforms. But the Pentagon establishment—civilian officials, career officers, defense contractors—has resisted nearly every idea from the military reform movement and has prevented most of its proposals from being implemented. This success in delay, however, is not a valid basis for dismissing ideas as "old" reforms. If a different way of doing things is rejected without a practical test, it can hardly be proven obsolete.

We need reform. Value received per dollar of military spending is not high. Use of the defense budget as a signal to the Soviets has outlived its usefulness. The defense budget now needs to become a signal to ourselves that we are spending sensibly and with real effect—a reasonable goal in return for $300 billion a year.

The Search for a Strategy

We, more than any of the other 200 million Americans, hold in our hands and in our daily work the potential to fortify or to erode the consensus in favor of a stronger defense. If we are perceived as wasteful, or unreceptive to new ideas of strategy and tactics, or if we do anything to lose the people's confidence, we might destroy the fragile national consensus so recently formed.
—Defense Secretary Caspar Weinberger, speaking to Air Force Academy cadets, May 27, 1981

DURING THE 1980 CAMPAIGN, 71 percent of Americans endorsed higher defense spending. By March 1982 the support level had dropped to 43 percent. In November 1982 it stood at 17 percent.[1] After a Korean jetliner was shot down by the Soviets in August 1983, pollster Lou Harris reported "a moderate increase in the backing for Reagan on defense. But that will not last, and erosion is already setting in."²

What happened? Part of the drop was due to the fact that defense spending did increase. This left fewer people in favor of further hikes. But the Harris Poll confirmed that "erosion" was also a factor. The terms of sustained support for a military buildup which Weinberger laid out in May 1981 had somehow not been satisfied.

To a remarkable degree, the Defense Secretary defined the causes of decline in popular backing for the program he directed. The most obvious problem was "waste," in the form of price gouging by Pentagon suppliers and dumping of usable spare parts by the services. But strategic inflexibility on issues such as the size of U.S. global commitments, the importance of arms control, and the uses of a 600-ship Navy added to the debate. Most basic, has increased spending translated into increased security?

Consider these terms:

Force. The amount and quality of military might at the nation's disposal.

Power. The ability to project force to achieve intended results in cases where our aims conflict with others.

Security. The ability to pursue vital national objectives while deterring rivals from resorting to war.

Strength. The combination of force, power, and security.

Cost. The portion of national wealth that must be allocated to achieve strength.

Force has increased. But it has not translated clearly into added power. More serious yet, there is a widespread sense that it has been accompanied by an actual decline in security.

The amount of force purchased per unit of cost is falling as the price of weaponry rises. Thus, given the propositions above, the amount of power and security purchased per unit of cost is falling even more rapidly.

The propositions just stated are not beyond debate. Indeed, they would be vigorously resisted by some key policy-makers. But they do reflect public perceptions which have brought about the erosion Weinberger warned of.

Military force exists both to be used and to deter situations which would require its use. The current buildup is intended to enhance our ability both to project force and to negotiate mutual reductions in force. To strike the right balance between these concepts is no easy matter even in calm contemplation, let alone in the chaos of politics.

The late Herman Kahn once likened defense planners to managers of a department store which was having a sale, with no way to tell when the sale would occur or what items would be featured.³ To plan for results is hard in any program. But in defense, your main customer (the enemy) seeks to render your plans misguided, even irrelevant.

Problems of military strategy are almost insoluble if war is treated as an activity apart, as an end in itself. In Clausewitz' words, "War should never be thought of as something autonomous but as an instrument of policy."[4] Military planning cannot be coherent unless it is part of a coherent foreign policy. Here is the root cause of public decline in support for the defense buildup.

President Reagan reaped an initial windfall by providing a sense of relief. People were grateful to be delivered from a foreign policy which seemed to waver in the face of moral superiority claims by "liberation" movements. If America could be pushed around by third world (read third-rate) powers, what chance did we stand against the Soviets? So ran the theme of unease.

Whatever the personal elements that shaped Carter's foreign policy, it looked in historical context like a bottoming-out of America's post-Vietnam retreat from power. The time for a turnaround had arrived. Reagan was resolute in his stated willingness to draw the line against aggression and in his certainty that America's political values were the best in the world. These themes were a tonic to the electorate.

Today, however, one fear has replaced another. Under Carter the danger was that Soviet miscalculation of American passivity would lead to adventurism that could provoke war. Under Reagan the danger is seen as Soviet miscalculation of American hostility, leading to preemptive action that could initiate war.

Admittedly, the electorate does not always make things easy for a President. The typical profile which emerges from poll data is of a public that wants the U.S. to "stand up to the Russians" without risking war: a tall order for any policy or force structure to fulfill.[5]

Force is an absolute concept: the number of planes, tanks, ships, men. Power is a relative concept: how does one's force compare with others, how much leverage does it provide? Security is a more complex matter: a combination of power and how one's intentions are perceived. Passivity and aggressiveness both diminish security. What maximizes security is a consistent posture regarding the use of force, based on criteria which one's foes suspect the world at large will find convincing—backed by force levels adequate to constitute a threat in any situation where they might be used.

There is no better way to focus these cosmic concepts than by looking at the defense budget debate. The fact that there are limits on resources means priorities must be examined. And priorities are the essence of strategy.

Almost from the beginning, Ronald Reagan's proposed defense budgets have been charged with eight related shortcomings:

1. The buildup is unfocused. It is Carter's program, only bigger, with no review of force structure.

2. There is a belief in "throwing dollars at defense" that parallels the liberals' approach to social spending in the 1960s.

3. The budget is driving policy, and weapons contracts are driving the budget.

4. The question "How much defense spending is enough?" has been approached in abstract and not realistic ways.

5. To the extent defense capability has been defined, it amounts to a "police the world" approach.

6. The buildup was intended above all to overawe the Soviets; instead it has galvanized them.

7. As a result of 5 and 6, there is a mismatch between U.S. strategy and affordable force levels.

8. The public is aware of these shortcomings, and its support for defense spending has eroded, imperiling the basis for a sustained buildup.

A sampling of the critique on each of these points:

An unfocused buildup. "Nothing has distinguished the Reagan defense build-up so much as its expanded size"—Gen. Brent Scowcroft.[6] "We're getting more disjointed in the sense of not having fully coherent programs. . . . Our total capability is less than the sum of the individual parts"—former Joint Chiefs Chairman Gen. David Jones.[7] "Our strategy is the best-kept secret we've had"—William Hoehn, the Rand Corporation.[8] "If you do not plan effectively, the only way you can spend money effectively is by accident"—John Collins, defense specialist, Library of Congress.[9]

Throwing dollars at defense. "The details of the Pentagon's spending proposals reflect so little selectivity that the budget may undermine the case for the big buildup being proposed. . . . The Pentagon has a particular responsibility to handle its funds carefully. It is seeking budgets so big they are almost impossible for the layman to grasp"—Walter Mossberg, *Wall Street*

Cartoon by Auth. Reprinted by permission: Tony Auth, 1982.

Journal.[10] "It is not easy to construct a scenario in which increased defense spending is unnecessary. But so far the need has not been supported by sufficient reasons and definition of purpose"—Walter Guzzardi, *Fortune.*[11] "I'm afraid the conservatives are in danger of making the same mistakes in defense policy that liberals made in social policy. We have to learn that you can't simply throw money at problems and expect them to go away"—Robert Pranger, American Enterprise Institute.[12]

Weaponry-driven strategy. "We've probably built ourselves into a position where we're going to erode . . . our combat forces starting about 1985. That's when all the bills come due for big hardware projects underway, and there won't be enough money . . . to pay for them"—former Defense Secretary James Schlesinger.[13] "Some people suspect the administration wanted multi-year contracts not because of the efficiency but to lock Congress into buying expensive new systems"—William Kaufmann, Brookings Institution.[14] "Unless tough choices are made, we are likely to end up in precisely the wrong place—with a portion of the forces needed to carry out each strategy, but not enough to implement any of them adequately"—Philip Odeen, former senior defense policy analyst, National Security Council.[15]

Abstract yardsticks. "The key question, the cost-conscious Weinberger said, is not the percent increase in future military budgets, but 'are we get-

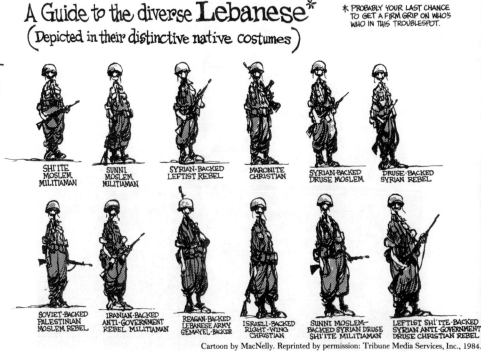

A Guide to the diverse **Lebanese***
(Depicted in their distinctive native costumes)

* PROBABLY YOUR LAST CHANCE TO GET A FIRM GRIP ON WHO'S WHO IN THIS TROUBLESPOT.

SHI'ITE MOSLEM MILITIAMAN

SUNNI MOSLEM MILITIAMAN

SYRIAN-BACKED LEFTIST REBEL

MARONITE CHRISTIAN

SYRIAN-BACKED DRUSE MOSLEM

DRUSE-BACKED SYRIAN REBEL

SOVIET-BACKED PALESTINIAN MOSLEM REBEL

IRANIAN-BACKED ANTI-GOVERNMENT REBEL MILITIAMAN

REAGAN-BACKED LEBANESE ARMY GEMAYEL-BACKER

ISRAELI-BACKED RIGHT-WING CHRISTIAN

SUNNI MOSLEM-BACKED SYRIAN DRUSE SHI'ITE MILITIAMAN

LEFTIST SHI'ITE-BACKED SYRIAN ANTI-GOVERNMENT DRUSE CHRISTIAN REBEL

Cartoon by MacNelly. Reprinted by permission: Tribune Media Services, Inc., 1984.

ting the strength we need'"—*Washington Post*, January 7, 1981.[16] "The answer to (fixed percent growth) arbitrary proposals is not for the defense experts to assure us they will provide 'the strength we need.' In fact, there is no such thing. . . . There are no defense programs, or at least no sensible ones, that will reduce the risk to zero"—former Council of Economic Advisors Chairman Herbert Stein.[17] "Because the answer to the question, how much is enough, is so nearly metaphysical, any number can play the game"—Jack Burby, *Los Angeles Times*.[18]

Unreasonable goals. "The strategy articulated by Weinberger is that the U.S. has to be prepared to fight an unlimited number of conflicts in an unlimited number of geographic areas for an unlimited length of time. . . . A universal conflict strategy cannot reasonably be argued . . ."—Norman Ornstein, Catholic University.[19] "Asked to which areas of the world he accords highest priority [Weinberger] answers, 'all of them,' which is to say he has no priority"—Morton Kondracke, *The New Republic*.[20] "The goals that the President set for the nation's defense are a logical extension of earlier concepts rather than a radical departure. But because [several major] goals were combined and adopted all at once, they require such a quantum leap in military commitment that they amount to a major shift in policy"—Robert Toth, *Los Angeles Times*.[21]

Faulty reading of the Soviets. "Early on, this administration argued that the Soviet economy was at or near the break point and that we could exact arms control concessions, or force a Soviet turn inward, by using our economic and technical advantage to force the pace of the arms race. . . . The

Cartoon by MacNelly. Reprinted by permission: Tribune Media Services, Inc., 1983.

results are in the glossy new book, 'Soviet Military Power, 1984'"—Stephen Rosenfeld, *Washington Post*.[22] "One of the dozen most important people in the administration on these issues offered the view that the net accomplishment . . . so far may have been to ignite another expensive round in the arms race"—Robert Kaiser, *Washington Post*.[23] "The real fight in Washington is not over the size of the defense budget but over differing views of the Soviet Union"—Charles Maines, editor, *Foreign Policy* magazine.[24] "It was the worst damn posture statement I've ever seen. He [Weinberger] went from 200 years of Russian history into the need for five new tanker aircraft, without any kind of rationale"—Congressman Les Aspin.[25]

Strategy-force mismatch. "The money's not enough and the projected program's not enough for the planned commitments around the world. That's a traditional failing . . . but it's worse this time partly because there's been less attention to priorities"—former Defense Secretary Harold Brown.[26] "These forces [proposed in the budget] will not in fact support either enduring nuclear war or full-scale conventional war in three theaters simultaneously. Fortunately, in all probability, neither can Soviet forces"—John Steinbruner, foreign policy studies director, Brookings Institution.[27] "The Reagan budget cannot buy all the President is trying to buy even if it got every dollar"—Senator Sam Nunn.[28]

Lack of public sanction for the troops. "The generals and admirals have learned and over-learned the lesson of Vietnam. They instinctively recoil from applying small doses of force in messy wars for obscure political reasons"—Joseph Kraft, *Los Angeles Times*.[29] "We must make the price of involvement clear before we get involved"—Gen. Frederick Weyand.[30] "It is wrong to have soldiers at the end of the string without support of the American people"—Army Chief of Staff Gen. Edward Meyer.[31]

Loss of public support for the program. "Another decision to spend more, taken in careless haste, could leave us worse off than we were before. It could set up a new wave of public dismay as the decisions began to hurt us economically while adding little of consequence, or the wrong things, to our military capability"—Walter Guzzardi, *Fortune*, September 1980.[32] "The worst thing that could happen would be for the nation to go on a defense spending binge that will create economic havoc at home and confusion abroad and cannot be wisely dealt with by the Pentagon"—former Defense Secretary Melvin Laird, November 1980.[33] "If Congress buys into all the major weapons programs now, the nation will end up slightly weaker, slightly more confused, with slightly less momentum, having unnerved the Russians, irritated our allies, and without having substantially increased the security of the American people"—Congressman Newt Gingrich, December 1982.[34] "The defense consensus has already been destroyed"—former Defense Secretary James Schlesinger, December 1982.[35]

The consistent theme in these concerns is that a democracy will sustain long-term growth in defense spending only if military power is seen as an instrument in the service of a coherent foreign policy. Ironically, the Reagan program has had to deal with mounting criticism, because it has based foreign policy too exclusively on the use of military power. Overemphasis on the instrument of force has undermined support for its increase. The weight given to military might suggests a hollowness of underlying policy, and this has unnerved the public.

In a double irony, the erosion of support has been abetted by the Pentagon's hesitation to use its augmented power, and the ambiguous success achieved when it has done so.

"Out of the trauma of Vietnam, generals and admirals have acquired a transcendent political sensitivity that demands muffled drums and muted trumpets if the military institution is to survive. The sum of those sensitivities is that never again should American forces be thrown into the horrors of the battlefield without popular political support. . . . Undeclared wars cannot be sustained. Resolutions of the Tonkin Gulf or Lebanon variety are frail and mischievous mandates." [36]

Col. Harry Summers of the Army War College sees a trend, beginning with Korea, of an unwitting return to the 18th century type of war repudiated by the great military thinker Clausewitz—and by the Founding Fathers. The "passions of the people" are deliberately not aroused—and the price is a lack of popular sanction for the troops. The commitment of force is called a "police action"—and the price is a lack of national war aims. The military role is defined in surgical terms—and the price is total muddle when things get messy, as they always do. "There are not military solutions and political solutions, but only the latter. Military force is one of several possible means of achieving a political goal." [37]

When the Long Commission urged President Reagan to pursue diplomatic alternatives as distinct from military operations in Lebanon, Secretary of State Shultz said this reflected a fundamental misunderstanding of the relationship between power and diplomacy. [38] He was of course correct—military strength is a definite part of diplomacy. But "no diplomatic payoff has followed the assertion of American power." [39] Why?

In one regard the Reagan Administration deserves considerable sympathy. Its own beliefs aside, it had every reason to feel it came to office with a mandate to "draw a line in the dirt" against aggression by the Soviet Union and its third world surrogates. Not only did Reagan win, but Carter lost, to a real degree on this issue.

It appears, though, that the American voter was standing midway between the two men on the "toughness" issue. Four years at one pole made some movement toward the other pole attractive. Under Carter, Americans were worried about the future of our place in the world. Under Reagan, Americans came to be worried about the future of the world itself.

This leads to the over-riding question: what is the nature of the Soviet Union? Is it an "evil empire" which can only be restrained by a level of force that guarantees retaliation in the form of damage above a high "pain threshold"? Or is it a "dismal empire" whose political history and tradition is sad to contemplate, and whose motives include self-justifying paranoia and archaic Russian imperialism, both cloaked in the fading raiments of an increasingly bureaucratic and perfunctory Marxism?

It might seem that there is not much to choose from in these two definitions. They both fit a metaphor used by the late Senator Henry Jackson. The Soviet Union, he said, was like a hotel burglar walking down the hallways to see which doors had been left unlocked.

Certainly, the Soviets found too many doors unlocked in Eastern Europe after World War II. Certainly they continue to outrage civilized standards— witness the jetliner attack, the Afghan war, the persecution of dissidents.

Perhaps the crucial distinction is this: the American people want the Soviets treated firmly, but on the basis of specific acts, not on grounds of incorrigibility. Not only does the latter approach run up against our standards of fair play, but people sense its potential for leading to war. The Soviets should fear our response to excesses, but they should not sense a perfervid hostility. The one course aims to correct and restrain; the other aims to obliterate.

The postwar pattern of presidential behavior toward the Soviet Union has been, in LBJ's words, "with one hand clenched to fight and the other hand open to shake."[40] This is a game for the strong of nerve but it is a pragmatic not an ideological game.

Critics charge that an administration of true believers over-reacted in money and hardware and invigorated the Kremlin's true believers. In consequence, more will be spent and less security will be achieved on both sides. The earlier theory, which was overdone but had a core of truth, was that Soviet and American strategies were mutually reactive ("apes on a treadmill"). The newer theory is that Soviet strategy is of spontaneous ideological origin. If, in Weinberger's words, the Soviets aim for "military domination, it's just that simple,"[41] it is only fair to ask whether the goals of American strength, deterrence, or strategic stability can be reached at all— or whether mutual bankruptcy will set in first.[42]

In line with the new theory of Soviet strategy, there has been a major change in American doctrine, abandoning the long-implicit belief that any war with Russia would be short. The standard model was one in which a conventional conflict in Central Europe ended rapidly as our side, fearing defeat, "went nuclear." At that point things would be resolved fast.[43]

The new strategy calls for us to be able to: (1) fight a prolonged conventional war; (2) fight a protracted nuclear war; (3) launch strikes at points remote from Soviet attack.[44] It is argued, correctly, that the first of these abilities will make escalation less likely, both because we will offer a stronger deterrent against Soviet attack and because we will be able to hold out longer before "going nuclear." The concern is that capability may not match policy. "If there is a 'window of vulnerability' in the 1980s, it lies far more in

Cartoon by MacNelly. Reprinted by permission: Tribune Media Services, Inc., 1984.

the conventional than in the nuclear area," says Robert Komer, a senior Pentagon official in the Carter Administration.[45]

As for gearing up to fight a protracted nuclear war, Secretary Weinberger succinctly answered critics by saying, "There's no point in planning to lose,"[46] raising the issue of what was meant by winning. Defenders of the plan argued that it is proper, even necessary, to prepare for a worst case because you thereby avoid setting a specific "threshold" at which you could be coerced.

Some analysts believe the major foreign policy goals—sending a signal to the Soviets, stiffening Europe's backbone, getting Syria out of Lebanon, making the Cubans "cool it" in Central America—were appropriate and attainable. But they each required "policies, not just postures."[47] In this view the Administration's goals were sound, if ambitious. The problem was that "it sees all the wrongs in the world but no rights; it demonstrates no political imagination to reach out and achieve anything positive."[48]

This orientation, the charge runs, caused the Administration to fall back on a foreign policy which used as its starting point the diplomatic tool of last resort—military force. And the tool was wielded by reluctant dragons, the officers who had been left "at the end of the string" in recent, unpopular wars. The paradox was of belligerent civilians, treating all interests—even secondary ones—as vital (the true "lesson of Vietnam"),[49] while those in uniform tried to beg off. It seemed a case of speaking loudly and carrying a stuck stick.

The talk was softer in each real crisis than in the abstract (witness President Reagan's restraint in the Korean airliner tragedy). And a pragmatic note is often sounded ("It's unreasonable to expect some crisp 'Reagan doctrine' that would describe the whole program in a phrase"—Defense Under Secretary for Policy Fred Iklé).[50] But there is an uneasy sense that the moderate responses have been ad hoc. They are not backed by the equivalent of LBJ's "one fist–one hand" doctrine. Indeed, each calm and prudent act appears as a victory won from a dark and consistent ruling theme—the vision of an "evil empire."

Fears of where this might lead were not eased by revelations of a possible link between religious belief and foreign policy. This subject falls in a category used on political broadsheets in the early days of the Republic: "Important if true."

Many fundamentalist Christians believe the Bible prophecy of an apocalypse is about to be fulfilled. Russia will attack Israel. A nuclear war will ensue. While the missiles are flying, those who have been saved through making a timely decision for Christ will be lifted off the earth in the rapture. For the rest, there will be the holocaust, then the Millennium—a thousand years of Christ's rule on earth, with Satan chained. And finally, the Day of Judgment.

Ronnie Dugger, publisher of the *The Texas Observer*, and Larry Jones, a graduate student in religion, claim to have found "at least five occasions in the last four years"[51] when President Reagan expressed a belief in the possibility or probability of the above events. Some of the references are murky. One was a private conversation between the President and the Rev. Jerry Falwell which Falwell first described and later repudiated.

As of this writing, the White House has not repudiated the purported harmony of belief between the President and religious fundamentalists on this subject. The real defense lies elsewhere. It is that, on a consistent basis, President Reagan coupled his statement of faith with an expression of personal responsibility to work against the coming of nuclear war, saying, "I believe that God will respect us for making all-out efforts toward world peace, and that is where my commitment lies."[52]

Linking theology and foreign policy is not an exercise to which Americans are accustomed. On one level, the President's stated position is tenable because he affirms a belief held in common with those he has generally identified as his coreligionists, while emphasizing that he is also committed to fill the duties of secular office which have been deemed most honorable throughout history.

The difficulty comes at a deeper psychological level. It deals in imponderables which the tools of public policy analysis are ill-suited to decipher. It comes down to a single question: If you believed that the events of the apocalypse would sometime occur, and if the elements of a current situation could be construed to fit the prophecy, and if the result of those events would be to spare the God-fearing (not even a night in jail, so to speak) while chastising the godless and, finally, ushering in a millennium followed by eternity; if you believed all this, would you work against the triggering event with all capacities of heart and mind as vigorously as you would do if you dwelt only on the nature of nuclear war and on the responsibilities of office? It is a question which cannot be answered.

Some knowledgeable analysts believe it is absurd to consider this issue. They find the case neither persuasive nor relevant. They point out that there is no evidence religion plays any part in the Administration's strategic policy, that the President is not particularly religious, and that he is the direction-setter but not the detailed policy-maker on such matters.

Indeed, they say that if religious arguments are to be taken seriously, the risk would have been much greater under Carter, who was an authentic, born-again Christian. President Reagan's August 1984 joke about outlawing and bombing the Soviets, they point out, suggests not the end of the world but destruction of the enemy with impunity.

There is much to be said for this latter view. A widespread belief among political conservatives is that the Soviet "empire" is decaying from within and that it is realistic to work toward a world for our children which is free of communism. They see U.S. intervention in areas such as Central America as an opportunity to prove we can work our will, thereby erasing the sense of impotence created by Vietnam.

The danger in this line of thought is not that it accepts the worst consequences but that it assumes there will be no bad consequences if the U.S. pushes vigorously on the premise that history favors us. The danger arises not from religious resignation but from political adventurism.

It is not easy to know what relative weight to assign to these two schools of thought. One hopes both fears are misplaced.

There are two basic problems in thinking about nuclear strategy. One is the horrible consequence if deterrence fails. The other, less obvious, is that deterrence itself has become an unmanageable concept. It has moved from paradox to contradiction to absurdity. Deterrent strategy continues to be treated as a serious and indeed impressive intellectual enterprise. The question must be raised whether in fact there has arisen a "fog of deterrence" which makes even the fog of war transparent. If, as may be the case, thinking about the unthinkable has become a muddle, we should also examine the negative feedback onto our planning and strategy for conventional war. Are the bizarre categories of nuclear conflict (both its avoidance and its prosecution) blunting our ability to talk sense about other kinds of conflict? Is there a mental unraveling in this twilight zone that is leading to "unthinking the thinkable"—losing our grasp on common sense and wisdom about war as it has been known through history?

There are three broad categories of conflict: (1) conventional war in which there is a "front" between opposing forces and firepower is based on bullets, shells, and explosives; (2) counter-insurgency (formerly "guerrilla war") in which opposing forces meet at a large number of scattered points, the "front" is poorly defined, and concentrations of firepower are seldom decisive; (3) unconventional war in which aerial delivery of nuclear, chemical, or biological weapons is the outstanding feature.

The categories of conflict become much more difficult to grasp as one moves from conventional warfare to counter-insurgency, or from principles of war (associated with non-nuclear weapons) to principles of deterrence (associated with nuclear weapons). The following definitions were developed by the Library of Congress' chief defense analyst John Collins: [53]

Counter-insurgency compared with conventional conflict

1. Comparative characteristics (U.S. experience)

	Conventional	Counter-insurgency
Threats:	Clearcut	Ambiguous
Decisive strategy:	Direct	Indirect
Decisive force:	Military	Reform
Decisive participant:	United States	Local people
Technological impact:	Telling	Trivial
Desired culmination:	Military victory	Political victory

2. Comparative aims

	Insurgents	U.S. in Vietnam
	Political	Military
	Strategic	Tactical
	Offensive	Defensive
	Positive	Negative
	Deferred	Immediate

3. Comparative negotiating techniques

	Insurgents	U.S. in Vietnam
True aims:	Concealed	Exposed
Aims stress:	Consistency	Compromise
	Concessions from foes	Conciliation
Tactics:	Deceptive	Straightforward
Armed forces:	Support talks	Separate from talks
Time:	Immaterial	Important

Principles of war compared with principles of deterrence

Principles of war	Principles of deterrence
Initiative	Preparedness
Concentration	Nonprovocation
Economy (of force)	Prudence
Maneuver	Publicity
Surprise	Credibility
Exploitation	Uncertainty
Security	Paradox
Simplicity	Independence
Unity	Change

Actual wars do not always fit neatly within one model. For example, the Lebanon conflict shows elements of both conventional and counter-insurgency warfare, while the potential NATO–Warsaw Pact conflict in Central Europe could include both a conventional and a nuclear exchange.

It's not only the generals who think in terms of the last war. And it's not always the war most recent in time that leaves the biggest impression. For millions of Americans, as well as for many politicians and military officers, the last "real" war was not Vietnam or even Korea. The last "real" war was the one that we fought the way wars should be fought and ended the way wars should end—the "big one," World War II. The very terms Collins uses for conventional warfare tell the story: clearcut, direct, telling, United States, military victory.

By comparison, counter-insurgency is part of a new era of ambiguity. The fight against guerrillas began glamourously enough with talk of special forces and slogans like "who dares, wins" and "the possible we accomplish quickly; the impossible takes a little longer."[54] But frustration set in when the enemy refused to stand and fight, and body counts took the place of ever-advancing front lines. Even when the troops were winning, it couldn't be explained to the folks back home. "The Viet Cong were decimated by search-and-destroy operations and virtually destroyed during the Tet Offensive in 1968. But these tactical victories were at the strategic price of the support of the American people."[55]

Even further removed from our historical experience are the shadowy measures of success in the world of nuclear deterrence. Only the first of Collins' nine principles has a meaning which is clear and sits easily with traditional notions of strength. Not one of the remaining principles deals with the things soldiers are trained to do. Instead, there is a blend of weapons capability and psychological manipulation—the objective and subjective facets of deterrence.

There used to be a continuum, workable if not smooth, from preparedness to war: if you aren't deterred by our strength, we'll use it. Nuclear weapons have changed that. "Thus far, the chief purpose of our military establishment has been to win wars. From now on its chief purpose must be to avert them. It can have almost no other useful purpose," wrote strategic analyst Bernard Brodie in 1946.[56]

In short, nuclear deterrence rests on an armory that is never to be used under operational conditions—but only because it is kept in such a high state of readiness for use that the enemy dare not provoke us. The other element of deterrence is a psychology that walks the razor's edge of gamesmanship—intimidating but not alarming, warning of consequences but not making specific threats.

How to think clearly while confusing the enemy—as we are dealing in the same facts and imponderables available to him—is a daunting challenge. Consider for example two statements in favor of the MX missile from sources of the highest competence:

Former Defense Secretary James Schlesinger: "We should prepare to match Soviet forces and for this reason we should proceed with MX deployment. The argument for modernizing the ICBM force has never been to provide invulnerability. . . . The argument [is] above all, throw-weight, which provides the prospect of matching Soviet counterforce."[57]

Former Defense Secretary Donald Rumsfeld: "We seem to be in danger of having identified a serious problem—Minuteman vulnerability—and then systematically rejected every conceivable solution because no single solution is perfect. . . . It is particularly imperfect over time as the Soviets take steps to counter it. But the way deterrence becomes healthy . . . is by fashioning pieces that fit together, each one of which is imperfect, but together they create a deterrent across the spectrum."[58]

The basis for this type of "healthy" deterrent is synergy: adding to the difficulty of calculation by piling up uncertainties, thereby diminishing a foe's confidence that he has taken everything into account.

The Office of Secretary of Defense has been consistently filled by men of the highest intellectual ability. When their statements do not make sense it may be a sign that the subject has become unmanageable. Schlesinger and Rumsfeld use arguments that illustrate Collins' principles of publicity, uncertainty, paradox, independence, and change. But these arguments also seem to lack compelling logic.

Piling up imperfect systems—Rumsfeld's scenario—suggests the image of an America tossing oranges at a Soviet juggler who must find a way to keep them all in the air. But Soviet defense analysts are not all one person who will break down under such a distraction. A separate team can be assigned to deal with each imperfect system. Does a flawed weapon become an asset by serving in an armory which includes a lot of other flawed weapons? It is not clear that this approach leads to a credible deterrent. The only sure result would seem to be a runaway arms race.

Schlesinger's "throw-weight" competition can be analyzed more briefly. As Henry Kissinger told NATO members in Brussels in 1979, "It is absurd to base the strategy of the West on the credibility of the threat of mutual suicide."[59]

This is not the phrase normally used to describe nuclear doctrine. Instead, it is known as "mutually assured destruction" (MAD). Those who find MAD credible argue that its strength lies in this proposition: to challenge the balance of terror through war, what you do must not only work, it must work brilliantly; if you fail at all you have failed catastrophically.[60]

The argument is that nuclear weapons have changed the basic nature of war by giving the loser power to inflict a punishing level of damage. Only a deadly handful of warheads has to get through the winner's defenses to wreak havoc. In this sense, nuclear bombs are the ultimate equalizer, granting both sides the capacity for unacceptable harm. Thus the balance is preserved.

Defenders of MAD laud its "unusual success" in preventing a direct confrontation during 40 years of unremitting superpower conflict. The fear of escalation has deterred conventional war. The impossibility of either side gaining a decisive technical edge has prevented a nuclear exchange. As for war itself, "the gravity of the evil must be discounted by its improbability."[61]

Not surprisingly, large segments of the public do not share this sanguine view. The experts "are much more optimistic about the chances to avoid nuclear war in the next 50 years," says former Defense policy planner Walter Slocombe.[62] To what degree this optimism is due to superior knowledge rather than to such factors as faith in the logic of deterrence theory and habituation to thinking about war cannot be assessed.

Slocombe sees a "public revulsion" against deterrence. It is based on "doubts that the Soviet military threat is real and stronger doubts that our own nuclear threats are moral, but most of all on the belief that the risk of war has grown." This revulsion translates into support for repudiating alliances, renouncing first use or any use of some weapons, retreat from insistence that mutual force reductions be verifiable, and even disbanding our forces.[63]

U.S. nuclear doctrine is expressed in a number of guises. The three most important are "extended deterrence"—the general threat that we will use nuclear weapons to defend against a wide range of Soviet actions; "horizontal escalation"—the general threat that if we cannot respond directly to what the Soviets are doing somewhere, we will get back at them somewhere else; and "limited nuclear war"—the general threat that we will prevail on any battlefield by using an armory that assures decisive tactical advantage without provoking an all-out exchange.

Earl Ravenal of the Cato Institute says: "Extended deterrence is at the heart of America's strategic dilemma. Nuclear weapons are used to deter all kinds of threats, conventional and nuclear, to ourselves, our allies, and even to other objectives of less than vital interest. By committing the U.S. to the defense of numerous allies and clients abroad, this strategy has stretched the capacity of our general purpose forces to the breaking point and has relied on threats of nuclear retaliation to close the breach. . . .

"What is wrong in the Reagan version of U.S. strategy is what has been wrong with that strategy for 40 years—reliance on nuclear threats to buttress an over-extended structure of global commitments. The task now is to find an alternative to the framework of deterrence and alliance that has become so burdensome and unstable."[64]

Cartoon by Stayskal. Reprinted by permission: Tribune Media Services, Inc., 1983.

The current status of the second key concept, "horizontal escalation," is not easy to determine. This capacity was to be added as part of an "intellectual reform" Weinberger launched in 1981. Previous doctrine called for the U.S. to be able to fight a specific number of wars at once. The number was set by comparing potential threats with existing budget realities. Weinberger rejected this approach. "The decision on how large our overall defense effort ought to be must be based on much broader and more fundamental judgments than some arbitrary and facile assumption about the number of wars or fronts."[65] Instead, planning was aimed at acquiring specific capacities, one of which was horizontal escalation—counter-attack on Soviet targets remote from the field of battle. The Navy found this concept particularly attractive.

Among the critics was former Defense Secretary Harold Brown, who argued that horizontal escalation "fails the first test of deterrence—reminding a potential enemy that aggression will cost more than it gains."[66] Brown pointed out that even if the Navy could carry it out, the policy would leave only one target more valuable to the Russians than the Persian Gulf oilfields are to the U.S. and Europe—the Soviet homeland. Thus, unless the U.S. was willing to launch World War III, the policy would lack credibility, and would implicitly abandon important battlefields to Soviet attack.[67]

It appears that horizontal escalation as a doctrine is now "inoperative" to some undefined degree. The inventors of the idea deserve sympathy. They were looking for a way to limit America's global commitments without making the error of declaring specific areas to be beyond our "defensive perimeter." But in practice the new approach turned out to be another version of extended deterrence if important military objectives were at stake.

The third key concept is "limited" nuclear war. It too is part of Secretary Weinberger's "intellectual reform," the latest step in a 30-year evolution from massive retaliation to "flexible response."

In 1982 there was a storm of criticism when Weinberger's first Defense Guidance became public knowledge. This document, the Secretary's instructions to the services, called for the ability to fight a protracted nuclear war if deterrence failed. The 1983 Guidance toned down the rhetoric but refined and expanded the concept. "Our nuclear forces must be governed by a single coherent doctrine," was expressed in an order to integrate plans for using long-, medium-, and short-range nuclear weapons so the President could "execute controlled-response options."[68]

The document noted the Soviet Union has not isolated the role of long-range nuclear weapons from those of other nuclear arms. "Thus we must not impose any arbitrary division between categories of nuclear weapons systems which could constrain their effective, coordinated employment in retaliation," the Guidance concluded.[69]

Supporters argue that "flexible response" is preferable to the all-or-nothing choice implied in massive retaliation, where the U.S. either initiates a devastating exchange or allows the Soviets to act with impunity. They see the new doctrine as a contribution to our deterrent ability by giving the U.S. a usable capacity to react at the proper level, to "make the punishment fit the crime."

To Slocombe, the doctrine is part of an "assault from the right" against deterrence. "The aim is to use nuclear weapons more flexibly, to find a way to fight limited nuclear wars. But in the chaos of an exchange, could nuclear war be kept both short and restricted? Could it avoid such mass destruction as would set off a chain of retaliation?"[70]

The scenario most often used by proponents of tactical nuclear weapons is a Warsaw Pact attack on NATO that could not be resisted with conventional forces. But "some nervous Europeans, hearing American talk about 'limited war,' began to suspect it meant war limited to them."[71] One item that doesn't show up in U.S. military budgets is that West Germany supplies free real estate and facilities for American forces. In wartime, "West Germany would even provide the battlefields."[72]

The concern about planning for use of tactical nuclear weapons is that it ups the odds on an all-out exchange, and defers action in the real solution in Western defenses—better conventional capability.

"There is less and less willingness to redress conventional shortfalls with nuclear forces," says former Assistant Secretary of Defense "Bing" West. "Kissinger and Schlesinger have spoken out on this theme; it is spreading throughout the military. There is less assumption by all NATO members that a conventional conflict will 'go nuclear' in Central Europe."[73]

West says there is also a felt need to do more mobilization planning, "which either means a benign capacity for a sustained buildup or less benignly, ability to fight a long conventional war."[74]

"The failure to upgrade command and equipment pushes us to go nuclear," says Army Reserve Major Lance Sterling. "To be strong in conventional forces is like being able to stop a fight before it starts because people know you can use your fists. Reliance on nuclear forces is like having to decide whether to use a knife or gun to stop that fight."[75]

Walter Slocombe believes "the surest way to avoid nuclear war is to avoid a conventional war, because the most likely way for a nuclear exchange to develop is through escalation of a conventional conflict."[76] Thus, the fists that deter are the best insurance against ever having to draw the gun.

No subject is more fundamental to deterrence, or to strategy generally, than the nature of our foe. Is the antagonist crafty and unscrupulous, but sane? Or are we up against latter-day heirs to the Nazi doctrine of "world power or ruin"?

The requirements of deterrence are upped considerably if one accepts a premise seldom seen in print but held by a number of persons involved in defense planning and analysis. It is that Soviet leaders are willing to suffer at least the 20–30 million in civilian casualties that they suffered in World War II, if America can be eliminated as a threat. This view is said to be corroborated regularly by escapees from the Soviet system. It pictures Russian strategy as going beyond a rule of thumb to an active premise which says that as soon as civil defense is at the point where casualties can be held below X level, there will be a nuclear exchange.

This assumption complicates defense planning, casts doubt on the sincerity of our arms control efforts, and mutes the hope that any deterrent will be effective. The assumption is "important if true." But if true, it may leave us facing "death with dignity" as our most prominent remaining option.

Ultimately, the nature of Soviet intentions cannot be known. As with the question of whose military force is more powerful, or who is adding crucial capacity most rapidly, the final brush strokes, the statements at the margin,

" LOOK ON THE BRIGHT SIDE ... THE ARMS RACE IS OVER ! "
Cartoon by Stayskal. Reprinted by permission: Tribune Media Services, Inc., 1984.

come not from facts but from one's own inclinations and beliefs. Even if in the dark recesses of the Kremlin there exists a doctrine based on an acceptable level of slaughter, we still cannot know whether those charged with the decision would put it into effect or step back from the brink.

For older Americans, an indelible impression of under-rating a maniacal enemy's intentions was left by the Nazi experience. Chamberlain at Munich has become a paradigm of how not to behave. But there is also a risk in assuming one's foes are mad. This risk goes beyond the matter of a war brought on by mutual exasperation. Mental health and moral strength are also involved.

The danger for America is that "we become what we hate." To entertain nightmare assumptions about the Soviets, to equal tough mindedness with tough guy-ness, to practice thinking about the unthinkable as a fitness program for doing the unthinkable, is to lose the candle. It is to forfeit our role as champion of human opportunity, and exchange it for a theory of conflict.

Our defense leadership has been made up of intelligent and distinguished men. When their programs are resisted, it is time to reexamine the basic premise. This is not a case of an indifferent public failing to support a sustained buildup in peacetime. It is a case where vast additions of force are accompanied by an apparent decline in security. Those who direct our defense are in a different position from that of critic or analyst. They do not want a judgment of history which says they left the nation less than fully prepared. But prepared for what? For acquitting ourselves well in a devastating exchange? Or to redefine capability in a form which is both usable and can help deter such an exchange?

The argument is not for submission but for a strenuous dialogue to buy time, to seek levers, to determine courses of action. If not strictly speaking an argument for peace, it is an argument for war on sufficient grounds, if there is to be war. Those grounds must be proportional to the chance of an awful result, and against war undertaken in a moment of absentmindedness, pique, or error. "The most likely path to nuclear war today is through a crisis which escalates out of control because of miscalculation, miscommunication, or accident," say William Ury and Richard Smoke in a study commissioned for the U.S. Arms Control and Disarmament Agency.[77]

The United States, land of human opportunity, has a particular responsibility not to be an agent in the interruption of history. Doctrines of nuclear strategy have become unmanageable. We must refashion them or risk becoming what we hate.

There is a broad consensus in the defense community that "we are over-prepared for nuclear war and under-prepared for conventional war."[78] Nuclear doctrine has moved from paradox—an uncomfortable but workable category—to absurdity. Yet our obligations remain: to define the role that we can fill and to fill it effectively. A revitalized conventional force is the only means to this objective.

Strategic reform thus has two dimensions: mission definition and force structure. America's mission—the interests we are committed to defend, the threats we are prepared to meet—requires separating vital and secondary issues. Failure to make such a distinction creates the risk that a "universal conflict" strategy will trap us between a mismatch of implied commitments and the force levels that can be built without busting the economy.

We also must be willing to treat Soviet leaders as cunning but not crazy. It is impossible to fashion an effective deterrent at any price if one's foe is mad. And if progress on arms control is to be pursued, we must make it clear to the foe that we do not believe him to be mad.

However irritated and even outraged we may be at our reliance on a balance of terror, it is something we will move away from only by degrees. There are very useful things that can be done. But they will take years, even decades. During that period, a commitment to steady progress in a clear direction can best preserve peace.

One major step is to separate tactical and strategic nuclear weapons, and to set about replacing the former with high-accuracy conventional weapons. The technology has to be thoroughly tested and matured. We cannot assume it works just because we badly want it to work. High-accuracy technology is not a magic answer—but it does define the right direction. If it can be perfected, the U.S. can disband its tactical nuclear arsenal without engaging in unilateral disarmament. Tactical weapons are meant to achieve specific objectives, not to be doomsday machines. If conventional warheads can be guided with high accuracy to do the job, they will meet the need while avoiding the risk of nuclear escalation.

On the strategic side, the goal is to seek a world in which neither side has the capacity to use nuclear weapons first, and both sides have the ability to use them second. The result is a level of stability that could cause nuclear weapons to drop out of the equation.

There are specific ways to move in this direction. Crucial to success is lowering the warhead-to-target ratio. Experts agree that a first strike would be very high risk if the attacker had less than two warheads for each target. This low ratio can be attained by moving from multiple to single warheads and by putting our eggs in the highest possible number of baskets—i.e., numerous, dispersed launch sites. The concept can be illustrated by what would happen if the U.S. replaced its 550 Minuteman IIIs with 1,000 Midgetman missiles. Our warhead count would drop by 650—making America less of a first-strike threat to the Soviets. But they would have 450 more points to target—making them less of a first-strike threat to us.

Our arms control proposals can be consistent with our modernization efforts. This would force the Soviets to signal hostile intentions to the world if they did not join us in a clearly stabilizing course of action. If the warhead-to-target ratio could be brought down low enough, verification would be possible because either side would need to take drastic steps (i.e., doubling its force) that the other side would be sure to notice.

In the past there was a continuum in conventional weapons planning that moved from preparedness to use. This helped foster realistic planning and training. Massive retaliation created an abyss in thinking between deterrence and retaliation. One result has been an over-extension of U.S. commitments under the nuclear shield. Another result has been "monopoly war"—the invention by defense consultants of scenarios in which you can "win" by plugging in the right strategy or weapon.[79]

We must carefully reforge the missing links which have appeared between foreign policy, grand strategy, and weaponry. The strains imposed by "thinking the unthinkable" have taken an intellectual as well as a moral toll. It is time to make our way back to realistic commitments and usable weaponry.

Triumph of the Careerists

> The prevailing ethic of modern American defense is the 'managerial' view . . .
> which assumes that organizing for conflict is similar to organizing for other human
> activities. . . . That mentality leads to tactics based on over-simplified, abstract
> models; to an emphasis on machinery rather than on men and strategies; and to a
> tendency to neglect those human elements which, throughout history, have often
> determined the outcome of conflict.
> —James Fallows, *National Defense* [1]

A REVITALIZED MILITARY FORCE may require changes in doctrine, leadership, and organization which are even more significant than changes in equipment. More precisely, the crucial element may be a style of combat leadership which emphasizes human factors over equipment, and demands equipment which is flexible, tractable, and suited to maneuver warfare.

The dominant doctrine of the army still reflects the concept of attrition dominated by massive firepower and designed to destroy an enemy physically. This was the ruling theme in World War I. The Germans demonstrated in World War II that a concept based on maneuver is far more effective (they almost proved this in August 1914), especially for the side with fewer men and less equipment.

As late as January 1981, Senator Gary Hart noted in the *Wall Street Journal*, "One can place the U.S. Army's field manuals side by side with those of the French in 1940 and find remarkable parallels." [2] In the fall of 1981, the Army's chief strategist, Brig. Gen. Donald Morelli, requested to meet with Congress' military reform caucus (of which Senator Hart was a founder). Morelli revealed there for the first time that the Army planned a major change of doctrine, to emphasize the capability of lightly armored, highly mobile units, with tactics stressing maneuver and deception. [3]

The concept of light (i.e., maneuverable) divisions is still in the pilot phase. It is viewed as promising, but as of the 1985 budget it represents only a fraction of the Army's force level. The 9th Infantry Division at Fort Lewis, Washington, is the main test unit. [4]

When the Air Force put out a high-tech prospectus on how it would fight in the year 2000, a group of Air Force and Army National Guard officers responded with "Vista 1999," a long-range plan calling for greater emphasis on maneuver warfare and less on the "purchase of high-cost, high-technology systems that have uncertain reliability and significant difficulties of maintenance above the operator level." [5]

A leading apostle of the new doctrine is "right stuff" fighter ace John Boyd, who uses a four-hour slide-illustrated briefing to make his points. The prime object of war, Boyd contends, is not high body counts or holding terrain. It is to destroy the enemy's will to fight. This means the ability of commanders to observe the enemy, deploy units, and then attack in a faster tempo and less predictable pattern than used by the enemy.[6]

Boyd and many other reformers of doctrine cite as a source the writings of Sun Tzu, whose *Art of War* appeared in 500 B.C. His concepts are the equal of deterrence theory for subtlety, with the crucial distinction that they relate to the active prosecution of war.

Sun Tzu's principles stress deception, indirection, deviation in thrust—the opposite of slugging it out toe-to-toe. Indeed, he goes so far as to say that "supreme excellence [in generalship] consists in breaking the enemy's will without fighting." Best of all "is to baulk the enemy's plans; next best is to prevent a juncture of his forces; next in order is to attack the enemy's army in the field; worst of all is to besiege a walled city."[7]

The flavor of this doctrine recalls our frustrations in Vietnam with an enemy who would not come out in the open. An irony is that only half the enemy's success came from following the principles of Sun Tzu in specific engagements. The other half came simply from the existence of the doctrine. It baffled the American people. An enemy who would not stand and fight was incomprehensible. This was refusal to abide by the rules of the game. It sapped the base of support for the war so that even when there was a decisive victory (Tet) it could not be seen as such. A sense of disgust had set in over trying to beat "the little men in black pajamas."

That America finally gave up rather than being defeated in Vietnam is no disgrace for the victors under Sun Tzu's rules. It's just as fair and honorable to win through your opponent's forfeiture as if you had played all four quarters. In fact, it reflects favorably on your shrewdness to have won it this way.

American military reformers do not stress an esoteric, Zen-like reading of Sun Tzu. Instead, they seek a blend of western and eastern wisdom on war. For example, his praise of "victory without fighting" is seen as encouraging economy of force rather than as a literal goal. Sun Tzu's ideas are used as a leaven to the traditional emphasis on firepower and attrition, as a way to put more weight on maneuver and deception in strategy, and perhaps most important, as a reminder that history bestows greater credit on commanders who have outfoxed the enemy than those whose motto is "blow him away."

In a distinctly western note, equipment is seen as an asset, enhancing the capacity for maneuver and deception. But it should be equipment which is "simple, reliable, and relatively abundant," to quote another reformer, defense consultant Pierre Sprey.[8]

Emphasis on the wrong kind of weaponry not only defeats sound strategy but undermines morale. Joseph Kraft writes, "Warriors fight badly or not at all when the political and spiritual atmosphere discounts the value of sacrifice. . . . The administration shows no signs of squeamishness about the use of force. . . . But when it comes to deeds that denote a willingness to pay for beliefs in blood and money, a different theme prevails. . . . The clear emphasis is on the easy way—on buying the most sophisticated weapons available, regardless of the capacity to use them."[9]

"Politicians are trying to substitute technology for bodies, promising the home front they won't commit men to fight and promising high-tech industry big contracts. In contrast to Israel and other successful armies, it's the 'white shirt and tie' generals in the Pentagon who are in command," says Army Reserve Major Lance Sterling. "We're lying to ourselves. We need an 'attack of honesty.'"[10]

A vehement critic of the values and performance of the U.S. military is Jeffrey Record of Georgetown University. Among the chief weaknesses he sees are "an unbridled, though historically unwarranted, faith in technology as the solution to most problems on the battlefield" and a proneness "to disregard the fact that war remains first and foremost a human encounter. . . . The outcome of combat is still determined less by . . . power than it is . . . by such intangibles as generalship . . . training, morale, unit cohesion, combat experience, and, of course, chance. . . ."[11]

Record compiled a listing of America's battlefield performance since MacArthur's successful 1950 landing at Inchon. His conclusion: "The U.S. seems to have lost touch with the art of war."[12] Record's litany of failure has been challenged by former Army Chief of Staff Gen. Maxwell Taylor, who cites three major achievements in Korea, and the Tet offensive in Vietnam.[13] The Ia Drang Valley and Cambodian offensives were added by Robert Cocklin, executive vice president of the Association of the U.S. Army.[14]

Perhaps the key concern is not the ability to win our share of battles in a long war, but the capacity to gear up quickly. "As the political outcome in a confrontation has become increasingly dependent on an impressive initial performance at the outset of a conflict, we are no longer able to bear the luxury of arrangements which preserve institutional roles but work against the execution of military plans."[15]

Reinforcing NATO is an obvious example of a major mission requiring quick reflexes. In previous wars, America's geographic isolation was an advantage. It gave us time to gear up. But today our distance from European front lines has turned into a handicap. "The assumption is that the Soviets have an edge in moving over land, at least initially," notes Bing West. But in conflicts that require both superpowers to reach a remote point, "we have the advantage in moving over sea lanes or in the air."[16]

Such conflicts are likely to become more frequent if, as West predicts, "the focus is shifting back to Third World conflicts requiring special forces. The theory is that the Soviets will be 'nibbling at the edges' rather than launching a direct assault."[17]

Some argue against this model. "Are the Marines organized for police work in Beirut? No. Is our force designed to conduct an Iran rescue? No. That doesn't mean they can't give a good account of themselves in a place where it counts—in Europe or Korea, for example," says former Defense Under Secretary Robert Komer.[18]

The pattern of conflict in the near-term suggests, however, that the U.S. must have an ability to deal with what might be called "prolonged incidents." Inability to do so would not only damage our prestige but forfeit the opportunity which small conflicts provide to learn lessons applicable to larger wars.

What are the lessons we and our allies learned in the Falklands, Iran, Lebanon, Grenada? British Defense Minister John Nott said the Falklands War "stressed the value of professional, well-motivated forces capable of responding quickly and imaginatively to the unexpected." Most British attacks were made at night, requiring a high degree of planning and coordination.[19]

Israel's attack on the PLO was a highly coordinated movement of ground troops, air raids, helicopter-borne combat units, and sea landings. Edward Luttwak of the Center for Strategic and International Studies believes that "both the British and Israeli armies were successful because they encouraged elite forces that emphasize maneuvers and tactics rather than attrition warfare. Both armies pursue the art of war rather than the science of war, developing weapons to suit combat conditions and tactics geared to specific objectives rather than to computer models."[20]

Examples: the British Harrier jump-jet, whose hovering abilities enabled it to settle in with the motion of a carrier heaving on stormy seas that would have prevented landings by "hot" U.S. Navy fighters;[21] Israeli destruction of Syrian T-72s, sophisticated Soviet-built tanks, by roving teams in open jeeps using small but effective anti-tank weapons.[22]

But above all: "The split-second timing required could never have been achieved by the U.S. military because of deep divisions created by interservice rivalry."[23]

In the Iran rescue mission, because of turf rules only the Navy could command carriers and the aircraft to fly off them. But the Army and Air Force had forces better trained and equipped for a ground mission. Planners decided that moving Army or Air Force craft to a Navy ship (as was done for Doolittle's famous raid on Tokyo) might compromise the mission's secrecy, because of the effort required to create a joint command. So Navy and Marine pilots less well-trained for the mission than their land-based counterparts were assigned to use Navy minesweeping helicopters. In addition, to avoid the stress involved in creating a new, mission-based structure, there was no single ground commander at the spot where helicopters landed and the mission was aborted.[24]

In Lebanon many of these problems reappeared. A Marine force was deployed which was ill-equipped to deal with the main threat: terrorist bombings and sustained artillery fire. Army units could have dealt better with the artillery, but would have been less mobile. In fact the U.S. had no ready force for this mission.[25]

The Marines received their orders from European Command in Stutt-gart, via London. Some analysts believe that Command failed to properly weigh the threat of terrorism because its chief concern is a Soviet tank at-tack in Germany. Others cite a more basic cause. The Long Commission which investigated the Beirut bombing found "a general attitude through-out the chain of command that it would somehow be improper to tell [the Marine commander] how best to protect his force."[26]

Defense analyst Steven Canby describes the problem: "All the way up the chain of command, every officer gets a chop. We get the lowest common denominator, so we end up doing something very predictable and take losses."[27] The daylight attack on Syrian positions in which Lieutenant Goodman was shot down is an often-cited example. The local Navy com-mander argued for a nighttime raid to avoid defensive fire. He was over-ruled by a staff officer thousands of miles away in Europe.[28]

The Iran mission and the Beirut bombing have something else in com-mon: no one was punished. The 1980 Department of Defense report highly critical of planning and execution in the hostage rescue attempt cautioned that "no judgment of the able men who planned this mission nor the brave professionals who executed it is intended nor should it be inferred."[29]

The Long Commission was more courageous. It recommended disciplin-ary action against those whose negligence contributed to the disaster. But it is unlikely any action will be taken since the President, on the eve of release of the report, issued a statement that pardoned everyone in advance.[30]

The system seems unable to distinguish between culpability and respon-sibility. When the British executed Admiral Byng for losing a fight with French men-of-war, Voltaire commented they had done it "to encourage the others." Byng was treated as if he were culpable, and as if this were tanta-mount to treason. Obviously, such a code is not compatible with contempo-rary standards.

But we have gone to the other extreme. "This should not be surprising, since bureaucracy compartmentalizes responsibility to the point that ex-empts most individuals from accountability for doing anything more than meeting the internal requirements of the bureaucracy itself."[31]

There is one recent case where even culpability went unpunished. Grip-pingly retold in Fallows' *National Defense*,[32] it is the saga of the M-16, to whose notorious undependability under combat conditions many American troops in Vietnam owed their deaths.

The M-16 began life as a brilliant, privately developed design, the AR-15, a rifle which set a world standard for lightness, reliability, and destructive power. The design was arbitrarily modified by top brass in Vietnam, mostly to make it look more like an M-14. This added unnecessarily to its weight. Much more serious were equally arbitrary changes forced by the Army's firearms bureaucracy. A higher muzzle velocity was imposed, conforming to a traditional standard. This change made the gun vulnerable to overheating. The jamming which resulted in the field was often blamed not on a design error but on the troops' alleged failure to keep the gun cleaned.

Elite units in Vietnam contrived to get their hands on the AR-15 while infantrymen were stuck with the degraded M-16. Many died with the malfunctioning weapon in their hands. As word from outraged troops filtered back home, congressional hearings were held. The testimony indicated that the firearms office knew the weapon was jamming, and that its design changes were the cause. Bureaucratic obstinacy prevented rescinding the adverse modifications. The hearings themselves were a model of evasion and obfuscation by witnesses. No one was punished for one of the most shameful chapters in American military history.

What of the successful invasion of Grenada? This operation does differ from others in that it produced clear-cut victory—"We blew them away," to quote a participating admiral.[33] But many of the same problems were evident.

Joint Chiefs of Staff Chairman John Vessey did achieve a notable advance by turning over broad authority to the commanders at the scene. The night before the invasion he packed his briefcase and headed home after the order was handed down, and he recommended that members of his staff do likewise.[34]

Once again, the problem was lack of a standing force designed and trained for the specific mission. Ad hoc planning was necessary, and this produced a curious command situation. Two distinct ground forces invaded a tiny island: Army Rangers backed by Air Force tactical support, and Marines backed by Navy aircraft. There was no single commander. The limited capability of opposition prevented the lack of coordination from having serious consequences. Only 18 U.S. servicemen were killed.[35]

Even so, the invasion was far from a classic operation. The Navy's original plan was overruled by the Joint Chiefs, who demanded that all four services be involved. It is said the Army was particularly eager for a "piece of the action" to justify its request to Congress for a new Ranger batallion.[36]

The resulting "pie-dividing contest" allowed a relatively small number of Cuban defenders to regroup, and to form and maintain a fairly effective resistance. The famed 82nd Airborne Division advanced across the island with such caution (partly due to an inflated estimate of Cuban strength) that Vessey complained, "We have two companies of Marines running all over the island, and thousands of Army troops doing nothing. What the hell is going on?"[37]

The Marines and Army Rangers were in their element and performed superbly, laying the basis for victory. Regular units were improperly organized and equipped, failed to gain most of their objectives, and fell victim to critical lapses in combat communication. Yet the Army, in contrast to the Marines, showered itself with medals: 8,663 awards and decorations for 7,000 actual Army combatants. This compares with 679 medals distributed by Britain to its 28,000 member Falklands force, 255 of whom lost their lives.[38]

"What the nation suffers from is not militarism, but serviceism," says Samuel Huntington, director of Harvard's Center for International Affairs.[39] To Defense research consultant Richard Garwin, "the biggest game in town is not the U.S. versus the Soviets; it's the Navy versus the Air Force."[40] Former Joint Chiefs Chairman Gen. David Jones sees Defense budget planning as "an intramural scramble for resources." Only after the services have divided up the money do they "clean up the battlefield by writing strategy."[41]

Among the major harmful effects are: (1) major costs from needless duplication of roles, missions, and weapons; (2) underemphasis on crucial missions requiring inter-service cooperation, including airlift, sealift, and tactical air support; (3) investment in weapons systems of doubtful effectiveness which provide one service with a capability it doesn't trust the others to deliver.

The current allocation of roles and missions among the services is based on a 1948 agreement reached between the Chiefs and Defense Secretary James Forrestal. Despite the fact that World War II had demonstrated military operations were increasingly complex and interrelated, the agreement based service assignments on traditional distinctions between land, sea, and air warfare. The result was to encourage each service to focus on defeat of enemy counterparts (i.e., services) as its core function. These separate and often disconnected plans do not add up to a coherent national strategy.[42]

Consider for example this insiders' description of the 1979–80 debate on creation of a Rapid Deployment Force: "The Navy said we could do it with sea power. The Air Force said air power would work like a charm. The Marines were big on amphibious landings. The Army said ground troops would do the trick. We had four parochial strategies."[43]

"None of the services trust the others to support them in battle. The Army doesn't believe the Air Force will provide the needed air support for troops, so it goes in for attack helicopters. The Navy won't commit its ships close to land for fear that, in wartime, the Air Force will concentrate on its own missions rather than protect the fleet. And so on. You've got to have a referee in there, and you don't now."[44]

There is nothing wrong with the services' dedication to their traditional combat roles. This is a natural tendency, and damage could be done by trying to dissuade people from devotion to their specialty. The problems just cited are the result of poor planning and resource allocation. They must be resolved by "superiors." Unfortunately, it is not now clear who those superiors should be (see pages 89–91).

Not surprisingly, there are mismatches between the design of new Army equipment and the design of Air Force planes to transport them. The M-1 tank is ready-made for Central European defense. But it is so big and heavy that only one tank at a time can be carried in our largest transport, the C-5.

At the start of the current buildup, the Pentagon wanted 7,000 M-1s but had only 77 C-5As. Fifty new transports will be added in 1985.[45]

The situation with regard to sealift is even more serious. Since 1981 the number of "mobile logistics ships" which carry ammunition, fuel, and other resupply cargo has increased only from 72 to 73.[46] Yet, Britain's defense secretary John Nott reports that "in light of rates of consumption during the Falklands campaign, both of ammunition and stores, Britain is reviewing the size and composition of its NATO stockpile, with a plan for a substantial increase."[47]

The shortage of airlift and sealift capacity has been brought on by decades of the Air Force and Navy spending their dollars on "primary mission" hardware rather than transports. As a result, the U.S. today has more active, trained, and equipped combat forces than it can send overseas rapidly.[48] William Kaufmann of the Brookings Institution predicts we will end up with "a very bright, shiny force that's all tied up at the docks and grounded."[49]

From 1979 to 1981 the concern was that this lack of mobility would mean it would take weeks to move a Rapid Deployment Force to the Persian Gulf. More recently, the focus has returned to NATO. In the opinion of many analysts, the greatest risk of nuclear war would be in the interval between a Soviet attack in Central Europe and the arrival of American reinforcements. The oceans, a defensive barrier in the pre-ICBM age, now are a strategic disadvantage for America, a distance we must traverse to the most important battlefields—above all, Europe. It would be ironic if interservice rivalry, by starving a vital mission, denied us the ability to play a crucial role that is otherwise within the reach of our forces.

The issue is all the more vital because the U.S. and its NATO allies may have a far better prospect of holding out against Soviet attack than has often been assessed. The major reason is that when the chosen point of attack is obvious or restricted, the defense gains a major advantage.[50]

John Keegan of Britain's Sandhurst academy has analyzed invasion routes across the "inner German frontier." Here in the center of Europe, with its history of wars, is a region that was never before a military dividing line. Keegan finds only three major and six secondary highway routes suitable for the mass of Soviet armor required to sustain an all-out attack. Given the existing concentration of force along this frontier, Keegan argues that the number and dispersion of alternate routes may not be sufficient to provide the Soviets with a decisive advantage leading to breakthrough.[51]

There is some history to back up this thesis. In 1943 the Russians and the Germans met in the Battle of Kursk for the greatest tank combat in history. The combined forces equaled NATO's entire tank inventory—12,000 late-model, large-gun weapons. First the Germans attacked carefully prepared Russian defensive positions, arranged in five overlapping parallels. After a furious exchange, they were rebuffed. The Russians, thinking to follow up this repulse with an annihilating counter-attack, charged hastily prepared German defensive positions. The Panzers, in shallow trenches and using cover afforded by low hills, decimated hundreds of Russian tanks. In short, the defense carried the day—first the Russians, using superbly prepared positions, and then more surprisingly, the retreating Germans.[52] As Keegan says, the best thing NATO could do with the inner frontier is "take a pick and shovel to it."[53]

In addition to the natural advantage of defending forces, other factors argue that NATO's conventional forces may be able to hold out. The French are excluded from most NATO counts. They have 315,000 troops—50,000 of them in West Germany. The loyalty and reliability of Warsaw Pact troops to the Soviets are open to question. And Soviet command has suffered even more than American from a structure inadequate to wars of maneuver.[54]

According to congressional defense specialist Terry Freese, "NATO does best in war simulations if neither side goes nuclear or chemical in Central Europe. There is enough uncertainty in this course of action that it is not a useful strategy for the Soviet Union."[55] There is no better investment the U.S. can make to deter nuclear war or enhance our security than to assure that taking on NATO is an unappealing prospect for the Soviets.

The Army and Navy are each working on new tactics. The Army's plan calls for falling back, the Navy's for pushing forward.

The inner German frontier presents a condition unusual in military history: large forces in direct contact with each other for long periods of time—the equivalent of an alert without war. The troop dispositions which reflect this condition are inconsistent with emerging Army doctrine. Political logic calls for holding forward positions so as not to yield ground; military logic calls for tactical withdrawals to gain room for maneuver.[56]

There is a strong parallel between this and a conflict which arose between Hitler and his most capable strategist, General von Manstein. "Where the German soldier puts his foot, there he stays," said Hitler. Manstein argued that a flexible defense which allowed tactical retreats would have permitted an indefinite stalemate in the East. To hold forward positions was to enable the enemy to plan his attack precisely and to encircle the defenders. To fall back would have permitted feints, counter-attacks, and in turn, encirclements by the Germans.[57]

Hitler's approach was political, based on ideology and image; Manstein's was strategic, based on final outcomes.

The Navy's new doctrine uses principles of maneuver and counter-attack rather than simply "defending the sea lanes." But it is much more controversial than the Army's because it calls for more rather than less forward positioning. (The strategy is discussed on pages 108–12, in the context of its chief instrument, the nuclear carrier battle group.)

In practice, there may be a conflict between the Army and the Navy in pursuing a flexible, maneuver-based, counter-attack strategy. The problem is in the budget, not on the battlefield.

Even the most cursory review of World War II brings out the importance of sealift and airlift capacity, which was vital both to our "island-hopping" campaign in the Pacific and to gaining a firm foothold on the Continent. Today, "the problem isn't readiness; it's sustainability," says Congressman Norman Dicks.[58] To maximize NATO credibility, our capacity for rapid reinforcement is crucial.

Why not just station more troops in Europe, to obviate the need for more transports? "The history of U.S. military budgets is that they vary in size with just one factor—the number of American troops overseas," observes William Niskanen of the Council of Economic Advisors. "The marginal cost of each soldier stationed abroad is $125,000."[59]

The U.S. Maritime Sealift Command has 60 ships under its control—half as many as during Vietnam and one-sixth the number available during Korea.[60] Capacity is being added at a glacially slow rate because sealift is a "low priority" inter-service function.

A major opportunity exists to retarget naval investment toward what in fact is a high priority. The Navy wants to build 29 new *Arleigh Burke*-class destroyers at a cost of $1.1 billion for the first ship and $700 million apiece thereafter. When the class was first proposed, it was a particular point of contention with Defense Under Secretaries Paul Thayer and Richard De-Lauer, who argued the ship was too expensive and potentially vulnerable in wartime. But knowledgeable officials said chances for cutting the program were always dim because "it offers the only hope for struggling West Coast shipyards."[61]

The West Coast shipyards could be saved by building transports and logistics ships which would enhance our largest military investment: NATO resupply. It is also a capacity which could balance our naval force structure for dealing with any "protracted incidents" in the third world that have similar requirements to those the Royal Navy faced in the Falklands.

In opposition to this approach is what might be called the "Navy League argument"—an example of inter-service rivalry carried to the point of predicting an American defeat which can only be staved off by relying on the "right" service. The argument runs like this: The Army will lose in Central Europe. Therefore, don't waste money on sealift. Spend it instead on strategic naval forces which will strike back at the heart of the Soviet Union.

The problem with this argument is that it leads to a harmful kind of self-fulfilling prophecy. Increasing the portion of the budget devoted to nuclear weapons means we will inadvertently decrease our options to protect vital interests without recourse to such weapons.

DIVIDING THE PIE

Service shares become fiscal reality through a Planning, Programming, and Budgeting System (PPBS). The phrase is McNamara's. The system has four phases:

The *planning* phase culminates in the publication of the Defense Guidance, sent by the Secretary to the services. The Guidance is based on a Joint Strategic Planning Document (JSPD) prepared by the Joint Chiefs. It describes "the strategy and force structure requirements needed to attain national defense objectives."

The *programming* phase culminates in Program Objective Memorandums (POMs) submitted by the services to the Secretary. The POMs are intended to reconcile defense objectives and resource constraints, with the result expressed in the form of mission statements and force structures.

The *budget estimating* phase culminates when all the services submit budget estimates to the Secretary. This is done after the Office of the Secretary has advised each service on changes required in their POMs to bring them in line with the Defense Guidance.

The *budget development* phase culminates when the Defense Secretary submits the defense section of the President's budget to Congress. This is done after the Secretary's proposal has been reviewed by the Office of Management and Budget, and both DOD and OMB comments have been reviewed by the President.[62]

"The Defense Guidance is so broad you could drive a truck through it," says former Joint Chiefs Chairman Gen. David Jones.[63] The Guidance requires so many more weapons than the budget can afford that each service "does its own wish list in its own cocoon,"[64] targeting dollars at traditional missions and short-changing inter-service programs.

The POMs are reviewed by the Defense Resources Board (DRB), whose members are the 16 highest-ranking Pentagon civilians and the Joint Chiefs chairman. DRB review is limited by the volume of data and detail, and the fact that "no service understands the language, needs, missions or systems of the others."[65] DRB's role is to provide a coordinated overview. But in practice, "what comes out is just what the services put in."[66]

Retired Vice Admiral Thor Hanson says "the pressure is to defend that POM." Lost in the process is broad, integrated strategic thinking that would link goals and spending. Instead of evaluating the effectiveness of proposed weapons, the Chiefs operate under "negotiated treaties" whose basis is "I won't question your pet system, and you won't question mine."[67]

"The recommendations and plans of the Chiefs must pass through a screen designed to protect the institutional interests of each service," writes former Defense Secretary James Schlesinger. "The general rule is that no service ox may be gored. If, on rare occasions, disputes do break out, the subsequent turmoil within the institution will be such as to make a repetition appear ill-advised."

Schlesinger says the system will be readily recognized by members of Congress because it is designed to achieve long-run political consensus through "log-rolling, back-scratching, marriage agreements, and the like." But he asks whether this is the right approach to producing urgent military decisions. "Our political system is designed to force compromise even at the expense of rapidly achieving certain national goals. . . . One can only ponder whether such a system for forcing compromise in such a manner is appropriate for our military establishment."[68]

What resources does the Secretary have to knife through the services' consensus process and extract crucial issues? His main tool for this task is the Office of Program Analysis and Evaluation (PA&E). It studies items of defense spending with an eye to fiscal efficiency. But each issue is focused on separately, the antithesis of viewing the budget from a broad strategic perspective.

PA&E was set up by McNamara and staffed with his "whiz kids." Weinberger has played down its role and shifted decisions back to the services. "'Decentralized management' has actually led to centralized management by the services," says Congressional defense specialist Terry Freese. "A lot of decisions never leave the military contingent of each service."[69] Former Defense Secretary Melvin Laird adds, "If you give the services that kind of parameter within which to operate, they will come in with letters to Santa."[70]

Freese also charges that "elimination of 'micro-management' has become a rallying cry for the services' desire to elude civilian oversight."[71] Foes of "micro-management" claim they are doing battle on behalf of all defense planners, uniformed and civilian, against the intrusions of an over-zealous Congress.

One reason Congress has thrust itself into such an active role is concern that "the Office of Management and Budget has almost no capability to review the Defense budget and has abdicated as a watchdog in this area."[72] Other portions of the budget are critically reviewed by OMB examiners for three months. But its Defense team actually "lives" in the Pentagon and works with DOD budget staff during that period. There are few formal hearings. Those which do occur are chaired by the DOD Controller's office. Some fear that once David Stockman lost the battle of the budget to Weinberger in September 1981 (see pages 150–51) OMB took a hands-off approach—just at the time when exploding defense spending made outside review even more important.

Even a Defense enthusiast like Navy Secretary John Lehman complains of the 6,000-person bureaucracy in the Defense Secretary's office. "They have their own agenda; they are accountable to no one."[73]

Gen. David Jones believes "the civilian leaders in the Pentagon are not given good advice on alternative policies and programs." All the advice comes in "vertically" from the services and from specialists. But the crucial problems cut across these lines. Jones notes that "within the office of the Secretary, you don't have the knowledge of all the war plans, the fundamentals of strategy and weapons and so forth, so the services can just chew you up."[74]

James Schlesinger seems to have learned this lesson during his tenure: "A wise Secretary of Defense will turn for crisis management involving military forces primarily to the uniformed military. All those civil engineers, scientists, systems analysts, logisticians and the like, who aspire to be field marshals, should be gently cut out of the process during the handling of the immediate crisis."[75]

Without strong advice to sort out parochial interests from national interests, "a gaggle of kibitzers has formed throughout the government on these issues," says former Navy Under Secretary James Woolsey. "For years, the only central voice in defense has been provided by the civilian staff of the Secretary of Defense. Lacking military expertise, it has largely failed."[76]

James Schlesinger agrees that "the Office of the Secretary has grown substantially and sometimes has strayed beyond the appropriate bounds of its authority. But the growth in the office is largely a reflection of weakness in the military command system."[77] Robert McNamara feels "you can't run this thing by committee. The Secretary of Defense has to do it personally."[78] Another former Pentagon chief, reflecting on his experience, expresses the same view: "These pressure groups (in defense) aren't disloyal; they're just following their own parochial interests. But that's why you have to have somebody in there to control the thing."[79]

What to do? An important element is reform of the Joint Chiefs, discussed below (pages 88–92). Nuclear submariner, Admiral Hyman Rickover, with his usual acerbity, offered this proposal for streamlining DOD: "I would split the officers into three groups. One-third would do the work. The other two-thirds would sit in offices with no secretaries or aides and would write letters to each other in longhand and get replies in longhand, but nothing more."[80]

Realistically, it would seem a Secretary has to strive for the right balance between two sets of extreme inputs. One polarity is between policy and knowledge. "The most accurate and detailed knowledge is at the bottom of the DOD bureaucracy. As it flows upward through each layer of decision-making, it is increasingly diluted by policy considerations. At the top you have one hundred percent policy and no knowledge; at the bottom you have just the reverse. In between, there is a collision between knowledge and policy."[81]

In short, the Secretary must avoid relying on either dilettantes or technical "gnomes." He must find people who are both broad-gauged and well-informed.

The second and related polarity is between military wisdom and military "secrets." The "national security" argument has been used to denigrate OMB's role in analyzing defense budgets, believes Terry Freese.[82]

"Too many people get wrapped up with acronyms and use them to dismiss good work," says Department of the Army budget analyst Rebecca Paulk. "The unfortunate result is to downplay valid input from 'outsiders.'"[83] Paul Feldman of the Center for Naval Analysis sums it up: "The pros can always beat down critiques by non-specialists. They just keep tossing technical objections at you."[84]

There are four levels of facts about weaponry. First and most likely to be secret is how weapons work, the technology that makes them function. Next is how well they have performed in tests and whether the design concepts are practical. Third is their intended mission. Fourth, how does each weapon fit into an armory related to strategic or tactical goals?

These four levels span the entire range from the stuff of espionage to the topics of public debate. There is a strong tendency to classify more than national security requires. No one with a clearance wants to face the charge of laxness in letting information get out. Besides, keeping it "in the profession" adds to the stature of those holding specialized knowledge.

Within the Pentagon, there is a pecking order of those who hold higher or lower security clearances. Like karate belts, the top-rated is "black." Franklin Spinney of Defense's Program Analysis and Evaluation office says the fastest growing portion of military spending is in super-secret programs requiring a black clearance. Although he has access to highly classified documents, Spinney lacks authority to see black-rated material. "This top clearance is very restricted. Slap it on a program and you've got a great way to limit access to test results. You can really hide mistakes."[85]

The combination of rapid cost growth and restricted review is disconcerting. Not just specific facts but even the budget numbers on many super-secret programs are not made available to Congress. Almost without doubt, a lot of information which is available to any conscientious Soviet analyst is effectively denied to the American public and often to Congress by a combination of over-classification and the use of technical mumbo-jumbo and acronyms.

Reform must begin within the defense establishment. The crucial distinction is not between civilians and uniformed personnel but between "gnomes" and broad-gauged thinkers. By making defense planning more realistic internally, Pentagon leadership could help make budgets more believable.

THINKERS, WARRIORS, BUREAUCRATS

"The services value the manager, tolerate the troop leader, but have virtually no place for the theorist," Sen. Gary Hart told readers of the *Wall Street Journal* in January 1981.[86] This theme has been sounded by many others. From field commanders, the note is one of resentment toward the dominance of deskbound generals. From students of defense planning, there is concern that we have misread the "lesson of history" offered by the German General Staff.

The U.S. employs eight times as many admirals per ship as it did at the end of World War II. Seven times as many Air Force generals per aircraft and two to three times as many Army generals per soldier are also on the rolls.[87] It is the case that today's hardware is more "capable" per unit, which justifies a smaller inventory per officer. The cost of this capability also reduces the number of units of hardware, leading to the same result.

However, the evidence suggests Parkinson's Law is at work. The Army has twelve lieutenant colonels for each one in field command; the Navy has twelve captains for every command slot at sea.[88] What do the others do? "In the peacetime military, procurement is the path to promotion. The only major success for general officers is in the development of weapons systems. As the number of officers multiplies, so does the number of projects. There's a need for more pyramids to accommodate the officer hierarchy," says Joseph Burniece of the Project on Military Procurement.[89]

Many analysts believe that "massive arms development and procurement programs have promoted explosive growth in the officer corps."[90] If this view is combined with Burniece's it produces a perfect circle of cause and effect. Defenders of the officer structure argue that "there is no obvious remedy. The job the bureaucracy is designed to do—administer weapons programs and logistics operations—will in large part bring success in the first months of a conflict."[91]

Defense critic Jeffrey Record suggests just the opposite: "America's military malaise stems largely from the substitution of technocratic and managerial values that has taken place since World War II. The U.S. military has become a bureaucracy in which winning wars has been supplanted by career advancement, maintaining an orderly flow of people and paper within the system, and protecting it from outside disturbance."[92] Adds Burniece: "Officers make general either as businessmen, lobbyists or PR men—not as warriors in the peacetime military."[93]

Those who are field commanders add extra emphasis to this point. "'Mission, men, and me'—that's the order of priority. But in the Pentagon, it's reversed," says the Reserve's Major Sterling. "A lot of hatred is felt in the service toward those officers who don't care about mission or men. That's why some were 'fragged' in Vietnam—not because they tried to lead their men on dangerous duty."[94]

Record's analysis of Vietnam supports this reading. "Too many military men forgot why they were in uniform. Promotion-hungry officers more interested in 'punching the ticket' too often forgot to lead their men and treated them like interchangeable parts in some vast machine."[95] The problems arising from this have been summed up in the oft-quoted phrase, "Men cannot be managed to their deaths; they must be led there."[96]

Sterling believes ticket-punching skills reached such a high level that "most top brass have shuffled their way to the top without having actually commanded." Once they arrive there, "it takes about one month to forget the details of life at the battalion level." Then the bureaucrats take over.

"Deskbound generals are getting a lot of bad advice. A pencil hole isn't a bullet hole. It flunks."[97]

The picture presented by Sterling and Record undercuts what might otherwise be a convincing argument for an expanded peace-time officer corps. "The military intentionally keeps itself top-heavy with officers so it can mobilize a much larger force in a crisis. Without a surfeit of officers, a far longer period would be required to build up to wartime strength."[98]

Germany's post-World War I Reichswehr operated on this model to build the nucleus of an army of millions from the 100,000 cap imposed by the Treaty of Versailles. But obviously, an officer corps of "businessmen, lobbyists and PR men" is hardly the nucleus which can lead millions in battle. "In peacetime, there's no place for wartime commanders," says Sterling, who adds that on a day-to-day basis, "it's the NCOs who keep the Army going."[99]

Within the ranks, morale has taken a battering from "personnel turbulence," the constant shuffling of troops from unit to unit by a highly centralized personnel management system. This practice has "catastrophic effects on the social bonding critical to the cohesion of small units under the stress of battle."[100] At the officer level, the effects are just as damaging. Put a stop to frequent transfers, said Admiral Hyman Rickover. "In addition to high cost, they are disruptive and cause inefficiency. How well would industry run if all the CEOs played constant musical chairs?"[101]

The Army has begun testing a promising new manpower system to increase unit cohesion. Called "cohort companies," the new approach is one of the best ways to add value without adding cost. Building up unit pride and stability is expected to contribute to morale, effectiveness, and mutual trust, while reducing training and rotation costs.[102]

Another major reform thrust is greater reliance on the Guard and Reserve, which provide far more manpower per dollar of expense than do the regular forces, yet frequently outperform them in competitive field exercises. One reason, say a number of analysts including Burniece, is that "right stuff" captains and majors get frustrated and leave the service. Then they join the Guard or Reserve where they get more time to train on equipment.

How can this be? The paradox is that, although the fancy gear goes to Regular forces, it is too expensive to practice upon. So it is Reserve fighter pilots who often best their Air Force counterparts in mock dogfights because they have had hours of flying time in old "clunkers," cast-off jets whose top speed is around 1,000 miles per hour instead of 1,500.[103]

This says something about the fabulous cost of new weaponry, which is too scarce to train on. It also suggests that full attention should be given to maximizing the pool of trained military manpower represented by the Guard and Reserve. There is almost certainly an optimizing strategy which would insure units a better shake on weaponry in an emergency, without going to the extreme of equipping them with exotic, "too valuable to lose" hardware—which we couldn't afford to do in any case. This subject is receiving a good deal of current attention.[104]

The cost-effectiveness of the Guard and Reserve also raises the issue of the All Volunteer Force. How good is it? How well is the concept working?

These questions are worthy of more detailed discussion than can be supported by the research done by this writer. However, a couple of facts stand out strongly. One is that the skill levels in the Force have steadily improved, as measured by IQ tests and percentage of high school graduates. The services' greatest personnel problem parallels that faced by the public schools: holding on to "science and math" skills; in this case, primarily operators of sophisticated equipment who get their training in the service and then are tempted to leave for higher private sector pay.[105]

The increase in average ability of military personnel is heartening. But critics charge a major part of it has been "recruitment by recession." The sharp downturn during all of 1982 and parts of the adjoining years led to job shortages and losses that made military service attractive. Can the Force compete in a more robust job market?

One answer is: no, if military pay levels are frozen or are hiked by less each year than living costs go up. Indeed, pay is always a ready target of budget cutters seeking quick fixes, and should be guarded against erosion.[106]

Much more dubious is the argument that today's military retirement benefit levels must be maintained to assure adequate recruitment and retention in the All Volunteer Force.[107] We have a vastly overstaffed officer corps and a pension plan whose upper-end benefits are most striking. Existing military retirement law does not bear a cost-effective relationship to the kind of specialists the Force badly needs to attract and hold in its ranks.

The All Volunteer Force is expensive. The yearly cost of maintaining competitive pay scales has been estimated at about $28 billion.[108] The alternative is universal national service. In economists' language, that would mean a transfer of the $28 billion burden from taxpayers to 18-year olds who would work at substandard wages. In the opinion of a number of people, it would also mean a much healthier body politic and military service. The body politic would benefit by eliminating a class division and exposing all youth to the democratizing experience of national service. In some cases this would be military; in others medical or humanitarian.[109]

If patriotic duty no longer depended on economic choice, the character of the service would change. Currently it has to attract enlistees on the basis that this is "a great place to start." By making the All Volunteer Force compete with other jobs, we encourage those who sign up to think of themselves as employees rather than soldiers. As a result, there is a tendency for everyone to want training as an electrical engineer and no one to expect that they will have to slog through 20 miles of mud with a 50-pound pack unless they so choose.

There is a common expectation that the Army owes something to its volunteer in terms of choice of occupation, career training, even a good lifestyle (off-base living). Under compulsory national service, those called up would be more likely to share the attitude, "We've got to get through this thing together." One overlooked source of esprit de corps is shared misery. One undercutting factor is the unmet expectations which arise when someone enters the service feeling "the Army will take care of you," that it cares about a soldier's personal well-being.

Those generals who have called forth the most devotion from their troops, who could when necessary lead men to their deaths, have cared about soldiers' well-being. But they have also known there are times when the Army can't care about much more than whether, as the horn goes off at six in the morning, you are standing there with your toes on the line.

This is more difficult for the All Volunteer Force, which is in some regards a social program whose objectives include job training for the poor and freeing those better off from the burden of asking their sons (and in some cases their daughters) to carry rifles. This brings us back to the basic issue: All benefit from freedom but all are not called upon to share in the burden of preserving it. How democratic is a policy which dictates that it is patriotic for the have-nots to volunteer for military service and equally patriotic for the haves not to do so?

Directly relevant to military reform is the question of what effect national service would have on making the officer corps less bureaucratic. Certainly it would test officers' ability to lead. It would also bring into the military people who might never have thought to join on their own but would find a true calling. It would also give talented officers more people of topflight intelligence and ability to work with and to show their stuff.

These are attractive possibilities with the flavor of reform about them. Only a few among elected officials are open in talking about restoring the draft. Compulsory service is a political disaster if a democracy gets involved in a long and unpopular war. Vietnam set the stage for the volunteer force. It is hard to see a way back to conscription.

The current system carries its penalties, however. Along with those just noted, perhaps most important is that a volunteer force increases the temptation and the danger of government employing a professional army to fight undeclared wars that do not "arouse the passions of the people." It is a convenient system if one doubts that a war he wants to fight has mass appeal. But it does circumvent the spirit of reform embodied by the U.S. Constitution against 18th century practice (see above, pages 54–55).

If the fighting man has felt reduced to second-class service by the dominance of military bureaucrats, the officer whose gift is "thinking about war" has found himself in limbo.

John Collins, defense specialist for the Library of Congress, has given the subject definitive treatment in his *U.S. Defense Planning: A Critique.* Military education and service promotional paths alike ignore vital areas of skill. "Concept formation should be the forte, since it affects all defense plans. In fact, it is not. . . . Many decision-makers, unschooled in strategy, focus on forces, funds, and associated issues, which take precedence over concepts.

"Without solid backgrounds on which to build, [officers] become technicians and managers, rather than masters of military art. They suffer from a syndrome identified 200 years ago by Marshal de Saxe, who said, 'In default of knowing what should be done, they do what they know.'" [110]

In 1981 Sen. Gary Hart summed up the findings and proposals of Collins and other like-minded reformers: "The military education system—service academies, command and staff schools, war colleges—gives little emphasis to ideas about warfare. It emphasizes the study of management and lower-level leadership. . . . We must give our officers a chance to think about war both in our service schools and while on regular duty assignments.

"This means changes in the school curricula, much greater emphasis on military history and theory, and possibly longer school terms. It means upgrading and revising military journals. It means reducing the administrative load of officers in the field, to give them time to think.

"And we should consider providing a formal career path for those officers who excel in military theory, to parallel those paths already existing for the troop leader and manager." [111]

Why has this dimension of capability been so strongly down-played, to the point where U.S. law actually denies the Joint Chiefs of Staff the planning role of a general staff? [112]

The reason appears to be a rereading of the German experience. The Germans had a powerful General Staff. It was the very devil at planning. The Germans started two world wars. Therefore, general staffs start world wars.

But this rereading may be a misreading. In both wars the German Army lagged behind the political leadership in its eagerness for war. A key factor in launching World War I was indeed the mobilization program, which was based on linking railroad timetables to troop concentrations. This schedule took on a life of its own which previewed such nuclear age concepts as the "doomsday machine" and the "failsafe point." But to arrive at a juncture where a planning assumption could wreak havoc required 20 years of belligerent posturing and unwise alliance commitments by Kaiser Wilhelm and his corps of post-Bismarckian diplomats. [113]

The General Staff played even less of a role in launching World War II. They gave serious thought to a coup d'état that would dump Hitler rather than run the risks involved in taking on a nation with the best defended frontier and best equipped army in Europe: Czechoslovakia. But Hitler pulled the Munich rabbit out of the hat.

The Wehrmacht marched away past eerily silent crowds in 1939 and 1940—a fact no more lost on the generals then than it would be today. The General Staff was so hesitant about invading Russia that Hitler was furious.

He took revenge six months into the campaign and named himself supreme commander as well as head of state.

After the officers' plot against Hitler in 1944, he carried out a reign of terror against the military brass, whom he saw as a "reactionary element" lacking fervor for Naziism.[114]

The German General Staff was very good at what it did. For this reason, it is easy to assume an eagerness to prove its instrument. But military planners, like most craftsmen, are reluctant to let their tool be used if it may be blunted. Such a risk always exists in war; thus we have the paradox that the shrewdest generals, even those who may be tactically bold, are usually cautious in initiating a conflict.

Building into law a misreading of the German experience has produced a strange result. "Today defense is run to a large degree neither by career officers nor by visible civilian appointees but by invisible 'experts,'" says Congressman Norm Dicks' chief aide Paul Roberts. "The Beltway bandits [defense consulting firms that ring Washington] have replaced the thinkers and are playing 'Monopoly war.'"[115]

It is not a healthy situation. The Beltway bandits serve up an endless menu of exotic scenarios, most of which can be dealt with only by equally exotic—and expensive—weaponry. Budgets soar while accountability for results declines. To correct the situation requires rewriting the charter of the Joint Chiefs of Staff, to emphasize what it should be rather than focusing, as in the past, on what it should not be.

Currently, tours of duty by officers serving the Joint Chiefs are limited to three years. No emphasis is placed on "thinkers." Indeed, JCS staff duty is avoided because "it removes participants from service mainstreams and affects careers adversely."[116] For some officers, "JCS assignments are sought as a pre-retirement post." This fits the needs of those who want to stay in the D.C. area.[117] About 80 percent of JCS staff officers were talented combat commanders decorated for bravery under fire. Few had experience in high-level strategy or interservice planning.[118]

Lack of technical background, combined with legal ceilings on staff size, has left the Joint Chiefs at a disadvantage. The Office of the Secretary (OSD) has expanded partly because JCS could not provide the expertise to deal with the services' own vast planning and budget staffs.[119]

A major deficiency is that only the Chairman speaks for all the services and has explicit responsibility to provide "cross-cutting" advice to the Secretary and the President. General Vessey has improved on past practice by rotating the "acting chairman" (deputy) role quarterly among the service chiefs, so all have experience in this broader assignment.[120] But even under this arrangement, a majority of the Joint Chiefs will, at any one time, speak only for their branch of the service.

"In all our military institutions, the principle of 'unity of command' is inculcated," says former Defense Secretary James Schlesinger. "Yet at the national level it is firmly resisted and flagrantly violated. . . . The Chairman of the Joint Chiefs should be the link between the unified and specified commands."[121]

An awkward structure has led to bad practice. Gen. Volney Warner, former head of the Readiness Command, wrote the President in 1982: "The Joint Chiefs . . . have subverted the unified command system in creating ad hoc headquarters to meet each new military crisis. This proliferation of headquarters without any attendant increase in forces . . . creates a facade of readiness that simply does not exist."[122]

JCS reform leads directly to the question of restructuring the services themselves. "Traditionally the services were organized on a 'corporative model.' Each officer was inculcated with, and worked to advance, the overall goals and purposes of his service. Today only the Marine Corps adheres to this model. The other services have adopted the bureaucratic model in which the officer specializes in narrow functions and the overall goal of the organization is supposedly attained by linking the 'boxes' which define each individual job."[123]

But many reformers believe it is not enough to return each service to the "corporative" model. "The root cause of all these problems is an inefficient division of missions and roles among the services," write David and Morton Halperin. "The U.S. ought to reorganize its forces into units trained and equipped for specific missions such as large-scale ground combat, counterterrorism, control of the seas, and delivery of strategic warheads."[124]

The Halperins see two advantages: (1) "Such units would not have to rely on other units for support." (2) "Chains of command could be short and firmly established."[125] *Plowshares Into Swords* author Jack Stockfish sounds a similar note: "No one knows how much each service should receive. But there is a way to deal with this by making major allocations, for example, Army land-based forces, and applying only broad guidelines to achieve maximum capability. The proper level of detail would be worked out by each service on the basis of specific missions. Thus the guidelines would be oriented toward performance rather than compliance with regulations."[126]

This approach is endorsed by retired Army Lt. Gen. Harry Kinnard: "What we need is a restructuring of OSD so it is kept out of detailed management. We need a broad policy-making body to set basic plans among land, sea, and air missions. But then let the services go ahead and carry out these plans."[127]

Council of Economic Advisors member and former defense analyst William Niskanen believes the Joint Chiefs "should be reconstituted into regional and functional commands. All weapons development would report to them. The services would then be competing to supply forces to the commands. Buyer and supplier would no longer be the same."[128] In other words, a "market" would be created for defense services.

There might be considerable differences between the Halperins, Stockfish, Kinnard, and Niskanen if they all sat down at the table to divide up the missions. Who got what, and how much the existing services would change, might be an issue. But there is a common theme: match structures to missions; don't overmanage from above. Have a planning capability which is strong but broad.

"The current awkward command system is a deliberate response to two deeply felt American fears. First, going back at least to George Washington's time, the 'man on horseback.' Second, the German General Staff blamed, rightly or wrongly, for two World Wars. That the thing functions at all is because of the ingenuity of a corps of military and civilian bureaucrats who have found ways to work around the system and a succession of strong-willed individuals who have gotten things done despite roadblocks." [129]

We owe those folks a debt of gratitude. Perhaps it's time to give them a helping hand.

"Pressure to fundamentally reorganize our national security apparatus has come from the failure of higher defense budgets to translate into military impacts," says former Pentagon official Bing West. He sees a big push coming for changes in the Joint Chiefs and Office of the Secretary. West, himself a skeptic about the dangers of box-shuffling and illusory reforms, believes "reorganization will be resisted from the inside. There is no belief it is required." [130]

West's caveats are well taken. But this is one case where the structure itself seems to generate perverse incentives which promote rivalries instead of building joint capability, and which have precisely inverted the pyramid used by successful armies: strategists, fighters, support officers.

Box-shuffling is indeed irrelevant. But Pentagon reform which encourages inter-service cooperation is not. Investment in weapons, career paths and promotions, plans and exercises, must be melded so the services are not preparing to fight separate wars—against each other in peacetime, against their Soviet counterparts in a conflict. This is not the Army-Navy game; the team uniform is lettered "United States of America."

How would reform lead to more coherent advice and more "hard choices"? This is where the experts in organization incentives, issue identification, and conflict resolution must apply their skills—with the backing of the President and his Pentagon chief.

There is probably no issue on the reform agenda that can be so directly and beneficially affected by top political leadership as that of inter-service cooperation. The Commander-in-Chief can remind career officers of the vital role played by combined land, air, and sea power in the past. He alone, with more ease than everyone else acting without him, can recognize and reward those who work to break down the walls of servicism.

Lacking such positive attention, the natural processes of bureaucracy hold sway. The result is a fragmented and needlessly costly defense effort whose performance is likely to disappoint the nation in cases which require inter-service trust and coordination. These cases constitute a virtual roll call of U.S. military operations since the end of the Vietnam War. The challenges which lie ahead—"low-intensity" conflicts in the third world—are expected to fall in a similar category.

Technology: Savior and Seducer

Equipment should be designed by geniuses to be used by idiots.
—Russian saying [1]

We are pricing ourselves into unilateral disarmament.
—Defense consultant Pierre Sprey [2]

THE U.S. MILITARY is charged with being driven by a "technological imperative." [3] The result is pictured in such terms as "gold-plating," [4] "gee whiz" weaponry, [5] "bells and whistles," [6] and "feather edge" of technology. [7]

Complex, exotic weapons are attractive for three reasons. First, "It is axiomatic that technical superiority can cancel out overwhelming numerical superiority." [8] With Soviet production of some weapons estimated at three times that of the U.S., [9] this logic is appealing. Second, the idea of a capital-intensive war, substituting machinery for men, seems both productive in the industrial sense and sane in minimizing the risk to human life. Both values find strong confirmation in American economic experience. And "ultimately, there is no performance ceiling for weaponry; you simply want the best you can get." [10]

The most obvious problem with this approach is cost. In 1952, $7 billion bought 6,300 jet fighters, [11] a number equal to the total U.S. inventory deployed around the world today. [12] In 1983, the Pentagon paid $8 billion for 270 fighters, [13] a number far below the 400 planes that wear out or are destroyed each year in accidents. [14]

Quality-improvement costs in weaponry have been steadily growing 5–6 percent faster than the general inflation rate, more than doubling the average cost per weapon every 15 years. [15] If the existing trend continues, the entire defense budget in the year 2054 will purchase just one tactical fighter plane which "will be shared 3½ days a week by the Air Force and Navy and made available to the Marines for one day each leap year," in a now-famous illustration developed by Norman Augustine, president of Martin Marietta Aerospace. [16]

Gen. Volney Warner, former chief of the U.S. Readiness Command, criticizes "the super-weapon philosophy, the gold-plated mousetrap, always holding out for the last 10 percent of capability. We have been captives of technology. There is always some development, promised for tomorrow, that we ought to attach to a weapons system."[17]

Warner worries that this leaves us with old equipment while the new system "stays out there 10 years or more being perfected."[18] But it also has an exponential cost impact. "Squeezing the final 5–10 percent of performance improvements out of new systems usually adds 20–50 percent to their total cost," says defense analyst and former Pentagon official Jacques Gansler. He advocates "slight reductions in performance" to cut costs dramatically. "The marginally reduced performance of each individual weapon would be more than offset by the far greater quantities the Pentagon could purchase."[19]

Gansler's views are supported by Dina Rasor, head of the Project on Military Procurement, an independent watchdog group that has analyzed why weapons costs are soaring. "The basic use of high tech should be to improve the design features of standard kinds of arms. Otherwise, we end up with equipment so costly that it is not available in adequate quantity for either training or combat."[20]

The technology push seems to have taken on a life of its own. But it began sensibly enough. In World War II there seemed to be an entirely positive relationship between advanced design and capability. Technology extended the "reach" and effectiveness of the human combatant.

Perhaps the first evidence of a break in this linkage came in Vietnam. U.S. Phantom jets had the ability to fly at over 1,600 miles per hour. But despite more than 100,000 sorties, not one minute of recorded flight time was at more than 1,250 miles per hour, and only a tiny fraction—a few hours—was at more than 900 miles per hour. "The vast majority of military operations and all heavy combat maneuvering was done in the domain of speeds below 1.2 Mach (885 miles per hour)."[21]

The reasons for avoiding high speed were excessive fuel consumption, stress on delicate parts, and inability to make quick course changes required in dogfighting.

The impact of technology on weaponry can be illustrated graphically:

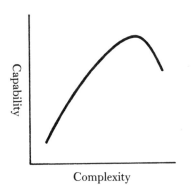

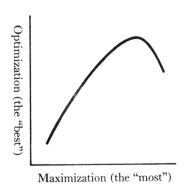

World War II and Korea were fought in an era when the curve was assumed only to have an upward slope. In those days, it was possible to define a weapon's capability simply in terms of lethality = destructive power. But today the equation may be: capability = lethality × reliability × availability × usability in which sheer power is qualified by both human and mechanical factors.

The speed and complexity of some weapons systems may exceed the human capacity to utilize them—weapons designed to be used by geniuses, calmly, amidst the chaos of combat. "Feather edge" technology can take so long to debug that experts sometimes talk as if test failures are supposed to occur, at least in the early stages.[22] And when a new weapon is finally operational, "if it works, it's obsolete," to quote an anonymous general.[23]

A weapon's capability can no longer be equated with its theoretical lethality because the attempt to extend technological reach, if overdone, can degrade combat worthiness. Quantum-leap design features are likely to increase the risk of breakdown and to require that a weapon be off the line and in the shop more often for routine inspection.[24] Yet these features may not justify themselves as fitting the hard realities of battle.

Secretary Weinberger and many others argue that our lead in technology is what keeps the West's outnumbered conventional forces competitive with the Soviets. This is the argument for complex, highly "capable" weapons systems. It is supported by some real world experience, perhaps most notably the consistent, high success ratio enjoyed by Israeli over Syrian pilots. But setting aside the role that training and morale play in such victories, there is another, more specific question: How can we best distinguish between the latest technology and the latest usable technology, so that we may have the latter in the field while we are testing and figuring out what to do with the former?

Failure to make this distinction is reflected in the failure of new weapons to work. Some problems are in the design concept itself. Weapons that require pilots or infantrymen to risk grave danger in order to fire them are not "user-friendly." Weapons whose awesome capabilities can be neutralized by obvious countermeasures are "smart-stupid." Weapons whose capabilities are "proven" in phony tests are "Mickey Mouse."

Such weaponry has given rise to a genre of mordant humor. Consider the Maverick air-to-surface heat-seeking missile, which can be thrown off by an enemy setting ground fires. "It would probably get more pilots killed than it would kill targets," says Anthony Battista of the House Armed Services Committee.[25] Or the Viper, a high-tech bazooka. For weight and cost reasons its power was cut below specs. No longer could it penetrate the front armor of a Soviet T-72 tank. The "Kafkaesque" solution to the Viper's degraded performance: redefine the mission. Now troops are supposed to let the tanks pass and fire on them from the rear. The comment of Senator Warren Rudman on this tactic: "We want a weapon that hurts the enemy, not just pisses him off."[26] Then there is the Division Air Defense Gun (DIVAD): "We have taken a relatively inexpensive, inaccurate Soviet weapon and turned it into a relatively very expensive, inaccurate American weapon," says a congressional staff specialist.[27]

The new weapons also have to contend with an attitude problem. "Battlefield commanders tend to be conservative about reliance on star wars weaponry. They fear it won't work—and many officers suffer from their own brand of computer phobia," notes former Rand analyst Mark Menchik.[28]

This hesitation has a sound basis in the opinion of George Kuhn, a former Army captain and defense consultant to the Heritage Foundation. Kuhn argues that complex technology is "not only busting the budget but detracting from the military's ability to fight. Tactics have been driven by technology" yet high tech is "usually comparatively ineffective."[29]

Jeffrey Record of Georgetown University concludes that "technology proved indecisive in Korea, ultimately irrelevant in Vietnam, and unreliable in Iran. But this seems not to have shaken that faith [in] technical advance as the solution to most problems on the battlefield" even though a price must be paid in the form of unreliability and prohibitive unit costs.[30]

Thus the danger is of a "triple whammy" from high tech on the size of America's combat-ready weapons inventory. First, the amount of hardware that can be purchased is cut sharply by the rise in unit costs. Then, the planes and tanks that have been built break down too often. And as a final touch, the high cost and heavy use of spares squeeze the budget further.

An argument continues to be made that "those who criticize complex weapons across the board miss an important point: America's chief military advantage over the Soviets is its technical supremacy."[31] But the response is that we are in a negative spiral and risk becoming like the mythical bird which, to put it politely, flew up behind itself, and disappeared. "If present trends continue, America's technological edge will soon be too small to offset Soviet numbers," says Gansler.[32]

"The whole Russian system is a game of numbers. Each of their weapons is restrained in technology and performance, and as a result is cheaper," observes Rand Corporation's Soviet specialist Arthur Alexander.[33] The end product is often a weapon that is simpler than its American counterpart and thus is easier for a soldier to operate. "They settle for incremental improvements while we strive for the quantum leap."[34]

Defense Secretary Weinberger takes no comfort from our supposed technical edge. "The Soviets are also building highly sophisticated weapons, and the U.S. cannot send its men into battle with weapons it knows would be inferior to some it would face."[35]

Weinberger is surely right that the most advanced Soviet designs are not to be dismissed. But his emphasis differs from that of most analysts, and it can be read as meaning that all our troops must be equipped to match a capability provided only to some Soviet forces. In addition, there is concern that U.S. defense officials may overstate what the "other team" can do.

In technical areas such as the performance of Soviet weapons, much of the Pentagon's evaluation work is shipped out to private analysts on the theory they have the expertise required. The result, according to one high-ranking Defense official, is "the government ends up contracting out to counter an emerging threat to the very people who will profit from it."[36] The companies doing the analysis are then asked for a weapon to counter the Soviet weapon whose features they describe.

One result is "threat inflation," the exaggeration of Soviet weapons' capabilities. An example is the MiG-25 "Foxbat" fighter plane. "It had been portrayed as the most serious of all threats to U.S. security," says Rand analyst Arthur Alexander. Then a Russian defector supplied the plane to us. Its performance was lower than estimated in every major regard. "If the MiG-25 had been properly evaluated, the U.S. response would have had design consequences leading to a simpler machine" on our part.[37] In a double irony, the MiG-25 was originally developed to counter the U.S. B-70 Valkerie bomber, which was never put into production.

In recent years, American and Soviet defense officials have taken to producing slick, magazine-like catalogues of the other's weaponry. The first edition of "Soviet Military Power" appeared in 1981 on Weinberger's instructions. Using illustrations, photographs, and charts, the publication described Soviet weapons in dramatic, occasionally admiring terms.

Less than a year later, the Russians responded with their own version, "Whence the Threat to Peace." It listed American weapons in equally respectful terms. This inverse competition sometimes reaches absurd heights. "It's like Macy's advertising for Gimbel's," jokes one Soviet expert.[38]

In the 1981 U.S. publication, the huge Nizhniy tank plant was shown in a superimposed image over the Mall in Washington. Editors of the Soviet publication responded with an outline of the even larger Detroit tank armory, over the Nizhniy plant, over the Mall. In 1983 Weinberger released an even more elaborately illustrated version of "Soviet Military Power," but the tank factory was left out. In 1984 the Russians responded with an updated version of "Whence the Threat to Peace."[39]

A "scientific-technical elite" of the type foreseen by Eisenhower in his Farewell Address has arisen. Members of this elite move easily between private industry and government jobs, carrying with them their expertise but also their preference for high-tech weaponry which is increasingly expensive and may be too sophisticated for the realities of war.

"Weapons acquisition is out of control because the R&D (Research and Development) cartel is able to spend $20 billion a year on 'technical hobbies,' advanced systems that don't relate to operational conditions," says Jack Stockfish. "There is no internal critique of current R&D; indeed there

Cartoon by Stayskal. Reprinted by permission: Tribune Media Services, Inc., 1983.

is a suppression of any critique. You find what might be called 'information failure'—the unwillingness to pursue analyses that would reveal shortcomings. The reason for this is that the very people who have the information needed to clarify certain issues have a stake in their not being analyzed."[40]

The process now begins when a group in the "R&D cartel" proposes a new set of technical standards which usually calls for a substantial increment of added performance. These standards are given to the suppliers who must generate technical advance. The hoped-for capabilities tend to precede and determine the requirements ("technology drives tactics").

"There is no incentive to go for simplicity when the Defense research and development branch is striving for maximum technical advance. Cost overruns are almost inevitable, especially since there is no penalty for experiments that don't pan out," says Stockfish.[41]

It might seem that the services would reject so much investment in weapons that may not fit operational realities. But "perverse incentives drive the services to seek expensive weapons, even if they fail to meet practical needs. The reason: service budgets are viewed as a zero-sum game: If we don't get the money, some other branch, or a domestic program, will."[42] Thus, the R&D office is viewed as a source of dollars, and operational testing is seen as a threat that could imperil the go-ahead.

IBM defense consultant Richard Garwin finds the U.S. "keeps starting all kinds of weapons but doesn't have the money to finish them and seldom buys enough of any one kind. . . . We end up with a miserable capacity." Garwin says a major problem is the parallel development, purchase, and maintenance of similar weaponry by each service. The extra cost has been put at $20 billion a year.[43]

Ironically, the current system tends to downplay design changes that would increase usability and reliability, but to encourage those that incorporate emerging high-tech features. The latter procedure is called "concurrent testing"—altering specifications after production has begun. "You finish a job 50 percent through, then rip it out and put in a lot of revisions," says an Electric Boat Division draftsman.[44]

Obviously, in a mission context, realistic performance information becomes a plus. But so long as the focus is to protect budgets, the system leads to "lying and evasion."[45]

In 1983 Congress acted on an idea from the Project on Military Procurement. It created an independent weapons testing office. The intent was to assure that evaluators of performance tests did not have a vested interest in results that looked good.

The Department of Defense has responded by setting what may be a record for foot-dragging. The appointment of personnel to staff the office has been a model of delay. Instead of being treated as a welcome reform, independent weapons testing is seen as awkward and inconvenient.[46]

After six wars in 35 years of independence, Israel is probably the world leader in battlefield testing of new equipment. Careful records are kept on the performance of major weapons in combat. This information is used to modify existing equipment and is built into the design of new weapons. Zvi Yarom, director of the weapons division of Israeli Military Industries, has said "the burden about quality which lies on us is tremendous. . . . The product we are making is to protect our sons. . . . The connection between a faulty or over-priced weapon and battle casualties in a country the size of the U.S. is much more remote."[47]

The Israeli-built Uzi submachine gun is used by the Secret Service to protect the President. They laud its firepower and compact size. In their own army, Israelis have replaced the U.S. made M-16 with an indigenous design, the Galil. It is slightly heavier but has fewer problems in the field. For instance, if more than 120 rounds are fired rapidly by an M-16 and a cartridge is left in the chamber, it will be fired by heat generated from earlier rounds. The Galil can be fired more than 400 times without developing a similar problem.[48]

The Israelis hesitate to claim that their experience has lessons for us. But in fact, the most important thing that can be done for the morale of the fighting man is to assure him the equipment and training best designed to preserve his life. This requires the kind of "close in" attitude Israelis show about battlefield realities.

The effect of high tech on tactics seems to be just the opposite. Weapons become "too valuable to lose" or even to use in training. Heritage Founda-

"I have a dream . . . ."

Cartoon by Auth. Reprinted by permission: Tony Auth, 1983.

tion consultant Kuhn assails the Pentagon for its "pre-occupation with fighting wars at a distance. Highly technical equipment has its place, but its expense has crowded out fulfillment of other needs. Acquisition has gone ahead of reliability and outstrips the training of people to operate it."[49]

Jack Stockfish agrees: "The Army has been shortchanged by our high-tech bias. A capital-intensive strategy failed in Vietnam. It's difficult to replace labor inputs in a land war. 'All the king's helicopters' were no substitute for an adequate infantry."[50]

Indeed, even basic force structure is affected by the "technological imperative." Army budgets are starved by soaring Navy and Air Force bills for hardware. So the Army strives to become high tech. "In all this, there is a tendency to go 'tactical nuclear,' a dangerous course," says Stockfish.[51] If our weaponry precedes and to some degree shapes strategy, then any conflict that arises as a result of such technology "is something that has happened to us—a kind of natural catastrophe. . . . If strategy comes first, then the nature of the confrontation is more likely to be something we have deliberately chosen," observes Thomas Powers in *Thinking About the Next War*.[52]

The premier example of a weapon that is the ultimate in high tech, has the capacity to determine strategy, and is designed to fight wars from a distance is the proposed space-based missile defense system.

Debate among scientists about the feasibility of "Star Wars" lies beyond the judgment of the layman. Defenders of the idea call it a "high frontier" while critics speak of a new U.S. triad: Reagan, Teller, Rube Goldberg.

The appeal of a remote defense cannot be denied. If it worked, the plan would seem to remove the nightmare of an ICBM exchange. The problems seem to lie in three areas: the cost, the impact on deterrence, and the impact on strategy.

"Space lasers—the price is not right," observes *Business Week*, which puts the cost of deploying lasers in all strategies and modes at $300 billion by the end of this century.[53]

The impact on deterrence shows up the painful paradox in a balance of terror. Prior to the nuclear age, the best weapon was the one that was so effective it defied countermeasures. But today, the prospect of one side developing such a weapon invites preemptive attack by the other side. "Star Wars" is a combination of dazzling capability and protracted development. This is the worst formula for destabilizing deterrence and giving the enemy plenty of time to decide whether he must act.

As for its impact on our strategic thinking, "it is an illusion to think we can render nuclear weapons obsolete simply by spending enough dollars and being patient enough," suggests Walter Slocombe. "The ultimate danger is this approach, if it were believed, could make us careless with regard to all other strategic readiness issues. It is one thing to protect selected military targets. It is quite something else to protect 'the country' when the offense need only get a small number of its missiles through to impose a Carthagenian peace."

"A 'high frontier' just over the horizon—this is a delusion," Slocombe concludes.[54] It is also the supreme testament to the seductive power of a technological imperative.

Weapons on Parade

Selecting the right mix of equipment is especially difficult in an era of rapid technical advance. Four major weapons systems illustrate various aspects of the challenge: the B-1 bomber, the F-14–F-18 generation of fighters, the nuclear carrier battle group, and the MX missile. A fifth system, precision-guided munitions, is either the latest high-tech fad or one of those rare developments that could change the nature of warfare.

The B-1B bomber: Problem of the "interim generation." More than 20 years separate the production of the last new B-52 and the first B-1s issued to squadrons. Perhaps no major weapons system in American history has generated so much controversy over so many years. At various times, the Air Force, the Pentagon, the Congress, and three Presidents have pronounced the B-1 vital to national security. With equal conviction, members of Congress, one President, two former Defense Secretaries, and a host of others have declared it not worth producing.

Without question, the B-1 is an awesomely graceful and lethal piece of machinery. Swing-winged and needle-nosed, about the size of a Boeing 707, the craft was designed to cross the Arctic or Atlantic like a javelin, befuddle Soviet air defenses with sophisticated electronics, thunder over

Russian territory to drop nuclear bombs on strategic targets, and return home.

The history of B-1 development is a fine example of a problem which Secretary Weinberger eloquently described in a July 1983 interview: "It is very difficult to get a decision and then it's very difficult to keep it together. Divergent views are represented with great vigor and freedom, as they should be. But this has an effect on the ability to come to closure and make a lasting decision."[55]

The striking thing about the B-1 is that it illustrates equally well the opposite aspects of inertia. In the decade of the 1970s, when the new plane's features would have represented a timely advance, progress was slow as policy makers disagreed on how rapidly, or whether, to proceed. The debate and the false starts and stops confirm Weinberger's point.

But as the process ground away, the plane was being overtaken by military events. Manned bombers had been part of the U.S. "strategic triad" along with missiles launched from silos and submarines. But now, cruise missiles, which like ICBMs can be launched from outside enemy air defenses, were said to make manned bombers unnecessary. If all you need is a flying platform to launch these missiles, then B-52s will do and the B-1 is "like taking the family Ferrari to the corner grocery"[56]—an extravagance.

As the plane's offensive mission was being called into question by the cruise missile, its survivability was threatened by developments in Soviet air defenses—an inevitable result of the terrific delay in development. Even in 1980 it was reported that Russian fighters will be equipped with "look-down, shoot-down" radar-guided missiles and the Soviets will deploy arrays of superfast, ramjet-powered SA-10 missiles. "Both systems pose a grave near-term threat to a low-flying 'penetrator' such as the B-1."[57]

The ultimate argument against the B-1, however, was the impact of its cost on timely development of a new generation of bombers which could cope with the Soviet air defense threat. The price tag of each B-1 went from an estimated $50 million in the late 1970s to $250 million in the early 1980s. Concern arose that building a fleet of 50 to 100 planes would generate cost pressures and starve the budget for "Stealth," a new plane using radar-absorbing materials, radar-elusive, rounded airframe shapes, heat-disguising engines, and electronic countermeasures.

"To forgo or defer Stealth technology would be a very serious mistake," concluded Carter's Defense Secretary Harold Brown. "No one today has the slightest idea how to win a war without radar," added Stansfield Turner, retired CIA director and four-star admiral. "With Stealth, radar may not be usable any more. It could mean a revolution in warfare."[58]

By 1980, skeptics gave the B-1 only a two to three year jump over Stealth in reaching the squadrons, and a similar time period to penetrate Soviet air defenses. "After that," said one Air Force general, "it will be used for dropping hay to stranded yaks."[59] Harold Brown argued that "the Soviets have been working for 10 years on weapons to shoot down the B-1. But Stealth would force them into a totally new air defense system, presumably using heat sensors or optical surveillance rather than radar. The diverted funds would be unavailable for other weapons or adventures."[60]

The Air Force's feelings were schizophrenic. Brown's fears about delaying Stealth were shared, but the B-1 was seen as a bird in the hand. A two-track strategy developed: build the B-1 in case Stealth technology bogs down *and* try to apply Stealth technology to the B-1.

The former approach has a curious budget history. At one point in 1981, Weinberger reportedly was about to give up on the B-1 and recommend concentrating entirely on Stealth. But then the Air Force let it be known that it would accept even a cut in fighter production to get the B-1. Members of Congress insisted on a go-ahead.[61]

In 1984 the Air Force privately circulated its own cut list in Congress—a practice used when the services know large cuts are in the offing and they have priorities which differ from the Secretary's. This list suggested trimming $325 million from Stealth R&D funds, to stave off cuts in the F-15 and F-16 fighter programs. A coalition headed by Weinberger and Capitol Hill aides, and ironically including B-1 lobbyists, turned back the proposal. Instead, the purchase of fighters was reduced.[62]

This was perhaps the first evidence that B-1 funding, by adding pressure to the Air Force's budget needs, might risk delay in development of Stealth. The twist was an alliance of "bomber men" from both B-1 and Stealth camps lining up against and beating "fighter men" in preventing the risk from becoming reality.

The attempt to apply Stealth technology to the B-1 was dealt a setback in February 1984. At a Pentagon briefing, Air Force Vice Chief of Staff Gen. Lawrence Skantze reported: "If you were to take the B-1B and maximize Stealth characteristics, it still would not come anywhere near what you can do with an advanced technology bomber. . . . You have to begin the design with a clean slate."[63]

This leaves the B-1 back where it started from in 1981, as a short-life penetrating bomber or as an expensive launch platform.

Almost everyone agrees the B-1 is a decade late. Its history confirms Weinberger's point about getting a program started. Yet, despite obsolescence, the B-1 is being built. This highlights the other aspect of inertia, expressed in an often-quoted "law" of defense procurement: "A weapons program in motion tends to stay in motion."

Perhaps the biggest reason projects keep rolling is that "once suppliers' geographic locations are known, the pork barrel sets in."[64] In 1980, three years after Carter had killed the B-1, Congress was ready to go ahead. The plane had been under discussion for so many years that members knew who would get the contracts and where the jobs would be. "If Reagan is in the

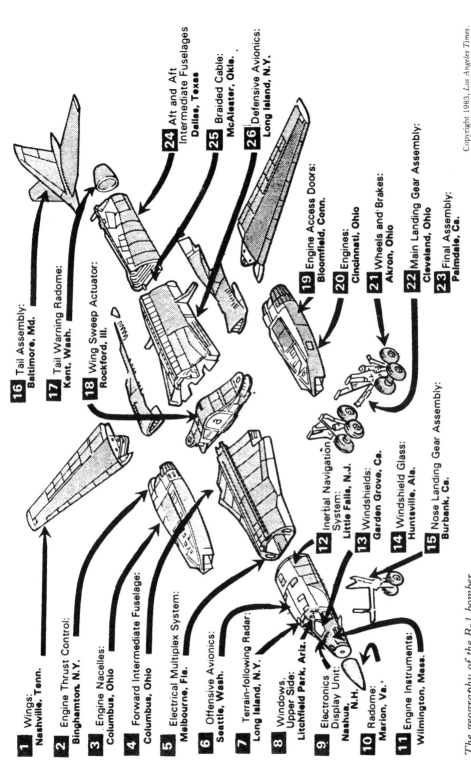

The geography of the B-1 bomber

1 Wings:
Nashville, Tenn.

2 Engine Thrust Control:
Binghamton, N.Y.

3 Engine Nacelles:
Columbus, Ohio

4 Forward Intermediate Fuselage:
Columbus, Ohio

5 Electrical Multiplex System:
Melbourne, Fla.

6 Offensive Avionics:
Seattle, Wash.

7 Terrain-following Radar:
Long Island, N.Y.

8 Windows, Upper Side:
Litchfield Park, Ariz.

9 Electronics Display Unit:
Nashua, N.H.

10 Radome:
Marion, Va.

11 Engine Instruments:
Wilmington, Mass.

12 Inertial Navigation System:
Little Falls, N.J.

13 Windshields:
Garden Grove, Ca.

14 Windshield Glass:
Huntsville, Ala.

15 Nose Landing Gear Assembly:
Burbank, Ca.

16 Tail Assembly:
Baltimore, Md.

17 Tail Warning Radome:
Kent, Wash.

18 Wing Sweep Actuator:
Rockford, Ill.

19 Engine Access Doors:
Bloomfield, Conn.

20 Engines:
Cincinnati, Ohio

21 Wheels and Brakes:
Akron, Ohio

22 Main Landing Gear Assembly:
Cleveland, Ohio

23 Final Assembly:
Palmdale, Ca.

24 Aft and Aft Intermediate Fuselages
Dallas, Texas

25 Braided Cable:
McAlester, Okla.

26 Defensive Avionics:
Long Island, N.Y.

White House next January [1981], the B-1 will go into production; if Carter is still there, it will not," said a Pentagon strategic planner.[65]

The support structure for the B-1 has set what must be a record for geographic dispersion. Parts of the craft are being built in 48 states and 400 congressional districts. Thus, only 35 members of the House and four members of the Senate don't have a jobs stake in the project (see chart, page 103, for the location of 26 principal suppliers).

The bill for the B-1 is coming due: 34 of the planned 100 aircraft to be built in fiscal 1985 will cost $8.2 billion. That is almost double what the B-1 program cost in 1983 when only seven planes were funded. In 1986 the Administration hopes to fund 48 more to complete the B-1 fleet by 1988. Congress is not expected to cut it back—55,000 jobs are involved, spread in virtually every state.[66]

William Kaufmann of Brookings argues the schedule proves the Administration is not worried about short-term exposure and has delayed solving long-term problems. "The window of vulnerability is not closing. It has simply been moved."[67] Thus the problem of an "interim generation" of weaponry in an era of technical change.

The F-14 – F-18 fighters: "Everybody wins." Building front-line fighter planes in an era of advanced technology is not a line of business which firms begin easily or abandon casually. Highly specialized skills, knowledge, and equipment are required. In practical terms, there is little chance for major new producers to enter this field. To hurdle the requirements of competence from a dead start is nearly impossible.

Nor is it desirable to lose any of those now in the game. Design competition is very real, and the existing production base is thought to be minimal for "surge" capacity—a rapid hike in output needed to replace attrition in a long conflict.

Thus each firm comes to be seen as a defense resource whose continued existence should be nurtured. But there is a conflict between encouraging "let the chips fall where they may" design and bidding contests, and keeping all the players fit for the next round. Two means have been found to cope with this. One is that the losers wind up as major subcontractors on winners' projects. The other is that a greater number of aircraft types are kept in production than is strictly required.

The United States has four front-line fighter/interceptor craft, any one of which is arguably superior to any other plane built outside this country. Their key features include:

	F-14	F-15	F-16	F-18
Top speed (mph)	1,584	1,676	1,333	1,190
Weight empty (lbs)	39,930	28,700	14,567	28,000
Combat radius (mi)	725	975	360	480
Engines	2	2	1	2
Cost per plane ($mil)	$40	$40	$20	$30

The F-14 Navy and F-15 Air Force craft are fast air-superiority interceptors. Both planes became so expensive it seemed they could not be acquired in needed quantities. The F-16 and F-18 were developed as still hot but less expensive alternatives.

Each of the latter suffered production delays which raised unit costs. A cause of delay, and a result of it as well, was the addition of expensive equipment to what began as "simpler" designs. The process worked both ways: new gear required revisions which set back production, and the passage of time itself suggested a need, or at least the opportunity, to plug in fancy features that had not been in the original design.

The F-18 began life as the loser (to the F-16) in a contest to replace the F-15. The Navy picked it up because long flights over water have led to a doctrine expressed in the quip, "When an engine flames out on a one-engine aircraft, it becomes very quiet." [68] Critics have called the F-18's range disappointing, possibly deficient, and certainly below specs. Skeptics have been countered by test pilots who proclaim, "In this plane, we own the sky." [69]

The planned production runs of the F-14 and F-15 are over. But the F-14 has been hanging on at increasing cost per plane. Politics has kept the line open while its proponents looked for a mission. The F-15 has been aggressively promoted in new roles. One looks as if it may stick. The "E" version was victorious in a competition with the F-16 to perform the deep strike role in the Air Force's AirLand 2000 doctrine. [70]

American and NATO doctrine hinges on close air support, which defense consultant Pierre Sprey calls "the single most important mission of maneuver warfare." [71] Only in the last decade has the Air Force had a good close-support plane available: the A-10, which is sturdy enough to take hits, can fly slowly enough to find the enemy, and is armed with a simple but effective 30mm cannon to hit tanks.

Pilots have ridiculed the A-10, joking that they fear being hit from the rear by birds. [72] This reflects the generally low esteem in which tactical missions are held by high-flying pilots. The Air Force has stopped adding the A-10 to its inventory, and launched a competition between the F-15 and F-16 for the tactical role. The use of hot interceptors as ground-attack craft has been a subject of strong controversy since the F-104 Starfighter was loaded with ordinance, and suffered a rash of crashes, in NATO service two decades ago.

Even if the mission is proper to these planes, the competition is being pursued in a manner which insures that "everybody wins" or, at least, all options are kept open. In January 1984 the director of the General Accounting Office (GAO) wrote Secretary Weinberger a letter of concern about the contest. The GAO noted that separate statements, tailored to the differing traits of the F-15 and F-16, had been used by the Air Force. These were sent to each aircraft company as a request for proposal (RFP).

Normally, a common request is sent out. The GAO rejected use of tailored instructions and also refused to accept the Air Force argument that "ranking the evaluation criteria and further refining and quantifying them might predetermine results."[73] In other words, one plane was probably better suited for the tactical role. Had a uniform standard been applied, that would have been clear. And at least in this case, such a method was contrary to keeping both craft in the running for future assignments.

Despite such accommodations to the industry, there is widespread anxiety about a shake-out. The reason: a ferocious new competition is beginning over what is likely to be the last new fighter jet the Defense Department will buy for the rest of the century.

The Air Force has awarded contracts to seven firms to develop design concepts for a new warplane called the Advanced Tactical Fighter (ATF). It will eventually replace the F-15 and F-16 in the air defense role. Test flights are slated for 1991 with production two years later. Industry analysts expect development costs to exceed the $38 billion required to design, test, and build the F-15.

At stake for the big firms is their ability to continue as prime contractors. Each of these firms has at least one multibillion dollar program in hand, but in many cases only brief bursts of production are called for. Failure to win part of the ATF program could force one or more companies out of the aircraft business or relegate them to roles as subcontractors or subsidiaries of other firms. "There is too little dish to feed all the dogs and the question is who will starve," says Wolfgang Demisch, aerospace analyst at First Boston Corporation.[74]

As in past contracts, the Air Force has set its sights on a quantum leap in technology, according to Lt. Gen. Thomas McMullen, whose Aeronautical Systems division will manage the project. The new fighter may feature such advances as voice activated cockpit controls, supersonic cruising capacity, and use of epoxy graphite, and other non-metals in more than half its components.

Most important, the Air Force wants the new fighter to be capable of detecting and destroying enemy aircraft at such long distances that its own safety will never be in question. This means new radars and computers, coupled to longer-flying missiles.[75]

Many of these features are the subject of serious technical and philosophic criticism. The general concern is that the craft will be too complex. Perhaps to meet this objection, McMullen has included a major reduction in maintenance and higher reliability among the advances called for in the ATF.

Of the main competitors, a Rockwell spokesman has said, "All these firms are giants, but where are the giant programs coming from? Everything is very tenuous these days and we want to be sure we are one of the survivors." The rivals are jealously guarding details of their design efforts. Several firms refuse to discuss their approach.

Rockwell, Lockheed, and Boeing are the "serious money boys" with the engineering talent to overpower virtually any competitor, Demisch says. "But there are seven competent design teams, most with 70 years' experience. How the Air Force is going to eliminate any of them is not obvious."[76]

High tech creates a dilemma. It requires the building of a superb capacity. But even this capacity is put at risk in a "quantum leap" environment. The Air Force and Navy have tried to meet firms' economic needs in a number of ways: by paying $20–$40 million per fighter plane, by taking risks on experiments that may not pan out and picking up the tab if they fail, by keeping four major fighters in production at once, and by encouraging "everybody wins" subcontracting. Yet, with the end of current runs and advent of the ATF, the industry is on a spear point. The costs of maintaining a "quantum leap" industrial structure may outstrip budget realities.

One company took a bold step to escape the trap. Northrop, at a cost of $625 million, developed the F-20 as a private venture. The craft is an improved version of the F-5, which captured nearly a world monopoly on low-cost fighter sales. The F-20 is intended solely for export and costs $11 million.

Not a single F-20 has been sold and none may ever be. The episode is viewed as a cautionary tale, a dismal experience that raises doubts about efforts to make the defense industry more competitive and willing to take risks to market superior products. Analysts say Northrop got caught in "a defense contracting environment that is a morass of conflicting allegiances and ideology" and had to contend with more than half a dozen federal agencies and congressional committees that push their special perspectives on weapons exports.[77]

In theory the U.S. is only supposed to provide the frontline F-14–F-18 series fighters to its closest allies. In 1979 the State Department told aerospace firms they could develop a fighter with "intermediate capabilities" for export. The phrase came to haunt Northrop. "Being intermediate in capability does not sound like the best chance of winning," says Demisch. "In peace, it sounds expensive, and in war it sounds like losing."[78]

The concept arose partly as a "second-class fighter for second-class friends." But another factor was simpler maintenance to avoid the need for thousands of American technicians to be stationed around the world to support weapons sold by U.S. firms. The F-18 repair manual now being developed will have an estimated 500,000 pages—judged too long for use by personnel in "technically backward" nations.

The F-20 got caught in a double crunch. First, sales to its most promising prospect were blocked. President Carter hesitated and President Reagan refused to allow sales to Taiwan because of U.S.-China relations. Then, a number of third world allies were allowed to buy front-line jets. This was against the theory, but "policy by exception" became the rule. For example, "the F-16 was the lynchpin of our new relationship with Pakistan," said a State Department official.

Northrop claims the F-20 is fully competitive, with an optimal mix of high performance and low cost of purchase and repair. It has gone to some lengths to prove this, including securing the endorsement of legendary "right stuff" test pilot Chuck Yeager. One problem has been the services themselves. Recently when Turkey was shopping for new jets, Air Force Secretary Verne Orr and Navy Secretary John Lehman wrote Ankara promoting their respective craft, the F-16 and F-18. In addition to service pride, export sales increase production runs and lower unit costs.

Congressman Bruce Vento asks, "What sort of Defense Department policy allows the Navy and Air Force secretaries to act as hucksters for private defense contractors?"[79] Northrop is asking what happened to its export fighter program. The craft would have at least served to mitigate a problem described by Noel Koch, a top Defense official in international security affairs: "Everybody wants lethal and very expensive weapons, and we don't always see the threat that would justify it. Often the demand arises from a military that wants toys and a dictator who tries to get them through foreign arms purchases so the generals will help keep him in power."[80]

The F-20 might have reduced the amount of funds squandered in this fashion—and might also have had some kind of positive impact on U.S. weapons costs if it is as capable as Northrop says.

Nuclear carriers 14 and 15: Strategic contradiction. The most expensive items in the Defense budget are two new *Nimitz*-class carriers. Each costs $3.4 billion and is the nucleus of an armada of other vessels and aircraft whose price totals $17 billion. The two new battle groups would join thirteen now in existence.

The $34 billion investment has been called "wildly wasteful" and "perhaps the most striking example of procurement without regard to grand strategy."[81]

At issue is a new "forward position" doctrine for the Navy. In the event of a war in Europe, the fleet would not restrict itself to guarding Atlantic sea lanes. Instead, it would seize the offensive, sealing off Soviet naval forces in their bases, bottling up Soviet submarines in the Arctic Sea, and launching deep air strikes into the Russian land mass.[82]

There are two basic concerns. One is the value of the strategy, and the other is whether the mission involves risks that would doom the battle groups.

"How do you defeat a great land power like Russia? Not by nibbling at the edges with carrier strikes," says former Under Secretary of Defense Robert Komer. "The contention that we can defeat Russia by being supreme at sea, even if the Soviets are supreme in Eurasia, is simply nonsense. If the Soviets take over Eurasia and we have only the seas, we've had it."[83]

Forward positioning is in the spirit of Admiral Farragut's injunction: "The best defense is a well-directed fire from your own guns." It is also related to the ambiguous doctrine of horizontal escalation; in this case, how to make the Soviets pay if NATO is overwhelmed by Warsaw Pact forces.

But an ominous indication already exists that, in extreme cases, the huge investment would not be risked. The admirals declined to send a nuclear carrier to the Persian Gulf during the Iran hostage crisis. It appears that naval strategists also rule out the use of even one of the existing 13 battle groups to contest an event as serious as Russian seizure of the Gulf oilfields. "Not wanting to lose it, they decline to use it."[84]

The Persian Gulf scenario would seem a paradigm for the maximum use of naval power. The military objective being contested is the most valuable in the world apart from major power homelands. The objective is uncomfortably convenient to Soviet land forces but is also accessible by sea. Yet the peril posed by putting a $17 billion task force in harm's way is judged too great. And even more hazard would be involved if a battle group sailed into the teeth of Soviet naval power, as forward positioning calls for.

Either the investment would not be used or—and here the admirals' fears seem justified—it would be destroyed. Vivid scenarios picture the latter result.

As the British experience with the Exocet makes plain, "our Navy has a horrendous problem, and the situation will only get worse." The Exocet's range is only 45 miles; the Navy's Harpoon is "a much better, long-range anti-ship missile." A new version of the Tomahawk will extend that range to 700 miles. A similar missile is already carried on Soviet Backfire bombers assigned to naval operations. A high-ranking Navy officer says, "Once those missiles are launched, there will be hell to pay."[85]

The defensive plan calls for spotting the Backfires before they come within range to fire, and diverting or destroying them far from the carrier battle group. If an enemy plane manages to evade and launch, close-in anti-missile defenses would either destroy the Soviet weaponry or "seduce" it into attacking a false target. And even if the missiles hit, the Navy says it could cope with the damage that destroyed the *Sheffield*.

The new generation of anti-ship missiles will "raise the stakes substantially." Their range may exceed the defensive "bubble" around the ships. They will have anti-jam gear and jammers of their own. And in a ballistic rather than a cruise mode, the Soviet AS-4 travels at 2,500 miles per hour, meaning that the only effective defense is to shoot down Backfires before they launch.

Of all large warships, carriers are the most vulnerable. One old-fashioned bomb can put them out of commission as launch platforms. "No post-World War II surface ships have armored hulls comparable to the *Iowa*-class battleships or *Baltimore*-class cruisers," writes Navy Captain Charles Pease, "nor are they designed to stand near-misses by nuclear warheads." Pease says a "leakproof" aircraft and missile defense would be "difficult to establish and maintain in conventional war and almost impossible in nuclear war."

In an era of satellite surveillance, individual ships might cruise unde-
tected on the open seas, but a battle group would be picked up, Pease believes. Then he offers this nightmare scenario: "Saturation raids of cruise
missiles arriving simultaneously from many axes would be most stressing.
But ballistic nuclear weapons change the odds dramatically against Allied
surface ships. Traditional ship spacings for air defense present an attractive
target for a nuclear barrage. However, wide dispersal would prevent concentrated area defense against Soviet aircraft and cruise missiles." A likely
scenario: nuclear ballistic missiles are used to disable the active defense.
Then Backfires and subs are sent in to finish the job from close up. It's
"Sink the Bismarck" on a grand scale.

Pease argues there is only one way to carry out the mission against such
opposition: build a "semi-submersible" Navy—in itself, an awesomely expensive project.[86]

In early 1984 a Soviet submarine collided with the nuclear carrier *Kitty
Hawk*, which was surrounded by its screen of support craft. Critics jumped
on the incident as a timely warning on the battle groups' vulnerability. So-
nar contact with the sub was lost two hours before the collision despite the
presence of five to ten vessels.

Navy Secretary John Lehman said not to worry. "The significant thing
about the *Kitty Hawk* incident was not that the sub surprised the carrier. In
the course of the previous three days it had been located and 'killed' more
than 15 times and had been ignored thereafter as the exercise proceeded
beyond the sub-hunting phase." Lehman added that "the role of the aircraft
carrier in particular is not to defend itself against Soviet attacks but rather
to defend our lifelines against those attacks."[87]

One can only wonder why, even in a training exercise, there would be an
end to the "sub-hunting" phase and loss of contact with a Soviet vessel
which was trailing the battle group. One must wonder even more how a
nuclear carrier "defends our lifelines" if it cannot defend itself.

This raises a point which is perhaps the most damning fact that exists
about any American weapons system: "It is generally accepted that 70–90
percent of the ships that accompany the carriers and planes they carry are
for self-defense."[88]

In a bizarre twist, Lehman has now reversed the argument and says the
carriers are needed to protect the accompanying planes and ships. But he
has admitted the battle groups are not self-sustaining. The plan to pin the
Soviets back on their Arctic bases requires a heavy degree of cooperation
from Air Force radar planes, interceptors, and tankers. "If NATO airpower
can cover the same areas in or near the Soviet Union which Lehman wants
to cover with carriers, why employ such a high-risk, high-cost approach?"[89]

The forward positioning strategy indeed seems to be galvanizing the
Russians. This is heightening the risk to NATO ally Norway, according to
that country's defense chief, Gen. Sven Hauge. In fact, there is evidence the

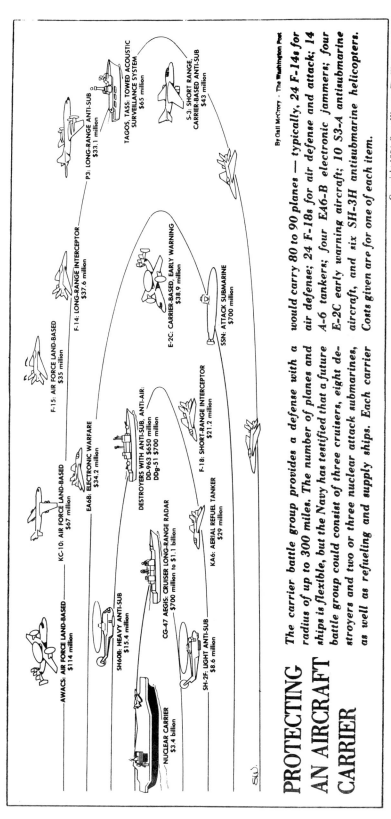

PROTECTING AN AIRCRAFT CARRIER

The carrier battle group provides a defense with a radius of up to 300 miles. The number of planes and ships is flexible, but the Navy has testified that a future battle group could consist of three cruisers, eight destroyers and two or three nuclear attack submarines, as well as refueling and supply ships. Each carrier would carry 80 to 90 planes — typically, 24 F-14s for air defense; 24 F-18s for air defense and attack; 14 A-6 tankers; four E46-B electronic jammers; four E-2C early warning aircraft; 10 S3-A antisubmarine aircraft, and six SH-3H antisubmarine helicopters. Costs given are for one of each item.

AWACS: AIR FORCE LAND-BASED
$114 million

KC-10: AIR FORCE LAND-BASED
$67 million

F-15: AIR FORCE LAND-BASED
$35 million

P3: LONG-RANGE ANTI-SUB
$33.1 million

TAGOS, TASS: TOWED ACOUSTIC SURVEILLANCE SYSTEM
$65 million

S-3: SHORT RANGE, CARRIER-BASED ANTI-SUB
$43 million

EA6B: ELECTRONIC WARFARE
$34.2 million

F-14: LONG-RANGE INTERCEPTOR
$37.6 million

SH60B: HEAVY ANTI-SUB
$15.4 million

DESTROYERS WITH ANTI-SUB, ANTI-AIR:
DD-963 $650 million
DDg-51 $700 million

E-2C: CARRIER-BASED, EARLY WARNING
$38.9 million

CG-47 AEGIS: CRUISER LONG-RANGE RADAR
$700 million to $1.1 billion

KA6: AERIAL REFUEL TANKER
$29 million

F-18: SHORT-RANGE INTERCEPTOR
$21.2 million

SSN: ATTACK SUBMARINE
$700 million

NUCLEAR CARRIER
$3.4 billion

SH-2F: LIGHT ANTI-SUB
$8.6 million

By Gail McChory — The Washington Post

strategy plays directly into Soviet hands. Adm. Sergei Gorshkov, chief of the Russian Navy, has written, "a single submarine is capable of destroying a major surface ship with a salvo of cruise missiles."[90] One U.S. admiral asserts, "Cruise missiles are categorically the most revolutionary development in naval warfare since nuclear power."[91]

In an era when new weapons have made every surface ship much more vulnerable, the Navy has come to depend on just 15 vessels—the nuclear carriers. The result is "a Navy built around a mission it cannot perform—and needlessly expensive for lesser missions."[92]

This is the heart of the problem: a strategic contradiction. Since thirteen battle groups already exist, a burden is placed on advocates of two new ones to explain the use of this $34 billion investment. It turns out to fit only a "universal conflict strategy" where a lot of trouble is happening at once, or a major U.S.-Soviet clash where very bad trouble is happening in one place. In either event, the very condition that would make the enlarged inventory desirable also implies a level of enemy attacks that would place the battle groups in gravest peril.

Navy Secretary Lehman has forged ahead in pursuit of the 600-ship fleet, apparently taking comfort in every new contract commitment as a defense against any scaling back of the program. Indeed, the claim has been made that cancellation fees would be so great as to exceed the cost of completing the ships.[93] But there are options. It should be recalled that the *Lexington* and *Saratoga*, our first two large carriers, were built on the hulls of two canceled battle cruisers. The other two vessels in the class were scrubbed entirely.[94]

In addition, "even if the two new nuclear carriers cannot be stopped, construction of support ships and aircraft can be avoided by Congress by legislating early retirement for the oldest carrier, the U.S.S. *Coral Sea*. This could save up to $500 million a year in operating expenses and tens of billions in procurement costs" by holding the Navy to 12 or 13 battle groups.[95]

The MX missile: Weapon as bargaining chip. As in the case of other strategic weapons, we hope never to use the MX. Unlike our other nuclear arms, the missile is not primarily seen as an addition to U.S. striking power but as an inducement for negotiations. It is a case of building up our force to spur talks on a mutual reduction of force. The MX is meant to deter not merely the ultimate use, but the initial production, of nuclear weapons.

The missile thus represents a double paradox. We will have failed if we have to use it. This is the paradox of deterrence generally. But we will also have failed if we have to produce and fully deploy 100 or more MXs. This is the paradox of arms control psychology.

Surely, one must walk a tightrope of alert prudence if a force-in-being is to enhance deterrence. Equally, one must strike a fine balance if a new weapon is to promote arms control. A skeptical, rival power must see resolve but not recklessness. One's willingness to build the system must be beyond doubt; one's regret at the prospect must be equally certain.

The Carter Administration began the MX project for modernization. The plan became mired in a dispute over the "race track" basing mode which would have required vast expanses of land in Nevada and Utah. The Reagan Administration succeeded in removing this obstacle by endorsing the recommendation of the Scowcroft Commission, which was a model exercise in bipartisan cooperation and use of experts to fashion a compromise.

Even with the breaking of this impasse, the MX could gain vital support in Congress only as a bargaining chip. Some felt the system was defective; others saw no reason to enlarge our nuclear armory. Their votes for the MX were forthcoming solely in order to add arms control leverage for the U.S. in talks with the Soviets.

Thus the MX, as a weapon, took on a somewhat shadowy existence. It turned out the new basing mode—use of old ICBM silos—was "explicitly non-survivable."[96] The Russians could take out the missiles on a first strike. Still, the MX's value was presumed undiminished "as a demonstration of U.S. willingness to proceed with force modernization."[97]

Critics charged that the difficulty in finding a basing mode should have been a warning sign that the MX was deeply flawed. "Instead, the President committed himself, at great cost in political capital, to a system dreamed up in previous administrations by an unholy alliance of defense interests and arms controllers.

"Reagan is playing the same old game of backing a white elephant whose main utility is as a bargaining chip with the Russians. . . . On the one hand, we're told the Soviets have been building up their forces to a war-footing level and we can't trust them not to use what they've got. On the other hand, we are told we can negotiate arms control treaties with them, while they're violating the ones they've signed. . . . The threat needs to be defined more clearly."[98]

A technical debate rages on whether the MX can do what it is supposed to do. One argument against it is that the same first strike which demolishes the MX would also empty Soviet silos of the ICBMs that are its justification, since the prime use of its 10-warhead design is against hardened targets.[99] A more basic objection is that the MX is simply the latest, and last, attempt to perpetuate what is now the vulnerable leg of our strategic forces, our land-based ICBMs in "soft" silos. "The triad is not the trinity," says Congressman Charles Bennett.[100] Others flavor the debate with interservice humor: "One of the MX's chief attractions to the Air Force is the sonofabitch is so big it won't fit in a Trident sub," claims a Capitol Hill defense specialist.[101]

The Soviets walked away from the bargaining table in late 1983 to protest installation of U.S. Pershing II missiles in Europe. Will MX bring them back? "This missile is a marginal improvement in a type of system we already have," believes Terry Freese. "The Soviets may well be more interested in what we do with tactical and theater systems in Europe."[102]

In the spring of 1984 the Soviets began what appeared to be a counterproductive attempt to influence the U.S. election by refusing to deal with President Reagan. Part of the ploy was an indefinite extension of their arms control talks boycott. This made the role of the MX secondary to other factors until at least November 1984.

A compromise plan was fashioned by Congressman Les Aspin to the Administration's request for 40 MXs funded in fiscal 1985. Money for 15 missiles would be approved, not to be spent until April, and not to be spent at all if the Soviets had come back to the bargaining table.[103]

The interim may bring about new developments in arms control. It may also be a chance to evaluate whether we ought to proceed with a weapon that is at best controversial, and at worst is an offensive or first-strike missile which cannot itself survive a first strike by the other side. This latter argument is raised by those who view the MX not only as wasteful but as profoundly destabilizing. Critics charge that its only use would be to start a nuclear exchange and that its deployment would raise the ratio of warheads to targets, which also creates a greater risk of war (see page 69).

No weapon is ever designed to be a bargaining chip but rather to attain a military objective or to serve as a deterrent. At some point we may decide to trade the weapon away if other nations will abandon or restrict a given capability in return. The MX began as a modernization of our land-based ICBM force. But the problem of a basing mode and the progress of our thinking on arms control and deterrence have made the MX a marginal addition to our arsenal and a step backward in terms of stability.

Precision-guided munitions (PGMs): Dawn of the post-nuclear age? In theory there are at least three ways to end the nightmare of nuclear war: (1) arms control; (2) an invulnerable defense; (3) evolution of new weapons superior to nuclear arms.

The first of these approaches has received great attention but has found little success. The second is the subject of lively controversy, but is decades and hundreds of billions of dollars away from proving itself. The third has hardly been discussed, except by a small group of enthusiasts who see a way to hit targets over great distances with great accuracy, but without the unpleasant side effects of a nuclear explosion.

Joseph Kraft once wrote that in some cases the way to overcome problems created by technology was to apply more technology. This is a belief shared by advocates of precision-guided munitions, "smart" bombs that would land at ground zero and do their damage with conventional warheads.

Highly accurate, non-nuclear missiles are seen by proponents not just as a new weapon to be added to our armory, but as *the* new weapon which will replace other systems. They will cut costs, focus the defense effort, and re-define warfare.

The argument runs like this: The U.S. is fast approaching a crisis of de-fense planning. The nation cannot afford a $1.6 trillion buildup. But even severe critics admit few cuts can be made in manpower, operations, and maintenance. That leaves procurement.

Unless weapons that are just entering production (such as the B-1, the MX, the nuclear carriers) are halted soon, they will be increasingly difficult to stop. A political and economic vested interest will arise to keep them go-ing, and the military will argue that cancellations would waste big money.

But the sheer cost of these systems threatens to shoulder aside newer weapons that could defend the U.S. effectively and at much less cost. R&D programs now promise such swift advances in microelectronics that "smart" missiles could be the dominant weapon in tomorrow's arsenal. Richard De-Lauer, Under Secretary of Defense for Research and Engineering, says that the U.S. "absolutely must become more selective" in deciding which sys-tems to produce, and he leaves little doubt that super-accurate missiles are high on his priority list.[104]

In 1982 DeLauer predicted it would take five years to develop the sen-sors and microcomputers that would give U.S. missiles "zero probability of error" in striking targets at both short and intercontinental ranges.

The missiles would cut costs in two ways. First, their efficiency would reduce the number of ships, aircraft, and land vehicles needed to carry them. Second, because of electronic component design, a single missile air-frame could be fitted for different missions. This would drastically reduce the variety of missiles each service needs.[105]

Proponents see an opportunity for dramatic strategic and budgetary gains. Some call for a Manhattan-style project to integrate precision-targeted mu-nitions, conventionally armed missiles, and other modern systems. They call it "a real opportunity for the West to offset much of the Soviet buildup and reduce its dependence on nuclear weapons."[106] IBM's defense specialist Richard Garwin claims that speedy development of all state-of-the-art mili-tary technologies, plus rapid construction of new mixtures of weapons and missions, would enable the Pentagon "to do a better job with one-half its present budget."[107]

The *Wall Street Journal* offers this comprehensive case for precision-guided munitions: "You can avoid killing civilians if you have weapons that can actually hit the target. In fact, as nuclear weapons systems have im-proved in accuracy over the last 20 years, the gross megatonnage of the U.S. nuclear force has steadily declined. . . . We are now at the point where, if the Pentagon could be made to fully exploit dawning technologies, many targets could be hit with advanced conventional weapons, vastly raising the nuclear threshold." Overcoming the prejudice in deterrence theory against accuracy is "the first prerequisite for an effective and affordable defense; the second is taking on the Pentagon. The outcome in the Falklands and Lebanon leaves little room for doubt that the warfare of the future will be dominated by precision-guided conventional weapons. . . . Pentagon procurement only sporadically reflects these developments.

"The Reagan defense policy has been to throw money at the Pentagon, relying on the generals and admirals to compile shopping lists. . . . This is a recipe for an expensive and clumsy defense apparatus. . . . The command for a thorough-going emphasis on smart conventional weapons has to come from the top down. . . . This is an ambitious menu. . . . Probably it exceeds the will and capacity of the Reagan administration. . . . But the risk of the present course is that . . . program after program will be crushed between budget pressures and its own defects."[108]

In sum, precision-guided munitions (PGMs) enjoy a unique appeal. They promise to give weapons development a sharp focus which will restore affordability to the defense budget. They also offer the vision of "clinical" strikes which will restore the prospect of civilized warfare in which non-combatants are spared.

Movement toward PGMs is slowed by familiar causes. The services resist giving smart missiles higher priority than ships, planes, and tanks—"things people can ride on." DeLauer finds "we don't seem to be able to cut down on the number of missile-carrying platforms."[109] In 1984 the services' intransigence again defeated the search for a common missile airframe. The flexible use of modular components would in theory permit the same projectile to house equipment for air-to-ground, air-to-air, and ground-to-air roles, cutting production costs. As usual, each branch claimed its own "unique mission" made such coordination impossible.[110]

Even deterrence theory has helped to bollix up progress on the new systems. It might seem that better conventional systems could bolster deterrence, since it would be seen that the U.S. was doing all it could to make nuclear weapons a last resort.[111] But instead, "the biases and prejudices of mutually assured destruction (MAD) against new and more accurate systems have been built into our negotiating posture." Smart missiles are seen as destabilizing in two regards: they use technology that could be applied to nuclear weapons, and paradoxically, they aren't "horrible enough" to insure they wouldn't be used. Indeed, clean and accurate bombs could be just the thing to launch a conventional war that would escalate into an all-out exchange.[112]

Read critically, precision-guided munitions may be the icing on the cake of "flexible response"—the ultimate fine-tuning in an array of arms that the U.S. would claim to apply with finesse to each situation. The concern is that fine-tuning in war is an illusion. Once launched, a conflict is a greased slide on which rising passions and damage already done insure a swift passage to use of one's full armory.

Nor should the destructive power of these weapons be overlooked. They create no Sunday school picnic vision of war. Indeed, there is no reason why enough smart missiles couldn't create vast wreckage, especially if they were directed at targets such as chemical plants whose destruction would lead to environmental damage.

Another objection is the cost. "Nobody is going to pay the price to develop precision-targeted munitions," says Bing West. "There's always some new superweapon on the horizon. This is just the latest."[113] The cost argument gains force if PGMs are simply added to our armory on top of other items. Consider this assessment by a top White House weapons technology specialist: "Radically new systems should be able to replace or at least reduce our investment in older systems, and also in manpower in some cases. There is new weaponry in this class. I could play an ace and get an hour with the President to talk with him about this. But before he made the decision to cut an existing program, he'd call in the Joint Chiefs. They'd tell him not to eliminate anything. To agree with me, he'd have to set aside their pleas."[114]

The biggest problem, however, is the simple fact that most PGMs have not proven themselves yet. Indeed, they may be the latest example of weaponry which is vigorously promoted before it has passed the test. The paralysis of deterrence theory, and the increasing cost and design problems in ships, planes, and tanks, together with the apparent lessons of recent wars, have made it seem that smart missiles "must" work. This could set the stage for rushing hardware into production before its performance in the field is reliable. If this happened, PGMs would be a mirage, not a solution.

The issue is whether specific weapons are achieving test results that provide a reasonable basis for production. Here, once again, some of the record reads like a script for the Keystone Cops.

Indeed, the story begins with America's first PGMs in World War II—the torpedo and the bazooka. The submarine torpedo with which our "silent service" began the war had three flaws: a defective depth setting, and both magnetic and contact fuses reluctant to detonate. Early results in firing on the enemy were so poor that desk-based Navy officers in the U.S. accused sub skippers of cowardice in failing to approach close enough to make a hit. Slowly, the weapon was debugged. The contact fuse took longest of all. As a backup system, its nonperformance was concealed unless the magnetic detonator was turned off.

The bazooka could have been tested easily against the steel of captured German tanks. In European combat, it proved unable to penetrate the Panzers' armor. The solution, which saved American lives in the Battle of the Bulge, was to employ the captured German bazooka (*Panzerfaust*) using translated German manuals to operate it.[115]

One of the most highly touted PGMs is the "assault breaker." Sensors are dropped by parachute into an area where the enemy is expected. When the tanks arrive, the sensors guide missiles into their targets.

One successful assault-breaker test went like this: A section of the Mojave Desert was raked level. On it was placed a tank whose gasoline engine, vertical exhaust pipes, and baffle plates put out a stronger "heat signature" than the diesel engine and horizontal exhaust used on Russian tanks. Then the sensor was dropped next to the tank and the motor given time to run. All on a winter morning. The missile was fired and, sure enough, it hit the target. The results were written up in a form that obscured these assists, and were released.[116]

The DIVAD air-defense gun is another example. It uses the doppler effect—the radar signature of an object approaching and receding, such as a helicopter blade. In a test, a drone whirlybird flew into the target zone. DIVAD was activated. It turned, leveled its twin barrels, and locked onto a portable latrine. Investigators searched the target and found the cause—a fan above the john, whose "signature" had proven more attractive to DIVAD than the blades of a helicopter propeller.[117]

DIVAD is not central to any current tactical plan. Assault-breaker would probably have some role in the AirLand 2000 strategy. More serious are the development problems of two PGMs which are crucial to the success of our two largest hardware investments: the carrier battle group and the next generation fighter plane.

Even those who argue carriers could survive in a general conflict with the Soviets base their belief on the effectiveness of the Aegis cruiser missile-defense system. In April 1983 the Navy held carefully rehearsed warm-up tests with the engineers and program managers who built the ship at the controls of the Ticonderoga. Ten days later there was a realistic operational test with an independent Navy team facing tough, unrehearsed battle scenarios.

After the first test, the Navy's public relations apparatus rushed to tell the good news to reporters and congressmen: the $1.2 billion ship had hit 13 out of 13 targets; it would be able to protect the carrier battle group. After the second test, the Navy issued a statement that the ship was "setting the standards of excellence." The results of the test were classified secret. They leaked: the ship missed 11 of 17 targets because of serious computer, hardware, and crew malfunctions.[118]

In May 1984 the Navy announced that the Ticonderoga in a new test had downed 10 of 11 drone missiles in a simulated attack on a carrier battle group. One missile launched from 70,000 feet managed to get through. "We feel that 91 percent success on these targets is more than we ever planned," said Chief of Naval Operations Adm. James Watkins. He compared the hit ratio with 1983's figure of 33 percent, i.e., the score for the second, realistic test held that year.[119] But critics of the 1984 test pointed out that a Navy aircraft was flying above the ship on a course parallel to the missiles. By radar-tracking the plane, gunners could also track the target.

In the words of a naval weapons consultant, "the results of tests that suc-

ceed tend to get publicized; the results of tests that fail tend to get classified."[120] And the details on some tests that succeed get sanitized, as in the
case just noted.

The other PGM system crucial to a major hardware investment is the
"fire and forget" missile. It is intended to be so far-ranging and accurate that
a pilot can launch before he even sees the enemy. This is a design assumption for the Advanced Tactical Fighter (ATF). To fight out of sight is an
attractive concept, given the ATF's probable cost per plane.

The PGM is known as Advanced Medium-Range Air-to-Air Missile
(AMRAAM). At issue is whether the Air Force should commit several
hundred million dollars to buy 100 to 3,000 AMRAAM's as a starter—
before tests have shown the weapon will work, and even before its design is
fixed.

Hughes Aircraft has a development contract called "weak" and "miserable" by the Air Force's Thomas Amlie, who was a project manager on the
successful Sidewinder missile. Amlie's associate James Ririe finds "rather
chilling similarities" between AMRAAM and the Maverick, another
Hughes missile project plagued by expensive delays and doubts about its
combat effectiveness. Endorsing these concerns is Amlie's boss, famed analyst of the C-5A cost overruns, Ernest Fitzgerald.[121]

Who is correct? Those who see a surge in microcomputer technology that
will make PGMs the wave of the future? Or those who say that we confuse
"must work" with "will work" and "is working"? The answer is probably
both. A bright prospect exists. But we must move prudently or PGMs
could be an added cost burden before they are a breakthrough.

The electronic battlefield: Dawn of the post-warrior age? In 1982 Israel
wiped out more Syrian missile launchers in one battle than had been used to
fell 150 Israeli jets in the Yom Kippur War. Syria sent up 60 MiGs to defend the batteries; 90 U.S.-made Israeli jets pounced and shot down 36 of
them without a single loss. The next day, Syria dispatched 50 more MiGs
and Israel claims not one of them returned to base.

Rumors of a secret weapon quickly cropped up. But the consensus among
Western military experts is that the only secret weapon was a "bold and superb" battle plan based on experience and exploiting a new category of
weaponry called "unconventional," which utilizes the tools of electronic
warfare (EW).

A key example is intelligence-gathering drones, pilotless aircraft which
collect vital data on enemy forces and help guide attacks on targets by using
a standard TV camera.[122]

The Pentagon's DeLauer is pushing for EW-based weapons systems.
They are also the basis for the AirLand 2000 plan whose aim is "to disrupt,
deceive, and destroy" an enemy. Soviet planning is moving in exactly the
same direction, aimed at fighting a protracted conventional war without recourse to nuclear weapons. The deputy chief of the General Staff Academy

in Moscow says, "When conducting an offensive using conventional weapons, achievement of penetration can require concentration of large masses of artillery, aviation, and tanks, and reliable suppression of the numerous anti-tank weapons of the enemy. To increase the tempo of the offensive, it will be essential to make missile and air strikes over the entire depth of his defenses and to make wide use of airborne assaults." [123]

Western analysts believe recent improvements in Soviet air, artillery, and rocket fire support systems could substitute for tactical nuclear weapons in a Warsaw Pact assault. A Polish military theorist calls for "elimination of nuclear missiles during the conventional phase of the battle" as the key element in the success of a Soviet offensive. In pursuing their own AirLand 2000, Eastern forces are enhancing their capability to fight the kind of war for which NATO is least prepared. Says NATO Supreme Commander Gen. Bernard Rogers: "We have mortgaged the defense of NATO to a nuclear response because members have not been willing to pay the cost of a credible conventional force." [124]

Maj. John Hines and Phillip Peterson, Soviet specialists at the Defense Intelligence Agency, believe "reliance on an essentially all-or-nothing nuclear retaliation tends to invite the very strategy the Soviets are apparently refining: early and, if possible, pre-emptive destruction of NATO's in-theater nuclear arsenal with conventional weapons, accompanied by a high speed offensive that would exploit Soviet superiority in conventional forces. The speed of such an offensive might render a NATO response with global nuclear systems pointless." [125]

A vigorous spirit of reform is evident in NATO, and a major thrust is to redress the deficiency in conventional arms. One striking feature is that both sides are working off very similar battle plans based on deep strikes and simultaneous assaults in all modes. When all factors are taken into account (see pages 77–78), the stage may be set for an awesome exchange of firepower, followed by a stalemate if each side hesitates in "going nuclear."

Precision-guided munitions, intelligence-gathering drones, pilotless tanks, and other features of the electronic battlefield raise questions not only of strategy but of the human role in a future "unconventional" non-nuclear conflict. Not a post-war age, but a post-warrior age, is at issue.

Military historian John Keegan offers this perspective: "One wonders if it is not now the great armored armadas that tremble on the brink of being old-fashioned, and another form of warfare which the progress of technology is about to bless.

"The Soviet Army, through its obsession with speed, is bound to cling to the tank as the means of winning in Europe before NATO's reinforcement program redresses the balance. But it may be that the tank is coming to resemble the battleship. . . . Even generals of the most traditional cast of mind now talk of the front being defended by fleets of aircraft firing precision-guided ordinance from long distances, at targets on the move and at lines of communication. On the ground they foresee soldiers with target-indicating lasers that will play on tanks or combat vehicles until a missile rides on their beams to the point of destruction. Overseeing all will be the wizards of electronic warfare, clearing the air for their own side's transmissions while jamming the other's."[126]

Keegan puts this vision at least 10 or 20 years in the future. But the electronic battlefield will profoundly affect, and perhaps greatly diminish, the role of human warriors in an all-out "unconventional" war. The military's preference is to give first place in the budget to "things people can ride on"—ships, tanks, planes. In the age of EW, they may be the horse cavalry of the future.

There have already been battles so devastating that not a blade of grass, let alone a man, was left standing. The first day of the Somme was one. Sixty thousand British soldiers fell in a futile assault on entrenched German machine guns. The Battle of Kursk was another, a veritable "storm of steel." But in both world wars, courage, initiative, and combat leadership were still very relevant.

It may be that future wars will require two kinds of warriors: the warrior-tactician who can keep his head and move men in the midst of chaos, and the electronic warrior who can exercise, if you will, leadership over the most sophisticated equipment.

The two concepts need to be carefully related. One involves conventional, and the other non-conventional, non-nuclear warfare. Ultimately we may need top-level commanders competent to make decisions on when to use one capability or the other. But it may turn out that technology has played another trick on us. First, it created a form of weaponry so horrible that its use is unthinkable; then it led to arms of such lethality on the battlefield that the human combatant was banished. Today, this is the stuff of science fiction. But for the future, we cannot rule out the possibility of a paradox: the very technology which is bringing advances in speed, mobility, and detection capability may also bring with it a volume of accurate firepower so deadly that the carnage of a war in the trenches is attained on a battlefield that is both deep and fluid. The geography of war will resemble World War II; the attrition of war will resemble World War I, but achieved much more rapidly. If not the end of war, it could be the end of the warrior.

There is a very real chance that this is where the technology of full-scale "unconventional" war is taking us. If this happens, the psychological adjustment for the profession of arms will be even more painful than giving up the horse. In the interim, it would be most unwise to treat the quality of courage with contempt. It is admirable in itself; it may always be needed. But two great "reform" themes must be melded: inculcating the "warrior" virtues, and facing the reality of the electronic battlefield. This is the next great challenge of strategic theory, a challenge created by the "technological imperative" in its onward march.

There is a tendency in any age to view technology the way Hegel viewed history. When we look back we see dramatic change with each development stimulating some other innovation. When we look ahead we tend to believe we are at or near the end of development, and that beyond a certain point there will be little change.

When World War I began, the automobile had only been in existence for about twenty years and the airplane for ten. Both, especially the airplane, represented experimental technology. Radar had existed for only about five years before World War II began, and jet aircraft were introduced seven years before the start of the Korean War.

Today we take all these technologies for granted. Precision guidance systems, electronic warfare, and lasers represent our threshold technology. There is no reason to doubt the odds that the battlefield of the future will be as different from today's as today's is from that of 1914. Nations which advance most quickly into that world will continue to have an advantage over their adversaries.

This argues for a vigorous research and development program. But it also argues for patience. The basic difference between "enthusiasts" and "reformers" in their view of technology is that the former are more likely to dream of possibilities, to plan on the basis that what is desirable is also feasible, and to look with favor on production commitments which push the state of the art; the latter are more likely to call for investing in prototypes, to advocate rigorous testing which measures how systems react to realistic conditions, and to insist that any delay will be recouped by not having to debug weapons after they are built.

The spirit of the former is an invaluable prod, but the method of the latter is inescapable good sense. One expert who is sometimes portrayed as a high-tech skeptic, Pierre Sprey, offers this defense of technology's proper use: "It is true that at any point in time, complexity tends to rise in proportion to inputs of technology. But this is not true over time. Technology can be superbly simplifying. This can and should be a major thrust of technology." [127]

We must be bold in imagining possibilities but prudent in managing that period of transition between the latest technology and the latest usable technology. Human maturity of judgment is required to permit the scientific maturing of discoveries. Failure to observe this rule leads to enormous costs and risks misplaced faith for which we could pay dearly in combat.

The Price of Procurement

If a color television set were built by the Hughes Aircraft Company using the same rates and shop time relative to product as on its military electronics, the retail price would be $100,000.
—Computation of Defense analyst Ernest Fitzgerald [1]

Defense procurement needs a dose of 'creeping capitalism.'
—Senator Charles Grassley [2]

JUST BEHIND THE COCKPIT in the world's most sophisticated radar plane, on the leg of a folding blue and gray stool, sits the world's most expensive plastic cap. What distinguishes this cap from any other lump of white nylon is that the Air Force paid $1,118.26 for it, which is roughly the cost of the plastic plus $1,118.

In commercial mass production the stool cap would probably have cost less than a dollar. In small quantities ordered irregularly, experts say the Air Force should pay no more than $10 each. How one minor spare part grew in price and how a staff sergeant in Oklahoma finally put a stop to it is a story of how the military procurement process does and does not work.

The stool cap, which weighs less than half an ounce, may be the most unimportant piece of equipment of the millions of parts on the E-3A Airborne Warning and Control System (AWACS), a $92 million aircraft that is a flying surveillance center on the cutting edge of reconnaissance technology.

Routinely on January 12, 1983, Sgt. Charles Kessler of Tinker Air Force Base called Billy Manning, the base's director of distribution, with a replacement order for two plastic caps that were missing from planes in his charge as crew chief in the 552nd Airborne Warning and Control Wing. This request set in motion a procurement request much like thousands of others handled at Air Force bases every day.

Manning, a civilian, pulled out Air Force form 2005 to make the requisition. He did not know the request was for plastic caps. What he did know was that Kessler had asked for item 27 from Figure 205-03-13A in Technical Order 1E-3A-25-1. But in military parts parlance, Manning could not simply put those numbers on his form. Suppliers would not understand them. Instead, Manning had to call the stool cap by its National Stock Number: NSN-5340-01-040-4512.

At the receiving end of Manning's order was the Defense Industrial Supply Center (DISC) in Philadelphia, a central parts purchaser for all three services. DISC got the order February 2. A supply officer found the microfiche catalogue card for NSN-5340-01-040-4512 and slipped it onto a display screen. What he saw was not a plastic cap but a code which revealed that the item was "proprietary." This meant the prime contractor owned the rights to its design and was therefore the "sole source" of the item.

The Air Force code was in error. The Boeing Company, maker of the cap, did not have a legal monopoly on its design. But the code meant the supply center was not authorized to advertise its need for stool caps and buy from the lowest bidder. (Thousands of parts, according to Defense Inspector General Joseph Sherick, are unnecessarily listed as "sole source" items.)

As the supply center officer looked at the screen, he found that to get the part he would have to contact supplier 81205. The Boeing Company received the request and located the item, listed internally as P-N-204-40797-3. Two plastic caps were in storage at a depot in Memphis. These were sent to Tinker Air Force Base.

Two days after Kessler requisitioned his stool caps, he checked his "daily document record." He noted with approval that his order had been logged and the item would be available from storage. Then he noticed the price: $1,118.26 for each cap. Kessler, by all accounts, was shocked and angry. He called Manning and said, "I want my money back." Then Kessler wrote Manning: "Hopefully, this item has never been ordered before. The current exorbitant price for this item is beyond all realistic thought."

Manning passed Kessler's complaint to Barbara Jones, "zero overpricing" official for Tinker AFB, who sent the complaint to Robert Swartz at the defense supply center. On January 18, Swartz asked for the stool cap's technical drawings and specifications from Air Force officials in Washington. These were shipped the following day. By March 24, after "cost engi-

Cartoon by Stayskal. Reprinted by permission: Tribune Media Services, Inc., 1984.

neers" had studied the sample and the drawing, the supply center decided that all future purchases would be made by competitive bid. It estimated that the cost "should not exceed $10."

In 1979, long before Kessler had met his first stool cap, the item had been priced by Boeing at $219.18. This cost estimate was part of a large "provisioning package" for the AWACS, in which the company priced hundreds of parts that were expected to need replacement or maintenance in normal use. The Air Force approved the package, and in reviewing the stool cap case said, "the overall price [for all items] appeared reasonable; minute details of the provisioning package were not assessed." In other words, no supply officer specifically reviewed or approved the line item that said a plastic stool cap would cost $219.18. Given the number of items, such a process could be completely impractical. Nor did the buyer from DISC—or even the Boeing employee who opened the letter—know what was being bought and sold. It was all in code. Only in the Memphis depot did someone actually reach for a plastic cap.

All the same, how did the price rise to $1,118.26? Boeing's 1979 estimate called for acquiring little cubes of plastic and grinding them into caps, being sure to cut the cross-shaped notch in the end where the stool leg fits. In 1981 when initial supplies ran out, the supply center ordered three caps from Boeing. There was a cost overrun. Instead of $219.18 the company charged the Air Force $916.55 per cap. This was based on 66.71 labor hours to make the three caps, including 8.01 hours for inspection, at $833.49; employee fringe benefits of $354.23; manufacturer's overhead of $1,376.83; and a profit fee of $358.65, or $119.55 per cap.

No one in the Air Force actually paid as little as $916.55 for a stool cap because the supply center slapped on a standard surcharge to cover "such costs as inflation, transportation costs, special packaging, obsolescence, breakage, deterioration, pilferage, etc." The total charge to a stool cap user in 1981 would have been $1,086.17. In 1982 the supply center raised its surcharge, creating the new total of $1,118.26. One cap was sold to Tinker in 1981; the other two were stored until Kessler's request.

"We feel chagrined; it's obviously too high a price to pay for something like that," said Boeing spokesman Peter Bush. The company's explanation in part blamed the Air Force for ordering its spare parts in small quantities, thereby raising unit costs. The house organ *Boeing News* compared this practice to "the guy who tries to save money by ordering a la carte, and finds himself paying $5 for a second helping of cranberry sauce." Boeing spokesmen in an interview also talked about the precision equipment they said is required to make the stool cap.[3]

"The problem in procurement is not being charged $435 for a claw hammer [another case] but the nature of what Defense buys. They commit to a 'unique buy' before they know what they need. Some idiot MILSPECS [creates a military specification for] a screw that can't be turned with an ordinary screwdriver," says an expert on Pentagon budgeting. "Defense procurement is one of the dirtiest funnels in the world."[4]

"It doesn't take directives to correct the $9 screw situation [yet another case]; it takes managers," believes Dale MacComber, former chief civil servant at OMB. "A climate has to be created and incentives have to be changed. Whistle-blowers point the finger at symptoms, but the basic problem is more complicated."[5]

Part of the MILSPEC problem is that "arcane requirements justify military expertise."[6] Another part is that "thousands of unique items are in production. Many are made by small subcontractors—one item, one firm."[7]

In June 1984 a Pentagon audit of 2,300 spare parts found over half were definitely or potentially overpriced. A Defense inspector general said reforms put in place the previous year should correct most of the abuses. The Office of Management and Budget agreed. Deputy Defense Secretary William Howard Taft IV said further reforms proposed by Congress were sensible but the department would prefer to attack the problem itself.[8]

Defense procurement has been marked over the years by a loose contracting environment in which companies have often escaped any penalty for cost overruns. Periodic payments have been made for expenses they have incurred rather than the progress they have made. Attempts at reform nibble around the edges of a bloated pricing structure, and victories in the war against waste would be accounted as defeats in any other sector of the economy. The common interest of companies wanting business, services wanting weapons, and congressmen wanting jobs for their districts leads to chronic underestimates of cost.

In this way, the maximum number of new projects is fitted under budget ceilings. Cost overruns far in excess of inflation become the norm. At a time of rapid buildup as is currently underway, another impact is added by the natural growth curve of weapons programs—slow during tooling up, steeply upward as production hits its stride. The combined effect is a "bow wave" of massive spending commitments which threaten to preempt defense budgets for future years. To stay within spending ceilings, the Pentagon responds by cutting operations, maintenance, and personnel expenses and stretching out production runs. The first set of actions imperils readiness and the quality of the volunteer force; the second sends the unit costs of weaponry still higher.

A running debate of charge and counter-charge has been carried on for several years about why weapons costs are rising so fast and whether reforms launched by Secretary Weinberger can correct the problem.

In March 1982 a stir was created when Defense released a revised estimate on the 15-year acquisition cost of 44 major weapons. The total was $114.5 billion higher than in a report released just three months earlier. It cited two factors behind the increase. First was inflation, whose cause and components are at the heart of the debate. Second was larger purchases.

The report did not explain why it would be buying more weapons but simply said this was one reason costs were rising.[9]

Two months earlier a major flap had erupted when an estimated $750 billion gap between the Administration's $1.6 trillion buildup plan and actual "needs" was revealed. Pentagon Under Secretary for Research and Engineering DeLauer said the "most probable" figure for the gap was $300 million, with the higher number a top-end estimate.

Weinberger denounced the report in these words: "To take a preliminary, highly classified report on all the wish lists, to publish it without any regard to the classification and without any indication that it is simply a wish list and nothing more and is based on the assumption there aren't any fiscal restraints, is not presenting a fair picture of what we are trying to do."[10]

" WHAT A FRUSTRATING DAY. THE READOUT ON MY CALCULATOR WOULD ONLY ALLOW ME TO GO UP TO $999 BILLION! "

Cartoon by Stayskal. Reprinted by permission: Tribune Media Services, Inc., 1983.

The question which has never been clearly resolved is whether the $750 billion was a gap between what service chiefs felt they needed and what the Administration was willing to provide, or a gap between official estimates and potential costs of items that were scheduled for purchase. Using the latter approach, a $200 billion gap over five years was projected by John Steinbruner, foreign policy program director for Brookings. He derived this estimate on the basis of an "imbalance" between the average 14 percent real growth in procurement for fiscal 1981–87 and a comparable 3 percent for operations and maintenance.[11] The thesis is that acquiring new equipment carries with it proportional hikes in support costs. This is part of a great debate on whether there is a "readiness gap" (see pages 135–38).

Defense consultant Jacques Gansler found that from 1976 to 1982, inflation for Pentagon purchases of military hardware outstripped rates for civilian durable goods by 40 to 100 percent. Gansler notes that "on average, program costs double during the acquisition cycle" for each weapon. He says the causes are "initial economic optimism" in planning; lower cost estimates "to make the program appear more attractive"; the fact that Congress permits and even "demands" unrealistic projections to justify programs; and finally, a "winner take all" bidding policy which gives the low bidder sole rights on a new item for up to 20 years. "Real competition virtually ends after the initial contract is awarded. From then on, the Pentagon finds itself stuck with a single supplier that can raise prices almost at will." [12]

The two leaders in documenting and measuring these forces at work are Pentagon analysts Ernest Fitzgerald and Franklin "Chuck" Spinney. Fitzgerald became famous for his exposé of huge cost overruns on the C-5A transport. But within the Department, he was harassed rather than praised by his superiors. Spinney showed how the soaring inflation rate for weapons was built into the system and was not due simply to individual cases of mismanagement. His reward: the Pentagon began marking some documents "no spin"—not to be shared with him [13]—and Secretary Weinberger deigned not to see Spinney's widely noted briefings, "Defense Facts of Life" and "The Plans/Reality Mismatch." [14] Cost accountant George Spanton had his job ratings lowered, was confronted with a transfer and pressured to quit, after he completed an audit accusing a major Defense contractor of padding labor costs by $150 million, and another for incurring a $1 million entertainment bill while courting Pentagon officials. News reports caused Weinberger to intervene on Spanton's behalf, but internal pressures dissuaded the Secretary from disciplining those who had harassed him. [15]

Spinney believes that, despite recent reforms, the Pentagon continues to make optimistic assumptions about the inflation rate, the amount Congress will appropriate, and the "learning curve"—a decrease in the cost of each weapon as it is produced in volume over time. He puts underfunding of the current program at $500 billion, raising the total cost from $1.6 trillion to $2.1 trillion. [16]

Spinney's supervisor is David Chu. The new system of making separate inflation estimates for each major program should improve accuracy and avoid cost overruns, Chu argues. He notes that 75 percent of Defense cost growth over budget in the 1970s was caused by poor inflation estimates. [17] The dispute is focused on whether new techniques have corrected the problem or whether, in the words of Army Under Secretary James Ambrose, weapons program managers are still "sliding costs forward into future years." [18]

Defense specialist George Kuhn of the Heritage Foundation believes the problem persists. "Weapons program costs are underestimated because experience with expensive design changes is often ignored. The future cost of spares, ammunition, and maintenance may be treated lightly. In at least one case, estimates that threatened to kill a proposal were withdrawn and rewritten." Kuhn concludes that "our defense establishment has stagnated. Unrealistic cost planning and force-development decisions contribute directly to the escalation of costs even beyond the capacity of generous budgets."[19]

Ernest Fitzgerald's focus is on the defense industry. An industrial engineer by training and an auditor by profession, he concentrates on "what's going on in the factories." In his book *The High Priests of Waste*, Fitzgerald notes that a company could abide by the rules and still run up huge costs. The solution: change the rules to impose standards similar to those which discipline the market economy.

"Ernie thinks we could get everything we want for far less. I think we'll never have enough money to do the job. It's not just the production line, but the whole system of incentives, that needs revision," says Chuck Spinney.[20]

Jerome Storalow of the General Accounting Office combines the two emphases: "The Pentagon is often too quick to charge cost increases to inflation when management foul-ups are more to blame. The effect of inflation isn't as great as DOD would lead you to believe. But it is substantial, because they tend to be highly optimistic with respect to costs, technical development problems, and operational characteristics. They want to show that the proposed weapon will do wonders at a very low cost." Adds Deputy Under Secretary of Defense Dale Church, "We haven't pinned very many medals on program managers who have stepped up and said, 'My program is a disaster—kill it.'"[21]

To change incentives and reduce mismanagement, the Administration introduced the "Carlucci initiatives"—32 reforms developed by former Deputy Secretary of Defense Frank Carlucci.

The initiatives attempt to encourage realistic weapons pricing, economical (i.e., higher) rates of production, and killing marginal programs rather than ordering stretch-outs or shorting funds for support functions. Even critics agree there has been some progress. The Departmentwide Inspector General's office has launched a fraud crackdown. Some small contractors have been blacklisted for overcharging or for quality defects. At least one large firm has been given a criminal fine. Sperry sold microchips after their shelf life had expired. The chips could cause critical failures endangering the lives of military personnel.[22]

There have been tough price negotiations, with the threat to cancel programs—most notably in the case of the F-18 fighter, which Navy Secretary Lehman "jawboned" down to $22.5 million per plane when McDonnell Douglas claimed its unit cost was $24 million.[23] Then there was a spirited competition for the F-15 and F-16 jet engines, with General Electric the surprise winner over long-time dominant supplier Pratt & Whitney.[24]

Perhaps the most notable reform is also the most controversial—use of multi-year contracts. This is a reasonable thing to do on purely economic grounds. It creates the efficiencies of sustained production. It gives contractors the incentive to expand a shrunken industrial base. It is also shrewd politics, making program cancellations much harder by transforming them into a "breach of contract" carrying large penalties.[25]

The controversy arises because "the feeling is widespread that the administration has allowed every major weapons project on the books, old and new, to go forward, cutting nothing of consequence, giving the military a free hand."[26] "By granting every important hardware request of the top brass, the budget suggests that no amount of escalation in price or shortcomings in performance seem enough to disqualify a weapon from production."[27] In other words, multi-year contracting is a step backward unless it is preceded by a review of one's commitments. Lacking this, it simply locks one more firmly into an unexamined program.

Is such a critique fair given, for example, the Navy's stance on the F-18? By agreeing to pay less than the maker's price, was the Pentagon finally moving away from cost-plus contracts and demanding that contractors share the burdens of inflation? It is not really clear. By the time Lehman put his foot down in mid-1982, the F-18's price had already risen from $5.4 million to $24 million. And if one divides the F-18 budget for 1985 by the number of planes ordered, the unit cost comes out to be $30 million—far above the price the Navy insisted on.[28]

A parallel case is the B-1B, which has been hailed as a "procurement success story" because it is two months ahead of schedule and $550 million under budget. The plane is being built on a fixed-price incentive program in which the makers and the government evenly split any savings. It is an approach that seems to be working.[29]

To put the story in perspective, however, requires a bit of history. In 1973, three years after Rockwell International had won the B-1 development contract, a Pentagon report found there was no way the project could be completed with the funds Rockwell had requested. The report said the program was "unrealistically austere" and that "significant funding over that presently planned will be required."

This was after Rockwell had reported a $75 million cost overrun, after the Air Force had cut back the number of planes on order, and after the B-1's performance had been reduced to save money. The price of each bomber was pegged at $45 million in 1973. A decade later the estimate had risen to $280 million. Since then the price has bounced around in a somewhat lower range.[30]

Thus, both the F-18 and the B-1 were subject to modest price rollbacks, but only after costs had exploded above original levels. And while the B-1's on-time testing schedule is good news, it is hardly surprising. The plane has been around a long time. Its delayed development should lead to smoother-than-normal progress in working the craft up for operational use.

The move to fixed-price incentive contracts may, however, bear fruit in the future. Pentagon officials in the past had been willing to sign cost-plus contracts under which companies can charge Defense for increases in everything from labor costs to the price of fuel for executive jets. Now the Pentagon is no longer willing to pay on this basis. Weinberger believes that past practice inflated the price of weapons and the new policy will force prices down. Aerospace executives fear that fixed-price incentive contracts will be very hard to get rid of once they become commonplace.

The President made a personal plea for the new policy in September 1981. He called the chief executives of the top eleven Pentagon contractors to the White House to discuss rising weapons costs. That was the highlight of a day-long, top secret seminar in which Air Force officers revealed their long-range plans will go for naught unless money is available to carry them

"YOU'D LIKE TO SEE GENERAL HIGDON IN PROCUREMENTS? WHICH SECTION IS HE IN...MILLION, BILLION OR TRILLION?"
Cartoon by Stayskal. Reprinted by permission: Tribune Media Services, Inc., 1983.

out. One aerospace exec grumbled, "The administration is out to show it's being tough with us so it can keep public support for its military budgets." [31] Another said, "When the Pentagon gets pressured, it kicks the only dog it owns—industry." [32]

The new policy calls not only for a fixed price but disallows costs that were paid in the past, including exorbitant wages paid to industry workers (25–30 percent above private sector norms), firms charging all overhead costs to Defense even for non-military work, the cost of lobbying Congress, and "golden parachute" pay settlements for executives caught up in aerospace mergers.[33]

The spirit of the Carlucci initiatives is sanctioned by no less a figure than former Deputy Secretary and electronics billionaire David Packard, who called for "a sensible 'Dutch Uncle' approach. . . . The fact is there has been bad management of many defense programs in the past . . . large cost overruns by both the services and industry contributed to an antidefense attitude. . . . There is no way to avoid this criticism except to do a better job in the future."[34]

How successful has the reform effort been? "The administration's public statements on its management of the Pentagon tend to make its program appear more successful and efficient than it really is," reported the *Wall Street Journal* in July 1983. It said test failures and cost increases in major weapons systems had been "glossed over and misstated in what might kindly be called half-truths and exaggerations." Despite reforms, the *Journal* found "signs that the old ways persist" and cited a Navy order to its professional cost estimators that they lower the projected expense of planned new ships over the next five years to make the figures more optimistic.

The General Accounting Office estimated that Defense would realize only one-fourth of the $40 billion it claimed reforms would save in future years. The Department's own inspector general found the Navy engaging in the widely condemned practice of using funds intended for testing equipment and support gear to cover F-18 cost increases.

As for the Carlucci initiatives themselves, they weren't put into official regulations until the summer of 1982 and few officers ride herd on them. One, since departed, was quoted as saying, "Either they didn't know how to put the initiatives in place or they didn't want to." Another retired officer who had major control over weapons buying said the new rules hadn't been enforced and were easy to ignore. "We saw them more as a statement of aspirations, to which all could subscribe, than as a radical change in the game plan. . . . Not much has really happened."[35]

A major reason why costs continue to soar and the shopping list stays long is that Weinberger has tried to impose centralized management changes at the same time he was handing back to the services the very authority which Secretaries have needed to temper the appetite for weaponry. "None of the high-cost items most prized by the generals and admirals have been excised—regardless of cost overruns or performance problems—because Mr. Weinberger has delegated much authority over weapons choices to the military services."[36]

There is a sense that the Secretary has been bedazzled by brass and gold braid. "Why should we drop more money into the Pentagon when the place is rotting with bad management?" asks Senator Charles Grassley. Former Air Force officer and aerospace executive David Smith comments, "The full Reagan defense program as it stands now can't be funded for any price they put on it, let alone the amount Congress will grant. They won't even be able to afford the upkeep of the things they want to buy." Senator Sam Nunn sums up: "It is now obvious that the Reagan program cannot be fully implemented."[37] To defense consultant Larry Smith, "Putting out a hit list on individual weapons systems is like chasing bees with sticks. You have to go after the hive, the system."[38] And "in the scale of things, Pentagon veterans say Weinberger's reforms amount to little more than tinkering with the system."[39]

What is a fair and just assessment? One somber conclusion is that "over the long run, the varying styles of Defense Secretaries may make little difference. The bureaucracy knows in its heart it can outlast almost any appointee or administration."[40] But there are differences. A just-retired general who handled billions of dollars in weapons buying says, "This administration has done less pruning than its predecessors. The approach is to assign a high priority to everything. It's not a well thought-out buildup."[41] And a top civilian aide notes, "Cap hasn't done very well in riding herd on the services. He delegated much of that to Carlucci and Frank in turn made his only serious mistake—he deferred too much to the services on budget matters."[42] Carlucci was followed by hard-charging Paul Thayer, who had a skepticism about standard practice that reformers found refreshing. But Thayer became involved in charges of irregularity in securities trading. His successor, William Howard Taft IV, owed his rapid rise to Weinberger and "will march in step" with the Secretary of Defense.[43]

Perhaps the lesson is this: modest management reforms, even aggressive crackdowns on fraud and waste, cannot significantly offset the budgetary impact of policy decisions which call for a massively expanded program. And when a buildup lacks clear priorities or focus, the result is disappointing. "The increased spending secured by President Reagan should permit a marked improvement in force size. It does not," concludes Kuhn.[44]

"The yawning gulf between what leaders of both parties say the U.S. needs to protect its security and what the country can afford to spend [adds] new urgency to the need for effective controls. . . . Costs continue to outstrip funds, and the real combat power of the U.S. lags behind its global commitments."[45]

THE BOW WAVE, THE READINESS GAP

The weapons buying surge has impacts that go beyond budget numbers. It threatens to preempt defense spending options for years to come and to starve programs that are vital if new hardware is to be a useful part of our military force.

The "bow wave" is a term that describes the typical curve of expenditure on a weapons program. Outlays begin slowly and years pass as a project moves from the drawing board through tooling up to full production. Each phase is more expensive than its predecessor. As a result, during a rapid buildup, many projects are in a relatively low-cost part of the process.

For example, the two new nuclear carriers required only $165 million in fiscal 1983 and $790 million in 1984, even though their combined cost is $7 billion. The really expensive work starts in 1985.[46] The Office of Management and Budget in 1982 found that killing every procurement item worth over $500 million would reduce eventual outlays by $49 billion, but would trim spending for 1983 by only $6.5 billion.[47]

Defense industry and military service lobbyists often use this poor payoff ratio as an argument against any cuts in big ticket weapons systems when Congress is scrambling to fit total outlays within ceilings. But there is a reverse implication. Small initial outlays on a big program mean "the camel's nose is under the tent." If caution is not used in making commitments, an unsustainable level of spending can accumulate. As procurement programs mature, they bump against budget ceilings. Hard choices are then forced, choices which a more prudently planned buildup might have avoided.

The biggest bills for weapons Reagan requested and Congress approved in 1981 and 1982 will not fall due until the second half of the decade and beyond. We are now entering that period. The 1985 budget contains no major new program. But procurement costs are up 25 percent in one year.[48] The Congressional Budget Office warns that by 1987 almost 40 percent of the defense budget will go for weapons systems ordered in the past, up from 25 percent in 1980.[49] Not since World War II has military spending climbed in real terms four years in a row.[50] The bow wave could insure continuous growth for at least twice that long.

Mounting resistance against defense budget increases has forced down the rate of change. Adjusted for inflation, the 1982 hike was 12 percent. This dropped to 7 percent in 1983 and 3.7 percent in 1984.[51] These figures are on a collision course with the spending curve in the bow wave.

Three unattractive options arise: (1) "Congress is locking itself into heavier and heavier defense budgets in the future as the final bills come due for expensive new weapons"; (2) defense planners may be forced to curtail or abandon some of the projects that were liberally funded in the "downpayment" phase; (3) the Pentagon may decide it must "starve other programs to pay" for weapons contracts.[52]

One former high-ranking defense official warns, "The fundamental trouble is that we're seeing only one slice of a program that's going to get bigger and bigger. If the money Reagan wants now and down the road is not fully available, something big is going to have to go."[53] An active-duty officer says, "I wonder whether this is a one or two year shot that will fizzle when the President sees how much the strategic [nuclear] forces and the Navy are going to cost in the end."[54]

Senator Carl Levin observes, "We are creating military 'entitlement' programs by ordering weapons today that will have to be paid for tomorrow."[55]

A top Senate staffer adds: "Our options are becoming narrower and narrower. You quickly reach the point where you are chained to these programs."[56] Even Secretary Weinberger laments, "We are prisoners of past decisions,"[57] suggesting the process has taken on a life of its own.

To turn back the wave of spending would require interrupting programs in which Congress has invested billions of dollars. Not only sunk costs, but termination penalties are involved. Defenders of the current program sometimes cite the latter as a compelling reason why nothing should be scrubbed. For example, the Air Force had to pay Rockwell and other firms $271 million when the B-1 was canceled in 1977.[58] However, this is the approximate price of a single bomber today.

A good part of the bow wave is the cost of deferred modernization in the 1960s and 1970s when hardware was not replaced or upgraded on a timely basis. "A crucial question is how long the current generation of weapons will be in the front lines," says congressional defense specialist Terry Freese. "As the M-1, the B-1, the Trident are completed, how extensive a breather will they give us from the next round of modernization costs?"

To Freese the catch-up challenge is aggravated by "pushing the technological edge." He is among those who believe "we are so far into this bow wave we may have to follow through. The alternative is ever bigger bow waves due to the cost of technology." Delay means longer "quantum leaps" to produce state-of-the-art weaponry. Freese cautions against the hope that such costs can be avoided by going to simpler weapons advocated by military reformers, whom he calls "the bow and arrow lobby."[59]

It is impossible to weigh exactly the role of two factors which have built bow wave costs into the budget: first, the push by contractors and the services to sharply reverse the 1970s decline in real levels of defense investment; second, errors in estimating the total price for new systems. The former was an enthusiastic rush to get as many camels' noses under the tent as possible. The latter was a compound of wishful thinking, inexperience, and omission.

A near consensus exists that the greatest threat created by bow wave costs is that of a readiness gap. The defense budget, it is feared, will be kept within bounds by starving accounts for operations and maintenance. Training, ammunition, and spares are particular areas of concern. Examples: Congress approved 820 M-1 tanks but the Army asked for only 740 because it doesn't have the funds to keep 820 in working order.[60] The M-1 is 36 percent more expensive to operate than the M-60 it replaces. The new tank uses 4 gallons of fuel per mile compared to 2 gallons for the older model.[61]

The Bradley fighting vehicle has risen in price by 27 times since 1972 and the Army is planning to buy 7,000 Bradleys. Yet there is a $1 billion shortfall in training ammunition for each of the next five years. The Army's antitank gunners have so little ammunition that they can fire only one live round per year in training exercises.[62] The Air Force is $4 billion short of

"WELL, ANOTHER DAY, ANOTHER SIX HUNDRED MILLION DOLLARS!"

Cartoon by Stayskal. Reprinted by permission: Tribune Media Services, Inc., 1982.

spare parts. As a result, 25 to 40 percent of its F-15s, at $40 million a copy, are unable to fly at any given moment. Yet Weinberger's budgets have requested planes for four more attack wings.[63] "We can't go on like this," says Air Force Lt. Gen. Hans Driessnack.[64]

"This administration has done some good things for readiness but it's planted the seeds for a real disaster," believes former Defense Secretary Harold Brown. "It is committed to a force structure that makes sense only if we can count on continued real growth in the defense budget, and no one really expects that. So we'll have difficulty maintaining the forces already built and there'll be a readiness squeeze, particularly in the Army."[65]

Former Council of Economic Advisors Chairman Charles Schultze says the defense buildup will create a squeeze on certain sectors of the economy. But the "unwanted side effects" of price run-ups "may be more military than economic. . . . The main result may be to force out of the defense budget a large part of the non-glamorous but vital increases in spending for the deployment and combat capability of our conventional forces." Schultze sees an "inevitable collision between substantial cost over-runs on contracts already under way and a defense budget that is unlikely to be further revised upward." The victim will be readiness.

"Paradoxically, the insistence on continuing this very rapid buildup . . . may leave our armed forces with too small a quantity of very high-priced weapons and with . . . less capability to deploy, use, and maintain them in combat. The total defense budget will rise sharply, but the increase for some of its most critical elements may be squeezed out."[66]

One way in which this process reveals itself is the early retirement of older weapons, to avoid maintenance costs and pour more dollars into procurement. Administration plans have called for retiring seventy-five B-52Ds before the B-1B is operational and fifty-four Titan ICBMs before the MX is deployed.[67] The Navy has been mothballing ships, including vessels recently reconditioned at great cost, to free up funds for the 600-ship fleet. The rate of retirements so outstrips new additions that some wags suggest Secretary Lehman is "slip-sliding away" from his goal.[68]

In recent years the rate of growth in spending for procurement has outstripped that for readiness by about three to one. This imbalance suggests that "if the buildup proceeds as planned, it will be increasingly difficult to cut back substantially on defense outlays in later years without cutting the operating accounts that contribute to defense readiness."[69]

Why should the starving of an account increase the odds that it will be squeezed further? The reason lies in the nature of each account. "We're buying too few of too many things because we committed to purchase so many systems at once. No one wants to lose 'their' weapons system," says Congressman Norman Dicks. "Procurement is driving costs through the roof."[70] Hardware purchases are "hard" accounts; support functions are "soft."

When the Office of Management and Budget made its big run on defense spending in September 1981, it went after funds for fuel, training, spare parts, ammunition, maintenance, and personnel benefits. These cuts show up rapidly in actual outlays, and have historically been more acceptable because they are less visible and more politically digestible than slashing weapons programs.[71]

In early 1984 there was a highly publicized debate about the emergence of a "readiness gap." The debate was set off by reports that the services' own internal measures showed lower readiness levels than existed prior to the current buildup. The Pentagon responded by noting that the numbers were based on factors that could be easily misconstrued. For example, more new tanks meant more tank crews which had not been fully trained on the new gear. But it did not mean less capability to go into combat. After an indecisive exchange, the debate cooled.[72]

Perhaps the most serious challenge to the concept of a readiness gap was offered by Les Aspin, a congressman respected for his analyses of defense issues. Aspin's thesis was that "the administration's buildup for the most part involves modernization and replacement of weapons systems, rather than a large expansion of the force. Thus, increased maintenance costs would only be expected on the basis that new weapons are more complex. It is likely that new weapons will cost more to maintain, but not as much more as they cost to buy." Examples: An F-15 costs three times as much as an F-4 but its operating costs may be only 40 percent higher. The ratio for the new M-1 tank and the older M-60 is almost exactly the same.[73]

Aspin notes that while procurement outstripped operations and maintenance (O&M) by 91 percent to 35 percent in fiscal 1981–85 cost growth, the ratio for 1985–89 is 15 percent for procurement and 28 percent for O&M. "Whether this margin is sufficient is unanswered, but the reversal may be adequate."[74]

There are two concerns with Aspin's line of argument. First, all of O&M isn't readiness. More than 25 percent of it goes to pay civilian salaries and benefits. Almost one-half of all federal employees work for Defense, and Secretary Weinberger has added 72,000 job slots to his department. Another 10 percent of O&M goes just to move people and their furniture around the country.[75] Thus, the account does not translate directly into a budget for readiness.

A more basic concern is whether Defense can hold the intended outlays in the range Aspin cites. The evidence of chronic underestimates of hardware costs, and the steep curve on the bow wave for fiscal 1985–89, makes it highly doubtful that procurement will decline to one-sixth its previous growth rate. Indeed, the proposition is as nearly impossible as one could imagine.

PROCUREMENT AS A PUBLIC WORKS PROJECT

When Harold Brown reviewed the Pentagon's proposed 1983 budget, he concluded that the level was proper but that "Congress ought to insist" on a spending plan "that lays more emphasis on present and future readiness and on the ability to move conventional forces over great distances, as against proposed commitments to major procurement increases in some marginal new weapons systems."[76] Congress did no such thing. Indeed, it has not canceled a single major program in conventional or nuclear weaponry. What is meant by Congressman Dicks' observation that "no one wants to lose 'their' weapons system"?

It is an overstatement to refer, as some have, to a "congressional-industrial" complex. But it probably is true that Congress is the most under-rated player in the defense budget game—especially as a force in continuing any project that has begun. "The record of Congress is quite mixed," says Jack Stockfish. "Sometimes they treat the military budget as a pork barrel that has a defense aspect to it. At other times, they raise the hard questions."[77]

With the enormous power over military spending exerted by the Armed Services, Appropriations, and Budget committees, and with a proliferation of military specialists on committee staffs, Congress involves itself in the smallest details of the defense budget. This is a mixed blessing. Former Joint Chiefs Chairman Gen. David Jones notes, "We have ended up with six different committees in Congress which are in competition with each other on defense issues. They get into tremendous detail without tackling any of the more general issues."[78]

Some critics charge that frequently Congress feels free to brush aside the views of its fellow players and acts as it sees fit. Examples: between 1978 and 1981, Congress authorized the production of 58 A-7 fighters, even though neither the Air Force nor the Navy had requested them and President Carter termed the craft "obsolescent at best." The reason for the program: 10,000 jobs in Texas.[79]

In 1982 a House Armed Services subcommittee cut back some weapons programs but added $300 million for work at military bases the Pentagon didn't want done. About two-thirds of the bases were in districts of committee members.[80]

A particularly blatant example of leveraging came when Representative William Gray spoke to the issue of whether the new Airlift Command base would be located in New Jersey or in his home state: "The awarding of MAC is essentially a test of the Reagan Administration's commitment to Pennsylvania, which has not gotten a major defense contract since the Saratoga aircraft carrier, and that was in the Carter Administration. It will be interesting to see if the Reagan Administration is going to try to help its Republican Governor and two Republican Senators."[81]

If the services don't get what they want from the Secretary of Defense, they can turn to Congress, pointing out to members the benefits for their districts if projects appear in the budget. Congress often responds. Senator Barry Goldwater has said, "I don't care what the piece of equipment is, or how bad it is, if it's done in his state, the Senator has to get up and scream for it."[82] Paul Nisbet, a defense securities analyst, agrees: "Why, despite the rhetoric, can we assume that even dovish politicians will vote for potentially aggressive weapons systems whenever their votes are crucial for passage—even strategic nuclear weapons? The answer: jobs."[83] Examples abound, but perhaps none is more striking than that of Senator Cranston's support for the B-1B bomber, whose prime contractor is California-based Rockwell International.

"If the administration declines to make serious choices, Congress won't do it for them," believes Carnegie Endowment for Peace Senior Associate I. M. Destler. "Congress isn't set up to choose among weapons programs on the basis of an overall defense plan. Instead, it is likely to fix on some gross budget reduction number and achieve it through arbitrary cuts based on the principle of 'share the pain.'"[84] Such an approach can easily reduce Pentagon efficiency by hiking unit costs. Ultimately, Congress cannot use a "cheese paring" approach year after year while continuing to authorize all weapons systems. At some point, the accumulated spending restraint will require a budget that is done fairly specifically. The alternative is an increasingly illogical force structure—"too few of too many things," to quote Congressman Dicks.

The current system operates to aggravate existing imbalances. "The most efficient way to trim military budgets is the one most often avoided in the past—to fund long-term procurement projects fully in order to optimize the Pentagon's bargaining leverage with contractors. . . . However, this policy trades large apparent costs now for large savings in the future, whereas the instinct in Congress is to do exactly the opposite."[85]

There is broad agreement by analysts that a long-range focus is crucial. "If Congress finds it cannot swallow the defense spending balloon, it should make future year costs the primary target. Rather than seeking reduction in near term spending, priority should be given to serious but selective cuts in the broad range of weapons development and modernization programs. The main bill will come due in fiscal 1985 and beyond."[86] "What is important in assessing the behavior of Congress is the dynamics of the buildup. The greatest financial impact of what lawmakers decide on military spending this year will be felt a few years down the road."[87] "Attempts to trim a single year's budget can lead . . . to shortsighted cuts that over time only make an adequate defense effort more costly."[88]

Nothing is more unfortunate than the fact that Weinberger's sensible procurement-reform push for long-term contracts is in the context of commitments that do not seem well thought out. A valuable management tool is not being taken up with enthusiasm because it could easily serve to lock in a program that fails to inspire confidence.

"The legislative system is not set up to determine long-term strategy, so it defers to the Joint Chiefs. But the Chiefs' 'strategy' often reflects interservice rivalry more than clear, impartial thinking. Until decisions are made across service lines and a coherent strategy is prepared, Congress, like the taxpayer, will continue to be at the mercy of the process."[89] But responsibility cuts both ways. "Hearings on reorganizing the Joint Chiefs have avoided

" . . . WORLD WAR II . . . KOREA . . . VIETNAM . . . THE BIGGEST SPENDER AT THE PENTAGON . . . "
Cartoon by Stayskal. Reprinted by permission: Tribune Media Services, Inc., 1983.

the crucial issue of the budget process because of Congressional responsibility for pork-barrel politics," says Jack Stockfish. "They focused instead on 'whiz kid' failures in decision-making. JCS reform rests ultimately on management and budget issues which tend not to be raised openly by either Congress or military officers. Procurement reform may be needed to make JCS reorganization effective."[90]

Is reform possible? In 1980, *Fortune* magazine reported that "Congress continues to act in the old, sickeningly familiar patterns we can no longer afford. It encourages the military passion for new weapons because plants in the right districts help the right constituents."[91] In 1983, *Business Week* said "Congress is copping out on defense cuts. . . . Instead of considering weapons programs on their merits, Congress is ducking the responsibility of deciding which ones to lop off. The reason: programs bring big money to districts, and the politicians would rather have the Pentagon do the chopping." The magazine found Congress trying a new tactic: freezing manpower at current levels. Denying the military personnel needed to operate the new gear is "an oblique way of getting at weapons programs." The result of not facing the issue squarely: "Congress could be doing the country a great disservice."[92]

There is some hope of a new direction. A military reform caucus of several dozen Senate and House members was formed in 1981. It met with Secretary Weinberger several times that year and one member, Representative William Whitehurst, reported that "So far, the dialogue we've had has been very constructive."[93] Within the military establishment, the caucus has been viewed with considerable skepticism. One Air Force general at the Pentagon described it as "an internal threat."[94]

The caucus has lost some of its early vigor but it has helped keep issues alive, including overall force structure and more efficient procurement. A leading defense reformer in Congress is Senator Sam Nunn, who says, "We have got to the point where we must come up with new military priorities."[95]

It seems likely that Congress' approach to defense will continue to be a mix of three themes that sometimes conflict: the desire to "send a message" to the Pentagon that its buildup fails to provide a coherent link between strategy and force structure; the desire to respond to "horror stories" about high prices and poor performance of military hardware; and the desire not to eliminate any defense-related jobs in any congressional district. Thus the dominant pressures will be for budget restraint and procurement reform, but against the cancellation of any program. This translates into slower production runs and higher unit costs, which can easily cancel the savings from better contract practices. Even during the height of the Vietnam backlash, Congress failed to scrub a single weapons system. Its ability to do so will test the strength of reform sentiment as it collides with traditional pork-barrel priorities.

MODEST PROPOSALS

Changing the force structure is an "ambitious menu" which may "exceed the will and capacity" of Congress as it now operates.[96] More within reach are proposals which have been worked out in some detail to create a more businesslike contracting environment. The dollars involved, even without strategic reform, are very much worth saving. Key concepts include (1) more competition, (2) fixed-price incentive contracts, (3) warranties, and (4) multi-year contracts.

More competition. When Weinberger took office, fewer than 10 percent of the Pentagon's procurement dollars were being spent on contracts won by competitive sealed bid.[97] A mid-1983 estimate showed no rise in this ratio. It pegged at one-third the portion of outlays tied to "competitive negotiation"—bids limited to a handful of "qualified" corporations. Another one-fourth was spent on extensions or expansions of contracts already awarded, and a final one-third was "no competition"—sole-source business where Defense went to a single firm.[98]

The potential savings from competition are immense. Hughes Aircraft, which has one of the worst cost-control records of any contractor, found that for every dollar it invested in finding a second supplier for electronic components, it saved $20 in lower item costs. This is a special kind of competition called "dual sourcing" which relates not to the development phase but to the later and more costly production phase.[99]

Defense manufacturers are up in arms about Pentagon plans to change the rules on "data rights." The Air Force has told contractors that five years after it receives any new product, it intends to circulate the blueprints for competitive bids on the parts. If only one company makes a bid and it is too expensive, the Air Force will make the part itself. Corporations have maintained that if the policy is enforced it will not only curtail industry-funded R&D but will give away sensitive technical information to the competition, including the Soviets.[100]

This is a thorny problem. But the rewards are too great to prevent continuing attempts toward competition. The issue is not new. In 1967, Secretary McNamara estimated as much as one-fourth of every procurement dollar was wasted by Defense's failure to take advantage of competitive bids—a statistic quoted by Senators Goldwater and Metzenbaum in a 1981 letter to Secretary Weinberger.[101]

Acting on a proposal from the Project on Military Procurement, Senator Grassley has introduced a bill to require steady movement toward the use of competition. A yearly increase in the number of contracts awarded on a sealed bid basis would occur over a 13-year period until it reached 70 percent of procurement funding. Grassley calls it "creeping capitalism."[102]

Fixed-price incentive contracts. In the initial struggle to win a development contract, the competition among defense firms can be as fierce as in any American business. But once the award has been made to a single producer, competition tends to vanish and incentives for cost control fade. The practical result is that in the production phase, prices rise—the reverse of what is supposed to happen in a free market. "High technology is not inherently cost-explosive; just look at consumer electronics," notes Pierre Sprey. "The market knows what it wants and culls what it wants. In a cost-plus environment, there is no buyer demanding price reductions."[103]

The lure of an enormous cost-plus contract leads to "buying in"—understating actual R&D costs in the hope these will be recouped through the production contract. This has typically not been difficult. Consider for example the Air Force's discovery that it might face a $4 billion spare parts shortage.

A report by retired Gen. Alton Slay blamed the Air Force itself: "We could not identify anybody who had sufficient management information and authority to control the problem. . . . No one is held accountable." Some Air Force officers, however, took a different view. They noted that Pratt & Whitney, the largest supplier of military spare parts, had increased its prices for some items by 300 percent in one year. The company was apparently making no "significant efforts to control indirect costs or drive costs downward."[104] The Air Force may have understated its needs, but without doubt price increases far outran the spare parts budget.

Especially with spares, the lack of competition arises from thousands of unique items in production—one part, one firm. Defense advances dollars to prime contractors so they can get subs "on line." Now the Department has found it needs to send its own people, called "competition advocates," directly to subcontractors to eliminate price mark-ups by the primes.[105]

Industry has strongly resisted fixed-price contracts, even though they provide that any savings be shared with the producer rather than being recouped entirely by Defense. Corporations must realize that price discipline is the minimum "price" they have to pay for the stability and efficiency provided to them by multi-year contracts.

Without such discipline, there is no basis for government to make long-term commitments to industry. "Prime contractors have one client, Defense, which buys large, unique systems and is interested primarily in performance, not price. For each of these systems there are a few large sellers who often engage in monopoly pricing even when they have excess capacity, because they also have huge debts. These traits mark an inefficient industry," says Jacques Gansler."[106]

When the General Accounting Office reported the price of 14 major weapons systems had jumped 30 percent in 1980, Senator Sam Nunn, over the military's objections, secured adoption of a law requiring Defense to notify Congress if the projected cost of a new weapon climbs by more than 15 percent.[107] This law ties in sensibly with Weinberger's move toward fixed-price contracts. The short-term benefit is better control of costs on projects under way. The long-term gain may be even greater: an end to "buying in" and a more realistic match between available dollars and program commit-

Cartoon by Stayskal. Reprinted by permission: Tribune Media Services, Inc., 1983.

ments. There is even a benefit for the companies in greater price discipline. Many major defense contractors have divisions operating in the competitive private economy. Management problems would be eased if all parts of the firm were governed by the same sense of market realities.

Warranties. When Paul Thayer was Deputy Defense Secretary, he estimated that as much as 30 percent of the cost of new weapons was caused by "contractors' slipshod work that has to be redone." [108] The most obvious solution is to require warranties. But the issue has become one of fierce debate. Barely three months after Congress forced a reluctant Pentagon to demand warranties on new weapons, a repealer clause was tucked into the 1984 supplemental appropriations bill. [109] "All I can figure out is they assumed no one would be looking," said Paul Hoven of the Project on Military Procurement. The Administration must have hoped that Congress would repeal the warranty requirement without realizing what it was doing, Hoven claimed. [110]

Why all the fuss? Wouldn't Defense want the protection such a law provides? Indeed, the previous week the Air Force had congratulated itself for obtaining broad guarantees from engine manufacturers rather than following the usual practice of bearing the risk of product defects. A warranty requirement would have saved a $1.4 billion repair bill on the Lockheed C-5A when an Air Force request to make the plane lighter led to wings so fragile they wobbled, and later had to be removed and rebuilt.

The Boeing Company, alone among the largest Defense contractors, gains more revenue from commercial than military sales. It routinely offers warranties not only on airliners but on the air-launched cruise missile it builds for the Air Force. Boeing's Harold Carr sees no objection to applying the concept to some products or weapons: "But a warranty specified for every system isn't feasible."[111] Indeed, the law permits the Secretary to make exceptions for overriding reasons of national security or cost-effectiveness.[112]

When Congress wouldn't pass the repealer, the Secretary simply authorized Defense officials to void the law by making an exception of every case. The Pentagon argued that the addition of a warranty to cost-plus contracts (there are still plenty around) would enable manufacturers to treat the expense of repairing defects as chargeable to the government. Indeed, they could even tack on their standard profit fee to such billings.[113]

Another problem is that Pratt & Whitney, the sullen loser in the great jet engine war of February 1984, complied with the warranty provision by slapping on a "prohibitive" charge of $53 million for forty F-15 fighter engines—about one-third the cost of the engines themselves. Foes of warranties say this reveals their unworkability. But they neglect the fact that a major reason General Electric won the engine competition was that it offered a warranty at a reasonable cost.[114] This was why Air Force Secretary Orr could state in making the award: "Our primary purpose in conducting this competition was to encourage the contractors to produce and deliver to the government a quality product, at a price the taxpayer can afford, that does not require frequent removal, repair, or replacement. We have achieved our goal."[115]

Clearly in this context, and in the new era of fixed-price incentive rather than cost-plus contracts, warranties have an appropriate place. They represent the quality dimension of putting an end to the disastrous practice of "buying in."

Multi-year contracts. Behind problems in weapons procurement, analysts see a unifying cause: time. It takes 50–100 percent longer to build weapons now than it did in the 1950s and 1960s. The General Accounting Office estimates that each year added to the production cycle adds 25–30 percent to the cost.[116]

A major cause of delay is political "gridlock" between the Pentagon and Capitol Hill. Congress has expressed its basic lack of confidence in the Weinberger programs by "over-oversight." It held 407 review hearings with 1,200 Defense officials testifying for more than 5,000 hours during one 8-month period in 1983. Paul Thayer estimated that 40 percent of the amount his firm charged the Pentagon for weaponry when he was an executive there came in response to "micro-management"—unnecessary controls which aimed at compliance with detailed reporting rather than performance to a broad standard.

Perhaps most crucial is the need to maximize prudence in a decision stage which selects weapons, and maximize speed in an action phase which produces them. The current system seems to be reversed. "It's hard to cut back on any weapon once it's out of R&D, and sometimes before then. Yet, operational testing can occur only after a considerable investment has been sunk. The early decisions on technical capability are made by people with no interest in cost. There is no overview in Defense of performance requirements to produce the best possible design for a clearly defined mission. We need a gatekeeper on R&D projects to match missions, weapons, and budgets. This would force a decision. If you must have something but can't pay for it, you must decide what to eliminate in order to stay within the budget."[117]

This proposal is offered by Terry Freese, who also believes "Congress only starts to pay attention after a couple of billion dollars have been spent. Currently, it's easier to fight battles on procurement programs for weapons already chosen than to get into the choice of weapons"[118]—again, a reversal of logical process.

What typically happens is that "exaggerated claims about capability and low cost are encouraged in the bid stage because this is when the only real competition occurs," says Defense specialist Daniel Goldfarb of Senator Slade Gorton's staff. When the inevitable disappointment sets in, the response is to stretch out production. Goldfarb calls for "a commitment to large runs of a small number of weapons, avoiding the use of multiple systems for the same function."[119] Again, this is a reversal of current practice.

Charles Mohr of the *New York Times* estimates "very few weapons programs are even near economical production rates." Therefore, further reduction in output increases unit costs.[120] Stretch-outs have been widely condemned, but Congressman Les Aspin offers a word on their behalf. He says first of all they have been proposed so often by Defense itself that the Pentagon has implicitly accepted them. But more compelling is the fact that "there is an unspoken understanding" which assures no major contractor will be left without work. "Therefore, to use an 'efficient,' i.e., high, production rates is simply to speed the day when the next contract will be let. Thus the effect in the long run is not to save money, but to cost money by creating a 'need' for new production runs." Aspin says the real cure is to prevent the defense industry from tooling up rapidly in the first place. "If in the end we decide we want more production, we can always add a second shift."[121]

Aspin's views are somewhat heretical. They may be more convincing as an argument against the protected nature of the arms industry than they are in proving the case for stretch-outs. It is true that slower production saves money in any budget year by reducing the number of units purchased. But part of the saving is canceled by higher unit costs. And long-term expenses may actually be driven up by exposure to inflation and design changes, which increase in direct proportion to the length of a production run.

If stretch-outs are a way of life, multi-year contracting becomes especially valuable. By providing increased stability and a longer planning horizon, it offers one of the few ways to offset higher unit costs. Since industry knows it will be freed from boom-or-bust cycles, there is no need to allow for wide swings in the amount of overhead that has to be charged to each unit of production. This provides a basis for negotiating fixed-price contracts. Such stability, says Gansler, could cut costs 20 percent.[122]

A satisfactory procurement system begins with a coherent strategy. Then it defines the missions related to implementing that strategy. Design proposals are sought for weapons which can perform the missions. Test models from each competitor are put through their paces. When performance is proven, a multi-year production contract is signed on a fixed-price incentive basis. The weapon carries a warranty.

Currently, few of these pieces are in place. As a result, the price of procurement is too high—"more bucks, less bang."[123] There is one over-arching reform that is also needed to get the maximum benefit from competition, fixed-price and multi-year contracts, and warranties. It is to establish a Defense Procurement Agency or its equivalent.

As put forth by Senator William Roth and others, the Agency would be modeled on the practice in West Germany, Great Britain, and Canada. Procurement would be managed by a corps of highly trained, well-paid civilians who are career professionals on the model of the Foreign Service or Public Health Service. The two qualities the agency would provide are continuity (each project would be guided by a single manager), and competence (each manager would be required to complete a course of specialized training).

Currently, each major new weapons program is handled by a succession of uniformed officers who are rotated in and out of their assignments. In a multi-year program, as many as nine or ten project officers may be in charge at different stages. No one builds up the necessary knowledge or experience, and no one is clearly responsible for either successes or failures.

Roth notes that the C-5 transport has had nine different program managers during its problem-plagued life. In many other major programs, the tenure of managers averaged only two years, the first half of which could be fairly called on-the-job training. A survey of the Pentagon's 26,000 procurement specialists found that over two-thirds had not completed "mandatory" training requirements.

A special Defense Procurement Service would base promotions on experience, expertise, and success in quality and cost control. Roth would require those who sign up to agree they would not accept a job with any defense contractor for at least five years after leaving the service.

The chief merit of the plan is that if one team stuck with a project from the concept stage to completion, continuity and accountability would be assured. If the weapon didn't work or costs soared, we would know who to blame. If the project was a success, we would know who to praise and reward.

Roth says the change would also leave military officers free to do the work they are trained for: formulating strategy and developing weapons requirements. Currently, he says, some uniformed project managers regard such tours of duty as unwelcome detours on the road to higher rank.

Ironically, the proposal has never had a full hearing because of strong opposition from the services. They fear a centralized Defense Procurement Agency would interfere with the freedom of the Army, Navy, and Air Force to develop separate armories. The fear is warranted but it may have to yield to larger concerns. "With defense spending at an all-time high, it's time to make fundamental changes," says Roth, who notes that only one other major military power (the Soviet Union) continues to procure prime weapons systems through a process controlled by the military services.[124]

The Permanent War Economy

Nothing is more essential than that permanent, inveterate antipathies against particular nations . . . should be excluded. . . . Antipathy in one nation against another disposes each more readily to offer insult and injury . . . and to be haughty and intractable when accidental or trifling occasions of dispute occur. . . . The nation which indulges toward another an habitual hatred . . . is to some degree a slave.
—George Washington, Farewell Address, 1797

There is no way in which a country can satisfy its craving for absolute security. But it can easily bankrupt itself, morally and economically, in attempting to reach that illusory goal through arms alone. The military establishment, not productive of itself, necessarily must feed on the energy, productivity and brainpower of the country, and if it takes too much, our total strength declines.
—Dwight Eisenhower, Farewell Address, 1953

There is not the slightest evidence of . . . any visible, large, effective lobby made up of any conjunction of military people and business people who are skewing American policy in any way.
—Caspar Weinberger, 1983[1]

THE CRUCIAL STRUGGLE within the Reagan Administration over defense spending happened a long time ago. The climactic event was a meeting in mid-September 1981 at which Budget Director Stockman and Secretary Weinberger offered the President their views. The roots of issues they debated lie in the late 1970s; the ripples from Reagan's decision to go with Weinberger persist to this day.

As long ago as June 1978, not mid-way through the Carter years, *Los Angeles Times* editorial writer Ernest Conine could describe the contents of a looming "battle over national priorities." The cause of conflict: "an effort to cut spending" which "points to a new competition between defense and social programs."

Conine judged the public to be "in a conservative mood" because of "the widespread impression that a lot of the tax dollars spent on poverty and urban programs had been wasted" and due to the "disturbing behavior of the Soviet Union." The likely outcome was that "pro-Pentagon forces" would win "any new battle over national priorities that occurs in response to the taxpayer rebellion." But he cautioned, "The danger is that the struggle, if it comes, will arouse passions and bitterness of a sort that no American should want to see."[2]

In 1980, the Carter Administration, "those born-again proponents of American military might,"[3] offered a "hyped-up, election-year defense budget"[4] of such dimensions that its five-year outlay projections marginally exceeded those used by the Pentagon under President Reagan. Carter's proposal for fiscal 1981 might be thought of as a "Satchel Paige" budget— "Don't look back; somebody might be gaining on you." And somebody was.

The Carter plan called for 1982–86 outlays of $1.199 trillion. The Pentagon's 1984 estimate for the same years was $1.196 trillion. When Reagan took office, he asked for $1.318 trillion. It is striking how close Carter's 1980 paste-up turned out to track what Congress would actually grant his successor (amounts in billions):[5]

	1982	1983	1984	1985	1986
Reagan outlay request	$189	$226	$256	$304	$343
Congress-approved amount	187	210	238	266*	295*
Carter outlay request	184	210	238	268	299

* estimate

The coincidence appears uncanny if seen in the light of the mix of forces that produce budget numbers, since these forces no longer have much to do directly with Carter. The close fit has been used by defenders of Reagan's budgets to ask, in effect, whether we would be attacking Carter for the same numbers if he were still in office. But the fit is a coincidence caused by the interplay of two forces pushing the numbers down and one pushing them up. Congress has trimmed the Reagan request, as the table shows. Had Carter stayed in office and stuck with his program, his projection would have been trimmed by the drop in inflation produced by the monetary policies of Carter appointee Paul Volcker. The Reagan budgets represent a much larger "buy" in real terms because they are based on much lower inflation.

In the summer of 1981 it looked as if Reagan might be driven inexorably

Cartoon by MacNelly. Reprinted by permission: Tribune Media Services, Inc., 1983.

toward military outlays that were in a consensus midrange. On August 31, White House Chief of Staff James Baker revealed that "the President is ready to slash the Pentagon budget for 1983 and 1984 by 20–30 billion dollars to reach his goal of balancing the budget by the end of the present term." Baker said Reagan was "totally committed to this concept and anticipates taking the additional action required."[6]

Meanwhile, the Secretary of Defense was reported to have ordered the military services to prepare a "reverse wish list" of cuts that could be made.[7] These were not actual reductions in spending but trims in the growth rate originally set at 7 percent above inflation. In its devotion to the balanced budget goal, the White House was said to be "bucking pressure from the Pentagon and defense-minded congressmen."[8]

On September 7 *Business Week* reported, "Even defense will feel the axe" as cuts were readied "aimed at calming a jittery Wall Street" which feared deficits would lead to higher interest rates and bring on a recession.[9] On September 8, a deputy to David Stockman told the *Wall Street Journal* that "getting onto the right track to a balanced budget without cutting defense is so difficult as to verge on the impossible." Budget officials contended that the Pentagon spending hikes proposed in March were "so huge the President can afford to trim them and still argue that he has increased the defense budget more than Carter planned to do." This, said the *Journal*, would fill "a major campaign pledge."[10]

Some budget officials even echoed arguments used by the Carter Pentagon: "We started with a false perception that defense spending was flat under Carter. Actually, it went up a lot in his last year."[11]

On September 12, Stockman and Weinberger went head to head before the President. Afterwards, Reagan announced a compromise: $11 billion in defense cuts over three years—$2 billion in 1982, $3 billion in 1983, and $6 billion in 1984. This compared with the $60–90 billion that was Stockman's original goal, and the $26 billion which he fought for at the meeting. Weinberger came in with a "maximum" $7–8 billion cut and Reagan ordered the two officials to reach agreement. The $11 billion plan resulted.[12]

Sounding a theme that was to become familiar, Weinberger called the $2 billion cut for 1983 "the deepest possible, consistent with national security."[13] Senate Budget Committee Chairman Pete Domenici stated that "on purely budgetary grounds, the overall cut in defense should be on the order of $30 billion. The Administration plan will make it very difficult to get where we have to go."[14] *Time* found "the President's problem is painfully real: how to convince a sudden rush of skeptics he can balance the budget in fiscal 1984."[15]

The argument Weinberger used to clinch his case to the President was that "to achieve Stockman-sized spending cuts, the Pentagon would have to make eye-popping cuts in appropriations"[16] (new authority to sign contracts and keep money in reserve for multi-year programs).

Though Weinberger's biggest battles with Congress lay ahead, the internal war was ebbing. Stockman's leverage with the President was hit when on November 11 early reports of the *Atlantic* interview became public. "Stockman said he plans to attack the 'blatant inefficiency' and 'contracting idiocy' of President Reagan's sacred cow, the Pentagon, for savings of up to $30 billion," said one wire service. The budget director predicted that "defense is setting itself up for a big fall. If the Pentagon isn't careful, they are going to turn it into a priorities debate in an election year"[17]—the Conine scenario.

In early March 1982, President Reagan announced his complete conversion on the relative importance of Weinberger's planned buildup and a balanced budget. Claiming "the very survival of our nation" required greater spending, Reagan said, "as much as I detest the idea of large deficits, as President I must accept them if that is what it takes to buy peace for the rest of the century." Reagan also offered this caveat to members of the public who were inclined to dispute his decision: "This is one subject on which the man holding the job I hold is practically the only one who has all the facts with regard to our national security."[18]

In June 1982 the President strongly supported a congressional resolution which contained spending ceilings for all programs including defense. One month later he announced that he did not feel bound to curbs on military outlays. The President said he would stand by the overall ceiling while reserving "flexibility" on individual programs. He left no doubt that meant defense.

Republican congressional leaders warned the White House that the Administration's tax cut plan and domestic cuts were both threatened by Reagan's reversal. What touched off the fight was a memo from Weinberger to the President saying that any commitment to defense ceilings "would give the wrong signal to the Soviet Union and be the wrong tactic in dealing with Congress."

The Defense Secretary was opposed by White House aides Baker and Darman, by Treasury Secretary Regan, and by Stockman. They argued that backing away from defense spending cuts "would be interpreted as reneging on a commitment" to Congress.[19] But Weinberger prevailed.

In October, the Secretary "infuriated" Senate Defense Appropriations Subcommittee Chairman Ted Stevens by initially refusing to discuss cuts in the 1983 budget. "His heavy-handed tactics may have alienated many key Senators, leading to White House fears of far deeper defense cuts in the future." Weinberger's response was to map "a preemptive strike against critics . . . a plan to raise defense appropriations by $200 billion over the next years."[20]

In December the Secretary offered a tactical retreat—a claimed $11.3 billion in cuts for fiscal 1984. Further trims would be "a risk to our security."[21] The President lauded this plan: "I'm pleased. . . . Cap did it!" and warned that any action by lawmakers to deepen the cuts "would endanger our country."[22] The stage was set for the 1983 session.

In February, Stockman, presenting the Administration's budget request, encountered "mockery, ridicule, and very little encouragement" from the House Appropriations Committee. The basis for claiming a five-year, $55 billion cut was described by Representative Mickey Edwards as "ludicrous." The defense budget as a whole was judged out of proportion with other spending needs. "The American peole are not going to support this program without some level of equity"[23]—the Conine scenario again.

A week later, members of the House Appropriations subcommittee on defense expressed "anger and frustration" at Weinberger's "unwavering refusal" to discuss any change in his budget. The Secretary "rejected, in a stern lecture that has become a litany on Capitol Hill, the idea that looming federal deficits require cutting defense spending" and "declared his budget effectively sacrosanct from cuts, even with a sagging economy."[24]

But the initial blast from Congress did not discourage the Pentagon. Indeed, the more they looked at the structure of their spending plan, the more it seemed "the budget axe may only graze defense."

Procurement was the only area which offered sufficiently large savings. A Pentagon aide mused on the strategy: "Nobody is going to be willing to cancel anything big, like carriers or bombers. But we could give up little

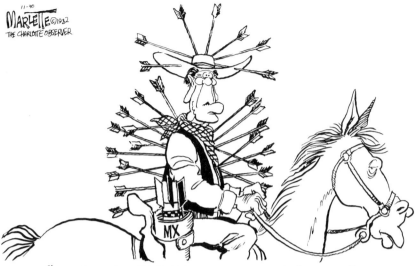

" I BELIEVE I JUST HEARD A DISCOURAGIN' WORD!..."
Cartoon by Marlette. Copyright 1982, King Features.

pieces of the procurement budget—fairly marginal items—to get a political accommodation with Congress."[25]

Defense industry lobbyists mounted an impressive campaign to save embattled contracts. "They appear to be scoring gains," reported *Business Week.* "They are capitalizing on the proclivity of many congressmen to engage in log-rolling on defense contracts by supporting another member's pet program in order to save their own."[26]

In April it was rumored that Weinberger had urged the President to bypass the budget process and fight for his defense program in individual appropriation bills. To Senate budget chief Domenici, "Anyone who thinks that's the way to do it is living in ancient times."[27] Weinberger reportedly wanted the President to "hang tough" and prevent a budget resolution in Congress. He argued that the appropriations committees would then give the Pentagon much more money. "Perhaps," wrote Joseph Kraft. "But in the process, the budget procedure would collapse."[28]

To David Broder, it was "extraordinary to find Weinberger, of all people, inviting and urging members of Congress to subvert the congressional budget process. This is the same Cap Weinberger who, in his earlier incarnation, was budget director for the Nixon Administration. In those days, Weinberger understood the importance of enforcing spending ceilings."

Indeed, Broder cited a letter written by the then-OMB chief to the *Washington Post* in October 1972 lamenting the fact that "Congress has proved beyond any reasonable doubt it is incapable of exercising effective control over total spending. The Congress . . . pays virtually no attention to the effect of individual, separate acts of spending on budget totals. This is the very antithesis of fiscal responsibility."[29]

Broder contrasted this stern assessment with a letter written by Weinberger to Senate Armed Service Committee Chairman John Tower in July 1983 urging him to ignore the 5 percent real growth target agreed to by House-Senate conferees and instead adopt the Administration's 10 percent boost. Then the Secretary turned his attention to Broder, writing the *Post* to say, "I do not worship at the altar of the congressional budget process. I never have . . ." His reason, somewhat puzzling in light of his request to Tower, is that "I understand the importance of enforceable spending ceilings, which the congressional budget process does not provide"[30]—a thesis which Weinberger seemed to be doing his best to test through an "end run."

Cartoon by Marlette. Copyright 1983, King Features.

In October, the Secretary informed the White House he intended to ask for a budget increase of 17 percent or more for fiscal 1985 to make up for earlier cuts by Congress in his five-year plan. Pentagon officials estimated an increase of no more than 16–17 percent would bring spending back in line with the original $1.6 trillion program. But White House staff anticipated that Weinberger would ask for $320 billion—a hike of over 20 percent.[31]

At the end of November, the Secretary "startled" Senate Republican leaders by informing them that he would seek a $55 billion increase, about 22 percent.[32] "It's not an arms race," Weinberger said. "What we're engaged in is an attempt to regain deterrent strength."[33] Weinberger's presentation was met with "disbelief" by Senators Baker and Domenici. Senator Dole said, "If we're talking about shrinking the big deficit and coming in with a big defense increase, I would just say to Secretary Weinberger, in all kindness, 'You're going to lose.'"[34]

The Secretary's comment on Congress: "They did not respond the way we would have liked in [fiscal] 1984. They certainly did much better in 1981, 1982 and 1983. But dropping way back down in 1984 will have a serious and unfavorable impact, and we'll try to regain and recover from that just as quickly as we can."[35] An Administration official familiar with Weinberger's budget request said it was "wildly out of the question as far as enactment by Congress is concerned."[36]

In mid-December the Pentagon announced a "scrub" of its proposal— many small changes that brought the total down to $305 billion. Three elements produced the $17 billion "cut." First, inflation was reestimated downward—increasing the risk of understatement in costs. Second, a $5 billion "reserve" was poured into the 1985 budget, relieving the requirement for more new appropriation authority. This $5 billion was money allowed to the Pentagon but not obligated by previous budgets.

Finally, small amounts were cut from hundreds of unglamorous items, yielding $10 billion. The "scrub" cut into ammunition, maintenance, and spares. "We're doing just what we accuse Congress of," said an Administration official. "Eventually you reach a point where you have more modern systems, but they're just not as ready as they should be."[37]

Even with these reductions the defense budget was much bigger than David Stockman wanted. But insiders said he devoted less energy than in the past to what "has become a largely fruitless effort to curb the Weinberger buildup." Stockman's supporters argued that if Weinberger had compromised on the 1984 budget he might have won 5–7 percent real growth instead of the 3 percent which Congress ended up approving. For the time being, however, the services were pleased with a "share the pain" approach, because the pain was less than expected. Bitter disputes appeared to be brewing in the Pentagon during the summer of 1983 but "it appears that every service will be a winner again this year." The Army in particular was relieved to avoid the prospect of a no-growth budget season.[38]

In January 1984 defense analysts looked at spending commitments and announced the triumph of the Weinberger strategy. The nation was now inexorably locked in to his program, many believed. While Congress cut the request for 1984 and 1985, the cuts "don't really mean much in the out years" due to the "bow wave" of procurement contracts. One Administration official noted: "This year on the Hill they will hold the defense buildup to 5 percent real growth. Ask what the out-years are going to be: 10 percent."[39] To save $10 billion in 1985 spending would require $50 billion in contract cuts.[40]

Cartoon by Mauldin. Reprinted by permission: Bill Mauldin and Wil-Jo Associates, Inc., 1981.

In February, the Secretary assured Congress that, if two more years of sharp growth were funded, the defense budget could start to level off. While military spending more than doubled between 1981 and 1985, the $47 billion increase requested for the latter year was "the absolute minimum needed to defend the nation."[41]

Even allowing for inflation, the 1985 budget was the largest submitted by the Pentagon since World War II, outstripping real spending during Vietnam and Korea. In late February 1984, former President Gerald Ford proposed taking six years to reach the goals of the Pentagon's five-year plan. The Congressional Budget Office estimated this would save $227 billion over five budgets. On February 22, Weinberger said to reporters that he had told Ford that the former chief executive "clearly should know better" than to make a proposal which "would yield only an illusory, one-time saving."[42]

Why are abstract numbers so often the focus of defense spending debates? Why is it that budget totals and, even more often, budget growth rates take the place of basic policy questions about strategy and force structure? "Presidents are faced with a large number of individual decisions in regard to defense—decisions that are invariably so difficult that Presidents are driven to express their policy in the form of percent changes in spending levels," says former OMB senior civil servant Dale MacComber.[43]

Herbert Stein observed the process first-hand as chairman of the Council of Economic Advisors in the Nixon Administration. Fixed annual percentage increases in real defense expenditure or in defense's share of Gross National Product (GNP) are "crude rules of thumb which ignore most of the facts insiders know and which do not explicitly balance costs and benefits." But bad as they are, scrapping these benchmarks doesn't always lead to a better result. "The alternative to an arbitrary rule has not in fact been the ideal, rational decision-making process, but has been a real-world process shot through with ignorance, uncertainty, myopia, inertia, and special interest. The outcome may be errors more serious than those that would result from admittedly arbitrary rules."[44] The approach Stein developed for Nixon was to spell out the economic consequences of different levels of defense spending, including the effect of financing options (taxes and deficits) in the context of other budget decisions.

Stein has been a consistent advocate of steady defense spending increases to reverse the decline in real outlays that marked the 1970s. But he has called for "explicit tax increases to fund defense." These would be, in effect, a designated account in the General Fund[45]—an idea that has been picked up by some liberal congressmen as a means of enforcing accountability on the Pentagon by linking taxes and military outlays.

In September 1981 James Schlesinger joined Stein in focusing on the defense-tax link. "The arbitrary cutting of the tax base endangers defense funding today as much as the unrestrained growth of entitlement programs endangered it in the past."[46] Among those who felt the risk would be minimized was National Bureau of Economic Research President Martin Feldstein: "Nothing is written in concrete for [the] 1983 [budget] and beyond.

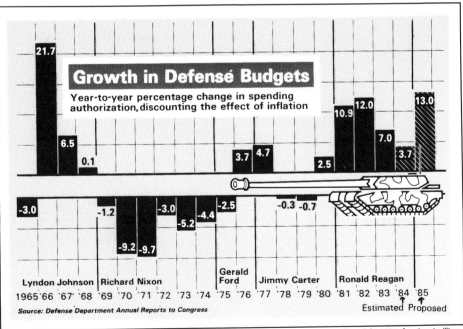

Growth in Defense Budgets
Year-to-year percentage change in spending authorization, discounting the effect of inflation

21.7   6.5   0.1   3.7   4.7   2.5   10.9   12.0   7.0   3.7   13.0

-3.0   -1.2   -3.0   -5.2   -4.4   -2.5   -0.3   -0.7   -9.2   -9.7

Lyndon Johnson | Richard Nixon | Gerald Ford | Jimmy Carter | Ronald Reagan

1965 '66 '67 '68 '69 '70 '71 '72 '73 '74 '75 '76 '77 '78 '79 '80 '81 '82 '83 '84 '85

Source: Defense Department Annual Reports to Congress   Estimated Proposed

JOHN SNYDER

Only a maniac would mindlessly pursue a long-range plan that events had shown was threatening to become dangerous. Mr. Reagan is not a maniac, and neither are his advisors."[47]

Shortly before he took office, the new "cost-conscious" Secretary of Defense "shied away from the spending standard to which conservatives have tried to hold the Carter Administration for the last few years: that the Pentagon budget rise each year by some fixed percentage beyond inflation." Weinberger said he was "concerned about the impact" this approach could have on future budgets. The Secretary said his standard would be, "Are we getting the strength we need?"[48] A week later, Stein warned that the answer to arbitrary hikes "is not for the defense experts to assure us they will provide 'the strength they need.' In fact, there is no such thing. There are only programs of different sizes which reduce the risk in greater or smaller degree."[49]

As it turned out, Weinberger's five-year spending plan was "a gusher of cash that stunned even conservatives in Congress and quickly erased" his reputation as "a ruthless enemy of fiscal excess." One Pentagon official joked that "'Cap the Knife' should be known henceforth as 'Cap the Shovel.'"[50]

It also turned out that percent growth targets played an important role in the process, and continue to do so. Only the most strenuous intellectual effort to base spending on a coherent strategy can move the defense budget away from a primary focus on numbers. The accumulation of service wish lists will not do the job. Indeed, they add up to a budget-busting total and thereby insure the debate will be on dollars and growth rates.

In early 1981 the Pentagon called for a 7 percent real growth in defense outlays "to adequately maintain national security." An independent analysis by *Fortune* magazine came up with the same number. Yet the Administration's first five-year plan called for outlays to rise at a 9.2 percent real rate. It inserted the higher number "without mentioning what it was doing, let alone explaining why so much more was needed."

By the fall of 1982 *Fortune* analysts had returned to the scene with a new reading. The drop in inflation had been sharper than predicted. This meant that the budget numbers generated not 9.2 percent, but nearly 12 percent real yearly growth. Several policy advisors urged the President to declare an "inflation dividend"—a cut in the defense budget that would save money but leave actual purchases unscathed. If Reagan simply scaled back the hike to a real 9.2 percent, he would have saved $75 billion between 1984 and 1986, *Fortune* argued. Going back to the original 7 percent target would net $114 billion. The 1986 deficit alone would be trimmed by $55 billion.[51]

In Congress, Senator Slade Gorton hammered on this theme in the climactic debate on the 1983 budget. Gorton proposed to make adjustments for the lower inflation rate, excepting operations and maintenance ("readiness") which was feared underfunded relative to weaponry. Weinberger's belated response was the January 1983 cut of $11.3 billion, half of which reflected a revision in the inflation rate.[52]

More recently, the Pentagon may have fallen into the reverse trap—understating the rate to make the long-term program look more affordable. Its 1985–89 projection is based on a modest 4.6 percent annual rise in procurement inflation. The Congressional Budget Office said in March 1984 that a 6.5 percent rate was more likely. The difference over five years is $90 billion.[53]

The dilemma Stein posed between arbitrary, abstract benchmarks and messy, illogical packages continues unabated. "Even the real growth concept itself has turned out to be maddeningly complex" because of different ways of measuring inflation and errors made in estimating the rate.[54] There is a major philosophic problem as well. "Debating percentage growth rates in the defense budget amounts to indexing spending in this area, at the very time we are moving to de-index transfer payments in the domestic budget," notes Carol Cox, president of the Bi-Partisan Committee for a Responsible Federal Budget.[55]

A frequent criticism of target numbers is that "no one can itemize exactly what 5 percent 'real growth' is going to buy that we cannot have at 4 percent, or what more we could get if we went to 6 percent."[56] One analyst who has tried to be specific is Jacques Gansler. He says the total defense budget must grow by 4.5 percent a year just to purchase the same amount of equipment bought during the previous year, and without any investment in modernizing a larger part of the force, catching up on "gaps left during the post-Vietnam period" or adding forces for new missions.[57]

Many analysts believe a steady growth rate is the only way to rebuild strength without bankrupting the economy. Congressman Jim Jones cites the comments of "high-ranking Pentagon officials" who told him they could live with as little as a 4 percent increase if it were assured over an extended period "because they can plan and set priorities in a more orderly way."

Defense is the only agency whose budget is built from the top down—through ten control numbers specified by the budget office. In other agencies, programs are added up to set spending levels.

"There is a tremendous decision-making apparatus working under the total numbers for defense," says MacComber. Another budget specialist calls the system satisfactory. "At first Defense yo-yo'd us somewhat by switching back and forth between numbers and missions. Now we have 'top line' budgeting at its finest. They are required to fit the cost of unexpected missions under the ten numbers."[58]

The fact that any extended mission would "blow" these numbers is not a serious criticism. Actual wars (as contrasted with buildups) can be expected to carry unpredictable costs. What is more crucial is the lack of a true "bottom line" for the total defense budget. Such a measure "would derive the dollar value of each program from data on weapons systems, forces and tactics, and in turn from military strategy and foreign policy."[59]

Lacking such a measure, Congress turns to "arbitrary measures desperately conceived to cap the rise in defense spending." Such fiscal guidelines have been described by former Congressional Budget Office Director Alice Rivlin: "You put an arbitrary limit on the amount of money available, and tell the practitioners to do the best they can. The best rule for political dealings with generals and admirals may be: put the money on the stump and run."[60]

The system does not work well. "Once the overall spending level is set—surely a congressional prerogative under the Constitution, not just the Budget Act—the Pentagon has a responsibility to honestly advise Congress on how to meet . . . the end of adequate military strength. . . . If it fails in that duty, there is no alternative to the kind of congressional micro-management of the military establishment that a series of Defense secretaries have rightly denounced," says former Deputy Under Secretary of Defense Walter Slocombe.[61]

Ultimately, using arbitrary fiscal guidelines as a "top line" and micro-management as a "bottom line" will not produce a defense which satisfies anyone for long. Earl Ravenal of the Cato Institute has summed up the challenge of creating a better system:

"Defense budgets are not for nothing; they are for something. Dollars buy forces; the forces have missions; the mission are in regions where the U.S. has commitments or supposed interests. Strategic involvements, in sum, are practically equivalent to the nation's foreign policy. . . . Those who would cut must decide what they would have us do without. This predicament cannot be solved in a few budget sessions. It involves nothing less than the dilemma of a . . . power that is facing multiple challenges but is unable to generate sufficient resources for the defense of its extended perimeter. Will our leaders have the vision and courage . . . to confront questions of national strategy?"[62]

THE ECONOMICS OF DEFENSE: BOON OR BURDEN?

Supporters of the current buildup would dispute Ravenal's claim that the U.S. "is unable to generate sufficient resources" to fund an expanded defense effort. Indeed, some enthusiasts of military spending argue that it is not only affordable but is positively good for business.

The job of one out of every ten Americans depends directly or indirectly on defense spending. The Pentagon is the largest single purchaser of goods and services in the nation. There are twice as many defense workers as farmers. Eleven percent of the nation's computer programmers, 25 percent of the scientists and engineers, and 47 percent of the aerospace technicians work in this field.[63] In 1983, the increase in defense procurement spending created 420,000 jobs compared to only 50,000 created by a jobs bill signed by the President that year.[64]

But using military outlays to add jobs is very expensive. One estimate by the Council on Economic Priorities is that a billion dollars spent by the Pentagon will create direct and indirect work for 28,000 persons. The same amount of money would produce 32,000 jobs in public transit, 57,000 in consumer goods and services, and 71,000 in education.[65]

Michigan-based analyst Marion Anderson sets the numbers lower—27,000 private sector jobs and 18,000 defense industry jobs for each $1 billion spent. Anderson argues that the difference should be considered a job loss—work that would have been available if economic resources had not been drained off for military outlays.[66]

Alice Rivlin rejects Anderson's estimates as "inconsistent and outdated." She puts defense job creation at 25,000 per billion dollars spent. Secretary Weinberger says it's 35,000. Rivlin believes, however, that this debate is beside the point. "The real question is whether we need this much investment in defense, not whether defense spending creates more jobs or not."[67]

It is certain that the types of jobs are high skilled and the types of companies are high technology. New defense contracts have flowed not to the "rust bowl," an industrial heartland hard hit by recession, but to firms and regions which were less prone to downturns to begin with. "There isn't much steel in $1 million of electronic communications equipment, and it doesn't add any jobs down at the foundry," a Midwest steelman says.[68] This raises one of the more important questions about the defense buildup: is the Pentagon competing for the economy's scarcest resources rather than propping up sectors that would otherwise sag. Unlike the goals for the Korean and Vietnam wars, the aim is not to equip armies of infantrymen but to acquire a relatively small number of very sophisticated and expensive weapons.

Those who argued in 1980 that the economy could stand a defense spending hike included Murray Weidenbaum, who tracked the trend of declining military effort in the 1970s:

Factor	1970	1979
Defense spending in 1972 $	$90 bil	$63 bil
Defense share of GNP (%)	8.4	5.1
Military manpower (mil)	3.2	2.0
Military % of labor force	3.7	2.1

Weidenbaum judged that "the slack in the economy should enable reasonable increases in military demand with less additional inflationary pressures than those that characterized the Vietnam buildup."[69]

Two and a half years later, Weidenbaum had served as chairman of the Council of Economic Advisors, and resigned. His first public statements afterwards had to do with defense spending: "These crash efforts rarely increase national security. They strain resources and create bottlenecks." Weidenbaum said that "in a weak economy [i.e., 1980] higher defense spending might provide some worthwhile stimulus" but the long lead times in weapons acquisition could produce "big resource demands . . . in years when we're hoping for a strong demand in private investment."

His conclusion: "The military economy and the civilian economy could end up competing for the same resources. We need to learn from our own history. Crash programs usually do just that: they crash."[70]

On its face, how could an increase in the defense share of GNP from about 5½ percent to 7½ percent over five years create a crunch? The answer: "What look like small increases from the standpoint of a $3 trillion national economy are very large increases for the specific industries that must produce them," observed another former CEA chairman, Charles Schultze, in 1982. Schultze pointed to the increase in defense procurement and R&D over the five-year period: a full 100 percent. "An increase of this magnitude will give rise to shortages within the defense industry itself of skilled labor and specialized components. . . . The almost certain result will be substantial cost over-runs."[71] There was widespread agreement among economists that the stage had been set for the phenomenon of "bottleneck inflation."[72]

Competition for scarce resources bids up their price. It also means there may be losers: sectors of the economy which are denied access to factors of production that are in short supply. In such a case, those who cannot keep pace with the highest bidder may find themselves falling ever farther behind, especially when the shortage is in skilled brainpower which designs technical advances.

"Very few people will admit what I believe to be a real connection between our over-emphasis on military technology and our lagging civilian economy," says Jerome Wiesner, former president of the Massachusetts Institute of Technology.[73] A study by the Congressional Research Service shows a steady decline of spending on civilian science in the U.S. and other countries with big defense establishments, with a dramatic increase in Japan and West Germany, which are our major high-tech rivals and have relatively small defense budgets (see chart, page 163).[74]

There is impressive evidence that Japan in particular is moving aggressively into every product market in which major U.S. firms have lost vital engineering talent to military projects. In the all-important machine-tool industry (a basic producer's good) equipment has been designed with special emphasis on the aerospace market. Many firms in this market work only for the government, and private sector norms of cost and price "don't matter," according to industrial engineering specialist Seymour Melman, who points to a Japanese take-over of half the market in certain crucial classes of machine tools used by competitive private industry. "You are looking at a calamity right there," he says.[75]

Defense Spending and R & D Costs vs. Productivity

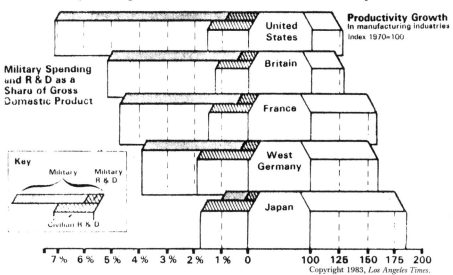

Copyright 1983, *Los Angeles Times.*

Economist Lester Thurow asks, "If the brightest engineers in Japan are designing video recorders and the brightest engineers in the U.S. are designing MX missiles, is it surprising if Japan conquers the video recorder market?"[76] Thurow believes, "Defense conducts an industrial policy, but it's very narrowly focused."[77]

Even attempts to put a good face on the situation attest to a serious problem. *Fortune* assured its readers not to worry, in an April 1984 article: "In semiconductors and computers, defense needs are indeed clashing with zooming civilian demand. But this will disrupt neither sales nor prices. In the short run, foreign competition will eagerly seize opportunities to gain a market share. Japanese shipments of semiconductors to the U.S. doubled in 1983 and should double again this year, to $1 billion. And chipmakers are rushing to add new plants. Most gloomily anticipate a slump as early as 1986."

The same article cheerfully advised that "most demand created by the defense budget is for [items required only by the military]. The higher prices that result [from high Pentagon demand] will apply mainly to the military; there is little overlap between [civilian and military needs]."[78]

In other words, the U.S. consumer won't pay more for anything he wants; he'll just buy more from foreign producers. And while the U.S. military will have to pay more for items in tight supply, it will not affect the consumer. Instead, only taxpayers will be hit with the bill for Pentagon purchases. There is little comfort in this vision. It suggests further economic decline brought on by defense spending.

In *The Permanent War Economy* (1974) Melman identified the trend that was to swell America's trade deficit: "As research in electronics was channeled into military applications, a few industries, notably computers, gained from government-sponsored research in their fields. But a host of consumer electronic industries, like radio and TV manufacturing, left to their own devices, have suffered massive depletion, closure of factories, transfer of work abroad, and loss of jobs in the U.S."[79]

Defense analyst Gordon Adams notes that "back in the 1950s and 1960s we had a tremendous capacity for growth in the economy as a whole and the inflation problem was minimal. . . . We could spend a nice piece of change on defense and still have a healthy, growing economy. Now the squeeze is on. We've got a tremendous need for rebuilding and restructuring investment and job training. . . . Defense spending is making it hard to find a solution."[80]

The concern is that heavy defense investment in R&D and in a few elements of large-scale manufacturing represents an industrial policy which is not only narrow but is "virtually opposite to that of every other Western nation and most American states."[81] The sectors hurt by this policy will be the two that have been engines of growth in mature industrial societies: consumer-oriented R&D, and small business start-ups and expansion. The former is at a competitive disadvantage in bidding for scientific and engineering talent; the latter inevitably suffers when capital is tight.

The pattern of investment under this policy "would most resemble the priorities of postwar Britain"; the centralized decision-making "would most resemble the Soviet Union," in the opinion of Stanley Weiss and James Morrison of Business Executives for National Security. They believe the current military buildup will have "a profound effect on the kind of goods and services our economy will be capable of producing." They see a one-two punch: "Diversion of resources diminishes the economy's responsiveness to private sector demand, and government raises funds to foot the bill [for this diversion] from the same diminished economy."[82]

During the current period of steeply climbing procurement, the Pentagon's share of total economic growth is startling. Defense provided 21 percent of the increase in GNP between late 1979 and the end of 1983.[83] In March 1984, U.S. factory orders rose by the largest amount in six months— 2.2 percent. But 99 percent of this gain was represented by military orders. The rest of this sector showed a sluggish 0.2 percent growth.[84] If these patterns persist, the relationship between surging military outlays and stagnation elsewhere in the economy could lead to a radical transformation in the structure of GNP.

But isn't it the case that defense research has civilian spin-offs? Didn't the transistor develop during World War II and wasn't Teflon invented for the space program? And didn't war mobilization finally put an end to the Depression?

To begin with the last point first, World War II in its peak years required 42 percent of America's GNP.[85] This is vastly more stimulus than was provided by any of FDR's domestic programs. Any spending of comparable magnitude would have had a dramatic effect on economic recovery.

It is true that some products of great value to the consumer market have been spin-offs of military R&D. But even an upbeat view of defense research and its impact on the economy can only manage a lukewarm conclusion: "The military isn't the best R&D game in town, but it's the longest running game—and for now, the one with the biggest pot. . . . Almost any other R&D program would be likely to yield a greater return on investment."[86]

World War II may have been an unusually favorable environment for the development of military technology that could be transferred to the private economy. For one thing, it was an actual war. The results of research were tested in combat. Technical advances had to be practical and workable. This raised the odds that breakthroughs might find a commercial use.

Another advantage was that the war ended and was followed by peace. Defense spending dropped to a fraction of its former level. The psychology and economics of the time supported a shift to consumer goods production. Military technology could be liberally "raided" for domestic purposes.

Today the case is far different. Much military research is on weapons that have not been tested in or out of combat. The design concepts are often so exotic that consumer applications are hard to imagine. Take for example VHSIC, Very High-Speed Integrated Circuits, which are needed to guide "smart bombs" as they make split-second decisions over targets. VHSIC calls for microchips that are 10 times as dense and 100 times as fast as current chips. "They don't seem to have much use elsewhere," is the typical comment of an industry executive.[87] In addition, "VHSIC requires the same resources we need for our commercial programs, particularly the kinds of people who are in short supply," says Perkin-Elmer Chairman Gordon Moore.[88]

Another problem in a permanent war economy is curbing exports to deny hostile nations access to militarily useful technology. At its worst this can lead to "reverse" technology transfer—the purchase by Defense of products developed for commercial sale and subsequent attempts to take these items off the market once they are in military use. The Apple computer case is an example.

American forces in West Germany had been using large, visible command centers to target tactical nuclear missiles. These facilities are hard to conceal or disperse, and thus are vulnerable to attack. By shortcutting the normal Pentagon procurement process, U.S. troops found a way to make an off-the-shelf Apple personal computer, and other components available at retail stores, into a $25,000 unit that replaces the command center. Fifty-five such units are in operation in West Germany.

Assistant Defense Secretary Richard Perle, a leading advocate of export restrictions, went before a Senate committee to report, "We are seeking a way to control the ease with which computers like this are made available to the Soviet Union."[89] This case of a private firm developing a product without government help and placing it on the consumer market, only to have Defense seek to pull the product as "military technology," brings the spin-off argument full circle.

There are a handful of exciting cooperative ventures between the Pentagon and industry. Perhaps most promising is a project to create "the factory of the future." It would use computerized machine tools, laser welding, photogrammetry (optical checks of the precision on machine cuts), and robotic assembly systems. The factory would move from awkward and uncoordinated "batch" production to simultaneous, integrated "serial" production. Through computers, efficient use would be made of all facilities all the time. "Down" time would disappear and productivity would soar.[90]

This effort is clearly to the good. But it is not in itself an argument for the cost-effective quality of defense spending. The "factory of the future" project is a highly effective leveraging of only $200 million in military R&D funds—less than the price of a single B-1B bomber. By contrast, the five-year buildup requires an amount of money equal to the total capitalization of all firms listed on the New York Stock Exchange. In other words, American industry could replace its total stock of plants and equipment if the Administration's $1.6 trillion plan (equal to $22,000 in taxes for every American family) were invested in the free enterprise economy.[91]

U.S. security at any moment in time may rest on the strength of our armed forces. But over time it rests on the strength of our economy—the source of revenues to pay for defense, and of productive resources to develop and build a military force.

A growing number of analysts believe the current program, based on an eagerness to rearm, fails to take the long view:

"President Reagan's record-breaking defense budgets might be good for the military, but they aren't good for the economy and therefore they aren't good for national security"—Representative Les Aspin.[92] "No branch of government can waste money easier, or in such large amounts, as the military. . . . Safety depends not only on the ramparts we watch but on the economic strength behind them. Conservatives also need to relearn old lessons now and then"—Vermont Royster, *Wall Street Journal*.[93]

"American technology development has been hurt rather than helped by our heavier investment in the military compared with other nations. We may reach the level of advance of the year 2000 that we would have reached two decades earlier if military research had been directed to those areas of science and technology promising the most economic progress"—Simon Ramo, president, TRW Systems, Inc.[94]

"The hard realities of economics, not sentiment, dictate that we must keep military spending within our means and make sure that our commit-

DE-FENSE! DE-FENSE! DE-FENSE! DE-FENSE!

Cartoon by Marlette. Copyright 1983, King Features.

ments are directly related to our security. . . . This means understanding the difference between a vital and a secondary interest. . . . The greatest military buildup in our peacetime history may or may not contain the spread of Marxism, but it will almost certainly undermine America's ability to compete economically with its major allies. We are told this is the price of meeting our foreign policy commitments. If so, then it is time to take a hard look at those commitments and the assumptions underlying them"— Ronald Steel, author of *Walter Lippmann and the American Century*.[95]

"A degree of risk is involved in a cutback or stretch-out of the defense program. But ignoring the economic and political facts entails even greater risks. If a world recession triggered the collapse of the world banking system and brought on another global depression, there is no way an adequate defense effort would be sustained by either this country or its allies. Third world countries would become more vulnerable to Cuban or Soviet-orchestrated revolutions. It is hard to imagine a greater windfall for the Soviet Union. The peril to the U.S. under such circumstances would far exceed that which might be engendered by modest restraints on defense spending"—*Los Angeles Times*.[96]

How about the idea that an arms race is a good way to force the Soviet economy to the wall and bring the Russians to the bargaining table? President Reagan has said, "I doubt if they could expand their military production any place beyond where it is right now."[97] The risk is that "the strength of our larger and more advanced economy may be counter-balanced in an arms race by the Soviets' superior ability to mobilize and direct resources in a strained but still vast economic machine."[98]

The volatility in patterns of U.S. and Soviet military investment makes it difficult to form judgments about economic capacity in an arms race. There was a surge of Soviet spending in the 1970s. But since then the growth rate has become far less clear. It may be as low as 2–4 percent in real terms, as the CIA suggests, or much higher, as implied in the "Macy's-Gimbel's catalogue war" that goes on between Weinberger and his Soviet counterpart. It is not clear that either side can bring the other to its knees—or even to the bargaining table—through an arms race. What we may well be able to do, however, is to produce mutually enfeebled economies. America's in particular will look more like its foe's than is our intent or would occur with a more moderate rate of defense spending growth.

By some measures the Soviet economy is indeed in alarming shape. In the 1950s GNP grew by about 6 percent a year; today it is 2 percent. Standards of living may actually have begun to decline. Alcoholism is clearly on the rise; infant mortality may be also. The dismal empire is becoming more dismal.

Will this promote an internal upheaval? Or will the Soviet people, denied an adequate supply of basic consumer goods, tighten their belts another notch? And will they be more or less vulnerable to the government's attempt to play on feelings of envy, resentment, and paranoia toward the West? This is probably a very dangerous game for us to play; almost certainly it is a dishonorable one.

Even from a narrow and selfish perspective, we must face the fact that an arms race in a high-tech era is a formula for bankruptcy. Qualitative advances are enormously expensive. Each side seeks a decisive advantage but can attain only a marginal edge, so the race is assured of perpetuity.

A basic fact not always visible to the public is that defense R&D dollars are spent by a group of people who know there is no end to what they are doing, who have no doubt they are right, and who, for the most part, are having a wonderful time. They refer to the Soviets not as the enemy but as "the other team." They arrive easily at conclusions carrying vast costs. Examples: "Stealth implies anti-stealth." "The other team is getting quieter. We have to learn to listen better" (anti-submarine warfare). "We need a big technological breakthrough so we'll know which direction to head" (precision-guided munitions).

The defense R&D community speaks with assurance. The choices it faces are simple. Economic trade-offs shrink to significance when compared to national security. Meanwhile, over in Moscow, someone is saying, "Comrade, we have just learned that the other team will soon have a startling new capability. . . ."

In his memoirs, Khrushchev recorded the following conversation with Eisenhower in 1959:

Eisenhower: "Tell me, Mr. Khrushchev, how do you decide the question of funds for military expenses? Perhaps first I should tell you how it is with us."

Khrushchev: "Well, how is it with you?"

Eisenhower: "It's like this. My military leaders come to me and say, 'Mr. President, we need such and such a sum for such and such a program.' I say, 'Sorry, we don't have the funds.' They say, 'We have reliable information that the Soviet Union has already allocated funds for their own such program. Therefore if we don't get the funds we need, we'll fall behind the Soviet Union.' So I give in. That's how they wring money out of me. They keep grabbing for more and I keep giving it to them. Now tell me, how is it with you?"

Khrushchev: "It's just the same. Some people from our military department come and say, 'Comrade Khrushchev, look at this! The Americans are developing such and such a system. We could develop the same system, but it would cost such and such.' I tell them there's no money; it's all been allotted already. So they say, 'If we don't get the money we need and if there's a war, then the enemy will have superiority over us.' So we discuss it some more, and I end up giving them the money they ask for."

Eisenhower: "Yes, that's what I thought."[99]

For the U.S. this game may be worse than "two apes on a treadmill." We flirt with forfeiting our prime advantage over the Soviets: an economy so strong that almost every nation wants a trade relationship with us. For the Russians, the burden of defense spending means further austerity in an already bleak society. For us, a permanent war economy could diminish our ability to influence events through the attractive course of trade and aid. By giving an outsized first priority to the tools of last resort, we could risk becoming what we hate—a nation which must rely too often on force because it is no longer able to offer an example others want to emulate.

Technically, it is impossible to charge that defense spending is busting the budget because, in the arithmetic of the deficit, all programs and all revenues are "fungible"—they are all part of the same pot. But, as we have just observed, the defense buildup has definite impacts on the economy, even apart from its impact on the budget. And the lack of a specific "war tax" to pay for the procurement surge makes military spending inseparable from the deficit.

Most large-scale policy disasters occur when short-term certitudes are allowed to block an awareness of destructive trends—in this case, the erosion of our economic health. The Soviets began the current arms race in the 1970s. We must be careful not to be the agents of its continuation by an "endless response" in the 1980s.

The crucial ingredients in a coherent defense are, first, the political will to project a firm and consistent posture on the use of force; second, a strategic doctrine to determine where that will is to be applied through force; third, the military capability to implement the use of force effectively. It should be especially noted that the first of these ingredients is not a substitute for the second.

For the United States, it would be unfortunate indeed to exchange the worst possible defense posture—the weakness and vacillation of the late 1970s—for the second worst—a vast but unfocused buildup of far less military benefit and far greater economic burden than, through foresight and purpose, might have been ours.

Democracy and Defense

Two over-arching problems seem to afflict the Pentagon: institutional corruption, and a lack of intellectual curiosity. At the outset, it is well to point out that the situation is one of "visible villains and hidden heroes." Some highly public figures have been highly disappointing; within the system are a notable number of obscure individuals working to make the system work better.

Institutional corruption is caused by perverse incentives which make people believe they are serving the national interest when they are subverting it. In defense, institutional corruption leads people to shift and hide funds, sanitize cost estimates, conceal damaging performance reports, ignore relevant findings and warnings, and overstate achievements.

The catch-all motive for these actions is to "maintain public support" for the military buildup. The result is of course just the opposite. The Pentagon leadership seems to have confused support for a strong defense with the sanctity of institutions and individuals in the system. It seems to have further confused support for the fighting man with the endorsement of wish lists from the top brass.

Most unfortunate is a frequent failure to recognize that the truth always gets out. It is better to acknowledge shortcomings and take the lead in reforming them than to believe that any admission of inadequacy is giving aid and comfort to the enemies of defense, domestic and foreign.

The Weinberger Pentagon has produced some notable improvements at the margin. Companies which overcharge or lose control of their costs are more likely to be blacklisted than ever before. Companies which sell defective merchandise are more likely to face criminal prosecution than ever before. Why, then do Congress and the media often treat these advances as anecdotal—Defense's version of the welfare Cadillac—rather than substantive?

One reason the Pentagon "can't get no respect" is that its own subverting and foot-dragging on implementing congressional reforms creates an impression of arrogance which hurts a lot.

The second and more serious reason is that improvements have been at the margin, not in the core of our enormous defense effort. Here is where the lack of intellectual curiosity comes in.

The Weinberger Pentagon has not seemed very interested in new developments in strategy, tactics, and force structure. The Secretary has shown a marked tendency before Congress to avoid any discussion over the pros and cons of major weapons programs and instead to reduce the issue to gross expenditure levels while protesting that any cuts will imperil national security.

"One of the dirtiest funnels in the world"—military procurement—has become the focus, even the basis, for our defense effort. Budget numbers have taken on a life of their own.

The result has been to impoverish the defense debate which began in 1981. Those who wished for a dialogue on finding the most effective options found they were talking to themselves. To read the record of congressional budget reviews from 1981 to 1984 is to experience, with the exception of only a few issues, a sense of winding down, a gradual emptying of content from an early look at specific choices to haggling over abstract percentage growth figures.

"The size of our expenditure on defense has become not just a measure of our strength but also an element of our discourse with the Soviet Union—a sign, a signal, a weapon of sorts in itself. . . . It is unfortunate that the money-test has been transformed into some kind of diplomatic message to the Russians. It could be our most expensive and least successful weapon.

"The whole military procurement and planning process, with its endless lead times and its pressures generated by congressional hearings and contractors and politicians, is a model of how not to get a weapons system, or any other, into being. It needs work, to understate the case. The condition of our economy [hardly unrelated to national security] imposes its own limit on what a prudent government should spend. . . . The President needs all the maneuvering room he can get in such a situation."[100]

As the years pass, we are increasingly locked into an existing set of contract commitments. The jobs that go with them, and the options they foreclose, both tend to sap the vigor of any continuing debate in Congress.

In addition, strategic vagueness and the contradictions of deterrence promote loose budgeting. To lack hard standards to evaluate the worth of weaponry is to lack any objective measure of whether we are spending "enough." The sense of overall ineffectiveness which lacks the energy for reforms also leads to spending more in the vague search for "enough" security. And finally, since the balance of terror assures there won't be a big war, it does not matter if you have the right weapons anyway—as long as you have enough of them to serve as a deterrent.

It is not surprising the quality of debate has declined, and the quality of our investment is in doubt.

The time has come to demythologize defense to set the stage for a revitalized debate. This is vital in order to correct "a very questionable policy assumption [which] is in control of the largest portion of the budget"—to quote "a high Administration official" interviewed by *Fortune*.[101] In the words of Congressman Les Aspin, "To make any numbers sacrosanct is to revere symbols and ignore principle."[102]

Demythologizing defense has two dimensions. Technical issues have to be demystified, and the place of defense within the role of government has to be desanctified. These steps are not only necessary to a fresh look; they also accord with the facts.

The average citizen—even one with unusual credentials—feels unable to participate in the defense debate in an era of high-tech and military secrets. There is a dilemma for both the public and the Pentagon: "In defense, strategy determines missions and missions determine weapons. But how much of this can we work out in a democratic, public dialogue? And in the absence of such openness, how can we develop public support for the notion that defense spending is effective and appropriate?" asks Irving Leveson of the Hudson Institute.[103] Former OMB Director James Lynn adds, "The defense consensus has shifted from the people to the defense industry, but it will return to the people for decision."[104]

The workings of our republic require, and the basics of the case justify, a faith by citizens in their ability to judge the quality of our defense effort.

The starting point may be this simple fact: the sum of information that is unclassified and non-technical is more important in evaluating whether our defense program makes sense than are all the military secrets in the world.

Of the three crucial ingredients to a coherent defense cited on page 169, the first is entirely political, the second cannot help but be widely known in its broad thrust, and even the third is largely on the record despite the tendency of Pentagon personnel to over-classify material.

If the public abdicates its role, then policy will be made by the system that designs, builds, and writes the checks for defense. Robert McNamara has described a vicious circle: "Neither political party can afford to challenge the military-industrial complex until the public understands the economic, social, and indeed military damage that the present system can do. But the public is not likely to grasp the danger unless the system is challenged vigorously, repeatedly, and credibly."[105]

Ultimately the military establishment itself must realize the price it pays if defense is treated as an arcane topic. The public is not likely to support prolonged hikes for a function that is treated as entirely beyond normal judgment. If defense is shrouded in mystery, secrets, acronyms, and technical mumbo-jumbo, it cannot be presented to the taxpayer as other than the most general sort of capability. This is not the way to build an intense popular commitment, or even to sustain tolerance for large outlays.

The second part of demythology has to do with restoring perspective. "One of the unfortunate parts of the budget business is the edge defense possesses in presenting its requirements. They are inherently more interesting, and seem more quantifiable, than other areas of spending," notes former OMB senior civil servant Dale MacComber.[106]

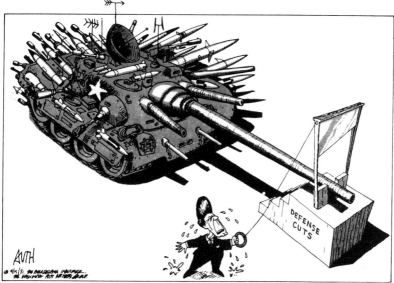

Cartoon by Auth. Reprinted by permission: Tony Auth, 1981.

In recent years, defense's unnatural advantage has been extended. Part of the reason is that we have been passing through one of the recurrent "gaps" (known this time as the "window of vulnerability") which mark defense budget history. But there is another factor. Many in government have mistaken a truism for a principle. The truism is that the most basic function of any nation is to protect its own existence. The principle is that spending for national defense, in any amount, under any circumstances, takes priority over any other use of public funds, and the Constitution and the Founding Fathers said so. This "principle" is partly a misreading of logic and partly an appeal to a past that never was.

The idea that the last dollar spent on defense must be of higher national priority than the first dollar spent on anything else is the faulty logic. There is a point of diminishing return on any expenditure, be its purpose ever so vital. In its rough way, the congressional budget process provides a yearly reminder of this fact.

More serious, because larger and vaguer, is the idea of historical sanction. The fact is that huge peacetime military outlays and a massive, permanent defense establishment are as foreign to the expectations and intent of the founders as is the welfare state. Indeed, the two are strikingly similar in their genesis and evolution. The "common defense" is the fourth and the "general welfare" is the fifth purpose named in the preamble to the Constitution. They are preceded by references to three other aims: union, justice, and domestic tranquility. Neither defense nor welfare have unique standing; indeed in their present form both would surely be seen by many of the Founding Fathers as threats to personal liberty and freedom.

Both purposes, as they have evolved in massive form, have legitimate causes. Both, however bloated they may be from a strict perspective, meet needs of the hour. Neither would magically rise to the top like cream if government were to return to some primal vision of the mythic past. One of the most cherished beliefs of many conservatives is pure fantasy: that a fresh and honest reading of the basic texts of the nation would strip government of all functions, save one: the military.

The farewell addresses of our two greatest general-presidents are devoted to dispelling this myth. Washington's words confirm his greatness; Eisenhower's reveal an eloquence and intelligence which may surprise some. Their theme is consistent. Washington counseled against long-standing enmities because he knew these were most likely to be the occasion for creating a large standing army, the bane of European monarchies. Washington himself was "Cincinnatus," the soldier returned to the plow after victory was won, the ex-commander who would talk only of farming with his guests at Mount Vernon.

Eisenhower's words are well known: "We have been compelled to create a permanent arms industry of vast proportions. . . . In the counsels of government, we must guard against the acquisition of unwarranted influence, whether sought or unsought, by the military-industrial complex. The potential for a dangerous rise of misplaced power exists and will persist."

Defense is a necessity; it is not the raison d'être for a government, still less for a society. Even in a stripped-down version of the world like Hobbes', the first role of government is to regulate an orderly society—an aim which corresponds to the first three purposes cited in our constitutional preamble. Defense is a function which takes on prominence during those unfortunate eras when one has external enemies. Washington's plea, cited on page 148, is to hold those eras to a minimum. The idea that there is something glorious in their perpetuation would be foreign to him as it is to Eisenhower who recognizes but is not comfortable with the persistence of hostile rivalries.

It is indeed remarkable that those who seem most ready to argue that defense is the basic function of government are also most ready to overlook the corollary of such a proposition: that everything done for this purpose must therefore relate to the national interest. The assumption of a special priority and the acceptance of slackness and waste do not sit well together. Indeed, if a function is vital, poor performance should be less tolerable.

The precondition of a badly needed effort to reconstruct the defense budget on coherent principles is to demythologize the function. Some would seek this by going back to the name which served for 150 years: "Department of War." That is a nice, clean, all-purpose designation. But whatever the label, military spending must take its place with all the rest so we may focus our eyes upon it and make some sense from it.

Those who would argue for a greater standing than this for defense must be reminded of the truth—there are no sacred texts supporting such a view.

If one wants to hold it, then let him frankly admit a personal preference. But even the Russians, "the ornriest neighbors on the block," should not cause us to forget that this outlay of resources has to justify itself on the basis of utility, not theology.

The American way is above all based on opportunity—keeping open diverse paths to the future, trusting in the choices of millions of people to shape the course, avoiding "end games" and obsessive visions. We face a hostile power that believes the opposite of these things. We must stubbornly resist becoming any more like our foe than we absolutely must to hold him at bay. Defense, if it is to coexist with democracy, must be the servant and not the master of our values.

Chapter 3

What Everybody Knows about Transfer Payments

UNTIL 1970 THE FEDERAL GOVERNMENT spent more on the military than for social programs. But in the decade of the 1970s a vast shift took place. By 1980 for every dollar spent on defense, $2.20 was spent on "human resources"—that part of the budget that covers Social Security, Medicare and Medicaid, welfare, education and training, and veterans' services.

The Reagan Administration put the brakes on this shift and in 1985 the $2.20 will have fallen to $1.56, because of both the surge in defense spending and the restraints on domestic programs.

Within "human resources" there have also been major changes since 1980. Social Security and Medicare have been "winners" whose value has continued to rise in real terms. Welfare, education, and training have been "losers" which have fallen under the budgetary axe.

One architect of recent policy changes observes, "To say publicly that Social Security and Medicare are welfare programs is to say 'the emperor has no clothes' because people honestly believe they paid for and have earned their benefits. Any fiscally sound proposal would be shot down so fast it would burn your eyes out. But any liberal proposal would cost so much it would fail, too."

To a striking degree, the "human resources" portion of the budget now goes for what has pejoratively but accurately been called middle-class welfare. It is dispensed largely on the basis of age without an income test. Programs that require proof of poverty by recipients are much smaller.

Social Security and Medicare are rising so fast in cost they are crowding out the rest of domestic spending. The budget for outlays other than defense, human resources, and interest on the debt peaked at almost 23 percent of total outlays in 1965. It is now at less than 8 percent—a two-thirds relative drop.

176

What is lost when this part of the budget is squeezed? The chief victim is "discretionary spending"—the choices and options Congress had for a long time to fund state-local assistance and federal domestic programs which covered the spectrum of services. Without doubt, some experiments launched by Johnson and Nixon in these areas outlived their usefulness—or failed to prove themselves in the first place. Rightly, they have gone into or are headed for the dustbin of budget history. But today's pressures on discretionary spending also sacrifice something of value: the capacity of a fiscally strong federal government to launch experiments appropriate to national needs.

To a degree, those programs which expressed the creative imagination of government are being ground to bits between two millstones: military spending and middle-class welfare.

Social Security and Medicare are often called "entitlements." The more neutral term "transfer payment" is used here because it is less mischievous. The very term "entitlement" has become part of the problem.

An entitlement is a program for which people qualify by meeting eligibility rules that are in law, and through which they are paid benefits from a formula also set in law. Instead of Congress making an appropriation each year of an amount that seems sensible, entitlement spending is driven by eligibility rules and benefit formulas. The budget for these programs is locked in by law.

In the late 1970s as outlays soared from the impact of inflation, some in Congress took to defending themselves by saying an ever-rising part of the budget was "uncontrollable." They and President Carter put the figure at about 75 percent. Some spending really fit the definition: paying interest on the debt, for example. Entitlements were called uncontrollable as well. Yet the only thing required to control them was to change the statutes on which they are based. Congress can and has done this many times. The characterization of entitlements as uncontrollable was not apt; it was misleading.

The term "transfer payment" has the virtue of being unemotional. As the following pages will show, programs like Social Security and Medicare have been paid for only in minor part by those who benefit from them. Retirement income security and health care are a national goal and a national commitment. But those who receive them are seldom "entitled" to what they get as if they were an insurance policyholder—even though this is exactly what many imagine themselves to be.

"Transfer payment" is a neutral phrase which describes what is going on: economic resources are being transferred from one sector of society to another. This implies neither a contract right nor a moral wrong, but an economic fact.

The use of this phrase permits us to examine corporate welfare as well as middle-class welfare. Transfer payments go not only to persons but to businesses, even to entire industries. Again, there may be reasons; there are always plausible explanations when such programs are created. But not all the reasons have held up well over time. Particularly in getting the most aid to those who need it most, many subsidy programs have drifted out of touch with current conditions.

While much smaller than defense and social services, corporate welfare is an expense the deficit forces us to examine closely. Many budget experts believe it could be a prime focus for reform efforts in 1985.

Medicare, Heal Thyself

We are witnessing the great demystification of health care, which now joins the 20th century as a business driven by market influences.
—John Bedrosian, National Medical Services, Inc.[1]

If the population were not ageing and if technology were static, costs could go down. But that's not the case.
—Philip Flame, American Health Management, Inc.[2]

THERE IS A PARALLEL between medical care and weapons procurement. Both deal with matters of life and death, which resist attempts to limit total spending. Costs for both are strongly affected by rapid technological change. Those who provide each type of service are presumed to be the only persons capable of defining need. As a result, suppliers largely determine the amount society should purchase and have often been able to set the price through cost-plus contracts.

It is not surprising that the rate of increase in spending for life-and-death delivery systems has been rapid. Expenses for medical and military technology are two of the fastest-growing items in the federal budget.

Since October 1, 1983, however, the parallel between health and defense has been more remote. On that date the 1984 fiscal year began, and a new era in Medicare finance began with it. Reimbursement is now based on the "reasonable" cost of care for some 467 diagnostic-related groups (DRGs) rather than on hospitals' actual costs. A DRG is a specific illness or medical condition. Medical facilities that treat DRGs for less than the benchmark amount will make a profit; those whose costs exceed this level will suffer a loss.

The old system was reimbursement after the fact, and it paid to cover whatever the costs were. Government remitted actual cost plus a profit. The new system is called "prospective reimbursement." It provides hospitals with an advance warning of the cost-control targets at which they must aim.

This change has produced a revolution in the economics of publicly financed health care. A new imperative for efficiency has been created.

How did such a dramatic event occur? The causes were three-fold. First, costs under the old system were rising so fast that rapid exhaustion of the Medicare trust fund was guaranteed. Second, prospective reimbursement had been tested by several states. Without this, "Congress probably would not have moved directly." With it, "the laboratory of federalism worked."[3] Third, the Administration originally proposed cost control in a form the health industry liked even less. TEFRA, the Tax Equity and Fiscal Responsibility Act of 1982, was to contain payment limits. Because hospitals felt this was an inequitable way to get at the problem, they rallied behind an even more revolutionary idea—prospective reimbursement.

In December 1982, Health and Human Services Secretary Richard Schweiker presented the plan. It got through Congress and became law in only four months. Shrewdly, the proposed change was attached to the Social Security rescue package, a tactic which helped assure rapid approval.

Medicare was created in 1965 as part of the Great Society program. It cost $3 billion in 1967, $49 billion in 1983, and is projected to cost $118 billion in 1988, "threatening to collapse of its own weight."[4]

In 1982 for the first time, payments for all public and private medical care exceeded 10 percent of gross national product. The $322 billion total averaged $1,365 for every person in the U.S.[5]

That year saw hospital rates climb by almost 16 percent when overall inflation was barely 6 percent.[6] Over the 1973–83 decade, consumer prices rose 124 percent while the cost of a hospital room jumped 234 percent— almost twice as much.[7] Doctors' fees rose by a more modest 148 percent. But the physician is the quarterback on the health care team playing a major role in hospital cost decisions—for example, the more than tripling in the number of hospital workers per bed since 1950. The cost of an average hospital stay grew from $1,172 to $2,493 in just six years, from 1976 to 1982.[8]

Trustees of Medicare's Hospital Insurance fund say that revenues must be increased 48 percent or costs slashed 32 percent by the early 1990s, or the fund will rack up deficits that would quickly mount to the tens and hundreds of billions of dollars. Medicare's Supplemental Medical Insurance fund, which pays mostly doctor bills, will not go broke. But the Congressional Budget Office sees it as the fiscal equivalent of Jack's beanstalk, ingesting 12 percent of the federal budget in the mid-1990s compared to less than 4 percent in 1984.[9]

Trends of this kind are never planned. In the case of Medicare, a mistaken assumption lay at the root of things. The public and its leaders "felt that demand for health care was independently fixed—occurring when people got sick—and that altruistic doctors and hospitals would not inflate costs." Now we know that demand also reflects "the availability of doctors and hospitals" and of "technology and services ordered by doctors."[10]

A dramatic factor is the continuing surge in MDs. Each year, seventeen thousand new doctors graduate from medical school. In 1960 there were 252 thousand; in 1970 there were 326 thousand; today there are more than 500 thousand MDs and the estimate for the year 2000 is that there will be 700 thousand.[11]

Doctors' average income is about $100,000, with pediatricians at the low end ($74,000) and anesthesiologists on top ($150,000).[12] Analysts are agreed that the virtual glut of physicians will cause stagnation in their income levels, but the surge in total numbers will add to health care spending simply because there will be more professionals diagnosing conditions and prescribing treatments.

Looking back, it was naive to expect that we could banish economic man from the medical profession by shielding doctors and hospitals from market forces. Instead, we created a one-sided situation. "From the beginning we should have had a system in which insurers negotiated rates with hospitals rather than permitting them to spend whatever they want and then get re-

"CLIMB UP HERE AND LET'S HAVE A LOOK AT YOU"

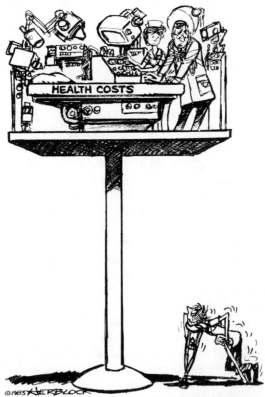

Cartoon by Herblock. From *Herblock through the Looking Glass* (New York: Norton, 1984).

imbursed for it. Cost-based reimbursement is really wasteful. We did not drive a hard bargain with the doctors and hospitals."[13]

The result was that "under both Medicare and private insurance plans, the more money providers spent, the more they got,"[14] a situation which "rewarded the wasteful and punished the efficient."[15]

"By immunizing the health care industry from market forces, government and insurance companies insulated consumers and providers alike from the true cost of care. Meanwhile, an open-ended reimbursement system rewarded excessive admissions and services and inefficient use of high technology. Fed by the lack of restraints and the government-supported conviction that health care is a God-given right, we became a nation of hypochondriacs bent on immortality."[16] Propelled by these forces, Medicare has grown to the point where, next to Social Security pensions, it is the single most costly government transfer payment.[17]

The nation's 5,800 community hospitals are a prime target for cost-control efforts. Since 1950, liberal insurance provisions have helped increase hospitals' share of personal-health spending from 36 percent to 47 percent.[18] With 100,000 excess beds nationwide, hospitals can easily slip below the 70–80 percent occupancy rate needed to break even.[19]

The new Medicare reimbursement system, with its fixed rates for treating each type of illness, has pushed hospitals into the "information age." A revolution is taking place in the facts hospitals need to know about themselves.

Under the old system, the costs for each department in the hospital were simply added up to produce a per diem rate that was applied to every Medicare patient. The new fixed-fee system, however, means they must be able to track costs patient by patient, doctor by doctor, and disease by disease. "Before, what was driving the system was quality; in effect, money was no object," says John McDaniel, president of Washington Hospital Center. "Now we're told the number one priority is cost-effective health care."[20]

Early findings have been startling, revealing vast disparities in costs among hospitals. One factor is how well a hospital is designed. The most modern have in-and-out ambulatory centers that offer quick, low cost surgery for up to 300 routine procedures. Patients recovering from more serious operations are moved to self-care "hotels" as soon as their condition permits. Free-standing clinics, located in shopping centers and residential areas, offer treatments not requiring central services.[21]

Most basic, however, is not physical plant but the decisions of physicians. This is the area of most radical disparity. The attempt to narrow the range of behavior brings on some of the most sensitive issues involved in medical economics.

"It is difficult to think of hospitals separately from physicians, since physicians largely determine medical costs by hospitalizing patients and ordering treatments," notes Carl Schramm, director of the Center for Hospital Finance and Management at Johns Hopkins University.[22]

A study by the National Academy of Sciences found dramatic variation in the rate for major operations. Even on a citywide basis, the rate of tonsillectomies among children age 15 ranged from 7 percent to 70 percent; hysterectomies among women age 55 ranged from 40 percent to 60 percent; prostate operations among men age 80 ranged from 7 percent to 40 percent.

Dr. Frederick Robbins, head of the Academy's medical institute, commented, "Nobody can get away from the potentially damning evidence that these great variations present. You can cover it up all you want, but it looks bad because it is bad, and it is bad because it is not an appropriate way for a profession to behave."[23]

The cost impact of these variations becomes explosive in combination with equally wide ranges in hospital markups for services. One analysis of rates at four typical hospitals showed profit margins from 25 percent to 2,797 percent on four commonly used services: complete blood count, IV solution, urinary catheter, and bedpan. For an IV, patient charges could be anywhere from $5 to $42.[24]

Even more worrisome, of course, is the cost of major operations: a stomach-cancer patient whose 37 days in a Boston hospital were billed at $239,089; an Iowa girl's treatment mandated by Medicaid at $12,000 a month—six times what home care would have cost; a Houston woman suffering a bad headache, kept two nights for observation at a teaching hospital and billed $1,226; a Los Angeles man undergoing a common operation and suffering brain death because of anesthesia problems—his bill for six months on life-support machines: over $1 million.[25]

The National Academy of Sciences study said 19 percent of Medicare admissions and 27 percent of patient-days were unnecessary.[26] A study done at Chrysler Corporation's request found a similar result in the case of its insured employees. For lower back pains, 2,264 out of 2,677 hospital days were "inappropriate" to actual need.[27]

What all this adds up to is a collision between hospital administrators and those doctors who are deemed "over-users" of services per patient. Fixed-fee reimbursement has forced the hospital into the role of cost-policeman. Smart administrators will step back and let the job be done by peer pressure within the MD community. This is proving effective because "doctors don't like to deviate from colleagues' norms."[28]

The change will not be painless. "Doctors are losing their preeminent position in deciding how hospital patients should be treated and what equipment a hospital should buy."[29] The fact that in some cases they are losing it to their peers rather than to outsiders is only partial compensation. Indeed, in some ways, being restrained by one's fellows could be the more ego-bruising experience.

Duke University law professor Clark Havighurst explains: "Doctors have had [read, the individual doctor has had] a monopoly, but not the traditional kind. It's a result of a long history, their shaping of their own beliefs and the belief of society that doctors . . . can be trusted to make decisions for the rest of us. Society has conceded a lot of power to doctors, and we're paying the cost for that."[30]

As we move to contain the cost, "erosion of the physician's autonomy will continue."[31] Hospitals are backing up peer pressure with information systems. One method, known as utilization review, monitors the doctor's use of hospital and lab facilities.[32] Computer-based tracking systems "will be able to spotlight who orders more tests than the average for a particular disease and who holds patients in the hospital for longer stays. This will give hospitals a chance to buttonhole doctors and encourage them to be more aware of costs."[33]

The result need not inevitably be a negative confrontation. One hospital cost-management consultant found that in a single hospital the antibiotic cost for hip surgery patients varied among 11 physicians from an average $34 per patient to $230. The surgeons decided the $34 treatment was adequate. One of the heavy users, Dr. William Kilgore, found himself persuaded that he was "using a cannon to kill a mouse."[34]

There are, however, three serious problems in moving to the new system. One is that hospitals in certain cases may actually seek out doctors who are "heavy admitters." Another is that the pressure to hold down costs will be resisted if it is pushed to the point of "doing less for the patient" than ethics suggest. And finally, controlled payments in one part of the system can shift costs to other users.

The rule on "high admitters" is simple. Hospitals have extra beds they want to fill. But they must fill them either with patients whose medical needs the hospital can provide at a profit under Medicare or with private pay patients who will bear the freight, whether directly or through medical insurance, in an amount that provides a profit. "Many hospitals, to maximize revenues, are going out to find doctors . . . who have high admission rates by virtue of their specialty or size of practice."[35]

What hospitals emphatically do not want is "high admitters" in Medicare categories that are losers. "Today, a physician who walks in and orders every test known to man tends to be the hero of the hospital. Tomorrow, he's going to be the bum," said a state Medicare director just before the new system began in 1983.[36]

There is concern that some doctors may turn Medicare losers into winners by manipulating patients' diagnoses to put them into "higher" DRG categories, or by discharging and then readmitting patients under a new DRG.[37] The inspector general for Health and Human Services believes hospitals are already skimming off an extra $327 million by "gaming" the catch-all DRG category 468. Patients enter the hospital for one condition and then undergo surgery for another. This automatically kicks the case into DRG 468, which pays more than 409 of the other 467 categories.[38]

The process is called "diagnosis creep." Some medical consulting firms are reputedly offering hospitals computer programs which show how to maximize "creep" potential.[39]

There will always be loopholes for the crafty. But it is doubtful they will have the same general cost impact as the old system whose motto was "the costs be damned." Large numbers of physicians will attempt to evade guidelines, however, if they believe patient well-being is truly at stake.

Comments from the 1984 American Medical Association convention include: "Physicians are patient advocates, not rationers of care" (Alaska delegation); "Rapid cures for patients are demanded, with pressure on physicians to adhere rigorously to guidelines" (Illinois delegation); "Physicians should not be deterred from aggressively treating conditions . . . unless it is clearly established that the patient is irreversibly terminally ill."[40]

These sentiments make clear the need for treatment norms that are soundly developed and persuasively offered. One example is a concept known as "best demonstrated cost." Developed by Travenol medical consultants, it compares treatment costs at different hospitals, and provides a composite for each particular treatment, built part by part from the lowest-cost parts of all the institutions. Thus it has a credibility with physicians that an externally imposed standard would lack.[41]

Another tool which assists doctors is a method of measuring the severity of illnesses, developed by consultants using computerized analyses of medical records. Such a system is vital if hospitals are to be fair in their evaluations of doctors' cost-effectiveness in treating patients. It can also be used by hospitals to identify services which none of their physicians can provide economically. "We have started looking at our hospital on a product line basis," says Jane Hurd, administrator of Children's Hospital in Los Angeles. "We have found several services that are better provided through out-patient programs."[42]

Of the nation's 5,800 hospitals, 30 percent are private for-profit, 30 percent are public non-profit, 26 percent are private non-profit, and 14 percent are teaching hospitals.[43] The medical care tab is paid 40 percent by government, 26 percent by private insurers, and 34 percent directly by consumers.[44]

Medicare pays an average of 80 percent of the billed changes. Blue Cross/Blue Shield, a non-profit, negotiates discounts up to 15 percent. Only commercial health insurers come close to paying full freight on hospital bills for patients they cover.

The shortfall in income is recouped by a Robin Hood approach. Hospitals jack charges even higher for private patients—at the rate of about $8 billion in 1983.[45] These are the people who are most likely and, it is assumed, most able to pay. There are limits to cost-shifting. The amounts involved are equal to only about 2 percent of total health care costs.

Congressional Budget Office analysts believe cost-shifting has not increased under the DRG system. Some in the insurance industry disagree.

They feel the strongest factor in producing cost-shifting is the pressure generated by tightening Medicare cost controls. Keith Stevenson of Aetna Life and Casualty claims that "Medicare, a government agency, is behaving far more like a private organization seeking to minimize its own costs than an organ of the people concerned about general social welfare."[46] Those in Congress and the executive branch who are pushing Medicare cost controls would dispute Stevenson's implication that government should not be businesslike.

Some proposed reforms aim at another problem: "balance billing." One reason the American Medical Association in 1984 agreed to a one-year fee freeze was to head off what they viewed as a worse provision pushed by the House Ways and Means Committee. It would require doctors to accept, as hospitals already must, the Medicare reimbursement as payment in full. Doctors currently can bill patients for any difference between what Medicare pays and what they think they should get. In half the cases, this means an extra bill to patients, averaging 27 percent of the total charge.[47]

There is also a subtler incentive for "balance billing." Even if the physician does not collect, it is still worthwhile to bill the maximum amount because it affects—in a small way—the computation of UCR. This is the calculation of "usual, customary, and reasonable" (UCR) fees on which the future DRG schedule is based.

The payment-in-full provision ignited a storm of protest by doctors and the House backed off. Representative Vic Fazio said the action reflected the political potency of doctors, who contribute heavily to congressional campaigns. But he predicted that "their strength will be lessened next year when Congress will have to deal with Medicare's problems comprehensively. Everybody in the system will be required to sacrifice."[48]

In the wake of the House stalemate, the Senate offered an explicit cost shift from the federal budget to Medicare members and employer-paid health plans, in the form of higher premiums and co-payments, and stricter benefit provisions.[49]

This illustrates the dilemma: cap Medicare fees and invite cost shift, or leave fees uncapped but move a greater portion of the cost off the government's books? The third approach, implied by Fazio, is for doctors and hospitals to accept lesser economic rewards as their part of a shared solution.

The cutting edge of the debate is the annual fee adjustment offered under the prospective payment program. When hospitals realized the 1985 fee increase would be the lowest in the 20 years since Medicare was created, they cried foul. They said the purported 5.6 percent hike was actually 4 percent when offsets were included.[50] Critics warned the Administration that the system needs a "soft landing" if the transition from cost-plus to fixed-fee is to avoid serious quality-of-care questions. Administration officials, however, emphasized that the new approach is a forcing mechanism. "Congress intended, through the prospective payment system, for inefficient hospitals to change the way they behave," said one spokesman, who added hospitals were well off compared to Medicare patients whose Social Security checks would rise only 3 percent, or doctors whose fees would rise not at all in the coming year.[51]

The current situation is being handled by the players in part as a game of "chicken." When the House considered mandatory assignment (requiring doctors to settle for a flat fee) the American Medical Association warned that its members might refuse to treat Medicare patients, as they have the right to do and as many have already done with Medicaid (welfare) cases.[52]

If the AMA acted on this threat, it might quickly find itself facing something akin to socialized medicine. Neither political party would tolerate the bulk of doctors being unavailable to serve patients enrolled in the government's huge program of health care for the elderly. The fee freeze provides a stalemate while each side rethinks its position.

The other part of the game of chicken is less crass. Prior to fixed fees, part of the "quality of care" was to do everything possible for the patient, even things whose likely payoff was low. But now, DRG rates will put the squeeze on treatments of marginal benefit. To some physicians, this is a genuine and meaningful decline in quality, either because of what they believe to be the need in individual cases or because time-honored ways of doing things are falling victim to a more austere approach.

The concept of a marketplace, and the logic of economics itself, rests on the allocation of scarce resources, on limits. The most basic medical resources—hospitals, doctors, nurses—are in over-supply relative to the financial resources that can be allocated to health care. The price per unit of service, or the number of units, or both, must stabilize or at least moderate in relation to the share of national wealth which they claim.

This is the message of the health care cost revolution. The game of "chicken" has to do with threats to withhold money vs. threats to withhold services, and with the specter of forcibly imposed standards vs. the specter of a decline in quality. Everyone is a potential recipient of Medicare, and millions earn their living in this, the second largest U.S. industry. "All the pulls and tugs of users and providers are felt," says health and welfare consultant Robert Carlson.[53]

CREATIVE RESPONSES

A lot of progress is being made toward more cost-effective, and simply more effective, medical care because the struggle is not just between government and the providers, but among all the players—with the private sector notably included—as health care goes through its industrial revolution.

"Any real solution must affect our entire health care delivery system. . . . We must remove the excessive intrusion of government and provide positive incentives for consumers and providers to be cost-conscious," believes

California's Health and Welfare Secretary David Swoap.[54] In the same spirit, California Roundtable health care task force chairman Edward Benson says business is "reaching out to our partners in the system—doctors, hospitals, insurance carriers, labor, consumers and government—in an effort to develop a solution to the cost/quality issue that all can live with and support."[55]

The fact is that over the years private insurance companies paid medical bills just as unquestioningly as did government. By 1983, business firms were paying $77 billion for employee health insurance, and $25 billion more for other worker health programs.[56] Auto companies' health bills now exceed their expenses for steel, and add $300 to $500 to the price of each car sold.[57]

Corporate medical costs continued to soar despite the recession. Then in the recovery they kept rising faster than the cost of living at a time when firms were struggling to become more competitive in world markets. In the auto industry, for 1983, American workers' hourly wages exceeded the Japanese only slightly—$11.80 vs. $10.27—but fringes were $10 vs. $3.25.[58] To compete means to control health care costs.

In practical terms, this means business negotiating with insurance carriers and medical providers in a new way. Under cost-plus payment, "administrators had no reason to be cost-conscious." Now "the incentives have changed rapidly and inexorably," says Los Angeles hospital administrator Richard Norling.[59]

These incentives have given a powerful boost to two new types of medical service delivery—health maintenance organizations (HMOs) and preferred

Cartoon by Skelly. Reprinted by permission: Skelly, *San Diego Union*, 1983.

provider organizations (PPOs). They have also pushed hospitals to form relationships with the new groups and to adopt some of the same innovations.

HMOs are group plans that provide care at a fixed rate. Because of the prepaid fixed fees, HMOs have an incentive to keep costs down and patients out of the hospital. Members pay up to 40 percent less than people with conventional insurance plans. And the savings come from the economies of group practice and out-patient and home care, not by providing less effective care.[60]

HMO enrollment grew from 3 million in 1973 to 14 million in 1984. Currently, only 3 percent of those over age 65 are in HMOs. But that could change rapidly. The government now allows Medicare to pay for HMO memberships. In a test of the concept, a group of Medicare recipients cut their hospital use 50 percent after joining an HMO. An estimated one-fourth of the Medicare population will eventually choose this form of coverage.[61]

For years it was argued that only fee-for-service practice would assure doctors professional independence. Today many MDs dismiss this view. Group practice in an HMO frees physicians from setting up their own business and offers them the prospect of regular business hours. Average salary is $75,000, three-fourths the median income of all MDs. But for those practicing in HMOs the trade-off is reasonable. "I happen to think I can do more for a patient when I am rested and leading a balanced life," says one.[62]

One option for physicians who want to work in a group setting is to start or join a "preferred provider organization." PPOs offer fee discounts to clients, usually corporations, who encourage their employees to become PPO patients by paying all of the fee vs. some lesser percentage of charges by outside physicians. An estimated 100 PPOs are in operation. Almost all are less than four years old.[63]

PPOs have been criticized for holding down costs by "skimming" patient loads, a practice which is the mirror image of "adverse selection." Skimming occurs when providers offer their services to patient groups with low-use profiles. Corporate employees tend to meet this standard. (Adverse selection occurs when patients choose the insurance option that offers the services they are likely to use most heavily.)

Another variation on group practice is the "independent practice association" (IPA). There is in fact no group setting. Services are provided by investor physicians who operate solo practices. The only link between them is the insurance plan. This enables physicians who want to retain fee-for-service and their own patients to combine the independence of private practice with the security and efficiency of group practice.

Then there are the free-standing clinics, known as "doc in the box." They have been popping up like fast-food franchises, growing from 55 in 1978 to 1,300 in 1984. The clinics offer everything from emergency care and minor surgery to kidney dialysis, alcohol rehabilitation, and diagnostic services.

What makes free-standing clinics ominous for hospitals is that they are owned by doctors and are capable of skimming off many highly profitable services.[64] (After all, it is doctors who determine the overwhelming majority of hospital admissions.)

Hospitals are responding with innovative approaches that parallel changes elsewhere in the system. "Self-care" units allow patients with relatively minor ailments to recuperate with minimal nursing, and thus minimal cost.[65] Hospitals are building their own free-standing clinics for eye and dental care, one-day surgery units, preventive medicine centers and other usually profitable out-patient services. They are opening neighborhood "emergicenters" which treat a walk-in trade seven days a week, making modest profits and providing substantial referrals to the hospital.[66]

The biggest thrust of the reform in medical service delivery, however, is to keep people out of hospitals. This is the most obvious way to cut costs. "We have an overbedded nation and we will not save any money unless we close down some of these hospitals," observes Dr. Richard Wilbur of the Council of Medical Specialty Societies. "Dehospitalization is unpopular, but I don't think we have a choice."[67]

The high-water mark for hospital use, as measured by in-patient days per capita, may have been as long ago as 1975. Since then the rate of growth has dropped below population increase, despite the rising portion of elderly.[68] Yet hospital construction has been booming. The value of contract awards in 1983 was 125 percent higher than in 1978 vs. 25 percent growth for all construction.[69]

Part of the boom is a drive to modernize for cost-effectiveness. But hospitals are currently carrying an inventory of 100,000 excess beds.[70] For each occupied bed, there are an average 3.7 full-time employees.[71] For every physician, there are seven allied health-care professionals.[72] The number of physicians has gone from a 50,000-person shortage in 1978 to a surplus estimated at 60,000 by 1990.[73]

These numbers imply a collision of forces which threaten the "soft landing" health care would like to achieve as it makes the passage from cost-plus to market economics.

The Minneapolis nurses' strike of June 1984 was viewed by analysts as "a harbinger of the hard times and labor problems that will soon hit hospitals across the country."[74] A hospital's main cost is labor. The trend toward shorter stays and more out-patient treatment had lowered the occupancy rate in the Twin Cities' hospitals to 65 percent—50 percent if wards that have been closed are counted. Seven of every ten registered nurses were working part-time.[75]

The strike was a protest by a group bearing the brunt of change. Demands were traditional: strict seniority, with full job security for those most senior; job retraining and reassignment for a group with mid-range seniority; all layoffs to fall on junior nurses[76]—not an inspiring agenda, or one that will have much impact in the revolution in medical care, but an agenda likely to add labor turmoil to hospitals' other management headaches in the coming period of transition.

Medicare's move to prospective reimbursement did not introduce a radical new concept. It built upon ideas that had already been road-tested in the private sector and by a few states. The impact of Medicare's new direction comes from the size of its service population, and the knowledge doctors have that there is really no way they can avoid or boycott the program.

Health maintenance organizations grew because of a federal requirement that companies above a certain size offer them as one insurance option. They prospered because of the cost control incentive created by a prepaid system. PPOs (preferred provider organizations) are coming on strong because they carry cost-cutting a step further.

Insurance firms, employers, unions—all groups that pick up the tab for worker health costs—can take bids on price and service and select the PPO that offers the best package. This marks the emergence of a true medical marketplace.

Health care is virtually unique in that government, business and individuals are all massive purchasers of the product. The kind of consumer behavior each sector chooses affects the mix of services and prices which providers are able and willing to offer to the other sectors. The interplay of forces, based increasingly on intelligent demand and hard bargaining, seems to be furthering both common sense and cost control in health care.

THE BRIEFEST BREATHER?

Many analysts believe medicine's industrial revolution came not a moment too soon. Indeed, it arrived just in time to deal with the new wave of challenges brought about by an exploding medical technology and a burgeoning aged population. Together they raise issues that threaten to disturb medical ethics and to send costs soaring. Some fear that today's gains in delivery systems will offer but a short respite before demography and technology swamp the nation's health spending-control hopes.

"The price of getting true cost containment is very great," warns Richard Egdahl of Boston University Medical Center. "It's not only less jobs, it's less access. It means in general that things just won't be as readily available." [77] Medical economist Dr. William Schwartz says "the public must give up the myth that rising health costs can be controlled simply by making the health system work more efficiently." [78]

The first of the two great factors driving costs up is the aging of America. When Medicare began in 1966, those over 65 were 9.4 percent of the population. By 1982 that number was 11.6 percent. By the year 2000 it will be 13.1 percent. [79]

The ratio of working taxpayers to retirees follows a reverse pattern—4 to 1 in 1965; 3.3 to 1 in 1980; 2.7 to 1 in 2015. [80]

Perhaps more important than total growth in the over-65 age group is the increase in the number of the very old—people in their 80s and beyond. From 1960 to 1980, those over 85 showed the fastest growth among all Americans—141 percent. Census Bureau economist Barbara Torrey says the $51 billion spent on federal health and pension benefits for those over 80 will grow 67 percent by the turn of the century, to $85 billion, even if medical costs are somehow held to the general rate of price increases.[81]

The problem will be even more acute in those decades when the baby boom generation—those born between 1946 and 1960—reaches old age. "The numbers then are stark and dramatic," says Kenneth Manton of Duke University. "I quite frankly don't know how one plans for such rapid growth."[82]

Management analyst Peter Drucker points out that Medicare was designed on the assumption that the overwhelming majority of its recipients would be 65 to 70 years old. In his view, "what is sinking the system is not primarily that so many more Americans are living to age 65 than in the past." Indeed, Drucker believes there is probably still an actuarial surplus in the fund for those age 65 to about 73. The problem is explosive growth in the number of members over age 75, whom Drucker estimates accounted for two-thirds of the increase in days of hospital care during the 1970s.[83]

In 1981, U.S. life expectancy reached a new high of 74.2 years—77.9 years for women, 70.4 years for men.[84] But those are the averages at birth. If you live to age 65, you can expect over 16 more years of life.[85]

In 1982 the average American was 30.6 years old. That mythical individual will be 36.3 years old in the year 2000 and will reach 40.8 years in 2030. For the latter year, 21.2 percent of Americans are slated to be members of the post-65 age group.[86]

The 1982 age-adjusted death rate was the lowest in history.[87] The Census Bureau's analysis predicts that the cost of caring for those over age 80 will exceed the benefits going to any other group by the year 2000.[88]

When these trends are related to health costs, the impact is dramatic. The post-65 group, an eighth of Americans in 1984, required a third of all health expenditures—$120 billion. The share of elderly health care paid by taxpayers was 67 percent of the total in 1984, up from 64 percent in 1977. Medicare was 49 percent of the total, Medicaid was 13 percent, and other government aid accounted for 5 percent.[89]

One of the more remarkable facts about the world of medicine is that as of December 1983 there was but a single department of geriatrics among U.S. teaching hospitals. The honors go to Mount Sinai Medical School in New York City. The explanation given is that many doctors do not consider aging as a separate specialty.[90] There may be a connection between this attitude and the fact that one-third of Medicare is spent on patients in the last year of life.[91] So long as doctors make no distinction between the terminally ill (especially the very old) and others in applying heroic surgical procedures and technology-intensive treatment, hospitals will be places where, "in a very real sense, one may speak of the prolonging of dying rather than the prolonging of life."[92]

This brings us to the second great factor driving up health care costs: the explosion in medical techniques. Together with an aging population, exotic and expensive new treatments challenge us to define medical ethics for the future—unless we intend to leave our wallets on the table and be ready to devote an unprecedented share of national wealth to pay for the things that are now possible.

Roughly a third of the 14 percent average annual increase in hospital costs since 1970 is "the price of progress." It represents the use of new methods and technology which did not previously exist.[93]

Coronary-bypass surgery was unknown 15 years ago. Now it is the most frequently performed heart operation, at an estimated total cost of $4 billion a year.[94] Patients with severe hip disease used to be given a walker, aspirin, and some physiotherapy; now they can have the hip replaced with an artificial joint—in an expensive but frequently performed operation.[95]

Noninvasive diagnostic methods are those which do not require breaking the skin. Best-known is the CAT scanner, a major addition to the inventory of medical hardware in the last few years. But on the way is a new "prestige" technique—nuclear-magnetic resonance (NMR)—which can help detect tumors that even CAT scans won't find. NMR machines cost $2 million and require $1 million more to enclose them in a special room protected from outside rays.[96]

Perhaps even more exotic are monoclonal antibodies, under development by the biomedical industry. They could be injected into the bloodstream to seek and knock out cancer-causing tumor cells. If the product can be developed as a cancer-killer, its sales will zoom. Experts predict a "megabucks possibility"—U.S. sales of $1 billion to $2.6 billion annually by 1990.[97]

The best example of what technology can do to Medicare costs is provided by the kidney dialysis program. In 1974 this became the first and only government medical program to single out a disease with catastrophic costs and offer to bear the burden for all patients, regardless of age, income, or other eligibility for government aid.

First-year cost was $172 million. A decade later it was $2.1 billion. Ninety percent of the patients receive dialysis treatment for end-stage kidney failure. The other 10 percent participate in the program through perhaps the most dramatic and controversial area of medical technology—organ transplants.[98]

In 1983, only 172 heart transplants were performed in the U.S., at an average cost of $107,000 each; only 163 liver transplants were performed, and they cost $240,000 apiece (these figures cover first-year post-operative costs but not the cost of any complications).[99]

There are several reasons for using the word "only." First, the technique is being perfected. Second, insurance companies are being pushed to offer coverage. Third, the current method of retrieving organs is rudimentary. It captures only a fraction of healthy hearts, lungs, and kidneys from persons who are in hospitals with brain death. The total number of organs available each year may be 20,000 to 23,000, according to Dr. Roger Evans of Battelle Research Center.[100] This provides the basis for an estimated 10,000 heart and 5,000 liver transplants a year, even with strict criteria denying transplants to older people and those with other medical problems.[101]

The impact of age criteria is profound. Dr. Evans calculates a "need" for 14,200 hearts, based on standards for recipients age 10 to 54. But if the eligible age were raised to 69, the required number of hearts would rise to 64,000.[102]

Here is a case where rationing would occur even if cost were no object. Demand simply exceeds supply if age eligibility for transplants extends beyond a certain point. But how would a life-respecting, democratic society develop a basis to ration life-prolonging operations?

The answer may well be that the more explicit the criteria, the larger the risk of social division. As an alternative, Great Britain for many years has provided an example of how the issue might be diffused.

Britain spends half as much per capita on hospital care as we do. Physicians, either consciously or not, have shaped their criteria for diagnosis and treatment to fit the reality of scarcity—in this case, of economic limits.

In the kidney program, the rate of dialysis and transplants is nearly the same as the U.S. up to age 45 or 50. But only a handful of patients over age 55 are in the program. There is no cutoff. Instead, internists do not refer elderly people who are ill with other diseases such as diabetes or heart disease to dialysis centers. Rather, they are told such treatment would be "inappropriate." Doctors are able to live with such decisions because, in the words of one, "virtually everybody over age 55 is a bit crumbly."[103]

One can imagine the political life expectancy of any elected official who offered this as an explanation. In the words of OMB Executive Associate Director and health care authority Don Moran, "government is relatively capable of picking the right way to do something, but it is not very capable of choosing to do nothing rather than to do something."[104]

Informally, however, the British process may be under way in the U.S., though not in the case of the dialysis program which is already established. Liver transplants are an example. The term "experimental" is being used to explain why there has not been generous funding for this operation, even though it is clear many patients' lives could be saved. "I'm quite convinced that this is the first of the rationalizations we are going to use to avoid pouring an enormous number of additional dollars into the system," says Dr. Schwartz.[105]

Any attempt to make the criteria explicit would probably result not only in social stress but in the huge costs which Moran and Schwartz imply in their comments. There will be broad pressure for "transplant egalitarianism,"[106] however, not only because America is hooked on gold-plated medicine but because, in some notable cases, transplant operations have been the occasion for a political circus.

In one case, the governor of Massachusetts was threatened with a full-page ad in the Boston newspaper, paid for by the parents of a child requiring a transplant. The governor gave in and ordered the operation performed at state expense. In another case, an insurance company paid for a transplant after the family's plight was aired on television news. The President of the United States has intervened personally in some cases.[107]

A medical indigent is a person who may not be poor enough to qualify for welfare but lacks the money to pay for the care in question. For treatment as costly as a transplant operation, a lot of people qualify as medically indigent. And the kidney dialysis program has set a precedent. It doesn't apply an ability-to-pay test at all.

"Basically, poor people are pretty powerless politically," says UCLA public health professor Richard Brown. "But a transplant case can become a cause celebre, and then it's politically hot."[108] Many legislators, however, "are growing weary of life and death dramatics." For them, "it is hard to defend a haphazard system that provides new organs to those who are savvy enough to go to the White House, resourceful enough to get themselves on television, or lucky enough to live in the right state."[109] Sarah Rosenbaum of the Children's Defense Fund calls it "medical care by anecdote. You can get care if you have money or insurance—or if you have the 'disease of the moment' and are resourceful enough to get on the Today Show."[110]

There are three ways to end this unstable situation. One is to pay for every operation that could be performed. This means permitting health care costs to grow by 30 percent or more in real terms. A second is to give absolute priority to transplants and high-tech operations over all other kinds of care, including routine surgeries and basic public health. But this would mean providing "more and more health care for fewer and fewer people,"[111] a clearly illogical approach. The third path is, to Dr. Schwartz, "the only answer." It is "to limit the use of new technology as it comes on stream, even if that means some people must forego the medical benefits that are newly possible. In other words, rationing."[112]

If government decides to do *everything* possible in an area of medical technology, the burden falls on the taxpayer. If government decides to do *nothing*, the burden falls on the political process—specifically, on elected officials. If government decides to do *something*—part but not all—of what is possible, the ultimate burden falls on doctors.

This prospect disturbs the medical profession for both ethical and legal reasons. Most doctors feel they are in the business to help prolong life and enhance patients' capabilities, not to decide who shall die or suffer from a continuing impairment. Seen from this viewpoint, every technical advance is an absolute victory which enhances MDs' sphere of action and effectiveness. And if one withholds forms of treatment that might help, can a malpractice suit be far behind?

In this traditional framework, doctors' ethical motivation, ego satisfaction, financial well-being, and legal prudence were all served by a single standard—maximal application of medical technique. It was a standard which worked so long as all applications of technique were assumed to take precedence over any consideration of cost.

There is one way out of the dilemma, a way which could minimize or rule out rationing even of fabulous new possibilities. It is, however, a way doctors are unlikely to take. That is to drastically modify their income expectations, to in effect adopt new fee schedules, particularly in the specialties most directly involved in the new technology. But the average doctor comes out of medical school with a personal debt of $28,000. As an intern he or she has worked awful hours. And now there is a glut in the profession, raising immediate fears of diminished income. The likelihood that MDs will create financial slack in the system out of their own pocketbooks is not great. So they are left with the probable dilemma of rationing medical care.

Nor can this prospect be headed off by the new and efficient forms of service delivery. HMOs and PPOs reduce only the basic costs of health care, not the costs that stem from new technology, whose use is growing by an estimated 6 percent a year. The reduction in hospital admissions from use of HMOs only offers a "transient euphoria." A drop in the hospitalization rate provides a one-time respite, but this will be eaten up by the compounded annual increases in use of expensive new techniques[113]—again, unless rationing occurs.

The term "triage" is central to the debate on rationing. But there is an irony here. Triage grew out of the experience of the French army medical corps. It meant: Separate those who don't need help, save those who can be saved, and don't spend time on those who are beyond help. This was a tough but sensible doctrine applied on the battlefield in cases when doctors were too few to treat all the wounded.

But in practice, the U.S. and British systems practice a form of reverse triage. Medicare spends a third of its funds on terminal cases, but won't pay for some things needed to keep people healthy, such as eyeglasses and dental work. In Britain, the biggest savings come from severe controls on elective surgery, not from refusing to perform emergency operations.

Britain, however, has made a decision which is crucial to medical cost control. Its system has been in effect for decades, so one must assume the decision has received some sort of social sanction. The decision is, basically, to accept death at or near the age of life expectancy.

The previous sentence may read like a truism. From a statistical point of view, it is. But from an individual point of view, Americans often believe, in this regard as in many others, that they can "beat the system." Collectively, of course, such an outcome is impossible. But we live life with a strong sense of being unique, even with regard to mortality.

Ultimately, the weight of public opinion will determine how America treats the terminally ill. Doctors will not play God in defiance of social mores. Elected officials waver at writing the rules in any case where, politically, "there will be no heroes. The best you can do is be a survivor."[114]

Public opinion on this issue is in transition; at times it seems to be in turmoil. But a direction is evident. A growing number of Americans no longer believe medical science should "keep alive the bodies of persons whose biographies have ended."[115] They are rebelling against "equating length of life with quality of life." They are observing that "sometimes the question isn't whether to pull the plug but whether the plug should be put in in the first place." They are asking, "Why does every hospital have to have every machine?"[116]

Some politicians, sensing the shift, have begun to speak out. "How much money do we want to spend on cases where death is inevitable in a short period of time?" asks Representative William Thomas.[117] Colorado Governor Richard Lamm set off a furor by using the phrase "duty to die." But his point was seconded by many senior citizens when he explained with greater care: "It is not right to impose life on people who are suffering beyond our ability to help them, or who have lost the capacity to understand what is happening to them and whose suffering is being increased and prolonged by those machines."[118]

Lamm does not appear to have overstated the point. A study at one of Harvard Medical School's main teaching hospitals found that at least one patient in three would reject medical intervention if they were about to die. But only one physician in ten asks patients whether they want doctors to take extraordinary steps.[119]

In April 1984, ten prominent doctors proposed a "bill of rights" for terminal patients. Doctors should tell patients the truth and inform them of their choices, rather than "leaving them adrift in a mass of medical fact and opinion"—or leaving them in the dark, since "anxiety of the unknown" can be more upsetting than the truth.

Doctors should respect a patient's wish to refuse treatment rather than viewing it as a sign of incompetency. A doctor who isn't sure about a patient's chances should consult specialists, and should not give undue weight to rare cases of "miracle" recoveries. Doctors should give priority to "appropriate and compassionate care" over undue fears of malpractice liability.[120] Indeed, by one estimate, "defensive medicine" caused by society's litigious nature is "the greatest waste of the medical care dollar"—accounting for 15 to 20 percent of total expenditures.[121]

The toughest cases, of course, are not those in which a patient reconciled to death tells the doctors to let him slip away quietly. The toughest cases are those where the patient can't speak to the question.

In the "bill of rights" the ten doctors said aggressive treatment should be reduced or halted if it would only prolong an uncomfortable process of dying. But discomfort and the certainty of death are not always clear issues. And they do not involve just the elderly.

"The costs of treating and tending badly deformed babies of the Baby Doe variety can easily amount to millions of dollars over a normal lifetime. Earlier these babies usually died quickly because we didn't have the capabilities now available. . . . It is strange that the Reagan administration, so sensitive to medical care costs for other patients, is pursuing a policy that seems to many physicians to demand no limits on expenditures to keep a deformed baby alive," observes medical writer Harry Schwartz.[122]

Governor Lamm, with his usual candor, has also questioned the value of "spending thousands of dollars to educate mentally retarded children when, after four or five years, all they do is roll over."[123]

Lamm's comment and his assertion that in the future "euthanasia is going to be our next searing issue"[124] reveal why many politicians prefer to intervene in dramatic rescue operations rather than to hammer out a new policy. The search for such a policy carries with it the risk of appearing to play God at His most severe. It is much more gratifying to play God at His most benevolent.

But the result is not policy; it is anecdote, even illusion. "The scandal is that political leaders won't face the central issue: Who shall live and who shall die in the new dispensation that puts economics first in health care? The current chaos is causing some to live who might otherwise die, and some to die who might otherwise live. Often there is no reason why one person is lucky and another unlucky," says Schwartz.[125]

Is it true that economics come first, or is it still the case, as Robert Samuelson asserts, that "the central problem in controlling health costs is imposing economic limits where people think them immoral"? Samuelson says health care remains "the supreme entitlement: It's due everyone on demand; no expense should be spared."[126]

How can we prevent health care from becoming a focus of unrest as it struggles to balance cost pressures with "rationing roulette?" The answer lies in another kind of balance. The opposite of an entitlement-based society is a personal responsibility-based society. We will never have either in pure form. But in the area of health care, a balance must be struck between the two principles.

The only doctrine workable over the long-term might read something like this: Every American shall have equal access to those forms of medical treatment consistent with reasonable expectations regarding span of life, difficulty of treatment and odds of survival in severe situations, and personal responsibility for the basic maintenance of one's health.

These notions are not utopian. A growing segment of the public has as its health goal "a lifetime of vigor followed by terminal collapse."[127] A growing segment of the health profession is interested in "a concept of full partnership between doctor and patient,"[128] replacing one in which "the patient does not question the doctor and the doctor does not voice his uncertainties."[129] And many Americans on grounds of responsibility reject, for example, liver transplants for those whose cirrhosis is due to alcoholism.[130]

Perhaps most important, a growing number of people find repellent the idea of being attached to a life support system which can only prolong, and not reverse, the process of terminal collapse. The knowledge that such care is so costly it may deny needed treatments to those with a future is one factor. Another is awareness of "near death experiences." Their positive rather than harrowing character suggests to many that the body has a wisdom about death, a wisdom with which intensive terminal care may interfere. It also suggests that the soul is preparing itself for a reality which we profess in our religious beliefs but against which we often struggle by demanding every aid science can provide.

Personal responsibility for one's good health, mature doctor-patient relationships, faith about what lies on the "far shore," aversion to becoming the appendage to a machine, a conscience that relates resources to the health needs of those with a biological future—these factors may lead us to a changed view on what is meant by medical entitlement.

The alternative is to permit the ideal of health care to be ground down between cost pressures and arbitrary decisions. It is not spectacular interventions which require moral courage. It is not the pretense that we can afford to follow a technological imperative and to perform an unlimited number of heroic procedures which expresses compassion. Moral courage requires an honest definition of what we should do, and compassion requires making care equally available to all persons whose medical problems and prospects are similar.

It would of course be ideal to have a stated consensus on these matters, to which all in the nation would subscribe. But it is more likely we will reach the same point by the working through of social attitudes which express a new maturity toward health care. The fatal error is to interrupt this process by enshrining in law the demands of the most clamorous claimants. Such a course would either be fiscal folly or moral hypocrisy. Far better to let the "market" of public opinion evolve along the broadest lines and to avoid explicit policies where they are untenable.

This is what Britain has done. We need not choose exactly the same mix they have. But we do need to choose flexibility and moderation, or demographics and technology will saddle us with a burden of soaring costs and ad hoc ethical dramas no American would wish to see.

TOOLS FOR COST CONTROL

Isn't there an obvious objection to the hopes expressed above that the political system will be guided by a broad evolution in public opinion? Isn't it a fact that government in general and the budget in particular reflect precisely the "demands of the most clamorous claimants" in all areas of spending? Why should health care be an exception?

There is a basis to hope for a sensible outcome, partly because, in the area of health, government is only one of the purchasers and can benefit by common sense decisions made by private-sector buyers. Another factor is that the search for cost control spans the political spectrum. The debate is over how, rather than whether, the health budget is to be contained.

An over-simplified distinction is that liberals favor more effective regulation, and conservatives favor more effective competition, as means of cost control. One method would use the discipline of law; the other, the discipline of the market. Each approach has a particular merit. Regulation has an important role in assuring equal access and in maintaining quality of care. Competition is an elegant and appropriate way to express, through consumer choice rather than political warfare, the emerging national sense of health care norms and expectations. Both approaches are being marketed primarily as means of controlling costs.

Senator Edward Kennedy and Representative Richard Gephardt propose to extend the use of prospective payments based on specific diagnoses. They have offered a bill to apply this reimbursement plan to privately insured as well as Medicare patients, and to doctors' as well as hospitals' fees.

Their aim is to tighten up Medicare financing by reducing the shifting of unreimbursed hospital costs onto private patients and by strengthening hospital administrators' ability to impose cost controls on doctors who, for the most part, determine what services will be provided.

The bill requires states to set ceilings on charges to patients, through voluntary means or regulations. If the states do not set their own limits, a federal cap would be imposed. The proposed level of cost restraint would save consumers an estimated $74 billion over a five-year period.[131]

A major alternative, a different route to the same savings goal, is California's experiment in competition. Under a new system being closely watched by other states and the federal government, and also being tested in Arizona, the state's Medicaid program and private insurers are negotiating with health care providers to set payment levels for specific services. Hospitals and doctors offering care at the most favorable terms will get the patients.[132]

The state's Secretary for Health and Welfare, David Swoap, said in 1983 the California plan should be copied. "Medicare's reimbursement system should be transformed gradually to a prepaid rate for the entire care of each beneficiary, as in a private insurance plan. . . . This rate should not exceed the average rate, adjusted regionally, that Medicare now pays. . . . The elderly would then choose any private plan that offers them the best mix of services, thus inducing further competition among plans to create efficiencies. The government could require that, to qualify, a plan must offer the same level of benefits now available to Medicare beneficiaries. . . . Each state could be responsible for establishing a means to qualify and monitor plans, as is now done for private insurance." [133]

Swoap, who served as under secretary of the federal Department of Health and Human Services, did not argue in vain. In May 1984 the government proposed that all Medicare recipients be given the choice of joining private health care groups whose charges are set in advance and billed as a monthly fee. The enrollee would have to use the HMO or PPO doctors and hospitals, but would not be billed extra regardless of the number of doctor visits or amount of hospitals time.

The federal government would save money because the health care group would receive a payment equal to 95 percent of the average cost for a Medicare recipient. The provider would try to make a profit through preventive care, lower hospitalization rates, and the economies provided by group practice. The hope is held out that a combination of fees from members and direct payments by government would cover not only basic care but also dental and eye care not offered by Medicare.

The program is voluntary, with about 600,000 persons expected to enroll in the next three or four years. Enrollees would be in the position of a person buying an insurance policy, weighing the unknown of future medical bills against the certainty of monthly fees. [134]

The proposal is less radical than it sounds because Medicare is far less comprehensive than is often realized. As a result, millions of Medicare members are forced to shop for extra protection. Private plans tailored to plug the holes in coverage are known as "medigap" insurance. A dizzying array of such plans are available, and shopping for one is not an easy task.

The biggest reason why many elderly are consumers in the medigap market is that "Medicare coverage is really great in the beginning but lousy in the end. It doesn't cover your expenses." [135]

Medicare Part A pays all costs in the first 60 days of hospitalization, except for a single deductible of $304 paid by the patient. For the next 30 days, the patient pays $76 a day and Medicare covers the rest. After the 90th day, the patient pays $152 a day. After the 150th day, the patient pays everything. Medicare Part B is voluntary supplemental coverage, which costs about $15 a month. It will pay 80 percent of all "reasonable" charges for physicians' services. [136]

In the opinion of many analysts, the structure of Medicare benefits is almost the reverse of good sense. Initial costs are generously covered. But as expenses for an illness climb to the point of catastrophic impact on an individual's financial resources, Medicare helps less and less.

The system is currently so unbalanced that the Reagan Administration in 1983 found it would be possible, by raising annual member premiums only $98 a year from $146, to provide an unlimited number of days in the hospital and financial protection to defray the cost of catastrophic illness, while *reducing* program costs by $41 billion over a ten-year period. [137]

This seemingly impossible feat is feasible simply because of the enormous cost of reimbursing routine expenses which people could pay themselves. The result of doing this is to strip the resources that could cover the much smaller number of situations for which everyone most needs insurance—the harrowing cases of catastrophic personal expense.

Such a change in the federal government's health care plan would parallel a major trend under way in the private sector. Not only are management and labor coming to unite in seeking coverage that pays the big medical bills, but some unions are agreeing that higher deductibles and even co-payments may be a reasonable price for catastrophic coverage.

The issue is far from resolved. 1983 saw some bitter labor disputes, and even some strikes, over these concepts. But the public may be ahead of the negotiators. A Harris Poll done for Equitable Life Assurance found American consumers "remarkably willing to accept a broad range of cost-containment policies." Among the most acceptable were higher deductibles and paying a greater share of the premium (co-payments).

Support for such ideas comes not because people want to get stuck with more of the tab, but because they recognize that greater personal responsibility for payment is an "incentive for lower utilization of non-essential health care services." It would also promote "comparison shopping" among providers, which only 16 percent of consumers do in the case of doctors, according to the Harris Poll.[138]

In June 1984 a business and labor coalition asked the Congress to pass a bill that would provide federal technical assistance to employers, unions, and other major purchasers of health care seeking to compare price, services and quality offered by competing providers. The bill was denounced by the American Medical Association as "a waste of the taxpayers' money."[139]

When deductibles and co-payments have been seen by labor as part of a general "give-back" strategy by management negotiators, they have been rejected. When they are seen as tools to promote consumer awareness, they have been accepted. And even when labor disputes have ended in stalemate, firms and unions have agreed to join in efforts to control health-care costs.[140]

A proposal which has been most resisted is to tax the value of employer-paid health plans as ordinary income. The intent behind the idea is, however, the familiar theme of creating consumer awareness. In 1983 the Reagan Administration proposed to limit tax-free employer-paid health insurance to $175 per family per month. "This would be enough to pay most of the cost of a good, comprehensive health insurance plan," says Alain Enthoven of the Stanford Business School. "Employees who choose more costly plans should pay the extra amount out of their own incomes."[141] In other words, the tax-free concept should cover only a basic plan. If gold-plated benefits are also tax free, then the consumer has less stake in cost control and is more likely to allow some providers to escape the discipline of a competitive market.

Cartoon by Meyer. Reprinted by permission: Meyer, *San Francisco Chronicle*, 1984.

The collision of demography, technology, and ethics is rich in possibilities for grim political confrontation and fiscal-economic stress. However, it is possible to see the elements of an emerging consensus on a workable health care system.

The emphasis would be on catastrophic coverage. Each person would be liable for medical bills and insurance fees up to a certain percentage of personal income. The extra revenue this provides the system would be used to pay all expenses above that threshold level of income.

The federal government's medical care for the elderly, state governments' care for the poor, companies' care for their workers, and individuals' care for themselves would all be purchased from the same group of providers, who would compete with one another by offering packages of services at agreed-upon rates, payable in the form of fixed fees. Some total spending cap might also be set annually by federal and state governments on their health outlays, representing a limit within which contracts must be negotiated. The private sector might conform and one assumes it would be happy to do so, in setting a comparable cap to prevent cost shifts.

Liberals like the regulatory discipline of a cost cap for the same reason conservatives like the market discipline of competitive bids: these are ways to contain spending without making direct benefit cuts. There is political wisdom in this kind of broad control, just as there is political folly in dramatizing specific medical problems. The latter approach invites a medical pork-barrel, the former lets the system work things through.

Of all government services, health care may be the one best suited to solution by broad mechanisms and the evolution of an accommodation with the future, rather than by forcing an explicit philosophy of care and treatment. A tolerance for diversity, and some faith in the common-sense choices of millions of consumers, is merely a reaffirmation that the American way of decision fits this most basic of all public services.

There is much truth in Lester Thurow's comment that "health care costs are not a federal budget problem. They are a social problem. Spending limits are the same regardless of whether the money is spent through the federal budget or private insurance. Somehow we are going to have to learn to say 'no.' . . . How much are we as a society willing to spend on prolonging life? The easy answer is 'any amount,' but that answer is neither true nor feasible." Thurow notes that if just half of those in their last year of life were given a Barney Clark-type artificial heart operation, the cost would equal one-third of GNP.[142]

Thurow, a social liberal, worries that leaving health care norms to the market will "let the capitalistic part of our ethics dominate the egalitarian part." Specifically, the rich will have access to treatment not available to the poor. As he notes, "when it comes to that famous bottom line, few are real believers in the market unless they would be willing to see themselves die if they could not afford available treatment."[143]

In wrestling with the issue, Thurow is unable to find a solution even through regulation. And the fact is, the rich will always be able to buy more things than the poor—even things as valuable as life-sustaining treatment. It is at least worth considering the possibility that the most effective way of narrowing the gap is to use the market, equally with regulation, as a means to evolve norms of care. The market will tend to squeeze out treatments which only marginally prolong life, and it will discourage applying treatments all the way to the point where their added payoff has fallen to zero.

When this happens, we will have achieved the most we can hope for in dissuading the rich from availing themselves of exotic and fabulously expensive care. On the one hand, there will be a social norm in which millions of people have made the heroic decision not to demand heroic treatments. On the other hand, the diminished practice of such procedures will tend to dry up the supply of specialists. Both "thinkability" and availability of costly care will be lessened.

This may well be all the egalitarianism we should hope for unless we are willing to change our system and move toward forms of coercion America has never employed.

Postage Due on the Chain Letter

We seem to be on a five-year cycle for fifty-year 'solutions' to Social Security.
—William Niskanen, member, Council of Economic Advisors[1]

IF DEFENSE IS A PROGRAM where the beliefs of conservative politicians have led to massive outlays of questionable value, Social Security is a program where the unwillingness of liberal politicians to level with the people has prevented an honest discussion of the problems and choices.

Social Security is not and never has been an actuarially sound insurance program whose members' contributions pay for their own benefits. Nor is it a system whose supposed "self-financing" is a cause for satisfaction and complacency. Nor do all proposals to amend its provisions involve a decline in the real value of future pensions and consequently a "breaking of faith" with the people. Indeed, acting as if everything is all right may be the more serious violation of public trust.

Strangely, the best-known threat faced by Social Security is the one least likely to occur: the fear that it won't be there for workers retiring ten years or more in the future. According to the Gallup Poll, more than half the people under age 55 hold this fear.[2] But the truth is better expressed in George Will's words: "The problem with Social Security's multi-trillion dollar deficit is not that it won't be paid off, but that it will."[3]

Social Security is a basic part of the American economic and political fabric. Its benefit structure and the revenue this requires—not its possible repudiation—form the issue realistically before us.

If Medicare is a program whose political problems are serious and whose real world problems are crucial, Social Security is a program whose real world problems are serious and whose political problems are crucial.

The political strength of Social Security finds its roots in the same event that has led to its political problems. When the system was launched in 1935, Franklin Roosevelt, that master of political psychology, made sure the program was designed to assure its popularity—and its perpetuation. In the process a fierce loyalty was created which, over time, has become a bulwark against reasonable change.

"To soothe conservative qualms, Roosevelt demanded that his planners draft a scheme that was not 'the same old dole.' That ruled out any use of general revenues, meaning primarily income taxes. . . . The system had to be funded entirely by a payroll tax . . . so that it could be presented to the nation as a sort of contributory insurance plan."[4]

One account from an eyewitness is that when FDR was asked whether Social Security should be a welfare or an insurance program, he replied, "If it's welfare, the Republicans will repeal it the first chance they get. It's got to be something everyone has a stake in because everyone's paid his share into it."[5]

This strategy worked brilliantly. And what turned out to be crucial was not that each recipient had paid for his or her own benefits, but that each had contributed toward them. This distinction is at the heart of the Social Security dilemma, but even politicians willing to embark on reform are reluctant to speak of it. Instead, the political history of the program has been "a story of demographics and demagoguery."[6]

The program began modestly. Enacted in 1935, it began collecting taxes in 1937 at the rate of 1 percent of the first $3,000 of earnings—$30 per worker, and an equal amount from the employer. This tax did not change until 1950, when it was raised to $45 per year.

Social Security pension check No. 1 went to retired legal secretary Ida May Fuller of Brattleboro, Vermont, in January 1940. Fuller had paid $22 in payroll taxes over her last three years of work. Her first check was for $22.54. Fuller's last check was drawn in December 1974, shortly after her 100th birthday. It was for $112.60. In return for her $22, she had collected a total of $20,944.42.[7]

Fuller's return of 952 times her contribution was exceptional due to her great age and her short period of taxpaying employment. And neither her first nor her last check was large in absolute dollars. But Social Security recipient No. 1 had set a pattern for those who would follow. She received from the system far more than she paid into it, and the amount of monthly support was modest, "not intended to guarantee a comfortable retirement, but to ward off destitution."[8]

In microcosm, Ida May Fuller's case history reveals the two great themes that have dominated debate ever since: Is Social Security meant to be an income floor or a complete pension? How much of each worker's pension should be paid in advance by himself and his employer, and how much should be paid by those who are in the workforce while he is retired?

Fuller's years as a recipient spanned the important milestones in extending coverage. Originally, only workers in commerce and industry (excluding railroads) were beneficiaries. In 1939, before the first checks went out, Congress broadened the 1935 concept by adding a 50 percent benefit for spouses, and for surviving dependents of retired workers.[9]

In 1956, women were made eligible for early retirement, with reduced benefits, at age 62. Disability insurance was added to cover those age 50 or over who were removed from the workforce by injury or chronic illness. In later years, Congress greatly liberalized the eligibility rules for disability pensions. Retirement at age 62 was extended to men in 1961, and over a period of years the base was broadened to include military personnel, the self-employed, and farm workers. Hospital insurance (Medicare) was created by a 1965 law which took effect in 1966.

In 1940 Social Security had covered only 58 percent of the labor force.

By 1975 the system included 90 percent of all workers. Federal workers were exempt, while state, local, and nonprofit agencies were in or out by choice. Benefits flowed to 89 percent of those over age 65, showing the system's intended coverage had become reality.[10]

By January 1983 Social Security had a membership and payout picture that looked like this:

Category	No. of recipients	Average $/month
Male retirees	11,110,705	$471
Female retirees	9,777,337	363
Retirees' spouses	3,050,073	213
Retirees' children	559,990	166
Disabled male workers	1,735,650	485
Disabled female workers	853,874	349
Disabled workers' spouses	361,444	129
Disabled workers' children	993,339	128
Deceased workers' widowed parents	514,751	303
Deceased workers' children	2,323,093	286
Workers' widows and widowers	4,491,731	379
Disabled workers' widows and widowers	113,871	242
Deceased workers' parents	12,370	335

The total of the above was almost 36 million checks a month in an average amount of $373—$156 billion a year.[11]

In 1940 the first checks went out to 222,488 persons. By 1945 the system had 1.3 million beneficiaries. The number grew to 3.5 million by 1950, to 15 million by 1960, and to 26 million by 1970.[12] The years from 1940 to 1975 might be thought of as an era of good feelings. "In theory the system was always supposed to be 'pay as you go,' but in fact, a strong bipartisan coalition was formed in Congress dedicated to expanding benefits every two years. Throughout the late 50s and 1960s, Social Security debates were a pleasure for Congress."[13]

In that golden age, recipients were numerous enough to form a large and grateful voting block. But they were comfortably outnumbered by active workers contributing to the system. And inflation was low enough that comparatively modest hikes in pension amounts were enough to make retirees' purchasing power whole again.

A fateful moment came in 1972. Congress raised the basic benefit by 20 percent and provided automatic, full adjustments whenever inflation, as measured by the Consumer Price Index (CPI), rose more than 3 percent a year.

For years the Social Security retirement fund had run a large surplus, and actually served as a useful source of loans to the general Treasury. In 1972, inflation was only 3.3 percent. But it had been 5.9 percent in 1970 and 4.3 percent in 1971. Automatic cost-of-living adjustments (COLAs) appealed not only to liberals worried about pensioners' real income. They also made sense to conservatives as a way of insuring that future hikes merely held the value of benefits steady. This seemed to foreclose the risk of ad hoc generosity the nation could not afford.

As for the one-time 20 percent increase, defenders said it must be measured against the relatively austere beginnings of Social Security. Critics said it would transform the system into "exactly what Franklin Roosevelt never intended it to be: the primary source of income for most of the aged." Did this not go far beyond what FDR meant when he said the plan would provide "some measure of protection to the average citizen . . . against poverty-ridden old age"?[14]

Political analysts looked at the prime movers behind the boost. They saw House Ways and Means Chairman Wilbur Mills embarking on what proved to be a brief and futile quest for the presidential nomination. They saw incumbent Richard Nixon only too happy to sign the bill and siphon off the credit.

The new CPI-based COLA took effect in 1975. Murphy's Law stepped in. From 1975 to 1981 America saw some of the fastest inflation rates in its history. The maximum annual benefit climbed 200 percent. Not only inflation, but an expansion in wages covered by Social Security, and a defect in the CPI, were also involved in this explosion. The CPI overstated the impact of soaring home prices and mortgage rates on retirees, only 9 percent of whom were even still paying on a mortgage.

The next effect of these factors was to raise the value of the average Social Security check, for persons retiring at age 65, from one-third of final pay in the early years of the system to 55 percent in 1981, all of it tax free.[15]

Looking back on the years 1940–75, it is tempting to divide this era of good feelings in two parts: the years of moderation (1940–64) and the years of extravagance (1965–75). The surge in covered employment and in benefits during that decade could not be sustained.

Indeed, the reversal was sharp. "Within a few short years, the combined effects of a faulty benefits formula, double-digit inflation, and the deepest postwar recession had pushed the system close to insolvency."[16] Stagflation illustrated some brutally simple arithmetic: for each 1 percent increase in unemployment, the system loses $3–4 billion a year in revenue.[17] For each 1 percent rise in inflation, the system pays out $2 billion more in benefits.[18]

In 1977, amidst estimates of the date funds would run dry, President Carter and the Congress adopted changes intended to carry the system comfortably into the next century.

First, they corrected a provision which had proven enormously costly in a period of high inflation: the "double indexing" of benefits for growth in both prices and wages. Then they took steps to make early retirement less attractive in the future (by granting a COLA that equaled but did not exceed inflation) and late retirement a better deal (by providing a pension bonus and by raising allowable earnings). These changes were important because delaying the average age a person leaves the workforce is a major "lever" on pension costs.

But most of the gap between Social Security spending and income was covered by hiking the payroll tax on workers and their employers. That negligible $30 a year, which had gone to $45 in 1950, had already risen to $1,071 for 1978. What the new law did was to change the future maximums. By 1981 the bite would be 43 percent bigger, and by 1987 more than 50 percent bigger, than previously scheduled. Specifically, the maximum $1,071 for 1978 would have gone to $2,012 in 1987 under the old law. Now it was headed for $3,046—or $6,092 if both worker and employer shares were included.[19]

Predictably, there was an outcry. Aside from the obvious complaint about taxes, analysts concluded "the Social Security time bomb is still ticking." A major concern was that the extra revenue came mostly from raising the wage base subject to taxes. This meant more money in the short term, but more of an obligation for the system to replace working income in the long term. Higher paid members would have more of their final pay covered by Social Security because of the change.[20]

Critics saw a heavy new burden imposed on workers' incomes and then even greater funding pressures down the road. Looking at the added taxes in the coming ten years, the *Wall Street Journal* observed, "A few more $227 billion victories like this one and we are undone."[21] To *Business Week*, "the ineluctable lesson of recent events is that Social Security can no longer be a positive sum game in which everybody wins and nobody loses."[22] The era of good feelings had ended.

PIN THE TALE ON THE ELEPHANT

From January 1981, President Reagan's political skills discomfited the Democrats. But there was one issue on which they almost always were able to catch him at a disadvantage: Social Security. Because it provided such guaranteed gratification at a time when such satisfactions were rare, the program became a political lightning rod. But as zinging the President grew to such sport it came to carry the risk of zapping the chances for reform.

In fairness, some admixture of genuine moral outrage was always present in congressional Democrats' attacks, as the White House showed itself unusually inept by springing "solutions" that could be portrayed as insensitive. The Social Security debate of 1981–84 was long on color and short on candor. The new "negative sum game" put key players in an ill humor.

THE DETROIT FREE PRESS

SHAPE UP, BUDDY...

HOUSE SOCIAL SECURITY PLAN

REAGAN SOCIAL SECURITY PLAN

Cartoon by Hyman. Copyright 1982, The Tribune Company Syndicate.

Reagan's problems began immediately. Even before he took office, the specter of 1977 was being raised: "Social Security four years later—it's time for another rescue." [23] Analysts vied with one another in estimating which calendar quarter the fund would run dry, and by how many tens of billions it would be in deficit in each future year. These numbers were to fly back and forth in bewildering profusion until early 1983 when yet another "solution" was adopted to carry Social Security into the next century—and quickly fell under the analytical knife for a dissection of its defects.

The 1977 reforms didn't do the job because Social Security was hit by the arithmetic of the "misery index." The four hard years which followed that rescue drained the fund as soaring prices boosted benefits while rising joblessness cut receipts. 1981 and 1982 were marked by deepening recession and uncertainty over whether the Reagan-Volcker anti-inflation plan would work. These years formed a dark background for a bitter debate.

In December 1980, all the experts were laying their proposals on the table. "The trouble is that for every idea that sounds reasonable, there are a dozen arguments by critics about why it won't work or why it shouldn't be done." [24]

On January 1, 1981 the biggest Social Security tax hike in history went into effect—a legacy of the 1977 rescue. Workers at the top end were hit with almost $300 in added withholding. Yet, "the extra $15 billion in revenue is not likely to offset the fund shrinkage caused by inflation and unemployment." [25]

"The Social Security system hovers over the revelries of the new Reagan administration like the ghost of budgets future," observed an editorialist.

"Nowhere in Washington is there a sharper reminder of how tough it can be in hard times to keep promises that were made in good times."[26]

A special commission Carter had appointed in 1979 made three "radical" proposals, two of which would later become law. Their suggestion for taxing benefits was rejected by Reagan "in 40 seconds," according to the White House. "No, they paid taxes on that money when they sent it in," said the President. As for the suggestion that the normal retirement age be raised from 65 to 68 some time between 1990 and 2002, it was dismissed by congressional spokesmen as "voguish." A third idea, to establish minimum, mandatory private pensions funded by a 3 percent tax on employers only, was bizarre enough to vanish without comment. Thus it was that the work of the President's Commission on Pension Policy sank like a stone.[27]

In March 1981 *Business Week* contrasted the Reagan Administration's avowed "commitment to a comprehensive, long-range economic program" with its inability to "come to grips with . . . Social Security." The problem was an "aversion to tampering with basic retirement benefits on the one hand and to raising taxes on the other"[28]—an aversion that was to be only too well justified by political events.

Meanwhile, Congressman J. J. Pickle, who with Senator Robert Dole was a beacon light of sanity and moderation during the dreary debates of 1981–84, warned against projections which technically would allow the system to squeeze by. "The last four administrations have told us 'the situation is bad now but it will be all right in three or four years.' We just don't believe that anymore."[29]

On May 8, 1981 the Senate voted to save almost $8 billion in fiscal 1982 outlays by making unspecified cuts. The betting was these would turn out to be mostly delays or other trims in the COLAs, suggested by Senator Ernest Hollings. While backing the changes, Dole said half-jokingly, "Voting to cut Social Security benefits is the last thing you do on your last day in the Senate."[30]

May 12, 1981 was a fateful day in the Social Scurity debate. President Reagan announced his proposal. Some saw "a program drawn with careful attention to the political power of . . . a segment of the population with unusually high voter participation." The plan avoided permanent COLA reductions (though there was a one-time delay) or payroll tax increases. But in skirting these mines it stepped on another. The big savings, $17 billion between 1982 and 1986, would come from slashing the benefits for those who retired at 62. Instead of 80 percent of the amount available at 65, they would receive 55 percent. And the change could take effect in 1982.[31]

Congressional reaction was swift. Senator Moynihan produced a resolution to condemn Reagan's "breach of faith" (a phrase that was to enjoy all-purpose use in the coming debates). How could the White House imagine rewriting the rules for those whose retirement was only a few months ahead? The President was "saved" from Moynihan's blistering rebuke only by a scarcely less sharply worded resolution drafted by Senate Republicans. By a 96-0 vote, this passed as a vow that the upper house would reject any proposal which would "precipitously and unfairly penalize early retirees." With elegant understatement, Senator Dole commented, "Some of the things the President suggests have great merit, some have less, a few have little." [32]

Why did the White House not sense its proposal would blow up? The case was one which every administration has known—secrecy in planning, haste in preparation, inadequate briefings. The process was driven partly by fears that Pickle would produce a bipartisan House bill without Administration input, and partly because of the hope that swift cuts in Social Security spending would help calm financial markets upset about a growing deficit. [33]

This latter theme caused great mischief. It led to the idea that Reagan was interested in cutting pension costs not to make the system sound again, but to balance the budget. This was a major reason why "the Congressional opposition abandoned its policy of appeasement and began to gear up for total war." Said Speaker Tip O'Neill, "I'm not talking about political issues. I'm talking about the decency of it. It was a rotten thing to do." [34]

The swift crackdown on early retirement was a blunder from which the Administration quickly retreated, and which faded into the general background of political ill-will. But reform of disability retirement, authorized

Cartoon by Haynie. Reprinted by permission: *Louisville Courier Journal*, 1981.

under an existing law, became a sort of ongoing nightmare for Reagan's policymakers. It generated fresh shockwaves for years to come.

The inception of what was to become an infamous crackdown occurred under Carter's presidency. The disability rolls had grown from 1.2 million at the program's start in 1967 to 2.8 million by 1980, when Congress passed a bill calling for careful review of the caseload. The General Accounting Office in 1979 estimated from a sample of cases that about 20 percent of the caseload was ineligible and $2 billion in improper payments were being made each year.

The specific problem was a failure to review cases where disability wasn't permanent. The law said this was to be done every three years. But the review cycle slipped; hence, GAO's finding.

Enter the Reagan team. Armed with the 1980 mandate, caseworkers studied the files of over 400,000 recipients between March 1981 and June 1982. Almost half, 191,000, were ordered dropped from the rolls. Some 64,000 of these had their cases overturned on appeal. An added 800,000 cases were set for review in fiscal 1983.

The explosion in workload caused reviewers to take shortcuts. They held few face-to-face interviews with those about to be cut off. They worked from files and did not obtain proof of medical improvement before disqualifying beneficiaries. Not surprisingly, a minor industry arose within the legal profession encouraging claimants to file appeals. A backlog of cases before 700 administrative law judges grew to 143,000 by June 1982. As a result, many of those terminated saw their three-month grace period of benefits dry up before they got a hearing.[35]

The horror stories were, of course, dramatic. They included a dozen suicides—one from a shotgun blast in front of the local Social Security office.[36] Social Security Administrator John Svahn conceded that "mistakes have been made. . . . We're very concerned about this." An effort would be made to avoid removing eligible clients from the rolls, such as the person who died while making an appeal and was reinstated post mortem.[37]

But somehow the reviews continued at what was felt by many to be an excessive, even zealous, pace. Congress was torn between three concerns. First, there really were many ineligible people on the rolls. Deputy Commissioner of Social Security Paul Simmons put the ratio at one-third of all recipients—$4 billion in annual benefits for 1982.[38] Second, the appeals process was severely clogged. Congressman Pickle introduced a bill in July 1982 which would sharply limit the use of new evidence on appeal and would curtail the power of judges to overturn lower-level decisions disqualifying recipients.[39]

Finally, the rate of initial denials was almost half the cases reviewed, not the one-third estimated as the ineligible portion. Senator William Cohen remarked, "The implementation of this law has created chaos and inflicted pain that Congress neither envisioned nor desired when it enacted what was meant to be a sound management tool."[40]

In September 1982 the Administration ordered a partial halt to the reviews. However, this turned out to mean a 20 percent drop in the cases scheduled for 1983. Instead of 806,000 reviews, there would be 640,000. But this was over 100,000 above the 1982 workload.[41]

In June 1983 District Judge William Gray of the 9th Circuit Court ruled the government had been operating "outside the law" because it had not obtained evidence of medical improvement before removing people from the rolls. He ordered Social Security to send notices to all those who had lost benefits in the last three years, telling them they could reapply for monthly payments.[42]

Administrators resumed payment of monthly disability income checks, but refused to include medical costs. Without Medicare coverage, recipients would be unable to hire their own doctors and prove they were disabled. At that point, they would be removed from the rolls.[43]

The Administration asked the 9th Circuit Court to block Gray's order. It also obtained a ruling from Supreme Court Justice William Rehnquist, later upheld by the entire Court, that Social Security could delay payment to the 30,000 to 35,000 persons affected by Gray's order, until the 9th Circuit made its decision.[44]

On February 22, 1984 the Circuit Court said administrators had been "evading" and "flouting" the law by terminating benefits without proof of medical improvement. The court said that many recipients were being "deprived of the very means with which to live" and "either died or suffered further illness" after losing their benefits.

Health and Human Services Secretary Margaret Heckler responded to the ruling with a "non-acquiescence" order, saying HHS disagreed with the Court's holdings and would not follow them. The government was expected to obtain a further delay in making payments by asking to extend Rehnquist's ruling to await the Supreme Court's own decision on the case.[45]

As the controversy became more intense, 26 states under court order or on their own refused to continue processing terminations (state agencies handle much of the initial casework).

On March 23 sources at HHS revealed plans for an 18-month moratorium on further reviews. Anyone whose case was on appeal could continue to receive benefits.[46] On March 27 the House passed, by a vote of 410 to 1, a bill by Congressman Pickle barring terminations if the government cannot show medical improvement. The bill also required a face-to-face interview before the initial removal decision and permitted receipt of benefits until an appeal has been heard.

Pickle said, "The disability program is in total chaos. . . . A moratorium cures nothing; it merely postpones reform."[47] The Administration opposed the bill, saying it had already moved to cure the problem.[48] The Senate passed its own bill by a lopsided margin but placed the burden of proof on the recipient, not on the government, as the House had done.[49]

The disability controversy has been like a poison gas attack on the Social Security front. It has made civilized warfare much more difficult. Compared to its protracted damage, the 1981 debate on minimum benefits (another overkill solution to a genuine problem) and even the exchange that year over early retirement penalties were no more than cameo fiascos for the Administration.

While these topics absorbed political energies, the fund's financing crisis ground steadily on toward D (for deficit) day. From the announcement of Reagan's package on May 12 to his naming of a bipartisan panel on De-

Cartoon by Borgman. Copyright 1982, King Features.

cember 16, 1981 was a period of growing stalemate. Analyzing the May 12 plan, the *National Journal* noted, "Students of the Social Security system have said that many of the proposals are reasonable and have credited the Administration with political courage for having advanced them, bringing an important issue to center stage." But the *Journal* found that "the general reaction has been highly critical" and was focused on aspects of the plan most vulnerable to attack, such as early retirement penalties.[50]

The President acknowledged his problem and, in a May 21, 1981, letter to congressional leaders, volunteered that he was "not wedded to any single solution" and invited them "to launch a bipartisan effort to save Social Security."[51]

Representative Pickle responded with characteristic forthrightness: "Congress just doesn't have any choice but to act." A contrasting theme, picked up by Representative Claude Pepper, was sounded by former Social Security Commissioner Robert Ball: "There is no reason for the severity of these cuts except to balance the budget." Liberal ranks split over these positions. The UAW and AFL-CIO sided with Ball; the American Association of Retired Persons went with Pickle. AARP's legislative counsel Peter Hughes called Ball's position a "head in the sand approach. I don't think anybody on the hill believes that something isn't going to have to be done."[52]

Hughes was wrong. On July 18 Senator Moynihan led off, challenging HHS Secretary Richard Schweiker, "Are we not being told, take away from the retired people of America, take it out of their household budgets, and put it into the President's budget, to make him look good?" Schweiker, angered by the implication that Social Security benefits would be cut to balance the budget, responded: "Not a penny of the trust fund will be used for anything other than Social Security checks." Noting the pension fund was by law separate from the general fund, Schweiker added, "I think you're trying to create the impression that one offsets the other. It doesn't."[53]

The President and Speaker O'Neill traded the coin of the realm on July 21, as the minimum benefit bill was coming to a vote. Reagan's "Dear Tip" letter said House Democrats were engaged in "opportunistic political maneuvering, cynically designed to play on the fears of many Americans." Reagan said O'Neill had brought the bill up "to exploit an issue rather than find a solution." In a letter of reply, the Speaker observed that it was "unconscionable" for the President "to create and exploit fears about the [financial] fate of the Social Security system so as to make deep cuts in benefit levels."[54]

On September 16, Reagan demanded "blood, sweat and tears" in a new round of budget cuts, including a three-month delay in the Social Security COLA (from July 1 to October 1, 1982). Budget Director Stockman signaled other cuts in food stamps, Medicaid, housing, welfare, and other programs. "We cannot fund the Great Society. Substantial parts of it will have to be heaved overboard." O'Neill's comment: "We will not let the President wreck the Social Security system."[55]

The Administration found itself in a growing bind. "On the one hand, the public and congressional furor that greeted its proposals to cut back drastically on early retirement pensions and other benefits has made it reluctant to offer any new substantive proposals. On the other hand, cutting the massive federal budget has become the acid test of credibility [for its] economic program."[56]

Why should the Democrats rush in to help extricate the President? "There's nothing we would like more than to see the Republicans slip on the old banana peel again. I don't think the Democrats want to strut the bipartisan tango quite yet," said a House majority staffer.[57]

In October 1981 the President "hit upon the only approach to the high-strung issue of Social Security that has any chance of success." He would create a commission, whose members would be appointed one-third each by the White House, the Speaker, and the Senate Majority Leader.[58] On December 16 the Greenspan Commission was announced.

The war of words continued through the Christmas season. Reagan warned: "For too long, too many people . . . have been frightened by individuals seeking political gain through demagoguery and outright falsehood. This must stop."[59] O'Neill shot back: "Social Security is not in the dire, disastrous circumstances the Reagan people would have you believe."[60]

Each accused the other of scare tactics. The President said the Speaker wanted to scare off any talk of reasonable reforms by implying benefits would be ravaged. The Speaker said the President wanted to scare off those who found the current level of benefits proper so he could free up money to balance the budget.

The period from Reagan's 1981 inaugural to the 1982 congressional elections may be divided up like this on the issue of Social Security:

January 20 to May 11, 1981: Something must be done.

May 12 to December 15, 1981: Democrats sense an issue that can stop the Reagan juggernaut. They hammer on controversial parts of his May 12 plan. He seeks to shift the focus to bipartisan agreement. Mutual accusations, deepening stalemate.

December 16, 1981 to November 2, 1982: Democrats feel sure they have a winner. Notwithstanding their participation on the Greenspan Commission (which by design won't report until after the election) they decry Social Security reform as a Republican plot. In "one of the more egregious examples of partisanship" Speaker O'Neill orders Congressman Pickle to cease drafting a bill for the gradual phase-in of an increase in the normal retirement age. The reason: "O'Neill saw an opportunity to assail Reagan as an enemy of Social Security and he did not want the issue to be clouded by anything that could be interpreted as a Democratic plan to reduce benefits to anybody."[61]

The box score on November 2: Republicans lose 26 House seats, 8 to 10 of them on the Social Security issue. Recalls senior GOP Representative Barber Conable, "It was a disgusting experience. My opponent would say, 'Conable wants to cut your benefits!' and I would shout, 'No I don't.' Then afterwards, the little old ladies would come up to me and say in a quivering voice, 'Why do you want to cut my benefits?' It was . . . no dialogue, just accusation and denial."[62]

After the election, longer-term effects were assessed: "The Republicans deserved to have the Democrats try to wring their necks with the Social Security issue during the 1982 campaign. But the Democrats overdid it and

Cartoon by MacNelly. Reprinted by permission: Tribune Media Services, Inc., 1982.

possibly created a monster—a political panic so powerful that Congress may be unable to enact the Social Security reforms that all its leaders know are necessary."[63]

The Commission had of course been doing its work in this increasingly heated political atmosphere. During the campaign season, its meeting schedule was leisurely: one session a month. After the election, it began to close in on proposals. But fears arose that the Commission, created to resolve a stalemate, would fall victim to a stalemate of its own. Republicans opposed higher payroll taxes and Democrats resisted changes in automatic cost-of-living increases. Commission member Senator Dole urged his colleagues to "fashion a compromise in which every one of the special interests would be displeased."[64]

Politicians began to speak of Social Security as the "third rail"—touch it and you're dead. Rudolph Penner of the American Enterprise Institute recalled "dozens of seemingly equitable and efficient solutions . . . have disappeared without a trace, and any politician who touches the issue faces the danger of disappearing with them."[65] But Penner also noted that "the most hopeful thing about the Commission is that it has politicians on it." This was vital because "the only changes that can be made are changes that will not provoke violent revenge by the voters on legislators who enact them."[66]

In late November, there was movement. Senator Moynihan, who had "long made political hay" from the issue, offered to break a growing deadlock by agreeing to lower COLAs if the Republicans would go for accelerated tax hikes.[67]

But stalemate set in again as the panel tried to move toward details. It was felt that only the personal intervention of the President and the Speaker could restore momentum. They demurred. The President said, "For me to impose myself on the commission and say, 'Hey, fellows, this is the way I want you to go,' I would then stand back, cock my ear and wait for the loud outcry from Capitol Hill, and the same old political football would be seen going up into the air like a punt on third down."[68]

From O'Neill there was silence. From Claude Pepper, the 82-year-old, newly named Chairman of the House Rules Committee who stumped the country for other Democrats in the fall of 1982, came this informative comment: "Fifty-two of those Democrats got elected and all of them pledged not to cut benefits." Pepper then gave a new definition to what was meant by cuts: "My interpretation is future benefits as well as present benefits."[69] In debate Pepper has extended the concept to its limits: no reduction in the rate of growth scheduled for any benefit, and no recipient, no matter what his or her age today, to be affected negatively by any future changes in law.

Such a view may seem to be nothing more than "after me the deluge." But it is made politically tenable because of the way issues have masked one another. The cash-flow crisis had to wait upon the bitter exchanges over Reagan's 1981 plan and the outcome of the 1982 congressional elections before it could get the attention it needed. And the awesome challenge of the next century, when the baby boom becomes the senior boom, has little chance of stepping into center stage in a decade of crises over cash flow, first in the pension fund and then in the health care fund.

The Greenspan Commission's recommendations were announced on January 15 and were quickly embraced by both Reagan and O'Neill. The 1977 plan was a "$227 billion solution"; this was a "$169 billion solution," which in the by now familiar phrase would "insure the solvency of the system" for 75 years.

Why was it that "both sides blinked" and enabled the Commission to approve a plan by 12 votes to 3? "Some of the Republicans were willing to give up the idea of a far-reaching solution. Democrats seized on the offer and, mindful of an economic outlook of less than abundance, proved willing to give on details. The product was a fairly straightforward compromise."[70]

The plan boosted revenues by adding rates above those scheduled in the payroll tax and boosting the rate for self-employed persons. It delayed the next cost-of-living hike from July 1, 1983 to January 1, 1984. These two steps were controversial, dealing with the two things politicians least like to do to Social Security—raise the payroll tax and trim the benefits.

But its other two major planks were almost revolutionary. They proposed doing things political wisdom said couldn't be done. One was to bring new federal workers into the system over the objections of a powerful union. The other was to tax half the benefits (representing money put in by the employer rather than the retiree) when a recipient's total income topped a given amount.[71]

Those skeptical of the plan's survivability warned that "a catalogue of those who would bear increased burdens under the compromise is almost a Who's Who of potent political constituencies."[72] Specifically:

—Each of the 115 million covered workers would pay substantially higher taxes.

—Employers would pay matching tax increases.

—Current recipients would face a six month COLA delay. Some would pay taxes on half their benefits.

—Newly hired federal workers would have to join Social Security instead of the more generous pension program that previous government workers enjoyed.

Chairman Alan Greenspan defended the plan in terms that have become the norm on pressure group issues: "None of this is any good except the conclusion. . . . That's why it is so terribly important that there be agreement that the total is acceptable even though none of the individual parts are."[73]

Greenspan's politic but excessively humble statement is eloquent testimony to the tactics necessary when one is about to be fire-bombed by groups only too willing to focus on the "individual parts" of a plan. In fact, every part of the compromise had its own merits. But because the obstacles were political, not technical, the chairman had to pretend he was offering a bunch of bad ideas that somehow in counterpoise added up to a good idea. This was the olive branch for those who were sure to be offended by one or more specifics.

"The Commission's proposals will now go to the Congress, where they will be attacked by interest groups. Their demands will be modest: simply eliminate the proposals affecting them," observed a voice of experience, Milton Gwirtzman, who chaired the National Commission on Social Security from 1979 to 1981.[74]

Speaker O'Neill found some provisions "an injustice to the golden-agers and senior citizens."[75] Chairman Pepper said "I will not support the package if we put one item in there cutting benefits."[76] What may have saved the plan was that "opponents have no common interest around which to build an alternative."[77] To Representative Conable, "It is the kind of gut-wrenching agreement which often translates into legislation that sails through Congress."[78] And that is basically what happened. The Commission's suggestions were adopted with few changes.

Seen from the perspective of the bitter debates over Reagan's 1981 package, of the hard feeling left by O'Neill's use of the issue in the 1982 elections, and of conventional wisdom about the politically possible, the Commission's plan boldly broke new ground and, more notably, proved able to dodge the silver bullets and win approval. Seen from the longer term, its claim as a 75-year solution rested on thin margins of error in the assump-

'THIS IS NO POT OF GOLD, HENRY—THERE'S NOTHING IN HERE BUT THESE TWO SILLY LEPRECHAUNS!'

Cartoon by Oliphant. Copyright 1983, Universal Press Syndicate.

tions made for Social Security costs and income. "Major concessions had to be made to get bipartisan agreement," observed one analyst. "The result was a weak solution."[79]

Except for the festering disability review problem, Social Security puttered along politically for a year and a half after the rescue package was enacted. In March 1984, Reagan made a vague reference to "revamping" the program to make sure it was fair to younger workers. O'Neill shot back, "President Reagan has had a lifelong itch to tamper with Social Security. This week he started scratching again."[80]

In May Treasury Secretary Regan suggested it might be necessary in the future to curb benefits for high-income retirees. This set the Democratic hounds off in full cry. Senate Minority Leader Robert Byrd called Regan's comment a "pre-election glimpse" of GOP intentions. "Trusting the Reagan administration to protect Social Security after the November election is like hiring a self-proclaimed pyromaniac to guard your firewood," Byrd said. Claude Pepper solemnly intoned that adopting Regan's idea would mean "the program has changed from social insurance to welfare."[81]

In reality the benefits of upper-income recipients are already being siphoned off—through the 1983 tax change. And the system is not social insurance but an "intergenerational transfer"—a term akin to welfare (see pages 223–24).

Playing off the Reagan and Regan comments, O'Neill and Pepper on July 10 demanded the President make what they called "a full disclosure statement" of his intentions, before the election.[82]

Reagan did not respond directly to O'Neill and Pepper, whom insiders say are the only two politicians "able to get under the President's skin."[83] Instead, the President took direct action to show "the golden agers and senior citizens" he could be trusted.

In 1972 when automatic annual benefit hikes went into law, a little-noticed provision said that if inflation was below 3 percent, there would be no COLA. Benefits would stay where they were, but in the first year that the total price jump was 3 percent or more, the entire COLA would be made up. Thus, low inflation would delay but not deny a full hike.

This provision was a dead letter in the economy of the 1970s. But along comes the Reagan-Volcker anti-inflation program. It works so well that by 1984 Administration economists are looking at a possible annual rate of 2.9 percent. It so happens the number would be announced in late October—just days before the 1984 election. To have no hike for the first time in history would be bad news. "Politicians hate a benefit vacuum and President Reagan rushed to fill this one."[84]

Faster than a Democrat could say, "betrayal of trust," the President called on Congress to amend the law and grant a 1985 COLA no matter how low the rate of inflation. Senator Moynihan popped in a bill which his colleagues were persuaded to pass by a vote of 86 to 3. The House contemplated delicious options. If a 3 percent hike was fair game, why not the 4.5 percent originally budgeted, or even more, based on some new principle of equity for the "golden agers"?

The dark side is that a 3 percent hike equals a one-time net cost of about $3 billion, with $300 million in added interest payments each year until the federal debt is paid. To grant the COLA meant forcing a tax hike of about $2 billion on some 7 million workers. This offset part of the $5 billion increase in benefits.[85] But "Reagan's action raised anew the question of whether he or any other President can conquer the problem of reining in entitlement programs. . . . By seeking to waive a benefit restraint already in law, Reagan has jeopardized . . . the difficult job of bringing the budget under control."[86]

From the perspective of fiscal responsibility, the case is indeed a melancholy one. But as a historical footnote, all the players are perfectly in character. The actions of 1984 were an exact replay of a forgotten chapter in 1981.

The existing CPI badly overstated the rise in seniors' living costs in the late 1970s. In March 1981 the Senate Budget Committee was ready to make a change. The President personally quashed the move, saying he had promised in the campaign not to change the basis for benefit hikes. Among those expressing their dismay was Alan Greenspan. That year the formula was based on inflation of 11.2 percent, or about $20 billion for Social Security recipients. Scarcely a week later, the White House dismissed a proposal by Senate Republican leaders for a two-year freeze on COLAs as part of a deficit-cutting package. Budget Director Stockman strongly defended the

President's action: "Indexing is a good thing in the kind of inflationary environment we live in today, unless you want to totally destroy the value of those benefits that people earned and solve the inflation problem at the expense of those who can least afford to pay the price."[87]

This was Stockman the presidential spokesman, using many of the same words Reagan was to use in 1984. Stockman the fiscal analyst might have noted the over-stated index, the small portion of benefits paid by the recipient (see page 233), and the actual economic condition of the elderly vs. other age groups (see page 231). But in March 1981 he was speaking to placate the largest voting block in America—23 million senior citizens.

Cartoon by MacNelly. Reprinted by permission: Tribune Media Services, Inc., 1982.

"Which political leader is willing to bite the bullet?" asked *Time* magazine in May 1982. "The answer right now seems to be nobody, because every suggested solution will offend some powerful group. But the reconciliation of conflicting interests is the real art of politics. In this case, some form of reconciliation is a social necessity."[88]

Since 1982 there have been some relatively bright moments, the Greenspan Commission for example, and some backsliding such as the benefit bidding of July 1984. The "social necessity" for responsible action remains. As Congressman Pickle commented of President Reagan's stunning move on the COLAs, "Good election-year politics is not always responsible public policy."[89]

PENSION PROMISES AND THE SOCIAL FABRIC

What is fair? What is responsible? These are the crucial questions. To answer them one must step back from the politics of the moment and, to the degree possible, one must also seek distance from the ideologies that drive political debate.

What was Social Security meant to be? What has it become? Do either match what it should be?

These questions would be easier to answer if the system had begun and remained an insurance program in which workers' contributions were deposited to earn interest and held in trust for their own retirement. It would then have been possible to build in both a mandatory basic pension plan and an optional plan that would pay extra in return for higher payroll tax contributions over the years. Some experts, as we shall see, are struggling to create these features—no simple task half a century into the system's history.

"The aged have been misled for two generations into believing that Social Security payments constitute no more than a return to them of the payroll taxes that they have paid during their working years. This is dramatically untrue. From the very first, benefits have been paid out of taxes deducted from the paychecks of people working that year. They in turn have to rely at their retirement on benefits from taxes paid by their children's generation."[90]

Things have worked out this way partly because the early cost estimates were wrong (example: in 1935 the system was projected to spend $1.2 billion in 1980; instead, it spent $103 billion). But in part Social Security was designed from the outset to transfer income.

The 1935 law said benefits would begin to flow in 1940. Thus, the first recipients had paid in for only five years. Yet they received pensions based on 35 years of contributions. Not until the end of the 1980s will a majority of beneficiaries have actually paid in the system for that many years.[91] This is one reason why the average retiree gets his or her contributions back five times, with interest.

Other decisions were made on the basis of compassion and clearly waived the so-called "equity" policy—that recipients were being paid in proportion to their own deposits. The 1939 amendments added survivors and dependents; the 1956 amendments added disabled workers forced into early retirement; the 1972 amendments transferred existing welfare programs for the needy elderly, blind and disabled into Social Security.

None of these additions could be self-financing. But the term "Social Security" was becoming synonymous with freedom from want. The last of the three cases is most interesting. Supplemental Security Income (SSI) is funded from general revenues, not the payroll tax. Its benefits are based on need, not on previous earnings or contributions. The transformation of the

Aid to the Aged, Blind and Disabled program into SSI was simply to give it the dignity of an "entitlement" and make it vanish as "welfare." The symbolism of Social Security is so powerful that not only are its own welfare aspects denied but other programs that are explicitly welfare lose their "taint" when covered by the Social Security umbrella.

"Despite all evidence to the contrary, the system is still regarded by many as a pure contributory pension plan and not as transfer payments from the young to the old," observes Rudolph Penner. "All the jargon surrounding the system perpetuates this myth. Officially, payroll taxes are called 'contributions.' You 'earn' benefits by working. . . . Recipients feel that they bought their benefits; they paid highly for them by the sweat of their brows; and, by golly, they own and want to keep every last penny of their entitlements.

"One makes no impression whatsoever with arithmetic analyses which show that benefits received by current retirees imply a rate of return . . . far in excess of what could have been earned on private investments and far higher . . . than will be earned by future retirees." Penner calls it the Panama Canal syndrome: we bought it and we're going to keep it.[92]

Statements from spokesmen for the elderly bear Penner out. Harold Sheppard, associate director of the National Council on Aging, has a one-word description of benefits paid now and all the increases that may be needed to keep those payments abreast of inflation. The word is: sacred.[93]

Former Social Security Commissioner William Driver says, with a flourish, "Americans are rugged individualists who believe they've paid their own way for Social Security. . . . Any suggestion of financing this program through general revenues taints it as welfare-oriented."[94]

James Hacking of the American Association of Retired Persons says taxing the benefits of the well-off "could eventually turn Social Security into a welfare system. This is outrageous."[95]

An Associated Press-NBC News Poll taken in 1981 showed Americans opposed, by nearly three to one, to basing payments solely on need rather than primarily on payroll contributions.[96]

A series of events has nearly severed any link between reality and these attitudes and beliefs. First, contributions have always been based on what the fund needs now, not on what would be required to pay the member's own pension (this has kept the payroll tax far lower than it would have been). Second, none of the eleven categories of recipients added to the pension fund since 1935 have any hope of paying their own way. In nine of the cases, they make no contribution at all; in the other two, their working life is cut short by disability (see page 206). For this 40 percent of the caseload, self-funded benefits are not even a theoretical possibility.

Third, the surge of inflation, especially in the 1970s, "destroyed the current value of contributions made before 1970 and has eroded significantly the current value of contributions made since, while benefits have been fully indexed against inflation."[97] Rampant growth in the cost of living will undermine almost any pension plan. Social Security has been saved by its power to tax.

Finally, 1983 amendments began to tax half the Social Security benefits of upper-middle income retirees. The extra $227 billion brought in by the 1977 rescue plan came mainly from hiking the wage base subject to payroll taxes. But the plan obligated the system to eventually pay more in pensions to those at the upper end of the wage base. Now the higher-income bonuses from the 1977 law will largely be taxed away, after they are paid as benefits, by the 1983 law. Simply put, upper-middle income workers will pay more and get less than they would have in the past. The arithmetic clearly moves the system in the direction of welfare.

Some critics charge that "if we wanted a welfare system for the old, we should get it by means other than the regressive payroll tax."[98] What does this mean? Is it true?

A regressive tax takes a larger part of smaller incomes. The payroll tax is regressive in that it is not applied above the wage base ($37,800 in 1984) and thus the effective rate declines above that level. The tax also fails to touch investment income, which is often substantial for the well-to-do.

But there are also ways in which the tax is not regressive. First, it takes a constant share of earnings (7 percent in 1984) up to the maximum. For the 90 percent of workers earning income less than $39,300 in 1984, the tax was proportional, not regressive. More important, the tax code provides a break for low-income workers, the Earned Income Credit, which cuts their tax bill by as much as 10 percent. A basic purpose of the credit is to refund all or part of the payroll tax paid by the working poor.

On the benefit side, the impact is dramatically progressive. Social Security returns much more for each dollar paid by low-income than by higher-income workers.

Benefits are computed using AIME (average indexed monthly earnings). The mechanics of AIME make it clear that those better off won't get their money back as many times over as those down scale. This was true even before 1983, when a tax on benefits was applied to single retirees with income above $25,000 and couples with incomes above $32,000.

The aim of AIME is to make sure that as many recipients as possible are guaranteed an income floor for necessary living costs. Above that level, the portion of a worker's last paycheck replaced by his pension is much smaller. AIME is computed by excluding the member's five lowest-earning years. Then, twenty-eight remaining years are averaged and adjusted for inflation. This monthly income is replaced on a sliding scale that determines what the member's monthly check will be. As of 1984, the formula worked roughly like this:

—90 percent of the first $267 of AIME was replaced.
—32 percent of the next $1,345 of AIME was replaced.
—15 percent of all AIME over $1,612 was replaced.

A worker whose AIME is $1,000 will get a monthly check for $475. If AIME is $2,000, the pension rises to $728. The portion of income replaced is 47.5 percent in the first case and 36.4 percent in the second.

This is the way the system is supposed to work. Basic support dollars are the crucial part of income insurance. It is logical and proper that more should be replaced at the low end. But this progressive weighting of benefits should be kept in mind when critiques are made of the tax's regressive impact.

Indeed, we cannot have it both ways. The benefit structure already makes Social Security a much better return for those at the low end than for others. The tax could be similarly shaped for "fairness." But then we would have to finally admit that Social Security is indisputably welfare, clean and simple.

Here we come upon the need to be free of ideology. The preceding pages may seem to be building a case that the system is a rip-off or fraud, with the implication that benefits should be cut. But the system is neither a rip-off nor a fraud; it is a basic part of America's social contract.

Social Security does suffer, however, from being based on a myth: the myth of earned benefits. This myth was invented by the master politician who created the system. It was perpetuated eagerly by his liberal successors who approved the sentiment behind the myth, and defensively by conservatives who feared—all too correctly—that they would be fire-bombed if they dealt in alternative concepts.

What has proven crucial in political psychology is not that anybody actually paid for his benefits through his contributions. That happens only if a person is unlucky enough to die soon after retiring (in the first year if he is married; in the first 18 months if he is single). No, the crucial point is that everyone knows they have paid *something* into an earmarked fund which is obligated to pay a pension in return. The general public are not accountants or actuaries. Ratios of return mean little. Contracts mean a lot.

If one sets ideology aside, an interesting and important question can be examined: Would the needs of the elderly be as well or better met if it could be admitted that Social Security is a program into which vast amounts are paid and from which vast amounts are disbursed, with wide variations in taxes and benefits among the members of each generation, and even greater variations between the members of different generations?

The taxation of benefits brings the insurance concept to a final point of absurdity, if by insurance one means a monthly payment which bears a fixed ratio to one's prior contributions. Where Social Security really is insurance is in providing an income floor. It has succeeded in its original purpose. But to best match that purpose to the future we must come to grips with the most potent force in politics: fear.

The old assert their entitlement rights because they fear economic destitution. The young resent that assertion because they fear the system won't be there for them. Social Security is an intergenerational transfer system.

Cartoon by Meyer. Reprinted by permission: Meyer, *San Francisco Chronicle*, 1984.

Yet the generations have a vastly different picture of what it means for them. This is not a healthy political situation; it carries seeds of instability. But the steps required to restore confidence in both the adequacy of benefits and the affordability of taxes are modest indeed. They violate none but possibly the most extreme interpretation of the system's intent.

Let us examine the fears of the old and the fears of the young, and then look at the facts of their economic experience and their prospects. And let us imagine for the moment that Americans have let go of the myth that their benefits are based on an insurance contract instead of a social contract. Let us imagine we are all willing to figure out the best way to collect and spend $200 billion a year for retirement income security.

Rudolph Penner wrote objective, analytical pieces on Social Security when he was on the research staff of the American Enterprise Institute. His articles generated "much hostile mail" from older readers. Penner asked himself why.

One cause was the Panama Canal syndrome discussed on page 224. "The second strong emotion derives from a profound sense of insecurity among the elderly. . . . The threat of financial disaster because of serious illness or economic instability is ever-present. Many have a profound fear of becoming financially dependent on their children or on welfare. . . ."

A "curious statistic" regarding the elderly "may provide additional evidence of intense feelings of insecurity." They do not stop saving, but continue to accumulate assets. Rejecting the idea that they do this for their heirs, Penner says, "I suspect that they become more and more worried about the possibility of a financial disaster related to illness or other events, and they are saving for precautionary reasons."[99]

Time magazine reporters came to the same conclusion: "This opposition [to changes in benefit laws] is not driven by economic calculation but by plain fear of a poverty-ridden old age." They added that "the trouble for politicians, of course, is that the only people who are likely to vote for or against a candidate on the basis of this one issue are the aged, and they are passionately opposed to any tampering with COLAs."[100]

Penner's conclusion on the politics of reform: "It is time to underplay the Social Security problem. . . . The public discussion has been confused and irrational. It has left the impression that a drastic reform of the benefit structure is required. In fact we do not need a revolution. An evolution will do. I expect that even an evolution will be strongly resisted. . . . But the chances of success will be much greater if we stop making people believe we are about to deprive them of a very large part of their economic sustenance."[101]

How can fears be calmed? Perhaps we must consider making one admission and then taking two steps. The admission is that part of the problem lies in the realm of psychology and is beyond politics. It is that, for some, saving as a hedge against the unknown is wrapped up in a dread of the greatest unknown: death. Penner notes with amazement that "some evidence suggests [the] propensity to save *rises* with age!" Public policy cannot assuage those anxieties which spring from an attempt to outwit the adage "You can't take it with you."

But there are two policy changes which should be considered. First, the threat of catastrophic illness is real and it does carry the specter of economic destitution. There may be a useful link between reform of Medicare to do the job that most needs doing (see pages 200–1) and a reasoned dialogue on Social Security. If Medicare shifted its coverage to those costs that are truly destructive of financial well-being, it could remove a major fear that, among other things, works against pension reform.

Second, as Penner notes, no drastic reform of the benefit structure is required. What we do need is a gradual phasing-in of some changes to put long-term cost growth on a different path. These changes will in no case reduce the purchasing power of any current retiree's monthly pension check. Indeed, the impact on them and on those about to retire will be either slight or nil.

This raises a possibility. If discussions of long-term reform continue to be blocked by the fears of today's retirees, perhaps they should be explicitly held exempt from any change in the system. A defined group of those already retired or about to be retired could be "held harmless" so they would have no concern about the impact of any debate.

If this sounds extravagant, consider that the political system currently rushes to crank out benefit increases for this group, but agonizes to act on any restraints. Little would be forgone in savings opportunities; much might be gained in freedom for reform.

Would this lead to a two-tier system? We have already begun creating one through the 1977 and 1983 changes. Indeed, because the system was not soundly financed at the outset, there was a virtual guarantee that some workers later on would be picking up a bigger tab, both in absolute dollars and relative to their own benefits.

But isn't it dangerous to make this unequal treatment explicit? The question is probably best answered by looking at poll data. The fact is, today's younger workers have sensed the problem but have drawn a conclusion even more disturbing than what the facts warrant. In any number of polls, those under 50 have said, by margins of 55 to 75 percent, that they "have little or no confidence" that the Social Security system will provide benefits to them or to their spouses when they retire.[102]

To these Americans, the system is a fraud. It takes their money; it will vanish before they qualify for benefits. It is a Ponzi game: you collect the money in one window and shovel it out the other and, as in Charles Ponzi's concept, at some point the out window slams shut while the cashier runs off with the receipts.[103] Among other things, this cynical view is a great excuse for younger workers to get as much of their income as possible from the underground economy.

Which is better? To maintain a fiction nobody any longer believes—that retirees will forever get five times as much from Social Security as they paid into it? Or to admit that the rate of return will gradually decline—yet will still translate into a monthly check whose purchasing power equals those going out today? In short, it seems probable younger workers, if the case were clearly presented, would be willing to trade a moderate reduction in theoretical benefits for the assurance that the benefits which are promised will actually be paid.

The risk would seem to be worth it. Today, Americans' view of Social Security is, to borrow Mario Cuomo's phrase, "a tale of two cities." In the city of the old, there is a clinging to the status quo, a fear of change driven by an underlying fear of financial destitution. In the city of the young, there is rampant cynicism about a rip-off that takes their money and plans to disappear before they cross the finish line. The two cities do not form an enduring basis for America's most expensive social contract.

THE WELLDERLY

Whenever a congressional committee holds a hearing on any problem which government is supposed to help cure by legislation, the committee will not be lacking in an adequate supply of witnesses, from our 230 million citizens, whose personal experience illuminates that problem in the most heart-rending detail. The challenge for lawmakers in such cases is to balance between relieving individual hardship and the pitfalls of government by anecdote. More precisely, does the witness's story represent a large and general condition requiring relief through national law, or is it an atypical hand of low cards from the deck of life?

In the judicial branch, hard cases make bad law. In the legislative branch, hardship cases make bad law. The "hold harmless" strategy for change proposed above is offered despite certain facts: the elderly are much better off than they or most other Americans realize. They have improved their economic condition faster than any other group and now stand higher than several other groups.

The gap between perceptions and reality is dramatically revealed in a 1981 Harris Poll done for the National Council on Aging. Harris asked those over 65 to rate serious problems for the elderly, on the basis of their own experience. The same group, and another sample age 18 to 64, were asked to give their beliefs regarding how serious various problems were for the elderly in general. The findings show a large gap between the reality of problems experienced and the perception of their threat: [104]

Type of problem	Persons over 65: Is a problem for them	Persons over 65: Think it hurts others	Persons under 65: Think it hurts elderly
Lack of money	17%	50%	68%
Lack of health care	9	34	45
Poor health	21	40	47
Poor housing	5	30	43
High energy costs	42	72	81
Lack of transportation	14	43	58
Lack of jobs	6	24	51
Loneliness	13	45	65
Fear of crime	25	58	74

These numbers are a tribute to the compassionate nature of the American people. Those over 65 were two to six times more likely to mention a problem on behalf of someone else than in terms of their personal experience. Younger people showed a level of concern for others that was one-third higher still.

Thus, there is an objective cause for the gap between column 1 and columns 2 and 3. Each of us is one person who knows many persons. Column 1 can be read as "tell us about yourself," the other columns as, "tell us about everybody (and anybody) you know." The respondent has to keep in mind that he is being asked to measure a general condition. That's tough to do if you know of a vivid example. We're back to the problem of hardship cases and national laws.

A 1983 survey by the American Council of Life Insurance found that 70 percent of all adults do not expect that their retirement income will let them live comfortably.[105] Do the facts bear this out?

The 1970s were a time of dramatic improvement in the well-being of the elderly. Ironically, the cause was inflation, a force which is often assumed to hit retirees hardest because of their dependence on "fixed incomes." But it turned out that the value of Social Security was less fixed than were workers' wages. It not only kept pace with inflation, but outstripped the real cost-of-living rise for most seniors.

During the decade 1970–79, the average annual increase in income for households headed by a person over age 65 was 8.8 percent. This was matched by no other group. For those age 25 to 34, the gain was only 7.3 percent; for those age 34 to 45, it was 8.1 percent; for those age 45 to 64, the rise was 8.2 percent.[106]

Thanks largely to Social Security, the rate of poverty among the elderly dropped from 29.5 percent in 1967 to 15.7 percent in 1980. Says liberal economist Lester Thurow, "Social Security was a system designed to move us toward a world where the elderly were treated equally with the non-elderly. We have virtually reached that world."[107] Today, the gap in the poverty rate for seniors and that for all Americans is negligible.

The reliance of older Americans on earnings for retirement income dropped in half between 1950 and 1978, from 50 percent to 23 percent; meanwhile, their reliance on asset income fell from 29 percent to 19 percent. Social Security, the source of a mere 3 percent of the average retiree's income in 1950, rose to be the largest single source—38 percent of the total—by 1978. One measure of seniors' rising well-being was that public assistance fell from 9 percent to 2 percent of income over that period.[108]

During the 1970s wages for all workers doubled, Social Security benefits tripled, and the payroll tax quadrupled.[109] Even before the 1983 amendments, Social Security taxes were scheduled to triple again in the 1980s.[110]

Martin Feldstein estimated in 1982 that the benefits of an average recipient rose 55 percent faster than inflation in the 1970s, while average worker income stayed ahead of prices by only 2 percent.[111] Using a slightly different method, *Wall Street Journal* analysts came up with less favorable numbers for everyone, but the same pattern:[112]

	In constant 1977 $		
	1971	1981	$ Change
Average monthly Social Security benefit	200	256	+ 28
Average weekly earnings before taxes	191	170	− 11
Average weekly earnings after taxes	168	147	− 13

Clearly, in comparative terms, there has been an enormous increase in the value of grants and in the income gains of the elderly relative to other

Americans. But are the amounts enough? Thomas Borzilleri, a consultant to the American Association of Retired Persons, cited 1980 average Social Security benefits of $3,792 for single persons and $5,922 for couples. "Benefit levels this low are not sufficient to provide a particularly lavish standard of living, nor should they give rise to concerns that we are shovelling dollars at our affluent elders." [113]

These monthly grant levels seem modest, but they contain a striking amount of income replacement power. In the earlier years of the system, the percentage of a worker's last paycheck that was replaced by his first Social Security check hovered between 30 and 34 percent at the median income level. By 1973 it had reached 39 percent; by 1981 it had mounted to 55 percent.[114] And since Social Security benefits were and remain tax-free for any retiree whose total income is below $25,000, the replacement of actual, spendable income has been even greater. Feldstein sets it at 60 percent in 1970 and no less than 90 percent in 1982.[115]

Indeed, any retiree at this level of income replacement is likely to have more real income than the average worker. The reason is home mortgage costs. The surge in home prices and interest rates in the late 1970s gave a big boost to the Consumer Price Index. This translated into Social Security hikes. Ironically, the same surge tore into the disposable income of working families who were buying homes during those years, and tore into the hopes of families that could not afford to buy in a runaway market.

The CPI didn't adjust for the reality of reduced sales. Fewer people could qualify, fewer of those who were able to buy could stomach double-digit mortgage rates. But the CPI assumed the market was as active as before.

Seniors benefited from this error because, while 54 percent of all Americans make mortgage payments, only 9 percent of those over age 65 do so. They are either not in the homebuyer market or, more likely, have "burned the mortgage"—an experience not likely to be shared by many younger Americans. Those who are still paying have far lower payments than most other buyers.

The CPI overstatement was so bad that it was finally removed from the index—after most of the damage had been done. For example, of the $22 billion in federal budget costs to index transfer payments in 1980, an estimated $8 billion was due to exaggerations in the formula. Yet this benefit hike created a new base that was built in for all time.

Social Security has lifted many of the aged from poverty. This was intended. Social Security has wiped out the income gap between the average retiree and the average worker. This may also have been intended; it surely would satisfy the most ambitious hopes of those who launched the system. Social Security has proved a fabulous investment for those who have enjoyed a normal span of retirement. Here we encounter a difficulty—the "chain letter problem." Can anything that has been such a good deal in the past continue to be a fair deal in the future?

Cartoon by Wright. Copyright 1981, Jim Wright.

"What about a retirement plan to which one contributes at most $14,300 over a period of 30 years, and is able to retire at age 65 on $753 a month, or $9,000 a year, for as long as one lives? Sounds good, no? Anyone would want in, yes? It's Social Security, or at least it was. This particular plan is not available any more," writes S. J. Diamond of the *Los Angeles Times*.[116]

Diamond's figures are for a worker retiring in 1981 who put in the maximum payroll tax and is eligible for the maximum benefit. He has a life expectancy of over 16 years. This will return him about $220,000 if inflation averages 5 percent a year. He will get back over three times what his contributions would have earned on an interest-bearing investment. A worker at the average, rather than the maximum, level of tax and benefit will reap a fivefold return.[117]

These lopsided shares are of course reduced by half if the employer's contribution is included. Some economists believe this is not only good accounting but is required for fairness because the employer's share represents wages that would have otherwise been paid to the worker. Other economists dispute this and argue that the payroll tax on employers merely leads to fewer jobs because it makes workers so expensive to hire that companies are pushed to buy labor-saving machinery instead.

In short, it is clear that the employer's payroll tax represents income to the fund. Whether it also represents forgone earnings which the worker has the right to get back through Social Security is less certain.

If a worker pays into the fund from age 20 to age 65 and earns an average wage, his contribution plus that of his employer will nearly match the amount that would be needed to accumulate an equal nest egg through saving—$34,124 in taxes vs. $94,074 in benefits, as of 1982.[118] But even this arithmetic is blown by the fact that the bulk of his deposits didn't come in until those recent years when the payroll tax soared. And of course (this is the system's fault, not the worker's), when he did pay, the money was not invested at interest but shipped out to a then-current retiree. And if our average-income, 45-year worker has a spouse, the payback will be almost twice as great—$171,063, putting him safely on the plus side of the game.[119]

Can this go on? Or is it a chain letter that will run short of addressees, a pyramid game that will topple? The answer is already known. The return on investment for future recipients of Social Security is undergoing an inexorable deceleration. Stanford economist Michael Boskin calculates as follows: [120]

Year of birth	Net transfer received
Before 1913	$59,445
1913–22	41,126
1923–32	31,894
1933–42	18,242
1943–52	− 375
After 1952	"Large, negative"

Another estimate was made by Haeworth Robinson, former chief actuary of Social Security. He says those who are age 24 to 28 today will probably get back $1.15 per dollar paid by them and their employer. Tomorrow's new workers "should probably expect to receive less in benefits than can be provided by the total of employee and employer payroll taxes." [121]

"Until well into the next century, no Social Security recipient will have contributed more than a third—at most two-fifths—of what he will be entitled to in benefits," says Peter Drucker.[122] But after that there is a dramatic change. It is best illustrated by the exploding tax burden:

Year	Maximum income on which taxes are paid ("wage base")	Tax rate	Maximum tax
1937	$ 3,000	1.0 %	$ 30
1950	3,000	1.5	45
1960	4,800	3.0	144
1970	7,800	4.8	374
1975	14,100	5.85	825
1980	25,900	6.15	1,588
1985	39,300	7.05	2,771
1990	52,800	7.65	4,039

The escalation mirrors the pattern of outlays—46 years passed before the system spent $1 trillion; the five years ending in 1986 will require its second trillion.[123] But in fact the tax rate explosion is even more dramatic than the spending surge because the chain letter is running short of addressees. As recently as 1950, there were over 16 active workers paying taxes into the fund for each pensioner. In 1980 there were only 3.2 workers backing each check. This ratio is expected to drift slowly downward and reach 2 to 1 in the year 2030.[124]

The 1983 rescue plan was based on an estimated revenue need equal to 1.8 percent of the wage base. Congress ignored an estimate from the American Society of Pension Actuaries that the need equaled 2.5 to 3 percent of payroll for the pension fund and twice that for Medicare.[125] No one can be sure where these numbers will finally come to rest in the "twilight zone" of 75-year forecasts. But those who urge further reforms cite as a benchmark the prospect that if today's benefits are continued, the children of today's younger workers will have to contribute three times as much as their parents, a total employee-employer share equal to 25 percent of covered wages. The levy is now set to surpass 15 percent in 1990.

There is a fear that the tax is already so high it is aggravating the decline in number of workers per retiree. The Congressional Budget Office estimated the 1977 tax hike cost 500,000 jobs. Data Resources put the job loss at almost 1 million from the $82 billion added tax on employers during 1983–89 as a result of the 1983 law change.[126] Prior to that increase, the National Association of Wholesaler Distributors said the payroll tax bill for its average member was equal to 43 percent of net profits.[127] The new rates added about 5 percent more.

KEEPING FAITH

Social Security is an intergenerational transfer system. Today's workers agree to have money taken from their paychecks to fund the pensions of yesterday's workers. In turn they trust tomorrow's workers will do the same for them. For the agreement to hold, there need not be a promise that "every day in every way, things will get better and better." But there must be a sense of fairness and of stability. If experts report that they have "seen the future and it does not work," a vital element of trust is eroded.

"It is bad for this generation, blessed by a relatively small population of aged persons, to tie the hands of the next generation by leaving in place a set of benefits that will require ever higher taxes," said economist Henry Aaron, chairman of a 1979 federal panel that explored the future of Social Security.[128] Martin Feldstein pointed out that "as long as Congress can raise taxes to increase current benefits, it is open to pressure from beneficiaries to increase payments." Feldstein noted such pressure "would have been less effective had a trust fund been established."[129] Arthur Laffer argued that, "in general, moral solutions to economic problems also entail economically efficient solutions."[130]

Henry Aaron looked ahead in late 1980: "The short-term problem (cash flow) is critical but not serious because so many solutions are at hand and no one doubts Congress will act. The long-term financial problem on the other hand is serious but not critical."[131] Rudolph Penner came to the same conclusion in late 1982: "The funds need a cash infusion or a benefit reduction of between $60 billion and $127 billion between 1983 and 1987 to . . . pay all obligations without suffering severe cash flow problems. While these amounts appear large, they are not overwhelming relative to total benefits. In fact, current deficits pale beside those that will emerge under current law during the first half of the 21st century."[132]

What to do? One analyst who has probed the problem deeply and treated it as a social contract is Charles Schultze, former chairman of the Council of Economic Advisors. He asks to what extent Social Security should be an absolute guarantee and to what degree recipients should be asked to share with workers "the vicissitudes that periodically afflict the whole nation."

Schultze summarized his conclusions in the following way:

	Recipients should be protected	
Type of problem	in principle	automatically
Supply shocks	No, or partially	No
General inflation	Yes	Only partially
Long-term productivity slowdown	No, or partially	No
Recessions	Yes	Yes

In the above, "supply shocks" are special cases of inflation like the Arab oil embargo. "In principle" means in an ideal world without economic limits. "Automatically" means legally in a world of finite financial resources.

Schultze argues that the elderly poor should be given full protection against all four types of economic event. But other recipients can be made immune only by leaving the average worker to bear a double burden: from adverse events, and from the tax level needed to pay for undiminished pensions. Schultze has provided a superior framework for seeing the problem in terms of a social contract. He would leave to Congress the job of balancing between the benefits that would be extended in an ideal world and those that represent a fair sharing between workers and retirees in hard times.[133] Given the effective political organization of the elderly, this reposing of trust could defeat his intent.

A similar framework is used by University of Wisconsin economist Burton Weisbrod, who says "long-run feasibility demands we immediately begin to recognize that Social Security is not, and cannot be, a conventional insurance program. It is a profit-sharing program and, as such, will not pay a fixed level of benefits."[134]

The concepts of Schultze and Weisbrod may lack only one brand of logic: the political. One must hope that out of crisis may come the maturity which will give them that virtue of realism.

Congress may be able to take a cue from the people. A 1983 survey by Senator Slade Gorton found a surprising level of support for tough reforms. Some 33,000 Washington State residents replied to a long list of options. There was no yawning chasm of disagreement between those over and under age 60. Twenty concepts, all of which would cut benefits or raise revenues, were endorsed by 44 percent to 95 percent of respondents. Only two ideas were supported by less than half the survey and only one—taxation of benefits—got more "no" than "yes" votes from either age group. The other choices ran the gamut of virtually everything Congress has dared consider.[135]

The willingness to accept reasonable change, and the moderate degree of change required to make the system whole, argues for applying Schultze's framework and Gorton's list to the job of reform. Continued drift will deepen the darkest fears of the next generation: that Social Security is a trap, a snare, and a delusion.

The baby boom of 1946–60 has been likened to a pig moving through a python. This inelegant image first arose in the 1960s when the number of people age 14 to 24 grew by 50 percent in one decade vs. the typical 10 percent rate of increase. As the baby boom generation retires in the years after 2010, a "demographic twilight zone" is created because of the "senior boom"—a tidal wave of demand for health services and retirement income. Nobody needs a weatherman to see the storm coming.[136]

Former Social Security chief actuary Robert Myers believes "doomsday is so bad that, politically, it will never be allowed to happen." Congress will always do something to postpone the day of unthinkable tradeoffs between tax hikes and benefit cuts.[137] But a frustrated Michael Boskin hears a siren song from those who somehow believe 21st century fears are a fantasy. Boskin and others ask whether Claude Pepper, for example, really thinks there is no problem or whether he believes the best line of defense against benefit curbs now is to deny the prospect of difficulties later. As for a man who has joined Pepper in resisting long-term cuts "designed to solve a problem they say they doubt will ever materialize," Boskin comments of former Social Security Commissioner Robert Ball: "He has ruled out every severe option except the most severe of all—doing nothing about the long-term problem."[138]

In the same vein, Arthur Laffer finds "abhorrent and immoral" a commitment by government "to a specific course with specific promises and then, after people have, as a consequence, relinquished reasonable alternatives, reneging on that commitment."[139]

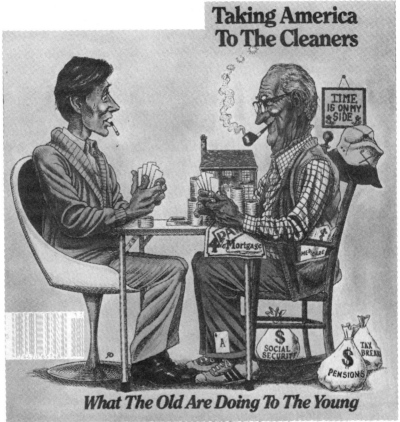

Reprinted by permission: *The Washington Monthly*, Washington, D.C., 1982.

Economist George Perry makes the same point in more detached language: "A surplus would head off the kind of [cash flow] problem Social Security confronts today [in 1982]. But it would not avoid the real hard choice for 2025, which will be to curtail either retirement benefits or other demands on the economy of that day, such as investment, housing, or consumption by workers. An individual can draw down accumulated assets without noticeable sacrifice by others in the economy. But the entire retired population cannot."[140] After peaking about 2020, the fund's assets are expected to plunge due to the surge in qualified retirees.

Some hopeful analysts see America's demographic shift as a problem that carries its own solution. Money will be freed up for pensions because less of it need be spent on families. Sociology and fiscal needs will mesh. The case is put forth by Ball and others that "an increasing number of elderly people to be supported will be offset by a smaller number of children to be cared for. That will allow more money to be spent on the elderly."[141]

The assumption is that the personal satisfaction and the social equity involved in this shift are at worst neutral. But for most people, there is a world of difference between taking on the responsibility of raising children and having the government remove an ever-larger payroll tax from one's earnings. It is the difference between choice and compulsion, between a personal and an impersonal relationship, between concluding the biography of yesterday's workers and launching the biography of tomorrow's.

Furthermore, the two functions may soon, may already, be at odds. Not in this context but in a statement of general concern against further payroll tax hikes, Rita Ricardo-Campbell of the Hoover Institution noted, "Many young families are paying such high taxes that they do not perceive they can afford to have children." [142]

This hints at a negative spiral: the higher the payroll taxes, the fewer the children, and thus the fewer workers tomorrow among whom the payroll tax might be spread.

A major benefit of Social Security thus far has been the reduction in intergenerational tension by giving the retired their own income base and reducing parents' dependence on their children. As the arithmetic of the system becomes more strained, timely adjustments are called for to avoid a new form of stress in which parents don't become grandparents because their children don't feel they can afford to have children of their own.

An unrestrained increase in the cost of Social Security can mortgage the future of tomorrow's young workers in an even more basic way: by adding to the deficit. There can be little doubt that this is the case, but it is often denied because the impact is at one remove.

Social Security is a "self-financing" system. Despite recurrent crises, the system has not relied on the Treasury for either general revenues or loans to more than a minor degree. The pension fund has shown huge projected deficits, before the 1977 and 1983 rescue plans were passed, and the hospital fund shows a huge projected deficit today. But except for a short period in late 1982 and early 1983, neither fund has actually run in the red.

Not only has Social Security not been in deficit, but the system is scheduled to be removed from the unified federal budget in 1992, at which time its financing should have no link at all to that of other federal programs. How, then, can one speak of an impact on the deficit?

The most obvious connection is Social Security's appetite for revenues that might otherwise have been used to reduce red ink in the federal budget. Payroll taxes rose from less than a tenth of federal revenues in 1950 to less than a fifth in 1970 to one-quarter of all receipts by 1981. [143] In the last four years, while other tax burdens eased, Social Security surged. Its share is now about 30 percent of the total and could reach a remarkable one-third of federal revenues by decade end.

This tax rise has been paced by the growth in Social Security and Medicare outlays as a proportion of all federal spending: from 1.8 percent in

1950 to 12 percent in 1960 to 18 percent in 1970. For 1980 the share was 26.4 percent; for 1982, it was 28.2 percent; for 1984, an estimated 31.5 percent.[144] These gains are still more striking when one recalls they are being scored within the same budget that includes a record defense buildup.

The result of such growth is "fiscal pre-emption," a foreclosing of other options. Many analysts believe the combined growth of defense and Social Security has the rest of the budget in a squeeze that will virtually eliminate discretionary spending on domestic programs or state-local assistance.

Fiscal pre-emption on the revenue side is equally potent. If there is a political rule of thumb that says taxes shall not exceed some share of GNP (roughly between 18 and 22 percent), then applying 6 to 7 percent, or even more of GNP, to social insurance taxes simply precludes their use to close the deficit within the taxing power that is available.

Payroll taxes have exploded because the system has no reserve funding. "A pay-as-you-go system is vulnerable to the slightest blip."[145] Blips come in the form of departures from the forecasts of inflation, unemployment, and longevity on which the system's costs are based.

Here is why the $227 billion rescue plan of 1977 was good for six years instead of seventy-five:[146]

Year	Consumer prices		Unemployment	
	Estimate	Actual	Estimate	Actual
1977	6.0%	6.5%	7.1%	7.1%
1978	5.4	7.7	6.3	6.1
1979	5.3	11.3	5.7	5.8
1980	4.7	13.5	5.2	7.1
1981	4.1	10.4	5.0	7.6
1982	4.0	6.1	5.0	9.7

Each 1 percent error in either inflation or joblessness costs the system $2 billion in higher payments or lost revenue. Even Robert Ball, a leading optimist on the system's prospects, said in 1981, "the problem is that the contingency fund wasn't kept large enough to see us through the kind of economic situation we've had in the last few years. The income has been less than anticipated, and benefits have been running higher than expected."[147] Former chief actuary Hayworth Robinson predicted in 1983 that "10 years from now . . . we [will] frantically search for solutions to [the next] 'surprise crisis.' We will resort, one more time, to hastily designed compromises."[148] Another former actuary told pension specialist Richard Styles that "because of the political climate, assumptions at times were used to ensure that the projections arrived at the desired results."[149]

The impact of such razor-thin margins on fiscal resources is an ever-present threat. Social Security is self-financing because it has been able to claim a vastly increased share of these resources. The tax capacity that might have been used for deficit reduction dwindles under these conditions.

Another danger is the lure and the potential trap involved in huge inter-fund transfers. This may be the trickiest matter in federal finance.

The pension fund, the hospital fund, the disability fund are separate. In the "good years" until the mid-1970s, each fund accumulated a substantial surplus. This was used in part to "bank" Treasury bills which could have been covered otherwise only by monetizing the debt (printing money) or selling more bonds to the public (with the risk of crowding out other borrowing).

From the war debt of the 1940s, through the 1960s, this operation of the social insurance funds was an important anti-inflation tool for debt managers. Now, of course, the situation is reversed. Fund balances have been drawn down. The Treasury can no longer look to the system to hold its notes.[150] Indeed, Social Security taxes and payouts have become part of the "budget problem."

Enter phase two of the interfund borrowing saga. Amazing as it may seem in light of today's concerns, part of the 1983 rescue plan was to permit the "sick" pension fund to borrow from the "healthy" hospital fund. That was a short-term cash flow device. Now it is Medicare that is looking at red ink—by 1990 if nothing is done, and a shortfall in the 21st century three times that predicted for the pension fund.[151]

The situation is made politically interesting and fiscally dangerous by a peculiar event heading our way. From 1990 to 2010 there will be a "false era of good feelings" for the pension fund. The baby boomers will be in their prime earning years, and payroll tax dollars will flow into the coffers. Meanwhile, retirements will come from the low-birthrate, Depression-era babies. The result will be an oasis between the cash crises of the 1970s and 1980s, and the "demographic twilight zone" of the 21st century.

Social Security actuaries project the reserve (loosely called a "surplus") to exceed $1 trillion in the late 1990s. There are three fears. One is that Congress will spend the money on benefit hikes, as happened in 1972 when the assumed flushness of the fund played a role in the 20 percent boost. Such an action at the turn of the century would set the stage for a senior-boom funding crisis after 2010.[152]

A second fear is that the fund would have so much money it could not invest such amounts without disrupting, perhaps even controlling, the economy. Not many share this concern, but one who does seems to suggest that for this reason alone, "we must see to it that the huge fund buildup . . . never takes place."[153] This is a peculiar conclusion, based on the inability to find an economic answer to a problem created by steps taken to meet an inescapable fiscal need.

The third danger is that, since the Medicare fund goes bust just as the pension fund gets flush, a great temptation will exist to "return the favor" of

1983 and start arranging ever-larger interfund transfers. This would lead to an appalling collision between combined resources and combined requirements after 2010.

Over a 20-year period beginning in 1990 the pension fund will accumulate a surplus equal to about one-half the national debt on the rest of the federal budget.[154] Is there a way to take prudent advantage of this remarkable event? Perhaps the safest course is for the fund again to become a major holder of Treasury bills, as it was for more than two decades after 1945.

This could be a useful strategy if three things of uncommon farsightedness are done. First, the breathing space thus provided will be used to work the budget out from under whatever deficit problems remain as of 1990. Second, the cost control steps required in health care will continue to be pursued. And third, the tax-and-benefit balance to fund pensions after the year 2010 will be worked out and set in law no later than the early 1990s.

This is a tall order. But it deals with the largest and most inescapable fiscal issues. When Social Security moves off-budget in 1992, its house should be in order. "Many congressional defenders of Social Security believe independent status would help protect it from budget cutters and politically motivated administrative decisions."[155] Behind these soothing words lies the potential for runaway fiscal pre-emption by the system unless reasonable ground rules are set beforehand.

TREND-BENDERS

There is some good news about Social Security. It is that small changes in provisions can generate big savings over time. The earlier these changes are made, the smaller they need be. We have started down the road on a number of reforms. Further movement along the same lines can bend the trends far enough to keep the system affordable in the 21st century.

Every rescue plan begins with an estimate of the gap between outgo and income if current laws were left in place for the next 50 to 75 years. The gap is expressed in terms of the added tax rate that would have to be applied to the wage base during that time to balance the system's finances.

This doesn't mean all the gap-closers are on the revenue side (though about 75 percent of the 1977 and 1983 rescues were based on higher taxes). Changes that reduce benefits are also expressed in terms of the pressure they would take off payroll tax rates.

Social Security actuaries produce three sets of estimates based on the best, most probable, and worst trends for major cost drivers such as inflation, unemployment, and life expectancy. The variation among the three sets can be 3 or 4 percent of payroll, or one-fourth to one-third the current total tax burden. The 1983 plan was said to solve not only a short-term cash crisis, but two-thirds of the long-term shortfall which was pegged at 1.8 percent of payroll. Other analyses put the problem as high as 6 percent of payroll.

There is a growing consensus that future rescues cannot be based 75 percent on taxes. Analysts have no trouble projecting hikes in existing rates to the point where they take 20 to 25 percent of payroll, or even more. The concern then becomes whether wage levels and job opportunities would actually hold up under such a tax burden.

The long-term problem can be dealt with entirely on the benefit side. Potential areas of change are reviewed below. But before examining specific ideas, let us consider a basic question: who should be affected by laws which reduce benefits below where they would be without a change in law?

There are three groups: the retired, the about-to-be retired, and those whose retirement is more distant. It is clear that those who have the most time to plan can, in fairness, be asked to accept the most significant changes in existing benefits.

But does this mean that those now or nearly retired are exempt from any share in the sacrifice? In Charles Schultze's thought-provoking social contract framework, the answer is that they are prudently shielded, but not exempt.

This is surely the most mature and just approach. Can the political system handle it? The American Association of Retired Persons has not been intransigent on all reforms. But it has lobbied hard for its members and has been uncompromising on many issues. There is no comparable Association of Unretired Persons which lobbies on 21st century pensions. But consider this comment of a respected congressman: "Barber Conable, weary and bent from previous battles (the year is 1980), is despondent about the prospects for heading off the long-term crisis. 'We should be able to design a system based on the facts of the baby boom. But it's going to take a Congress that's politically accountable, and this Congress is not. This craven collective will break and run as soon as they get 300 letters on a subject.'" [156] Make that three million letters and you have the AARP.

The years since 1980 have been no better. At times, House Speaker Tip O'Neill has seemed to be a sort of Caspar Weinberger of Social Security, championing the sanctity of the status quo and quick to equate the search for a better way with the betrayal of a public trust. He has alternated between insisting everything is all right and asking for more money to put in the system.

Today's retirees receive benefits based on overstated cost-of-living adjustments in the decade after 1972. The accident of double indexing was removed in 1977, but five years of its impact are permanently imbedded in the base. Tomorrow's retirees are caught in a cruel dilemma of funding this generation's pensions and then funding a share of their own as well.

All this argues for providing a COLA of something less than inflation

Cartoon by MacNelly. Reprinted by permission: Tribune Media Services, Inc., 1982.

over the next few years. This would represent current retirees' modest "give back" of benefits to those who must bear the double burden that is coming. Will such a sacrifice be made willingly? Almost certainly not. Will it be imposed? Not if Congress is unable to grow beyond Conable's "craven collective."

At a certain point, those who want to get on with the business of reform may have a decision to make. The ability to make adjustments in the systems' provisions has been limited by seniors' lobbying power. Sometimes this power acts against the direct impact of change. At other times it seems to be based on a "domino theory." Representative Pepper, for example, appears to hold the view that today's benefits are best protected by denying any need for tomorrow's reforms.

The freedom to move ahead can be purchased at the price of sparing current retirees from the impact of proposed changes. This creates a basis for removing the senior lobby as a central party in the debate on what those changes ought to be.

The price of a "hold harmless" clause is significant in financial and even in moral terms. But it might be worthwhile if the price of further delay appears greater. Some experts feel the need for reform is already acute. "The next Social Security crisis is already on the horizon," says Peter Drucker. "It will hit us no later than 1987 . . . and it promises to be quite a bit nastier than the one we just 'solved.'"[157] Robert Myers, on the eve of the 1983 rescue plan's adoption, warned that "the system could still encounter a financial crisis in the mid-1980s under adverse economic conditions."[158]

Other analysts see the price of delay as much more subtle. The risk is not so much another cash crisis before we reach the oasis of the 1990s. It is to forgo the chance to fairly phase in a down-sized deal for the retirees of the 21st century. Says Penner, "We have given the impression of an impending disaster in public discussions of the problem [but] very modest changes can greatly reduce the burdens." The sooner they begin, the more modest these changes can be. Penner points out that if the annual growth rate of average benefits were trimmed by 1 percent for each year between 1983 and 2025, the payroll tax rates of 1985 might cover the entire cost.[159] The longer one waits after 1983 to achieve that saving, the larger it must be in each year until 2025.

There are three very powerful tools for achieving the trend-bending that is required: raising the average age of retirement, keying the starting level of each pension to inflation but not to growth in wages, and changing the basis for yearly hikes in benefits. Indeed, these tools are so potent that one can easily compile a combined impact that would put the retirement fund's costs below what currently scheduled payroll tax rates will produce. This may be essential, however, because of pressures for added financing in the hospital fund. Let us examine each of these tools.

Perhaps the most clearly justified change is a gradual increase in the age at which a worker is eligible for full Social Security benefits. The program throughout its history has been providing an automatic benefit increase that is seldom mentioned. Each year, those who retire can hope to receive a pension for longer than their predecessors. Rising life expectancy assures this.

The drafters of Social Security could look at the 1930 census and find an average life expectancy at birth of 59.7 years. It was to grow to 62.9 years in 1940, when the system's first checks went out. Both ages are below the longevity which qualified a member for full benefits. It is fair to say that Social Security began not only as an income floor, but was intended for that handful of people who reached age 65. You can fund a good program at low rates when it appears your average member will die before he retires.

As of 1980, however, life expectancy had reached 73.8 years. Those who reach age 65 can look forward to an added 16 years of life. "I made a mistake," said the man who picked 65 as the normal retirement age. Frank Bane, then age 90, said in 1981, "I believed old man Solomon. . . . Three score and ten? He didn't know what he was talking about." Bane would move the normal age up three years to 68, and adjust early retirement an equal amount to age 65. This would be done at the rate of six months a year for six years.[160]

Bane's figures are "ballpark" for nearly all reformers. The 1983 reform administered this medicine with an eyedropper. It raised the full benefit age to 66 by the year 2009 and 67 by 2027. This change will not begin until the year 2000. The rate of change is about 22 times slower than Bane's and only goes two-thirds as far. Early retirement would still be permitted at age 62, but benefits would be 70 percent rather than 80 percent of the full amount.

Any number of variants on Bane's theme have appeared. The private National Commission on Social Security would push the age to 68 by the year 2012.[161] Former Commissioner John Svahn said such a change would save 1.3 percent of payroll,[162] more than the amount Penner says would keep the pension fund in the black. Martin Feldstein would raise the age in six month steps each year until it reached 70. This, says Feldstein, would give the average retiree a decade of pensions benefits.[163]

It would also match the normal retirement age with the minimum age at which a person can be forced to retire. In 1978 Congress raised the mandatory retirement age from 65 to 70. It "recognized . . . that the same advances in medical science and health care that have been lengthening the lives of the retired . . . permit them to keep working for more years."[164]

This highlights the fact that there are incentives, carrots as well as sticks, to delay the average age people leave the workforce. Beginning in 1982, those who stayed on the job past their 65th birthday got a 3 percent bonus in eventual pension benefits for each year of continued work. The 1983 plan calls for raising this bonus gradually to 8 percent a year by 2008.

The reason some older workers retire is that up to 96 percent of their earnings are taxed away. Take the case of William Hassler, a 66-year-old Virginia biologist. His last dollar of earnings is in the 22 percent federal tax bracket and in a state tax bracket whose net rate is 4.5 percent. He loses 50 percent of every dollar earned above $6,960 because the law requires such a reduction in Social Security benefits, the so-called "income offset." And even though he is building a late retirement bonus of only 3 percent a year, he pays 11.3 percent to Social Security as his self-employment tax. Finally, Hassler is caught paying an added 8.25 percent on bonds that he thought were tax exempt, but are included as income in determining his Social Security benefits.

Total tax and benefit costs of working: 96 cents on the dollar. "That's a disincentive," Hassler says dryly. And he notes that friends have solved the problem by retiring—or by going into the underground economy of unreported income.[165]

Peter Drucker estimates the average rate for people in Hassler's position is 75 to 85 percent. Drucker would exempt workers over 65, and their employers, from Social Security taxes. He calculates the Treasury would reap a substantial net benefit from income taxes paid by those still working or who had surfaced from the underground economy.[166]

The objection might be raised that this helps the general fund of the Treasury but hurts the pension trust fund. There is already considerable melding of the two funds. This would increase if, as many advocate, general revenues are brought in to help support the hospital fund. Ultimately, the well-being of Social Security and of general federal finances are not separable.

American University economist Bradley Schiller would eliminate both the earnings test and the eligibility of older persons to receive Social Security while still working. He notes those still in the labor force get 20 percent of the system's dollars—an amount in excess of the trust funds' projected deficits. Public opinion polls show as many as 40 percent of retired workers age 62 to 65 would work "if economic incentives were better," Schiller claims. In place of the value of a pension, he would offer a refundable tax credit to those who stay in the labor force.[167] House Majority Leader Jim Wright endorsed this concept in 1982. His plan would add $1,000 to the credit for each year's delay in retirement.[168]

These changes fit in logically with insuring the long-term political viability of taxing Social Security benefits. The 1983 law applying the tax did not "index" the income thresholds for future inflation. Eventually, nearly all single retirees will receive $25,000 and all couples $32,000 a year. Some time before then, indexing will probably be applied. But even after that happens, the taxation of benefits needs to be coordinated with the tax treatment applied to seniors' total income.

Once it is realized that Social Security is an income transfer system and not a normal economic return on members' contributions, the goals of the system can be directly addressed: income adequacy, social equity. "The only way to apply a means test to Social Security is through the tax system. The result should not be thought of as a revenue increase, but as a way to hold down costs," says Carol Cox.[169]

The same concept of fairness that calls for taxing the benefits of higher-income recipients also calls for not taxing, at rates of 75 percent or more, the earnings of those who want to work. One meaning of fairness is that Social Security should be neutral in its impact on individual decisions regarding continued work. It is ironic that the mandatory retirement age has been raised to 70, but the tax system may force people to quit their jobs. This is neither fair nor helpful to the system's finances.

The percentage of older workers staying in the labor force has plummeted. For men age 60 to 64, the rate dropped from 82.5 percent in 1955 to 61.8 percent in 1979. For those age 65 to 69, the drop was from 57 percent to 19.6 percent. The cost impact on Social Security is large. Early retirement, like increases in life expectancy, simply adds to the average length a person draws benefits. This is a major driver of costs. Some recent data suggest that the trend toward early retirement is reversing, an encouraging shift that should itself be encouraged.

The "stick" is to raise the age for full benefits and to reduce the percent of benefits available at age 62. These changes are not punitive, but offset the impact of life expectancy on the length of pension payouts. The "carrot" is increased rewards and fewer penalties for continuing to work.

Restraining eligibility (the number of recipients) is one major tool for cost control. The other tool is containing growth in the size of future pension benefits (the number of dollars spent per recipient). There are two aspects: How big is the retiree's first check? How fast do benefits grow each year?

The 1972 boost "double indexed" annual hikes to both wages and prices. This bonus was removed in 1977. But through the AIME formula, an initial pension check still reflects both factors. By replacing a fixed portion of each worker's average pay, it not only covers wage hikes based on inflation but those made possible by productivity growth. This means that to replace a constant portion of the average worker's earnings, Social Security will not just keep up with inflation but will steadily increase in purchasing power.

The Congressional Research Service estimated in 1979 that if America's economic performance continued at expectable rates, the real value of benefits per worker would triple in the next 75 years. This sounds wonderful, but it is a prime reason for the system seeming to resemble a pyramid scheme or chain letter.

Many analysts propose "decoupling" the initial benefit formula from future wage growth. This would hold constant the buying power of the average retiree's first check. But the percentage of final earnings that check replaces would decline because it would not reflect any rise in his pay due to productivity gains.

Decoupling is a "big ticket" item, one of the most potent cost control tools. Those who favor it point out that it explicitly protects the purchasing power of future retirees while saving the system a lot of money. They also note that although there would be a downward drift in the portion of final pay that is replaced, this would only mean a gradual return to the ratios that prevailed before 1972. And since the basic gains of 1972–85 would still be in the formula, actual buying power for the newly retired would start at a level 50 percent or more above the pre-1972 era.

Decoupling has another virtue. In return for allowing the average replacement of final pay to again be 35 or 40 percent rather than today's 45 percent, it would take a huge amount of pressure off the payroll tax. This could help the system return to what many feel is its true purpose: to be one leg of a three-legged stool whose other legs are private pensions and personal savings.

The explosion in payroll taxes has made it more difficult for workers to save for retirement, while the explosion in benefits has made it seem less important for them to do so. But in the process, what might have been a larger pool of savings is taxed away for immediate consumption. There is no way to make this problem go away, given the system's immense funding needs. But decoupling would offer some long-term relief of pressure on the tax.

This would not only permit workers more choice in how to build retirement income. It also is a precondition for the most ambitious reform some propose in the system: to have sound and separately funded plans for basic benefits and for an optional annuity. This would involve a fundamental clean-up of Social Security's books on each member and would add a true insurance feature. It is possible only if the system is free from recurring cash crises and from tax rates so steep they could discourage members from buying added coverage.

The highly progressive shape of the AIME formula would assure that workers too poor to save, and unlikely to have much of a company pension, still receive an adequate basic grant. Future inflation will translate into revisions for the specific numbers in AIME, but need not diminish its effect in targeting dollars at the low end of the scale.

The final big ticket item is how pensions are adjusted each year to reflect inflation.

Currently, growth in the Consumer Price Index each year translates into a full adjustment in Social Security checks for the following year. The one exception in law, delaying these hikes when the CPI goes up less than 3 percent, is an apparent casualty to the 1984 political campaign season.

Ways to save money on the annual adjustment abound. They include delays and freezes, offsets against the CPI or wage growth, and "fail-safe" formulas designed to protect the fund if it falls below a minimum level.

"Cost-of-living adjustments (COLAs) have become a major focus of debate in Congress," says Carol Cox. "Ways to lessen their annual growth have become a stand-in for changes in the structure of the program that would save money. But COLA freezes are politically unsupportable over time." Cox sees a use for formulas like CPI less 2 or 3 percent. "They may help stem the tide of red ink while we figure out what to do." Rather than a fixed percent offset, Cox believes it might be better to provide 60 percent of whatever the CPI is. "This helps the most when retirees need it most."[170]

Some experts including Robert Myers and Haeworth Robinson favor hiking grants by last year's average wage growth minus about 1.5 percent. This is estimated to cover price increases over time, but not productivity gains won by the active workforce. This approach also is a good way to keep the system's outgo in line with its income, since future increases in the payroll tax base are keyed to average wage growth. Such a link would help overcome the unfairness Robinson notes in a system where 36 million beneficiaries are fully protected against inflation while 116 million people paying taxes aren't protected (these were the figures for 1982). It is noteworthy that the largest lobby for the retired didn't oppose the idea when it was discussed by the Greenspan Commission.[171]

Another idea is akin to Charles Schultze's concept to decently protect but not immunize retirees against conditions which affect workers. A formula would adjust pensions each year by the lesser of wage or price growth. In years when real income increased, benefit hikes would offset inflation. But if pay failed to keep pace with prices, the value of pensions would slide by the same amount.

A "lesser of" formula was proposed by the Greenspan Commission, but only as a fail-safe device when the fund was in trouble. The provision would kick in whenever Social Security had an amount on hand that was less than 20 percent of annual benefit costs. The new rule would take effect in 1988.[172]

Congress approved the idea, and added a three-year start-up period beginning in 1985 when the trigger would be only 15 percent. It seemed in late 1983 that the new law might actually go into effect in 1985. Higher disability and old-age payments, and lower tax collections from the self-employed, were pushing the fund toward the trigger point.[173]

A more difficult and ambitious fail-safe provision is offered by Peter Drucker. He would set up a benchmark ratio of no less than four-to-one between workers and retirees. The ratio would be maintained by calling into play the entire range of laws on retirement age and inducements to stay in the work force. "The current 3½-to-1 ratio is probably already more than the economy and society can stand for long periods without serious strain," Drucker believes.[174]

A PUBLIC TRUST

Social Security is a fundamental part of America's promise to itself. The explosion in membership, average benefits, and total cost of the program; political courage and political posturing; the imponderables of sociology, demography, and economics; fears of destitution by the old and fears of betrayal by the young; reforms that are technically sound and politically perilous; far-sighted vision and short-sighted bargains; retirees' security and workers' opportunity; intergenerational promises, duties, and burdens; the sanctity of a social contract and the reality of a practical problem—all these have been part of the story of our national pension system.

By picking our way through the emotional and analytical challenge aroused by Social Security, we can come safely to the high ground of moderate and prudent change. There is no excuse for not putting the pension fund clearly in the black over the long term. Additional steps would also enable the tax resources it now requires to help meet the more difficult cost problem in health care, and to play a positive role in coping with the deficit.

The Gravy Train Robbery

> If American taxpayers had told Congress many years ago, "Federal employees are doing an excellent job and we want a retirement plan for them that is comparable to the best in the private sector—equal to typical plans in the top Fortune 500 companies" and Congress had provided just that, in the last 10 years the two biggest federal retirement systems would have cost taxpayers $103 billion *less* than they actually did and $314 billion *less* than they will cost in the next 10 years.
> —Grace Commission Report[1]

THE PRESIDENT'S PRIVATE SECTOR SURVEY ON COST CONTROL, popularly known as the Grace Commission, was the largest project of its kind in history. Two thousand executives were loaned to the project by major firms. They spent 500 person-years studying federal agency operations, at an estimated cost to their companies of $75 million in salaries and expenses. This scale of effort dwarfs the Hoover Commissions of the past and may never be matched in the future.

The work product was a six-foot shelf of books on every aspect of federal management. It is probably fair to say that never have so many potential improvements and cost-saving ideas been uncovered in a single exercise. In fact, there were 2,478 ideas.

The Commission's work was criticized on two general grounds. One was its claim that $424 billion would be saved over a three-year period if all recommendations were adopted. The Congressional Budget Office and General Accounting Office trimmed that to $97.9 billion by focusing on 396 recommendations which contained 90 percent of the total savings. CBO and GAO said 122 of the ideas were "too vague" to be assigned a value. The remainder were downsized because of a different method of estimating savings. The Commission had calculated what each idea would be worth when in full operation and had then expressed the saving in 1983 dollars. CBO and GAO by contrast had shown what the idea would actually have saved in the first three fiscal years after its adoption. Since some reforms take a decade to reach full impact, the two approaches produce quite different results.[2]

The other general ground for criticizing the Commission was that it had exceeded its charter by wandering from "management" to "policy." Indeed, a review of the more important proposals reveals that most of them would involve a change in law, not just a change in administration. But this is hardly a damning criticism. The Grace Commission felt it had a job to do and did it, without being put off by a fine distinction. As professionals in public management soon learn, the line separating procedure from policy is often invisible.

Those in the CBO and the GAO who critiqued the Commission report surely had mixed feelings. On the one hand, they found a concern for efficiency and cost control which was congenial. On the other hand, they encountered an unfamiliarity with government ways which must at times have seemed naive. Calling upon bureaucrats to act more like businessmen is reasonable, but there are also reasonable exceptions which "outsiders" may overlook.

If there is one issue on which the Commission's work seems likely to have lasting impact, it is federal pension reform. About one-sixth of the total savings identified by Grace were in this area of the budget. The funding trends are frightening enough, and the comparable benefits are impressive enough, to make federal pensions a top-drawer issue. Grace helped draw attention to this fact.

The most startling fact about federal pensions is that they contain a "hidden debt" in excess of $1 trillion. What this mind-bending number means is that federal employees are accumulating the right to pension benefits whose value will outstrip pension fund assets by $1 trillion. These numbers cover the next forty years. To bring the civil service and military retirement systems into balance would require an added $41 billion in taxpayer and employee contributions to the funds during each of those forty years.[3] That is close to double the current rate of financing.

The Grace Commission blamed the huge unfunded liability on a failure to adjust payments into pension accounts for the improvements made in retirement benefits over the years.[4] Inflation was a culprit. It swelled paychecks on which starting pension levels were based. And large cost-of-living adjustments (COLAs) were needed to offset its effects for those already on a pension.

Between 1970 and 1982, civil service retirement (CSRS) costs rose an average 17.5 percent a year while military retirement (MRS) costs rose almost 15 percent a year.[5] These growth rates produce a doubling every five years.

The deterioration in financial condition is starkly evident if one compares the CSRS trust fund balance sheet for 1970 with that of 1982:[6]

Source of income (in billions)	1970	1982	Average annual growth
Employee contributions	$1.7	$ 4.2	7.8%
Agency contributions	1.7	5.0	9.4
General Treasury contributions	0.2	14.5	42.9
Interest and profits	1.1	7.8	17.7
Total receipts	4.7	31.5	17.2
Total outlays	2.8	19.5	17.6

To speak of deterioration may seem at first glance to be an overstatement. Receipts have grown almost as fast, and interest earnings have grown slightly faster, than outlays. This suggests balance.

But look at the figure for general Treasury contributions. These are simply taxpayer dollars that have been shifted into the fund to keep it afloat. Agency contributions are also from the taxpayer, but have the merit of being planned as part of agency budgets. The Treasury share is what might be called a quiet emergency transfer. Without these funds, CSRS would show a current deficit of $2.5 billion. In theory this means some pension checks could not be mailed. But in fact such a failure to pay earned benefits would put CSRS under a court order to ante up.

Why, if the taxpayer has to be hit, did CSRS take $14.5 billion in 1982 general revenues rather than just the $2.5 billion it currently needed? The answer is that the remaining $12 billion is a pathetically thin cushion against future cost growth. Many public pension funds with appalling long-term imbalances enjoy an attractive excess of current income over payments. Local police and fire funds are an outstanding example. But the arithmetic is due to be swamped by predictable future outflows that will drain away existing balances.

One clear way funding pressures can be expressed is in terms of how much pensions add to salary costs. Indeed, the most frequent way of budgeting for public pensions is as a "percent of payroll." The numbers are startling. Currently-earned civil service retirement benefits add an average 30 percent above basic pay to the cost of each employee. This is built into agencies' budgets. For military personnel, the add-on is 41 percent. If an amount were also included to cover previously-earned but unfunded benefits over the next 40 years, these figures would rise to 85 percent and 118 percent of salary for the two groups.[7]

In other words, the average federal worker's pension now costs as much as his or her paycheck. Not all these costs are being covered on a current basis, however. Grace estimated the growth in unfunded liability at $94 billion annually during 1979–82.[8] In September 1982 the total size of these unfinanced obligations was $515 billion for civil service and $527 billion for military pensions.[9]

BLOWING THE WHISTLE ON THE GRAVY TRAIN

A huge unfunded liability in itself is no evidence that a pension plan is excessively generous. It only shows that no adequate provision has been made to pay the promised benefits. But in fact federal retirement plans are generous. Grace concluded that CSRS returned three times as much, and MRS six times as much, as the best private plans offered by blue-chip corporations.[10]

These numbers compare the amount of retirement income an employee can expect for each dollar he earned while on the job. Federal plans have a high rate of return because of three unusual benefit provisions: an enriched formula, young retirement, and cost-of-living protection.

Enriched formula. In the private sector, an employee typically earns the right to a pension worth about 1.2 percent of his salary for each year of work. A 30-year employee, for example, would build up rights to a check 36 percent the size of his working pay. In the government, benefits accumulate at the rate of 1.7–1.9 percent a year. This generates a pension equal to 51–57 percent of pay.[11]

The meaning of "pay" differs to the advantage of federal workers. Private sector employees usually have their last five years of salary averaged. For those in government service, it's the last three years. This average, not an actual paycheck, is used to compute the percent of income replaced. If annual pay hikes are 5 percent, a formula based on the last three years provides a pension 4.8 percent higher than one using the last five years. If pay goes up 10 percent a year, the three-year formula generates an advantage of 8.9 percent.

When the rate of benefit buildup is combined with the base for computing pay, federal pensions have an edge anywhere from 48 to 72 percent over their typical private counterpart in generating retirement income per dollar of earnings on the job.[12]

But, it will be objected, federal employees are paid less. Clearly, this once was the case. But in the last two decades the federal government has used a salary survey whose explicit purpose is to eliminate any gap. In the opinion of many analysts, this goal has been attained. "For the most part, civil service and military salaries are now reasonably competitive with salaries in the private sector," say Brookings Institution economists who add, "so there is less justification for retirement benefits that are more generous."[13]

It is true that within the civil service various groups fare differently. Grace judged that top-level federal managers were underpaid by about 50 percent relative to the private sector.[14] They simply did not receive the executive income and "perks" that industry provides. For years this gap has been widely known. It is assumed that the satisfactions of a high post in the public service are sufficient to offset the differential. But surely some capable people become unavailable to federal agencies as a result.

For the rest of government's labor force there is a pay edge, according to Grace. White-collar workers enjoy a "bonus" which averages 4 percent; blue collar, 8 percent; postal workers, 28 percent.[15] If these pay differentials are applied on top of the pension formula edge, retirement checks would appear to be an average 52 to 92 percent higher for federal workers than for those who hold comparable jobs in the private economy.[16]

Young retirement. The civil service system allows employees to be paid a full pension at age 55 with 30 years of service. The military system permits retirement at age 40 after 20 years in uniform. Private firms typically will not grant a full pension until about age 63.

There is a dramatic cost impact when people retire younger. Grace calculated the following:[17]

Age of retirement	Relative cost of pension (retirement at age 65 = 100)
62	130
60	150
55	220
45	340
40	400

The enormous multiples of cost for younger retirees arise not only from the obvious fact of a longer pension payout period but also from its mirror image: the shorter time for asset accumulation. In a fully funded pension plan, 70 percent of total needs can be met by interest earnings on assets. When the time period for making deposits is shortened, it means that not only fewer dollars go into the fund but the "miracle" of compound interest has less time to work. Thus, more of the pension must be funded the hard way—in this case, from tax dollars.

The fact that CSRS permits retirement with full benefits at age 55 is not an abstraction. It has a powerful impact on when people quit working. Grace cited these data:[18]

Age at retirement	As percent of total retirements		Cumulative percent of total	
	CSRS	Private	CSRS	Private
Under 55	9.5%	1.1%	9.5%	1.1%
55–59	39.6	6.3	49.1	7.4
60–61	14.5	12.6	63.6	20.0
62–64	18.1	42.1	81.7	62.1
65 and over	18.3	37.9	100.0	100.0

Only one private worker in five retires before age 62; more than three civil servants in five do so. The federal Office of Personnel Management found that only 10 percent of employees who were eligible to retire before age 60 remained in active service at age 60.[19]

Young retirement is not just an option with enormous mathematical effects; it is an option that is exercised by the vast majority who qualify. Grace believes it "is a major contributing factor to the 1,891 percent increase in CSRS costs over the 1960–81 period—more than nine times the rate of inflation."[20]

Cost-of-living protection. Civil service and military pensions provide a full adjustment (COLA) for inflation. The typical private plan covers only one-third of erosion in the value of a dollar. But Social Security is integrated with most private plans, and it offers a full COLA. This brings the combined adjustment to an average 70 percent of inflation.[21]

Since 1968, COLAs for federal retirees have exceeded both the cost-of-living rise and pay hikes for those still working in the civil service. How could the inflation adjustment exceed inflation? It happened by granting COLAs twice a year, which allowed the "miracle" of compound interest to work on federal pensions. How could COLAs exceed pay hikes? Simply because the latter are adopted each year by Congress as part of the budget, and may be set at any level.

From 1968 to 1982, the civil service pay scale was raised by 131 percent. Consumer prices went up 178 percent. Government pension schedules gained by 198 percent.[22]

These differentials create some interesting results. A federal retiree would have seen his pension grow three times as large over the 14 years. But an employee working in 1982 at the job formerly held by the pensioner would have a paycheck only 2.3 times bigger. The retiree's COLA is 28.7 percent greater than if it had been applied to his active pay, and 7.2 percent greater than the actual rate of inflation.[23] This kind of arithmetic has led in a few cases to a pension which surpassed the paycheck of the retiree's successor.

An enriched basic formula, full benefits at a young age, and complete inflation coverage accumulate into an impressive advantage for the federal retiree. Grace made this comparison of average lifetime pension benefits:[24]

Preretirement salary	Civil Service benefits	Military benefits	Private pension and Social Security
$25,000	$ 542,000	$1,072,000	$266,000
50,000	1,085,000	1,679,000	398,000

The payoff for civil service and private pensions is based on retirement at age 55 after 30 years of service. The military pension payoff is based on 20 years service, with retirement at age 39 in the example with $25,000 final pay, and at age 43 in the example with $50,000 final pay. If a private sector worker retired at those young ages, his pension rights would fall to $176,000 and $252,000, in the two examples shown.

It is possible to quibble with Grace's figures. For example, the advantage of civil service over private plans is 2–2.7 times in the table, not three times as claimed in Grace's text. And not many of those who retire from the service at a $50,000 pay level do so at age 43. But as Grace Commission Executive Director J. P. Bolduc said more than once in congressional hearings when such arguments were raised, "We can give that point away and still make the case." By any reasonable standard, the federal pension system is a generous one.

MILITARY RETIREMENT: FACING THE X FACTOR

It is logical to compare federal civilian workers' benefits with those in industry. But can the same be said of the military, which involves unique working conditions and has many jobs which have no parallel in the private sector? This question is important because the supposed noncomparability of soldiering is used to defend enriched military pensions.

A decade ago the Pentagon's retirement plan was "universally regarded as being not only practical but virtually indispensable."[25] It served three aims: first, to compensate those in the service for pay scales substantially below private industry; second, to encourage men and women to retire after 20 years so the fighting force could be kept young and vigorous; finally, to reward those in uniform for the intangible sacrifices that they are called on to make—the X factor of frequent moves, inhospitable surroundings, long hours, family separation, and of course, personal danger.

Military retirees have accumulated pension benefits even faster than those in civil service—at the rate of 2.5 percent of final pay per year of service. This is far above the 1.7–1.9 percent rate for federal civilian workers, and more than double the 1.2 percent which Grace said was the private sector norm.

Retired military personnel are eligible for earned Social Security benefits with no reduction in their annuity, and may also collect earnings from a second career without a pension penalty. The Congressional Budget Office estimates that the lump sum value of military retirement benefits alone ranges from about $100,000 for a "very junior" enlisted member with 20 years' service to over $1 million for "very senior" officers with 30 or more years' service.[26]

The average enlisted member retires at age 42 after 22 years in uniform; the average officer retiree is 46 and has served for 25 years. Over one-third of all retirees leave active duty on the day they qualify for retirement benefits—upon completing 20 years in the service.[27]

Each of the three premises which have justified this unusually generous system are under attack. The clearest case is the first. "We made a terrific mistake in the early 1970s when we started raising military pay," says Congressman Les Aspin. "We should have changed the pension formula and we didn't. Now we're paying the price."[28] The price is not only that taxpayers failed to receive relief from a legitimate offset of costs, but found themselves committed to pay a huge increase for pensions tied to pay boosts.

The secret to success of an All Volunteer Force is competitive pay, not pensions. In the annual bidding by the military for capable personnel, it is "front money" that counts. A retirement plan which pays nothing to those with less than 20 years' service is not a major factor in job-seekers' short-run decisions. In fact, only 13 percent of people in uniform ever collect a military pension.[29] "Pensions cannot be an important incentive since so few recruits ever stay around to collect them."[30]

The second rationale for offering half-pay to those who retire after 20 years has come under the harshest attack. This policy is viewed not only as unneeded but as perverse in its effects.

The key is the concept of a "young and vigorous force." The reality is pension incentives which distort the personnel profile the Pentagon needs.

The saying among servicemen is that anyone who stays on after 20 years is "working for half-pay" since he would get the other half just by retiring. The Brookings Institution looked at the system and saw this strange pattern: "Little inducement to reenlist after only a few years of service, big inducements for those getting close to the 20-year mark, and little additional incentive after that." Brookings concluded that "the result is an odd system of incentives that may bear little relationship to military manpower requirements."[31]

The rationale behind this pattern "is based on an antiquated concept of the military." Soldiers are not spending a large part of their 20 years on the front lines. The General Accounting Office found that retiring enlisted men had spent 92 percent of their time in nonhazardous duty, and four-fifths of them had served 20 years with no combat experience. "To treat supply clerks and combat veterans the same is unnecessary and inequitable."[32]

The incentive to serve 20 years and then get out conflicts with "current trends in manpower requirements [which] tend to emphasize skill and training while placing less emphasis on 'youth and vigor,'" says the Congressional Budget Office.[33] Admiral Rickover estimated that less than 5 percent of the Navy's jobs need to be performed by young men. Less than 25 percent of the Army consists of ground troops and artillery. A 1981 Brookings study found that "the U.S. military's insistence on youth and vigor has yielded armed forces too inexperienced to operate today's sophisticated weapons systems."[34]

Training and recruiting cost the Army an average of $15,000 for each enlisted person and $50,000 per officer in 1983.[35] This initial expense is another reason why it makes good sense to keep experienced people. But the CBO found that "the current retirement system will be of at best modest help in retaining these key personnel." The reason is that a plan requiring 20 years' service to qualify for benefits "does not appear to exert a strong retention pull" on the most crucial component of the force—those with

4 to 12 years in uniform. This group makes up to 60 percent of all career personnel, and "their retention would be critical in any expansion" required during a military alert.[36] But their pension rights are still far in the future.

Those who defend the current system tend to focus on monthly pension benefits rather than lifetime payout, and to ignore the strange shape of the system's incentive impact over the span of a career by talking in general about a "career force."

One statement receiving broad coverage was by two former officers and personnel specialists, Thomas Hale and David Evans. They said "an Army sergeant major, the top enlisted rank, can expect $990 a month after 20 years. And don't forget, these modest stipends are taxable."[37] Hale and Evans didn't mention that the expected lifetime payout would be $560,100[38] or that the "modest stipend" is more than double the average monthly Social Security benefit received by private sector workers retiring in their sixties.[39]

More serious than the numbers game are the foggy analyses of manpower needs which are used to defend the current system. In a typical phrase, Hale and Evans say, "We need to recognize that the retirement system supports the career force." They go on to argue that "the career force is a major distinguishing edge that the U.S. military has over a Soviet military machine that is numerically superior but depends on short-term conscripts for the bulk of its strength."[40]

In a remarkable lapse of logic, Hale and Evans also offer as an argument the fact that "even the Soviet Union has a more generous retirement plan after 30 years."[41] Thus in the same article we learn that U.S. military pensions give us a decisive personnel edge and that the Russians have a military pension system which in some respects is superior to ours. One is not sure what to think.

Nor is it clear whether Hale and Evans consider that group of U.S. personnel with 4 to 12 years experience, who make up 60 percent of the force, as "short-term conscripts" on the Russian model. They offer no comment on that group's pension rights or on the weak retention incentives mentioned by the CBO. But they do cite with disapproval Congressman Aspin's comment that the military retirement system has become "the ultimate special interest boondoggle."

More remarkably, Hale and Evans claim that "in a closed door Congressional hearing earlier this year [1984], Secretary Weinberger and Gen. John Vessey, chairman of the Joint Chiefs, expressed strong opposition to any changes in the present system."[42] Yet in that same year Vessey was quoted directly in a national publication as saying, "the changing nature of warfare may justify changes in military retirement."[43]

The Road to Reason

The CBO studied nine proposals offered between 1969 and 1984 to reform military retirement. It said that while Congress had focused on computing COLAs and final pay, these studies were much more sweeping. Their goal was "modifying military retirement to meet manpower goals at an acceptable cost." The CBO said that, "Should Congress opt for more far-reaching changes, the studies show a near-consensus on how the system should be modified."

Before offering specific comparisons, the CBO dealt with the X factor problem which has been a potent factor in preventing reform. The "dis-amenities" of military service—family separations, the Code of Military Justice, the perils of combat—"are sometimes cited as justifications for a generous retirement system." The CBO did not stress the fact that few in the service now must contemplate facing death. Instead, the CBO noted, "to the extent that [the X-factor argument] holds, it merely explains some of the difficulties of meeting military manpower requirements. It does not justify retention of the current retirement system in preference to other(s)."[44]

The CBO then compared four major proposals. The first would provide full pensions only after 30 years and would reduce COLAs. Those with 20 years could take a lump-sum payment, equal to two times annual pay for officers and three times for enlisted ranks.

A simpler option would provide a COLA equal to half rather than all of inflation for any military retiree under age 62.

A third plan would combine the half-COLA with a catch-up raise and full COLAs after age 62. It would provide vesting (earning the right to pension benefits) much earlier than the 20th year of service. Social Security would be integrated with military retirement in computing the size of the pension.

The fourth plan contains many features of the third but would also make a basic reduction in monthly benefits.

The first three plans were developed by federal agencies and regular advisory groups; the fourth comes from the Grace Commission.

The table on page 261 compares the four plans.[45]

The figures assume long-term inflation of 4.5 percent and wage growth of 5 percent. The reason plans 3 and 4 reduce average seniority while also increasing the incentive for longer careers is that in a period of transition they would reduce the size of the force, thus lowering average length of service. This effect, CBO says, could be offset by pay or other incentives. These would involve current costs, though probably less than the pension cuts would save. And the costs would be current, not part of the buildup in a trillion dollar "time bomb" of federal pension liabilities.

Impact	Plan 1	Plan 2	Plan 3	Plan 4
Reduction in typical retiree's total pension	20–25%	25%	18–22%	85–89%
Reduction in 1985 buildup of benefit rights	9.2%	25.2%	8.4%	76.7%
Savings in budget outlays (billions of $)				
1985–89 (5 years)	1,208	2,339	2,707	2,176
2020 (1 year)	257	5,816	4,123	15,994
Change in career force				
Size	+4.7%	−3.4%	−3.0%	−11.0%
Average seniority	+2.3%	−2.7%	−2.3%	−7.9%
Increases incentive for long (20+) careers	Strong	None	None	Strongest
Increases incentive for journeymen (4–20)	None	None	Strong	Strong
Makes involuntary discharge easier	No	No	Yes	Yes
Risk of unanticipated effects	Least	Modest	Large	Largest

Clearly, the time has come to strip away the mythology surrounding military pensions. Their extraordinary benefits do not flow solely to that fraction of those in uniform who do have to lay their lives on the line. More serious, their incentive appeal is weakest to that very group which is the backbone of the service's technical capability and capacity for wartime expansion. Nor does the system play a major role in attracting new recruits. Competitive pay is the key to that.

Military retirement is far off the mark in helping us "meet manpower goals at an acceptable cost." Alternatives like the four reform plans must be examined and enacted in some combination of provisions. Nor must Congress be lulled by the argument that savings will only occur far in the future since they would be limited to new recruits. That is simply a formula for perpetuating existing defects. Even the concept that current provisions are an absolute contract right needs careful review.

Pension experts agree that the already-earned pension rights of today's workers and retirees should not, and legally cannot, be changed. They also agree that the not-yet-earned rights of future employees can differ totally from today's provisions. All that is required is the use of legal authority to adopt changes.

But pension experts vary widely on the degree to which the not-yet-earned rights of current employees can be altered. Some take the view that these are absolute and cannot be modified. Others believe the only restriction is a general standard of fairness that requires changes to be phased in equitably. Given the fact that military retirees can begin a second career in their early forties with no reduction or delay in receiving full benefits, this would seem to be a situation where the issue should be put to the test. And even if the test fails, major changes are still worth making now for the impact they will have in the future.

As for the civil service, there is no reason why its retirees should have a pension advantage of 2–2.7 times over those in the private sector.

In April 1984 the National Commission on Public Employee Pension Systems, headed by a former Civil Service Commission director and a former congressman, warned Congress about federal pension levels. This warning included an analysis of how much the current "full benefit" system overshot the actual income replacement needs of retired civil servants. It calculated the impact of retirement on consumption patterns, tax liability, medical needs, dependents, charitable contributions, and the like. Then it compared the required with the actual pension that would be produced under the existing civil service plan, under a reformed plan proposed by Congressman John Erlenborn, and under the Grace Commission plan:[46]

Preretirement salary	Retirement equivalent	Current CSRS	Erlenborn	Grace
$10,000	$ 8,175	$12,050	$10,200	$ 9,408
25,000	18,028	24,500	19,862	19,422
50,000	28,999	38,100	28,850	30,936

These numbers cover the case of a person retiring at age 65 after 30 years service. Thus the figures for CSRS are higher than average because so many federal workers take young retirement. In only one case, Erlenborn at $50,000, is replacement below need.

This illustration reveals, as do the military pension options, an opportunity for careful, cost-saving scrutiny. The explosion in unfunded liabilities at the rate of nearly $100 billion a year during 1979–82 argues the necessity for such a review. Otherwise, federal pensions may turn into a promise we cannot keep.

The Least of These

IT MAY SEEM STRANGE in a book which claims to review the full range of ways to cut spending that welfare should not be a big topic. Public opinion surveys often find that people prefer "eliminating welfare waste" over all other trims as a way to save money and balance the budget.

Unfortunately, it turns out this poll response is about as practical as the high level of support people give to providing all the revenues their state needs by a lottery. It seems painless to solve the fiscal problem by "getting the bums off the dole" or by raising money from voluntary gambling. Neither idea remotely approaches a solution. Each is capable of delivering something like 2 percent of the impact that is imagined.

In March 1984 *Business Week* offered a plan to wipe out the deficit. $100 billion apiece would come from spending cuts and tax hikes. On the spending side, 8 percent of the budget was identified as being "welfare." Its contribution to the magazine's budget-balancing plan was even less: 2.5 percent of the total.

There are still budget issues in welfare: housing aid, school lunches for the affluent (back to middle-class welfare), and especially in moving retarded persons out of institutions and into lower-cost care. There are major cost-avoidance challenges in Medicaid, simply because it is part of a cost-explosive industry. But in the long-controversial Aid to Families with Dependent Children program, *Business Week* and others have concluded "there's no welfare fat left to trim."

The major reason is that the Reagan welfare reform program has been widely implemented. Expenses in 1985 for AFDC will be less than for the B-1 bomber: about $8 billion.

There is a paradox, however. Budget issues concerning welfare are now small; policy issues remain large. The nation has not yet solved the puzzle of how to meet the basic needs of those who are destitute without encouraging a dependence on welfare. It is true that, to a heartening degree, welfare assistance is a form of short-term emergency cash aid for those who have been caught by economic change and are in transition from one job to another. But there remains a hard core of semi-permanent poverty.

The challenge has been to strike a balance between two kinds of disincentives for people to make themselves financially independent. One extreme is a welfare system that is too "soft" and makes it too easy for people to stay on the dole. The other extreme is a system that is too hard on the working poor, which disqualifies them too quickly for income and health benefits as they begin to earn a few dollars. Such a system can make it so costly for the working poor to seek self-sufficiency that they are discouraged from doing so.

The Reagan welfare reform has enraged some by its stringency. Yet it must be seen not only as a reaction against a program some felt was too loose in extending benefits, but also as part of a continuing effort to find a system which will encourage those who might be able to make their own way without persecuting those who cannot. The balance point is not easy to find.

Even as we turn from the welfare portion of the budget as only a minor factor on the fiscal scene, we should anticipate that it deserves and will receive attention from some of our best policy minds in the years ahead. The issue in welfare today is not really a more balanced budget but a more perfect society.

Subsidies for the Strong

TRANSFER PAYMENTS FLOW not only to individuals but to economic interest groups. As in the case of a Medicare or Social Security recipient, business firms and entire industries have come to treat government assistance as an "entitlement."

Most subsidy programs began for the same reason as programs to benefit individuals. They were a response to hardship cases. In their early days, aid was targeted on the basis of an immediate need or a real national purpose. Over the years, many of these programs lost their focus as conditions changed. Instead of being phased out, they were expanded. No longer a lifeline to the distressed, they distributed their largesse indiscriminately.

Some businesses in peril continue to be the target for help. But all too often, the amount of aid received by any company in a favored field is proportionate to its size—not a very sure basis for determining need.

The examples given below illustrate but do not exhaust the range of government subsidies. Agriculture, synthetic fuels, water projects, and federal "off-budget" loan programs are described in the pages which follow. Other subsidies of equal interest for energy, public works, transit, and users of many federal services are not discussed. The review offered here is more than an hors d'oeuvres tray but less than the full seven-course meal.

Winds of reform are blowing over the budget for subsidies. The reform mood defies traditional distinctions of political philosophy. It often allies fiscal conservatives, environmentalists, and "free market" advocates against business, labor, and agriculture.

The more modest reforms are those which would "clean up" badly managed programs. The bolder reforms would dismantle subsidies and return protected sectors to a condition that all laud but many seek to escape: economic competition.

Agriculture has the highest potential of any American industry. But current policies are based on conditions in the 1930s, and we cannot expect them to work in the modern world.

—William Niskanen, member, Council of Economic Advisors[1]

The average American farmer produces enough food to supply 78 persons, compared with 53 as recently as 1972. American consumers spend a smaller portion of their income for food than anyone else in the world—an average $16.10 for every $100 in take-home pay.[2]

In the 1930s, farms employed more than 20 percent of the national workforce. Today, they employ 3 percent. During the Depression, farm families' average income equaled about 40 percent of the national level, compared with nearly 90 percent today.[3] Fifty years ago agriculture was the classic model of free-market competition. Each farmer produced a tiny fraction of total output. No individual was able to affect economic events. Today this is still the plight of the small farmer. In the words of North Dakota Congressman Byron Dorgan, "the invisible hand can shoot agriculture in the foot."[4]

But agriculture has become much more concentrated. Two-thirds of the food is now grown on big farms with a heavy investment in modern equipment. Twelve percent of farms with sales over $100,000 account for two-thirds of all production.[5] Half the food comes from the top 5 percent—those farms with more than $200,000 in annual sales.[6]

All is not well down on the farm. For the first time since the Depression, the U.S. recorded three straight years of decline in farmland values since their peak in 1981. The greatest loss of value was in the Midwest agricultural heartland. Three-year declines in Iowa, Ohio, Indiana, Nebraska, and Illinois exceeded 20 percent.[7] In September 1984 the Census Bureau reported that "the biggest farmers are getting bigger, small farmers are becoming more numerous, and the guys in the middle are getting squeezed out." The new small farmer tends to be of the gentleman variety, enjoying the agricultural life as a diversion. Vermont, a favored rural retreat for jaded city-dwellers, showed a 59 percent increase in small farms from 1978 to 1982.

Concentration of production was most evident in livestock agriculture.

Forty-three percent of the cattle market was held by the top 1 percent of firms, 70 percent of the hog market by the top 16 percent, and 79 percent of the poultry market by the top 2 percent.[8]

Those being squeezed out in the middle were the very group which U.S. farm programs are supposed to serve: family farmers of modest means, committed to the agricultural life.

Net farm income in 1983 was $27 billion. When this number is adjusted for inflation, it is the second lowest since the Depression. The drop in income, combined with high interest rates and increased operating costs, has buried farmers under a mountain of debt—$218 billion, up from $141 billion just five years ago.

Most of those who have gone bankrupt are younger operators mortgaged to the hilt and counting on constantly rising land values to provide collateral for loans. Some analysts believe the family farm can no longer compete and should be absorbed into larger, more efficient operations. But the fate of those farms has affected the entire business of agriculture as a career choice. In 1982 the number of college students pursuing degrees in this field was down—8 percent for B.A.s, 12 percent for M.A.s, and 5 percent for Ph.D.s.[9]

Remarkably, agriculture's downward economic spiral has been accompanied by an explosion in federal farm aid. For a decade, from 1972 to 1981, farm programs cost an average $3 billion a year. The tab for 1982 through 1984 was $34 billion.[10]

The combination of huge outlays and worsening conditions for many farmers has produced critical assessments such as these: "Farm policies have never worked very well, and the justification for them seems to weaken progressively."[11] "Almost everyone—members of Congress, bankers, main street merchants, supermarket shoppers and above all farmers themselves—agrees the system is badly out of kilter."[12] "From political left to right, there is near unanimity: the complex federal support system of farm loans, subsidies, reserves, and other controls is broken and needs fixing, reshaping, or just plain euthanasia."[13]

As recently as the 1970s, agricultural aid seemed to be meeting its economic goal of farm solvency, though critics even then deplored its cost and contradictory features. In the 1980s, with family farms in trouble, the program's defects stand out glaringly.

There is a basic conflict at the heart of federal policy. Some programs seek to cushion farmers from economic risk by providing higher and more stable prices than the market would pay for their crops over time. Other programs try to prevent the overproduction of food that results from these subsidies. They do this in a way that has always bothered many Americans: by paying farmers not to grow food.

"While the '70s were the decade of flash and cash, the '80s look to be weak and bleak."[14] What caused the boom and bust?

Ironically, the boom of the 1970s sent a signal which reversed previous agricultural policy and set the stage for the bust of the 1980s. Since the 1950s, the government had tried to deal with constant farm surpluses by paying to keep land out of cultivation. It didn't work. Farmers doubled their yields per acre on the land that remained. Thus they got paid for not growing on some acreage, and were covered by price supports for the crops they grew on other acreage.

The government's error was in restricting land rather than production. U.S. officials learned a lesson strangely similar to that of the U.S.S.R., where yields on small private plots are vastly higher per acre than those on collective farms. American farmers took their marginal land out of production and then applied more fertilizer, irrigation, and advanced cultivating techniques to the remainder.

To be paid to grow and paid not to grow was probably too good a deal to last. "Only the dramatic changes of the 1970s spared the programs from self-destruction."[15] There was a shift of focus from abundance to scarcity. Suddenly it seemed that everything American agriculture could produce would find a market.

The reason for this shift was the worldwide effort to improve diets by increasing meat production. This required huge amounts of feed grains, far beyond the capacity of local farms. The gap was filled by U.S. exports. Over the decade of the 1970s, grain and vegetable oil exports tripled. In the early 1950s, only 10 percent of these crops were shipped overseas; by 1979 the figure was 40 percent.[16]

The scarcity message was reinforced by concern about future threats to American farm productivity: soil erosion and depletion, water shortages, and fertilizer costs boosted by energy price hikes.

Government's role was reoriented toward preventing scarcity by accumulating surpluses in good years to neurtralize shortages in bad years. This seemed the best of all possible worlds, protecting farmers' incomes while protecting consumers against price shocks. But the situation proved too good to last.

In 1980 crucial changes took hold. Exports began to slow due to a sluggish world economy, international debt problems, and reduced population growth. President Carter's partial embargo on Soviet grain sales dealt exports a further blow. And while "demand" stagnated, "supply" surged due to renewed productivity growth. By 1982 corn yields were 25 percent above 1977.

In a return to the 1950s, surpluses skyrocketed. Reserves of grain held by government and in private hands tripled from 1981 to 1983. This glut sent prices down and farm subsidy costs up. The 1950s-era commitment to support minimum price levels caused farm payments to rise from $2.75 billion in 1980 to $21.8 billion in 1983—making them the fastest growing item in the Reagan Administration budget.[17]

In early 1983, Agriculture Secretary John Block thought he had found a way to get out of the swamp created by falling prices on the farm and huge food surpluses in government hands. Instead of being paid money to idle part of their acreage, farmers would be given ownership of surplus food in government warehouses. That would serve to reduce the cost of storage. It would also raise market prices by drawing down supplies, thereby relieving the budget of billions in price-support costs.[18]

The program was called payment-in-kind (PIK). To its supporters, it was a one-time effort to draw down huge reserves and to put economic assets in the hands of farmers who might otherwise go out of business or default on government loans. To its critics, PIK was "a massive giveaway"[19] and "a bureaucratic nightmare."[20]

The value of commodities given to farmers is expected to run as high as $12 billion, not counting administrative costs. The taxpayers' net loss is the amount government would have made on these sales minus savings on storage and price supports. An embarrassingly large part of the $12 billion has flowed into the coffers of large farmers, some of whom received over $1 million worth of commodities.

As PIK drove up grain prices, it hurt livestock and poultry producers who were counting on low costs for feed grains. As it slowed new planting, it hurt the farm supply industry. Main Street in Farm Country, U.S.A., is struggling to survive.

It is not even clear if PIK achieved its intended purpose. Once again, farmers took their worst acreage out of production while applying more fertilizer and pesticides to the remaining land. Record wheat yields of 40.7 bushels per acre were expected to make the 1983 harvest third largest on record despite an 18 percent reduction in acreage.[21]

Maddeningly, stocks of crops more dependent on summer rains were sent plunging by a severe drought. The 1983 corn crop was 38 percent below the 1982 crop. Thanks to the drought, "this surgical effort to trim government payments and stocks may boomerang into a major increase in retail food prices," said economist Robert Samuelson in September 1983.[22]

Wheat and corn are key feed grains. A rise in their cost reduces meat and poultry production, which causes retail meat prices to rise. The year 1983 illustrated the economic, technological, and natural factors affecting agriculture. "The devastating drought . . . did more than any government program to reduce surplus stocks." It also served as "a singular reminder . . . of the risks in reducing production in a world that remains vulnerable to unpredictable events."[23]

Far more farmers than anticipated agreed to idle their land. They took 83 million acres of grain and cotton land out of production, one-third of the total. That was more than Block figured. The Agriculture Department found it owned less wheat and cotton than needed to meet its obligations. Surplus stocks remained enormous, but it was now owned by farmers. The solution (final testimony to the upheaval caused by PIK): Foreclose on farmer-held surpluses and force some farmers to turn over part of their current crop at the government-supported price level.[24]

Angry cotton farmers protested the idea of selling to the government at 55 cents a pound when the market price was 70 cents. They got Congress to bail them out in July 1983. Taxpayers funded the purchase at prices as high as 77 cents a pound. Nearly 50 farms, many owned by large corporations, got a million dollars or more of free cotton. The other side of the program, promising to leave land idle, came as a bonanza for some 2,000 farmers in California's Central Valley. Spring floods covered the fields until well into summer. "To be paid for not growing cotton on underwater land is really something," marveled one Kings County farmer. "I couldn't have planted this year even if I'd been wearing scuba gear."[25]

The government won't be able to offer much in the way of PIK in the future. The program is being phased out because federal surplus stocks are running low. In the future, when reserves build up again, PIK is unlikely to be revived because of the criticism it has drawn.[26]

If PIK is a sort of one-time, non-repeatable policy disaster, the government's long-standing farm-aid programs are also up for reform.

A prime candidate is the system of "deficiency payments" for major crops, including wheat, feed grains, rice, upland cotton, and dairy products. The system is designed to close any gaps among three kinds of prices: actual *market* prices for which farmers sell their crops; *support* prices, which are used to determine value when farmers use crops in storage as collateral for federal loans; and *target* prices, which are set at a fixed level.

When the target price level is the highest of the three (and it often is) farmers are paid the difference between it and either the market price or the support price, whichever is smaller.

The problem is "this floor-setting means that no price received by farmers gets too low to discourage them from farming. Indeed, price floors encourage those who shouldn't be tilling to keep right on. Thus, the farm program produces too many farmers producing too much stuff."[27] Target prices give farmers economic insulation. But they do so by blocking the signals that market prices send, and thus they undermine the balance between demand and supply.

The federal program of target prices makes overproduction the norm. The federal program of crop loans is designed to discourage production. Farmers who agree to idle part of their land can borrow against crops they have in storage. These crops are valued at a specified loan rate, or support price. If the market price rises above the support price, a farmer can sell the grain pledged as collateral and repay the loan. If the market price is lower, a farmer can keep the loan and forfeit the grain, in effect selling it to the government at an above-market price.

Loan levels have been set so high by Congress that farmers have an incentive to overproduce even when demand is weak. And when large harvests reduce prices, the government is stuck holding a huge quantity of forfeited crops. In fiscal 1983, two bumper harvests drove loan value to a net cost of $8.4 billion, up 20 percent in one year.[28]

In August 1983 the government stockpile of surplus food was set at 1.3 billion bushels of wheat, 3.4 billion bushels of corn, 1.6 billion pounds of dried milk, 982 million pounds of cheese, 567 million pounds of butter, and comparably huge volumes of peanuts, honey, and soybeans. Total stockpile value was almost $24 billion.

The U.S. Conference of Mayors at the same time identified hunger as "the most prevalent and insidious" problem facing the nation's cities. Yet if the government distributed large amounts of the stored surplus to the poor, it risked cutting market prices and forcing federal purchase of still more surplus production.[29]

Meanwhile, family farms were going over the financial precipice in record numbers because government largesse had driven U.S. agricultural prices to a level that made them uncompetitive in the arena they needed for survival: the world market.

When world prices fall below government-set target prices, American farmers keep their output at home. They store it rather than sell abroad. When the biggest supplier sits on the sidelines, world prices rise. This encourages other nations to produce and export more. At the same time, price targets and supports get built-in (capitalized) as part of U.S. farmland values. The land is worth more because the price of its output is guaranteed. But this increases production costs and pushes them higher than competitive world prices.[30]

The problem is aggravated by two other factors: tax shelters and tight money. A number of bizarre tax shelters allow wealthy non-farmers to get involved in such activities as large-scale feeding facilities for cattle and hogs, and the planting of vineyards and orchards. Joined in some cases by large farmers, they have an advantage over smaller operators because the economics of the tax code subsidizes them. Sometimes even financial losses become attractive due to the tax consequences. This distorts market economics and drives up basic U.S. agricultural costs still higher.[31]

Monetary policy has kept the dollar expensive compared to foreign currencies. This has reduced American agricultural shipments abroad, just as it has hit industrial exports. The price premium on the dollar is created by its scarcity, and one cause of its scarcity is the deficit. A ravenous demand for dollars by the Treasury has not been accommodated by the Federal Reserve printing money, but by high interest rates rationing other users of dollars out of the market. Among those rationed out have been overseas buyers of U.S. goods. And among the goods are farm crops.

The combined impact of all this is that "the U.S. not only allows other nations to increase their market share, but renders its own exports less competitive. In short, we undercut ourselves. Rather neatly."[32]

The instinct among some in Congress is to deal with the "uncertainty and frustration which has swathed rural America" by adding yet another cost to government spending for agriculture. Defenders call it putting an end to "Reagan's pinch-penny handling of federal farm-credit programs."[33] Critics call it reopening the floodgates to pour largesse upon the land. The programs at issue are the Rural Electrification Administration (REA) and the Farmers Home Administration (FmHA).

The REA was founded in 1935 to bring electricity to rural America. Today, even though 99 percent of farms have electricity, the REA is as busy as ever. In 1949, after its basic mission was complete, REA was given authority to bring telephone service to rural America. Today, 95 percent of farms have telephones, yet REA made $560 million in new phone loans and loan guarantees in 1983. President Carter in 1979 secured yet another mission for REA: to "overcome isolation in rural areas through modern communications technology." And so was born REA community antenna television, which extended $58 million in loans and guarantees in 1980, its first year of operation.

Almost as important a duty for REA as advancing new services has been subsidizing the cost of existing services. The price of electricity is held down 8–12 percent below that for unsubsidized customers. In one region of the country, REA's role is filled by another agency, the Tennessee Valley Authority (TVA). It provides power at 60 percent the national average (and at less than half Frost Belt rates) by access to cheap federal loans, of which $2 billion are outstanding.

In 1984 the House ignored Administration opposition and voted to forgive a $7.9 billion federal loan to REA while expanding subsidies to rural electrical cooperatives at a total cost of $21 billion.

An even bigger source of loans is the Farmers Home Administration, which made more than $6 billion in loans in 1983 and has a total $51 billion outstanding. FmHA was slated to increase its activity 25 percent in 1984, with new loans of $7.8 billion. The Administration went after FmHA's budget in 1981 because the agency was offering 40-year rural housing loans at 5 and 7 percent, with no downpayment. Congress had continually expanded the program without limiting borrowers to those unable to get credit elsewhere. The Administration's stance could do no more than slow the rate of growth in loans outstanding.[34]

This "tight-fisted" policy of screening applicants more selectively created a "bitter backlash" as farmers were squeezed by declining land values, a credit crunch, reduced sales, the drought of 1983, and the freeze of 1984.

As farm failures soared, debt and loan deliquencies in FmHA programs climbed from 27 percent in 1980 to 56 percent in 1984. FmHA is supposed to be the "lender of last resort" for financially beset farmers. Inevitably, it became the focus of efforts to relieve a crisis in agriculture caused by factors that ranged from the weather to the perverse impact of government programs that had long worked at cross-purposes.

In the spring of 1983 two Democratic congressmen from California wrote Agriculture Secretary John Block asking that loan rules be relaxed for farmers in distress. Three months later they got a "no" from FmHA. The House passed a bill to require extra leniency in foreclosing on deliquent loans. Administration pressure stalled it in the Senate. In December 1983 a court ordered the release of $600 million in emergency farm loans which Congress had authorized but Block had refused to release.

In September 1984 some GOP strategists were urging President Reagan to court the farm vote by supporting a $35.7 billion budget appropriation for agriculture. One reason for the President's hestitation was Budget Director Stockman's opposition to $625 million in new emergency farm loans.

Suddenly, on September 18, the President announced FmHA would excuse borrowers from paying interest and principal on their loans for as much as five years, and would spend up to $650 million to guarantee troubled loans if banks agreed to write off 10 percent of any given loan. When asked about the timing of his announcement on the eve of a Farm Belt campaign swing, the President deadpanned, "I know that none of you . . . are going to believe this. It wasn't done with that in mind. It was done because there are people out there who need help."[35]

The question that arises is whether this form of help is anything more than yet another expensive band-aid on a program which has turned out to be an almost unique policy disaster. Perhaps nowhere else in the budget has so much money been spent on so few and yet done for them so little good. Total federal outlays for agriculture are at a level which equals or exceeds net farm income each year. Yet agricultural America is in severe distress.

Taxpayers subsidize farmers getting into business, lend them money if they go broke, and prop up prices at levels only the inefficient farmer needs. In the first three years of this decade, the budget burden for these assists soared while the economics of agriculture sagged.

To persist along the same lines, to follow the instinct toward subsidies and bailout, is to adopt a farm policy which is the rural equivalent of "lemon socialism"—that much-derided form of industrial policy where government props up the losers. What is really dangerous is that such a policy can end up making losers out of many who might have succeeded in a free market.

"Solutions must make American prices more, not less, competitive," writes Susan Lee of the *Wall Street Journal*. "This means getting the government out of agriculture." But is such a proposal from the "free market crowd" practical? Lee admits, "Even those who dislike the farm program are anxious about this solution."[36]

Those who believe such a dramatic change can occur point to ways in which market mechanisms could take the place of subsidies in providing farmers the degree of security and stability they need. The ranks of American agriculture might be thinned somewhat as those unable to survive without today's props left the fields. But the farming which remained would be stronger and healthier, more able to compete and far less costly to the taxpayer.

Free market advocates cite "private income buffers" which can fill the role of a government farm program: "to smooth out the boom-bust cycle of limiting the bust side of things."[37] These buffers include forward contracts, the futures market, and options. Each is basically a promise to sell a specific quantity at a specific price to be delivered at a specific time. The contract is firm on all provisions. The futures market is flexible on price. Options are flexible on timing.

Proponents of free market mechanisms say they will "help restore U.S. farming to a full and fierce competitive position in the world market." Government should pull back from its current level of intervention not only to make farming more efficient, but to encourage farmers to use private risk management. "After all, if the cost of risk can be transferred to the taxpayer, why not? It's no wonder the farm program's cost is out of control."[38]

Other reformers have more modest aims. They would scale back rather than abolish federal programs. Two key reforms have already been applied to one major crop, soybeans. Deficiency payments based on target prices have been eliminated, and loans based on support prices are set at 75 percent of the average market price for the previous three years. The result, analysts believe, is a system which provides "market stabilization" but does not attempt to raise prices above "long-term clearing levels."[39] What this means is that farmers in need are protected against hardship without an incentive for excess production being created.

The case for a change in policy is strong. Today's program distorts domestic markets, undermines our international competitiveness, is subject to huge cost surges, and pays half its benefits to the wealthiest 12 percent of farmers. Even $20 billion annual outlays have not sufficed to protect the family farmer from risk and even from bankruptcy. This is due both to a mistargeting of benefits and to competitive handicaps imposed by the program itself. To a degree, the hand that heals has become the hand that kills.

The Department of Agriculture was established in 1862 to distribute seeds to farmers. Its original budget was $64,000 and it had a staff of nine. In the America of those days, 78 percent of the people lived on the farm.

Today the Department is the fourth largest federal agency, with a budget exceeding $20 billion in "bad" years. Three percent of the people live on the farm. The seed distribution program was a success. The farm stabilization program needs reform.

This is probably the most productive day in the history of the Corporation.
—Edward Noble, Chairman of the federal Synthetic Fuels Corp., as the SFC approved $4.4 billion in subsidies[40]

This incredible enterprise was launched with the goal of committing $15 billion of taxpayer money to projects that would substitute expensive energy for cheap energy.
—*Wall Street Journal* editorial[41]

On April 5, 1984, the U.S. Synthetic Fuels Corporation (SFC) board voted to help fund six large energy projects. The $4.4 billion in total subsidies was 36 times the money spent by the board up to that point in its three-year existence.[42] It might seem that the word "productive" is a strange one for its chairman to apply. But "officials of the U.S. Synthetic Fuels Corporation face a dilemma seldom encountered by Washington bureaucrats: They have billions of dollars to hand out and no takers."[43] How this peculiar situation developed is part of the recent history of energy economics.

On July 4, 1980 President Carter signed legislation creating the SFC. A bipartisan groundswell of support had propelled the bill through Congress. Revolution in Iran had reawakened fears of widespread fuel shortages like those caused by the 1973 Arab oil embargo. Lawmakers predicted the corporation would became a unique "investment bank" able to cut through red tape and speed production of thousands of barrels of synthetic fuel daily from coal, tar sands, oil shale, and other unconventional sources.

The idea was praised as a model of cooperation between the public and private sectors; it was hailed as America's "ace in the hole" for achieving energy independence. Yet four years later, Energy Secretary Donald Hodel could characterize the synfuels effort as "absolutely moribund."[44]

True, the Corporation was eating up an operating budget of $35 million a year,[45] including staff salaries which ranged up to $108,000.[46] But by August 1984 only $740 million, aid to two relatively small projects, had been given out.[47] That "productive" day in April which so pleased the chairman did not actually commit $4 billion. It just approved a process by which contracts might be signed.[48] The agency's inability to spend money is highlighted by its original $15 billion appropriation and still more by its authorization to hand out $88 billion by 1992. These vast sums were to come from the windfall profits tax on oil companies.[49]

What caused the program to fall apart was that trends in energy prices didn't continue in the direction which seemed inevitable. Oil shortages made synfuels look sensible as a way to secure supplies in an unstable world. Oil price surges made synfuels look like they might soon be competitive on the open market. But in the 1980s both the fears and the hopes on which the logic of synfuels was based were to change a great deal. The result would justify the kind of biting assessment which *Wall Street Journal* editorialists applied with perfect hindsight on the preceding page.

Since 1980 an energy market unencumbered by price controls has mobilized the forces of oil exploration to increase supplies. At the same time, the 1970s price surge did make more attractive one alternative to petroleum: conservation. This reduced demand. In the early 1980s, U.S. imports fell 51 percent, from 5.3 million barrels per day to 2.6 million.[50]

More serious for the economics of synfuels, the price of oil fell by 30 percent, to $28 a barrel, by 1983.[51] In 1981, when the price seemed headed to $40 and was forecasted to rise rapidly beyond that level, "a price support only needed to be moderately above the market" to make synfuels feasible.[52]

In December 1983 the synfuels corporation extended $2.7 billion in price guarantees to Union Oil for its shale project at Parachute Creek, Colorado. Exxon had begun the project in 1981 and abandoned it two years later. Over 2,000 jobs were lost in an instant. Union took over the job and got a promise of $67 a barrel in December 1983.[53] Within eight months the guarantee was hiked to $92 a barrel—three times the world price and nearly double the $48 which SFC estimates oil will sell for in 1989 when Parachute Creek begins production.[54]

"The slumping world oil market . . . has dissipated the enthusiasm of private corporations for developing costly new technologies for producing fuel," said one analyst. "Generous financial incentives appear to be needed to attract firms willing to risk building the facilities to make synthetic fuels."[55]

The incentives did appear generous. In addition to a price guarantee that would run for 10 years, Union could receive as much as $3.4 billion in tax breaks for building the project.[56]

One area of difficulty is scientific as well as economic and political. The charter of SFC called for it to encourage and support development of synthetic fuels from both unconventional technologies and those which are proven but not yet commercially "on line." But only $200 million of the original $15 billion in funding was set aside for research and development activities. The rest was to backstop the construction of plants using proven industrial processes.[57]

Ironically, two of SFC's few projects have run afoul of this provision. Union Oil's plant uses technology similar to another federally subsidized project at Parachute Creek. Critics charge this means government funds are not advancing the state of the art. A countercharge is that the other plant isn't working. The General Accounting Office reported twenty unsuccessful attempts to get it in operation. Union Oil denies fundamental problems, but cannot say when full production will begin.[58]

A second example is the Cool Water coal gasification plant in California's Mojave Desert. Aside from the fact that there is no shortage of natural gas in the U.S., the project may actually be experimental, designed to test a new process said to be more efficient than those now in use. Under its original charter, SFC could give such a project part of the $200 million in research and development funds, but nothing from its operating account. Cool Water was turned down in 1981 because it was not a "commercial" synfuels plant.

Cool Water went ahead with blue-chip private financing: Texaco, General Electric, Bechtel Engineering, and the Southern California Edison Company. By late 1982 it was ahead of schedule and under budget. It utilized coal—an abundant American resource—and it had impeccable sponsors.

The synfuels corporation by this time was well behind schedule in handing out money. Cool Water looked more interesting. Its sponsors had continued to lobby the corporation, threatening to abandon it unless there was an infusion of federal aid. In July 1983, SFC put up $120 million in price guarantees. The agreement was structured to transform the plant from an experimental to an operating facility.[59]

Even more of an eyebrow-raiser is the largest synfuels project in the country, the Great Plains Coal Gassification Project in Beulah, North Dakota. It was granted a subsidy in 1984 after having already been blessed with the largest federal loan guarantee up to that time—$2 billion from the Department of Energy in 1981. The previous record was $1.1 billion to stave off New York City bankruptcy in 1976.

In October 1983 the five major energy companies which are backers of Beulah asked SFC for price supports like those given Union Oil at Parachute Creek. SFC analysts concluded, as had earlier studies by Congress and the Energy Department, that such aid was not needed. Even with low prices for energy, the project appeared profitable—especially when tax implications for the parent companies were considered. So SFC denied the request.

Following this decision, the corporation board chairman was "urged" to reconsider by the White House and by members of Congress including House Majority Leader Jim Wright. To underscore the appeal, the project's partners threatened to abandon Great Plains if price supports were not forthcoming.

SFC reversed itself. The corporation's directors did not mention any specific project. Instead they announced a new "competitive" solicitation for coal gasification projects. As it happened, the terms were such that they could be met by only one project: Great Plains.[60]

The original price support demand was $1.6 billion. By April 1984 this has been trimmed to $790 million. Great Plains was 95 percent complete and set to begin production in December 1984. But backers said they would cease all work without the subsidy. On April 27 the board approved a letter of intent. Even this did no more than "substantially mitigate"—not eliminate—the threat of shutdown.[61] Beulah's backers were seeking a zero-risk posture. As Congressman Mike Synar, chairman of the House subcommittee that oversees synfuels, had said, "taxpayers may have to pay through the nose for a decision based on little more than veiled corporate threats and back-room arm twisting."[62]

Parachute Creek, Cool Water, and Great Plains illustrate two key problems which have bedeviled the synfuels program: defining "appropriate technology" and avoiding corporate welfare.

The original SFC charter may have drawn an impossibly narrow technical line for the corporation to walk in sponsoring projects. On the one hand, only $200 million could go for research and development. This ruled out major aid to projects which seemed to be "experimental." On the other hand, plants which were commercially viable shouldn't be helped, because SFC's mission was to find marginal cases where it could make the difference. In practice, only a fine wedge seemed to exist between the two cases.

Parachute Creek provided a poetic illustration of the absurd dilemma which could arise. This single plant was charged with being an experiment in unworkable technology ("too risky") and a copy of proven technology ("not risky enough"). Logically, only one charge could be true. Legally, either would appear to disqualify the project from funding.

Cool Water seemed to be clearly in the experimental category while Great Plains looked like corporate welfare. Where was SFC's manuevering room for acceptable decisions?

The budgetary walls began to close in on synfuels during early 1984. In February the board, embarrassed that it had only passed out $123 million of its $15 billion budget in three years, adopted a "basic business" plan calling for it to unload the remainder within one year. But in the next few weeks, five major projects the agency hoped to finance were shelved by their corporate sponsors as either too expensive or technically unfeasible. SFC said this was progress; it reflected success in "weeding out" unrealistic projects. But critics noted that the dropouts were among the most advanced proposals before the corporation. "The private sectors is walking away from these projects as bad investments," said one SFC foe.[63]

An unusual coalition was forming against synfuels. Environmentalists wanted SFC abolished because they feared the physical impact of oil shale plants and other synfuel facilities. Economic conservatives felt SFC had become a nesting place for "energy radicals." The agency had an "aggressively liberal staff" which was reinforced by a group of academics who "bemoan the market's imperfections" and echo the alarmist sentiments of "exaggerationists" like Harvard energy specialist Daniel Yergin.[64]

What may have been decisive, however, was that some members of Congress began to cast a wistful eye at the corporation's unspent billions. Ideas began to pop up for reprogramming the funds to other domestic programs, demonstrating the truth of the saying that politics abhors a vacuum. This prospect gave a long-skeptical Office of Management and Budget the chance to step forward and urge decisive action to trim SFC's resources rather than see them dissipated in a series of congressional raids.

An earlier OMB initiative had caused the Reagan Administration to warn the synfuels board in December 1983 that it should not seek more money after it had spent the original $15 billion. SFC vice president for finance Edward Miller tiptoed around the threat. He said that when SFC gave Congress a "comprehensive strategy for the future" in 1984, it would "not necessarily" seek all the $68 billion in added funding envisioned by the 1980 act. This drew a blunt response from Energy Secretary Hodel's office. The board was told $15 billion was "adequate" and there was "no reason" to ask for more.[65]

The April 1984 commitment of $790 million to Great Plains was a sort of last gasp in new funding. It coasted through in overtime on the momentum provided by previous arm-twisting. But the surge of project abandonments in March really ended the game. On May 14 the new order of things was announced.

President Reagan asked Congress to slash $9.5 billion from SFC, about two-thirds of its total budget. He also proposed a new market-oriented test that would have the effect of eliminating nine of the ten projects before the agency for funding.

The test was simply that SFC could only fund projects "whose products will not cost significantly more than the projected market price of competing fuels." The intent, said the White House, was to "strike a balance between avoiding unnecessary and wasteful expenditures . . . and preserving a sound, sensibly scaled program." Energy Secretary Hodel added: "National security is supported by synthetic fuels, but not at any price. . . . The problem with these projects to date is that they never seem to achieve commercial viability." Under this new doctrine, the only survivor appeared to be Great Plains.[66]

The new market-oriented test gave SFC a much clearer focus. It would now be much easier to know whether a project should qualify for funding. Only two areas of dispute might arise between an applicant and the board. First, had a realistic estimate been made of a proposed plant's ability to produce at competitive prices? Second, did the plant really need federal assistance?

The second question went to the heart of a dilemma created by SFC's new and narrow role. When it was created in 1980, the corporation should have focused solely on research and development, many analysts believed. Of particular value would be grants to small, innovative firms and even to individual inventors. After the corporation was set up with a large operating budget, critics including Congressman Tom Corcoran pushed for SFC to be restricted along these lines.[67]

The policy change of May 14 moved in exactly the opposite direction. As a result, SFC was left with a single function which was embarrassingly close to dispensing corporate welfare: giving loan guarantees and price supports to big firms building plants with proven technologies.

At the same time, of course, billions were lopped off the SFC budget. This reduced its ability to have any impact at all on America's energy future and reawakened the debate on whether the country needs a government program on synthetic fuel.

Those who say "yes" believe the current oil glut is only temporary. They believe the U.S. should be working to build a synthetic fuels industry for the 1990s and beyond. SFC board chairman Noble says, "I think that now, when we don't have a crisis, we must go ahead and show the rest of the world we can" develop synfuels.[68] Ashland Oil Company chairman John Hall argues that "the nation faces a dilemma. . . . If we rely on the free market with only limited government assistance, synthetic fuels may not be available in the next crisis, when they will be badly needed."[69] The *Washington Post* believes that "to abandon synthetic fuels development now would be wanton. . . . Their purpose is not to protect consumers against another short, sudden disruption [but as] insurance against the slow, gradual tightening of supplies that may emerge over coming decades."[70]

In the summer of 1967, *Daedalus*, the journal of the American Academy of Arts and Sciences, published a reported titled, "Toward the Year 2000: Work in Progress." Energy did not make the list of issues. This serves as a cautionary note to today's widespread indifference about energy issues. The 1990s could end up resembling the 1970s more than the 1980s. If they do, the hedge against oil shortages that synfuels provide would look attractive.

But there is another cautionary note in the synfuels story. If it had actually spent the authorized budget of $88 billion, SFC would have been the biggest peacetime effort in American history, with a cost greater than combined outlays for the Marshall Plan, the Interstate Highway System, and the NASA moon landing.[71]

In May 1983 former SFC financial economist Elena Folkerts-Landau made this estimate of the program's potential fiscal impact: "If the appropriation is increased to $83 billion next year as planned, and if 80 to 90 percent of this is financed by the U.S. Treasury as predicted by senior officials of SFC, the effect on interest rates will be the same as an anticipated $66–$75 billion increase in the 1987–90 federal deficits. The SFC's potential outlays are nearly ten times the size of the Energy Department and equal to 35 percent of the 1983 defense budget."

Folkerts-Landau noted "the SFC is not a historical fluke or an outgrowth of some minority's misguided judgement. It was supported in 1980 by an overwhelming bipartisan vote" in Congress. "Born in a moment of impulse, it became quickly outdated by world events."[72] The awesome fiscal magnitudes Folkerts-Landau cited never became reality only because of an event virtually unique in the annals of bureaucracy. Here was an agency unable to spend more than a fraction of its budget. This incapacity violated a fundamental rule of survival and growth: if you spend all you have, you may get a bigger budget; if you spend less than you could, your budget will not grow; if you spend far less, you risk extinction.

In this case, the taxpayer can probably be grateful. The original concept of SFC was a massive exercise in industrial policy. Government gets generally low marks for its capacity to pick "winners." It either ends up helping those who would be winners without help from the taxpayer, or sticking with "losers" to save face—and to save jobs. Government gets much better marks as a source of support for research and development. At its best, the process manages to target funds toward projects that are almost profitable on their own. By providing that extra margin, government can achieve a high rate of "leveraging"—many dollars returned in economic benefit for each tax dollar spent on a project.

The first effort at a synfuels program searched in vain to find this sensible middle ground. Caught unprepared when energy economics changed, the SFC seemed unable to find projects where leveraging was possible. It alternated between backing "premature commercialization of ill-advised technologies"[73] and responding to corporate threats that plants using proven processes would be shut down unless subsidies were forthcoming. These should have been two extremes SFC sought to avoid; instead they became the substance of its program.

If and when America makes a fresh start toward developing a synfuels capacity, the focus should be on research and development, especially by small, innovative firms, and on aiding projects whose technology is neither premature nor proven, but at the edge of feasibility where a boost can help.

This is a large order. But then, $15 billion was a large sum of money. It is fortunate that this appropriation wasn't spent as planned—even if the day may come for a synfuels program.

> This [water projects bill] is a prime example of the type of big-spending, budget-busting bill that undermines confidence in our nation's ability to control spending and reduce the deficit.
> —Budget Director David Stockman[74]

> If you're spending, everybody loves you.
> —Congressman Trent Lott[75]

The term "pork barrel" has its roots in the days when slaves fought over the special rations of salt pork that plantation owners sometimes dispensed from a barrel. In a 1919 essay, the *National Municipal Review* recalled that such events would bring a rush in which each participant "would strive to grab as much as possible for himself." It continued: "Members of Congress, in the stampede to get local appropriations items into the omnibus rivers-and-harbors bills, behaved so much like slaves rushing to the pork barrel that these bills were facetiously styled pork-barrel bills."[76]

Even in 1919 it was possible to look back on the tradition of a phrase dating from the 1870s. That great tradition has continued unbroken to this day. As *Business Week* observed in October 1983: "Nothing juices up the reelection bid of a member of Congress quite like an infusion of federal construction funds into the home district."[77]

William Proxmire, the senator who hands out Golden Fleece awards, asserts that "pork is so popular on Capitol Hill there's no way to stop it. The hardest thing in politics is to get people who have been taking a free ride to pay their own way."[78] What Proxmire means by "free" is the vote-getting appeal of a big federal project. When a congressman grabs a plum for the district, home folks feel they count for something. They are "getting a return" on their taxes.

This points up one of the most insidious forces behind pork-barrel politics. Congress in 1984 had a bill before it to authorize spending $18 billion on some 300 water projects which were the pets of various members. The federal government has been subsidizing such projects since 1902. Many experts believe that "the cost-effective sites for dams and other water projects have been used up" and as a result, "collecting and diverting water has become very costly."[79] How can it be that the practice continues, and that indeed the 1984 bill was "easily the biggest piece of pork-barrel legislation in American history"?[80]

A major reason why economically unsound projects still seem politically attractive is that they are a "return on the tax dollar." The arithmetic works like this: Suppose there is an irrigation project which will return 20 cents of benefit for each dollar of cost. Suppose this project is located in a state whose residents pay 5 cents of each federal tax dollar. At this point the dollar disappears. It is 20 cents of benefit for 5 cents of cost—a good deal.

Pork-barrel bills are based on such arithmetic. Each project looks great in isolation. But collectively, the nation's taxpayers are forking over 100 percent of federal revenues and are underwriting many projects which will not pay for themselves. Yet, members of Congress still proudly "bring home the bacon" to their districts.

The extent to which taxpayers nationwide take the cost burden off the shoulders of project beneficiaries is startling. Analysts estimate that users pay an average 19 percent of the tab for irrigation and flood control projects,[81] and an average 10 percent for inland waterway projects.[82] There was consternation in 1984 when Congressman Thomas Petri introduced an amendment requiring up-front contributions of up to 50 percent from local users of Corps of Engineers water projects.

Petri's radical idea was in an amendment to a House bill which would allow beneficiaries up to fifty years to repay. In some cases, the U.S. tax-payer would pick up the entire cost. Budget Director Stockman said the Petri amendment would make it much more likely he could recommend the bill to the President.[83]

Corps of Engineers projects are spread over the country. Bureau of Recla-mation (BOR) projects are concentrated in the West. Petri's front-money rule would have affected only the former. The war on BOR projects had already been lost. The roots of that defeat lie as far back as the start of the Carter Administration.

Shortly after taking office, President Carter told Congress he would not support eighteen of the most wasteful and environmentally hazardous water projects then pending. Carter was told in return that any attempt to follow through on that threat would doom his entire legislative program. In the face of this friendly advice from the barons of Congress, the President backed down. This retreat proved politically disastrous—a sign that Carter could be intimidated.

Reagan's budget office campaigned for three full years to shift some of the cost of major water projects from the federal government to local interests. Stockman and others suggested that something like 35 percent of the bill should be covered by those who would benefit.

The important principle was a fixed share. The change would not only relieve federal taxpayers; it would also force local interests to find more eco-nomical ways of meeting their water needs. "This would take the pork right out of the barrel," said Brent Blackwelder of the Environmental Policy Institute.[84]

The effect of pricing water below its true cost is dramatic. Hundreds of thousands of acres of marginal farmland have been brought into cultivation, adding to crop overproduction and falling farm prices. Cheap water has an even more important impact. It discourages conservation, leading to waste that could be avoided with more efficient irrigation systems. The result is to set the stage for water shortages—and to create demand for yet more dams and canals.[85]

In early 1984, fifteen Republican Senators from the West struck back against the Stockman-environmentalist coalition. In a letter organized by Reagan's own campaign chairman, Nevada Senator Paul Laxalt, they warned the President that asking users to share the cost "would be viewed as anti-West as the infamous Carter 'Hit List.'"[86]

The President capitulated. Interior Secretary William Clark hand-delivered the President's response to Laxalt. The government would "work out" the beneficiaries' share of each dam and irrigation project on a case-by-case basis rather than following the "rigid, fixed-formula approach" he ini-tially supported.

At the same time, Secretary Clark asked Congress to lift the limit on the amount of federally subsidized irrigation water that farmers can receive. The Administration had originally supported this limit when it was enacted in 1982.

On each issue, the President offered a consolation to critics. Fixed-share financing had lost his support, but he believed users "should ultimately bear a substantial part of the cost." As for the water limit, it would be "small farmers" who would benefit by lifting the acreage restriction on subsidies.

Senator Howard Metzenbaum called the new cost-sharing approach "a blatant cave-in" and "a triumph of political expediency over responsible policy." Congressman George Miller commented on lifting the water subsidy limit, "A concrete, enforceable agreement was made with Congress that big farmers would pay the full cost of water. Nothing is sacred in their pursuit of greed." These two Democrats saw the not-so-fine hand of election year politics behind the Administration's policy reversal.[87]

Senator Ernest Hollings likes to point out that it was the East, not the West, that was developed without the assistance of the federal government. Certainly, that is true in relative terms. But the most bizarre public works projects are generously distributed throughout the nation. Every analyst has a favorite example.

To Neal Peirce, the "biggest outrage" is the $500 million Cross-Florida Barge Canal. It began in 1942 as a refuge for ships escaping Nazi submarines off the Atlantic coast. The man who secured its first authorization is still the canal's prime mover today: Congressman Claude Pepper. Even though the governor of Florida has called the project "dangerous, needless, and incredibly expensive," Pepper has managed to beat down repeated efforts to kill the canal.[88]

Then there's the Tennessee-Tombigbee project, which the *Wall Street Journal* describes as a $4 billion project that parallels the Mississippi River, "causing us to wonder why the country needs two separate waterways to the Gulf."[89]

One of the sharpest recent controversies was over a project which has succeeded wonderfully well: Hoover Dam. The dispute was not over the dam's cost-effectiveness but its "revenue run-off." When Hoover was built fifty years ago, the government decided to make its power attractive for purchase by agreeing that, in the first fifty years of operation, rates would only be high enough to recover capital and operating costs. There would be no profit.

In 1984 the dam had been paid off and power contracts were up for review. Over the fifty years, Hoover's rates had fallen far below those charged for power from more recently constructed dams. In a truly competitive market, the government would set its rates at the same level as the cost of adding new power in the region. This is called the "marginal cost."

When the Administration proposed to change Hoover's power rates from the original zero-profit formula to a modern, marginal-cost formula, the proposal was crushed in Congress. As a result, those lucky enough to have a piece of the action will save a total of $1.8 billion during the rest of the decade, compared to what they would have paid in a competitive market.

The claim is made that current recipients deserve this subsidy as a reward for their willingness to buy Hoover's power at the start and because two utilities in the region paid for some of the generating equipment. But critics respond that whatever equity claim this created has long since been satisfied, especially since the dam itself was built with U.S. tax dollars.

Letting the good times roll at Hoover created a familiar problem: "Underpricing of power . . . leads to a greater demand for electricity, which in turn will lead to construction of new power plants elsewhere."[90] The taxpayer is hit with a double whammy. Price breaks from power subsidies mean revenue losses and a bigger deficit. They also mean power waste and the demand for yet more subsidized construction of new dams.

In Hoover's case, the list of winners is completely arbitrary. It includes Los Angeles but excludes San Diego and San Francisco. It includes Arizona and Nevada, but excludes Utah, New Mexico, and Colorado. This allocation of rights is based, fifty years after the event, on what is now a historic accident, not on supply and demand.

Since the beneficiaries are a minority of U.S. taxpayers, why didn't the Hoover formula fail in Congress and give away to one of more general equity? The answer lies in log-rolling, the practice of voting "aye" on other members' dubious interests with the understanding they will vote likewise on yours. Log-rolling tends to honor existing arrangements as "the good old ways."

What is the answer to water project giveaways? It would seem to come in two parts. First, those who benefit from a construction project should have to pay a fixed share of the costs up front, as the Petri amendment called for. Second, those who hold title to water rights should be able to sell them.

This second idea may seem startling. It would enable users who now get cheap water from federal projects to reap a windfall by selling the rights to that water at their true value. But the economy as a whole would quickly benefit. "Perhaps people shouldn't be able to make a profit on what the government has given them," concedes Kenneth Frederick of Resources for the Future. "But unless we allow it, we lock water into low-value uses, and the nation is worse off."[91]

If, for example, a power plant can buy existing water rather than go out and tap the water table or force creation of another costly dam, everyone benefits: the current user (who sells at a profit), the power plant (which lowers the cost of new power), and the economy as a whole (which buys the power).

For a long time, water rights of any sort were not permitted to be sold in many states unless the use of water stayed the same. This normally meant agriculture, whose water needs are vast compared to residential and even industrial users. Too often, water which might have generated power or been applied to more valuable urban uses was keeping marginal land in production and swelling crop surpluses.[92]

Gradually economics is changing the picture by loosening the law. For example, the Metropolitan Water District of Southern California is helping the rural Imperial Irrigation District install more efficient irrigation systems which could cut Imperial's needs by an amount equal to one-fourth of Metroplitan's supply. The saving would be diverted to MWD, which currently pays $250 per acre-foot of water compared to IID's $10.

A coalition of environmentalists, free market economists, and taxpayer advocates believe legal restraints to considering water a commodity must be removed and water projects must be moved from the pork barrel to the discipline of a true price system.

> Congress wants to save the taxpayers' money *and* spend the taxpayers' money. How do you do both? Ah, there is a way! The name of the game is to get off the budget.
> —Paul Blustein, *Forbes*[93]

An off-budget budget is like a non-bank bank: a term which causes the mind to glaze over. But the glaze in this case obscures a neat $1 trillion in federal activity.

One trillion dollars is a lot of money. It is equal to the national debt in 1981, or to the unfunded liability of federal employees' retirement programs in 1982, or to the on-budget budget for 1985.

Fortunately, the net burden implied by $1 billion in off-budget programs is not comparable to the other three examples. The actual addition to outlays and deficits from this source is about $20 billion a year. But arriving at that figure is no simple matter. The numbers have to be smoked out.

Off-budget spending is due almost entirely to federal loan programs: direct loans, loan guarantees, and loans made by government-sponsored enterprises.

During the past two decades Congress has enacted more than 350 loan programs. Each was created with a specific purpose which seemed sound and even laudable at the time. Each began with a targeted group of beneficiaries. But over the years, most loan programs have lost their focus and swelled in size. Direct loans tripled to $142 billion between 1974 and 1983. They almost always involve a rate subsidy, which doesn't show up in the budget.[94]

Loan guarantees also enable borrowers to get money more cheaply than they could otherwise, since creditors know the government backs them. If a borrower defaults and the Treasury pays off, a strange thing happens. The federal budget records an outlay (an expenditure) that has not been preceded by an appropriation (legal permission to spend). The budget simply "eats" this added expense.[95] The annual volume of guaranteed loans also tripled, to $400 billion between 1974 and 1983.[96]

Finally, there is lending generated by government-sponsored but privately owned enterprises. Huge amounts are provided for housing and to the farm economy in this manner. Sponsored lending is even larger than guaranteed lending—more than $400 billion.[97]

The $20 billion in annual outlays comes in three forms. First, if new direct loan extensions exceed repayments, the difference is a net addition to the budget. Second, if a guaranteed or sponsored loan is in default, the cost of paying the creditor is an outlay. Third, some direct spending programs have been moved off-budget for no good reason except it is a cozy place to be. They are spared the normal review process, but turn up in outlay totals anyway. Most notable is the strategic petroleum reserve program.[98]

The off-budget budget has been called an underground federal economy[99] and a fiscal fig leaf—it defies close inspection.[100] The obvious problem is that it adds to the difficulty of controlling costs and deficits. The not so obvious problem is that federal loan subsidies and guarantees ration credit, giving some interests an advantage over others in securing loans. This may distort investment in a way that damages the economy.

Ironically, the pressure to get off the budget was spurred by 1974 reforms designed to start cleaning up the budget. The Congressional Budget Act passed that year sought to create enforceable spending ceilings. Instead of the budget being built up from the appropriations favored by its committees, Congress would now build the budget from the top down, dividing an agreed total among the committees.

Prior to this reform, there wasn't any real incentive to get off-budget. Fiscal discipline was so loose that every program came through virtually unscathed. Loan programs were chosen to be moved off budget in 1974 not because they were less popular than direct spending—instead, the reason was that by coincidence a new vehicle had just been created which could handle them off-budget. This shift relieved pressure on visible spending totals, freeing up room to fund other programs under the supposedly tighter system.[101]

The new vehicle for handling loans was the Federal Financing Bank (FFB). It had come into being in 1973 to clean up the accounting and centralize the management of all government debt. Now the FFB was given a quite different role: to purchase federal agency loans with money borrowed from the Treasury.

Some forty agencies were raising money by selling securities directly to the public. If the FFB backed these loans, it could relieve costly bidding for funds among agencies and reduce the interest rates demanded by lenders, since the "full faith and credit" of the Treasury was pledged in repayment.[102]

There was an alarming case of "creative accounting" involved in this transaction. Once the FFB relieved an agency of a loan, it was treated in the budget as if it had been repaid. This made spending appear smaller. But the full liability of the Treasury remained. It had simply been shifted off-budget to the FFB.[103]

The range of purposes for which loans were made covered the spectrum: housing, agriculture, energy, transportation, health, education, export assistance, and more. Scarcely any major area of federal spending was excluded.[104]

As agencies learned how to work the system, they were able to nearly reverse the FFB's original role of limiting and coordinating federal credit activity. FFB became the middleman for 85 percent of federal lending.[105] And in 1983 this bank, which had begun a decade earlier with twelve employees, surpassed the Bank of America as the nation's largest. Its assets were $136 billion compared to B of A's $121 billion.[106]

FFB's assets, of course, are almost wholly the loans it holds which someone is supposed to repay. Here is a major problem. Due to "a systematic record of mismanagement across a broad spectrum of government investments,"[107] the bank has lost nearly 10 percent of its portfolio. The synfuels program, the Farmers Home Administration, the Small Business Administration, and the Foreign Military Sales program were all involved. Amtrak defaulted on a billion dollars in loans, and the Department of Transportation forgave two-thirds of its loans to the plush D.C. Metro subway system, adding another $500 million to the taxpayers' tab for the FFB.[108]

An area of equal concern to these outright losses has been the slackness of FFB-backed agencies in collecting on loans that are delinquent. The government has been rapped in numerous studies for its poor performance as a bill collector. The data on private loans, and for those few on-budget federal loan programs, suggest much better performance.[109]

To Congressman Bill Gradison, FFB's off-budget status is the direct cause of these problems: "From a political perspective, FFB money is heaven sent. It mysteriously appears each year; it is spent; but it is not in the federal budget, not under the usual scrutiny, and not under the direct control of Congress or the President."[110]

It might seem that FFB can regain its appeal by applying that old bromide, better management. But there is another concern about federal loan programs that would persist even if borrowers had repaid every cent. Loans and loan guarantees are a way of allocating credit resources. At a time of large deficits, these resources are scarce. If FFB loan subsidies divert credit away from its most productive use, the loss in economic growth will be reflected in still larger deficits: a vicious circle.

As early as 1976, skilled budget-watchers like Rudolph Penner concluded that off-budget lending "is starting to run out of control." Penner contrasted political and economic aspects of backdoor spending: "There is a tendency to think that if these programs don't show up in the budget, they're not costly. But the real costs of the programs are that they redirect credit from general borrowers to an activity the government favors."[111]

Susan Lee suggests what effect this redirection might have: "By channeling credit flows, these loan programs cause injury in serious but subtle ways. . . . When government offers below-market rate loans to businesses, some of which could not raise financing on their own, it is in effect allocating credit to less productive enterprises. The government hands out the credit despite the market's assessment of risk and return. This distortion of investment flows both reduces funds available for more productive projects and keeps less productive projects afloat."[112]

Congressman Norman Mineta put the matter simply in 1980: "Credit subsidies are skyrocketing and driving up interest rates for everybody." Mineta suggested corrective action: "A control system is needed that will bring these programs into the budget process."[113]

That year Congress established an annual credit budget to capture the on- and off-budget direct loan obligations and loan guarantee commitments of federal agencies. But this document only details such spending. It has done nothing to control loan growth. From 1980 to 1983 the totals in the credit budget climbed 40 percent, despite heavy criticism and legislative initiatives by the Reagan Administration.[114] One reason for the lack of progress may be that "few lawmakers understand the complex system and those who do usually want to protect a favored agency's budget."[115] Berkeley economist George Break adds, "off-budget commands almost no public attention."[116]

Strong medicine has been prescribed by some experts for several years. Penner, then economic policy chief for the federal budget office (OMB), met with House Budget Committee staffers in 1976 to "use a special section of the Budget Control Act to impose some overall control on loan guarantees and other such financial sleights-of-hand."[117]

It has not proven sufficient to simply display a complete picture of federal credit activities. "It is time for fundamental budgetary reform. The federal government . . . must get all the programs that are outside the budget back in," says Steve Hoffman, executive director of the House Wednesday Group, a congressional caucus of House and Senate Republicans.[118]

Congressman Bill Gradison agrees. He lauds the fact that "in a historic policy change" the 1985 budget attributes FFB-financed outlays to the agencies that generate them, even though this spending is not added to deficit totals. Gradison calls for passage of a bill that would put FFB in the unified budget and make agencies accountable for the cost of loan programs. This would force credit programs "to compete for annual outlays just like all other government expenditures."[119]

Gradison and Senator Paul Trible have introduced another bill to implement a dramatic proposal from the Congressional Budget Office. Called the "market plan," it would require that direct loans made by government agencies be quickly sold to the private sector. Private sector lending that is guaranteed by government would be reinsured by private carriers.

The idea is to reveal the true cost of federal loans. This added visibility will dampen unwise lending, the CBO believes, and holds "the promise of saving the federal government billions of dollars."

The CBO has found $225 billion in loans it believes should be sold over a two-year period. This would produce an estimated one-time inflow of cash to the Treasury of $95 billion—an amount which could trim federal interest outlays by $10 billion a year if it were applied to reduce the public debt. Supporters claim the "market plan" could convert "a nightmarish tangle of uncontrolled federal lending activity into a series of efficiently managed credit programs" and also help reduce deficits.[120]

Not everyone shares this ambitious hope. But even those with more modest aims say the time is now to move credit programs onto the budget. "In the short-term the advantage is not so much deficit reduction as more effective review and restraint of growth in loan programs," says John Wills, staff economist for Senator Slade Gorton. Adds Wills: "The federal budget fails to conform to generally accepted accounting principles in so many ways."[121]

Chapter 4

The Fiscal Collision

by DAYNA HUTCHINGS

THE SPECTER OF GROWING DEFICITS does not evoke the same level of alarm as the more visible economic ills of high inflation and unemployment. Consumers are unsure of the impact of large deficits and are confused by the technical jargon used by economists to define the problem. Policymakers and business leaders argue about the impact of deficits on future economic growth and stability.

The basic story, however, is very simple and serious. The federal government spends far more money than it collects in taxes. This imbalance is bad for the economy because the deficit must be financed either by printing more money, which spurs inflation, or by floating government bonds, which diverts savings away from private investment needed for economic growth.

The deficit is also worrisome because it adds to the national debt, which is the accumulation of past federal red ink. Like private debt, the national debt requires interest payments. These federal interest payments must be financed by present and future American taxpayers. Large and rapidly expanding debt service payments are especially alarming because they add to pressures on the deficit yet fail to provide any goods or services in return.

Following is a series of graphs that look into the future to see what will happen if current policies remain unchanged. Economic and budgetary data are graphically projected. These projections do not predict future events; they merely extend current trends. Ignored are the ebbs and flows of the business cycle and the possibility of price shocks caused by unanticipated events, such as oil embargoes and bad crop harvests. Also not considered is the relief that would be provided by federal actions to control deficit growth.

Figure 1

Federal Budget Deficit

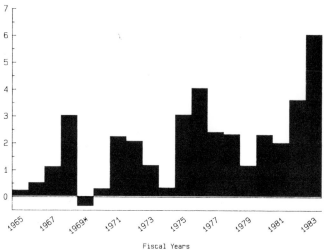

Percent of Gross National Product

Fiscal Years

* Budget Surplus in 1969

SOURCE: Office of Management and Budget, *Federal Government Finances*, February 1984.

This graph shows the federal budget deficit as a share of the economy's total output of goods and services, or Gross National Product (GNP). In 1983 the deficit constituted more than 6 percent of GNP, a level that is unprecedented in the postwar era.

The 1983 deficit of $195 billion is particularly disturbing because it occurred during a healthy expansion of 3.7 percent real growth. Economic expansions typically reduce deficits because growing personal incomes and corporate profits increase tax revenues while federal outlays for unemployment insurance and welfare programs decline. The budget imbalance in 1983 is projected to continue well into the future (see figure 7). This indicates the presence of a "structural deficit"—a fundamental imbalance between federal outlays and receipts that is not due to economic fluctuations.

Figure 2

Federal Budget Deficit

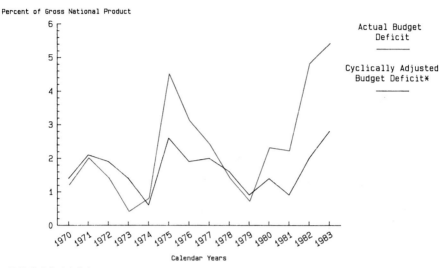

Percent of Gross National Product

Calendar Years

Actual Budget Deficit

Cyclically Adjusted Budget Deficit*

* Deficit Calculated at a
6% Unemployment Rate

SOURCES: Office of Management and Budget, *Federal Government Finances*, February 1984; U.S. Department of Commerce, *Survey of Current Business*, December 1983 and subsequent issues.

The structural deficit, illustrated above, removes the effects of the business cycle on outlays and receipts to form a clearer picture of the direction of federal budget trends. The graph shows the deficit which would occur at a steady and low (6 percent) rate of unemployment. This cyclically adjusted deficit reveals whether the budget would still be out of balance in a vigorous economy. The structural part of the deficit cannot be cured simply by an upswing in the business cycle.

The graph contrasts the large actual deficit in 1981 with a fairly low cyclically adjusted deficit. The gap between the two measures suggests that the deficit in 1981 was primarily due to sluggish economic growth. But in 1982 and 1983 the cyclically adjusted deficit rose sharply. A major factor was the enactment of large personal tax cuts which went into effect in 1982 and 1983.

Figure 3

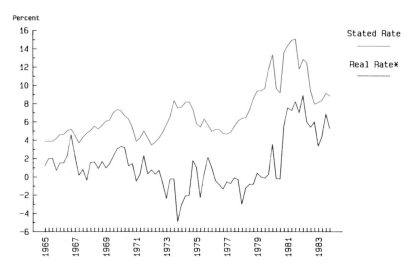

3-Month Treasury Bill Rates

* Real Rate is Stated Rate Minus
Inflation

SOURCES: Federal Reserve Board of Governors, *Federal Reserve Bulletin*; U.S. Department of Commerce, Bureau of Economic Analysis, *The National Income and Product Accounts of the United States, 1929–74 Statistical Tables*, a supplement to the *Survey of Current Business* and subsequent issues.

TECHNICAL NOTE: Quarterly Personal Consumption Expenditure (PCE) Deflator was expressed at annual rates and subtracted from preceding quarter's 3-month U.S. Treasury bill rate to compute a proxy for the real rate. Real rate is technically equal to nominal rate minus inflationary expectations.

In recent years, fiscal (budget) and monetary policies have taken the divergent paths of economic stimulus and economic restraint. Between 1979 and mid-1982, the Federal Reserve Board embarked on a tough anti-inflation campaign by restraining money supply growth (measured by M-1 shown on table 1). Fiscal policy was uncooperative in this effort and it became highly stimulative starting in 1982. Competition between private and public borrowers in the credit markets along with tighter monetary policy caused a sharp increase in both short- and long-term interest rates.[1]

Figure 3 illustrates the climb of the 3-month Treasury bill rate from an average of 10 percent in 1979 to 14 percent in 1981. The real Treasury bill rate (the stated rate after subtracting inflation) was similarly affected.

Figure 4

Long-Term Interest Rates
and Inflation

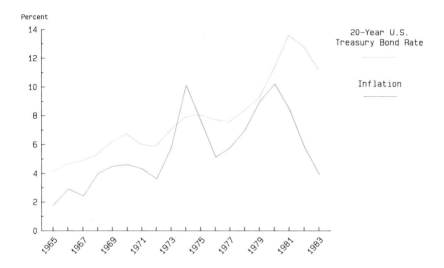

SOURCES: Federal Reserve Board of Directors, *Federal Reserve Bulletin*; U.S. Department of Commerce, Bureau of Economic Analysis, *The National Income and Product Accounts of the United States, 1929–74 Statistical Tables*, a supplement to the *Survey of Current Business* and subsequent issues.

TECHNICAL NOTE: Inflation is measured by year-over-year changes in the Personal Consumption Expenditure Deflator.

Figure 4 presents the 20-year United States Treasury bond rate, which rose from 9.3 percent in 1979 to 13.7 percent in 1981.

TABLE 1. Recent Economic Indicators

	1978	1979	1980	1981	1982	1983	1984*	
							I	II
Real GNP (annual growth rate)	5.0	2.8	−0.3	2.5	−2.1	3.7	10.1	7.1
Total consumption	4.5	2.7	0.5	2.0	1.4	4.8	4.6	7.9
Private fixed non-residential investment	12.9	7.4	−2.4	5.6	−4.7	2.5	20.5	21.4
Residential fixed investment	2.8	−5.2	−20.4	−5.4	−15.0	41.7	20.8	1.3
Money supply: M-1 (annual growth rate)	8.2	7.7	6.3	7.1	6.6	11.0	7.2	6.1
Inflation: CPI (annual growth rate)	7.7	11.3	13.5	10.4	6.1	3.2	4.4	4.4
GNP deflator (annual growth rate)	7.4	8.6	9.2	9.6	6.0	3.8	4.4	3.3
Unemployment rate— civilian workers	6.1	5.8	7.1	7.6	9.7	9.6	7.9	7.5

* First and second quarters expressed at annual rates.

Table 1 illustrates that high interest rates were not the only fallout from recent economic policy. The Federal Reserve's actions cooled inflation by sending the economy into a tailspin. Between 1980 and 1983, real GNP grew only a total of 3.8 percent while the unemployment rate climbed from 7.1 to 9.6 percent. Interest-sensitive sectors of the economy were especially hurt. The housing market staggered under the weight of high finance charges. Business fixed investment sputtered in 1980, rallied briefly in 1981, then plunged 4.7 percent in 1982.

The anti-inflation medicine administered by the Federal Reserve succeeded in easing price increases. Inflation, measured by the Consumer Price Index (CPI), dropped from its feverish annual growth rate of 11.3 percent in 1979 to a modest 3.2 percent in 1983.

Economic growth also improved. Real GNP advanced 3.7 percent in 1983 and accelerated to an annual rate of 10.1 percent during the first quarter of 1984 and 7.1 percent during the second, led by consumer spending and investment.

Figure 5

Net Exports

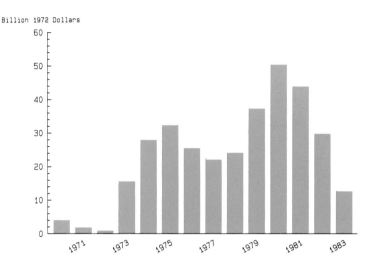

Billion 1972 Dollars

Note: Net Exports are the Excess of Exports
over Imports of Goods and Services

SOURCE: U.S. Department of Commerce, Bureau of Economic Analysis, *The National Income and Product Accounts of the United States, 1929–74 Statistical Tables*, a supplement to the *Survey of Current Business* and subsequent issues.

Unfortunately, the export sector did not participate in this economic recovery (see figure 5). Real net exports have deteriorated dramatically in recent years, plummeting from $43.8 billion in 1981 to $12.6 billion in 1983. Continuing their downward spiral, real net exports recorded a deficit of $8.3 billion in the first quarter of 1984 and $11.4 billion in the second.

Net exports equal the value of goods (merchandise) and services that we sell to the rest of the world, minus the value of what we buy abroad. The merchandise trade balance reveals the value of net exports of tangible goods, such as agricultural products and steel. The services account is based on the value of "intangibles" such as royalties, tourism, and interest earnings from foreign investments. The services account continues to maintain a large surplus because of interest receipts from American investments abroad. But the merchandise account has recorded a substantial and growing deficit caused, many believe, by the high value of the dollar.

Figure 6

United States Dollar Exchange Rate

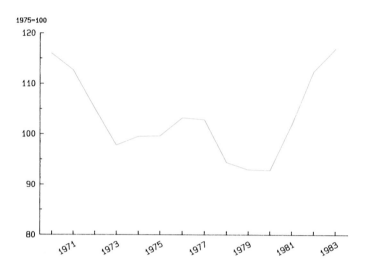

SOURCE: Morgan Guaranty Trust Company, *World Financial Markets*, and unpublished Morgan tabulations.

TECHNICAL NOTE: The dollar exchange rate is measured by the trade-weighted value of the dollar measured against 15 other major currencies.

The American dollar rose 26 percent from 1980 to 1983 in relation to the currencies of major United States trading partners. This increased prices of American export goods vis-à-vis foreign products and lowered prices of foreign imports in relation to domestic goods. As a result, imports to the United States have been far outpacing exports to foreign countries. This is expressed in a severe merchandise trade deficit.

One explanation for the currently strong dollar is that high American interest rates, caused partly by the credit demands of the deficit, have made U.S. investments attractive to foreigners. Demand for dollars has also been stimulated by the relatively low inflation and strong growth of the American economy. The current feverish demand for the dollar and its steady appreciation on international markets show no signs of abating at this time.

Projections

The projections which follow are based on the basic assumptions made by the Congressional Budget Office (CBO), a nonpartisan arm of the Congress.[2]

Projections assume 5 percent annual real increases in defense budget authority (the legal upper limit of new spending commitments). Nondefense discretionary spending levels assume that 1984 appropriation levels will be continued with increases only for projected inflation. All other expenditures, including Medicare and Social Security, are assumed to grow as dictated by current law. CBO projections from 1985 through 1989 have been altered here to accommodate higher inflation and interest rate assumptions. For the period 1990 through 1995, trends were simply extended based on the above set of assumptions.

Because economic conditions affect federal outlays and receipts, certain further assumptions must be made. Economic trends presented in table 2 underlie the projections in this chapter.

TABLE 2. Economic Trends (in Percent)

	Actual				Projected		
	1960	1970	1980	1983	1985	1990	1995
Real GNP (annual growth rate)	2.2	−0.2	−0.3	3.7	3.6	3.1	2.6
CPI (annual growth rate)	1.5	5.9	13.5	3.2	6.0	6.2	6.7
Civilian Unemployment Rate	5.5	5.0	7.1	9.6	6.7	6.3	6.3
3-Month Treasury Bill Rate	2.9	6.4	11.5	8.6	9.9	10.2	11.0
Corporate Bond Rate (Moody's AAA)	4.4	8.0	11.9	12.0	12.5	12.7	13.5

Figure 7

Federal Budget Deficit

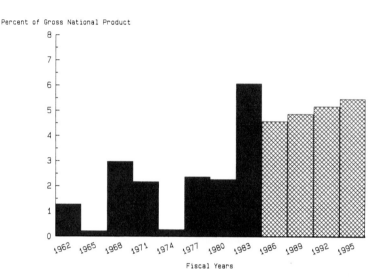

Percent of Gross National Product

Fiscal Years

SOURCES: Office of Management and Budget, *Federal Government Finances*, February 1984; Projections by Rainier Bancorporation.

As illustrated in figures 7 and 8, the present deficit problems are unlikely to disappear. The deficit reached 6.1 percent of GNP in 1983 and is projected to remain in the 4.5 to 5.5 percent range through 1995. Gone are the days when the deficit amounted to only 1 to 2 percent of the nation's output of goods and services.

Federal outlays and receipts began to part ways in the early 1980s and, if current budget policies remain unchanged, may never meet again. Led by defense and interest expenditures, total federal outlays will grow faster than the economy, thereby raising their share of GNP from a projected 23.5 percent in 1984 to 25.8 percent in 1995. Receipts will also outpace economic growth because rising real incomes will push taxpayers into higher brackets. Unfortunately, government coffers will not fill fast enough to finance burgeoning federal outlays, and the deficit will widen, as shown on table 3.

The Deficit Reduction Act of 1984 slightly improved the budget outlook. Signed into law by President Reagan in July 1984, the legislation, a complex package of revenue increases and spending cuts, stands a foot high in its published form. According to the CBO, the Act will raise $50.1 billion in revenue and save $13 billion in spending between 1984 and 1987.[3]

Figure 8

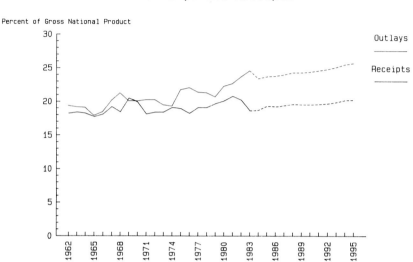

Federal Government
Outlays and Receipts

Percent of Gross National Product

SOURCES: Office of Management and Budget, *Federal Government Finances*, February 1984; Projections by Rainier Bancorporation.

Some of the Act's major tax provisions include postponing or repealing several previously scheduled tax reductions, tightening depreciation rules, diminishing the advantages of income averaging, and increasing the excise tax on liquor. This legislation has been billed as a "down payment" on the deficit, and there is wide agreement that much more work needs to be done.[4]

TABLE 3. The Federal Budget Deficit by Fiscal Year

	Actual		Projected			
	1982	1983	1984	1985	1990	1995
Billions of Dollars						
Outlays	728	796	845	941	1505	2476
Receipts	618	601	673	763	1197	1936
Deficit	111	195	172	178	308	539
Percent of GNP						
Outlays	23.8	24.6	23.5	23.8	24.7	25.8
Receipts	20.2	18.6	18.7	19.3	19.6	20.2
Deficit	3.6	6.1	4.8	4.5	5.0	5.6

Figure 9

Private Savings
An International Comparison

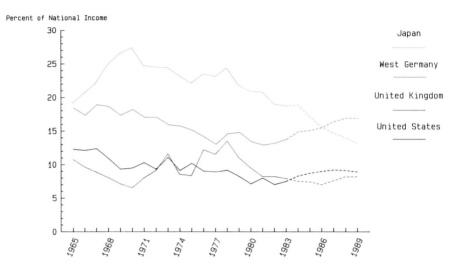

Note: 1986 — 1989 Values are Projections

SOURCES: U.S. Department of Commerce, Bureau of Economic Analysis, *The National Income and Product Accounts of the United States, 1929–74 Statistical Tables*, a supplement to the *Survey of Current Business* and subsequent issues; Foreign country sources for historical data. Foreign projections by Wharton Econometric Forecasting Associates, *World Economic Outlook*, July 1984, *Pacific Basin Economic Update*, June 1984; U.S. projections by Rainier Bancorporation.

The prognosis for a balanced budget is not good. But aside from annoyance over the government's mismanagement of its finances, why worry about the deficit? The basic concern among many analysts is that large and expanding deficits will threaten the long-term economic growth necessary to improve the quality of life for an expanding population. Growth, according to many observers, will be retarded because federal borrowing to finance the deficit will absorb savings, raise interest rates and "crowd out" private investment. Investment is important because it promotes growth by improving productivity, moderating inflation and encouraging business expansion and job creation.

Savings is the fuel for investment. An international comparison of savings and investment behavior shows that countries with high rates of private savings (personal savings plus after-tax corporate profits as a share of national income) typically have high levels of private capital investment (see figures 9 and 10). Japan and Germany, for example, have enjoyed comparatively higher private savings rates than the United States and the United

Figure 10

Private Fixed Investment
An International Comparison

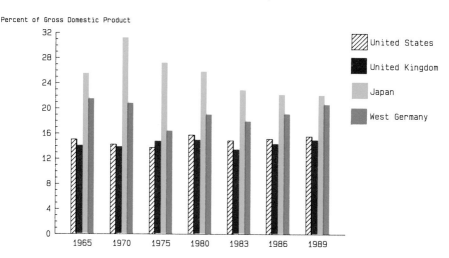

Percent of Gross Domestic Product

Note: 1986 and 1989 Values are Projections

SOURCES: U.S. Department of Commerce, Bureau of Economic Analysis, *The National Income and Product Accounts of the United States, 1929–74 Statistical Tables*, a supplement to the *Survey of Current Business* and subsequent issues; Foreign country sources for historical data, Foreign projections by Wharton Econometric Forecasting Associates, *World Economic Outlook*, July 1984, *Pacific Basin Economic Update*, June 1984; U.S. projections by Rainier Bancorporation.

Kingdom in recent years. As the figure 10 graph illustrates, they have also enjoyed relatively higher levels of private fixed investment. Not surprisingly, Japan's economy grew at a healthy average annual real rate of 5.1 during the 1970s and early 1980s. The rate for the average of the other three nations during the same period was only 2.4 percent. Without strong savings and investment it is difficult to achieve long-term economic growth.

The potential for a detrimental "crowding out" of investment has recently become a lively issue among policy analysts and corporate leaders. To fully understand the possible effects of the deficit on savings and investment, it is helpful to refer to some basic principles of economic accounting.

Total savings (both private and public) must equal total investment. Public savings consist, in theory, of federal, state, and local government surpluses. Recently, state and local governments have accumulated budget surpluses and thereby have contributed to total savings. Federal deficits, however, have negated these surpluses and have significantly reduced the level of total savings available for private investment.

Figure 11   Net Domestic Savings
                     and the Federal Budget Deficit

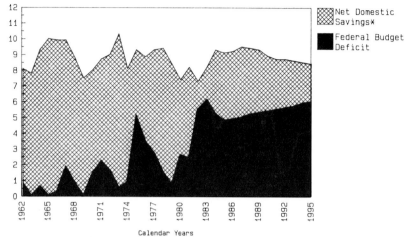

Percent of Net National Product

* Equal to Pers Svg + Undis Corp Profits +
St&Loc Govt Surplus – Federal Deficit
Note: Projections, 84–95; Fed Surplus 1963, 65, 69

SOURCES: U.S. Department of Commerce, Bureau of Economic Analysis, *The National Income and Product Accounts of the United States, 1929–74 Statistical Tables*, a supplement to the *Survey of Current Business* and subsequent issues; Projections by Rainier Bancorporation.

TECHNICAL NOTE: Net Domestic Savings and Net National Product equal gross values minus depreciation of existing capital.

Figure 11 illustrates the absorption of savings by the deficit. Net domestic savings are total domestic savings minus depreciation in the value of existing plants and equipment. During the 1960s, net domestic savings would have been 4 percent larger without the federal budget deficit, and during the 1970s 22 percent greater. In 1983, net domestic savings would have been almost three times its actual size, were it not for the deficit. Without future dramatic increases in private savings and state and local government budget surpluses, growing federal deficits will substantially reduce the net domestic savings available for private investment. By 1995, if no budget reduction actions are taken, the deficit may reduce savings by 75 percent.

A look at current economic indicators (see table 1) reveals that the United States enjoyed an investment boom during the first two quarters of 1984. Real private investment in plants and equipment grew at an annual rate of 20.5 percent in the first quarter and 21.4 percent in the second. Compare this performance with the pitiful 3.5 percent average annual growth which occurred during the previous six years.

A shrinking savings pool accompanied by rising investment appears to defy the economic accounting principles cited above. Figure 12 explains this apparent contradiction.

The current investment boom is being financed by the flow of foreign investment into the United States, which currently exceeds the flow of

Figure 12   Net Foreign Investment

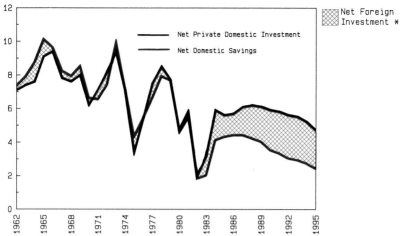

Percent of Net National Product

Note: 1984-1995 Values are Projections
* Equal to the Difference Between Net Domestic
Savings and Net Private Investment

SOURCES: U.S. Department of Commerce, Bureau of Economic Analysis, *The National Income and Product Accounts of the United States, 1929–74 Statistical Tables*, a supplement to the *Survey of Current Business* and subsequent issues; Projections by Rainier Bancorporation.

TECHNICAL NOTE: Net Private Domestic Investment and Net Domestic Savings equal gross values minus depreciation of existing capital.

American investment abroad. This net foreign investment closes the gap between domestic savings and domestic investment. When domestic savings are higher than domestic investment, this indicates that net foreign investment is flowing on balance from the United States to the rest of the world, as it did during the 1960s. Conversely, when domestic investment exceeds domestic savings, as it does today, foreign investment is flowing into the country from America's trading partners.

Net foreign investment is roughly equal to the current account deficit, the broadest measure of American trade with the rest of the world. As the dollar's rise widens the current account deficit, the United States goes deeper into debt with the rest of the world. This debt is satisfied by selling American assets to foreigners, thereby causing net inflows of foreign investment.

Without the currently large inflows of foreign capital augmenting the shrinking savings pool, interest rates would probably be higher than they are now and investment would be lower. However, the bolstering of investment by foreign capital has its price. The growing projected inflows, illustrated by figure 12, signify a huge current account deficit and a severe deterioration in our foreign trade position. If foreigners continue to be willing to invest a growing percentage of their portfolios in the United States and the dollar remains high, our export industry will continue to suffer. If foreigners withdraw such investments, there could be a domestic credit crunch.

Figure 13

Federal Debt Held by the Public

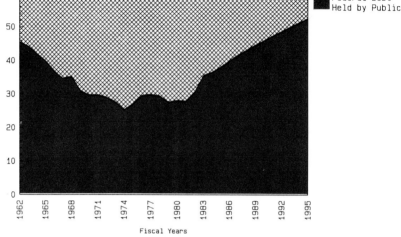

Percent of Gross National Product

Fiscal Years

Note: 1984–1995 Values are Projections

SOURCES: Office of Management and Budget, *Federal Government Finances*, February 1984; Projections by Rainier Bancorporation.

Federal debt held by the public is the current accumulation of past budget deficits. The public holds the debt in the form of government-issued, interest-bearing securities. (Total debt includes debt held by the federal government that is not included in budget deficits.) Without legislation to curb the projected deficits, the debt held by the public is projected to nearly quintuple from $1.1 trillion in 1983 to $5.1 trillion in 1995. To gain perspective on these enormous sums, it is only necessary to realize that the debt took nearly 200 years to reach $1.1 trillion.[5]

The size of the debt in relation to the economy is shown in figure 13. After steadily declining from its peak during World War II, the debt held by the public as a share of GNP began rising in 1982. From its average of 25–29 percent in the 1970s, the share rose to 35 percent in 1983 and is projected to exceed 50 percent by 1995.

Figure 14

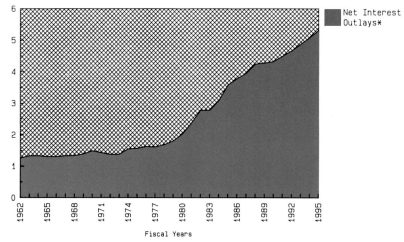

Net Interest Outlays
By the Federal Government

Note: 1984-1995 Values are Projections
* Net Interest Outlays are the Excess of Federal
Interest Outlays over Interest Receipts

SOURCES: Office of Management and Budget, *Federal Government Finances*, February 1984; Projections by Rainier Bancorporation.

The future burden of the federal debt becomes clearer with a look at the current and projected rise in federal net interest expenditures. Currently, this is the fastest growing category of federal outlays and is primarily composed of interest payments to the holders of federal securities. From an average annual share of slightly more than 1.5 percent of GNP during the 1970s, net interest expenditures are projected to mushroom to 3.3 percent during the 1980s and 5.3 percent by 1995.

The burden of these payments will fall on current and future generations of taxpayers. Without a swift and dramatic decline in the budget deficit, there will be a large transfer of wealth over the next decade from those taxpayers who do not hold government securities to those who do. To the extent that foreigners continue to hold a share of the federal debt, Americans will be taxed to enhance foreign portfolios.

The rising importance of net interest expenditures as a share of total outlays will also make the budget increasingly vulnerable to interest rate fluctuations. The CBO estimates that raising their interest rate projections by one percentage point every year between 1984 and 1989 would add nearly $100 billion to net interest outlays during that period.[6] The rise in net interest outlays due to the growing federal debt will render policymakers increasingly powerless over a growing share of federal expenditures.

Figure 15   The Composition of
                   Federal Government Receipts

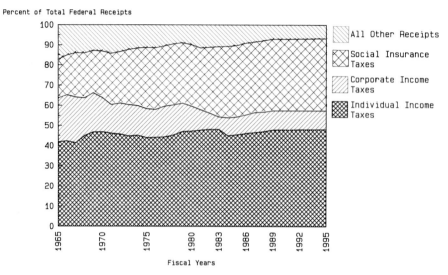

Percent of Total Federal Receipts

Note: 1984-1995 Values are Projections

SOURCES: Office of Management and Budget, *Federal Government Finances*, February 1984; Projections by Rainier Bancorporation.

To reveal the sources of the fiscal imbalance, it is helpful to divide budget receipts and outlays into their various components.

Tax receipts will rise slightly as a share of GNP over the next decade. Individual income taxes and social insurance taxes (including Social Security and unemployment insurance taxes) will be an increasing share of total receipts.

Personal tax collections will continue to rise because real personal income is projected to grow over the next decade, pushing people into higher tax brackets (tax indexing only protects against that part of "bracket creep" caused by inflation, not by real income growth). As a share of total receipts, individual tax collections are projected to rise from 44.9 percent in 1984 to 48.1 percent in 1995.

Social insurance taxes grow in importance as a source of revenue because of the payroll tax increases enacted in the Social Security Amendments of 1983. As a share of total revenues, social insurance receipts rise from 34.8 percent in 1983 to 35.8 percent in 1995.

Corporate income taxes strongly rebounded in 1984 from the recession, but once back on their long-term growth path, they continue to slightly diminish as a revenue source. According to the CBO, this decline basically results from the moderate growth of inflation and the 1981 tax law changes permitting accelerated depreciation.[7]

Figure 16   The Composition of
                        Federal Government Outlays

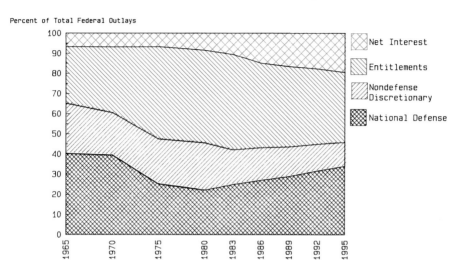

Note: 1984–1995 Values are Projections

SOURCES: Office of Management and Budget, *Federal Government Finances*, February 1984; Projections by Rainier Bancorporation.

Other tax receipts include excise taxes, estate and gift taxes, customs duties, and other miscellaneous receipts. The large reduction in this category over the projection period is basically caused by a drop in excise taxes due to the decline in windfall profit tax revenues. Revenue generated by this category is projected to fall as a share of total receipts from 10.9 percent in 1983 to 6.7 percent in 1995.

The composition of federal outlays will change radically over the next decade. Net interest and defense expenditures will grow as a share of total federal outlays while entitlements (transfer payments) and nondefense discretionary spending diminish in importance.

Net interest outlays are the fastest growing component of federal spending. As a share of total outlays, they will nearly double in twelve years, rising from 10.6 percent in 1983 to a projected 19.6 percent in 1995.

Defense expenditures, projected under the assumption of 5 percent real budget authority growth per year, also increase their share of outlays. They are projected to rise from 24.9 percent in 1983 to 34.1 percent in 1995.

Entitlements are outlays that federal agencies are legally bound to provide to those who meet the eligibility requirements. The CBO estimates that approximately two-thirds of entitlement spending is devoted to social insurance programs, such as Social Security, Medicare, and unemployment compensation.[8] Of the social insurance programs, Medicare outlays are increasing most rapidly. But, because net interest and defense expenditures are growing more quickly, entitlement outlays will shrink as a share of total expenditures from 47.4 percent in 1983 to 34.6 percent in 1995.

Nondefense discretionary outlays include all remaining expenditures and are subject to annual budgetary review. They fund a wide range of functions, including the operations of legislative, judicial, and executive branches, and various federal agencies; grants to states for education, employment and energy assistance; and federal programs to provide such services as air traffic control and operation of the nation's parks and forests. Projections assume that outlays for this category of expenditures would merely keep pace with inflation. Consequently, nondefense discretionary spending shrinks from 17 percent of total outlays in 1983 to 11.7 percent in 1995.

Figure 17

Defense Expenditures

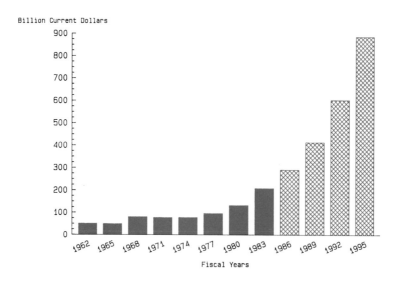

SOURCES: Office of Management and Budget, *Federal Government Finances*; Projections by Rainier Bancorporation.

The military buildup under the Reagan Administration is unprecedented at a time when no major conflict is underway. Current dollar expenditures have grown from $134.0 billion in 1980 to $209.9 billion in 1983. If current defense policies remain unchanged through the next decade, defense expenditures will reach $888.4 billion by 1995.

Figure 18

Defense Expenditures

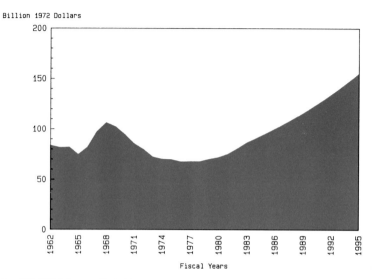

Note: 1984-1995 Values are Projections

SOURCES: Office of Management and Budget; Projections by Rainier Bancorporation.

Based on the assumption of 5 percent annual real growth in budget authority, defense projections expressed in constant 1972 dollars will grow
steadily over the next decade. From the 1983 level of $85.9 billion, real de-
fense expenditures are projected to reach $154.3 billion by 1995.

Figure 19

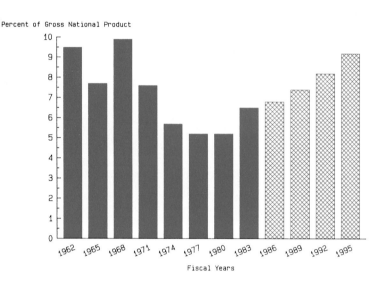

SOURCES: Office of Management and Budget, *Federal Government Finances*, February 1984; Projections by Rainier Bancorporation.

The defense share of GNP reached 9.9 percent at the height of Vietnam War expenditures in 1968, but fell to a 5–6 percent range during the mid 1970s and early 1980s. In 1983, defense expenditures rose to $209.9 billion, or 6.5 percent of GNP, and are projected to reach $888.4 billion, or 9.2 percent of GNP by 1995.

TABLE 4. National Defense Outlays by Fiscal Year

	Actual		Projected			
	1982	1983	1984	1985	1990	1995
Billions of dollars	185.3	209.9	230.0	261.6	469.5	888.4
Percent of GNP	6.1	6.5	6.4	6.6	7.6	9.2

Figure 20

The Composition of Defense Outlays

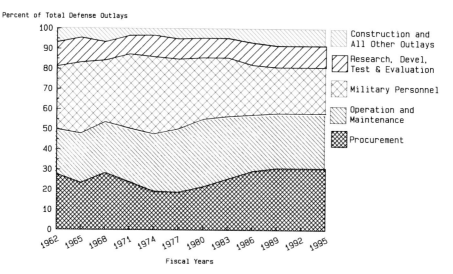

Percent of Total Defense Outlays

Fiscal Years

Note: 1984-1995 Values are Projections

SOURCES: Office of Management and Budget, *Budget of the United States Government FY 1985*; Projections after 1989 by Rainier Bancorporation.

Purchases of weapons systems (procurement) by the federal government have insured the future rapid rise of defense outlays because of the magnitude of contract commitments. As a share of total defense outlays, procurement will rise from 25.5 percent in 1983 to 30.9 percent in 1995.

However, outlays for maintaining the growing military arsenal will not keep pace with the rise in procurement expenditures. The account which funds the operations, upkeep, and repairs for facilities and weapons will shrink as a share of total defense outlays from 30.9 percent in 1983 to 27.2 percent in 1995.

Also diminishing as a share of defense outlays will be expenditures for military personnel, including allowances for pay increases. This category will continue its long-term decline, dropping from 29 percent in 1983 to a projected 22.8 percent in 1995.

The sum of the remaining categories will slightly increase as a share of defense expenditures in the future, led by military construction which will triple between 1983 and 1989.

Figure 21

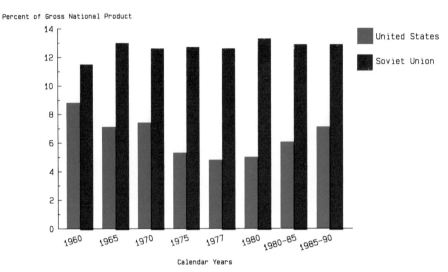

Defense Expenditures
United States and the Soviet Union

Percent of Gross National Product

Note: Projections for 1980–1985 and 1985–1990
are Annual Averages

SOURCES: *CIA Estimates of Soviet Defense Spending*, Hearing Before the Subcommittee on Oversight of the Permanent Select Committee on Intelligence, House of Representatives, Washington, D.C., 1980; Projections, "The Soviet Domestic Economy in the 1980s," July, 1983, by Daniel L. Bond, Wharton Econometric Forecasting Associates, and Herbert S. Levine, University of Pennsylvania (forthcoming).

One reason cited by both the Carter and Reagan administrations for the current arms buildup was that the United States was losing ground in military preparedness to the Soviet Union. The accuracy of this claim is uncertain because preparedness is a difficult concept to assess. Comparisons of military outlays do not necessarily indicate relative military capabilities. Expenditures measure the resources which are devoted to the military, but not the effectiveness of the defense effort.

According to the CIA, Soviet defense expenditures (measured in dollars) were 20 percent greater than American outlays in 1972, 55 percent greater in 1976 and 45 percent greater in 1981.[9] These figures can be misleading because of vast differences in military personnel policies, weapons investment programs, and strategic challenges faced by each nation. Even converting rubles into dollars is a source of disagreement among analysts.

Figure 22

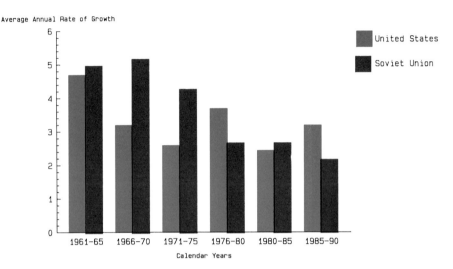

Gross National Product
United States and the Soviet Union

Note: Values are Expressed as Annual Averages;
1980–1985 and 1985–1990 are Projections

Sources: *CIA Handbook of Economic Statistics*, 1983; Projections, "The Soviet Domestic Economy in the 1980s," July, 1983, by Daniel L. Bond, Wharton Econometric Forecasting Associates and Herbert S. Levine, University of Pennsylvania (forthcoming).

While CIA estimates cannot be used to calculate the absolute magnitude of Soviet investment in defense, they can be used to compare the relative priority given defense spending in the U.S. and U.S.S.R. This can be done by examining the shares of GNP devoted to the military by the two countries. Figure 21 illustrates that the defense sector has consistently been given higher priority in the Soviet Union than in the United States. The allocation of American resources to defense diminished after the Vietnam War. But the Soviets continued to spend between 12 and 13 percent of their GNP on the military. Projections assume that the Soviet defense establishment will continue to garner approximately 13 percent of GNP in future years.

It will be difficult, however, for the Soviets to maintain their strong commitment to defense because, as shown on figure 22, their rate of economic growth is projected to diminish through 1990. Continued large defense expenditures will thus require even greater sacrifices by other sectors of the Soviet economy.

Figure 23

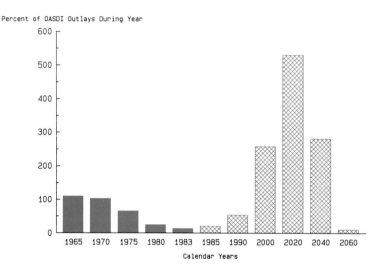

Social Security (OASDI)
Trust Fund Balance

Percent of OASDI Outlays During Year

Calendar Years

Note: Trust Fund Balance at
Beginning of Calendar Year

SOURCES: *1984 Annual Report of the Board of Trustees of the Federal Old-Age and Survivors Insurance and Disability Insurance Trust Funds.*

TECHNICAL NOTE: Alternative IIB assumptions in the above report.

The federal government contributes to the income security and health of aged and disabled Americans through the Social Security and Medicare programs. Together, the two programs constituted 28 percent of total federal expenditures in 1983 and absorbed 56 percent of the total federal budget for transfer payments.[10]

Social Security, officially known as the Old-Age, Survivors and Disability Insurance Program (OASDI), consists of two divisions which pay monthly benefits to workers and their families:

1. Old-Age and Survivors Insurance (OASI) pays benefits after a worker retires or dies.

2. Disability Insurance (DI) pays benefits after a worker becomes disabled.

The OASDI program, which had outlays of $167.2 billion in 1983, is financed for the most part on a pay-as-you-go basis. Payroll taxes, levied on current workers, are used to provide monthly pension checks to current retirees. In addition, the program maintains OASI and DI trust funds, which hold all assets not currently needed to pay benefits and administrative expenses.

The trust funds provide a reserve to absorb temporary fluctuations in the program's income and outflow. The fund balances are invested in United States government securities and add to the federal debt held by government agencies.[11]

The balance in the trust funds is one indication of the financial health of the Social Security program. Figure 23 shows the trust fund balance at the beginning of each calendar year as a percent of the total program expenditures during the year.

The program was in trouble in the early 1980s. In 1982, the OASI trust fund was forced to borrow $12.4 billion from the Medicare (Hospital Insurance) fund. The combined balances of the OASI and DI funds held a contingency reserve of only 14 percent in 1983, which is less than the expenditures needed for two months of operation.

According to actuarial estimates by the Social Security Administration, 1983 legislation restored the solvency of the program. In fact, the legislation is projected to create a large buildup in reserves until the year 2020. The trust fund balance will then begin to shrink and once again fall below recommended levels by 2060.

Figure 24

Maximum Annual Social Security Payroll Tax Paid By Employee

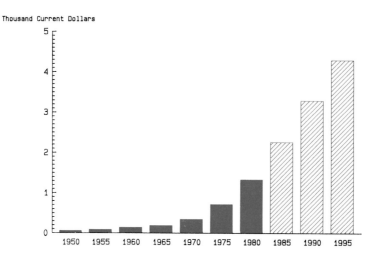

Thousand Current Dollars

SOURCES: Unpublished tabulations of the Office of the Actuary, Social Security Administration.

TECHNICAL NOTE: Alternative IIB assumptions.

Figure 24 projects the maximum annual payroll tax, which is the tax payment made by workers earning the highest income level subject to OASDI taxes. In 1983 these workers were required to pay taxes of $1,928 on the first $35,700 of their income. By 1995 the maximum taxable annual earnings level will be $69,000 and the corresponding payroll tax will be $4,278.

Figure 25

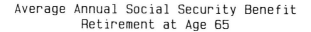

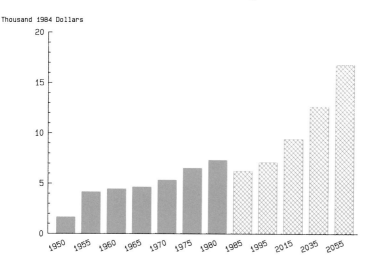

Average Annual Social Security Benefit
Retirement at Age 65

SOURCES: Unpublished tabulations of the Office of the Actuary, Social Security Administration.

TECHNICAL NOTE: Alternative IIB assumptions.

The receipts from payroll taxes are used to pay benefits to retirees. As shown on figure 25, the average annual real benefit (in excess of inflation) will rise from $6,342 in 1985 to $16,876 in 2055—an average real increase of 1.4 percent per year. This gain is caused by the fact that the initial benefit level is tied to the growth in real wage levels and not just to the rise in prices.

The drop in the value of benefit payments between 1980 and 1985 can be explained by the "notch" issue. The "notch" refers to the situation in which some workers who reach age 65 in 1982 (or later) have had their benefits computed under the more stringent provisions of the 1977 Social Security amendments. They may receive lower monthly benefits than those who reached 65 in 1981 (or earlier) and have their benefits computed under the previous system. A number of proposals are being considered to lessen this inequality.

Figure 26

Population Projections By Age Group

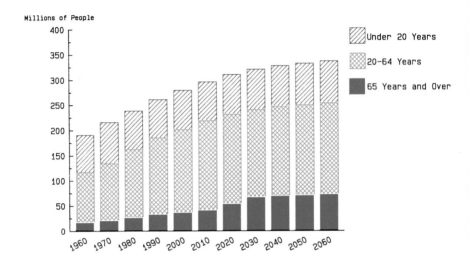

SOURCES: *1984 Annual Report of the Board of Trustees of the Federal Old-Age and Survivors Insurance and Disability Insurance Trust Funds.*
TECHNICAL NOTE: Alternative IIA and IIB assumptions.

Estimates of future demands placed on the Social Security program are highly dependent upon demographic assumptions. Figures 26–29 show the population growth trends which underlie Social Security projections.

Between the years 1980 and 2060, the population aged 65 and older will increase four times as fast as the average annual rate for those under 65. As a result, the proportion of population over age 65 is expected to double (see figure 26).

This demographic shift will accelerate as members of the "baby boom" generation (those born from 1946 to 1960) begin to reach retirement age around the year 2020. The aging of American society will put an increasing strain on the Social Security program soon after the beginning of the next century.

Figure 27

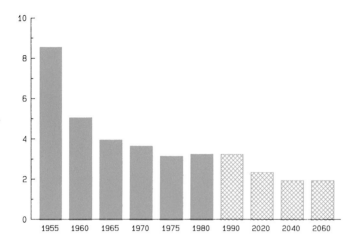

Number of Contributing Workers
Per Social Security Beneficiary

SOURCES: *1984 Annual Report of the Board of Trustees of the Federal Old-Age and Survivors Insurance and Disability Insurance Trust Funds.*
TECHNICAL NOTE: Alternative IIB assumptions.

The stress is evident in the decreasing number of contributing workers for every OASDI beneficiary (see figure 27). In 1980 there were 3.3 workers for every beneficiary. By 2060 the ratio is projected to be only 2 to 1.

Figure 28

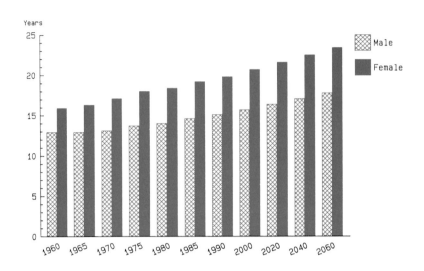

Life Expectancy at Age 65

Note: 1985-2060 Values are Projections

SOURCES: *1984 Annual Report of the Board of Trustees of the Federal Old-Age and Survivors Insurance and Disability Insurance Trust Funds.*
TECHNICAL NOTE: Alternative IIA and IIB assumptions.

Not only will more Americans enter the ranks of the elderly, but more people will be living far beyond age 65. In 1980 a man and woman both aged 65 could expect to live 14 and 18.4 more years, respectively. By the year 2060, a 65-year-old man is projected to have 17.8 years of life left and a woman, 23.4 years (see figure 28).

Figure 29

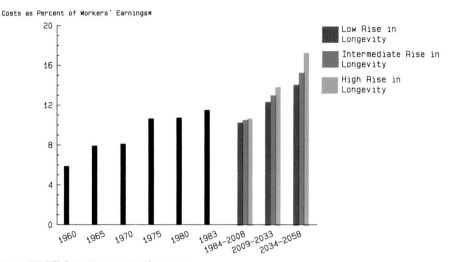

Impact of Longevity Increases
on Average Social Security Costs

Costs as Percent of Workers' Earnings*

Low Rise in Longevity

Intermediate Rise in Longevity

High Rise in Longevity

1960 1965 1970 1975 1980 1983 1984–2008 2009–2033 2034–2058

Note: 1984–2058 Projections are Annual Averages
* Workers' Earnings which are Subject to
Social Security Taxes

SOURCES: *1984 Annual Report of the Board of Trustees of the Federal Old-Age and Survivors Insurance and Disability Insurance Trust Funds.*
    TECHNICAL NOTE: Alternative IIB assumptions.

People living longer and remaining on the Social Security rolls will increase the amount of tax revenue needed from a relatively smaller population of workers. The effect on costs of differing longevity assumptions are captured by figure 29. Program outlays as a percent of contributing workers' taxable earnings during the period 1984–2008 initially decline as the baby boomers swell the labor force and provide increased receipts. However, the impact of longevity increases on costs becomes more pronounced during the 21st century. Figure 29 shows the impact of three different levels of longevity. High increases in longevity during the years 2034 through 2058 would raise costs as a share of taxable earnings 14 percent above those created by the intermediate longevity assumptions. Similarly, low increases in longevity would reduce this cost rate burden 8 percent below the intermediate assumptions.

Figure 30

National Health Expenditures

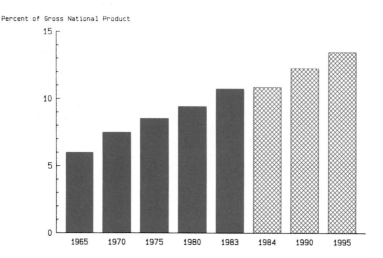

Percent of Gross National Product

SOURCES: "Health Spending in the 1980s: Integration of Clinical Practice Patterns with Management," by Mark S. Freeland and Carol E. Schendler, *Health Care Financing Review*, Spring 1984; Projections after 1990 by Rainier Bancorporation.

The Medicare program was established in 1965 to help finance medical care for those aged 65 and over. Beginning in 1973, beneficiaries of Social Security's disability insurance program (DI) were also eligible for Medicare benefits.

There are two basic programs under Medicare:

1. Hospital Insurance (HI), or Part A, accounts for the bulk of Medicare outlays (73 percent in 1983). This program pays for inpatient hospital care and other related health services for those aged 65 and over and for the long-term disabled.

2. Supplementary Medical Insurance (SMI), or Part B, is a voluntary program for aged and disabled Medicare beneficiaries who wish to purchase additional medical insurance. SMI pays for physicians' services, outpatient hospital care, and other medical expenses.

Medicare program outlays have mushroomed in recent years. The CBO estimates that the federal government will spent $70.1 billion on Medicare in 1985—a 25 percent rise from 1983.[12]

Health expenditures in general are absorbing a growing proportion of national resources, as shown on figure 30. National health expenditures have been rising as a share of GNP since the 1960s. In 1965 the proportion of GNP spent on health care was 6 percent. By 1980 the share had risen

Figure 31

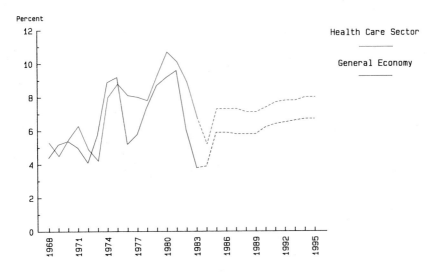

Inflation Growth Rates
Health Care Sector Versus General Economy

SOURCES: "Health Spending in the 1980s: Integration of Clinical Practice Patterns with Management," by Mark S. Freeland and Carol E. Schendler, *Health Care Financing Review*, Spring 1984; Projections by Rainier Bancorporation.

to 9.5 percent, and in 1995 is projected to be 12.7 percent. The Health Care Financing Administration (HCFA) cites the following reasons for the growth in health expenditures: a growing population, general inflation in the economy, rising per capita patient visits, and the increasing sophistication of services.[13]

As illustrated by figure 31, medical care prices typically rise faster than inflation in the general economy and decelerate more slowly. Factors which are specific to the health care industry, such as third party payments and fee-for-service reimbursement systems, contribute to the stubbornly high medical care costs.

In 1981 general inflation (measured by the GNP deflator) grew 9.6 percent, while inflation in the health care sector rose 10.2 percent. By 1983 the recession had reduced the growth rate of overall inflation to 3.8 percent, but prices in the health care sector were growing almost twice as fast.

The projections assume a continuation in the relationship between the two inflation measures. During the next decade, health care inflation is projected to outpace general inflation by an average of 1.4 percentage points per year.

Figure 32

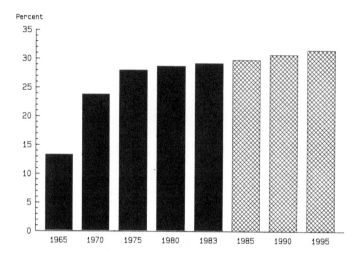

Federal Government Health Outlays
As A Share of Total National Health Expenditures

SOURCES: "Health Spending in the 1980s: Integration of Clinical Practice Patterns with Management," by Mark S. Freeland and Carol E. Schendler, *Health Care Financing Review*, Spring 1984; Projections after 1990 by Rainier Bancorporation.

Federal health outlays have grown both as a share of total federal spending and as a proportion of national health expenditures, as shown by figures 32 and 33. The establishment of the Medicare program in 1965 played a large part in expanding the role of the federal government in the health care sector. Medicare and Medicaid outlays account for the majority of federal health expenditures, but the government also finances health care through the Veterans Administration and medical research through the National Institutes of Health.

As a share of total national health expenditures, federal health outlays will rise steadily over the next decade from 29.1 percent in 1983 to 31.4 percent in 1995.

Figure 33

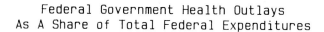

Federal Government Health Outlays
As A Share of Total Federal Expenditures

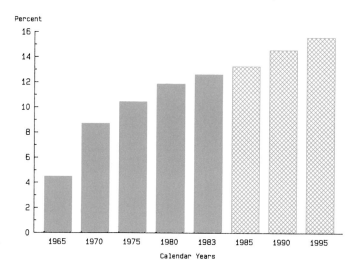

SOURCES: "Health Spending in the 1980s: Integration of Clinical Practice Patterns with Management," by Mark S. Freeland and Carol E. Schendler, *Health Care Financing Review*, Spring 1984; Projections after 1990 by Rainier Bancorporation.

Figure 33 illustrates that health outlays will continue to constitute an increasing proportion of total federal budget outlays, rising from 12.6 percent in 1983 to 15.3 percent in 1995.

Figure 34

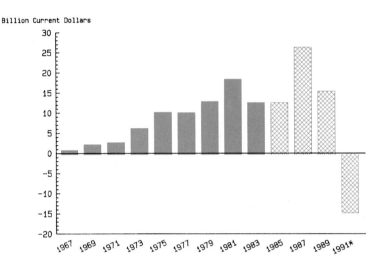

Medicare (Hospital Insurance)
Trust Fund Balance at End of Year

Billion Current Dollars

* Trust Fund Depleted in 1991

SOURCES: *1984 Annual Report of the Board of Trustees of the Federal Hospital Insurance Trust Fund.*
TECHNICAL NOTE: Alternative IIB assumptions.

Rising health care costs are taking their toll on Medicare trust funds. As shown on figure 34, the Hospital Insurance trust fund is expected to be depleted by 1991. The fund's trustees project that, to reestablish solvency for the next twenty-five years, either outlays would have to be reduced 32 percent or income increased by 48 percent.[14] In the absence of such changes, total income to the program is projected to grow at an average annual rate of 7.9 percent between 1983 and 1991, while total disbursements will rise at a 13.1 percent rate.

Figure 35

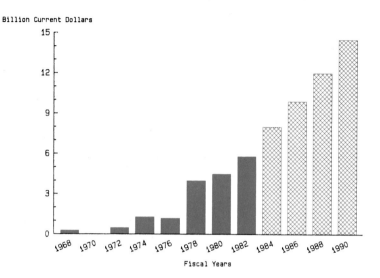

Medicare (Supplementary Medical Insurance)
Trust Fund Balance at End of Year

SOURCES: *1984 Annual Report of the Board of Trustees of the Federal Hospital Insurance Trust Fund*; Projections after 1986 from unpublished tabulations by the Health Care Financing Administration, U.S. Department of Health and Human Services.
TECHNICAL NOTE: Alternative B assumptions in the above report.

On the surface, the Supplementary Medical Insurance program appears to be in fine shape. The balance in the trust fund, shown on figure 35, appears to be growing rapidly with no sign of future problems. Between 1983 and 1990, it is projected to double to $14.5 billion. But inspection of figures 35 and 36 reveals that the SMI trust fund is a federal version of the bottomless pit.

Figure 36

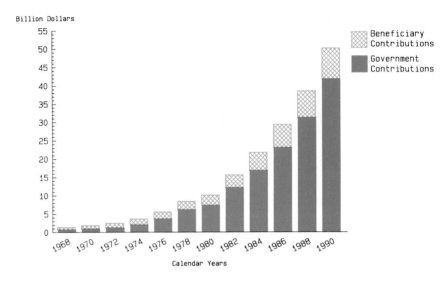

Medicare (Supplementary Medical Insurance)
Sources of Funding

Note: 1984-1990 Values are Projections

SOURCES: *1984 Annual Report of the Board of Trustees of the Federal Supplementary Medical Insurance Trust Fund*; Projections after 1986 from unpublished tabulations by the Health Care Financing Administration, U.S. Department of Health and Human Services.

TECHNICAL NOTE: Alternative B assumptions.

Financing of the SMI program comes from monthly premiums paid by participants and from contributions by the federal government. Between 1967 and 1973, premiums and federal contributions were roughly equal. In 1973 disabled Social Security beneficiaries became eligible for the program and the share of SMI contributions provided by the federal government began to increase. This share rose from approximately 50 percent in 1968 to 78 percent in 1983. Trustees of the fund project that by 1990 the federal government will provide $41.9 billion or 83 percent of program contributions.

Chapter 5

Renewing the Social Contract

We consider ourselves unauthorized to saddle posterity with our debts.
—Thomas Jefferson, 1813 [1]

If the system needs to be changed, as I believe it does with respect to fiscal policy and budgetary policy, the changes will have to evolve from a national public discussion that is only beginning.
—Herbert Stein, 1984 [2]

The world, in incredibly dark and devious ways, is headed toward salvation.
—Edward R. Murrow, 1950 [3]

IN A SENSE, AMERICANS are always of one party: the party of hope, experiment, and optimism. A majority never belongs to the other party: the party of austerity, prudence, and limits. When through personality or circumstance a Hoover or a Carter burdens his party with a cheerless philosophy, electoral consequences are sure to be close at hand.

Americans' preference for the positive has done us far more good than harm. It both reflects and promotes the dynamism of our historical experience. True, our booster spirit has often promoted and legitimized the whetting of material appetites through commercialism and a consumer economy. Some charge this has led to a demand for instant gratification which conflicts with the virtues our Founding Fathers considered essential in a republic. This is a valid concern; the demand for immediate results has made it harder to carry out long-term policies. But our economy and the quality of life it permits have set a standard which the world seeks to emulate.

The social contract is our agreement and promise, to those who follow and to ourselves, that no act of ours shall diminish the dream and hope this country has held out to its citizens and to the world. Renewing the social contract takes different forms at different times. Today it means removing the threat posed by deficits.

This chapter concludes with a list of proposals that would reduce the deficit by between $144 billion and $198 billion a year. More than 80 percent of the total comes from spending cuts and the remainder from increased user fees or tax changes closely related to the cost of providing government services.

Even the $144 billion plan, when combined with the debt interest savings it would produce, eliminates projected deficits without a general tax increase. To most Americans, the thought that the red ink can be wiped out so cleanly is refreshing. But to most budget experts, unless the details of such a proposal make sense, the idea itself may sound like it comes from a mad bomber. It flies in the face of widespread assumptions about what can be responsibly proposed. The remarkable fact is that the basis of this enormous impact is a review of recent reports from highly regarded sources of research on the budget.

Because the numbers cited above will startle many experts, it is important that the approach used here be explained precisely. This book was researched in the same order it was written. Program analysis preceded a look at deficit-cutting plans. When the focus turned to these plans, there was no attempt to work toward a target level of cuts in building the list of ideas. Instead, two criteria were applied: each proposal must come from a credible source, and each must be consistent with the apparent facts about program performance, budget priorities, and national goals.

At this point, it might be useful to restate the plan of the book. Chapter 1 examines how we moved from the fiscal comfort zone to the crisis zone. Chapters 2 and 3 examine the *quality* of spending in defense and domestic programs. Chapter 4 examines the impact of the *quantity* of spending and deficits on our economic present and future. Finally we come to the question, what shall be done?

The list of proposals offered here was built from several principles and concepts meant to insure it would be subject to a minimum of "discounting"—the loss of value from specific ideas because their impact is found to be overstated. Even the low-range total of $144 billion would over three years slightly exceed the $424 billion in deficit reduction claimed by the Grace Commission. Grace suffered the fate of having its estimate trimmed 77 percent by the highly credible General Accounting Office and Congressional Budget Office. Every effort has been made here to produce a list that is subject to a much smaller discount—indeed, one that will emerge virtually unscathed from such an analysis.

Each proposal on the list is credited to one or more of the following ten sources:

1. The Congressional Budget Office, *Reducing the Deficit: Spending and Revenue Options*, February 1984. This annually updated report has become a budget-cutter's bible.

2. The Congressional Budget Office and the General Accounting Office,

Analysis of the Grace Commission's Major Proposals for Cost Control, February 1984. This analysis is used in place of the Commission's own 600-page summary report in order to avoid any controversy over savings estimates. No Grace proposal judged "too vague" for evaluation by CBO-GAO is included on the list of cuts.

3. Senate Finance Committee, *Downpayment Budget Plan* options list, February 1984. This staff working paper has been augmented with ideas from individual senators' staffs.

4. The Heritage Foundation, *Slashing the Deficit,* February 1984. This study comes from a conservative group whose ideas led to many 1981 budget cuts. Heritage continues to review areas of spending that some other groups downplay. Even with a cautious approach to Heritage's ideas in education and welfare, its critique of subsidies and old-line programs has a logic with wide appeal across the political spectrum.

5. *Business Week,* Special Report: "How to Cut the Deficit," March 26, 1984. This plan balances equally between spending and taxes to eliminate the entire deficit. Within spending, defense and domestic programs are treated even-handedly.

6. The Brookings Institution, *Economic Choices 1984,* May 1984. This analysis and proposal was edited by Alice Rivlin, highly regarded former director of the Congressional Budget Office. Brookings' views have often helped to define mainstream moderate-to-liberal thinking.

7. Glenn R. Schleede, *Should You Care About the Federal Budget and Federal Deficits?,* June 1984. This paper by a former OMB executive was prepared for a group of business leaders in Massachusetts. It combines Office of Management and Budget and Congressional Budget Office material and ideas.

8. The Roosevelt Center for American Policy Studies, *Breaking the Deficit Deadlock,* September 1984. This is the report of a distinguished task force that was co-chaired by Arizona Governor Bruce Babbitt and Indianapolis Mayor William Hudnut, and included social scientists and economists as well as elected officials.

9. The Committee for Economic Development, *Fighting Federal Deficits: The Time for Hard Choices,* September 1984. This report by CED's Research and Policy Committee represents the views of chief executives from many of America's largest corporations.

10. Donald Lambro, "Who Says the Deficit Can't Be Cut?," *Washingtonian Magazine,* September 1984. This article comes from a public-interest muckraker, a sort of journalistic Senator Proxmire, who searches for the biggest golden fleece around. Lambro treated the same subject in a 1981 book, *Fat City.*

In addition to source credibility, other steps have been taken to help assure that the ideas offered here will deliver the promised impact. Some of these steps deal with technical pitfalls in making deficit reduction estimates: selecting a typical year; authorizations vs. outlays; and changes made by Congress in 1984.

Selecting a "typical" year. Some budget cuts take full effect immediately, while others rise in value with each passing year. A few even decline in impact over time. Examples of each case are: elimination of a program with stable funding; changes in transfer payment benefit formulas; accounting shifts.

The numbers given on the table that ends this chapter attempt to show what each change would mean in the second or third year after enactment. The value of the changes would be less in the first year, but more after the third year, than what you see here. The main reason for this is the fact that changes in benefit formulas begin small and grow every year. Because their cumulative impact is so significant, it is not possible to call any year "typical" with regard to the savings produced by amended formulas. The method used here is offered as a fair compromise.

Authorizations versus outlays. The United States uses a complex budget system which authorizes expenditures in each year that may differ from actual spending, known as outlays. The latter may be less than the former if an agency is unable to spend as rapidly as planned. In other cases, outlays may exceed current year budget authority, because an agency can spend not only its current year authorization but also any unused authority left over from previous years.

The U.S. system has been criticized for a number of reasons. It thwarts analysis because it is confusing. More serious, it can thwart budget control because the accumulation of unspent authority can lead to spending that is either too great or too erratic to meet program objectives and satisfy fiscal policy.

The problem is made more difficult by the five-year plan for Defense. Congress is often unable to determine whether the Pentagon has accepted budget trims made by lawmakers, or intends to roll forward the acquisition of weapons and other items of spending to future years after Congress has imposed reductions in the current year. Details of the five-year plan are firm only for the budget under discussion. The rest is uncertain.

As with the "typical year" problem, there is no wholly satisfactory solution to estimating savings, given the interplay of budget authority and outlays. On the table, outlay estimates have been preferred, but sources do not always specify which measure of savings they are using.

Changes made by Congress in 1984. All ten plans reviewed here were written before congressional adjournment. Several of them were published before the "deficit downpayment" plan was passed in the summer of 1984. In some cases, ideas from sources were removed because they seem to have been adopted. In four cases, the list indicates ideas which were substantially acted on in 1984. Because congressional adjournment was within a few days of the press deadline for this book, some other actions may have been taken which removed items from the list. The number, however, is not great.

Because of the three problems just cited, professional budget analysts will surely wish to make some adjustments in the list offered here. However, what you see is nearly correct in its order of magnitude—the dimensions of impact on the deficit which would occur if the list were converted into a program. Perhaps the most interesting fact which emerges from the list itself is the enormous total of cost savings that can be compiled by combining the areas of emphasis spotlighted by ten credible proposals. Even if areas of obvious disagreement are lopped off (as has been attempted here) the effect is so great that it defies conventional wisdom about the need for a general tax increase to close the deficit gap.

The magnitude of impact is large; what of the basis for the proposals? Are they sound changes in public policy? Do they involve responsible reductions in federal activity?

The best answer this book can give to these questions lies in Chapters 2 and 3, which analyze the substance and quality of major federal programs. That analysis reveals many cases of unwise spending which suggest the opportunity for major savings.

But what makes spending "unwise"? Hasn't every program passed some kind of policy test or received some mark of public approval? Doesn't its very presence in the budget demonstrate this?

In one sense, these questions must be answered "yes." To deny them weight is to dismiss the process of representative government. But in another sense, the budget swells because of a paradox. The budget is a Leviathan built from Lilliputs—a very big thing made up of a large number of small things. Each group cares very much about its small (and in some cases, not so small) things. The generally informed public cares about the awfully big thing which results and about the taxes they must pay to support it. But they know little and care little about the vast collection of bits and pieces which make up the whole.

It has long been observed that Congress is leaned on in specific ways by interest groups and in an unfocused way by the public. The difference has been compared to that between a laser beam and a ceiling light. Congress itself is divided and conquered. Its own committees, created to divide the workload and develop expertise, have become laser-beam targets. Bills are written to deal with specifics; that is the way of the law. It is not surprising that those who lean on Congress for detailed rather than general objectives so often prevail.

To each interest group, its programs return more than a dollar of benefit for each dollar of taxes its members pay to fund these items. To the taxpayer at large, the benefit in many cases—even the benefit of advancing the national interest—is less than a dollar. But, given the laser-beam ceiling-light problem, this fact often does not count for much.

The balanced budget amendment, despite its many defects and its potential for mischief, at least has the merit of being a general interest laser. Imposing a rule is an attempt to right a multitude of small, specific assaults on Congress with one big, specific assault.

But even if the mechanical and philosophic problems of the amendment do not bother you, "wouldn't it be better if Congress just got on with the job?," to quote former Congressional Budget Office Director Alice Rivlin.[4] Getting on with the job includes the kind of ideas found on the table which concludes this chapter. It has long since been time to eliminate federal programs which do not provide a decent return to the taxpayer or which represent a case of excessive generosity.

The deficit has added a powerful new reason for action, and equally, a powerful new way to frame the issue. Let us state the proposition at its boldest: If all items on the $144 billion version of the list were adopted, every interest group would give up something and most would give up things for which they had fought very hard. But could any group say that, if the entire program were enacted, its lost benefits would be more than a fair-share sacrifice?

By a happy coincidence it happens that the savings proposed from each area of the budget are in close proportion to the spending that each area bears to the whole budget. This establishes a fair-share principle. And what if the purpose of sacrifice is to lay the deficit monster to rest, not in economic theory and rhetoric, but in reality? What if the return for a fair-share sacrifice is a 4 percent decline in real interest rates, an end to the 25–30 percent overpricing of the dollar that is undermining our exports, and deliverance for us and the world from the threat which most elected officials, business and economic leaders, and citizens believe hangs over the future.

Even those who cherish the more-than-dollar of benefit their particular program delivers to them have to consider this new arithmetic created by the deficit. And even that rather small but vocal group which considers the deficit an abstraction must agree with Norman Ture's concern that, whether deficits matter or not in themselves, "an obsession with deficits is preventing us from focusing on the specifics we should include in spending reform and tax reform."[5] There is only one way to get rid of that obsession: remove its cause. The time has come to deal with deficits.

Before laying the list of actions before the reader, there are a few final points to consider about the "big three" building blocks in the budget: defense, Social Security, and taxes.

DEFENSE

Just as massive misinvestments do not add crucial capability to our military strength, so terminating these misinvestments does not detract crucially from our deterrent or our ability to fight conventional wars. We must keep this in mind so that we do not get cold feet when the moment to make justified cuts has arrived.

If we shift the focus from ourselves to our foe, the lesson is the same. In a general way the Soviets look at levels of U.S. military spending as a reflection of our national will. But they look much more carefully at what we are adding to our capability and whether it will make us more formidable in the situations that may actually arise. The dollars in the defense budget may interest the Soviets most as a measure of our intent to engage in a war of economic attrition. The contestants in that war would be America's fabled dynamism and growth versus Russia's equally fabled capacity for endurance amidst unrelieved hardship.

Weapons technology, more than any other factor, drives the defense budget. In July, August, and September of 1984, it seemed that experience was trying to tell us something. Stall-prone engines in the F-14 were cited in 24 accidents. Navy Secretary Lehman called the powerplants "terrible."[6] All F-18s were put on restricted maneuvers and ten were grounded because cracks turned up in their tail assemblies.[7] An automatic fuel-balancing system had been switched to manual, and the Air Force's premier plane, the B-1, crashed on a test flight only days before the roll-out of the first production model.[8]

Defects showed up in silicon chips which may have been used in as many as 15 million military and commercial parts in the last 15 years. The Pentagon stopped accepting shipment on thousands of weapons parts and other military hardware.[9] Its own effort to produce a "fifth generation" computer using fabulously condensed chips was reported delayed by logistical problems and infighting.[10]

A House subcommittee approved changes requested by the Pentagon to reduce warranty requirements on major weapons systems.[11] Yet, shortly before, Secretary Weinberger had pronounced the Trident submarine "under the worst contract I have ever seen. . . . It is evidence of gross neglect."[12]

Congressmen, citing pressure from their constituents, took the Pentagon to task for prematurely junking $2 billion in spare parts which it later had to replace. Defense officials blamed the error on "computer inventory problems."[13] Meanwhile, stockpiles of conventional tactical missiles were reported as low as 13 percent of need. This time the blame fell on troops firing the missiles in training. It was suggested simulators be used so pilots could be rated "combat-ready" without ever having fired a shot. As many as one-third of the missiles still in stock were rated as "unserviceable."[14]

Finally, there was one of those "tip of the iceberg" cases which are always so flashy. A coffee-maker for use in flight by Air Force crews was found to cost $7,600. The contractor was exonerated. He had been asked for, and had provided, a machine that would faithfully brew when all cabin pressure had been lost and the stress inside the plane was 40 g's—enough to kill every coffee drinker on board.[15]

This was an extraordinary spate of bad news in such a short space of time, even if all the themes were familiar. Does it mean that none of the affected weapons systems will ever make a contribution to America's defense armory? No. Does it mean that we are pushing the technological edge and badly need to get a handle on what we are doing before we surge ahead on all fronts? Yes.

The summer of 1984 also offered perhaps the most breathtaking budget ploy in defense history: the Star Wars Scam. It works like this: the assumption is made that a space-based ballistic missile defense will work. Therefore, the Soviets will step up all other forms of attack. Therefore, budgets for U.S. countermeasures in all these areas must increase. Take continental air defense: Intercepting Soviet bombers will now require many more F-15s, our most expensive and most "capable" craft for that mission. The classic quote from an Air Force general: "If you're going to fix the roof, you don't want to leave the doors and windows open."[16]

The ultimate budget ploy had been perfected: vast spending on a bold new system translated into greater spending on all the old systems that must defend against what the Soviets would do now that they had been thwarted in space. Not only could this mean a budget bonanza, it had the virtue of assuming Star Wars would work—indeed, in a sense, was already working—thereby shifting the focus away from any doubts that it would work.

The Soviet response was one they don't always manage. It actually made sense. They pointed out they planned to beef up their submarine force and to produce more cruise missiles—the same two weapons systems which U.S. planners feel deliver the most cost-effective attack potential.

Star Wars and the Soviet response to it demonstrate again the essentially futile character of an arms race where each side has vast nuclear capability and can add only increments over time. The facts of the case argue for a middle way between the arms race and the freeze—a path by which we neither rush to build new, mutually canceling systems nor lock ourselves into the existing force structure and rely on verifiable treaties. The middle way would move toward weaponry whose basic traits enhance stability (see section on "The Search for a Strategy" in the defense chapter).

With regard to military budgets as a whole, we must soon begin to cancel misinvestments in certain weapons systems by terminating them. The repeated attempt to contain defense spending by using percent growth caps is about to be thwarted by tremendous budget pressures arising from the buildup of the "bow wave"—the amounts that must be paid in the next few years if we go ahead with all weapons systems now on the books. To stick with abstract growth caps is to risk a starvation of funds for operations, maintenance, and personnel—or a costly stretch-out of production which gives us too few of too many weapons types each year. Both courses are condemned by defense analysts. The only escape from this dilemma is to make hard decisions on canceling contracts whose contribution to the armory does not match their cost.

SOCIAL SECURITY AND MEDICARE

Perhaps the most unedifying spectacle in the 1984 presidential campaign was the bidding war in which each candidate sought to outdo the other by promising to do nothing with Social Security. In an escalation of old battles, pledges were mutually exacted not to reduce benefits for future as well as current retirees.

The way the issue was handled suggests a combination of apparent unfamiliarity with the facts and hesitation to level with the people. This is less than what is now required from a chief executive.

The future of Social Security involves a tremendous paradox. In one sense, pension benefits are headed for a huge increase; in another, they are doomed to a huge decrease. Unraveling this paradox is part of the straight talk which tomorrow's retirees need in order to understand what will happen.

Because the current formula includes real wage growth as well as price growth in setting the initial pension level, future retirees can look forward to a monthly check which buys an ever-larger market basket of goods and services—assuming that real wage growth continues to be the norm as it has been with few exceptions throughout our history. Thus, a huge increase in benefits is assured over time.

Yet because today's young workers must not only fund a large part of their own benefits but also a major chunk of the underfunded pensions paid to their elders, there will be a spectacular hike in the ratio of lifetime contributions made by each worker compared to what he or she gets out of the system. In this sense, a huge decrease in benefits is scheduled simply because the "old deal" was too good to last.

If our leadership assumed it was possible to have a politically mature dialogue with today's younger workers, there would be a very fair and important question to set before them: Do they want the current law frozen forever in place, or is there a sensible trade-off between somewhat lower future benefits than are now scheduled, in return for some tax relief?

Ironically, "decoupling" (discussed at the end of the section on Social Security) would leave future grants just where they are today in terms of purchasing power, but it would take considerable financing pressure off the system. If one were both an optimist and knowledgeable about Social Security formulas, he or she might have prayed that when the candidates promised to preserve benefit levels, they were talking about things like decoupling and not a freeze of current law.

Further payroll tax increases are scheduled for 1988 and 1990. Prudent reform could permit these hikes to be lessened or forgone. We should not forget that if the entire federal budget were supported by a tax system which has increased its collections as fast as Social Security has, there would be no deficit. There would merely be a crushing tax burden. In this sense, Social Security is not sound. It has depended on an unsustainable rate of revenue increases. And even with these huge flows, some fear the assumptions that keep the system in balance are too optimistic about future costs.

The real question for the young, then, is the balance they wish to strike between tax hikes and benefit hikes. The days of the cushy deal are over; we must try to help the next generation achieve a soft landing on pension costs.

With regard to Medicare, the ideas on the table fall in three groups. Some are meant to beef up catastrophic coverage and fund the cost by asking the patient to pay a larger part of the bill on short illnesses. Others are meant to restrain over-use of private as well as public health care, recognizing that an excess in one part of the system spills over into the other. Both these changes affect patients. A third category is direct cost control imposed on providers.

The politics of the issue are relatively favorable. Both liberals and conservatives see merit in a shift toward catastrophic rather than short-term coverage. Both support cost controls on hospitals and physicians. Liberals tend to be less enthusiastic about using the tax system to restrain over-use of health care services. Yet the impact of taxing expensive employer-paid medical insurance, just like the impact of taxing Social Security and Unemployment Compensation benefits above certain levels, falls almost wholly upon well-to-do taxpayers. And in the case of health care, the tax is more than a revenue device; it is a way to help make the system more affordable for all.

Taxes

Oliver Wendell Holmes called taxes "the price of civilization." To John Marshall, "the power to tax is the power to destroy." The views of these two eminent Supreme Court justices define the poles of a debate which will never cease.

The $144 billion plan offered here is based on $121.6 billion in cuts, $13.8 billion in user fees, and $9.1 billion in program-related taxes. If such a plan were adopted, it would further reduce projected deficits by lowering interest costs about $15 billion in the first year, $30 billion in the second year, $45 billion in the third year, and so on. By relieving federal borrowing pressures, it could lower interest rates on "old" debt and could bolster revenues by upping the odds on long-term economic recovery spurred by the return of affordable credit.

The plan would come very close to dealing with the deficit problem without resort to an increase in the income tax or to creation of a major new levy such as a value-added tax. Does this mean that there is no place for a discussion of broad and basic changes in the tax system?

There are issues in the federal tax system which cry out to be addressed. Some of them are not related to revenue collection but to the ease of taxpayer compliance. We have nearly created an income tax which makes citizens feel they are fools if they haven't found a way to be tricky. To take the standard deduction is a mark of intellectual deficiency; to lack loopholes is to be unwise and unimaginative.

Such a system can only lead to resentment and contribute to evasion, for which the underground economy offers an excellent route. Indeed, the federal income tax is so complex and has so many quirks that it falls short on all the basic tests: equity, economic neutrality, ease of administration. Even revenue productivity, which has been a long suit of the system, is threatened by the rise in evasion and has been deliberately muted by indexing.

Revenue productivity is of course a double-edged sword. The supply-side critique was right in pointing out the crucial role of high, marginal rate brackets in depressing incentives and investment. The original movement to act on this insight came not from conservatives but from Democratic leaders in the House, who spearheaded the reduction from 70 percent to 50 percent in the top tax bracket on unearned income.

There are some very worthwhile tax reform ideas circulating just now, including tax simplification and changes in the income tax to increase savings incentives. The most attractive way to implement these reforms is to make them "revenue-neutral." They would not collect more dollars for the Treasury but collect the same dollars in a way that is more fair and less economically damaging.

Everyone who has closely studied proposals such as the Bradley-Gephardt simplified tax and the Brookings savings-incentive plan has found they are easier to design if the revenue impact is neutral. If a simplified tax is to raise more money, it must use rates which are too high to be an attractive trade-off for the elimination of current deductions and exemptions. For a savings-incentive plan to increase revenues, it must hike rates on taxable income doubly: to cover the loss from the new savings exemption and to boost collections.

The lesson, in brief, is that easing the pressure to bolster federal revenues will probably be a good thing for tax reform. It will aid the task of turning ideas into specific formulas and it will loosen up the discussion of alternatives. Norman Ture is right: with the deficit gun to our heads, we don't concentrate well on this sort of thing. Spending reform—making cuts and trimming deficits—could give tax reform a change it will not have otherwise.

There is another reason why spending reform should precede actions on the tax side, especially those which raise revenues. The issue is congressional credibility.

A number of conservatives, decrying Congress' free-spending ways, have found in federal deficits "the sweet uses of adversity."[17] The appalling prospect of a budget eaten alive by debt interest is an effective (and, some conservatives argue, the only) damper on Congress' inclination to create new spending programs. The conclusion: let's keep deficits forever. They quash initiatives for government to do new things and they lock in the existing pattern of spending which, with defense on the rise, isn't so bad.

This writer must admit to finding the above reasoning unpalatable and probably unpersuasive. It amounts to dismissing one branch of government as a ravening beast, incapable of self-discipline except when in the most dire peril. Evidence is not lacking for such a view. But there are notions one cannot defend without consequences, and this is one of them. To say that only a deficit can discipline Congress is to argue that representative government has proved to be a nonviable notion. This implies its replacement by something else. Those who prescribe the bitter medicine of deficits for the disease of runaway spending should take another look at the list of cures or admit they welcome the risk of killing the patient. If Congress has been part of the problem (as it has), the answer is not to render it impotent but to make it part of the solution.

However, Congress must take the first step in demonstrating it is ready for this positive role. The step is simple: Congress must move in a significant way to control spending before asking for tax dollars—even dollars that would be applied solely to reduce the deficit.

Congressional credibility requires that the people be asked for their tax dollars only if the deficit has, at least in a proposed plan, been beaten down to a level where taxes will materially reduce the remaining economic threat posed by deficits.

Suppose the current year deficit is $180 billion and there are to be $50 billion in spending cuts. Does a $130 billion deficit take the economy out of the woods? The answer is far from clear. And since the case cannot be made, there is no basis to ask for taxes to get the deficit down to $100 billion or $80 billion.

But suppose the deficit has been knocked down to $100 billion by proposed spending actions. At that point, $50 billion in taxes would take it down to one-fourth its current level, to where it was five years ago. The extra tax burden begins to "buy" something in terms of a real hope that the deficit is no longer an economic threat.

In this way, Congress would show it was asking for more revenue not because it had failed to make any headway on the problem, but because taxes would deliver a knockout blow to a deficit monster already on the ropes from spending cuts. By contrast, to ask for taxes before a punch had been landed on the spending side would be, as nearly every member of Congress recognizes, an admission of failure which plays into the hands of those who believe the time has come to radically reduce the legislative role and shift more power to the presidency.

POLITICAL STRATEGY AND DEFICIT CONTROL

The list of proposed actions is designed to serve as a flexible and realistic tool. Deficit reductions with a total value of $50 billion are marked with a single asterisk (*). Another $50 billion carries a double asterisk (**). Together, they provide $100 billion in impact. In several cases, multiple options are provided to achieve savings. If a topic on the list is judged too hot to handle, the lost impact can be made up by selecting one of the larger-value options in another area.

In the context of the thesis offered here, $100 billion in spending cuts with a $50 billion general tax increase is an acceptable course. But the preferable course is to act on the full $144 billion list, eliminating the deficit cleanly and leaving the tax-side focus on reform rather than revenue production.

Some experienced Washington hands believe the political arithmetic of a spending-side solution to the deficit won't work even if the fiscal arithmetic will. They argue that such an approach will appear unbalanced and unfair.

The assumption behind this belief is that any spending-side solution must involve cuts which are so deep they take away important services from some Americans. To avoid such cuts, and to balance the pain, tax hikes are said to be inescapable as part of any package that has the appearance of fairness.

This is a weighty concern. But it needs to be looked at in a new light. The list offered here suggests massive savings are possible without making cuts that are truly damaging. If this is true, why pursue fairness by retaining items of spending which are a poor investment? Wouldn't it be much better to focus on tax reform to enhance fairness?

For example, those below the poverty line could be completely relieved of any income tax liability for less than $5 billion. Doesn't it make more sense to ask higher-income taxpayers to foot this bill through tax reform than to pay $5 billion or more in added taxes for continuing programs which should be abolished and benefit formulas which should be changed?

If we don't pull our punches on spending reform, we maximize flexibility to enhance fairness in tax reform. Indeed, changes in the tax system could focus solely on fairness, unburdened by the stress of increasing revenue.

Such an approach gives both liberals and conservatives the very things each wants most: a slimmed-down government and a fair-share tax system. By contrast, the conventional wisdom leaves each side not with a breakthrough but with the cheerless and too familiar task of exacting a pound of flesh from the other. It is time to probe the possibility of rewriting the rules and discovering a new political equation.

Agreement on a package will not be easy to obtain even with proposals taken from the most credible sources. But a valuable lesson was learned in 1981. It suggests there is a way to move from today's logjam to the "reverse log-rolling" that would put a majority of Congress on the deficit-cutting bandwagon.

In 1981 there emerged a realization that, on fiscal policy as well as physics, there is a thing called critical mass. In politics, critical mass is the discovery that it is sometimes easier to make many cuts than a few cuts. This is no accident; there are specific reasons why it happens.

If a lot of cuts are made at once and none sticks out from the rest, there is a presumption of fair-share sacrifice. No one can justly utter the famous cry that the budget is being balanced on his back. And with so many interests affected at once, lobbyists from each interest group can capture only a few moments of any lawmaker's attention. Critical mass gives Congress the advantage in the game of divide-and-conquer. This is proper political hardball, used for the highest public purpose: to restore the general interest to its dominant position.

The $144 billion list offers the prospect of a grand solution—one of those rare, bold strokes by which the "crisis-driven institutions"[18] of our democratic government periodically restore balance to situations badly gone awry. Action in this case would restore the material part of America's priceless heritage: economic opportunity bequeathed by us, unmortgaged and undiminished, to future generations.

It is not morning in America; it is high noon. After two hundred years of history, we should find this fact a challenge rather than an embarrassment. The Founding Fathers were able to create a world anew; we must renew the American social contract.

If America is to retain a majority for the party of optimism, America must inject a bit of maturity and moderation to keep the optimism well founded. The party of pessimism usually pays with political defeat for voicing its fears, but only time will tell whether all its concerns should be dismissed. The best way to insure our optimism is justified is to remove any ground for charging it is reckless. The best way to keep hope forever alive is to keep it forever realistic.

At some point rhetoric, however elegant, and argument, however persuasive, must cease. Attention then turns to a specific basis for action. This book ends, as the political process itself must, not with words but with a plan. The pen must be laid down at last in the knowledge that, as the Latin phrase has it, "res ipsa loquitur"—the case speaks for itself.

Proposals to End Deficits without a General Tax Increase

(No item or issue with less than $400 million impact [.2% of $200 billion deficit] has been included)

Proposal (lowest value)	Savings ($ bil)	Source	Alternate proposals	Savings ($ bil)	Source
DEFENSE					
Weapons Systems					
MX: Limit production to 15 a year	2.0†	CBO, GS	MX: Cancel	5.0*	CBO, GC, *BW*, RC
B-1B: Cancel	8.0**	*BW*, BI, GS		8.0**	
C-5B: Cancel	2.0	CBO, BI		2.0	
F-18: Limit production to 72 a year	.4	BI		.4	
F-16: Limit production to 150 a year	.8	BI		.8	
F-15: Limit production to 36 a year	1.0	CBO	F-15: Cancel	2.3	CBO, BI

† = substance of proposal adopted by Congress in 1984.

* = elements of a $50 billion deficit reduction plan; * + ** = elements of a $100 billion deficit reduction plan; interaction has been accounted for in using different options on the * and ** lists.

SOURCES: CBO = Cong. Budget Office, Feb. 1984; GC = Grace Commission, analyzed by Cong. Budget Office and General Accounting Office, Feb. 1984; SFC = Senate Finance Committee staff and individual senators' staffs, Feb. 1984; HF = Heritage Foundation, Feb. 1984; *BW* = *Business Week*, Mar. 1984; BI = Brookings Institution, May 1984; GS = Glenn Schleede, June 1984; RC = Roosevelt Center, Sept. 1984; CED = Committee for Economic Development, Sept. 1984; DL = Donald Lambro, Sept. 1984.

Proposal (lowest value)	Savings ($ bil)	Source	Alternate proposals	Savings ($ bil)	Source
F-14: Halt production of A model; wait for D model	.8	CBO	F-14: Cancel A and D models	1.3	BI
AH-64 attack helicopter: Cancel	1.5	BI		1.5	
Army Helicopter Improvement Program (AHIP): Cancel	.5	CBO		.5	
Bradley fighting vehicle: Cancel	1.2	BW		1.2	
Division Air Defense gun (DIVAD): Cancel	.6	BW, BI		.6	
Copperhead, Maverick, Patriot, Phoenix, Sparrow missiles: Cancel	2.8**	BI		2.8**	
Nuclear carriers (Battle Groups 14 and 15): Cancel	2.0*	BW, RC		2.0*	
Defer production of DDG-51 and accelerate production of CG-47	.7	CBO	CG-47 cruisers: Cancel 3 ships DDG-51 destroyers: Cancel	3.2** 1.5**	BI BW, BI
SSN-688 nuclear attack submarines: Cancel 2 ships	1.5	BI		1.5	
Research & Development: Reduce budget request by 7%	2.6*	CBO		2.6*	

Competitive contracts (dual sourcing): Increase utilization	HF	1.0**	1.0**
"Procurement support" cost category: 1-year freeze	CBO	2.5	2.5
Total, Weapons Systems:		**31.9**	**40.7**

Operations, Maintenance, and Personnel

Close unneeded bases and facilities; consolidate support functions; coordinate Reserve and Guard activities; contract with private sector for commercial/industrial functions	HF	1.0**	1.0**
Close military commissaries in urban areas; eliminate subsidy and disqualify high-income ex-service personnel from use of remaining outlets	HF	.5**	.5**
Reduce growth in Operations & Maintenance to reflect smaller size of emerging force structure	CBO	3.5	3.5

† = substance of proposal adopted by Congress in 1984.

* = elements of a $50 billion deficit reduction plan; * + ** = elements of a $100 billion deficit reduction plan; interaction has been accounted for in using different options on the * and ** lists.

SOURCES: CBO = Cong. Budget Office, Feb. 1984; GC = Grace Commission, analyzed by Cong. Budget Office and General Accounting Office, Feb. 1984; SFC = Senate Finance Committee staff and individual senators' staffs, Feb. 1984; HF = Heritage Foundation, Feb. 1984; BW = *Business Week*, Mar. 1984; BI = Brookings Institution, May 1984; GS = Glenn Schleede, June 1984; RC = Roosevelt Center, Sept. 1984; CED = Committee for Economic Development, Sept. 1984; DL = Donald Lambro, Sept. 1984.

Proposal (lowest value)	Savings ($ bil)	Source	Alternate proposals	Savings ($ bil)	Source
Restore 1977 ratio of enlisted personnel to officers	.5*	CBO		.5*	
Charge units for cost of personnel and bill at standard cost rate	1.0*	HF		1.0*	
Reduce number of uniformed personnel by 144,000 due to elimination of unneeded weapons systems	2.9	BI		2.9	
Reduce number of Pentagon civilian personnel by 43,000 for same reason	1.0	BI		1.0	
Limit military pay hike to that granted civil service	1.0**	CBO	Freeze military pay for 1 year	1.9	DL
Replace All-Volunteer Force with draft; raise pay for technical positions and offset cost with cut for draftees	1.5	CBO	Replace All-Volunteer Force with draft; cut base pay in half and restore GI bill	23.0	SFC
Total, Operations, Maintenance, and Personnel:	**12.9**			**35.3**	
TOTAL, DEFENSE:	**44.8**			**76.0**	

MEDICARE

Hospital and Physician Reimbursement

Limit annual increases in prospective payment schedule to hospital inflation rate without adding 1% for new medical services	1.5	CBO, GS		1.5
Limit reimbursement to hospitals for admissions in excess of normal rates	1.2**	CBO		1.2**
Include nursing home and home health payments in basic hospital payment rates	1.0**	CBO		1.0**
Freeze physicians' fees for 1 year†	1.0*	CBO, GC, GS	Reimburse physicians on basis of fee schedule rather than using "reasonable charges" (ca. 5% cut in current level)	1.6	CBO, GS, DL
Limit physicians' fees for inpatient services to comparable charges for doctors' office visits	.5*	CBO		.5*
Total, Hospital and Physician Reimbursement:	**5.2**			**5.8**

† = substance of proposal adopted by Congress in 1984.

* = elements of a $50 billion deficit reduction plan; * + ** = elements of a $100 billion deficit reduction plan; interaction has been accounted for in using different options on the * and ** lists.

SOURCES: CBO = Cong. Budget Office, Feb. 1984; GC = Grace Commission, analyzed by Cong. Budget Office and General Accounting Office, Feb. 1984; SFC = Senate Finance Committee staff and individual senators' staffs, Feb. 1984; HF = Heritage Foundation, Feb. 1984; BW = *Business Week*, Mar. 1984; BI = Brookings Institution, May 1984; GS = Glenn Schleede, June 1984; RC = Roosevelt Center, Sept. 1984; CED = Committee for Economic Development, Sept. 1984; DL = Donald Lambro, Sept. 1984.

Proposal (lowest value)	Savings ($ bil)	Source	Alternate proposals	Savings ($ bil)	Source
Membership Coverage and Fees					
Increase member co-payments for short stays but provide full catastrophic coverage	2.0*	SFC, HF, BW, GS, RC		2.0*	
Charge deductible for first day of each stay during year rather than just once per illness; extend deductible to second day	3.0	CBO, CED		3.0	
Increase co-payments and deductibles each year by rate of medical cost inflation	2.0**	RC		2.0**	
Move part way back toward original 50% formula for physicians' services (Part B) by raising member share from 25% to 30% of cost:		SFC, BW, BI, GS, RC			
for high-income members ($25,000 single, $32,000 couple)	.5*		on a sliding scale from 25% at $25,000 single, $32,000 couple to 100% at $50,000 single, $75,000 couple	5.0	RC
			for all members†	(3.0**)	
			to 35% for high-income members	(.8)	

Limit use of Medicare by co-insured beneficiaries to the level of those who do not have co-insurance		2.0*	2.0
Total, Membership Coverage and Fees:		**9.5**	**14.0**

Cost Control–Related Tax Changes

Tax employer-paid health insurance benefits in excess of $80 a month for individuals and $200 a month for families	CBO, HF, GS	4.5**	4.5**
Tax, at 30% rate, "Medigap" insurance premiums used to pay any part of the first $1,000 of Medicare fees	CBO, GS	4.6	4.6
Total, Cost Control–Related Tax Changes:		**9.1**	**9.1**
TOTAL, MEDICARE:		**23.8**	**28.9**

[†] = substance of proposal adopted by Congress in 1984.
[*] = elements of a $50 billion deficit reduction plan; [*] + [**] = elements of a $100 billion deficit reduction plan; interaction has been accounted for in using different options on the [*] and [**] lists.

SOURCES: CBO = Cong. Budget Office, Feb. 1984; GC = Grace Commission, analyzed by Cong. Budget Office and General Accounting Office, Feb. 1984; SFC = Senate Finance Committee staff and individual senators' staffs, Feb. 1984; HF = Heritage Foundation, Feb. 1984; BW = Business Week, Mar. 1984; BI = Brookings Institution, May 1984; GS = Glenn Schleede, June 1984; RC = Roosevelt Center, Sept. 1984; CED = Committee for Economic Development, Sept. 1984; DL = Donald Lambro, Sept. 1984.

Proposal (lowest value)	Savings ($ bil)	Source	Alternate proposals	Savings ($ bil)	Source
SOCIAL SECURITY BENEFIT FORMULAS					
Recover cost of excessive inflation adjustments in prior years caused by defects in Consumer Price Index (CPI). Restrain cost-of-living adjustments (COLAs) by:					
having a COLA which is 1.5% less than the CPI for 5 years	7.0**	BW	having a COLA which is 2% less than the CPI for an indefinite period	9.3	CBO, CED
			having a COLA which is ⅔ of the CPI for an indefinite period	(7.6)	CBO, CED
			having no COLA for 1 year	(8.0)	CBO, CED
Recapturing COLA increases from high-income beneficiaries by a sliding-scale income tax which recovers 0 at $25,000 single, $32,000 couple, and 100% at $50,000 single, $75,000 couple	7.0	RC		7.0	

Description			
In addition to reduced COLA, "decouple" initial benefit formula so it is no longer affected by wage growth but only by prices (smaller savings initially, larger eventually)	2.0**	BI	2.0**
Adjust individual benefits at beginning of calendar year based on earnings estimates provided by beneficiaries	1.5*	GC	1.5*
Reduce by 2% a year the change in "bend points" used to compute percentage of income replaced by benefit formula	.5	CBO	.5
Limit inflation adjustment on survivors' benefits to amount to which deceased primary beneficiary would have been entitled	1.5*	CBO	1.5*
Use same maximum family benefit in OASI as is used for DI	.5*	CBO	.5*
TOTAL, SOCIAL SECURITY:	**20.0**		**22.3**

† = substance of proposal adopted by Congress in 1984.

* = elements of a $50 billion deficit reduction plan; * * = elements of a $100 billion deficit reduction plan; interaction has been accounted for in using different options on the * and * * lists.

SOURCES: CBO = Cong. Budget Office, Feb. 1984; GC = Grace Commission, analyzed by Cong. Budget Office and General Accounting Office, Feb. 1984; SFC = Senate Finance Committee staff and individual senators' staffs, Feb. 1984; HF = Heritage Foundation, Feb. 1984; BW = Business Week, Mar. 1984; BI = Brookings Institution, May 1984; GS = Glenn Schleede, June 1984; RC = Roosevelt Center, Sept. 1984; CED = Committee for Economic Development, Sept. 1984; DL = Donald Lambro, Sept. 1984.

Proposal (lowest value)	Savings ($ bil)	Source	Alternate proposals	Savings ($ bil)	Source
FEDERAL EMPLOYEES					
Retirement Benefits					
Reduce net costs of civil service retirement system (CSRS) and bring its provisions closer to private sector norms by:					
lowering initial benefits, raising retirement age from 55 to 62; half-COLA on benefits over $1,000/month	1.0	BI	having no COLA for 10 years; basing pension on highest 5 years of pay instead of highest 3; increasing employer/e contributions to 14% of salary; raising retirement age to 62	5.0	HF
			basing pension on highest 5 years; increasing period of service required to qualify for deferred pension from 5 to 10 years; changing formula for employees retired by cutbacks. For those under 45, change retirement age to 62, reduce the benefit formula, and require participation in Social Security	(2.5)	GC

Description	Value	Source
having no COLA for 1 year; basing pension on highest 5 years; increasing contributions to 9%	(3.0*)	GS
Reduce net costs and unique provisions of military retirement system (MRS) by:		
providing full pensions after 30 years and giving those with 20 years' service a lump-sum payment equal to 2–3 times annual pay	.2	CBO
deducting $1 of benefit for each $2 of earnings in excess of ⅔ of pension for "second career" members under age 62	1.6**	HF
providing a half-COLA to all retirees under age 62	(.4*)	CBO
half-COLA for those under 62; early vesting of benefits; integration of MRS with Social Security	(.4)	CBO
same as above plus reduction in basic benefit formula	(.5)	GC

Total, Federal Employee Retirement: 1.2   6.6

[†] = substance of proposal adopted by Congress in 1984.

[*] = elements of a $50 billion deficit reduction plan; + [**] = elements of a $100 billion deficit reduction plan; interaction has been accounted for in using different options on the [*] and [**] lists.

SOURCES: CBO = Cong. Budget Office, Feb. 1984; GC = Grace Commission, analyzed by Cong. Budget Office and General Accounting Office, Feb. 1984; SFC = Senate Finance Committee staff and individual senators' staffs, Feb. 1984; HF = Heritage Foundation, Feb. 1984; BW = *Business Week*, Mar. 1984; BI = Brookings Institution, May 1984; GS = Glenn Schleede, June 1984; RC = Roosevelt Center, Sept. 1984; CED = Committee for Economic Development, Sept. 1984; DL = Donald Lambro, Sept. 1984.

Proposal (lowest value)	Savings ($ bil)	Source	Alternate proposals	Savings ($ bil)	Source
Civil Service Pay and Benefits					
Delay pay increases within each GS grade	.8**	CBO	Freeze pay levels for 1 year	2.0	DL
Reduce overgrading of civil service jobs	.5**	GC		.5**	
Bring vacation rules in line with private sector	.4**	GC, *BW*		.4**	
Bring health benefits in line with private sector	.6**	*BW*		.6**	
Change overtime pay rules to conform with Fair Labor Standards Act	.6**	CBO		.6**	
Total, Civil Service Pay and Benefits:	**2.9**			**4.1**	
TOTAL, FEDERAL EMPLOYEES:	**4.1**			**10.7**	

FEDERAL BUREAUCRACY, Efficiency and Economy

Increase workforce productivity	1.0	GC, *BW*
Reduce travel costs by 10%	1.0	DL
Eliminate federal public relations programs except where vital to health and safety	1.0	DL
Sell unneeded federal properties, equipment, and buildings (one-time amount of $10 billion not included in total); resultant debt interest savings:	1.0	DL
Repeal Davis-Bacon, Walsh-Healey, and Contract Services Act provisions which inflate labor costs on federal projects	1.8*	CBO, GC, GS
TOTAL, FEDERAL BUREAUCRACY:	**5.8**	

† = substance of proposal adopted by Congress in 1984.
* = elements of a $50 billion deficit reduction plan; * + ** = elements of a $100 billion deficit reduction plan; interaction has been accounted for in using different options on the * and ** lists.

SOURCES: CBO = Cong. Budget Office, Feb. 1984; GC = Grace Commission, analyzed by Cong. Budget Office and General Accounting Office, Feb. 1984; SFC = Senate Finance Committee staff and individual senators' staffs, Feb. 1984; HF = Heritage Foundation, Feb. 1984; BW = *Business Week*, Mar. 1984; BI = Brookings Institution, May 1984; GS = Glenn Schleede, June 1984; RC = Roosevelt Center, Sept. 1984; CED = Committee for Economic Development, Sept. 1984; DL = Donald Lambro, Sept. 1984.

WELFARE, UNEMPLOYMENT, VETERANS ASSISTANCE

Proposal (lowest value)	Savings ($ bil)	Source	Alternate proposals	Savings ($ bil)	Source
Make permanent the provision set to expire in 1984 which penalizes states for excess Medicaid growth rates	.5*	CBO, BI			
Improve verification of income data used to determine welfare eligibility	.5*	GC			
Phase out school lunch subsidies for non-poor children	.5**	HF, DL			
Eliminate duplication in food programs	.5	HF			
Reinstitute food stamp purchase requirement dropped in 1977, and tighten program administration	1.3**	HF			
Maximize community-based (non-institutional) care of retarded Medicaid recipients	1.2	CBO, *BW*			
Require 2-week waiting period to qualify for unemployment compensation benefits	1.0	GS			

Item		Sources
Terminate supplemental coverage providing extended unemployment benefits	1.0	BI
Include all unemployment benefits in taxable income	3.3*	HF
Eliminate payments to veterans on the basis of "low-rated" (30% or less) disabilities	1.4*	CBO, GS, DL
TOTAL, WELFARE, UNEMPLOYMENT, VETERANS:	**11.2**	**11.2**

SUBSIDIES

Agriculture

Item		Sources
Eliminate deficiency payments based on target prices	4.0*	SFC, HF, BI, GS, RC, CED
Set support price at 75% of average market price for preceding 3 years	.5*	BI

† = substance of proposal adopted by Congress in 1984.
* = elements of a $50 billion deficit reduction plan; * + ** = elements of a $100 billion deficit reduction plan; interaction has been accounted for in using different options on the * and ** lists.

SOURCES: CBO = Cong. Budget Office, Feb. 1984; GC = Grace Commission, analyzed by Cong. Budget Office and General Accounting Office, Feb. 1984; SFC = Senate Finance Committee staff and individual senators' staffs, Feb. 1984; HF = Heritage Foundation, Feb. 1984; BW = Business Week, Mar. 1984; BI = Brookings Institution, May 1984; GS = Glenn Schleede, June 1984; RC = Roosevelt Center, Sept. 1984; CED = Committee for Economic Development, Sept. 1984; DL = Donald Lambro, Sept. 1984.

Proposal (lowest value)	Savings ($ bil)	Source	Alternate proposals	Savings ($ bil)	Source
Reduce milk price supports	1.0*	*BW*			
Terminate farm disaster payments	1.5	HF			
Reduce FmHA single-family home loans by 40%	1.3	CBO, DL			
Total, Agriculture Subsidies:	**8.3**			**8.3**	
Transportation					
Raise user fees on commercial aviation from 88% to 100%, and fees on general (private) aviation from 16% to 100% of costs imposed on federal government	1.0*	CBO, HF, GS			
Return unobligated balance in Airport and Airways Trust Fund to General Fund to reduce deficit (one-time amount of $3.4 billion not included in total); resultant debt interest savings:	.4*	HF			

Increase fees for use of inland waterways to full-cost recovery level	.6*	CBO, HF, GS, RC
Impose cost-recovery fees on commercial vessels and pleasure craft for Coast Guard services	1.0*	CBO, BW, BI, GS, RC
Increase fees for use of highways by heavy trucks from 70% to 100% of costs imposed	1.8*	CBO
Sell or shut down Amtrak	.7	DL
Reduce federal match for local transit construction grants from 75% to 50%	.8*	CBO, HF, BW
Terminate federal grants for local transit operations	2.5**	CBO, HF, BW
Total, Transportation Subsidies:	**8.8**	**8.8**

---

† = substance of proposal adopted by Congress in 1984.
* = elements of a $50 billion deficit reduction plan; + ** = elements of a $100 billion deficit reduction plan; interaction has been accounted for in using different options on the * and ** lists.

SOURCES: CBO = Cong. Budget Office, Feb. 1984; GC = Grace Commission, analyzed by Cong. Budget Office and General Accounting Office, Feb. 1984; SFC = Senate Finance Committee staff and individual senators' staffs, Feb. 1984; HF = Heritage Foundation, Feb. 1984; BW = Business Week, Mar. 1984; BI = Brookings Institution, May 1984; GS = Glenn Schleede, June 1984; RC = Roosevelt Center, Sept. 1984; CED = Committee for Economic Development, Sept. 1984; DL = Donald Lambro, Sept. 1984.

State and Local Government

Proposal (lowest value)	Savings ($ bil)	Source	Alternate proposals	Savings ($ bil)	Source
Target General Revenue Sharing only at jurisdictions in fiscal distress	1.4**	GS, CED	Freeze federal grants (except means-tested programs) at FY 84 levels and combine in single "mega-block"	6.0	RC
Abolish Community Services Block grants	.4**	HF	Abolish General Revenue Sharing	4.0	HF, *BW*
Abolish Urban Development Action grants	.4*	HF		.4**	
Target Community Development Block grants toward areas of greatest need	1.0*	CBO, HF, *BW*		.4*	
				1.0*	
Total, State and Local Government Subsidies:	**3.2**			**11.8**	

Miscellaneous

Abolish Small Business Administration	.6	DL
Tighten Section 8 Housing administration and utilize housing vouchers	1.1*	HF
Limit Education for the Disadvantaged to children who are both low achievers and from poor families	1.6*	HF
Target student loans at the poor and tighten program administration	.7*	HF
End Treasury support for Postal Service; change postal rates to reflect true cost:		CBO, GC, DL
Direct subsidy:	1.0	
Indirect subsidy:	1.2	

† = substance of proposal adopted by Congress in 1984.

* = elements of a $50 billion deficit reduction plan; + ** = elements of a $100 billion deficit reduction plan; interaction has been accounted for in using different options on the * and ** lists.

SOURCES: CBO = Cong. Budget Office, Feb. 1984; GC = Grace Commission, analyzed by Cong. Budget Office and General Accounting Office, Feb. 1984; SFC = Senate Finance Committee staff and individual senators' staffs, Feb. 1984; HF = Heritage Foundation, Feb. 1984; BW = Business Week, Mar. 1984; BI = Brookings Institution, May 1984; GS = Glenn Schleede, June 1984; RC = Roosevelt Center, Sept. 1984; CED = Committee for Economic Development, Sept. 1984; DL = Donald Lambro, Sept. 1984.

Proposal (lowest value)	Savings ($ bil)	Source	Alternate proposals	Savings ($ bil)	Source
Eliminate commercially oriented energy development projects	.8**	CBO			
Charge market rates for energy users in federal Power Marketing Areas (PMAs)	1.4*	HF			
Terminate Bureau of Recreation and Corps of Engineers construction and dredging projects with lowest cost-benefit ratios	.5*	SFC, HF, DL			
Increase charges for private sector and foreign government use of space shuttle and other NASA projects and facilities	.5*	CBO, DL			
Abolish direct loans by Export/Import Bank	1.5*	CBO, HF, BI			
Replace all direct loan programs with loan guarantees	.9*	GC			
Total, Miscellaneous Subsidies:	11.8			11.8	
TOTAL, ALL SUBSIDIES:	32.1			40.7	

CASH MANAGEMENT

Pay federal bills on due date and use check-paid letters of credit to slow cash disbursements	1.0**	GC
Hire private collection agencies to secure payment on overdue obligations	1.2*	GC
Offset IRS tax refunds to collect debts owed the government	.5*†	GC
TOTAL, CASH MANAGEMENT:	**2.7**	

TOTAL, ALL PROPOSALS:	**144.5**

2.7

198.3

Notes

Introduction (pages xv–xxii)

1. *Business Week*, 28 May 1984.
2. *Wall Street Journal*, 23 June 1984.
3. *Washington Post*, 22 July 1984.
4. Ibid.
5. Congressional Budget Office, Special Study: *Federal Debt and Interest Costs*, Sept. 1984, Table 7, p. 16.
6. *Time*, 5 Mar. 1984.
7. *Wall Street Journal*, 23 June 1984.
8. Ibid.
9. Ibid.
10. Interview with Van Ooms, 17 Jan. 1984.
11. Ibid.
12. Ibid.
13. Interview with James McIntyre, 17 Jan. 1984.
14. Interview with Ooms, 17 Jan. 1984.
15. Interview with Rudolph Penner, 5 May 1982.
16. Leonard Silk, *New York Times*, 11 May 1984.
17. Hobart Rowan, *Washington Post*, 4 Oct. 1984.
18. *Wall Street Journal*, 23 June 1984.
19. Office of Management and Budget, *Federal Government Finances*, Feb. 1984.
20. Interview with William Niskanen, 17 Jan. 1984.
21. Ibid.
22. Quoted by Carol Cox, interview, 26 Oct. 1983.
23. Hobart Rowan, *Washington Post*, 4 Oct. 1984.
24. Memo to the Hudson Institute, 5 Oct. 1984.

Chapter 1. Setting the Stage (pages 3–10)

1. *Los Angeles Times*, 22 Nov. 1983.
2. President's Council of Economic Advisors, *1984 Annual Report*, Table B-76, p. 251.
3. Washington State Research Council, *Agenda for the Eighties*, *Volume V*, p. 21.
4. This and many other of the observations that follow were offered by former and current career staff of the Office of Management and Budget.

The Carter Legacy (pages 10–21)

1. David Broder, *Los Angeles Times*, 26 Sept. 1978.
2. David Broder, *Sacramento Bee*, 6 Oct. 1976.
3. Ibid.
4. Remarks to Western States Taxpayers Association, 29 Aug. 1977.
5. *Fortune*, 3 July 1978.
6. Ibid.
7. Ibid.
8. Cited in *U.S. News & World Report*, 18 Aug. 1983.
9. *Across the Board*, Apr. 1978.
10. *Wall Street Journal*, 24 Jan. 1978.
11. Ibid.
12. *Across the Board*, Apr. 1978.
13. *Wall Street Journal*, 16 May 1978.
14. *Time*, 15 May 1978.
15. *Fortune*, 3 July 1978.
16. Ibid.
17. *Los Angeles Times*, 26 Sept. 1978.
18. *Fortune*, 3 July 1978.
19. Ibid.
20. *Business Week*, 13 Nov. 1978.
21. Ibid.
22. Citibank *Economic Week*, 13 Nov. 1978.
23. *Wall Street Journal*, 8 Jan. 1979.
24. *Los Angeles Times*, 18 Jan. 1979.
25. *Los Angeles Times*, 23 Jan. 1979.
26. Rudolph Penner, *Fortune*, 2 July 1979.
27. *Los Angeles Times*, 23 Jan. 1979.
28. Ibid.
29. Ibid.
30. *U.S. News & World Report*, 22 Jan. 1979.
31. Ibid.
32. Ibid.
33. *Los Angeles Times*, 23 Jan. 1979.
34. Ibid.
35. *Los Angeles Times*, 18 Jan. 1979.
36. *U.S. News & World Report*, 22 Jan. 1979.
37. *Wall Street Journal*, 21 Feb. 1979.
38. *Wall Street Journal*, 13 Apr. 1979.
39. *New York Times*, 28 Jan. 1979.
40. *Council of Economic Advisors* 1984 Report
41. *U.S. News & World Report*, 18 July 1983.
42. Rudolph Penner, *AEI Economist*, Feb. 1980.
43. *U.S. News & World Report*, 23 July 1979.
44. *Fortune*, 2 July 1979.
45. Ibid.
46. Ibid.
47. Rudolph Penner, *AEI Economist*, Feb. 1980.
48. *Los Angeles Times*, 11 Oct. 1979.
49. Ibid.
50. Rudolph Penner, *AEI Economist*, Feb. 1980.
51. *Business Week*, 11 Feb. 1980.
52. Rudolph Penner, *AEI Economist*, Feb. 1980.
53. *Across the Board*, Apr. 1980.
54. Rudolph Penner, *AEI Economist*, Feb. 1980.
55. *Wall Street Journal*, 29 Jan. 1980.
56. Rudolph Penner, *AEI Economist*, Feb. 1980.

57. *Business Week*, 11 Feb. 1980.
58. Ibid.
59. *Los Angeles Times*, 3 Feb. 1980.
60. *Tax Foundation News*, 19 Mar. 1980.
61. *Los Angeles Times*, 1 Apr. 1980.
62. *Tax Foundation News*, 19 Mar. 1980.
63. *Los Angeles Times*, 1 Apr. 1980.
64. Ibid.
65. *Los Angeles Times*, 8 May 1980.
66. *Los Angeles Times*, 12 June 1980.
67. Representatives Robert Baumann and Richard Ottinger in *Los Angeles Times*, 8 May 1980.
68. *Wall Street Journal*, 28 May 1980.
69. *Business Week*, 26 May 1980.
70. *Wall Street Journal*, 12 May 1980.
71. *Business Week*, 26 May 1980.
72. *Wall Street Journal*, 12 May 1980.
73. Citibank *Economic Week*, 2 June 1980.
74. *Los Angeles Times*, 12 Nov. 1980.
75. *Los Angeles Times*, 13 Nov. 1980.
76. *Wall Street Journal*, 14 Nov. 1980.

The Reagan Blueprint (pages 22–46)

1. Office of the Press Secretary, Official Briefing Packet, The White House, 18 Feb. 1981, pp. 1–2.
2. Ibid., p. 2.
3. Ibid., pp. 3–4.
4. Ibid., p. 5 (planned outlays), and Congressional Budget Office baseline projections for fiscal years 1983–86 (actual/estimated outlays) in Alice M. Rivlin, *Economic Choices 1984* (Washington, D.C.: Brookings Institution, 1984), p. 31.
5. Rivlin, p. 31.
6. Briefing Packet, p. 5 (planned share), and author's computation (actual share).
7. Briefing Packet, p. 8.
8. Ibid., pp. 6–7.
9. Briefing Packet, p. 8 (planned receipts), and Rivlin, p. 31 (actual receipts), with adjustments by the author.
10. Glenn R. Schleede, "Should You Care About the Federal Budget and Federal Deficits?," private printing, 25 June 1984, p. 17.
11. Briefing Packet, p. 2.
12. *Wall Street Journal*, 16 Jan. 1981.
13. Ibid.
14. Concept developed by Dr. G. N. Rostvold, Urbanomics Research, Irvine, California, in a conversation with the author.
15. David Stockman, "Avoiding a GOP Economic Dunkirk," private printing, Dec. 1980, p. 2.
16. Ibid., pp. 2–3.
17. Ibid., p. 3.
18. Ibid.
19. Ibid., pp. 13–14.
20. Ibid., p. 14.
21. Ibid., p. 15.
22. Ibid., p. 23.
23. *Los Angeles Times*, 16 Aug. 1984.
24. *Fortune*, 15 Oct. 1984.
25. *Washington Post*, 6 Oct. 1984.
26. *Wall Street Journal*, 1 May 1984.

27. Ibid.
28. John Berry, *Washington Post*, 22 Apr. 1984.
29. Berry, *Washington Post*, 17 June 1984.
30. *Wall Street Journal*, 11 Apr. 1984.
31. Berry, *Washington Post*, 22 Apr. 1984.
32. Berry, *Washington Post*, 17 June 1984.
33. Robert Samuelson, *Washington Post*, 5 Sept. 1984.
34. Ibid.
35. *Business Week*, 1 Oct. 1984.
36. James Fallows, "Endless Spending," *Atlantic Monthly*, Apr. 1984, and Robert Samuelson, *Washington Post*, 22 Aug. 1984.
37. *Business Week*, 24 Sept. 1984.
38. Samuelson, *Washington Post*, 22 Aug. 1984.
39. *Washington Post*, 31 Jan. 1984.
40. Ibid.
41. *Wall Street Journal*, 18 Sept. 1984.
42. *Washington Post*, 3 Aug. 1984.
43. Ibid.
44. Samuelson, *Washington Post*, 22 Aug. 1984.
45. Samuelson, *Washington Post*, 5 Sept. 1984.
46. *Los Angeles Times*, 27 Sept. 1984.
47. *Washington Post*, 3 August 1984.
48. *Washington Post*, 21 Sept. 1984.
49. *Washington Post*, 4 Oct. 1984.
50. Fallows, Apr. 1984.
51. Ibid.
52. *Fortune*, 5 Mar. 1984.
53. *Washington Post*, 3 Oct. 1984.
54. *Los Angeles Times*, 27 Sept. 1984.
55. *U.S. News & World Report*, 11 Oct. 1984.
56. *Washington Post*, 27 Sept. 1984.
57. *Washington Post*, 8 Oct. 1984.
58. *Fortune*, 5 Mar. 1984.
59. Fallows, Apr. 1984.
60. *Fortune*, 20 Feb. 1984.
61. *Washington Post*, 22 Aug. 1984.
62. *Business Week*, 25 June 1984.
63. *Los Angeles Times*, 16 Aug. 1984.
64. Ibid.
65. *Wall Street Journal*, 28 June 1984.
66. President Ronald Reagan, *Washington Post*, 7 Sept. 1984.
67. *Fortune*, 15 Oct. 1984.
68. Interview with William Niskanen, 18 Oct. 1983.
69. *Business Week*, 1 Oct. 1984.
70. Rivlin, p. 24.
71. *Fortune*, 5 Mar. 1984.
72. Ibid.
73. *Los Angeles Times*, 16 Aug. 1984.
74. *Washington Post*, 4 Oct. 1984.
75. *Washington Post*, 8 Aug. 1984.
76. *Los Angeles Times*, 16 Aug. 1984.
77. *Washington Post*, 22 Aug. 1984.
78. *Washington Post*, 29 Aug. 1984.
79. *Wall Street Journal*, 24 July 1984.
80. Ibid.
81. *Fortune*, 5 Mar. 1984.
82. Fallows, Apr. 1984.

83. *Fortune*, 15 Oct. 1984.
84. Ibid.
85. Rivlin, p. 21.
86. Lawrence Klein, *Los Angeles Times*, 11 Sept. 1984.

Chapter 2. What Everybody Knows about Defense

The Search for a Strategy (pages 48–69)

1. Business Week-Harris Poll, *Business Week*, 15 Nov. 1982.
2. *Business Week*, 12 Dec. 1983.
3. Interview, Paul Feldman, Center for Naval Analysis, quoting Herman Kahn, 8 Feb. 1984.
4. Quoted by Col. Harry Summers, *Los Angeles Times*, 14 Aug. 1983.
5. See for example, *Los Angeles Times* poll data, 20 Dec. 1983.
6. *Los Angeles Times*, 7 Feb. 1984.
7. *Seattle Times*, 7 Dec. 1982.
8. *Washington Post*, 14 Feb. 1983.
9. *Newsweek*, 20 Dec. 1982.
10. *Wall Street Journal*, 2 Mar. 1982.
11. *Fortune*, Sept. 1980.
12. *Los Angeles Times*, 30 Nov. 1980.
13. Author's interview with Carol Cox, 26 Oct. 1983.
14. *Los Angeles Times*, 7 Feb. 1984.
15. *Los Angeles Times*, 1 Feb. 1982.
16. *Washington Post*, 7 Jan. 1981.
17. *Wall Street Journal*, 15 Jan. 1981.
18. *Los Angeles Times*, 13 Mar. 1983.
19. *Los Angeles Times*, 26 Dec. 1982.
20. *Wall Street Journal*, 10 Feb. 1983.
21. *Los Angeles Times*, 7 Feb. 1984.
22. *Washington Post*, 13 Apr. 1984.
23. *Washington Post*, 15 Jan. 1984.
24. *Los Angeles Times*, 6 Feb. 1983.
25. *Seattle Times*, 7 Dec. 1982.
26. Ibid.
27. *Los Angeles Times*, 26 Jan. 1983.
28. *Newsweek*, 20 Dec. 1982.
29. *Los Angeles Times*, 9 Apr. 1984.
30. Quoted by Richard Harwood, *Washington Post*, 11 Mar. 1984.
31. Quoted by Col. Harry Summers, *Los Angeles Times*, 14 Aug. 1983.
32. *Fortune*, Sept. 1980.
33. James Fallows, *National Defense* (New York: Random House, 1981).
34. *Newsweek*, 20 Dec. 1982.
35. *Seattle Times*, 7 Dec. 1982.
36. Richard Harwood, *Washington Post*, 11 Mar. 1984.
37. *Los Angeles Times*, 14 Aug. 1983.
38. Quoted by Joseph Kraft, *Los Angeles Times*, 9 Apr. 1984.
39. Ibid.
40. Quoted by Charles Maines, *Los Angeles Times*, 6 Feb. 1983.
41. Stephen Rosenfeld, *Washington Post*, 13 Apr. 1984.
42. Ibid.
43. *Fortune*, 4 Apr. 1983.
44. *Los Angeles Times*, 7 Feb. 1984.

45. *U.S. News & World Report*, 13 June 1983.
46. *Newsweek*, 20 Dec. 1982.
47. Robert Kaiser, *Washington Post*, 15 Jan. 1984.
48. Ibid.
49. Ronald Steele, *Los Angeles Times*, 7 June 1981.
50. *Fortune*, 4 Apr. 1983.
51. *Washington Post*, 8 Apr. 1984.
52. Ibid.
53. John Collins, *U.S. Defense Planning: A Critique* (Boulder, CO: Westview, 1982), figures 23, 18.
54. British special forces mottoes.
55. Col. Harry Summers, *Los Angeles Times*, 14 Aug. 1983.
56. *U.S. News & World Report*, 13 June 1983.
57. *U.S. News & World Report*, 10 Jan. 1983.
58. Ibid.
59. Collins, p. 174.
60. Walter Slocombe, remarks to Hudson Institute annual meeting, 16 May 1984.
61. Ibid.
62. Ibid.
63. Ibid.
64. *Los Angeles Times*, 2 Apr. 1984.
65. *Newsweek*, 20 Dec. 1982.
66. Ibid.
67. Ibid.
68. Richard Halloran, *New York Times*, in *Seattle Post-Intelligencer*, 23 Mar. 1983.
69. Ibid.
70. Slocombe, 16 May 1984.
71. *Newsweek*, 20 Dec. 1982.
72. Ibid.
73. F. J. "Bing" West, remarks to Hudson Institute annual meeting, 16 May 1984.
74. Ibid.
75. Interview with Lance Sterling (the name is a pseudonym), 23 Jan. 1984.
76. Slocombe, 16 May 1984.
77. *Washington Post*, 31 Mar. 1984.
78. *Newsweek*, 20 Dec. 1982.
79. Interview with Paul Roberts, Office of Congressman Norman Dicks, 9 Feb. 1984.

Triumph of the Careerists (pages 70–92)

1. James Fallows, *National Defense* (New York: Random House, 1981), pp. xv, 18.
2. *Wall Street Journal*, 23 Jan. 1981.
3. *Wall Street Journal*, 13 Apr. 1982.
4. *U.S. News & World Report*, 20 Sept. 1982.
5. *Wall Street Journal*, 13 Apr. 1982.
6. Ibid.
7. B. H. Liddell-Hart, *Strategy* (New York: Praeger, 1965), p. 11.
8. *Wall Street Journal*, 13 Apr. 1982.
9. Joseph Kraft, *Los Angeles Times*, 25 May 1981.
10. Interview with Lance Sterling (pseud.), 23 Jan. 1984.
11. *Washington Post*, 29 Jan. 1984.
12. Ibid.
13. *Washington Post*, 5 Feb. 1984.
14. *U.S. News & World Report*, 27 Feb. 1984.
15. James Schlesinger, *Wall Street Journal*, 8 Feb. 1984.
16. Interview with F. J. "Bing" West, 16 May 1984.
17. Ibid.

18. *U.S. News & World Report*, 27 Feb. 1984.
19. *Los Angeles Times*, 4 Aug. 1982.
20. Ibid.
21. *Washington Post*, 8 Nov. 1983.
22. *Los Angeles Times*, 4 Aug. 1982.
23. Ibid.
24. David Halperin and Morton Halperin, *Washington Post*, 6 Jan. 1984.
25. Ibid.
26. *U.S. News & World Report*, 27 Feb. 1984.
27. Ibid.
28. Ibid.
29. Jeffrey Record, *Washington Post*, 29 Jan. 1984.
30. Ibid.
31. Interview with Lance Sterling, 23 Jan. 1984.
32. Fallows, pp. 76–95.
33. *Washington Post*, 10 Nov. 1983.
34. *Wall Street Journal*, 24 Mar. 1984.
35. Halperin, *Washington Post*, 6 Jan. 1984.
36. William Lind, *Washington Post*, 6 Apr. 1984.
37. Ibid.
38. Record, *Washington Post*, 15 Apr. 1984.
39. *U.S. News & World Report*, 27 Feb. 1984.
40. *Business Week*, 29 Nov. 1982.
41. *Newsweek*, 20 Dec. 1982.
42. See, for example, William Lynn, *Los Angeles Times*, 13 Apr. 1983.
43. *U.S. News & World Report*, 27 Feb. 1984.
44. *Los Angeles Times*, 7 Feb. 1984.
45. *Newsweek*, 8 June 1981, and *Time*, 7 Nov. 1983.
46. *Time*, 7 Nov. 1983.
47. *Los Angeles Times*, 15 Dec. 1982.
48. *U.S. News & World Report*, 27 Feb. 1984.
49. *Washington Post*, 6 Mar. 1984.
50. See, for example, Liddell-Hart, *Strategy*.
51. *Harpers*, May 1982.
52. Martin Caiden, *The Battle of Kursk* (New York: Ballantine, 1972).
53. *Harpers*, May 1982.
54. *Newsweek*, 20 Dec. 1982.
55. Interview with Terry Freese, 24 Feb. 1984.
56. Interview with West, 16 May 1984.
57. See Erich von Manstein, *Lost Victories* (New York: Praeger, 1956).
58. Interview with Norman Dicks, 9 Feb. 1984.
59. Interview with William Niskanen, 18 Oct. 1983.
60. *Wall Street Journal*, 4 May 1982.
61. *Washington Post*, 17 Dec. 1983.
62. Memorandum, Rebecca Paulk, Jan. 1984.
63. *Newsweek*, 20 Dec. 1982.
64. Interview with Freese, 24 Feb. 1984.
65. Ibid.
66. *Newsweek*, 20 Dec. 1982.
67. Ibid.
68. *Wall Street Journal*, 8 Feb. 1984.
69. Interview with Freese, 24 Feb. 1984.
70. *Los Angeles Times*, 31 Dec. 1982.
71. Interview with Freese, 24 Feb. 1984.
72. Ibid.
73. *Los Angeles Times*, 10 July 1983.
74. Ibid.
75. *Wall Street Journal*, 8 Feb. 1984.

76. *Los Angeles Times*, 10 July 1983.
77. *Wall Street Journal*, 8 Feb. 1984.
78. *Los Angeles Times*, 10 July 1983.
79. Ibid.
80. Ibid.
81. Interview with Paul Shannon, Science Applications, Inc., 9 Apr. 1984.
82. Interview with Freese, 24 Feb. 1984.
83. Interview with Rebecca Paulk, 24 Feb. 1984.
84. Interview with Feldman, 8 Feb. 1984.
85. Interview with Franklin Spinney, 23 May 1984.
86. *Wall Street Journal*, 26 Jan. 1981.
87. Congressman Les Aspin, *Los Angeles Times*, 26 Jan. 1982.
88. Ibid.
89. Interview with Joseph Burniece, 18 Jan. 1984.
90. *U.S. News & World Report*, 27 Feb. 1984.
91. Ibid.
92. *Washington Post*, 29 Jan. 1984.
93. Interview with Burniece, 18 Jan. 1984.
94. Interview with Sterling (pseud.), 23 Jan. 1984.
95. *Washington Post*, 29 Jan. 1984.
96. Ibid.
97. Interview with Sterling, 12 Jan. 1984.
98. *U.S. News & World Report*, 27 Jan. 1984.
99. Interview with Sterling, 23 Jan. 1984.
100. Jeffrey Record, *Washington Post*, 29 Jan. 1984.
101. *Los Angeles Times*, 10 July 1983.
102. Interview with Freese, 24 Feb. 1984.
103. Interview with Burniece, 18 Jan. 1984.
104. *U.S. News & World Report*, 2 Apr. 1984.
105. *U.S. News & World Report*, 13 June 1983.
106. Ibid.
107. Ibid.
108. Interview with Irving Leveson, 14 Nov. 1983.
109. See, for example, Charles Peters, *Washington Monthly*, Dec. 1984.
110. Collins, *U.S. Defense Planning: A Critique* (Boulder, CO: Westview, 1982), pp. 155–56.
111. *Wall Street Journal*, 23 Jan. 1981.
112. Collins, p. 58.
113. See Barbara Tuchman, *The Proud Tower* (New York: Macmillan, 1966) and *The Guns of August* (New York: Macmillan, 1962).
114. See William Shirer, *The Rise and Fall of the Third Reich* (New York: Simon and Schuster, 1959).
115. Interview with Roberts, 9 Feb. 1984.
116. Collins, p. 58.
117. Interview with Paulk, 13 Feb. 1984.
118. Collins, p. 49.
119. Collins, pp. 44–45.
120. *Seattle Post-Intelligencer*, 1 July 1983.
121. *Wall Street Journal*, 8 Feb. 1984.
122. *Seattle Times*, 8 Mar. 1982.
123. Sen. Gary Hart, *Wall Street Journal*, 23 Jan. 1981.
124. *Washington Post*, 6 Jan. 1984.
125. Ibid.
126. Interview with Jack Stockfish, 20 Jan. 1984.
127. *Los Angeles Times*, 10 July 1983.
128. Interview with Niskanen, 18 Oct. 1984.
129. *U.S. News & World Report*, 13 June 1983.
130. Interview with West, 16 May 1984.

Technology: Savior and Seducer (pages 92–122)

1. Cited by Arthur Alexander, Rand Corporation, *Los Angeles Times*, 10 July 1983.
2. *Wall Street Journal*, 13 Apr. 1982.
3. *Newsweek*, 20 Dec. 1982.
4. *Newsweek*, 8 June 1981.
5. Interview with Lance Sterling (pseud.), 23 Jan. 1984.
6. *Wall Street Journal*, 13 Apr. 1982.
7. Interview with Bruce Bishop, 18 Apr. 1984.
8. William Green, *Famous Fighters of World War II*, vol. I (New York: Macmillan, 1960), p. 117.
9. Jacques Gansler, *Foreign Affairs*, Summer 1983, p. 69.
10. Interview with Paul Shannon, 8 May 1984.
11. *Los Angeles Times*, 10 July 1983.
12. Gansler, p. 66.
13. *Los Angeles Times*, 10 July 1983.
14. Gansler, p. 66.
15. Ibid, p. 67.
16. *Los Angeles Times*, 10 July 1983.
17. *Los Angeles Times*, 27 July 1981.
18. Ibid.
19. Gansler, p. 81.
20. Interview with Dina Rasor, 18 Jan. 1984.
21. Everest Riccioni, quoted in James Fallows, *National Defense* (New York: Random House, 1981), p. 45.
22. *Wall Street Journal*, 4 Nov. 1983.
23. I. F. Stone, *Los Angeles Times*, 15 Mar. 1981.
24. Franklin Spinney, quoted in Fallows, p. 41.
25. *Newsweek*, 20 Dec. 1982.
26. Ibid.
27. Ibid.
28. Interview with Mark Menchik, Advisory Commission on Intergovernmental Relations, and formerly with Rand Corp., 11 Oct. 1983.
29. *Time*, 7 Mar. 1983.
30. Jeffrey Record, *Washington Post*, 29 Jan. 1984.
31. *Newsweek*, 20 Dec. 1982.
32. Ibid.
33. Interview with Mark Menchik, ACIR, 11 Oct. 1983.
34. Jeffrey Record, *Washington Post*, 29 Jan. 1984.
35. *Los Angeles Times*, 4 Sept. 1981.
36. *Los Angeles Times*, 10 July 1983.
37. Ibid.
38. Ibid.
39. Ibid.
40. Interview with Jacob Stockfish, author of *Plowshares into Swords*, 27 Oct. 1983.
41. Ibid.
42. Ibid.
43. *Business Week*, 29 Nov. 1982.
44. *Newsweek*, 8 June 1981.
45. Interview with Stockfish, 27 Oct. 1983.
46. Ibid.
47. *Los Angeles Times*, 10 July 1983.
48. Ibid.
49. *U.S. News & World Report*, 24 Jan. 1983.
50. Interview with Stockfish, 27 Nov. 1983.
51. Ibid.
52. *Newsweek*, 20 Dec. 1982.

53. *Business Week*, 29 Nov. 1982.
54. Slocombe, remarks to Hudson Institute annual meeting, 16 May 1984.
55. *Los Angeles Times*, 10 July 1983.
56. Ibid.
57. *Business Week*, 24 Nov. 1980.
58. *Business Week*, 7 Apr. 1980.
59. Quoted by Congressman Les Aspin, *Los Angeles Times*, 26 Jan. 1982.
60. *Los Angeles Times*, 21 Sept. 1981.
61. *Time*, 27 July 1981.
62. *Washington Post*, 29 Apr. 1984.
63. *Los Angeles Times*, 25 Feb. 1984.
64. Interview with Stockfish, 27 Oct. 1983.
65. *Business Week*, 7 Apr. 1980.
66. *U.S. News & World Report*, 13 Feb. 1984.
67. *Time*, 12 Oct. 1981.
68. *Washington Post*, 12 Feb. 1984.
69. *Los Angeles Times*, 12 Oct. 1983.
70. Interview with Terry Freese, 4 Feb. 1984.
71. *Time*, 7 Mar. 1983.
72. Ibid.
73. GAO letter of 19 Jan. 1984.
74. *Los Angeles Times*, 15 Apr. 1984.
75. Ibid.
76. Ibid.
77. *Los Angeles Times*, 26 Feb. 1984.
78. Ibid.
79. Ibid.
80. Remarks to the Hudson Institute, 16 May 1984.
81. *Business Week*, 29 Nov. 1982, and *Newsweek*, 8 June 1981.
82. Navy Secretary John Lehman, *U.S. News & World Report*, 22 Feb. 1982.
83. Robert Komer, ibid.
84. *Newsweek*, 20 Dec. 1982.
85. *Business Week*, 20 Sept. 1982.
86. *High Technology*, May 1984.
87. *Washington Post*, 3 Apr. 1984.
88. *Washington Post*, 25 Mar. 1984.
89. Ibid.
90. *Time*, 27 July 1981.
91. Ibid.
92. *Newsweek*, 8 June 1981.
93. *Fortune*, 4 Apr. 1983.
94. *Jane's Fighting Ships* (New York: Macmillan, 1942).
95. *Washington Post*, 25 Mar. 1984.
96. Congressional Budget Office, *Reducing the Deficit: Spending and Revenue Options*, February 1984.
97. Ibid.
98. *Wall Street Journal*, 30 Dec. 1982.
99. Walter Pincus, *Washington Post*, 18 May 1984.
100. *Newsweek*, 20 Dec. 1982.
101. Ibid.
102. Interview with Terry Freese, 24 Jan. 1984.
103. *Washington Post*, 16 May 1984.
104. *Business Week*, 29 Nov. 1982.
105. Ibid.
106. *Wall Street Journal*, 30 Dec. 1982.
107. *Business Week*, 15 Nov. 1982.
108. *Wall Street Journal*, 30 Dec. 1982.
109. *Business Week*, 15 Nov. 1982.

110. *Washington Post*, 17 May 1984.
111. *Wall Street Journal*, 30 Dec. 1982.
112. Ibid.
113. Interview with West, 16 May 1984.
114. A member of the Office of Science and Technology staff.
115. Interview with Pierre Sprey, 23 May 1984.
116. Interview with Spinney, 23 May 1984.
117. Ibid.
118. *Wall Street Journal*, 4 Nov. 1983.
119. *Washington Post*, 3 May 1984.
120. Interview with Andrew Borden, Center for Naval Analysis, 23 May 1984.
121. *Washington Post*, 15 Jan. 1984.
122. *Business Week*, 20 Sept. 1982.
123. Major John Hines and Phillip Peterson, Defense Intelligence Agency, quoted in *Wall Street Journal*, 7 Jan. 1983.
124. Ibid.
125. Ibid.
126. *Harpers*, May 1982.
127. Interview with Pierre Sprey, 23 May 1984.

The Price of Procurement (pages 123–48)

1. Quoted in an interview with Franklin Spinney, 23 May 1984.
2. *Time*, 7 Mar. 1983.
3. Barton Gellman, *Washington Post*, in *Los Angeles Times*, 27 Nov. 1983.
4. Interview, 2 Nov. 1983.
5. Interview with Dale MacComber, 17 Jan. 1984.
6. Interview with Daniel Goldfarb, Office of Senator Slade Gorton, 18 Jan. 1984.
7. Interview with Terry Freese, 24 Jan. 1984.
8. *Washington Post*, 2 June 1984.
9. *Los Angeles Times*, 20 Mar. 1982.
10. *Los Angeles Times*, 9 Jan. 1982.
11. *Los Angeles Times*, 26 Jan. 1983.
12. Jacques Gansler, *Foreign Affairs*, Summer 1983, p. 80.
13. *Time*, 13 Feb. 1984.
14. *Time*, 7 Mar. 1983.
15. *Washington Post*, 19 Dec. 1983.
16. *Time*, 7 Mar. 1983.
17. *Los Angeles Times*, 7 Feb. 1984.
18. *Los Angeles Times*, 5 Mar. 1983.
19. *U.S. News & World Report*, 24 Jan. 1983.
20. Interview with Spinney, 23 Jan. 1984.
21. *Wall Street Journal*, 7 Dec. 1979.
22. *Business Week*, 28 Nov. 1983; *Wall Street Journal*, 5 Jan. 1984; *Los Angeles Times*, 8 Mar. 1984.
23. *Business Week*, 20 Sept. 1982.
24. *Washington Post*, 3 Feb. 1984.
25. *Fortune*, 4 Apr. 1983.
26. *Seattle Times*, 7 Dec. 1982.
27. *Wall Street Journal*, 2 Mar. 1982.
28. *New York Times*, 23 Apr. 1983, and fiscal 1985 federal budget.
29. *Wall Street Journal*, 6 Feb. 1984.
30. *Los Angeles Times*, 10 July 1983.
31. *Business Week*, 15 Nov. 1982.
32. *Business Week*, 26 Mar. 1984.
33. *Business Week*, 15 Nov. 1982.
34. Quoted by Murray Weidenbaum, *Los Angeles Times*, 16 Dec. 1980.

35. *Wall Street Journal*, 6 July 1983.
36. *Wall Street Journal*, 9 May 1983.
37. *Wall Street Journal*, 6 July 1983.
38. *Business Week*, 15 Nov. 1982.
39. *Los Angeles Times*, 10 July 1983.
40. *Newsweek*, 20 Dec. 1982.
41. *Wall Street Journal*, 6 July 1983.
42. Ibid.
43. *Business Week*, 23 Jan. 1984.
44. *U.S. News & World Report*, 24 Jan. 1983.
45. *Los Angeles Times*, 10 July 1983.
46. *Seattle Times*, 5 Dec. 1982.
47. *Wall Street Journal*, 25 Mar. 1982.
48. *U.S. News & World Report*, 13 Feb. 1984.
49. *Los Angeles Times*, 22 Sept. 1982.
50. Ibid.
51. Department of Defense Annual Reports to Congress.
52. *Los Angeles Times*, 22 Sept. 1982.
53. Ibid.
54. Ibid.
55. *Seattle Times*, 5 Dec. 1982.
56. *U.S. News & World Report*, 13 Feb. 1984.
57. *Fortune*, 4 Apr. 1983.
58. *Seattle Times*, 5 Dec. 1982.
59. Interview with Freese, 24 Jan. 1984.
60. Ibid.
61. *Seattle Times*, 5 Dec. 1982.
62. *Time*, 27 July 1981, and *Los Angeles Times*, 10 July 1983.
63. *Los Angeles Times*, 11 Feb. 1982.
64. *Los Angeles Times*, 10 July 1983.
65. *Los Angeles Times*, 7 Feb. 1984.
66. *Los Angeles Times*, 20 Oct. 1982.
67. *U.S. News & World Report*, 13 Feb. 1984.
68. *U.S. News & World Report*, 22 Feb. 1982.
69. *Seattle Times*, 5 Dec. 1982.
70. Interview with Congressman Norman Dicks, 13 Feb. 1984.
71. *Wall Street Journal*, 9 Sept. 1981.
72. *Washington Post*, 5 Mar. and 7 Mar. 1984.
73. Congressman Les Aspin, *Washington Post*, 30 Apr. 1984.
74. Ibid.
75. Aspin, *Washington Post*, 26 Feb. 1984.
76. *Los Angeles Times*, 11 Feb. 1982.
77. Interview with Stockfish, 20 Jan. 1984.
78. *Los Angeles Times*, 10 July 1983.
79. Ibid.
80. Ibid.
81. Ibid.
82. *Newsweek*, 20 Dec. 1982.
83. *Los Angeles Times*, 10 July 1983.
84. *Los Angeles Times*, 15 Dec. 1982.
85. *Los Angeles Times*, 27 Aug. 1982.
86. *Los Angeles Times*, 15 Dec. 1982.
87. *U.S. News & World Report*, 27 Dec. 1982.
88. *Wall Street Journal*, 25 Mar. 1982.
89. *Newsweek*, 20 Dec. 1982.
90. Interview with Stockfish, 20 Jan. 1984.
91. Walter Guzzardi, *Fortune*, 8 Sept. 1980.
92. *Business Week*, 23 May 1983.

93. *Seattle Times*, 22 Dec. 1981.
94. Ibid.
95. *Business Week*, 29 Nov. 1982.
96. See, for example, *Wall Street Journal*, 30 Dec. 1982.
97. Stone, *Los Angeles Times*, 15 Mar. 1981.
98. *Time*, 7 Mar. 1983.
99. *Government Executive* magazine, May 1981.
100. *Business Week*, 26 Mar. 1984.
101. Stone, *Los Angeles Times*, 15 Mar. 1981.
102. *Time*, 7 Mar. 1983.
103. Interview with Sprey, 23 May 1984.
104. *Los Angeles Times*, 10 July 1983.
105. Interview with Freese, 24 Jan. 1984.
106. *Business Week*, 8 June 1981.
107. *Seattle Times*, 22 Dec. 1981.
108. *Los Angeles Times*, 10 July 1983.
109. *Business Week*, 20 Feb. 1984.
110. *Los Angeles Times*, 12 Feb. 1984.
111. Ibid.
112. *Los Angeles Times*, 13 Mar. 1984.
113. *Washington Post*, 16 Mar. 1984.
114. *Washington Post*, 11 May 1984.
115. *Los Angeles Times*, 12 Feb. 1984.
116. Gregory Fossedal, *Wall Street Journal*, 1 Mar. 1984.
117. Interview with Freese, 24 Jan. 1984.
118. Ibid.
119. Interview with Goldfarb, 18 Jan. 1984.
120. *Seattle Post-Intelligencer*, 21 Feb. 1983.
121. *Washington Post*, 26 Feb. 1984.
122. Gansler, p. 80.
123. See *More Bucks, Less Bang*, Project on Military Procurement (Washington, D.C.: The Fund for Constitutional Government, Apr. 1983).
124. *Washington Post*, 20 May 1984.

The Permanent War Economy (pages 148–75)

1. *Los Angeles Times*, 10 July 1983.
2. *Los Angeles Times*, 20 June 1978.
3. Walter Guzzardi, *Fortune*, 8 Sept. 1980.
4. *Wall Street Journal*, 30 Dec. 1982.
5. Data cited by Senator Rudy Boshwitz, *Wall Street Journal*, 10 May 1984.
6. *Los Angeles Times*, 1 Sept. 1981.
7. Ibid.
8. *Los Angeles Times*, 5 Sept. 1981.
9. *Business Week*, 7 Sept. 1981.
10. *Wall Street Journal*, 9 Sept. 1981.
11. Ibid.
12. *Time*, 21 Sept. 1981, and *Business Week*, 28 Sept. 1981.
13. *Los Angeles Times*, 24 Sept. 1981.
14. *Seattle Post-Intelligencer*, 14 Sept. 1981.
15. *Time*, 21 Sept. 1981.
16. *Business Week*, 28 Sept. 1981.
17. *Seattle Post-Intelligencer*, 11 Nov. 1981.
18. *Los Angeles Times*, 3 Mar. 1982.
19. *Los Angeles Times*, 30 July 1982.
20. *Seattle Times*, 3 Oct. 1982.

21. *Los Angeles Times*, 31 Dec. 1982.
22. *Seattle Post-Intelligencer*, 12 Jan. 1983.
23. *Los Angeles Times*, 2 Feb. 1983.
24. *Los Angeles Times*, 9 Feb. 1983.
25. *Business Week*, 14 Mar. 1983.
26. Ibid.
27. *Seattle Times*, 22 Apr. 1983.
28. *Los Angeles Times*, 26 Apr. 1983.
29. *Seattle Times*, 28 June 1983 and 12 July 1983.
30. Ibid.
31. *Los Angeles Times*, 7 Oct. 1983.
32. *Washington Post*, 2 Dec. 1983.
33. *Washington Post*, 23 Nov. 1983.
34. *Washington Post*, 2 Dec. 1983.
35. *Washington Post*, 14 Dec. 1983.
36. *Washington Post*, 2 Dec. 1983.
37. *Washington Post*, 17 Dec. 1983.
38. Ibid.
39. *Washington Post*, 31 Jan. 1984.
40. Les Aspin, *Washington Post*, 26 Feb. 1984.
41. *Washington Post*, 3 Feb. 1984, and *Los Angeles Times*, 7 Feb. 1984.
42. *Washington Post*, 22 Feb. 1984, and *Los Angeles Times*, 22 Feb. 1984.
43. Interview with Dale MacComber, 17 Jan. 1984.
44. *Wall Street Journal*, 15 Jan. 1981.
45. *Wall Street Journal*, 28 May 1980.
46. *Business Week*, 7 Sept. 1981.
47. *Newsweek*, 8 June 1981.
48. *Washington Post*, 7 Jan. 1981.
49. *Wall Street Journal*, 15 Jan. 1981.
50. *Newsweek*, 16 Mar. 1981.
51. *Fortune*, 15 Nov. 1982.
52. *Seattle Times*, 13 Jan. 1983.
53. *Business Week*, 26 Mar. 1984.
54. Guzzardi, *Fortune*, 8 Sept. 1980.
55. Interview with Carol Cox, 26 Oct. 1983.
56. Guzzardi, *Fortune*, 8 Sept. 1980.
57. Jacques Gansler, *Foreign Affairs*, Summer 1983, p. 67.
58. Interview, 2 Nov. 1983.
59. Earl Ravenal, *Los Angeles Times*, 2 Apr. 1984.
60. Ibid.
61. *Los Angeles Times*, 26 June 1983.
62. *Los Angeles Times*, 2 Apr. 1984.
63. *Los Angeles Times*, 10 July 1983.
64. *Newsweek*, 9 May 1983.
65. *Los Angeles Times*, 10 July 1983.
66. *Seattle Times*, 3 Oct. 1982.
67. *Los Angeles Times*, 17 Feb. 1983.
68. *Newsweek*, 9 May 1983.
69. *Los Angeles Times*, 5 Feb. 1980.
70. *U.S. News & World Report*, 22 Nov. 1982.
71. *Los Angeles Times*, 20 Oct. 1982.
72. *Los Angeles Times*, 14 Mar. 1982.
73. *Los Angeles Times*, 10 July 1983.
74. Ibid.
75. Ibid.
76. Ibid.
77. *Seattle Times*, 3 Oct. 1982.
78. *Fortune*, 30 Apr. 1984.

79. *Los Angeles Times*, 10 July 1983.
80. Ibid.
81. *Los Angeles Times*, 25 Sept. 1983.
82. Ibid.
83. *Fortune*, 30 Apr. 1984.
84. *Los Angeles Times*, 2 Mar. 1984.
85. *Los Angeles Times*, 10 July 1983.
86. *Fortune*, 30 Apr. 1984.
87. *Los Angeles Times*, 10 July 1983.
88. *Fortune*, 30 Apr. 1984.
89. *Washington Post*, 12 Apr. 1984.
90. *Fortune*, 30 Apr. 1984.
91. *Seattle Times*, 3 Oct. 1982.
92. *Los Angeles Times*, 26 Jan. 1982.
93. *Wall Street Journal*, 9 Sept. 1981.
94. *Los Angeles Times*, 11 Aug. 1981.
95. *Los Angeles Times*, 7 June 1981.
96. *Los Angeles Times*, 10 Jan. 1983.
97. *Washington Post*, 24 May 1984.
98. Walter Slocombe, remarks to Hudson Institute annual meeting, 16 May 1984.
99. *Khrushchev Remembers* (Boston: Little, Brown, 1971), p. 519–20.
100. Meg Greenfield, *Newsweek*, 1 June 1981.
101. *Fortune*, 15 Nov. 1982.
102. *Fortune*, 8 Sept. 1980.
103. Interview with Irving Leveson, 14 Nov. 1983.
104. Interview with James Lynn, 28 Feb. 1984.
105. *Los Angeles Times*, 10 July 1983.
106. Interview with Dale MacComber, 17 Jan. 1984.

Chapter 3. What Everybody Knows about Transfer Payments

Medicare, Heal Thyself (pages 178–203)

1. *Los Angeles Times*, 18 Mar. 1984.
2. *Business Week*, 25 July 1983.
3. Interview with Mark Menchik, 11 Oct. 1983.
4. Bedrosian, *Los Angeles Times*, 18 Mar. 1984.
5. *Seattle Times*, 17 July 1983.
6. *U.S. News & World Report*, 22 Aug. 1983.
7. *Business Week*, 27 Feb. 1984.
8. Robert Samuelson, *Washington Post*, 9 May 1984.
9. *U.S. News & World Report*, 26 Mar. 1984.
10. Samuelson, *Washington Post*, 9 May 1984.
11. *Business Week*, 16 July 1984.
12. *Los Angeles Times*, 21 Nov. 1983.
13. Paul Starr, *U.S. News & World Report*, 12 Sept. 1983.
14. *Los Angeles Times*, 11 Dec. 1983.
15. *Forbes*, 4 June 1984.
16. Bedrosian, *Los Angeles Times*, 18 Mar. 1984.
17. *Washington Post*, 8 Jan. 1984.
18. Samuelson, *Washington Post*, 9 May 1984.
19. *Washington Post*, 11 Mar. 1984.

20. *Business Week*, 18 June 1984.
21. *Newsweek*, 9 May 1983.
22. *U.S. News & World Report*, 9 July 1984.
23. *Washington Post*, 17 July 1984.
24. *U.S. News & World Report*, 22 Aug. 1983.
25. Ibid.
26. *Washington Post*, 17 July 1984.
27. *Washington Post*, 13 Apr. 1984.
28. *Wall Street Journal*, 19 Jan. 1984.
29. *Washington Post*, 18 June 1984.
30. *Newsweek*, 9 May 1983.
31. Starr, *U.S. News & World Report*, 12 Sept. 1983.
32. *Business Week*, 16 July 1984.
33. *Business Week*, 18 June 1984.
34. *Wall Street Journal*, 2 Dec. 1983.
35. *Washington Post*, 11 Mar. 1984.
36. *U.S. News & World Report*, 22 Aug. 1983.
37. *Wall Street Journal*, 6 Feb. 1984.
38. *Washington Post*, 22 Dec. 1983.
39. *Business Week*, 25 July 1983.
40. *Washington Post*, 19 June 1984.
41. *Wall Street Journal*, 2 Dec. 1983.
42. *Business Week*, 25 July 1983.
43. *U.S. News & World Report*, 22 Aug. 1983.
44. *Business Week*, 25 July 1983.
45. *U.S. News & World Report*, 22 Aug. 1983.
46. *Forbes*, 4 June 1984.
47. *Washington Post*, 10 Apr. 1984.
48. *Los Angeles Times*, 13 Apr. 1984.
49. *Washington Post*, 10 June 1984.
50. *Washington Post*, 21 June 1984.
51. *Business Week*, 9 July 1984.
52. *Washington Post*, 22 June 1984.
53. Interview with Robert Carlson, 26 Oct. 1983.
54. *Wall Street Journal*, 3 Jan. 1984.
55. *Los Angeles Times*, 2 Apr. 1984.
56. Ibid.
57. *Washington Post*, 13 Apr. 1984.
58. Lester Thurow, *Los Angeles Times*, 15 July 1984.
59. Ibid.
60. *Newsweek*, 9 May 1983.
61. *Forbes*, 4 June 1984.
62. *Business Week*, 16 July 1984, and *U.S. News & World Report*, 19 Dec. 1983.
63. *Business Week*, 16 July 1984.
64. *Forbes*, 4 June 1984.
65. *Wall Street Journal*, 2 May 1984.
66. *Business Week*, 9 Apr. 1984.
67. *U.S. News & World Report*, 22 Aug. 1983.
68. *Forbes*, 4 June 1984.
69. *Business Week*, 9 Apr. 1984.
70. *Washington Post*, 11 May 1984.
71. Ibid.
72. *Wall Street Journal*, 22 Dec. 1983.
73. *Washington Post*, 8 Jan. 1984.
74. *Los Angeles Times*, 10 June 1984.
75. *Washington Post*, 9 June 1984.
76. *Los Angeles Times*, 10 June 1984.
77. *Los Angeles Times*, 2 Apr. 1984.
78. *Los Angeles Times*, 13 June 1984.

79. *Business Week*, 6 Feb. 1984.
80. Ibid.
81. *Los Angeles Times*, 27 May 1984.
82. Ibid.
83. *Wall Street Journal*, 22 Nov. 1983.
84. *Washington Post*, 9 July 1984.
85. *Washington Post*, 1 Apr. 1984.
86. *Washington Post*, 21 June 1984.
87. *Washington Post*, 9 July 1984.
88. *Los Angeles Times*, 27 May 1984.
89. *Washington Post*, 18 July 1984.
90. *U.S. News & World Report*, 19 Dec. 1983.
91. *Business Week*, 6 Feb. 1984.
92. James F. Fries and Lawrence M. Crapo, *Vitality and Aging* (San Francisco and London: W. H. Freeman, 1981), p. 7.
93. *U.S. News & World Report*, 22 Aug. 1983.
94. Ibid.
95. Dr. William Schwartz, *U.S. News & World Report*, 25 June 1984.
96. Ibid., and *Washington Post*, 25 June 1984.
97. *Washington Post*, 25 June 1984.
98. Ibid.
99. Ibid.
100. Ibid.
101. Ibid.
102. Ibid.
103. Schwartz, *U.S. News & World Report*, 25 June 1984.
104. Interview with Don Moran, 22 June 1984.
105. Schwartz, *U.S. News & World Report*, 25 June 1984.
106. Daniel Greenberg, *Los Angeles Times*, 2 Jan. 1984.
107. *Wall Street Journal*, 12 Apr. 1984, and *Washington Post*, 23 Apr. 1984.
108. *Wall Street Journal*, 12 Apr. 1984.
109. *Washington Post*, 23 Apr. 1984.
110. *Wall Street Journal*, 12 Apr. 1984.
111. Ibid.
112. *Los Angeles Times*, 13 June 1984.
113. Ibid.
114. Rep. Hensen Moore, *Los Angeles Times*, 18 Dec. 1983.
115. Fries and Crapo, p. 38.
116. *Wall Street Journal*, 27 Mar. 1984.
117. *Los Angeles Times*, 18 Dec. 1983.
118. *Washington Post*, 1 Apr. 1984.
119. *Washington Post*, 26 Apr. 1984.
120. *Washington Post*, 12 Apr. 1984.
121. *Los Angeles Times*, 11 Dec. 1983.
122. *Wall Street Journal*, 3 Apr. 1984.
123. *Washington Post*, 1 Apr. 1984.
124. Ibid.
125. *Wall Street Journal*, 3 Apr. 1984.
126. *Washington Post*, 9 May 1984.
127. Fries and Crapo, p. 125.
128. Review of Dr. Jay Katz, *The Silent World of Doctor and Patient*, in *Business Week*, 9 July 1984.
129. Ibid.
130. *Wall Street Journal*, 12 Apr. 1984.
131. *Los Angeles Times*, 14 Feb. 1984, and *Washington Post*, 15 Feb. 1984.
132. *Los Angeles Times*, 11 Dec. 1983.
133. *Los Angeles Times*, 26 June 1983.
134. *Los Angeles Times*, 23 May 1984.
135. *Los Angeles Times*, 26 June 1983.

136. Ibid.
137. *Los Angeles Times*, 18 Dec. 1983.
138. *Los Angeles Times*, 14 Nov. 1983.
139. *Washington Post*, 16 June 1984.
140. *Seattle Post-Intelligencer*, 13 Sept. 1983, and *Los Angeles Times*, 19 Sept. 1983.
141. *Los Angeles Times*, 17 Aug. 1983.
142. *Los Angeles Times*, 15 July 1984.
143. Ibid.

Postage Due on the Chain Letter (pages 204–50)

1. Interview with William Niskanen, 18 Oct. 1983.
2. *Seattle Times*, 3 October 1981.
3. *Seattle Post-Intelligencer*, 14 June 1977.
4. *Time*, 24 May 1982.
5. As recalled by Dr. Frederick Mosher, relating comments of an eyewitness, in an interview with author, 2 May 1984.
6. James Kilpatrick, *Seattle Times*, 19 Aug. 1982.
7. *Time*, 24 May 1982.
8. Ibid.
9. *Wall Street Journal*, 22 Sept. 1981.
10. *Business Week*, 29 Nov. 1982.
11. *U.S. News & World Report*, 18 Apr. 1983.
12. *Los Angeles Times*, 9 Feb. 1984.
13. *Wall Street Journal*, 22 Sept. 1981.
14. *Time*, 24 May 1982.
15. Ibid.
16. *Business Week*, 9 Jan. 1978.
17. John Svahn, *U.S. News & World Report*, 15 Feb. 1982.
18. Computation by the author.
19. *Business Week*, 9 Jan. 1978.
20. Ibid.
21. Wall Street Journal, 14 Dec. 1977.
22. *Business Week*, 9 Jan. 1978.
23. *National Journal*, 20 Dec. 1980.
24. Ibid.
25. *Los Angeles Times*, 4 Jan. 1981.
26. *Los Angeles Times*, 22 Feb. 1981.
27. *Seattle Times*, 27 Feb. 1981.
28. *Business Week*, 16 Mar. 1981.
29. Ibid.
30. *Los Angeles Times*, 9 May 1981.
31. *Los Angeles Times*, 12 May 1981.
32. *Los Angeles Times*, 21 May 1981.
33. *Business Week*, 1 June 1981.
34. *Newsweek*, 25 May 1981.
35. *U.S. News & World Report*, 28 June 1982.
36. *Los Angeles Times*, 21 Mar. 1982.
37. *Los Angeles Times*, 19 Aug. 1982.
38. Ibid.
39. *Los Angeles Times*, 21 July 1982.
40. *Los Angeles Times*, 19 Aug. 1982.
41. *Washington Post*, 9 Sept. 1982.
42. *Los Angeles Times*, 19 June 1983.
43. *Los Angeles Times*, 10 Aug. 1983.
44. *Los Angeles Times*, 12 Oct. 1983.
45. *Los Angeles Times*, 23 Feb. 1984.

46. *Washington Post*, 24 Mar. 1984.
47. *Washington Post*, 27 Mar. 1984.
48. *Washington Post*, 14 May 1984.
49. Interview with Karen Trieger, Office of Senator Slade Gorton, 17 Aug. 1984.
50. *National Journal*, 13 June 1981.
51. Ibid.
52. Ibid.
53. *Los Angeles Times*, 8 July 1981.
54. *Los Angeles Times*, 21 July 1981.
55. *Los Angeles Times*, 17 Sept. 1981.
56. *Business Week*, 28 Sept. 1981.
57. Ibid.
58. *Los Angeles Times*, 5 Oct. 1981.
59. *Los Angeles Times*, 17 Dec. 1981.
60. *U.S. News & World Report*, 28 Dec. 1981.
61. *Time*, 24 May 1982.
62. *Wall Street Journal*, 10 Nov. 1982.
63. Morton Kondracke, *Wall Street Journal*, 11 Nov. 1982.
64. *Los Angeles Times*, 13 Nov. 1982.
65. *Public Opinion*, 11 Oct. 1982.
66. *Business Week*, 29 Nov. 1982.
67. *Los Angeles Times*, 6 Jan. 1983.
68. *Seattle Post-Intelligencer*, 10 Jan. 1983.
69. Suzanne Garment, *Wall Street Journal*, 23 Jan. 1983.
70. *Los Angeles Times*, 16 Jan. 1983.
71. *Los Angeles Times*, 23 Jan. 1983.
72. *Seattle Post-Intelligencer*, 17 Jan. 1983.
73. *Los Angeles Times*, 23 Jan. 1983.
74. *Seattle Times*, 27 Jan. 1983.
75. *Wall Street Journal*, 4 Feb. 1983.
76. *Business Week*, 31 Jan. 1983.
77. Ibid.
78. Interview with Office of Management and Budget senior staff.
79. *Washington Post*, 31 Mar. 1984.
80. *Washington Post*, 8 May 1984.
81. *Washington Post*, 1 July 1984.
82. *Washington Post*, 3 Aug. 1984.
83. *Washington Post*, 1 Aug. 1983.
84. *Los Angeles Times*, 28 July 1984.
85. *Business Week*, 6 Aug. 1984.
86. *Business Week*, 4 Mar. 1981; *Los Angeles Times*, 6 Mar. 1981; *Seattle Times*, 14 Mar. 1981.
87. *Time*, 24 May 1982.
88. *Los Angeles Times*, 28 July 1984.
89. *Time*, 24 May 1982.
90. Peter Drucker, *Wall Street Journal*, 11 Aug. 1983.
91. *Time*, 24 May 1982.
92. *Public Opinion*, Oct.–Nov. 1982.
93. *Time*, 24 May 1982.
94. *Seattle Post-Intelligencer*, 11 Jan. 1981.
95. *Wall Street Journal*, 21 Jan. 1983.
96. *Seattle Times*, 3 Oct. 1981.
97. Drucker, *Wall Street Journal*, 11 Aug. 1983.
98. *Wall Street Journal*, 21 Jan. 1983.
99. *Public Opinion*, Oct.–Nov. 1982.
100. *Time*, 24 May 1982.
101. *Public Opinion*, Oct.–Nov. 1982.
102. See, for example, *Seattle Times*, 3 Oct. 1981.

103. *Wall Street Journal*, 21 Jan. 1983.
104. *Public Opinion*, Oct.–Nov. 1982.
105. *Los Angeles Times*, 12 Nov. 1983.
106. Census Bureau data, *across the board* (monthly), June 1982.
107. *Time*, 24 May 1982.
108. James Storey of the Urban Institute, in *Seattle Post-Intelligencer*, 9 Jan. 1983.
109. Doug Bandow, *Wall Street Journal*, 25 Apr. 1983.
110. Senator William Armstrong, *Wall Street Journal*, 31 Jan. 1983.
111. *Los Angeles Times*, 2 Feb. 1982.
112. *Wall Street Journal*, 1 June 1982.
113. *Los Angeles Times*, 26 Mar. 1982.
114. *National Journal*, 13 June 1981.
115. *Los Angeles Times*, 2 Feb. 1982.
116. *Los Angeles Times*, 7 Feb. 1982.
117. Ibid.
118. Drucker, *Wall Street Journal*, 11 Aug. 1983, and *Time*, 24 May 1982.
119. Kondracke, *Wall Street Journal*, 11 Nov. 1982.
120. Ibid.
121. *Los Angeles Times*, 8 June 1981.
122. *Wall Street Journal*, 11 Aug. 1983.
123. *National Journal*, 13 June 1981.
124. Senate Finance Committee cost estimate in *Seattle Post-Intelligencer*, 9 Jan. 1983.
125. *Seattle Times*, 9 Feb. 1983.
126. *Wall Street Journal*, 25 Apr. 1983.
127. *U.S. News & World Report*, 21 Feb. 1983.
128. *U.S. News & World Report*, 12 Jan. 1981.
129. *Wall Street Journal*, 25 Apr. 1983.
130. *Los Angeles Times*, 2 Feb. 1982.
131. National Journal, 20 Dec. 1980.
132. *Public Opinion*, Oct.–Nov. 1982.
133. *Wall Street Journal*, 10 Aug. 1982.
134. *Los Angeles Times*, 7 Dec. 1982.
135. Senator Slade Gorton, "Washington Report," Mar. 1983.
136. *Wall Street Journal*, 18 May 1981.
137. *Wall Street Journal*, 22 Sept. 1981.
138. *Fortune*, 13 Dec. 1983.
139. *Los Angeles Times*, 2 Feb. 1983.
140. *Los Angeles Times*, 7 Dec. 1982.
141. *U.S. News & World Report*, 12 Jan. 1981.
142. *U.S. News & World Report*, 7 June 1982.
143. *U.S. News & World Report*, 12 Jan. 1981.
144. *U.S. News & World Report*, 7 June 1982.
145. Bandow, *Wall Street Journal*, 25 Apr. 1983.
146. *U.S. News & World Report*, 31 Jan. 1983.
147. *Los Angeles Times*, 4 Jan. 1981.
148. *Wall Street Journal*, 25 Apr. 1983.
149. *across the board*, May 1981.
150. Edward Sprague, *Tax Review*, Feb. 1981.
151. Michael Boskin, *Los Angeles Times*, 21 Mar. 1983.
152. Interview with Robert Carlson, 21 Nov. 1983.
153. Stuart Sweet, *Wall Street Journal*, 28 Mar. 1984.
154. Boskin, *Los Angeles Times*, 21 Mar. 1983.
155. *Washington Post*, 13 June 1984.
156. *Fortune*, 25 Aug. 1980.
157. *Wall Street Journal*, 11 Aug. 1983.
158. *Seattle Times*, 27 Jan. 1983.
159. *AEI Economist*, Oct.–Nov. 1982.

160. *Seattle Times*, 15 Jan. 1983.
161. *U.S. News & World Report*, 28 Jan. 1981.
162. *U.S. News & World Report*, 15 Feb. 1982.
163. *Los Angeles Times*, 2 Feb. 1982.
164. *Time*, 24 May 1982.
165. *Forbes*, 4 June 1984.
166. *Wall Street Journal*, 11 Aug. 1983.
167. *Wall Street Journal*, 7 May 1981.
168. *Los Angeles Times*, 8 Nov. 1982.
169. Interview with Carol Cox, 26 Oct. 1983.
170. Ibid.
171. *Fortune*, 13 Dec. 1982, and *U.S. News & World Report*, 7 June 1982.
172. *Wall Street Journal*, 3 Mar. 1983.
173. *Washington Post*, 14 Dec. 1983.
174. *Wall Street Journal*, 11 Aug. 1983.

The Gravy Train Robbery (pages 251–62)

1. President's Private Sector Survey on Cost Control (known as the Grace Commission), Summary Report, 15 Jan. 1984, p. III-281.
2. *Washington Post*, 29 Feb. 1984.
3. Grace Commission Summary Report, p. III-289.
4. Ibid.
5. Grace, p. III-282.
6. Ibid., pp. III-282 and III-290.
7. Ibid., p. III-287.
8. Ibid.
9. Ibid., p. III-288.
10. Ibid., p. III-286.
11. Ibid., p. III-284.
12. Computation of the author.
13. Alice Rivlin, ed., *Economic Choices 1984* (Washington, D.C.: The Brookings Institution, 1984), p. 60.
14. Grace, p. III-239.
15. Ibid., p. III-240.
16. Computation of the author.
17. Grace, p. III-294.
18. Ibid., p. III-293.
19. Ibid., p. III-294.
20. Ibid.
21. Grace, p. III-291.
22. Ibid., p. III-292.
23. Ibid.
24. Ibid., p. III-286.
25. *U.S. News & World Report*, 9 Jan. 1984.
26. Congressional Budget Office (CBO), *Modifying Military Retirement: Alternative Approaches*, Washington, D.C., Apr. 1984, p. xi.
27. Ibid.
28. *U.S. News & World Report*, 9 Jan. 1984.
29. James Bovard, *Wall Street Journal*, 20 Apr. 1984.
30. Ibid.
31. Rivlin, p. 60.
32. *Wall Street Journal*, 20 Apr. 1984.
33. CBO, p. xiv.
34. *Wall Street Journal*, 20 Apr. 1984.
35. *U.S. News & World Report*, 9 Jan. 1984.

36. CBO, pp. xiv–xv.
37. *Los Angeles Times*, 2 Sept. 1984.
38. *U.S. News & World Report*, 9 Jan. 1984.
39. *U.S. News & World Report*, 22 Aug. 1983.
40. *Los Angeles Times*, 2 Sept. 1984.
41. Ibid.
42. Ibid.
43. *U.S. News & World Report*, 9 Jan. 1984.
44. CBO, p. xiii.
45. CBO, p. xix.
46. *Washington Post*, 6 Apr. 1984.

Subsidies for the Strong (pages 264–89)

1. *Business Week*, 26 Mar. 1984.
2. *U.S. News & World Report*, 15 Aug. 1983.
3. Ibid.
4. *Washington Monthly*, Apr. 1983.
5. Alice Rivlin, ed., *Economic Choices 1984* (Washington, D.C.: The Brookings Institution, 1984).
6. Robert Samuelson, *Los Angeles Times*, 24 Aug. 1983.
7. *U.S. News & World Report*, 11 June 1984.
8. *Washington Post*, 4 Sept. 1984.
9. *U.S. News & World Report*, 15 Aug. 1983.
10. Ward Sinclair, *Washington Post*, 25 Mar. 1984.
11. Samuelson, 24 Aug. 1983.
12. *U.S. News & World Report*, 15 Aug. 1983.
13. Ward Sinclair, *Washington Post*, 17 Apr. 1984.
14. Susan Lee, *Wall Street Journal*, 8 Sept. 1983.
15. Samuelson, 24 Aug. 1983.
16. Ibid.
17. Ibid.
18. *U.S. News & World Report*, 15 Aug. 1983.
19. Samuelson, 24 Aug. 1983.
20. *U.S. News & World Report*, 15 Aug. 1983.
21. Ibid.
22. Samuelson, 24 Aug. 1983.
23. Ibid.
24. *U.S. News & World Report*, 15 Aug. 1983.
25. Ibid.
26. *Business Week*, 26 Mar. 1984.
27. *Wall Street Journal*, 8 Sept. 1983.
28. *Business Week*, 26 Mar. 1984.
29. *U.S. News & World Report*, 15 Aug. 1983.
30. Lee, 8 Sept. 1983.
31. *Washington Post*, 28 May 1984.
32. Lee, 8 Sept. 1983.
33. Ward Sinclair, *Washington Post*, 25 Mar. 1984.
34. *Wall Street Journal*, 9 May 1984.
35. *Washington Post*, 21 Sept. 1984.
36. Lee, 8 Sept. 1983.
37. Ibid.
38. Ibid.
39. Rivlin, p. 64.
40. *Washington Post*, 6 Apr. 1984.

41. *Wall Street Journal*, 20 Dec. 1983.
42. *Washington Post*, 6 Apr. 1984.
43. *U.S. News & World Report*, 17 Jan. 1983.
44. *Wall Street Journal*, 9 Aug. 1984.
45. *U.S. News & World Report*, 17 Jan. 1983.
46. *Wall Street Journal*, 13 May 1983.
47. *Wall Street Journal*, 9 Aug. 1984.
48. *Washington Post*, 6 Apr. 1984.
49. *U.S. News & World Report*, 17 Jan. 1983.
50. *Wall Street Journal*, 13 May 1983.
51. Ibid.
52. *Washington Post*, 1 Dec. 1983.
53. *Los Angeles Times*, 2 Dec. 1983.
54. *Washington Post*, 24 July 1984.
55. *Los Angeles Times*, 2 Dec. 1983.
56. Ibid.
57. Washington State Research Council, *Agenda for the Eighties, Volume VI*, p. 74.
58. *Washington Post*, 24 July 1984.
59. *Washington Post*, 12 Jan. 1984.
60. *Washington Post*, 2 Dec. 1983.
61. *Washington Post*, 27 Apr. 1984.
62. *Washington Post*, 2 Dec. 1983.
63. *Washington Post*, 17 Mar. 1984.
64. *Wall Street Journal*, 13 May 1983.
65. *Washington Post*, 1 Dec. 1983.
66. *Washington Post*, 15 May 1984.
67. *U.S. News & World Report*, 17 Jan. 1983.
68. *Wall Street Journal*, 13 May 1983.
69. *U.S. News & World Report*, 17 Jan. 1983.
70. *Washington Post*, 2 Aug. 1984.
71. Washington State Research Council, *Agenda V*, p. 74.
72. *Wall Street Journal*, 13 May 1983.
73. *Wall Street Journal*, 9 Aug. 1984.
74. *Los Angeles Times*, 29 Aug. 1984.
75. *Wall Street Journal*, 28 Sept. 1984.
76. *U.S. News & World Report*, 2 May 1983.
77. *Business Week*, 10 Oct. 1983.
78. *U.S. News & World Report*, 2 May 1983.
79. *Business Week*, 5 Mar. 1984.
80. Neal Peirce, *Los Angeles Times*, 29 Aug. 1984.
81. Ibid.
82. *Business Week*, 10 Oct. 1983.
83. *Washington Post*, 21 June 1984.
84. Ibid.
85. *Business Week*, 5 Mar. 1984.
86. *Washington Post*, 25 Jan. 1984.
87. Ibid.
88. Peirce, 29 Aug. 1984.
89. Washington State Research Council, *Agenda V*, p. 80.
90. Thomas Graff and David Marcus, *Wall Street Journal*, 30 Mar. 1984.
91. *Business Week*, 5 Mar. 1984.
92. Ibid.
93. *Forbes*, 15 July 1976.
94. *Business Week*, 10 Sept. 1984.
95. *Wall Street Journal*, 14 Dec. 1982.
96. *Business Week*, 10 Sept. 1984.
97. Ibid.

98. *U.S. News & World Report*, 4 Oct. 1982.
99. *Wall Street Journal*, 14 Dec. 1982.
100. *U.S. News & World Report*, 4 Oct. 1982.
101. *Wall Street Journal*, 14 Dec. 1982.
102. *Business Week*, 11 Feb. 1980.
103. Ibid.
104. *U.S. News & World Report*, 4 Oct. 1982.
105. Ibid.
106. Congressman Bill Gradison, *Wall Street Journal*, 15 May 1984.
107. Ibid.
108. Ibid.
109. See for example the three-part series in *Public Administration Times*, 15 Nov., 1 Dec., and 15 Dec. 1980.
110. Gradison, 15 May 1984.
111. *Forbes*, 15 July 1976.
112. *Business Week*, 7 Nov. 1983.
113. *Business Week*, 11 Feb. 1980.
114. *Business Week*, 7 Nov. 1983.
115. *Business Week*, 11 Feb. 1980.
116. *Business Week*, 7 Nov. 1983.
117. *Forbes*, 15 July 1976.
118. *Business Week*, 9 Mar. 1981.
119. Gradison, 15 May 1984.
120. *Business Week*, 10 Sept. 1984.
121. Interview with John Wills, 6 Oct. 1984.

Chapter 4. The Fiscal Collision (pages 291–330)

1. Alice Rivlin, ed., *Economic Choices 1984* (Washington, D.C.: The Brookings Institution, 1984), pp. 20–21.
2. Congressional Budget Office, *Baseline Budget Projections for Fiscal Years 1985–1989* (Washington, D.C.: 1984), pp. 2–5.
3. Congressional Budget Office, *The Economic and Budget Outlook: An Update* (Washington, D.C.: 1984), pp. 59, 65.
4. Ibid., p. 59.
5. Kathy Ruffing, "Federal Debt and Interest Costs," expanded version of paper presented at the American Economic Association meeting in San Francisco, 30 Dec. 1983, p. 1.
6. Congressional Budget Office, *Baseline Budget Projections for Fiscal Years 1985–1989*, p. 62.
7. Ibid., p. 19.
8. Ibid., p. 24.
9. U.S. Congress, Joint Economic Committee, *Soviet Defense Trends* (Washington, D.C.: 1983), p. 10.
10. Unpublished Congressional Budget Office tabulations.
11. U.S. Department of Health and Human Services, Social Security Administration, *1984 Annual Report of the Federal Old-Age and Survivors Insurance and Disability Insurance Trust Funds* (Washington, D.C.: 1984), p. 11.
12. Unpublished Congressional Budget Office tabulations.
13. Mark S. Freeland and Carol E. Schindler, "Health Spending in the 1980s: Integration of Clinical Practice Patterns with Management," *Health Care Financing Review*, Spring 1984, p. 17.
14. *1984 Annual Report of the Board of Trustees of the Federal Hospital Insurance Trust Fund* (Washington, D.C.: 1984), p. 38.

Chapter 5. Renewing the Social Contract (pages 331–44)

1. Saul K. Padover, ed., *Thomas Jefferson on Democracy* (New York: Mentor Books, 1960), p. 159.
2. *Wall Street Journal*, 28 Sept. 1984.
3. Recollection of the author.
4. Interview with Alice Rivlin, 21 Nov. 1983.
5. Norman Ture, remarks to Hudson Institute Committee on the Next Agenda, 19 Oct. 1984.
6. *Washington Post*, 19 July 1984.
7. *Washington Post*, 27 July 1984.
8. *Los Angeles Times*, 21 Sept. 1984.
9. *Los Angeles Times*, 11 Sept. 1984.
10. *Washington Post*, 5 Sept. 1984.
11. *Los Angeles Times*, 25 Sept. 1984.
12. *Washington Post*, 27 July 1984.
13. *Los Angeles Times*, 26 July 1984.
14. *Los Angeles Times*, 19 Sept. 1984.
15. *Washington Post*, 5 Oct. 1984.
16. *Washington Post*, 26 Aug. and 29 Aug. 1984.
17. Interview with John Shannon, 11 Oct. 1983.
18. Barber Conable, remarks to Hudson Institute Committee on the Next Agenda, 6 Sept. 1984.

Index

398   INDEX